THE RANDOM HOUSE

COMPACT
WORLD
ATLAS

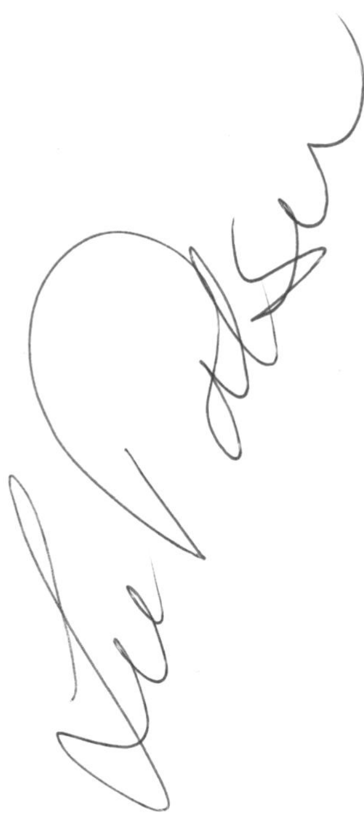

THE RANDOM HOUSE

COMPACT WORLD ATLAS

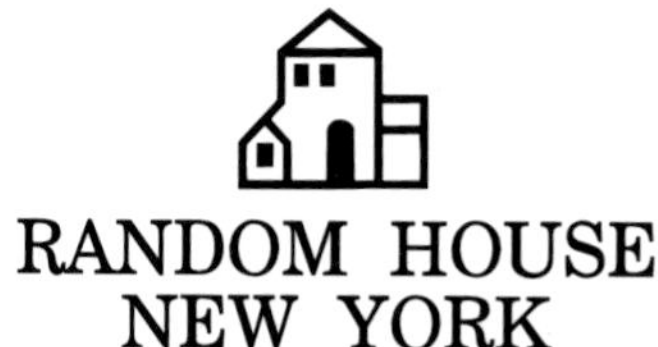

RANDOM HOUSE
NEW YORK

CONTENTS

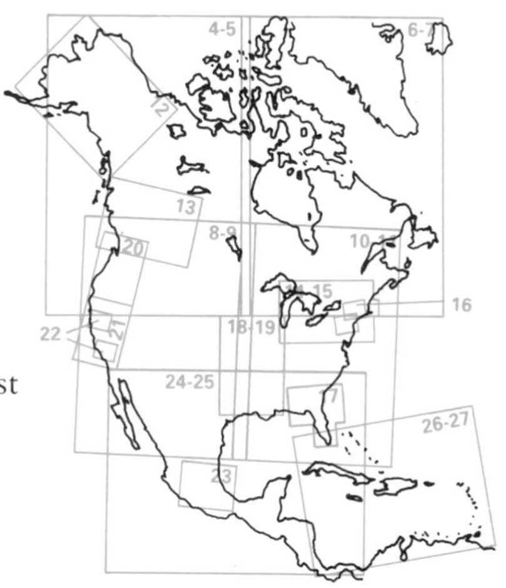

4-5
6-7
12
13
8-9
10-11
20
16
22
21
18-19
14-15
24-25
17
26-27
23

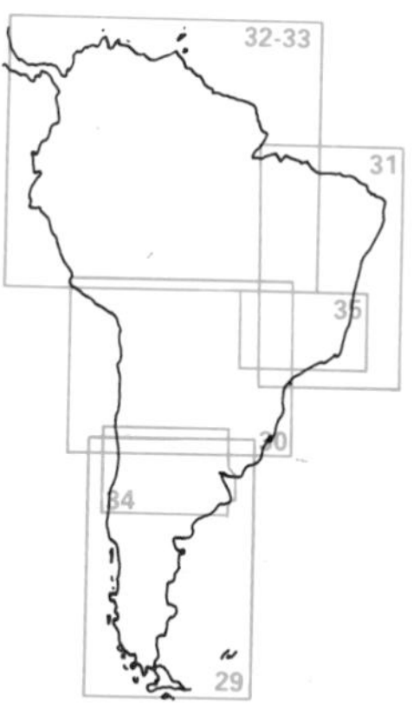

32-33
31
35
30
34
29

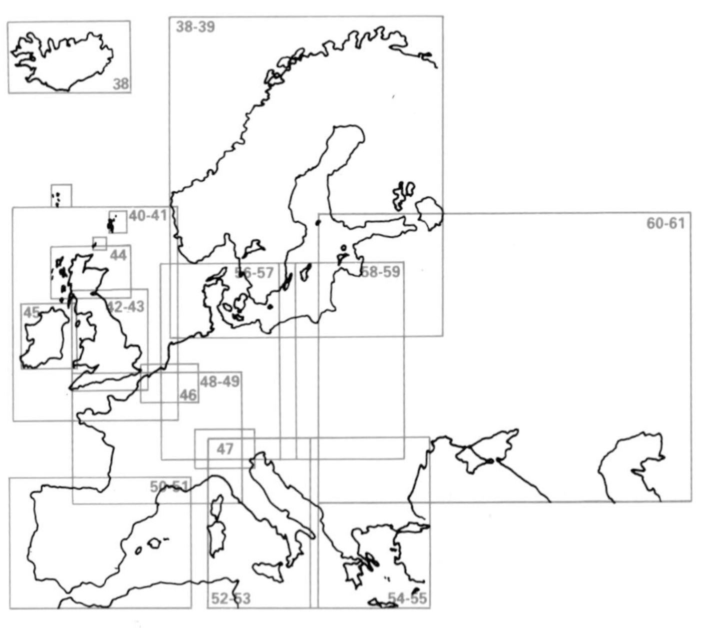
38-39
38
40-41
44
56-57
58-59
60-61
45
42-43
48-49
46
47
50-51
52-53
54-55

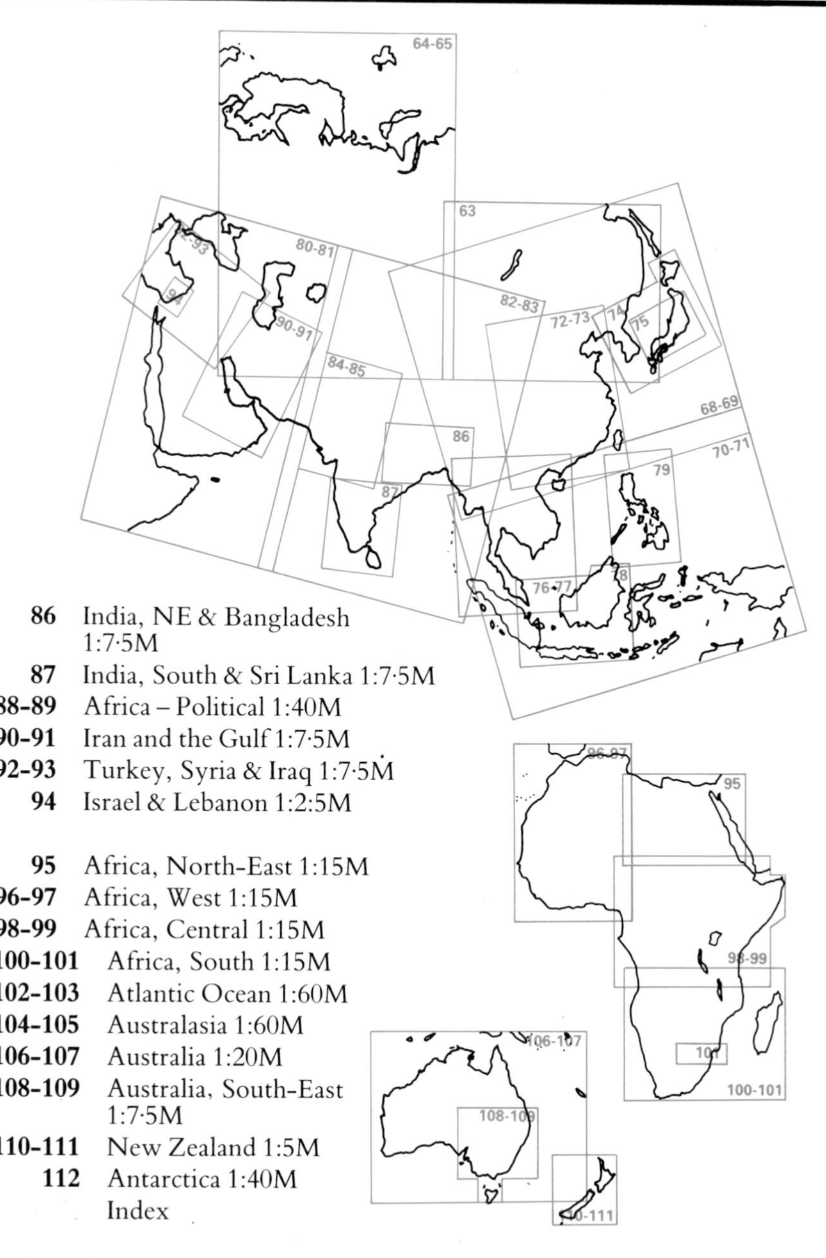
64-65
63
80-81
90-91
84-85
82-83
72-73
74
75
68-69
86
70-71
79
87
76-77
95
100-101

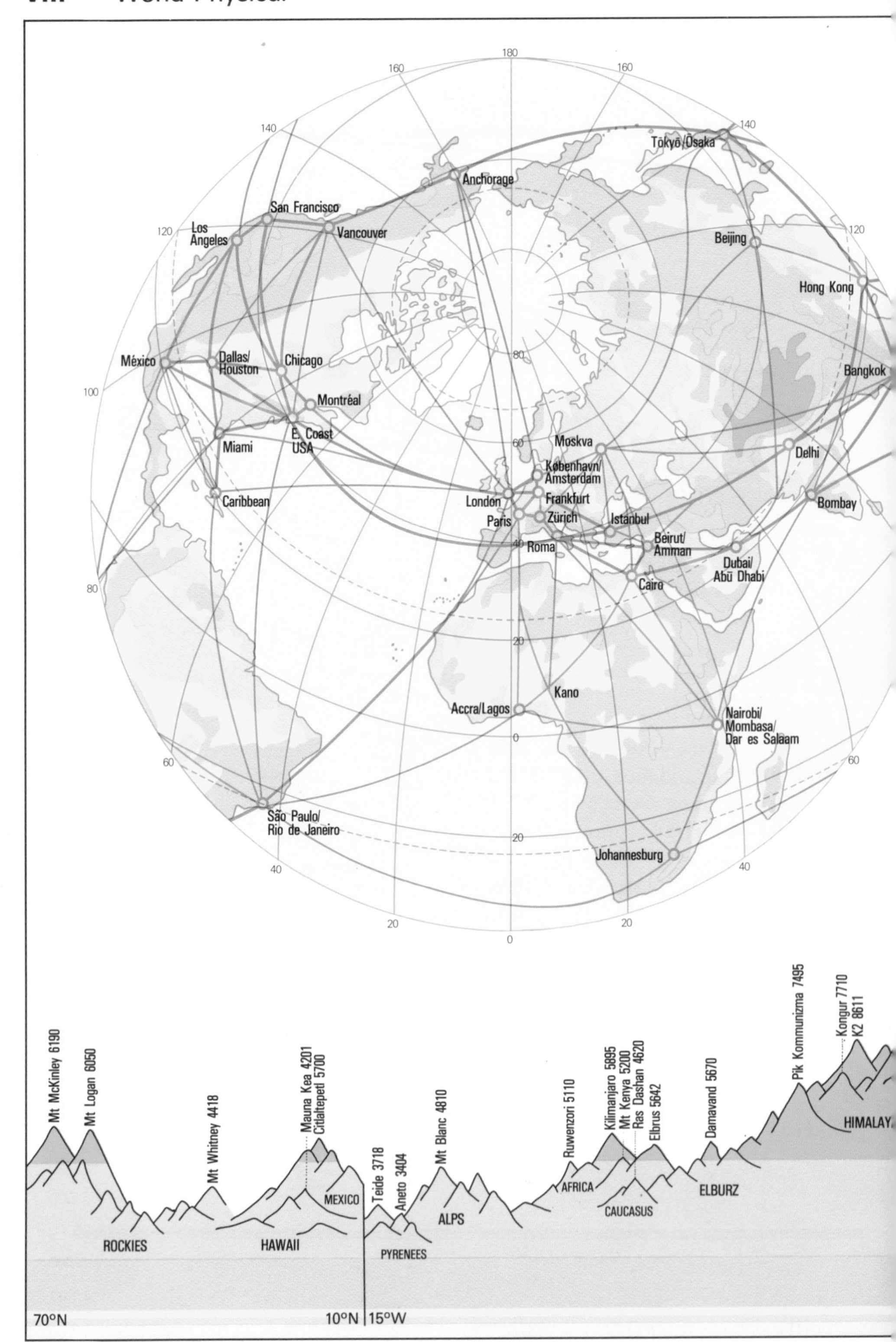
Tōkyō/Ōsaka
Anchorage
San Francisco
Los Angeles
Vancouver
Beijing
Hong Kong
México
Dallas/ Houston
Chicago
Bangkok
Montréal
E. Coast USA
Miami
Moskva
Delhi
København/ Amsterdam
Frankfurt
London
Caribbean
Bombay
Paris
Zürich
Istanbul
Roma
Beirut/ Amman
Dubai/ Abū Dhabi
Cairo
Kano
Accra/Lagos
Nairobi/ Mombasa/ Dar es Salaam
São Paulo/ Rio de Janeiro
Johannesburg
Mt McKinley 6190
Mt Logan 6050
Mt Whitney 4418
Mauna Kea 4201
Citlaltepetl 5700
Teide 3718
Aneto 3404
Mt Blanc 4810
Ruwenzori 5110
Kilimanjaro 5895
Mt Kenya 5200
Ras Dashan 4620
Elbrus 5642
Damavand 5670
Pik Kommunizma 7495
Kongur 7710
K2 8611
ROCKIES
HAWAII
MEXICO
PYRENEES
ALPS
AFRICA
CAUCASUS
ELBURZ
HIMALAY
70°N
10°N
15°W

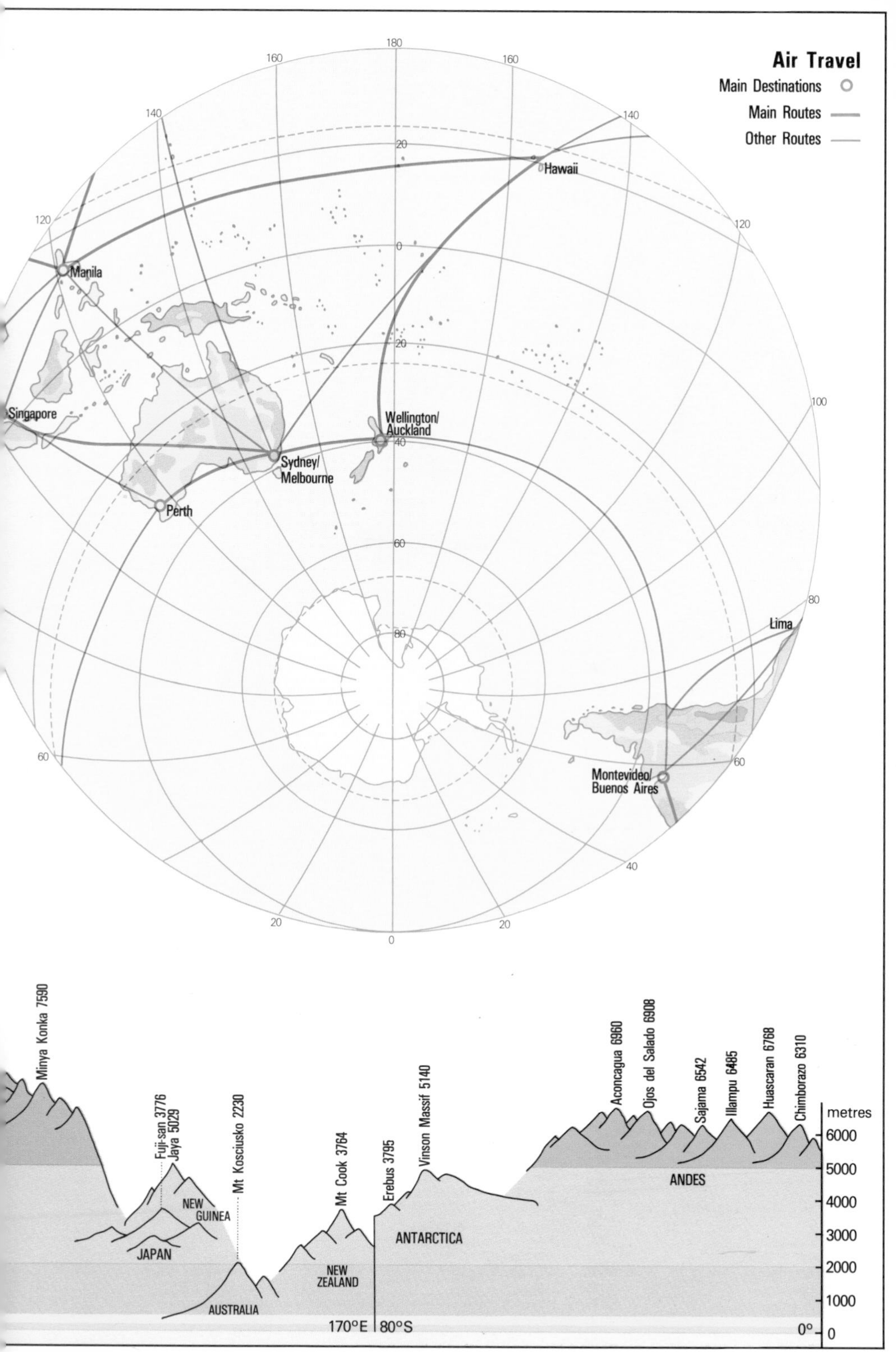

Air Travel
Main Destinations ○
Main Routes ——
Other Routes ——

Hawaii

Manila

Singapore

Wellington/
Auckland

Sydney/
Melbourne

Perth

Lima

Montevideo/
Buenos Aires

Minya Konka 7590

Fuji-san 3776
Java 5029

Mt Kosciusko 2230

Mt Cook 3764

Erebus 3795

Vinson Massif 5140

Aconcagua 6960

Ojos del Salado 6908

Sajama 6542

Illampu 6485

Huascaran 6768

Chimborazo 6310

metres

6000

5000

ANDES

4000

NEW
GUINEA

3000

JAPAN

ANTARCTICA

2000

NEW
ZEALAND

1000

AUSTRALIA

170°E | 80°S

0°

0

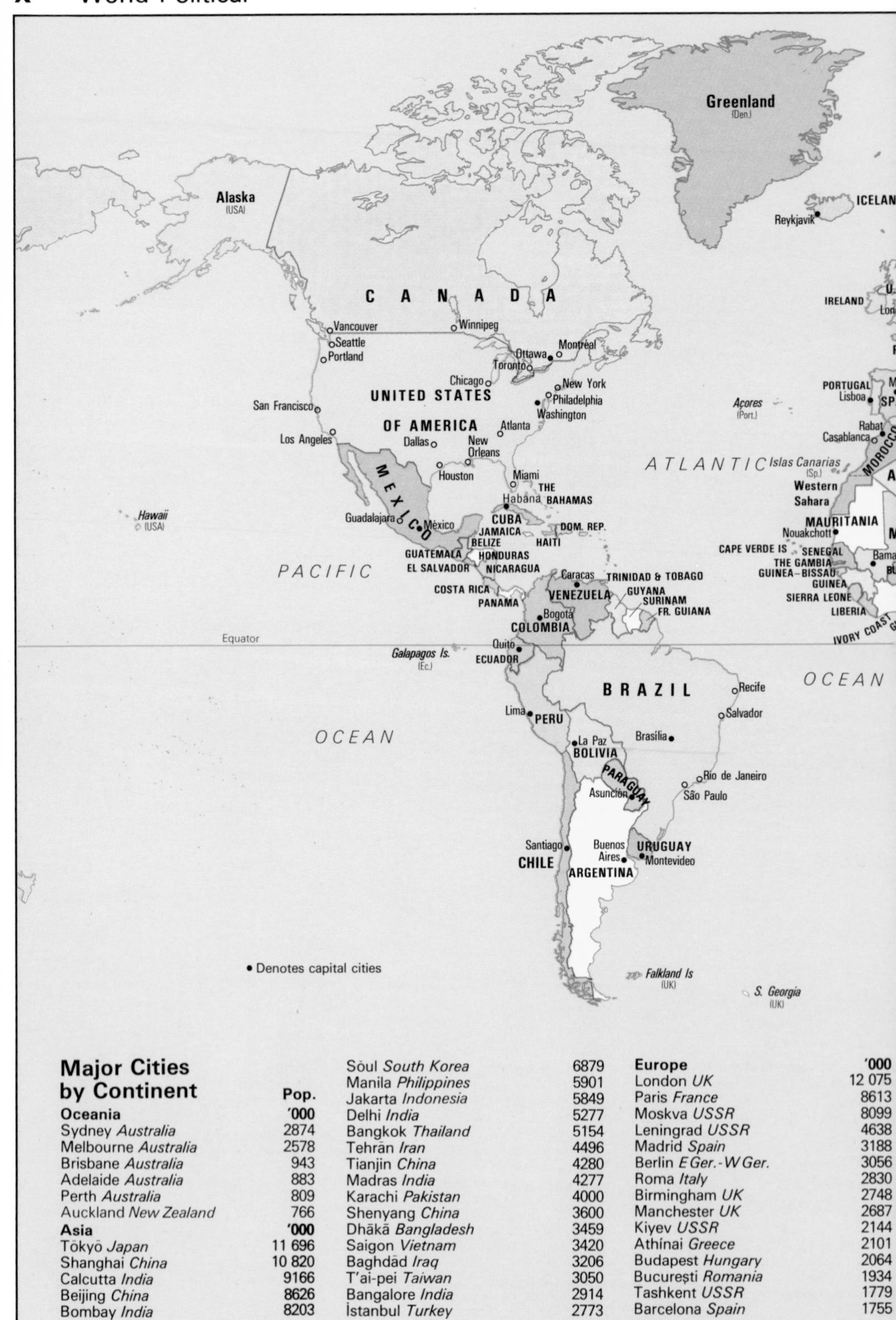

Greenland (Den.)

Alaska (USA)

ICELAN

Reykjavik

IRELAND   Lon

C A N A D A

Vancouver   Winnipeg
Seattle
Portland   Ottawa   Montréal
Toronto
Chicago   New York   PORTUGAL   M
UNITED STATES   Philadelphia   Lisboa   SP.
Washington
San Francisco   Açores   Rabat
OF AMERICA   Atlanta   (Port.)   Casablanca

Los Angeles   Dallas   New   MOROCCO
Orleans   ATLANTIC Islas Canarias   A
(Sp.)
Houston   Miami   Western
THE   Sahara
Hawaii   Habana BAHAMAS
(USA)   MAURITANIA
Guadalajara   México   CUBA   DOM. REP.   Nouakchott
JAMAICA   HAITI
BELIZE   CAPE VERDE IS   SENEGAL   Bama
GUATEMALA HONDURAS   THE GAMBIA   BU
PACIFIC   EL SALVADOR NICARAGUA   GUINEA-BISSAU
Caracas   TRINIDAD & TOBAGO   GUINEA
COSTA RICA   GUYANA   SIERRA LEONE
PANAMA   VENEZUELA SURINAM   LIBERIA
Bogotá   FR. GUIANA   IVORY COAST G
Equator   COLOMBIA

Quito
Galapagos Is.   ECUADOR   OCEAN
(Ec.)
Recife
B R A Z I L

Lima   PERU   Salvador

OCEAN   La Paz   Brasília
BOLIVIA

Rio de Janeiro
PARAGUAY
Asunción   São Paulo

Santiago   Buenos   URUGUAY
Aires
CHILE   ARGENTINA Montevideo

• Denotes capital cities   Falkland Is.
(UK)   S. Georgia
(UK)

Major Cities by Continent

	Pop.				
Oceania	**'000**	Sòul *South Korea*	6879	**Europe**	**'000**
Sydney *Australia*	2874	Manila *Philippines*	5901	London *UK*	12 075
Melbourne *Australia*	2578	Jakarta *Indonesia*	5849	Paris *France*	8613
Brisbane *Australia*	943	Delhi *India*	5277	Moskva *USSR*	8099
Adelaide *Australia*	883	Bangkok *Thailand*	5154	Leningrad *USSR*	4638
Perth *Australia*	809	Tehrān *Iran*	4496	Madrid *Spain*	3188
Auckland *New Zealand*	766	Tianjin *China*	4280	Berlin *E Ger.-W Ger.*	3056
Asia	**'000**	Madras *India*	4277	Roma *Italy*	2830
Tōkyò *Japan*	11 696	Karachi *Pakistan*	4000	Birmingham *UK*	2748
Shanghai *China*	10 820	Shenyang *China*	3600	Manchester *UK*	2687
Calcutta *India*	9166	Dhākā *Bangladesh*	3459	Kiyev *USSR*	2144
Beijing *China*	8626	Saigon *Vietnam*	3420	Athínai *Greece*	2101
Bombay *India*	8203	Baghdād *Iraq*	3206	Budapest *Hungary*	2064
		T'ai-pei *Taiwan*	3050	Bucureşti *Romania*	1934
		Bangalore *India*	2914	Tashkent *USSR*	1779
		İstanbul *Turkey*	2773	Barcelona *Spain*	1755

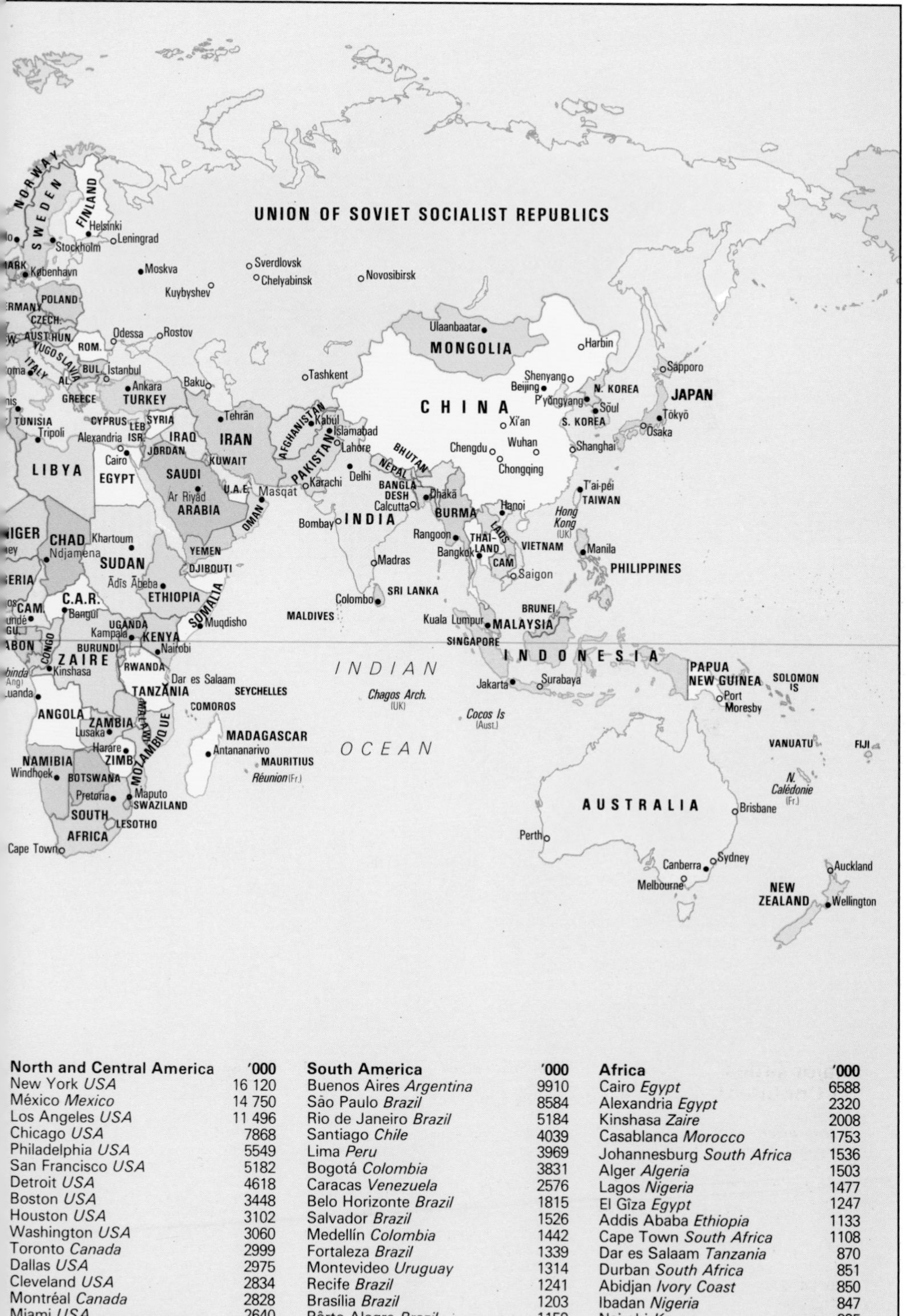

North and Central America	'000	South America	'000	Africa	'000
New York *USA*	16 120	Buenos Aires *Argentina*	9910	Cairo *Egypt*	6588
México *Mexico*	14 750	São Paulo *Brazil*	8584	Alexandria *Egypt*	2320
Los Angeles *USA*	11 496	Rio de Janeiro *Brazil*	5184	Kinshasa *Zaire*	2008
Chicago *USA*	7868	Santiago *Chile*	4039	Casablanca *Morocco*	1753
Philadelphia *USA*	5549	Lima *Peru*	3969	Johannesburg *South Africa*	1536
San Francisco *USA*	5182	Bogotá *Colombia*	3831	Alger *Algeria*	1503
Detroit *USA*	4618	Caracas *Venezuela*	2576	Lagos *Nigeria*	1477
Boston *USA*	3448	Belo Horizonte *Brazil*	1815	El Gîza *Egypt*	1247
Houston *USA*	3102	Salvador *Brazil*	1526	Addis Ababa *Ethiopia*	1133
Washington *USA*	3060	Medellín *Colombia*	1442	Cape Town *South Africa*	1108
Toronto *Canada*	2999	Fortaleza *Brazil*	1339	Dar es Salaam *Tanzania*	870
Dallas *USA*	2975	Montevideo *Uruguay*	1314	Durban *South Africa*	851
Cleveland *USA*	2834	Recife *Brazil*	1241	Abidjan *Ivory Coast*	850
Montréal *Canada*	2828	Brasília *Brazil*	1203	Ibadan *Nigeria*	847
Miami *USA*	2640	Pôrto Alegre *Brazil*	1159	Nairobi *Kenya*	835

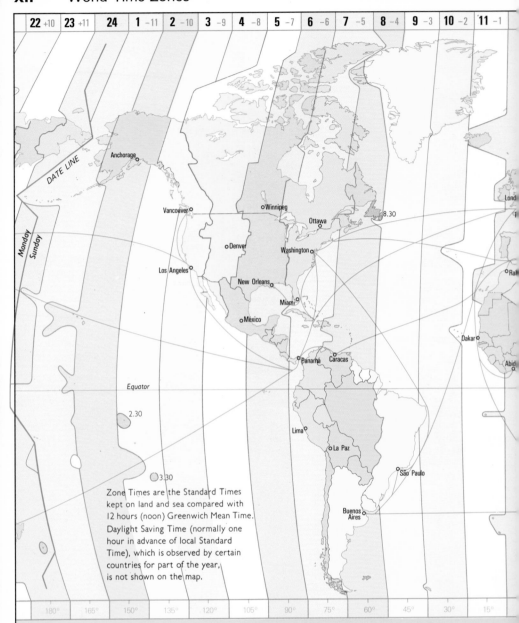

| 22 +10 | 23 +11 | 24 | 1 −11 | 2 −10 | 3 −9 | 4 −8 | 5 −7 | 6 −6 | 7 −5 | 8 −4 | 9 −3 | 10 −2 | 11 −1 |

DATE LINE

Monday
Sunday

Anchorage

Vancouver   Winnipeg   London

Ottawa   8.30

Denver   Washington

Los Angeles

New Orleans   Ra

Miami

México   Dakar

Equator   Panamá   Caracas   Abid

2.30

Lima

3.30   La Paz

São Paulo

Zone Times are the Standard Times
kept on land and sea compared with
12 hours (noon) Greenwich Mean Time.
Daylight Saving Time (normally one
hour in advance of local Standard
Time), which is observed by certain
countries for part of the year,
is not shown on the map.

Buenos
Aires

| 180° | 165° | 150° | 135° | 120° | 105° | 90° | 75° | 60° | 45° | 30° | 15° |

Journey Times

Sail (via Cape)
164 days

Steam (via Cape)
43 days

Steam (via Suez)
30 days

Supertanker
(via Cape)
28 days

Singapore ◀──

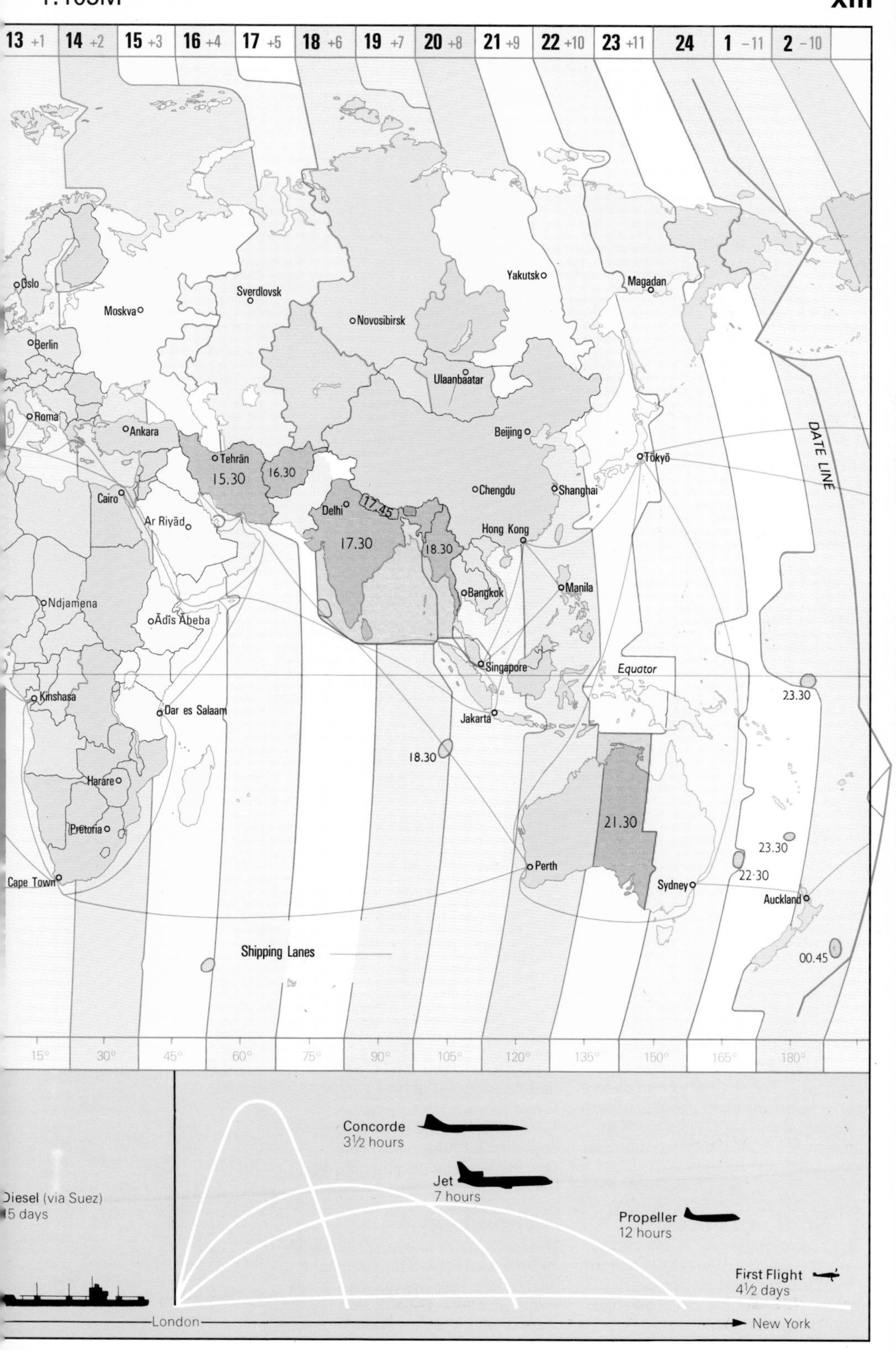

| 13 +1 | 14 +2 | 15 +3 | 16 +4 | 17 +5 | 18 +6 | 19 +7 | 20 +8 | 21 +9 | 22 +10 | 23 +11 | 24 | 1 −11 | 2 −10 |

Oslo

Moskva

Berlin

Roma

Ankara

Cairo

Ar Riyād

Ndjamena

Ādīs Ābeba

Kinshasa

Dar es Salaam

Harāre

Pretoria

Cape Town

Sverdlovsk

Novosibirsk

Tehrān 15.30

16.30

Delhi 17·45

17.30

18.30

Singapore

Jakarta

18.30

Ulaanbaatar

Yakutsk

Magadan

Beijing

Chengdu

Shanghai

Hong Kong

Bangkok

Manila

Equator

Tōkyō

DATE LINE

23.30

Perth 21.30

23.30

22·30

Sydney

Auckland

00.45

Shipping Lanes ——————

15° 30° 45° 60° 75° 90° 105° 120° 135° 150° 165° 180°

Concorde
3½ hours

Jet
7 hours

Propeller
12 hours

Diesel (via Suez)
5 days

First Flight
4½ days

London ————————————————→ New York

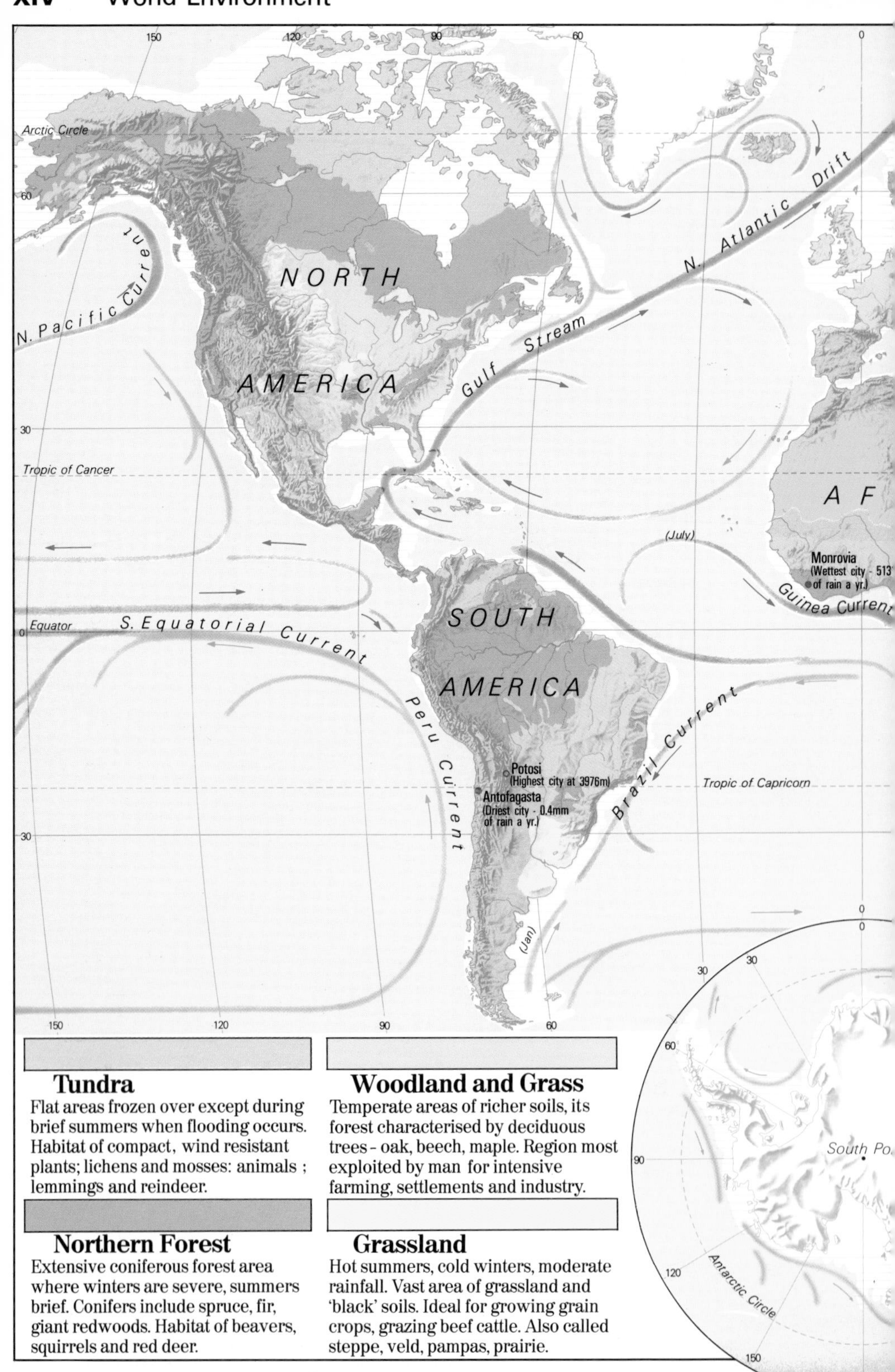

Tundra

Flat areas frozen over except during brief summers when flooding occurs. Habitat of compact, wind resistant plants; lichens and mosses: animals ; lemmings and reindeer.

Northern Forest

Extensive coniferous forest area where winters are severe, summers brief. Conifers include spruce, fir, giant redwoods. Habitat of beavers, squirrels and red deer.

Woodland and Grass

Temperate areas of richer soils, its forest characterised by deciduous trees - oak, beech, maple. Region most exploited by man for intensive farming, settlements and industry.

Grassland

Hot summers, cold winters, moderate rainfall. Vast area of grassland and 'black' soils. Ideal for growing grain crops, grazing beef cattle. Also called steppe, veld, pampas, prairie.

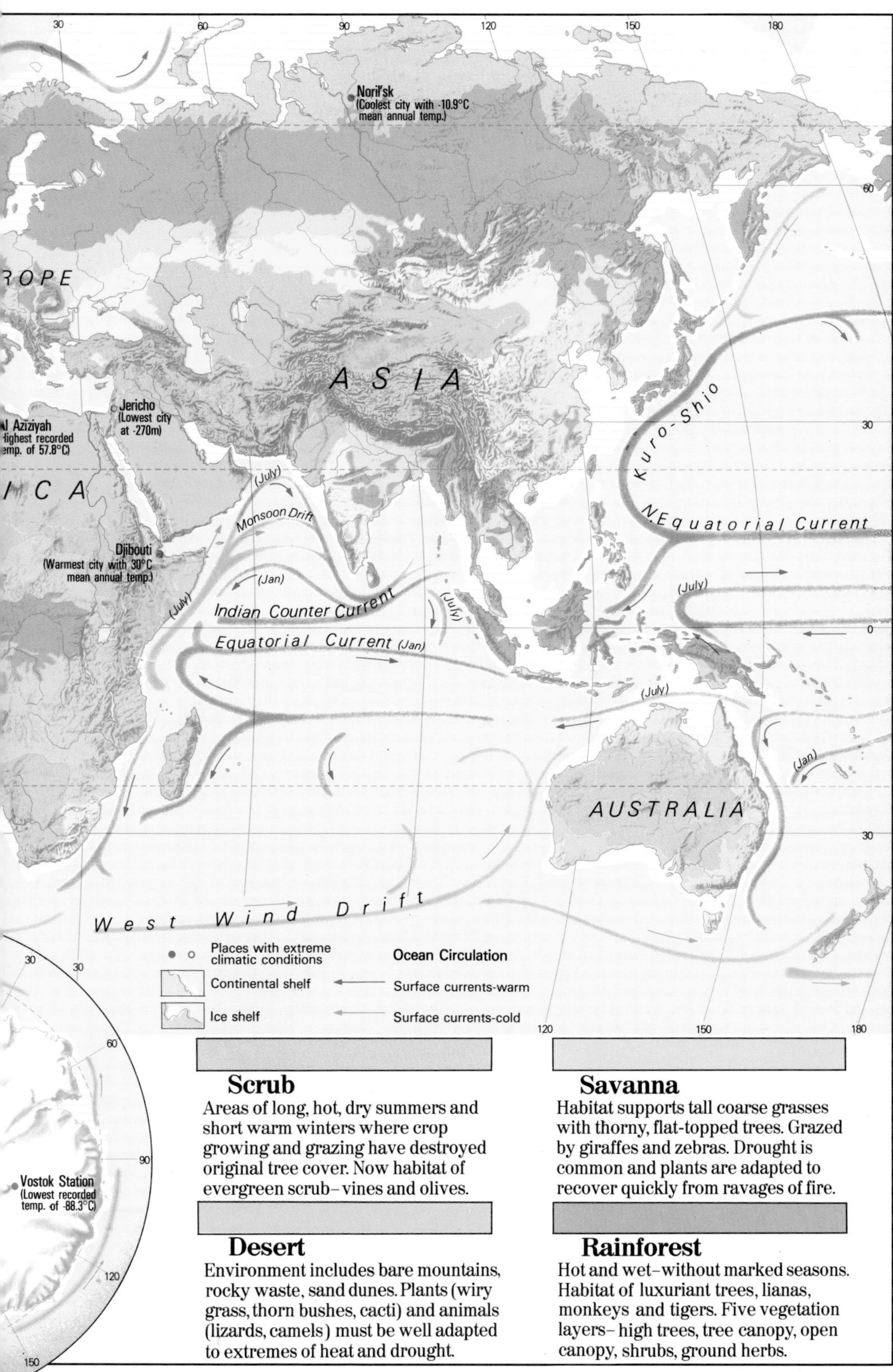

Places with extreme climatic conditions (● ○)

Continental shelf

Ice shelf

Ocean Circulation

Surface currents-warm →

Surface currents-cold →

Scrub
Areas of long, hot, dry summers and short warm winters where crop growing and grazing have destroyed original tree cover. Now habitat of evergreen scrub–vines and olives.

Desert
Environment includes bare mountains, rocky waste, sand dunes. Plants (wiry grass, thorn bushes, cacti) and animals (lizards, camels) must be well adapted to extremes of heat and drought.

Savanna
Habitat supports tall coarse grasses with thorny, flat-topped trees. Grazed by giraffes and zebras. Drought is common and plants are adapted to recover quickly from ravages of fire.

Rainforest
Hot and wet–without marked seasons. Habitat of luxuriant trees, lianas, monkeys and tigers. Five vegetation layers– high trees, tree canopy, open canopy, shrubs, ground herbs.

Noril'sk (Coolest city with -10.9°C mean annual temp.)

ASIA

Jericho (Lowest city at -270m)

Al Aziziyah (Highest recorded temp. of 57.8°C)

Djibouti (Warmest city with 30°C mean annual temp.)

Monsoon Drift (July) (Jan)

Indian Counter Current

Equatorial Current (Jan)

(July)

Kuro-Shio

N Equatorial Current

(July)

(July)

(July)

(Jan)

West Wind Drift

AUSTRALIA

Vostok Station (Lowest recorded temp. of -88.3°C)

BOUNDARIES

———————— International

— — — — International under Dispute

· · · · · · · · Cease Fire Line

———————— Autonomous or State/
Administrative

— — — Maritime (National)

— — — — International Date Line

COMMUNICATIONS

═══ ═══ Motorway/Under Construction

———————— Major/Other Road

— — — — Under Construction

· · · · · · · · Track

=)==== Road Tunnel

· · · · · · · · Car Ferry

———————— Main/Other Railway

— — — — — Under Construction

- - - - - - - Rail Ferry

—→——←— Rail Tunnel

┴┴┴┴┴┴ Canal

⊕　ㅅ International/Other Airport

LANDSCAPE FEATURES

Glacier, Ice Cap

Marsh, Swamp

Sand Desert, Dunes

Freshwater

Saltwater

Seasonal

Salt Pan

OTHER FEATURES

~~~~~→ River/Seasonal

≍ Pass, Gorge

Dam, Barrage

Waterfall, Rapid

———————— Aqueduct

~~~~~~~~ Reef

.217 ▲4231 Spot Height, Depth/
Summit, Peak

⌄ Well

△　▲ Oil/Gas Field

Gas / Oil Oil/Natural Gas Pipeline

Gemsbok Nat. Pk National Park

.·.UR Historic Site

LETTERING STYLES

CANADA Independent Nation

FLORIDA State, Province or
Autonomous Region

Gibraltar (U.K.) Sovereignty of
Dependent Territory

Lothian Administrative Area

LANGUEDOC Historic Region

Loire **Vosges** Physical Feature or
Physical Region

TOWNS AND CITIES

Square symbols denote capital cities			Population
▣	◉	**New York**	over 5 000 000
■	●	**Montréal**	over 1 000 000
▢	○	Ottawa	over 500 000
▪	•	**Québec**	over 100 000
▫	○	St John's	over 50 000
▫	○	Yorkton	over 10 000
▫	○	Jasper	under 10 000
			Built-up-area

Depth　　　　　Sea Level　　　　　　　　Height
0

8000m 6000m 4000m 2000m 200m

200m 500m 1000m 2000m 3000m 4000m 5000m 6000m

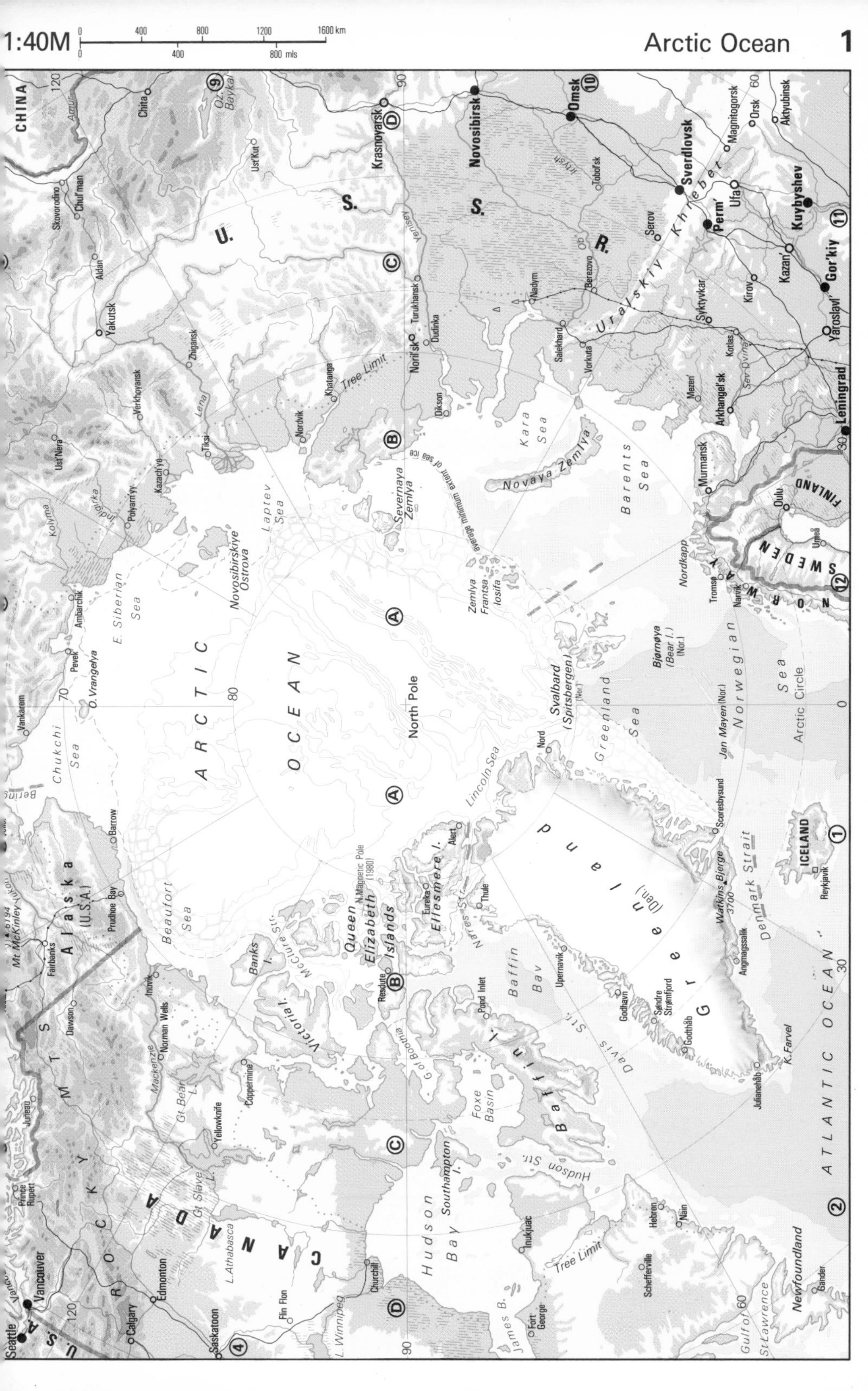
ARCTIC OCEAN
North Pole
U. S. S. R.
CHINA
CANADA
ROCKY MTS
Alaska (U.S.A.)
Greenland (Den.)
ICELAND
FINLAND
SWEDEN
NORWAY
ATLANTIC OCEAN
Chukchi Sea
E. Siberian Sea
Laptev Sea
Kara Sea
Barents Sea
Greenland Sea
Norwegian Sea
Beaufort Sea
Lincoln Sea
Baffin Bay
Hudson Bay
Foxe Basin
Denmark Strait
Davis Str.
Hudson Str.
Nares Str.
McClure Str.
G. of Boothia
James B.
Gulf of St Lawrence
Arctic Circle
Tree Limit
average minimum extent of sea ice
Novaya Zemlya
Severnaya Zemlya
Novosibirskiye Ostrova
O. Vrangelya
Zemlya Frantsa Iosifa
Svalbard (Spitsbergen) (Nor.)
Bjørnøya (Bear I.) (Nor.)
Jan Mayen (Nor.)
Queen Elizabeth Islands
Ellesmere I.
Banks I.
Victoria I.
Baffin I.
Southampton I.
Newfoundland
N. Magnetic Pole (1980)
Uralskiy Khrebet
Watkins Bjerge 3700
Mt McKinley 6194
Gt Bear L.
Gt Slave L.
L. Athabasca
L. Winnipeg
Oz. Baykal
Lena
Kolyma
Indigirka
Yenisey
Ob
Irtysh
Amur
Mackenzie
Yukon
Sev. Dvina
Moscow
Leningrad
Gor'kiy
Kuybyshev
Sverdlovsk
Perm'
Ufa
Kazan'
Novosibirsk
Omsk
Krasnoyarsk
Chita
Yakutsk
Aldan
Skovorodino
Chul'man
Ust'Kut
Zhigansk
Verkhoyansk
Tiksi
Kazach'ye
Ust'Nera
Polyarnyy
Ambarchik
Pevek
Vankarem
Khatanga
Nordvik
Noril'sk
Dudinka
Turukhansk
Dikson
Salekhard
Vorkuta
Nadym
Berezovo
Serov
Tobol'sk
Magnitogorsk
Orsk
Aktyubinsk
Syktyvkar
Kirov
Kotlas
Yaroslavl'
Arkhangel'sk
Mezen'
Murmansk
Nordkapp
Tromsø
Narvik
Oulu
Umeå
Reykjavík
Scoresbysund
Angmagssalik
Julianehåb
K. Farvel
Godthåb
Søndre Strømfjord
Godhavn
Upernavik
Thule
Alert
Nord
Eureka
Resolute
Pond Inlet
Barrow
Prudhoe Bay
Fairbanks
Dawson
Inuvik
Norman Wells
Coppermine
Yellowknife
Juneau
Prince Rupert
Vancouver
Seattle
Calgary
Edmonton
Saskatoon
Flin Flon
Churchill
Inukjuac
Fort George
Schefferville
Hebron
Nain
Gander
120
90
60
30
0
70
80

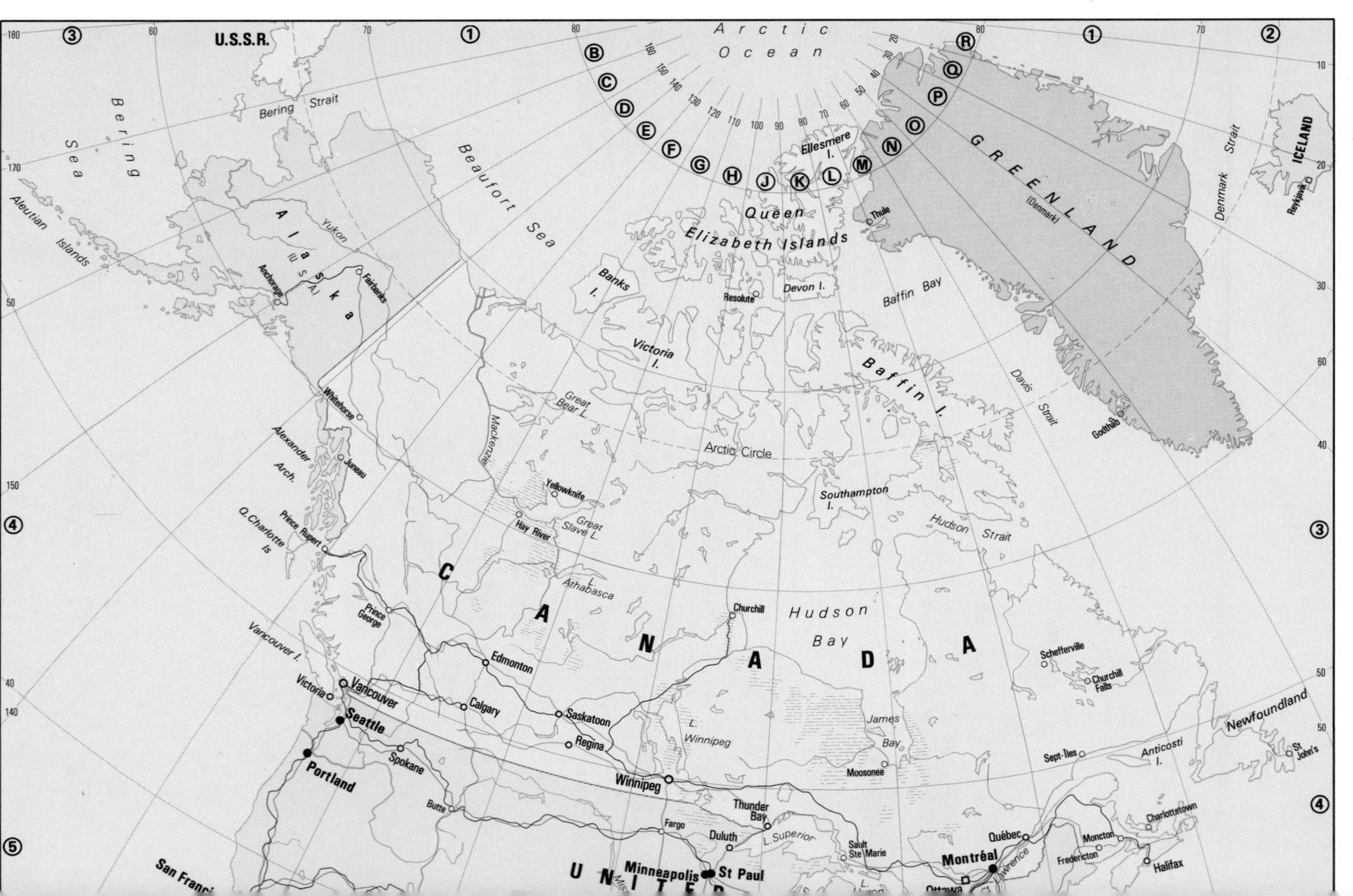
U.S.S.R.
Arctic Ocean
Bering Strait
Bering Sea
Aleutian Islands
Alaska
(U.S.A.)
Yukon
Anchorage
Fairbanks
Beaufort Sea
Ellesmere I.
Queen Elizabeth Islands
Thule
GREENLAND
(Denmark)
Denmark Strait
ICELAND
Reykjavík
Banks I.
Resolute
Devon I.
Baffin Bay
Victoria I.
Baffin I.
Davis Strait
Godthåb
Whitehorse
Great Bear L.
Mackenzie
Arctic Circle
Alexander Arch.
Juneau
Yellowknife
Southampton I.
Q.Charlotte Is
Prince Rupert
Hay River
Great Slave L.
Hudson Strait
C
L. Athabasca
Prince George
A
Churchill
Hudson Bay
N
A
D
A
Schefferville
Churchill Falls
Vancouver I.
Edmonton
Victoria
Vancouver
Calgary
Saskatoon
Seattle
L. Winnipeg
James Bay
Newfoundland
Regina
Portland
Spokane
Sept-Îles
Anticosti I.
St John's
Winnipeg
Moosonee
Butte
Thunder Bay
Fargo
Duluth
L.Superior
Sault Ste Marie
Québec
Moncton
Charlottetown
Fredericton
Montréal
Lawrence
Halifax
Ottawa
San Franc
UNITED
Minneapolis
St Paul

1:35M

| 0 | 250 | 500 | 750 | 1000 | 1250 km |

| 0 | 250 | 500 | 750 mls |

ATLANTIC OCEAN

Bermuda (U.K.)

New York
Philadelphia
Baltimore
Washington
Cleveland
Indianapolis
Norfolk

Charleston

Jacksonville

THE
BAHAMAS

Nassau

Miami

CUBA

Habana

Tampa

Gulf of Mexico

Atlanta
Nashville
Memphis
Birmingham
St Louis
Kansas City
Ohio
Mississippi

OF AMERICA
STATES

Dallas
Fort Worth
New Orleans
Houston
San Antonio

Albuquerque
El Paso
Chihuahua

Rio Grande

Tampico

Veracruz

Monterrey
Torreón

MEXICO

México

Acapulco

Guadalajara
Mazatlán

M

Phoenix
Tucson

Colorado

G. de California

Guadalupe (Mex.)

Is Revilla Gigedo (Mex.)

Los Angeles
San Diego

PACIFIC OCEAN

Tropic of Cancer

Pto-
Rico (U.S.A.)

DOMINICAN REP.
Sto Domingo

HAITI
Port-au-Prince

Guantánamo
Kingston

JAMAICA

CARIBBEAN SEA

Netherlands
Antilles

BAR-BADOS
ST LUCIA
ST VINCENT
GRENADA
DOMINICA
TRINIDAD & TOBAGO

Caracas

VENEZUELA

Maracaibo

Medellín
Bogotá
COLOMBIA

Sta Marta
Barranquilla

Panamá

PANAMA

S.José
COSTA RICA

I. del Coco (C.R)

Malpelo (Col.)

Quito
ECUADOR

PERU

BRAZIL

Negro

BELIZE
Belmopan

HONDURAS
Tegucigalpa

NICARAGUA
Managua

Mérida

GUATEMALA
Guatemala
S.Salvador
EL SALVADOR

Galapagos Is (Ecu.)

Clipperton (Fr.)

Equator

130 120 110 100 90 80 70 60

M L K J H G

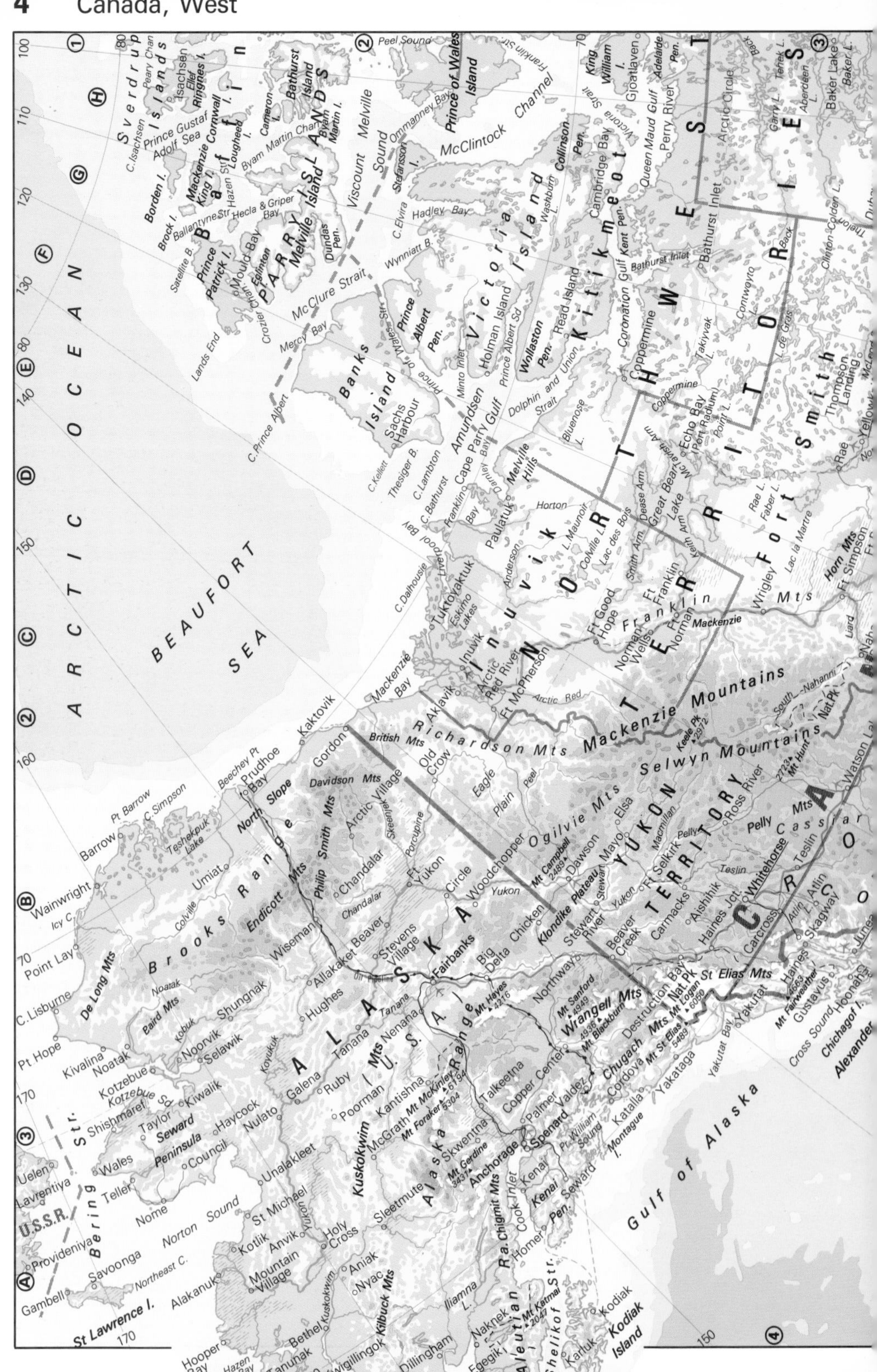
ARCTIC OCEAN
BEAUFORT SEA
Banks Island
Victoria Island
Prince Patrick I.
Melville Island
PARRY ISLANDS
Bathurst Island
Prince of Wales Island
Sverdrup Islands
Borden I.
Mackenzie King I.
Viscount Melville Sound
McClintock Channel
McClure Strait
Amundsen Gulf
Coronation Gulf
Queen Maud Gulf
Great Bear Lake
NORTHWEST TERRITORIES
Inuvik
Kitikmeot
Fort Smith
YUKON TERRITORY
Mackenzie Mountains
Selwyn Mountains
Richardson Mts
Ogilvie Mts
Franklin Mts
Cassiar Mts
St Elias Mts
Wrangell Mts
Chugach Mts
ALASKA
U.S.A.
Brooks Range
Alaska Range
Gulf of Alaska
Kodiak Island
Kenai Pen.
Seward Peninsula
Bering Str.
U.S.S.R.
St Lawrence I.
Norton Sound
Kotzebue Sd.
Barrow
Prudhoe Bay
Kaktovik
Fairbanks
Anchorage
Nome
Whitehorse
Dawson
Inuvik
Tuktoyaktuk
Aklavik
Ft McPherson
Norman Wells
Ft Good Hope
Ft Simpson
Wrigley
Coppermine
Cambridge Bay
Sachs Harbour
Holman Island
Paulatuk
Mt McKinley 6194
Mt Logan 6050
Mt St Elias 5489
Keele Pk 2972
Mt Hunt 2723
Mt Campbell 2489

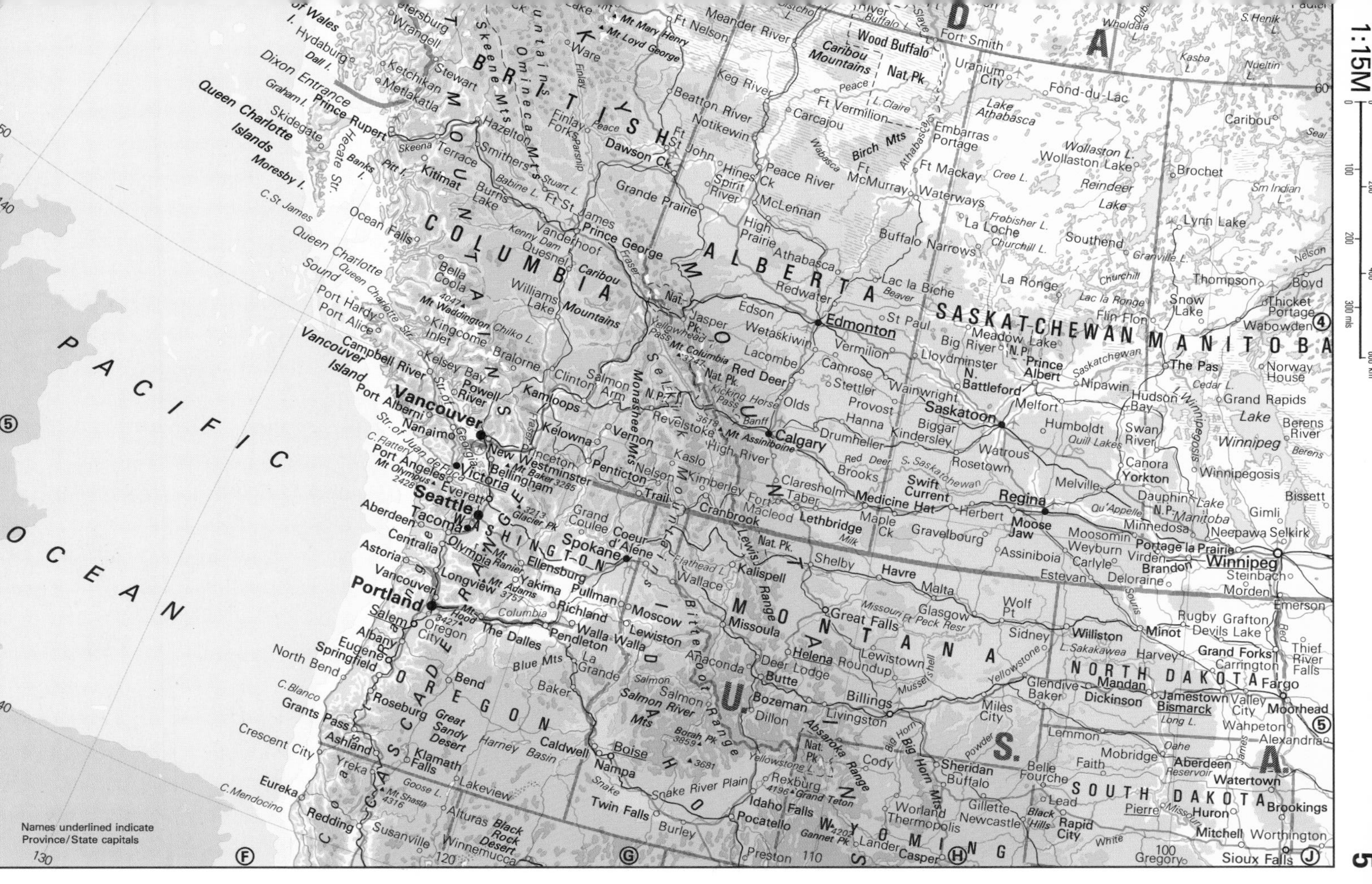

0	200	400	600 km
0	100	200	300 mls

PACIFIC

OCEAN

MANITOBA

SASKATCHEWAN

ALBERTA

BRITISH COLUMBIA

NORTH DAKOTA

SOUTH DAKOTA

MONTANA

WYOMING

IDAHO

WASHINGTON

OREGON

Winnipeg · Regina · Saskatoon · Edmonton · Calgary · Moose Jaw · Prince Albert · Lethbridge · Medicine Hat · Red Deer

Vancouver · Victoria · Seattle · Tacoma · Portland · Salem · Prince George · Kamloops · Kelowna · Penticton

Fargo · Bismarck · Grand Forks · Minot · Aberdeen · Watertown · Pierre · Rapid City · Brookings · Sioux Falls

Great Falls · Helena · Butte · Bozeman · Billings · Missoula · Spokane · Boise · Pocatello · Twin Falls

Caribou Mountains · Wood Buffalo Nat. Pk. · Rocky Mountains · Selkirk Mts · Monashee Mts · Absaroka Range · Bitterroot Range · Salmon River Mts · Skeena Mts · Omineca Mts · Cariboo Mountains

Lake Athabasca · Reindeer Lake · Wollaston Lake · Lac la Ronge · Cree L. · Lake Winnipeg · Lake Winnipegosis · Lake Manitoba · Dauphin Lake · Williams Lake · Great Slave Lake

Queen Charlotte Islands · Vancouver Island · Graham I. · Moresby I. · Banks I. · Hecate Str. · Dixon Entrance · Queen Charlotte Sound · Str. of Georgia · Str. of Juan de Fuca

Peace River · Athabasca River · Fraser · Columbia · Snake River · Missouri · Milk · Red Deer · S. Saskatchewan · N. Saskatchewan · Churchill · Nelson

Names underlined indicate Province/State capitals

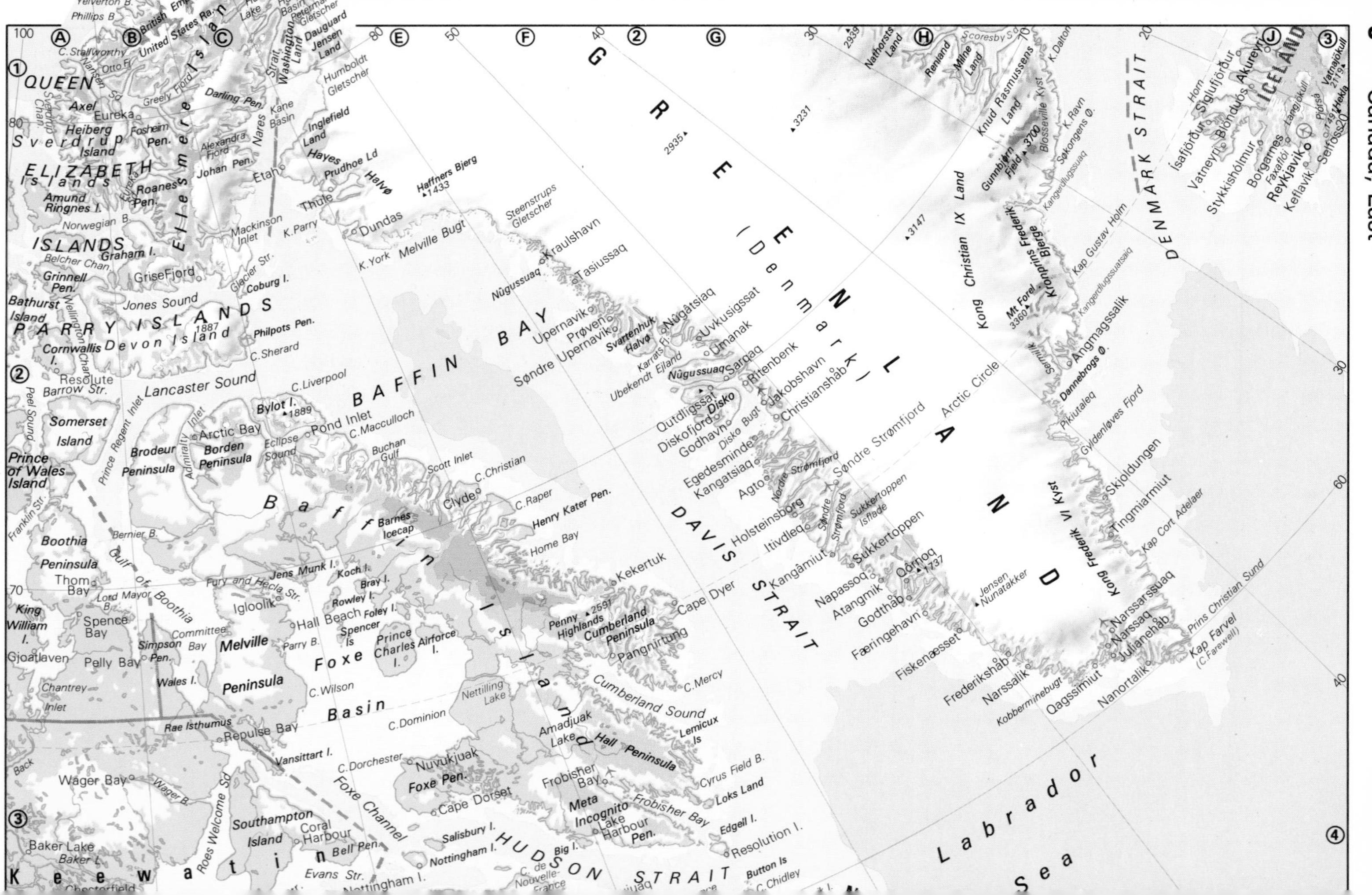
GREENLAND
(Denmark)
ICELAND
DENMARK STRAIT
DAVIS STRAIT
BAFFIN BAY
Baffin Island
Labrador Sea
HUDSON STRAIT
Foxe Basin
Foxe Channel
QUEEN ELIZABETH ISLANDS
PARRY ISLANDS
Sverdrup Islands
Ellesmere Island
Devon Island
Southampton Island
Keewatin
Reykjavík
Akureyri
Kap Farvel
(C. Farewell)
Prins Christian Sund
Nanortalik
Julianehåb
Narssaq
Narssarssuaq
Tingmiarmiut
Skjoldungen
Angmagssalik
Kong Frederik VI Kyst
Kong Christian IX Land
Kronprins Frederik Bjerge
Gunnbjørn Fjeld
3700
Knud Rasmussen Land
Scoresby Sd
Arctic Circle
Frederikshåb
Fiskenæsset
Færingehavn
Godthåb
Sukkertoppen
Holsteinsborg
Søndre Strømfjord
Christianshåb
Jakobshavn
Egedesminde
Godhavn
Disko
Umanak
Upernavik
Thule
Dundas
Melville Bugt
Kane Basin
Nares Strait
Lancaster Sound
Jones Sound
Pond Inlet
Clyde
Cumberland Sound
Pangnirtung
Frobisher Bay
Hall Peninsula
Meta Incognita Pen.
Resolution I.
Cape Dorset
Foxe Pen.
Nettilling Lake
Amadjuak Lake
Barnes Icecap
Prince Charles I.
Igloolik
Melville Peninsula
Repulse Bay
Gulf of Boothia
Boothia Peninsula
Somerset Island
Prince of Wales Island
Resolute
Cornwallis I.
Bathurst Island
King William I.
Gjoa Haven
Spence Bay
Pelly Bay
Wager Bay
Baker Lake
Coral Harbour
Roes Welcome Sd
Prince Regent Inlet
Peel Sound
Bylot I.
Admiralty Inlet
Arctic Bay
Brodeur Peninsula
Borden Peninsula
Axel Heiberg Island
Amund Ringnes I.
Eureka
Grise Fiord
Etah
Washington Land
Humboldt Gletscher
Inglefield Land
Hayes Halvø
Cape Dyer
Home Bay
Henry Kater Pen.
Penny Highlands
Cumberland Peninsula
Nottingham I.
Salisbury I.

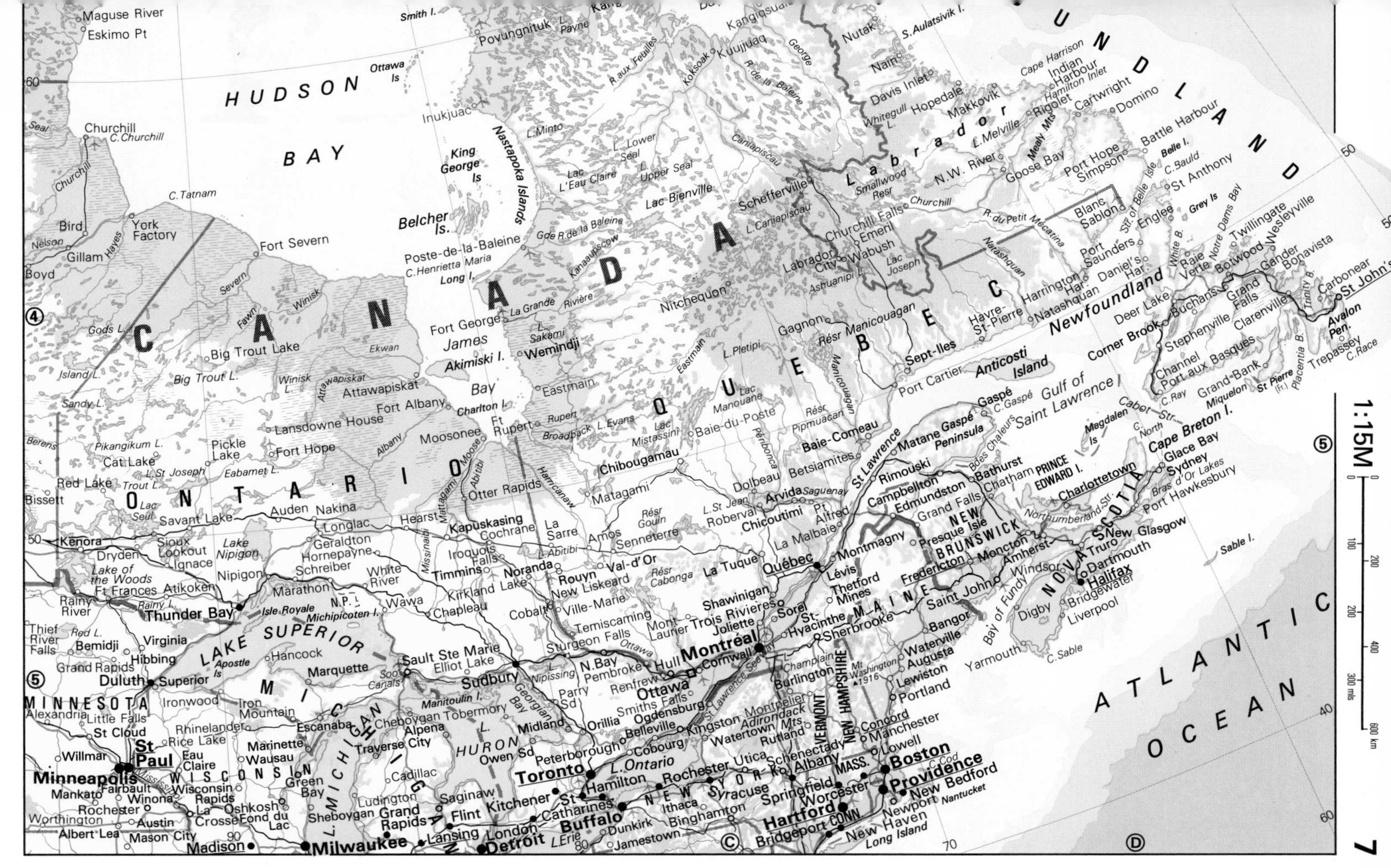
1:15M
0 200 400 600 km
0 100 200 300 mls
CANADA
ONTARIO
QUEBEC
NEWFOUNDLAND
Labrador
NEW BRUNSWICK
NOVA SCOTIA
PRINCE EDWARD I.
MAINE
NEW HAMPSHIRE
VERMONT
MASS.
CONN.
NEW YORK
MINNESOTA
WISCONSIN
MICHIGAN
HUDSON BAY
James Bay
ATLANTIC OCEAN
LAKE SUPERIOR
L. HURON
L. Ontario
L. Erie
Gulf of Saint Lawrence
Anticosti Island
Cape Breton I.
Nastapoka Islands
Belcher Is.
Akimiski I.
St John's
Gander
Corner Brook
Sept-Iles
Baie-Comeau
Gaspé
Charlottetown
Halifax
Sydney
Saint John
Fredericton
Moncton
Bangor
Augusta
Portland
Boston
Providence
Hartford
Québec
Montréal
Ottawa
Toronto
Hamilton
Buffalo
Rochester
Syracuse
Detroit
Milwaukee
Madison
St Paul
Minneapolis
Duluth
Thunder Bay
Sault Ste Marie
Sudbury
N. Bay
Timmins
Kapuskasing
Moosonee
Chibougamau
Churchill
York Factory
Labrador City
Schefferville
Goose Bay
Kuujjuaq
Inukjuac
Fort George
Sherbrooke
Trois Rivieres
Chicoutimi
Rimouski
Kingston
London
Lansing
Flint
Saginaw
Green Bay
Marquette
Kenora
Ft Frances

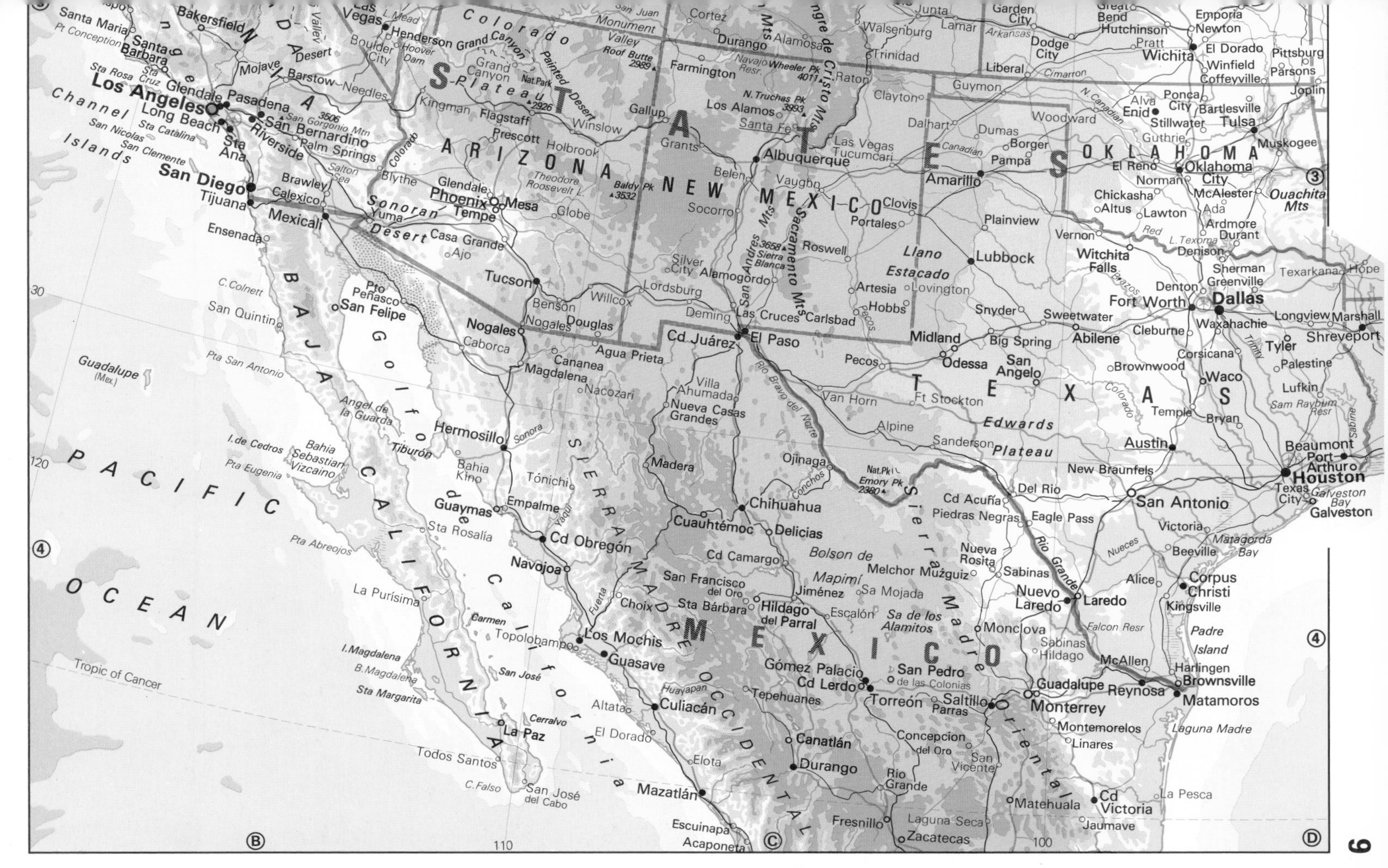
UNITED STATES
ARIZONA
NEW MEXICO
TEXAS
OKLAHOMA
MEXICO
BAJA CALIFORNIA
PACIFIC OCEAN
Golfo de California
SIERRA MADRE OCCIDENTAL
Sierra Madre Oriental
Colorado Plateau
Sonoran Desert
Painted Desert
Llano Estacado
Edwards Plateau
Sacramento Mts
Sangre de Cristo Mts
San Andres Mts
Ouachita Mts
Bolson de Mapimí
Channel Islands
Tropic of Cancer
Los Angeles
Long Beach
Glendale
Pasadena
San Bernardino
Riverside
Sta Ana
San Diego
Tijuana
Mexicali
Calexico
Brawley
Palm Springs
Barstow
Needles
Mojave
Bakersfield
Santa Barbara
Santa Maria
Pt Conception
Las Vegas
Henderson
Boulder City
Hoover Dam
Kingman
Flagstaff
Grand Canyon
Prescott
Phoenix
Mesa
Tempe
Casa Grande
Ajo
Tucson
Nogales
Benson
Douglas
Willcox
Globe
Holbrook
Winslow
Gallup
Grants
Farmington
Durango
Cortez
Albuquerque
Santa Fe
Los Alamos
Belen
Socorro
Las Vegas
Tucumcari
Clovis
Portales
Roswell
Artesia
Carlsbad
Hobbs
Alamogordo
Las Cruces
Deming
Lordsburg
Silver City
El Paso
Cd Juárez
Amarillo
Lubbock
Midland
Odessa
Big Spring
San Angelo
Abilene
Witchita Falls
Fort Worth
Dallas
Waco
Austin
San Antonio
Houston
Galveston
Beaumont
Port Arthur
Corpus Christi
Laredo
Nuevo Laredo
Brownsville
Matamoros
McAllen
Reynosa
Del Rio
Eagle Pass
Tyler
Shreveport
Texarkana
Oklahoma City
Tulsa
Muskogee
Wichita
Enid
Lawton
Dodge City
Garden City
Liberal
Monterrey
Saltillo
Torreón
Gómez Palacio
Cd Lerdo
Durango
Chihuahua
Delicias
Cuauhtémoc
Hildago del Parral
Culiacán
Los Mochis
Guasave
Cd Obregón
Navojoa
Guaymas
Empalme
Hermosillo
Caborca
Mazatlán
La Paz
San José del Cabo
Todos Santos
Ensenada
San Felipe
Pto Peñasco
San Quintin
Cd Victoria
Zacatecas
Fresnillo
Matehuala
Rio Grande
Rio Bravo del Norte
Guadalupe (Mex.)

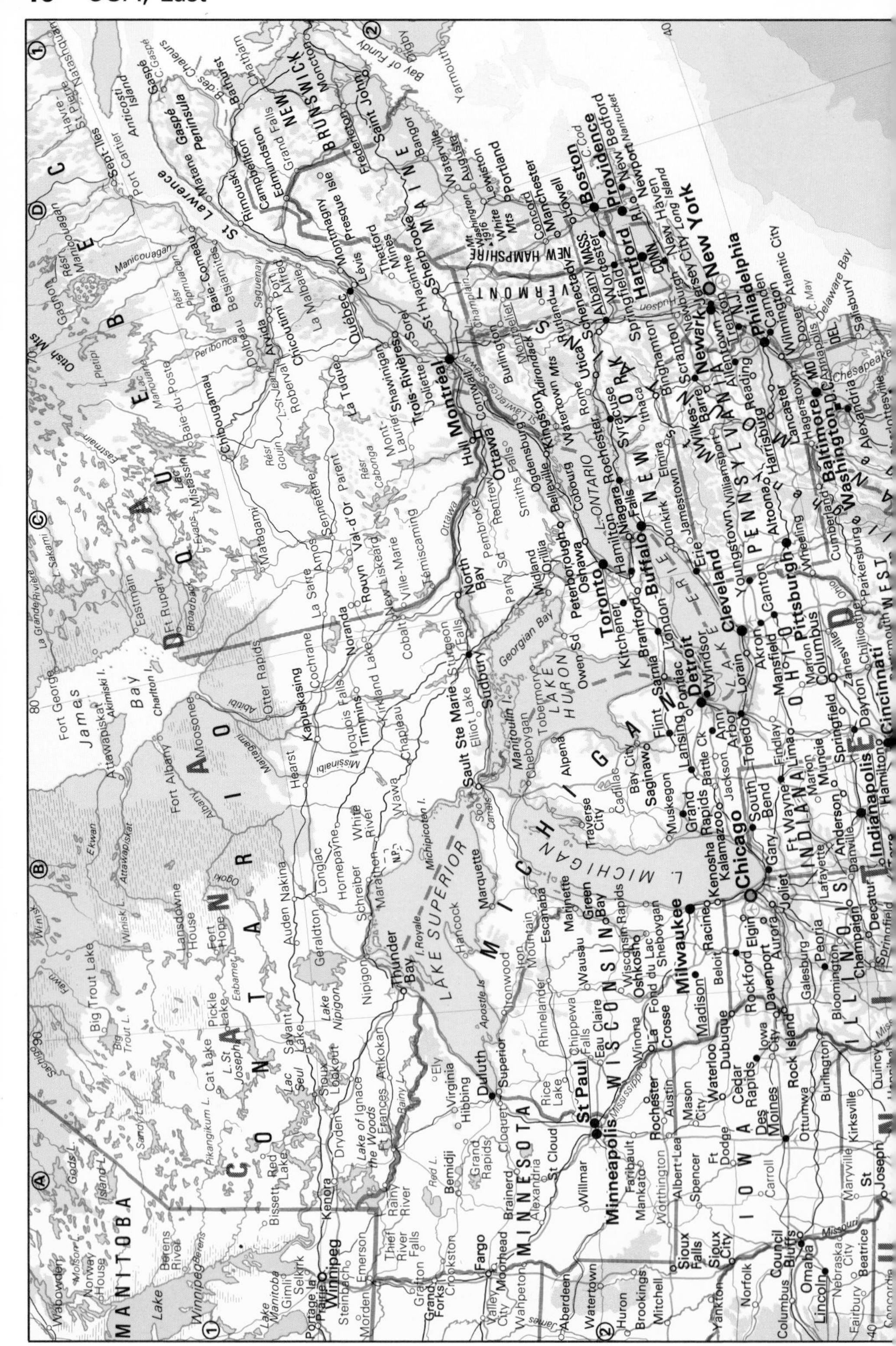

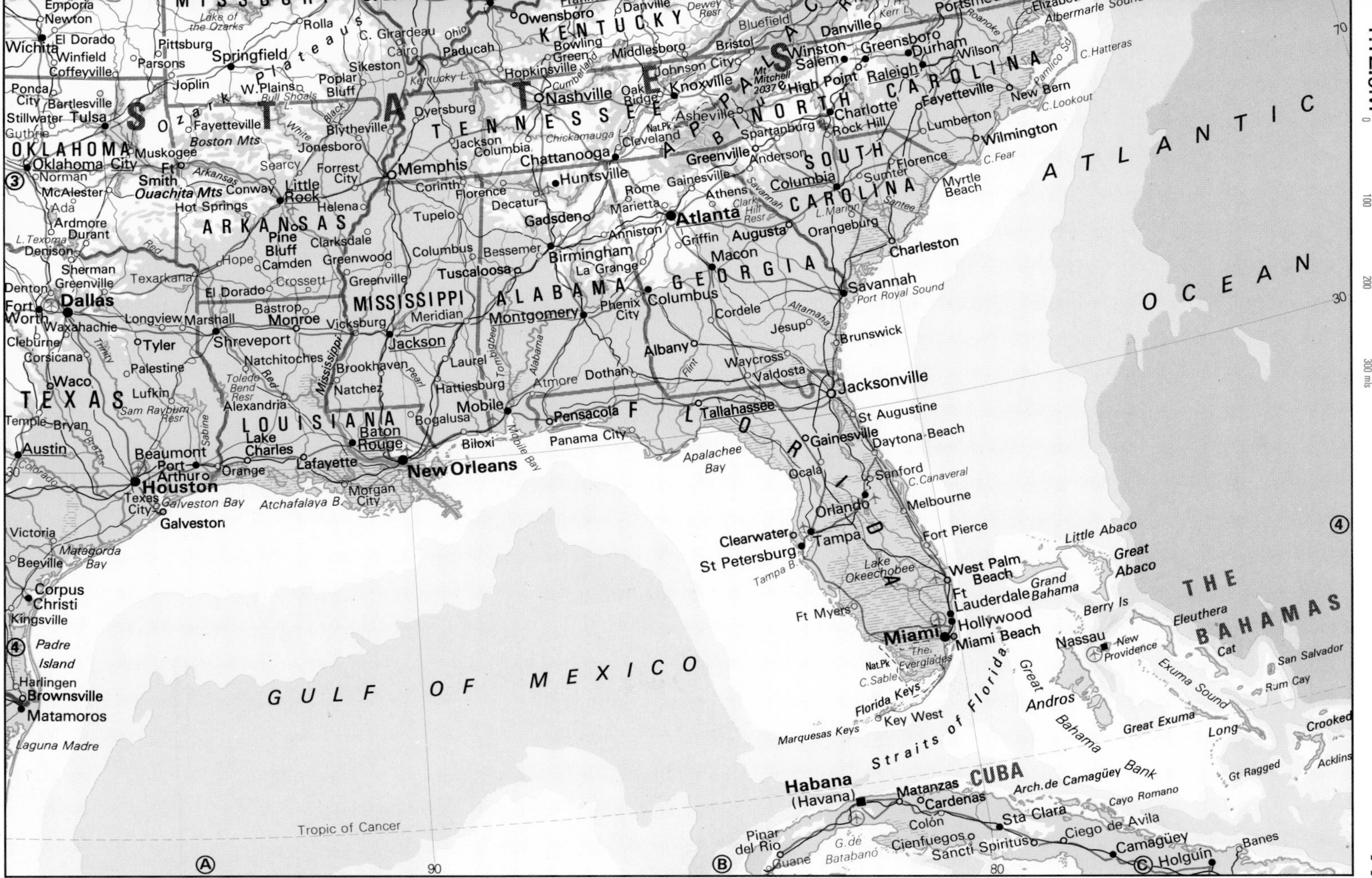

100 200 300 400 500 km
100 200 300 mls

ATLANTIC OCEAN

THE BAHAMAS

Albemarle Sound
C. Hatteras
Elizabeth City
Portsmouth
Roanoke
New Bern
C. Lookout
Wilson
C. Fear
Wilmington
Lumberton
Fayetteville
Jacksonville
Myrtle Beach
Florence
Charleston
Port Royal Sound
Savannah
Brunswick
St Augustine
Daytona Beach
Melbourne
Fort Pierce
West Palm Beach
Ft Lauderdale
Hollywood
Miami Beach
Miami

Acklins
Crooked I.
San Salvador
Rum Cay
Cat I.
Eleuthera
Great Abaco
Little Abaco
Grand Bahama
Berry Is
New Providence
Nassau
Andros
Great Bahama Bank
Exuma Sound
Long I.
Great Exuma
Gt Ragged I.
Banes
Holguín
Camagüey
Ciego de Ávila
Cayo Romano
Arch. de Camagüey
Sta Clara
Sancti Spíritus
Cienfuegos
Colón
Cárdenas
Matanzas
CUBA
Habana (Havana)
Pinar del Río
G. de Batabanó
Isla de la Juventud
Guane

Straits of Florida
Key West
Florida Keys
Marquesas Keys
C. Sable
Everglades
Nat Pk
Lake Okeechobee
FLORIDA
Ft Myers
Tampa B.
St Petersburg
Clearwater
Tampa
Orlando
Sanford
C. Canaveral
Ocala
Gainesville
Jacksonville
Valdosta
Waycross
Jesup
Tallahassee
Apalachee Bay
Panama City
Pensacola
Dothan
Albany
Cordele
Columbus
Phenix City
Macon
Griffin
Atlanta
Marietta
Rome
Gadsden
Anniston
Athens
Gainesville
Greenville
Anderson
Spartanburg
Rock Hill
Charlotte
Columbia
Orangeburg
Sumter
GEORGIA
SOUTH CAROLINA
NORTH CAROLINA

Raleigh
Durham
Chapel Hill
High Point
Greensboro
Winston-Salem
Salem
Danville
Asheville
Mt Mitchell 2037
Johnson City
Bristol
Bluefield
Kingsport
Knoxville
Oak Ridge
Cleveland
Chattanooga
Huntsville
Decatur
Florence
Tuscaloosa
Bessemer
Birmingham
La Grange
Montgomery
Alabama
Tombigbee
Selma
ALABAMA
TENNESSEE
KENTUCKY
Nashville
Murfreesboro
Columbia
Jackson
Dyersburg
Memphis
Corinth
Tupelo
Columbus
Greenwood
Greenville
Clarksdale
MISSISSIPPI
Meridian
Laurel
Hattiesburg
Mobile
Mobile Bay
Biloxi
Gulfport
Pascagoula
Bogalusa
Brookhaven
Natchez
Jackson
Vicksburg
Baton Rouge
New Orleans
Morgan City
Lafayette
Atchafalaya B.
Lake Charles
Orange
LOUISIANA
Beaumont
Port Arthur
Galveston
Houston
Galveston Bay
Texas City

GULF OF MEXICO

Tropic of Cancer

90

Emporia
Newton
Wichita
El Dorado
Winfield
Coffeyville
Ponca City
Stillwater
Tulsa
Bartlesville
Guthrie
Oklahoma City
Norman
OKLAHOMA
Ada
McAlester
Durant
Denison
Sherman
Ardmore
Fort Worth
Dallas
Denton
Waxahachie
Cleburne
Corsicana
Waco
Temple
Bryan
Austin
Victoria
Beeville
Corpus Christi
Kingsville
Padre Island
Harlingen
Brownsville
Matamoros
Laguna Madre
Matagorda Bay
TEXAS

Joplin
Springfield
Lake of the Ozarks
OZARK PLATEAU
Rolla
Pittsburg
Parsons
Fayetteville
Boston Mts
Ouachita Mts
Hot Springs
Little Rock
Conway
Searcy
Jonesboro
Forrest City
Helena
ARKANSAS
Pine Bluff
Camden
El Dorado
Hope
Texarkana
Bastrop
Monroe
Marshall
Longview
Tyler
Palestine
Lufkin
Shreveport
Natchitoches
Alexandria
Red River
Sam Rayburn Resr

MISSOURI
KENTUCKY
Paducah
Cairo
Owensboro
Bowling Green
Hopkinsville
Clarksville
Dyersburg
W. Plains
Poplar Bluff
Blytheville

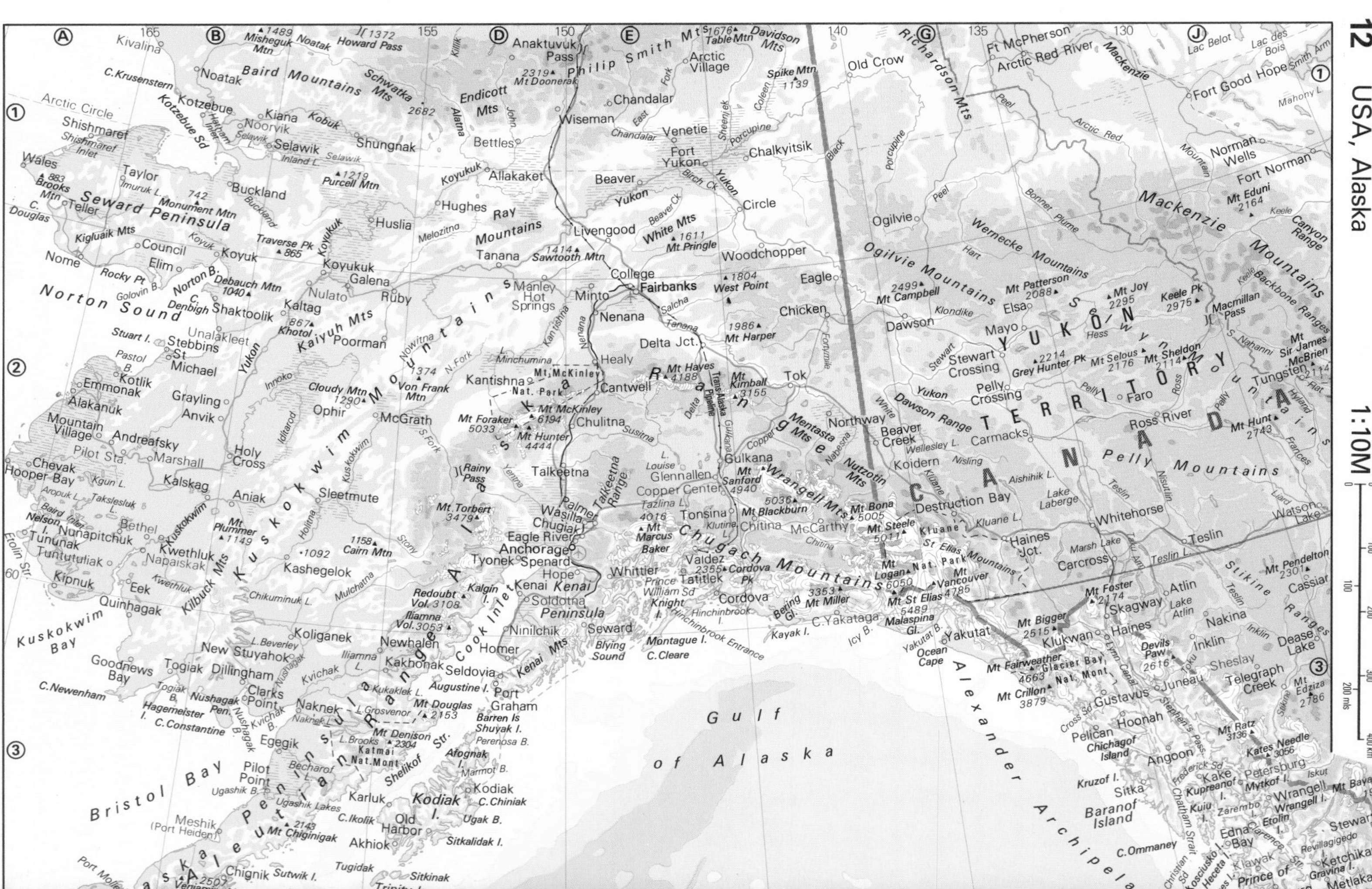

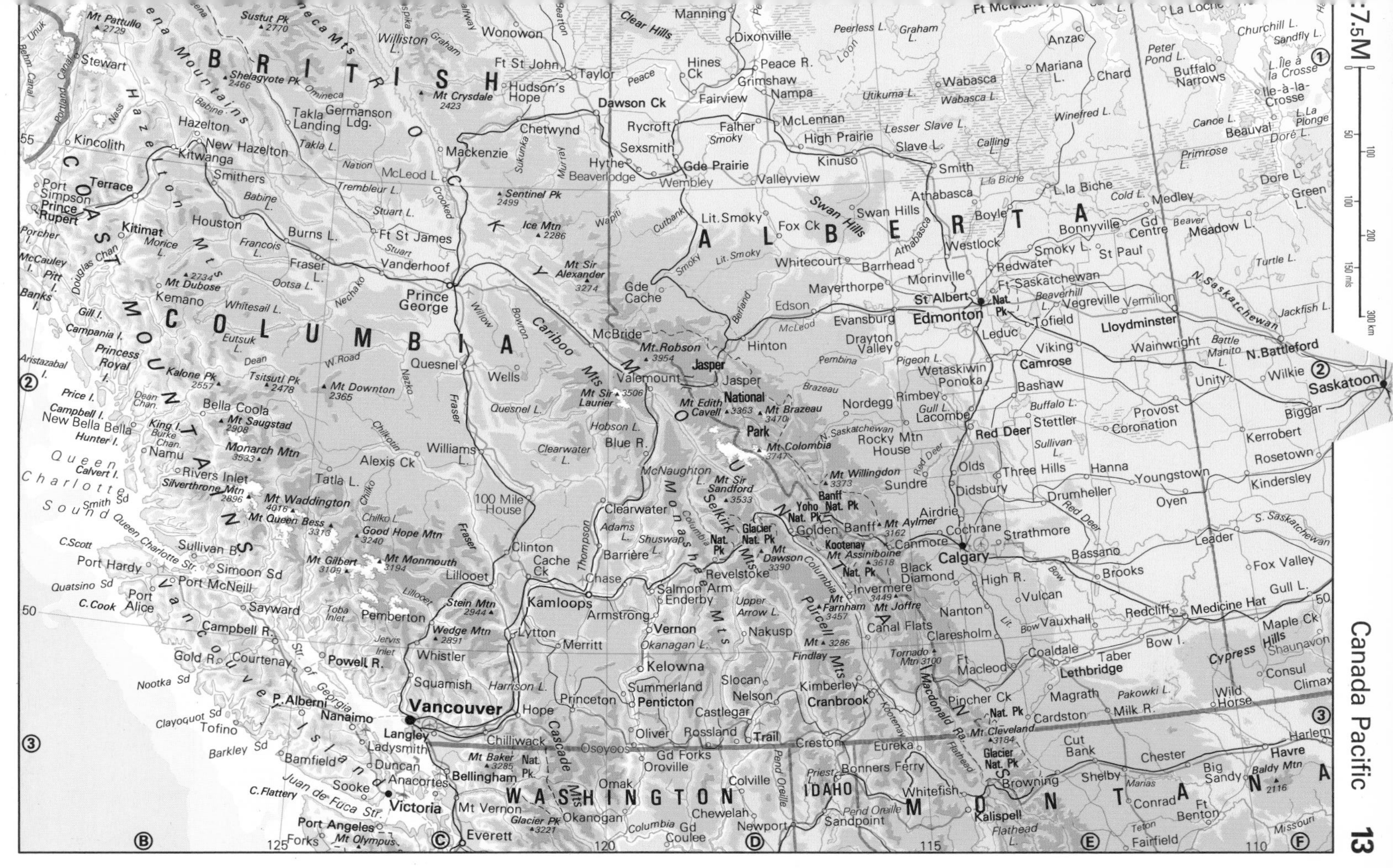
BRITISH COLUMBIA
ALBERTA
MONTANA
WASHINGTON
IDAHO
COAST MOUNTAINS
ROCKY MOUNTAINS
Cariboo Mts
Monashee Mts
Selkirk Mts
Purcell Mts
Cascade Mts
Hazelton Mts
Skeena Mountains
Swan Hills
Clear Hills
Cypress Hills
Vancouver Island
Queen Charlotte Sound
Str. of Georgia
Juan de Fuca Str.
Saskatoon
N. Battleford
Lloydminster
Edmonton
St Albert
Red Deer
Calgary
Medicine Hat
Lethbridge
Camrose
Banff
Jasper
Dawson Ck
Prince George
Prince Rupert
Kamloops
Kelowna
Vernon
Penticton
Nelson
Trail
Cranbrook
Vancouver
Victoria
Nanaimo
Kalispell
Havre
Mt Robson 3954
Mt Waddington 4016
Jasper National Park
Glacier Nat. Pk
Yoho Nat. Pk
Kootenay Nat. Pk
Banff Nat. Pk
N. Saskatchewan
S. Saskatchewan
Fraser
Columbia
Thompson
Peace
Athabasca
Smoky
125 120 115 110
50 55

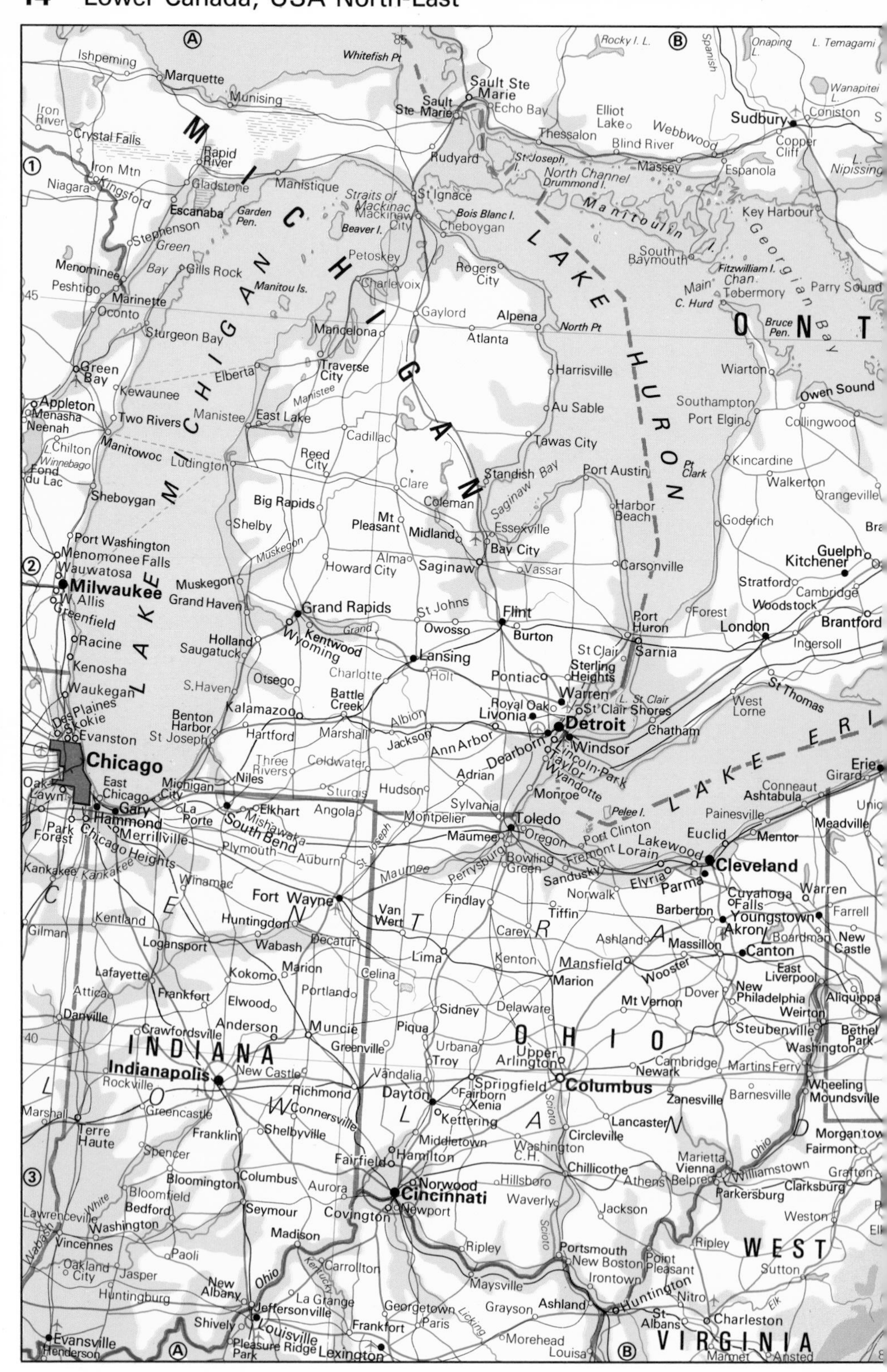

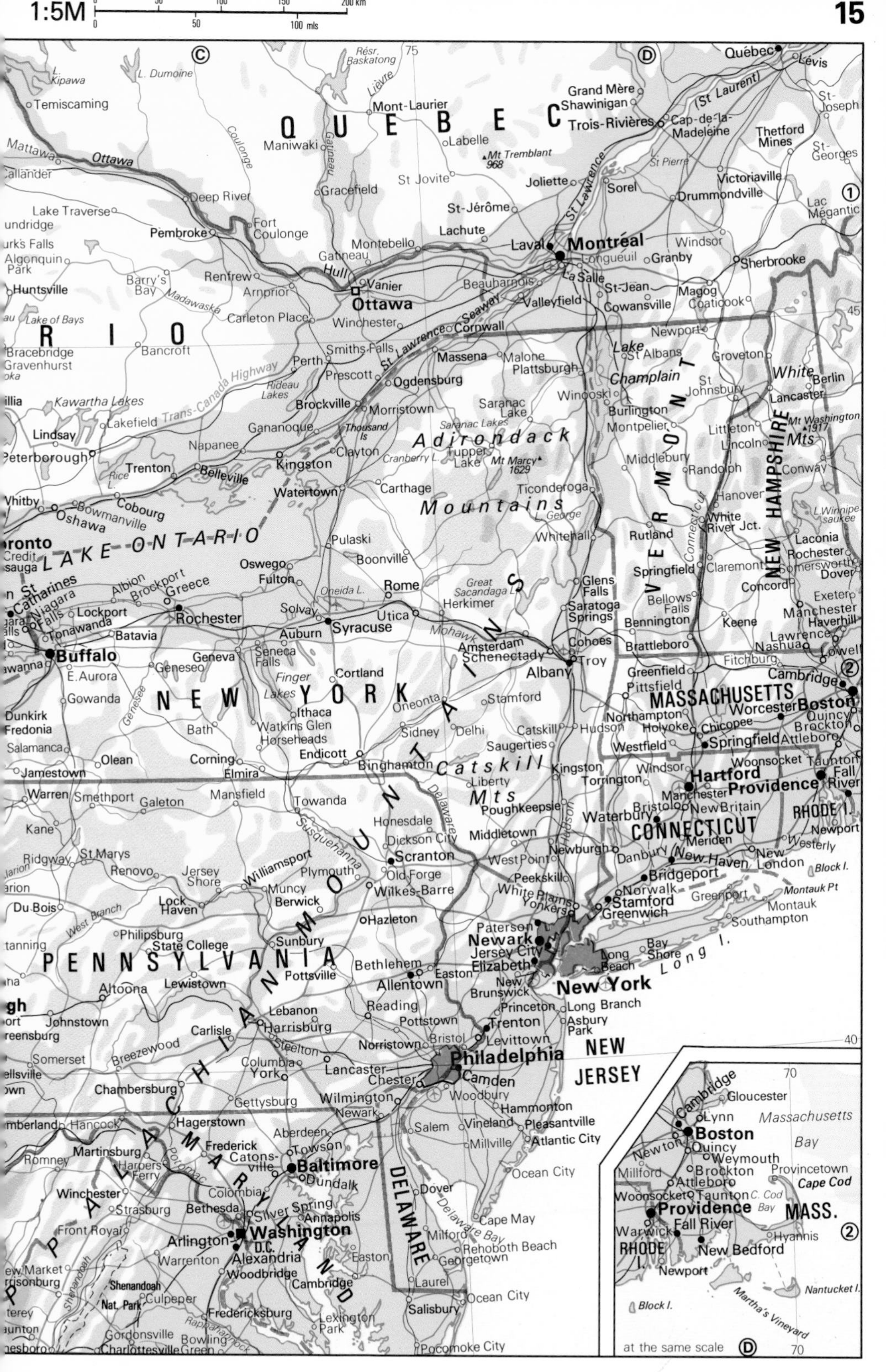
C
D
Résr. Baskatong
75
Québec
Lévis
L. Kipawa
L. Dumoine
Lièvre
Temiscaming
Mont-Laurier
Grand Mère
Shawinigan
(St Laurent)
St-Joseph
QUEBEC
Trois-Rivières
Cap-de-la-Madeleine
Thetford Mines
Coulonge
Gatineau
Labelle
Mt Tremblant 968
St-Georges
Mattawa
Ottawa
Maniwaki
St Pierre
Callander
St Jovite
Joliette
Sorel
Victoriaville
Gracefield
St Lawrence
Drummondville
1
Deep River
Lac Mégantic
Lake Traverse
St-Jérôme
Bundridge
Fort Coulonge
Lachute
Pembroke
Burk's Falls
Montebello
Laval
Montréal
Windsor
Algonquin Park
Gatineau
Longueuil
Granby
Sherbrooke
Hull
La Salle
Renfrew
Beauharnois
St-Jean
Huntsville
Barry's Bay
Vanier
Magog
Arnprior
Ottawa
Valleyfield
Cowansville
Coaticook
Madawaska
Lake of Bays
Carleton Place
Winchester
Seaway
Cornwall
45
RIO
Bancroft
St Lawrence
Newport
Bracebridge
Gravenhurst
Smiths Falls
Massena
Malone
Lake
St Albans
Groveton
Perth
Plattsburgh
Trans-Canada Highway
Rideau Lakes
Prescott
Ogdensburg
Champlain
White
Berlin
St Johnsbury
Lancaster
Kawartha Lakes
Brockville
Morristown
Saranac Lake
Winooski
Lakefield
Burlington
Mt Washington 1917
Lindsay
Gananoque
Thousand Is
Saranac Lakes
Montpelier
Littleton
Adirondack
Mts
Napanee
Clayton
Tupper Lake
Lincoln
Peterborough
Kingston
Cranberry L.
Mt Marcy 1629
Middlebury
Trenton
Randolph
Conway
Belleville
Rice L.
Carthage
Ticonderoga
Watertown
Hanover
Whitby
Cobourg
Mountains
VERMONT
NEW HAMPSHIRE
Bowmanville
L. George
White River Jct.
L. Winnipesaukee
Oshawa
Connecticut
Toronto
LAKE ONTARIO
Whitehall
Rutland
Laconia
Credit
Pulaski
Rochester
Mississauga
Boonville
Springfield
Claremont
Somersworth
Dover
Oswego
Glens Falls
Concord
St Catharines
Niagara
Albion
Brockport
Greece
Fulton
Rome
Great Sacandaga L.
Bellows Falls
Exeter
Oneida L.
Saratoga Springs
Manchester
Niagara Falls
Lockport
Rochester
Solvay
Herkimer
Haverhill
Tonawanda
Utica
Bennington
Keene
Lawrence
Batavia
Auburn
Syracuse
Mohawk
Lowell
Amsterdam
Cohoes
Nashua
Brattleboro
Buffalo
Geneva
Seneca Falls
Schenectady
Troy
Lackawanna
Geneseo
Albany
Greenfield
Fitchburg
2
E. Aurora
Finger Lakes
Cortland
Pittsfield
Cambridge
Gowanda
Genesee
NEW YORK
Oneonta
Stamford
MASSACHUSETTS
Worcester
Boston
Quincy
Dunkirk
Ithaca
Northampton
Brockton
Fredonia
Bath
Watkins Glen
Sidney
Delhi
Catskill
Hudson
Holyoke
Chicopee
Horseheads
Springfield
Attleboro
Salamanca
Endicott
Saugerties
Westfield
Olean
Corning
Binghamton
Catskill
Kingston
Windsor
Woonsocket
Taunton
Fall River
Jamestown
Elmira
Liberty
Torrington
Hartford
Providence
Warren
Smethport
Galeton
Mansfield
Towanda
Mts
Manchester
Bristol
New Britain
RHODE I.
Poughkeepsie
Hudson
Kane
Honesdale
Waterbury
CONNECTICUT
Newport
Susquehanna
Delaware
Middletown
Dickson City
Meriden
Westerly
St Marys
Newburgh
New London
Ridgway
Renovo
Williamsport
Scranton
West Point
Danbury
New Haven
Block I.
Jersey Shore
Plymouth
Old Forge
Peekskill
Bridgeport
Clearfield
Muncy
Montauk Pt
Lock Haven
Berwick
Wilkes-Barre
White Plains
Norwalk
Stamford
Greenport
Du Bois
Montauk
West Branch
Yonkers
Greenwich
Southampton
Hazleton
Philipsburg
Paterson
State College
Sunbury
Newark
Bay Shore
Long I.
Punxsutawney
Jersey City
Long Beach
PENNSYLVANIA
Bethlehem
Elizabeth
Pottsville
Allentown
Easton
Altoona
Lewistown
New Brunswick
New York
Pittsburgh
Lebanon
Reading
Princeton
Long Branch
Johnstown
Pottstown
Asbury Park
Greensburg
Carlisle
Harrisburg
Trenton
Steelton
Bristol
Levittown
Breezewood
Norristown
NEW JERSEY
Somerset
Columbia
Lancaster
Philadelphia
40
York
Chester
Camden
Chambersburg
JERSEY
Woodbury
Gettysburg
Wilmington
Hammonton
Newark
Pleasantville
Cumberland
Hancock
Hagerstown
Salem
Vineland
Atlantic City
Aberdeen
Frederick
Martinsburg
Towson
Millville
Romney
Catonsville
Baltimore
Harpers Ferry
Dundalk
Ocean City
Potomac
DELAWARE
Dover
Winchester
Columbia
Delaware Bay
Strasburg
Bethesda
Silver Spring
Annapolis
Cape May
Front Royal
MARYLAND
Milford
Arlington
Washington
Rehoboth Beach
D.C.
Georgetown
Alexandria
Easton
New Market
Warrenton
Harrisonburg
Woodbridge
Cambridge
Shenandoah
Laurel
Shenandoah Nat. Park
Culpeper
Ocean City
Salisbury
Fredericksburg
Lexington Park
Rappahannock
Gordonsville
Bowling Green
Charlottesville
Pocomoke City
APPALACHIAN MOUNTAINS
70
Cambridge
Gloucester
Lynn
Massachusetts Bay
Boston
Newton
Quincy
Weymouth
Millford
Brockton
Provincetown
Cape Cod
Attleboro
Woonsocket
Taunton
C. Cod Bay
MASS.
Providence
Warwick
Fall River
Hyannis
2
RHODE I.
New Bedford
Newport
Nantucket I.
Block I.
Martha's Vineyard
at the same scale
D
70

0 25 50 75 100 km
0 25 50 mils

Map labels (top section):

Cobleskill, Richmondville, Schoharie, Middleburgh, Cohoes, Watervliet, Troy, Rensselaer, Albany, Nassau, Ravena, Coxsackie, Chatham, Catskill, Catskill, Gt Barrington, Stockbridge, Lee, Lenox, Pittsfield, Dalton, Cheshire, Mt Greylock 1064, Adams, N. Adams, Williamstown, Readsboro, Hinsdale, Winchester, Greenfield, Shelburne Falls, S. Deerfield, Turners Falls, Northfield, Winchendon, Athol, Gardner, Leominster, Clinton, Fitchburg, Nashua, Greenville, Haverhill, Methuen, Lawrence, Dracut, Lowell, Newburyp, Ipswich, Gloucester, Beverly, Salem, Lynn, Marblehead, Cambridge, Boston, Waltham, Newton, Brookline, Quincy, Weymouth

Stamford, Grand Gorge, Prattsville, Catskill Mountains, NEW YORK, Shandaken, Slide Mtn 1281, Ashokan Res, Kingston, Saugerties, Woodstock, Liberty, Ellenville, New Paltz, Monticello, Otisville, Walden, Newburgh, Middletown, Port Jervis, Milford, Sussex, Warwick, Franklin, Newton, Hamburg, Haverstraw, Pompton Lakes, Suffern, Ramsey, Butler, White Plains, Paterson, Clifton, Passaic, Dover, Morristown, NEW Newark, JERSEY, Bernardsville, Somerville, Elizabeth, Jersey City

Otis, Ancram, Mt Everett 793, Mt Washington, Canaan, Winsted, Thompsonville, Windsor Locks, Stafford Springs, Putnam, Woonsocket, Attleboro, Central Falls, Pawtucket, Providence, Cranston, Warwick, RHODE ISLAND, Taunton, Brockton, Bridgewater, Plymouth, Middleb, Somerset, Warren, Bristol, Fall River, New Bedford

Millerton, Rhinebeck, Amenia, Torrington, Hartford, New Britain, Manchester, Rockville, Willimantic, Moosup, Jewett City, Colchester, Norwich, Uncasville, Mystic, Westerly, Newport, MASSACHUSETTS, Springfield, Holyoke, Chicopee, Westfield, Worcester, Framingham, Marlboro, Southbridge, Webster, Mansfield, Franklin, Milford, Norwood, Stoughton, Oxford, Ware, Barre, Amherst, Northampton, Easthampton, Monson, Quabbin Resv, Wachusett Res

Poughkeepsie, Hyde Park, Millbrook, Wappingers Falls, Beacon, Highland Falls, Carmel, Brewster, Danbury, Bethel, Derby, Bristol, Waterbury, Naugatuck, Meriden, Wallingford, Middletown, CONNECTICUT, Hamden, Seymour, Deep River, Old Lyme, Clinton, New Haven, New London, Stamford, Greenwich, Port Chester, Bridgeport, Milford, Stratford, Fairfield, Norwalk, New Canaan, Peekskill, Ossining, Tarrytown, Nyack, Yonkers, Bronx, Queens, Brooklyn, New York, Staten I., Long Beach, Huntington, Bay Shore, Sayville, Patchogue, Pt Jefferson, Riverhead, Center Moriches, Southampton, East Hampton, Montauk, Montauk Pt, Sag Harbor, Greenport, Mattituck, Kings Park, Great South Bay, Long Island, Long Island Sound, Block Island Sd, Block Island, Fishers I., Gardiners I., Rhode Island Sound, Martha's Vineyard, Nomans Land, Buzzards Bay

ATLANTIC OCEAN

Map labels (bottom section):

Milton, Bloomsburg, Danville, Catawissa, Hazleton, Lewisburg, Sunbury, Shamokin, Mt Carmel, Frackville, Mahanoy City, Tamaqua, Lansford, Lehighton, Palmerton, Stroudsburg, Bangor, Hackettstown, Netcong, Dover, Morristown, Butler, Paterson, Clifton, Passaic, White Plains, Po Ches, Yonkers, Newton, Bronx, New York, Queens, Brooklyn, Elizabeth, Milroy, McClure, Burnham, Lewistown, Mifflintown, Middleburg, Herndon, Minersville, Pottsville, Schuylkill Haven, Hamburg, Whitehall, Allentown, Bethlehem, Easton, Phillipsburg, Washington, Belvidere, Clinton, Somerville, New Brunswick, Perth Amboy, Raritan Bay, Amboy, Atlantic Highlands, Staten I., Long Branch, Newport, Duncannon, Dauphin, Lykens, Tremont, Pine Grove, Womelsdorf, Blue Mt, Reading, Boyertown, Emmaus, Quakertown, Flemington, Lambertville, South River, Red Bank, Highstown, Freehold, Harrisburg, Palmyra, Hershey, Lebanon, Shillington, Soudertown, Lansdale, Princeton, Trenton, Asbury Park, Manasquan, Point Pleasant, Steelton, Middletown, Lititz, Elizabethtown, Ephrata, Pottstown, Phoenixville, Norristown, Warminster, Morrisville, Levittown, Bordentown, Lakewood, Lakehurst, Breton Woods, Carlisle, Mt Holly Springs, Dillsburg, Manchester, Columbia, Lancaster, Coatesville, Downingtown, W. Chester, Philadelphia, Doylestown, Bristol, Burlington, Toms River, Seaside Park, York, Red Lion, Parkesburg, Kennett Square, Chester, Camden, Mt Holly, Willingboro, Chatsworth, Gettysburg, Hanover, Glen Rock, Stewartstown, Rising Sun, Wilmington, Newark, Woodbury, Atco, Barnegat Bay, Barnegat, Surf City, Waynesboro, Littlestown, Emmitsburg, Westminster, Reisterstown, Havre de Grace, Bel Air, Aberdeen, Elkton, Salem, Penns Grove, Glassboro, Woodstown, Hammonton, Egg Harbor City, Beach Haven, Frederick, Towson, Cockeysville, Edgewood, Middletown, Vineland, Mays Landing, Great Bay, Mt Airy, MARYLAND, Ellicott City, Damascus, Columbia, Catonsville, Baltimore, Dundalk, Glen Burnie, Cecilton, Bridgeton, Millville, Pleasantville, Atlantic City, Leesburg, Gaithersburg, Rockville, Laurel, College Park, Bowie, Queenstown, Centreville, Port Norris, Woodbine, Ocean City, Wheaton, Silver Spring, Bethesda, Queen Anne, Denton, Harrington, Smyrna, Dover, Milford, Stone Harbor, Wildwood, Somers Point, Great Egg Harbor, Arlington, Washington D.C., Fairfax, Alexandria, Mayo, St Michaels, Greenwood, C. May Pt, Cape May, C. Henlopen, DELAWARE Bay, Delaware, Frederica, PENN., NEW JERSEY

ATLANTIC OCEAN

72 74

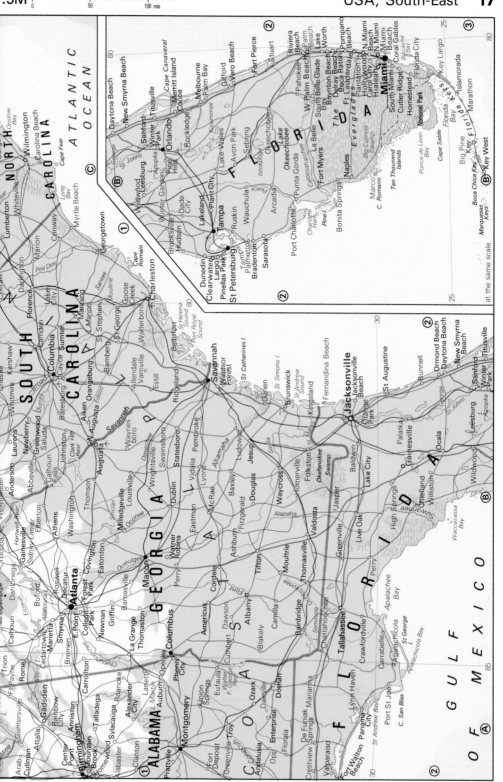

:5M

| 0 | 50 | 100 | 150 | 200 km |
| 0 | | 50 | 100 mls | |

ATLANTIC OCEAN

NORTH CAROLINA

Onslow Bay
Wilmington
Carolina Beach
Cape Fear
Long Bay
Myrtle Beach
Georgetown
Cape Romain
Charleston

Lumberton
Whiteville
Conway
Marion
Pee Dee
Darlington
Florence
Lake City

SOUTH CAROLINA

Kershaw
Camden
Sumter
Manning
St Stephens
Goose Creek
Summerville
St George
Walterboro
Beaufort
St Helena Sound
Port Royal Sound

Columbia
Cayce
Orangeburg
Bamberg
Allendale
Varnville
Estill
Ridgeland

Chester
Whitmire
Newberry
Saluda
Batesburg
Aiken
Augusta
Waynesboro

Anderson
Abbeville
Greenwood
Calhoun Falls
Johnston
Clark Hill Resr
Thomson
Washington
Elberton

Laurens
Westminster
Athens
Oconee

FLORIDA

Daytona Beach
New Smyrna Beach
Cape Canaveral
Merritt Island
Cocoa
Melbourne
Palm Bay
Gifford
Vero Beach
Fort Pierce
Stuart
Riviera Beach
W. Palm Beach
Palm Beach
Lake Worth
Boynton Beach
Delray Beach
Pompano Beach
Boca Raton
Ft. Lauderdale
Hollywood
N. Miami Beach
N. Miami
Miami
Miami Beach
South Miami
Coral Gables
Hialeah
Cutler Ridge
Homestead
Florida City
National Park

Titusville
Orlando
Winter Park
Sanford
Apopka
Leesburg
Wildwood
Winter Garden
Pine Hills
Kissimmee
Lake Wales
Avon Park
Sebring
Okeechobee
Lake Okeechobee
Pahokee
Belle Glade
South Bay
La Belle
Big Cypress Swamp
Everglades
The Everglades

Brooksville
Hudson
Dade City
Plant City
Lakeland
Winter Haven
Wauchula
Arcadia
Punta Gorda
Port Charlotte
Charlotte Harb.
Pine I.
Fort Myers
Naples
Bonita Springs
Marco
C. Romano
Ten Thousand Islands
Cape Sable
C. Sable

Dunedin
Clearwater
Largo
Pinellas Park
St Petersburg
Tampa
Palmetto
Bradenton
Sarasota

Ponce de Leon Bay

Florida Keys
Key Largo
Islamorada
Marathon
Big Pine Key
Boca Chica Key
Key West
Marquesas Keys

GEORGIA

Atlanta
Roswell
Marietta
Smyrna
Decatur
E. Point
Forest Park
College Park
Newnan
Griffin
La Grange
Thomaston
Barnesville

Macon
Covington
Eatonton
Milledgeville
Gray
Warner Robins
Perry
Dublin
Wrightsville
Swainsboro
Statesboro
Vidalia
Lyons
Eastman
McRae
Ashburn
Fitzgerald

Americus
Cordele
Dawson
Cuthbert
Albany
Camilla
Blakely
Bainbridge

Columbus
Phenix City
Opelika
Auburn
Union Springs
Eufaula
Ozark
Dothan

Savannah
Hinesville
Ludowici
Jesup
Baxley
Douglas
Waycross
Homerville
Valdosta
Moultrie
Thomasville
Tifton

Brunswick
St Simons I.
Kingsland
Fernandina Beach
Darien
Okefenokee Swamp
Folkston

ALABAMA

Montgomery
Prattville
Troy
Enterprise
Andalusia
Opp
Florala
De Funiak Springs
Crestview

FLORIDA

Jacksonville
Jacksonville Beach
Orange Park
St Augustine
Palatka
Gainesville
Ocala
Bunnell
Ormond Beach
Daytona Beach
New Smyrna Beach
Titusville
Sanford
Winter Park
Leesburg
Wildwood
High Springs
Lake City
Live Oak
Jasper
Greenville
Perry
Tallahassee
Crawfordville
Carrabelle
Apalachicola
Port St Joe
Panama City
Lynn Haven
Valparaiso
Fort Walton Beach

GULF OF MEXICO

St Johns
Suwannee
Waccasassa Bay
Apalachee Bay
St George
Apalachicola Bay
St Andrew Bay
C. San Blas
St Joseph Bay
St George Bay
C. St George

at the same scale

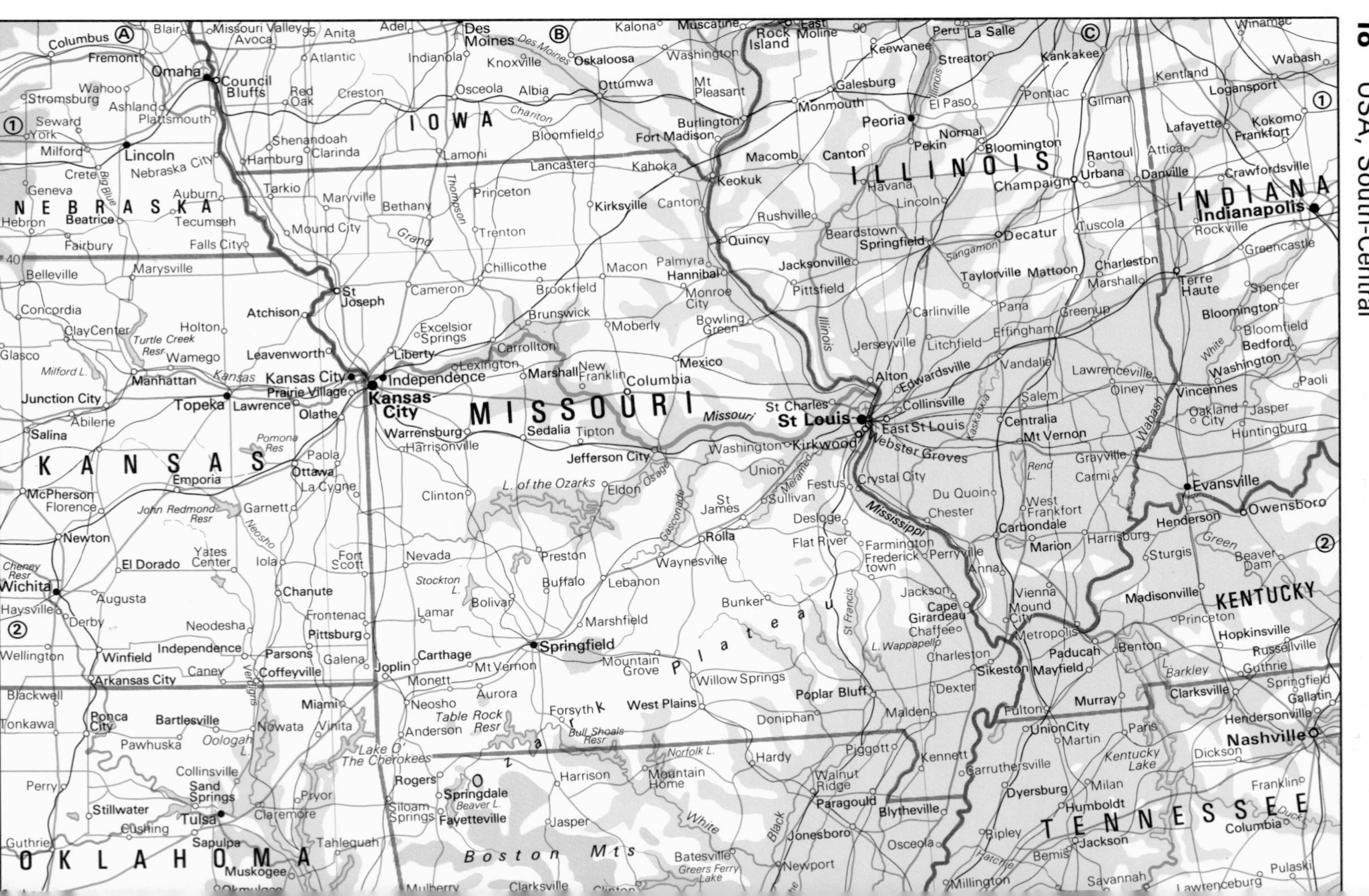
NEBRASKA
IOWA
KANSAS
MISSOURI
ILLINOIS
INDIANA
KENTUCKY
TENNESSEE
OKLAHOMA
Ozark Plateau
Boston Mts
Omaha
Council Bluffs
Lincoln
Des Moines
St Joseph
Kansas City
Independence
Topeka
Wichita
Tulsa
Muskogee
Springfield
Jefferson City
Columbia
St Louis
East St Louis
Peoria
Springfield
Champaign
Decatur
Indianapolis
Terre Haute
Evansville
Owensboro
Paducah
Nashville
Clarksville
Joplin
Fayetteville
Poplar Bluff
Cape Girardeau
Mississippi
Missouri
Illinois
Wabash
L. of the Ozarks
Table Rock Resr
Lake O' The Cherokees

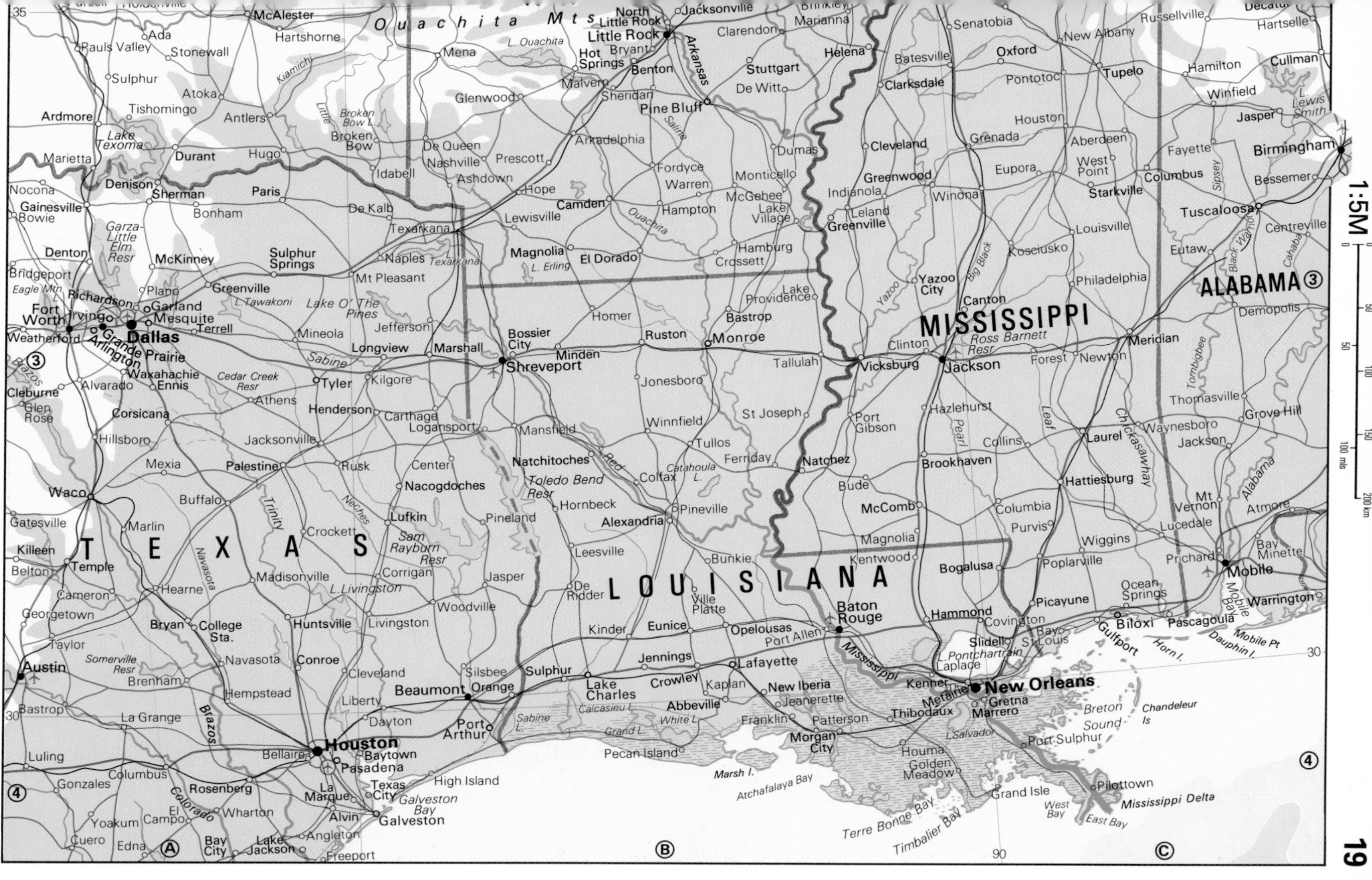
TEXAS
LOUISIANA
MISSISSIPPI
ALABAMA ③
Ouachita Mts
McAlester
Hartshorne
Ada
Pauls Valley
Stonewall
Sulphur
Atoka
Tishomingo
Ardmore
Antlers
Lake Texoma
Marietta
Durant
Hugo
Denison
Sherman
Nocona
Gainesville
Bowie
Bonham
Paris
De Kalb
Texarkana
Denton
McKinney
Sulphur Springs
Bridgeport
Eagle Mtn
Richardson
Plano
Garland
Mesquite
Greenville
Fort Worth
Irving
Dallas
Grande Prairie
Arlington
Weatherford
Terrell
Waxahachie
Ennis
Cleburne
Alvarado
Glen Rose
Corsicana
Hillsboro
Mexia
Waco
Gatesville
Killeen
Belton
Temple
Marlin
Cameron
Georgetown
Taylor
Austin
Bastrop
Luling
Gonzales
Cuero
Yoakum
Edna
Bryan
College Sta.
Hearne
Navasota
Brenham
Hempstead
La Grange
Columbus
Rosenberg
Wharton
El Campo
Bay City
Lake Jackson
Angleton
Freeport
Houston
Pasadena
Baytown
Bellaire
La Marque
Texas City
Galveston
Galveston Bay
Alvin
High Island
Mena
Broken Bow
Idabell
De Queen
Nashville
Prescott
Ashdown
Hope
Glenwood
Malvern
Hot Springs
Arkadelphia
Little Rock
North Little Rock
Jacksonville
Bryant
Benton
Sheridan
Pine Bluff
Stuttgart
De Witt
Clarendon
Marianna
Helena
Camden
Fordyce
Warren
Hampton
Monticello
McGehee
Lake Village
Dumas
Magnolia
El Dorado
Lewisville
Crossett
Hamburg
Naples
Mt Pleasant
Jefferson
Mineola
Tyler
Longview
Kilgore
Marshall
Henderson
Carthage
Logansport
Jacksonville
Athens
Palestine
Rusk
Center
Nacogdoches
Lufkin
Crockett
Madisonville
Huntsville
Livingston
Conroe
Cleveland
Liberty
Dayton
Beaumont
Orange
Port Arthur
Silsbee
Woodville
Jasper
Corrigan
Pineland
Sam Rayburn Resr
Toledo Bend Resr
Bossier City
Shreveport
Minden
Homer
Ruston
Monroe
Bastrop
Lake Providence
Tallulah
Jonesboro
Winnfield
Tullos
Ferriday
St Joseph
Natchitoches
Mansfield
Hornbeck
Colfax
Alexandria
Pineville
Leesville
De Ridder
Bunkie
Ville Platte
Eunice
Kinder
Opelousas
Port Allen
Baton Rouge
Jennings
Lafayette
Crowley
Kaplan
Abbeville
Lake Charles
Sulphur
New Iberia
Jeanerette
Franklin
Patterson
Morgan City
Pecan Island
Marsh I.
Atchafalaya Bay
Houma
Golden Meadow
Thibodaux
Kenner
Metairie
New Orleans
Gretna
Marrero
Laplace
L. Pontchartrain
Slidell
Covington
Hammond
Bogalusa
Kentwood
Magnolia
McComb
Bude
Natchez
Port Gibson
Vicksburg
Clinton
Jackson
Ross Barnett Resr
Canton
Yazoo City
Hazlehurst
Brookhaven
Collins
Columbia
Purvis
Picayune
Poplarville
Wiggins
Hattiesburg
Laurel
Bay St Louis
Gulfport
Biloxi
Ocean Springs
Pascagoula
Mobile
Prichard
Mobile Bay
Dauphin I.
Mobile Pt
Horn I.
Chandeleur Is
Breton Sound
Port Sulphur
Pilottown
Mississippi Delta
Grand Isle
Terre Bonne Bay
Timbalier Bay
West Bay
East Bay
Greenville
Leland
Indianola
Greenwood
Cleveland
Clarksdale
Batesville
Senatobia
Oxford
Pontotoc
New Albany
Tupelo
Houston
Grenada
Winona
Eupora
Aberdeen
West Point
Starkville
Columbus
Louisville
Kosciusko
Philadelphia
Meridian
Forest
Newton
Waynesboro
Jackson
Thomasville
Grove Hill
Mt Vernon
Atmore
Lucedale
Bay Minette
Warrington
Tuscaloosa
Eutaw
Demopolis
Centreville
Bessemer
Birmingham
Fayette
Jasper
Winfield
Hamilton
Cullman
Hartselle
Russellville
Mississippi
Arkansas
Red
Sabine
Neches
Trinity
Brazos
Navasota
Colorado
Pearl
Leaf
Chickasawhay
Tombigbee
Alabama
Big Black
Yazoo
Ouachita
Saline
Ⓐ Ⓑ Ⓒ
③ ④
30 35 90

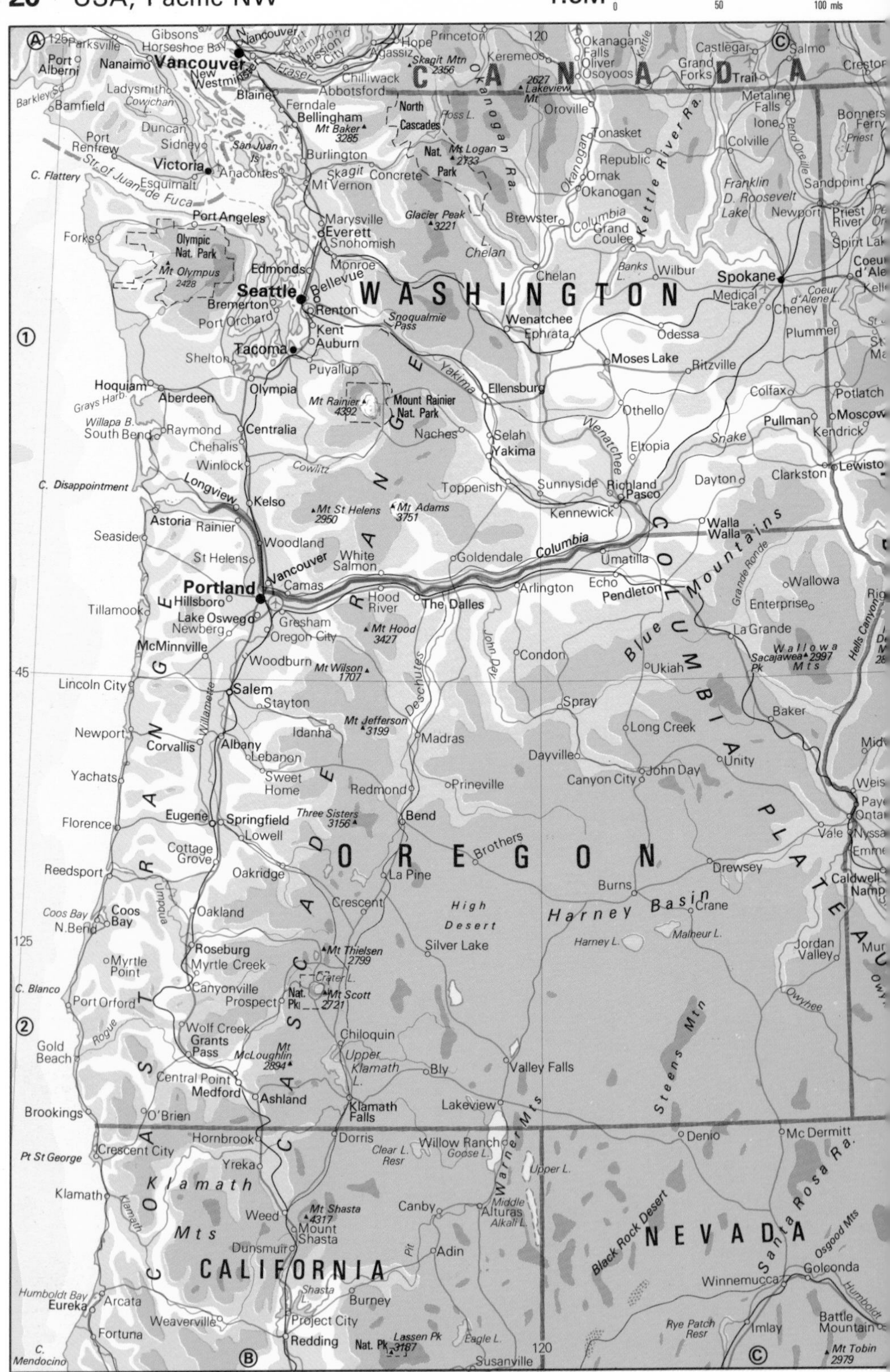

0 50 100 150 200 km
0 50 100 mls

PACIFIC OCEAN

California / Nevada map

Dunsmuir
Adin
120
Shasta
Burney
Arcata
Eureka
Fortuna
Weaverville
Project City
Redding
Nat. Pk.
Lassen Pk.
3187
Eagle L.
Chester
Susanville
Honey L.
Winnemucca
Goleonda
Humboldt
Emigrant Pass
Rye Patch Resr
Imlay
Battle Mountain
Mt Tobin 2979
berville
Red Bluff
L. Almanor
Quincy
Lovelock
Eastgate
Humboldt
Stillwater Ra.
Shoshone Mts
Austin
Summit Mtn 3188
40
ummings
Paradise
Chico
Feather Mid. Fork
Reno
Fernley
Fallon
Pyramid
Humboldt
Pt Bragg
Oroville
Grass Valley
Donner Pass
Sparks
Virginia City
Silver City
Carson City
Stewart
Yerington
Schurz
Gabbs
Wildcat Pk. 3203
Mt Jefferson 3642
Monitor Ra.
Ukiah
Lakeport
Clear
Russian
Williams
Marysville
Yuba City
Colfax
Tahoe City
Lake Tahoe
S. Lake Tahoe
Walker
Warm Springs
Healdsburg
Roseville
Auburn
Placerville
Coaldale
Tonopah
Bodega Head
Santa Rosa
Napa
Petaluma
Woodland
Davis
Carmichael
Sacramento
Sutter Creek
San Andreas
Sonora
Bridgeport
Mt Grant 3426
Hawthorne
Mono L.
Boundary Peak 4005
Piper Pk 2880
Goldfield
San Rafael
Berkeley
Oakland
Alameda
Hayward
Concord
Antioch
Lodi
Stockton
Oakdale
Galt
Fairfield
Vallejo
El Portal
Yosemite Nat. Park
White Mtn Peak 4342
(2)
San Francisco
Daly City
San Mateo
Redwood City
Sunnyvale
Santa Clara
Los Gatos
Livermore
Modesto
Turlock
Merced
Mariposa
Bishop
Big Pine
Beatty
San Jose
Gustine
Madera
Pinedale
Pine Flat Resr
Kings Canyon Nat. Park
Independence
Lone Pine
Owens L.
Santa Cruz
Watsonville
Salinas
Los Banos
Fresno
Sequoia Nat. Park
Mt Whitney 4418
Keeler
Death Valley
Panamint Range
Monterey Bay
Pt Pinos
Monterey
Gonzales
King City
Coalinga
Hanford
Exeter
Visalia
Lemoore
Tulare
Porterville
Telescope Peak 3368
Santa Lucia Range
Salinas
Paso Robles
Wasco
Earlimart
Delano
Inyokern
Morro Bay
San Luis Obispo
Grover City
Oildale
Bakersfield
Arvin
Johannesburg
Santa Maria
Tehachapi Pass
Mojave
Barstow
Yermo
Lompoc
Tehachapi Mts
Lancaster
Mojave Desert
35
Pt Conception
Santa Barbara
Santa Paula
Fillmore
Victorville
Mt San Antonio 3068
San Bernardino
Redlands
Beaumont
Santa Barbara Chan.
Ventura
Oxnard
Beverly Hills
Burbank
Glendale
Pasadena
Pomona
Riverside
San Jacinto Peak 3301
Palm Springs
Santa Cruz
San Miguel
Santa Rosa
Santa Monica
Los Angeles
Torrance
Long Beach
Huntington Beach
Laguna Beach
Anaheim
Santa Ana
(3)
Channel Islands
Santa Catalina
San Clemente
Palomar Mtn 1871
Oceanside
Carlsbad
Vista
Escondido
Ramona
Gulf of Santa Catalina
San Clemente
La Mesa
El Cajon
National City
San Diego
Chula Vista
Tijuana
Tecate
Descanso

COAST RANGES
Sacramento Valley
SIERRA NEVADA
CALIFORNIA
San Joaquin Valley
Diablo Range
NEVADA

USA, Hawaii inset

160
Hanalei
Kauai
1548
Mana
Lihue
(A)
Kauai Channel
Kahuku Pt
Kaena Pt
Wahiawa
Kailua
Oahu
1227
Pearl City
Honolulu
Kaunakakai
Molokai
Pailolo Chan.
Wailuku
Hana
Lanai
Lanai City
Nat. Pk.
3055
Maui
Kealaikahiki Chan.
Kahoolawe
Kapaau
Waimea
Upolu Point
Kailua
Hawaii
Mauna Kea 4201
Mauna Loa 4169
Hawaii Volcanoes Nat. Park 1243
Hakalou
Hilo
Kilauea Crater
Pahoa
Mililoli
Naalehu
Ka Lae (South Cape)
20 N
Alenuihaha Channel
155
160
USA, Hawaii
0 100 200 km
0 50 100 mls
PACIFIC OCEAN
(C)
(B)

0 25 50 75 100 km
0   25   50 mls

Upper map (San Francisco region):

Lytton, Calistoga, Woodland, Folsom, Placerville, Folsom, Camino, Diamond Springs, Markleeville, Topaz, W Walker
Healdsburg, L.Berryessa, Carmichael, Sacramento, Plymouth, Highland Pk 3333, Coleville
Forestville, St Helena, Winters, Davis, Elk Grove, Sutter Ck, West Pt, Mokelumne, Bear Valley, Devils Gate 2301
Santa Rosa, Yountville, Vacaville, Dixon, Galt, Jackson, Mokelumne Hill, Arnold, Dardanelle, Sonora Pass 2933, Bridge Resr
Sebastopol, Sonoma, Napa, Elmira, Fairfield, Clements, San Andreas, Pinecrest, Bridgeport
Petaluma, Isleton, Lodi, Angels Camp, Murphys, Hetch Hetchy Resr, Excelsior Mtn 3790
Novato, Vallejo, Pittsburg, Antioch, Oakley, Bellota, Sonora, L. Eleanor, Yosemite, Tioga Pass, Mt D 3978
San Rafael, S. Pablo B., Concord, Brentwood, Stockton, Farmington Resr, Melones Resr, Groveland, Mather, Tuolumne Mdws, Mt Lyell 3997
Mill Valley, Richmond, Mt Diablo 1173, Byron, Manteca, Stanislaus, Oakdale, Don Pedro Resr, Coulterville, El Portal, National Park, Mt Ritter 4010, Del
Golden Gate, Berkeley, Oakland, San Leandro, Tracy, Ripon, Riverbank, Modesto Resr, L. McClure, Del Paso
San Francisco, Daly City, S.San Francisco, Hayward, Livermore, Pleasanton, Modesto, Ceres, Turlock L., Wawona, Mariposa, Fish Camp, Kaiser P 3146
San Mateo, Fremont, Patterson, Turlock, Snelling, Merced, Yosemite, Mariposa Resr, Bass Lake, Lakeshore, Huntington L
Redwood City, Palo Alto, Mountain View, Sunnyvale, Santa Clara, Newman, Atwater, Merced, Planada, Shaver L
San Gregorio, San Jose, Coyote, Gustine, Mariposa, Raymond, Fresno, Millerton
Pescadero, Los Gatos, Morgan Hill, Volta, San Joaquin, Chowchilla, Berenda, Madera, Friant, Humphreys, Patterson P 2491, Pine Flat Resr
Boulder Creek, Santa Cruz Mts, Gilroy, S. Luis Resr, Dos Palos, Firebaugh, Friant Dam, Pinedale, Piedra
Davenport, Soquel, Laveaga Pk 1154, Herndon, Clovis, Minkler
Santa Cruz, Watsonville, San Juan Bautista, Hollister, Mendota, Kerman, Sanger, Badg
Monterey, Castroville, Tres Pinos, San Luis Canal, Helm, Selma, Reedley
Pacific Grove, Salinas, Alisal, Benito, Gabilan Ra., Kingsburg, Dinuba
Carmel, Seaside, Monterey, Gonzales, Pinnacles N.M.
Carmel Valley, Salinas
Monterey Bay, Diablo Range, San Joaquin Valley, Sierra Nevada, Yosemite

Mt Diablo 1173, Mt Hamilton 1284 (Lick Observatory)

Lower map (Los Angeles region):

Sta Ynez, Los Alamos, Los Olivos, San Rafael Mts, Big Pine Mtn 2081, Gorman, Piru Ck, Lake Hughes, Rosamond L., Helendale
Lompoc, Buellton, Solvang, L. Cachuma, Santa Barbara Resr, Castaic, California Aqueduct, Lancaster, Mirage L.,
Pt Arguello, Santa Ynez Mts, Ojai, Fillmore, Acton, Palmdale, Adelanto, Victorville
Pt Conception, Gaviota, Goleta, Carpinteria, Santa Paula, Santa Clara, Newhall, Wrightwood, Littlerock, Hesperia, Mojave
Santa Barbara, Ventura, Moorpark, San Fernando, San Gabriel Mts 3068,
Santa Barbara Channel, Oxnard, Camarillo, Burbank, Mt Wilson 1740, Pasadena, Upland, San Bernardino, Mt San Antonio 3068
San Miguel, Port Hueneme, Los Angeles, Glendale, Hollywood, Monrovia, Colton, High, Redlands
Santa Rosa, Sta Cruz Chan., Santa Cruz, Anacapa Is, Santa Monica, Beverly Hills, Whittier, Pomona, Ontario, Riverside
Santa Monica Bay, Inglewood, Torrance, Lakewood, Fullerton, Anaheim, Corona, Perris
Channel Islands, Redondo Beach, Long Beach, Garden Grove, Orange, Santa Ana, Santiago Pk 1736, Elsino
Santa Barbara, Huntington Beach, Newport Beach, Costa Mesa, Sta Ana Mts, Elsinore
San Nicolas, Laguna Beach, San Pedro Channel, San Clemente, S.Onofre, S Margarita
Gulf of Santa Catalina, Santa Catalina, Avalon, Oceanside, Vist
San Clemente, Carlsbad, Encinitas, Del Mar, La Jolla, San Diego
Outer Santa Barbara Channel

PACIFIC OCEAN

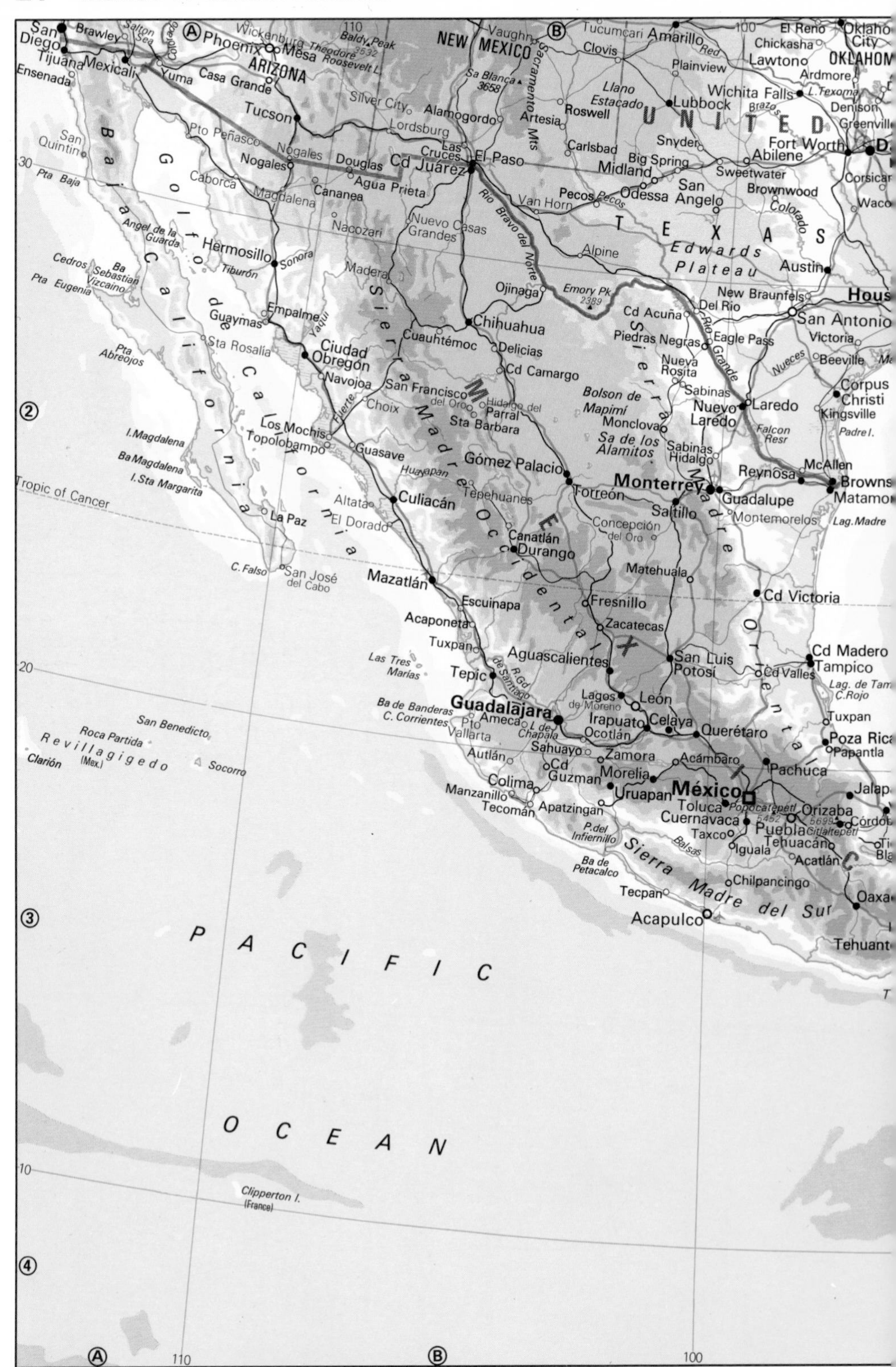

San Diego
Tijuana
Ensenada
Brawley
Salton Sea
Colorado
Mexicali
Yuma
Phoenix
Mesa
Wickenburg
Theodore Roosevelt L.
ARIZONA
Casa Grande
Tucson
Baldy Peak 3532
110
Silver City
Lordsburg
NEW MEXICO
Vaughn
Sacramento Mts
Sa Blanca 3658
Alamogordo
Roswell
Artesia
Las Cruces
El Paso
Cd Juárez
Tucumcari
Clovis
Amarillo
Red
Plainview
Llano Estacado
Lubbock
Carlsbad
Big Spring
Midland
Odessa
Pecos
Van Horn
Snyder
Abilene
Sweetwater
San Angelo
Brownwood
Colorado
El Reno
Oklahoma City
Chickasha
Lawton
OKLAHOMA
Ardmore
Wichita Falls
L. Texoma
Brazos
Denison
Greenville
Fort Worth
Corsicana
Waco
UNITED
TEXAS
Edwards Plateau
Austin
Alpine
Emory Pk 2389
New Braunfels
Del Rio
San Antonio
Cd Acuña
Eagle Pass
Piedras Negras
Victoria
Nueces
Beeville
Corpus Christi
Kingsville
Padre I.
Rio Grande
Nueva Rosita
Sabinas
Nuevo Laredo
Laredo
Falcon Resr
McAllen
Reynosa
Brownsville
Matamoros
Lag. Madre
San Quintín
Pta Baja
30
Pto Peñasco
Nogales
Douglas
Agua Prieta
Caborca
Magdalena
Cananea
Nacozari
Nuevo Casas Grandes
Rio Bravo del Norte
Ojinaga
Angel de la Guarda
Hermosillo
Sonora
Tiburón
Cedros
Ba Sebastian Vizcaino
Pta Eugenia
Madera
Chihuahua
Guaymas
Empalme
Yaqui
Sta Rosalía
Ciudad Obregón
Cuauhtémoc
Delicias
Cd Camargo
Pta Abreojos
Navojoa
San Francisco del Oro
Hidalgo del Parral
Sta Barbara
Bolson de Mapimí
Monclova
Sa de los Alamitos
Sabinas Hidalgo
Choix
Fuerte
Los Mochis
Topolobampo
Guasave
I. Magdalena
Ba Magdalena
I. Sta Margarita
Huayapan
Tepehuanes
Gómez Palacio
Torreón
Monterrey
Saltillo
Guadalupe
Montemorelos
Tropic of Cancer
Altata
Culiacán
El Dorado
La Paz
C. Falso
San José del Cabo
Mazatlán
Canatlán
Durango
Concepción del Oro
Matehuala
Cd Victoria
Escuinapa
Fresnillo
Acaponeta
Zacatecas
Tuxpan
Las Tres Marías
Tepic
R. Gd de Santiago
Aguascalientes
San Luis Potosí
Cd Madero
Tampico
Cd Valles
Lag. de Tamiahua
C. Rojo
20
Ba de Banderas
C. Corrientes
Pto Vallarta
Guadalajara
Ameca
L. de Chapala
Lagos de Moreno
León
Irapuato
Celaya
Querétaro
Ocotlán
Tuxpan
Poza Rica
Papantla
San Benedicto
Roca Partida
Revillagigedo (Mex.)
Clarión
Socorro
Autlán
Sahuayo
Zamora
Acámbaro
Pachuca
Cd Guzman
Morelia
Colima
Manzanillo
Tecomán
Apatzingán
Uruapan
México
Toluca
Popocatepetl 5452
Orizaba
Citlaltepetl 5699
Jalapa
Córdoba
Cuernavaca
Puebla
Taxco
Iguala
Tehuacán
Acatlán
P. del Infiernillo
Balsas
Ba de Petacalco
Sierra Madre del Sur
Chilpancingo
Tecpan
Acapulco
Oaxaca
Tehuantepec
Baja California
Golfo de California
Sierra Madre Occidental
Sierra Madre Oriental
MEXICO
PACIFIC OCEAN
10
Clipperton I. (France)
100

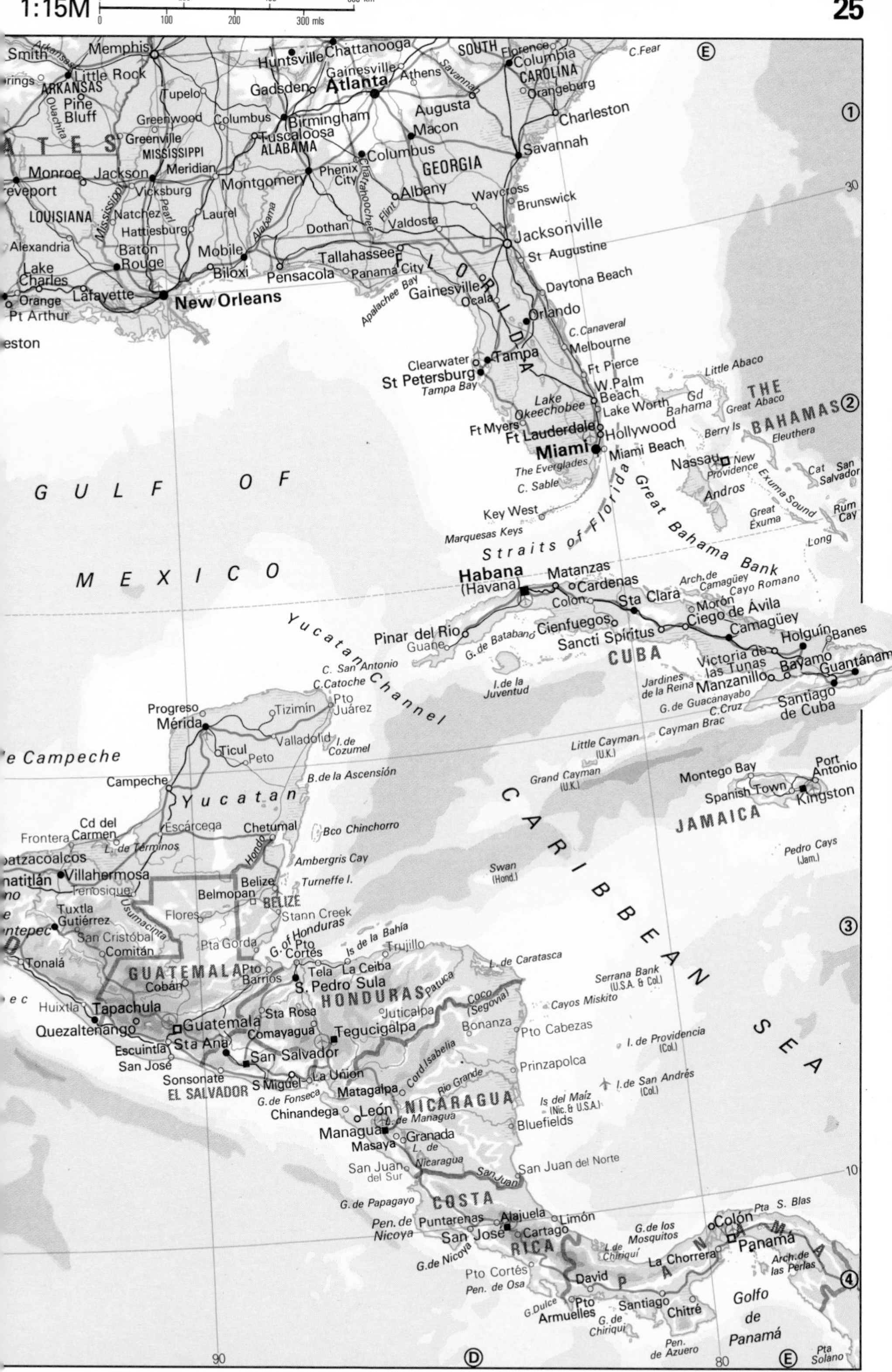

200 400 600 km
100 200 300 mls

Atlantic Smith
rings
Memphis
Huntsville Chattanooga
Little Rock
ARKANSAS
Pine
Bluff
Greenwood
Gadsden
Gainesville
Athens
SOUTH
Florence
Columbia
CAROLINA
C.Fear

Tupelo
Greenville
Columbus
Birmingham
Atlanta
Augusta
Orangeburg
①

Monroe
Jackson
Meridian
ALABAMA
Macon
Charleston

Vicksburg
Montgomery
Phenix
City
GEORGIA
Savannah

MISSISSIPPI
Tuscaloosa
Columbus
30

eveport
LOUISIANA
Natchez
Laurel
Albany
Waycross
Brunswick

Alexandria
Hattiesburg
Dothan
Valdosta

Lake
Charles
Baton
Rouge
Mobile
Tallahassee
Jacksonville

Orange
Lafayette
Biloxi
Pensacola
Panama City
St Augustine

Pt Arthur
New Orleans
FLORIDA
Gainesville
Daytona Beach

eston
Apalachee Bay
Ocala
Orlando

C. Canaveral
Melbourne

Clearwater
Tampa
Ft Pierce
Little Abaco

St Petersburg
Lake
Okeechobee
W.Palm
Beach
Gd
Bahama
Great Abaco
THE

Tampa Bay
Lake Worth
Berry Is
BAHAMAS
②

Ft Myers
Ft Lauderdale
Hollywood
Eleuthera

GULF
Miami
Miami Beach
Nassau
New
Providence
Cat
San Salvador

The Everglades
Andros
Exuma Sound

OF
C. Sable
Great
Exuma
Rum Cay

Key West
Long

MEXICO
Marquesas Keys
Straits of Florida
Great Bahama Bank

Habana
(Havana)
Matanzas
Arch. de
Camagüey

Cardenas
Sta Clara
Moron
Cayo Romano

Colon
Cienfuegos
Ciego de Ávila

Pinar del Rio
Sancti Spiritus
Camagüey
Holguín
Banes

Yucatan Channel
Guane
G. de Batabanó
CUBA
Victoria de
las Tunas
Bayamo
Guantánam

Progreso
C. San Antonio
I.de la
Juventud
Jardines
de la Reina
Manzanillo
Santiago
de Cuba

Mérida
C.Catoche
Pto
Juárez
G. de Guacanayabo
C.Cruz

Tizimin
Little Cayman
(U.K.)
Cayman Brac

e Campeche
Valladolid
I. de
Cozumel
Grand Cayman
(U.K.)
Montego Bay
Port
Antonio

Ticul
Peto

Campeche
YUCATAN
B. de la Ascensión
Spanish Town
Kingston

Cd del
Carmen
Escárcega
Chetumal
Bco Chinchorro
JAMAICA
Pedro Cays
(Jam.)

Frontera
I. de Términos
Ambergris Cay

atzacoalcos
Villahermosa
Belize
Turneffe I.
Swan
(Hond.)

natitlán
Tenosique
BELIZE
Belmopan

Tuxtla
Gutiérrez
Flores
Stann Creek
Serrana Bank
(U.S.A. & Col.)

San Cristóbal
Comitán
G. of
Honduras
Pta Gorda
Cayos Miskito

Tonalá
Pto
Cortés
Is de la Bahía
I. de Caratasca

GUATEMALA
Cobán
Pto
Barrios
Tela
La Ceiba
Trujillo

Huixtla
Tapachula
Sta Rosa
S. Pedro Sula
HONDURAS
Patuca

Quezaltenango
Guatemala
Comayagua
Juticalpa
I. de Providencia
(Col.)

ec
Escuintla
Sta Ana
Tegucigalpa
Coco
(Segovia)
Bonanza
Pto Cabezas

San José
Sonsonate
San Salvador
La Unión
Prinzapolca
I. de San Andrés
(Col.)

EL SALVADOR
S Miguel
Matagalpa
Cord Isabelia
Is del Maíz
(Nic. & U.S.A.)

Chinandega
León
NICARAGUA
Bluefields

Managua
Masaya
Granada
Rio Grande

San Juan
del Sur
L. de Managua
L. de
Nicaragua
San Juan
San Juan del Norte
10

G. de Papagayo
COSTA
Pen. de
Nicoya
Puntarenas
Alajuela
Limón
G. de los
Mosquitos
Pta S. Blas
Colón
Panamá

San José
Cartago
RICA
La Chorrera
Arch. de
las Perlas

G. de Nicoya
Pto Cortés
Pen. de Osa
David
G. de
Chiriquí
PANAMA

Pto
Armuelles
Santiago
Chitré
Golfo
de
Panamá

G.Dulce
Pen.
de Azuero
Pta
Solano

④

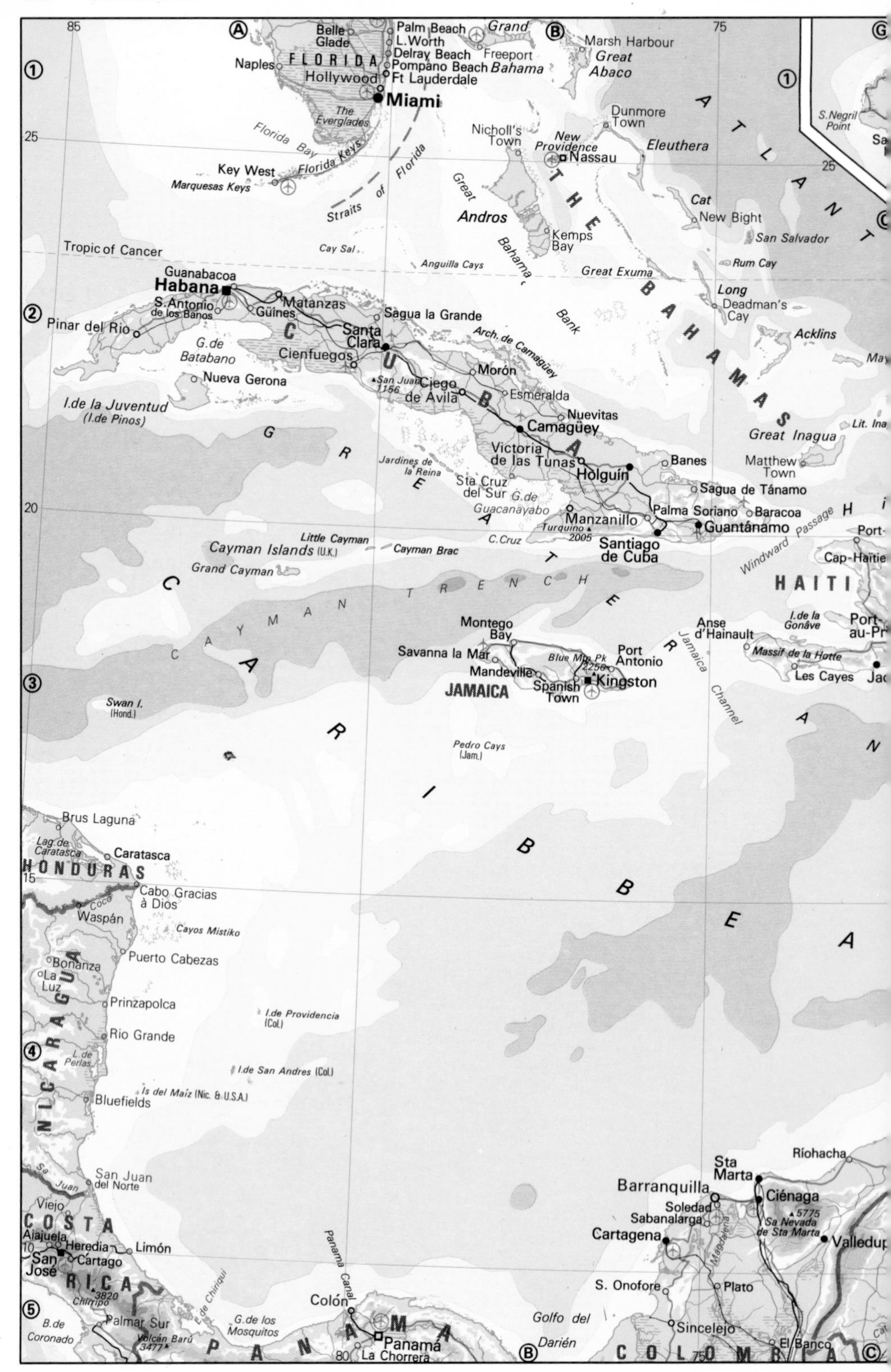

FLORIDA
Naples
Belle Glade
Palm Beach
L. Worth
Delray Beach
Pompano Beach
Ft Lauderdale
Hollywood
Miami
The Everglades
Florida Bay
Florida Keys
Key West
Marquesas Keys
Straits of Florida
Grand Bahama
Freeport
Marsh Harbour
Great Abaco
Dunmore Town
Eleuthera
Nicholl's Town
New Providence
Nassau
Andros
Great Bahama Bank
Kemps Bay
Cat
New Bight
San Salvador
Rum Cay
Great Exuma
Long
Deadman's Cay
Acklins
Great Inagua
Matthew Town
Lit. Inagua
THE BAHAMAS
ATLANTIC
Tropic of Cancer
Cay Sal
Anguilla Cays
Guanabacoa
Habana
S. Antonio de los Banos
Güines
Matanzas
Pinar del Rio
Sagua la Grande
Santa Clara
Cienfuegos
G. de Batabano
Nueva Gerona
I. de la Juventud (I. de Pinos)
Arch. de Camagüey
Morón
San Juan 1156
Ciego de Avila
Esmeralda
Nuevitas
Camagüey
CUBA
Jardines de la Reina
Victoria de las Tunas
Holguín
Banes
Sagua de Tánamo
Sta Cruz del Sur
G. de Guacanayabo
Manzanillo
Palma Soriano
Baracoa
Guantánamo
Turquino 2005
C. Cruz
Santiago de Cuba
Windward Passage
Little Cayman
Cayman Islands (U.K.)
Cayman Brac
Grand Cayman
CAYMAN TRENCH
GREATER ANTILLES
Montego Bay
Savanna la Mar
Blue Mtn Pk 2256
Port Antonio
Mandeville
Spanish Town
Kingston
JAMAICA
Jamaica Channel
Swan I. (Hond.)
Pedro Cays (Jam.)
Port-
Cap-Haïtien
HAITI
Anse d'Hainault
I. de la Gonâve
Port-au-Pr
Massif de la Hotte
Les Cayes
CARIBBEAN
Brus Laguna
Lag. de Caratasca
Caratasca
HONDURAS
Cabo Gracias à Dios
Coco
Waspán
Cayos Mistiko
Bonanza
La Luz
Puerto Cabezas
Prinzapolca
I. de Providencia (Col.)
Rio Grande
NICARAGUA
L. de Perlas
I. de San Andres (Col.)
Is del Maíz (Nic. & U.S.A.)
Bluefields
San Juan
San Juan del Norte
Viejo
COSTA RICA
Ajajuela
Heredia
Limón
San José
Cartago
Chirripo 3820
B. de Coronado
Palmar Sur
Volcán Barú 3477
L. de Chiriqui
G. de los Mosquitos
Panama Canal
Colón
PANAMA
Panamá
La Chorrera
Golfo del Darién
Ríohacha
Sta Marta
Barranquilla
Ciénaga
Soledad
Sabanalarga
5775
Sa Nevada de Sta Marta
Cartagena
Valledup
Magdalena
S. Onofore
Plato
Sincelejo
El Banco
COLOMBIA
S. Negril Point

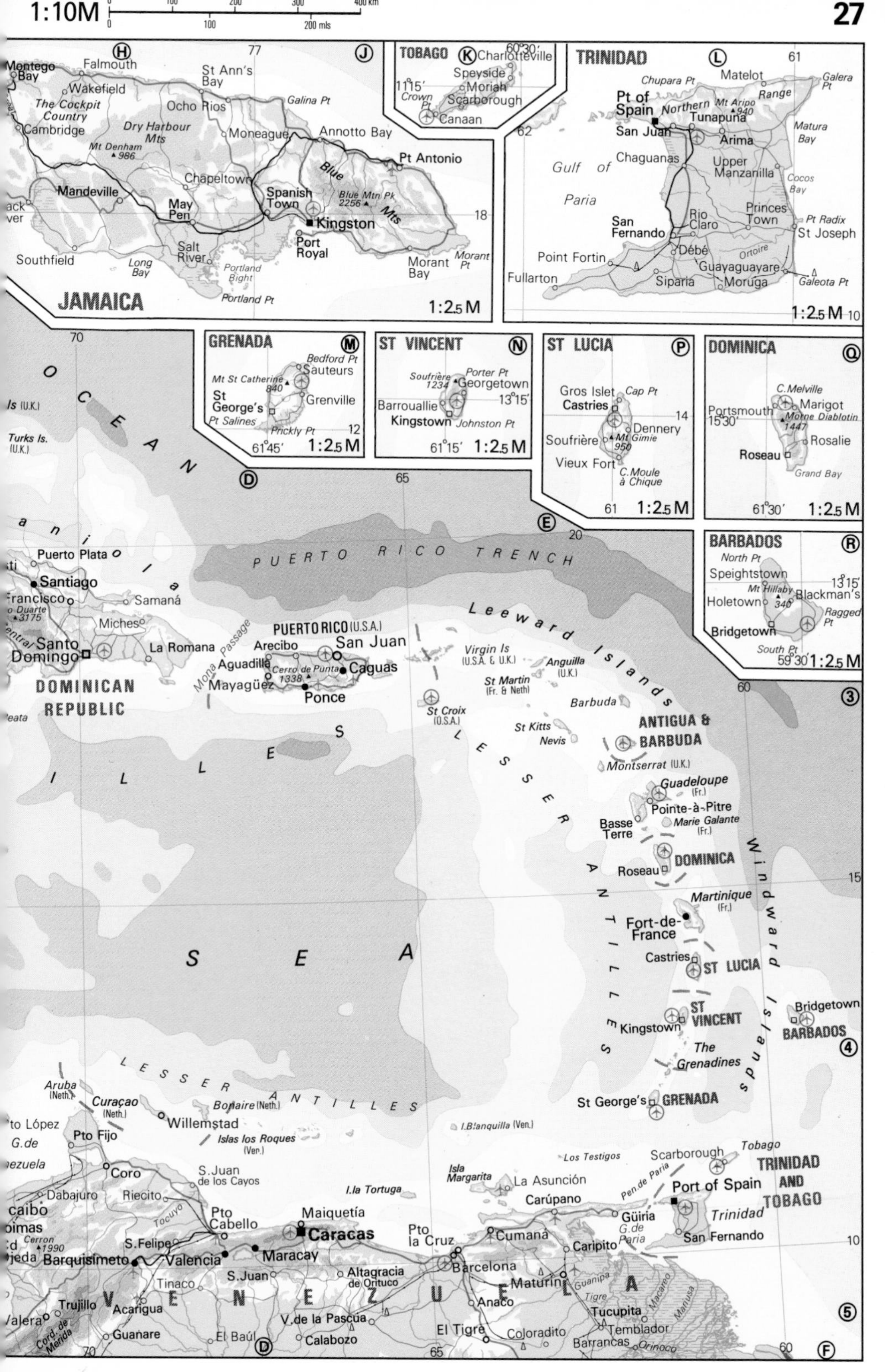
1:10M
JAMAICA
1:2.5M
TOBAGO
Charlotteville
Speyside
Moriah
Scarborough
Canaan
TRINIDAD
Pt of Spain
San Juan
Arima
Tunapuna
Chaguanas
Gulf of Paria
San Fernando
Point Fortin
Fullarton
Siparia
Moruga
Guayaguayare
Princes Town
Rio Claro
St Joseph
Matelot
Northern Range
GRENADA
Sauteurs
Grenville
St George's
ST VINCENT
Georgetown
Barrouallie
Kingstown
ST LUCIA
Gros Islet
Castries
Dennery
Soufrière
Vieux Fort
DOMINICA
Portsmouth
Marigot
Rosalie
Roseau
BARBADOS
Speightstown
Holetown
Bridgetown
Montego Bay
Falmouth
St Ann's Bay
Ocho Rios
Annotto Bay
Pt Antonio
Mandeville
May Pen
Spanish Town
Kingston
Port Royal
Morant Bay
Blue Mts
Puerto Plata
Santiago
Samaná
Santo Domingo
La Romana
DOMINICAN REPUBLIC
PUERTO RICO (U.S.A.)
San Juan
Arecibo
Aguadilla
Mayagüez
Caguas
Ponce
Mona Passage
PUERTO RICO TRENCH
Virgin Is (U.S.A. & U.K.)
Anguilla (U.K.)
St Martin (Fr. & Neth)
St Croix (U.S.A.)
Barbuda
ANTIGUA & BARBUDA
St Kitts
Nevis
Montserrat (U.K.)
Guadeloupe (Fr.)
Pointe-à-Pitre
Basse Terre
Marie Galante (Fr.)
DOMINICA
Roseau
Martinique (Fr.)
Fort-de-France
Castries
ST LUCIA
ST VINCENT
Kingstown
BARBADOS
Bridgetown
The Grenadines
St George's
GRENADA
Leeward Islands
Windward Islands
LESSER ANTILLES
OCEAN
SEA
Aruba (Neth.)
Curaçao (Neth.)
Willemstad
Bonaire (Neth.)
Islas los Roques (Ven.)
I.Blanquilla (Ven.)
Los Testigos
Isla Margarita
La Asunción
Tobago
Scarborough
TRINIDAD AND TOBAGO
Port of Spain
Trinidad
San Fernando
Pto Fijo
Coro
Dabajuro
Riecito
Pto Cabello
Maiquetía
Caracas
Maracay
Valencia
Barquisimeto
S.Felipe
Tinaco
S.Juan
Altagracia de Orituco
Pto la Cruz
Barcelona
Cumaná
Carúpano
Güiria
Caripito
Maturín
Anaco
Tucupita
Temblador
Barrancas
El Tigre
Coloradito
V.de la Pascua
Calabozo
El Baúl
Guanare
Acarigua
Trujillo
Valera
VENEZUELA

1:40M

0 400 800 1200 1600 km
0 400 800 mls

CARIBBEAN SEA

NICARAGUA
① COSTA RICA
S.José
PANAMA
Panamá

ST LUCIA
BARBADOS
TRINIDAD & TOBAGO

Ⓓ Ⓔ Ⓕ

Sta Marta
Barranquilla
Maracaibo
Caracas
Barcelona

S.Cristóbal
VENEZUELA
Cd Bolivar
Orinoco

Georgetown
Paramaribo
Cayenne
GUYANA
SURINAM
FR. GUIANA

Medellin
② Bogotá
Buenaventura
Cali
Popayán
COLOMBIA
S.Lorenzo
Boa Vista

Malpelo (Col.)

Quito
ECUADOR
Guayaquil
Iquitos

Negro

Santarem
I. de Marajó
Belém
São Luís
Equator

Manaus
Amazonas
Japurá

I.Fernan Noronha

③ PERU
Trujillo
Purús
Madeira
Tapajós
Xingu
Teresina
Fortaleza
Natal

Pto Velho
B R A Z I L
Recife
Maceió

Callao
Lima
Huancayo
Pto Maldonado
Cuzco
Arequipa

Cuiabá
Goiânia
Brasília
São Francisco
Salvador

④ La Paz
B O L I V I A
Cochabamba
Sucre
Sta Cruz
Arica
Corumbá
Belo Horizonte

Campo Grande
Ribeirão Prêto
Campos

⑤ S O U T H
Antofagasta
PARAGUAY
Asunción
Paraná
Rio de Janeiro
São Paulo
Santos

P A C I F I C
S.Félix (Chi.)
Salta
S.Miguel de Tucumán
Resistencia
Posadas
Curitiba
Tropic of Capricorn

O C E A N
A
R
G
E
N
T
I
N
A

Córdoba
Santa Fe
Paraná
URUGUAY
Pto Alegre
Pelotas

Valparaiso
Mendoza
Rosario
Santiago
Buenos Aires
Montevideo
R.de la Plata
S O U T H

Is Juan Fernández (Chi.)
Concepción
Mar del Plata
A T L A N T I C

⑥ Valdivia
Bahía Blanca
O C E A N

CHILE
Pto Montt

⑦ Cmd. Rivadavia
G.San Jorge

Falkland Is (U.K.)
Stanley

Rio Gallegos

Punta Arenas
Tierra del Fuego
S.Georgia (U.K.)

Ⓐ Ⓑ Ⓒ Ⓓ Ⓔ Ⓕ
S.Shetland Is (U.K.)
S.Orkney Is (U.K.)

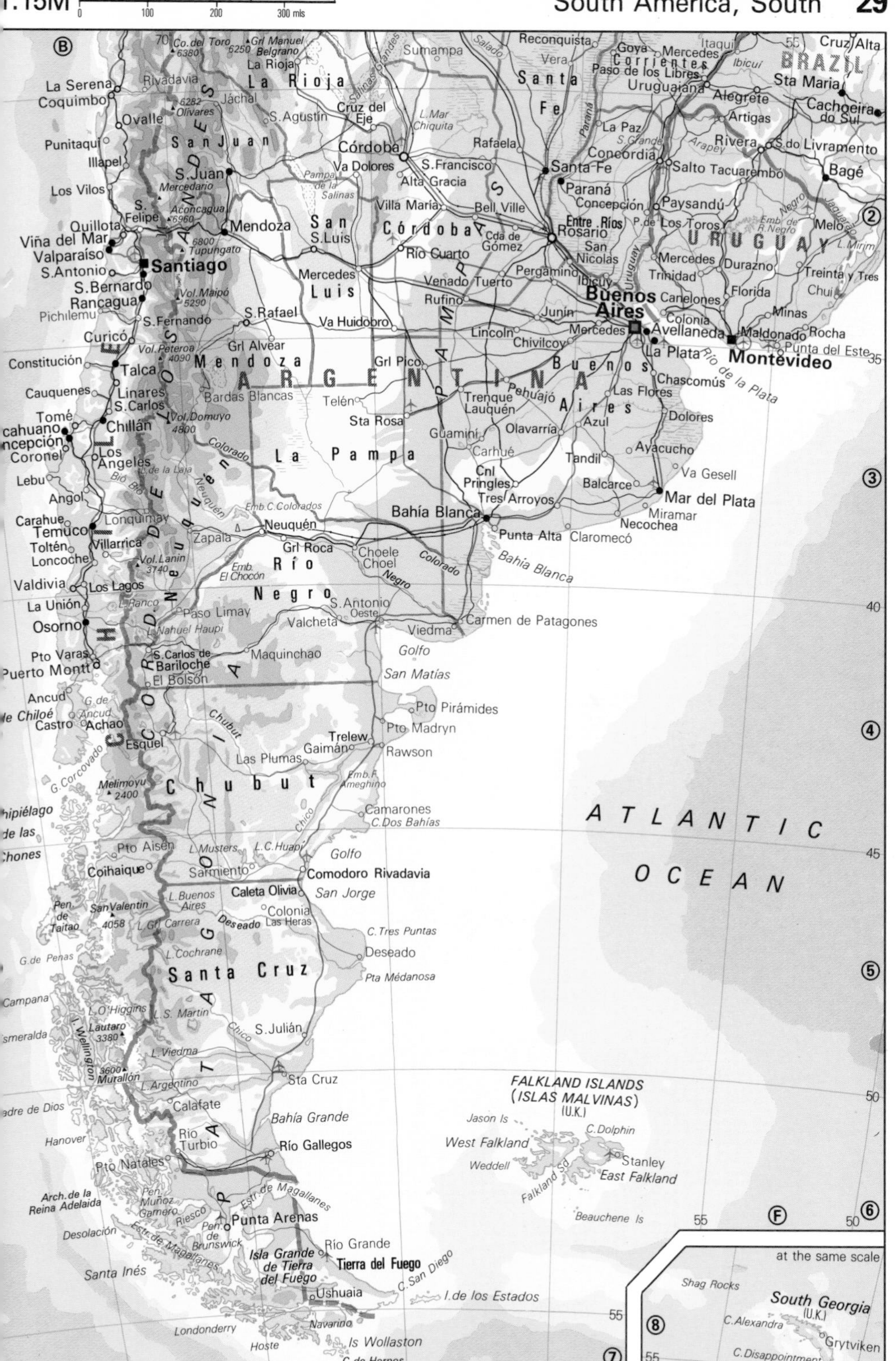

1:15M

200 400 600 km
100 200 300 mls

ATLANTIC OCEAN

FALKLAND ISLANDS
(ISLAS MALVINAS)
(U.K.)

Jason Is
West Falkland
Weddell
C.Dolphin
Stanley
East Falkland

Beauchene Is

at the same scale
Shag Rocks
South Georgia
(U.K.)
C.Alexandra
Grytviken
C.Disappointment

1:15M

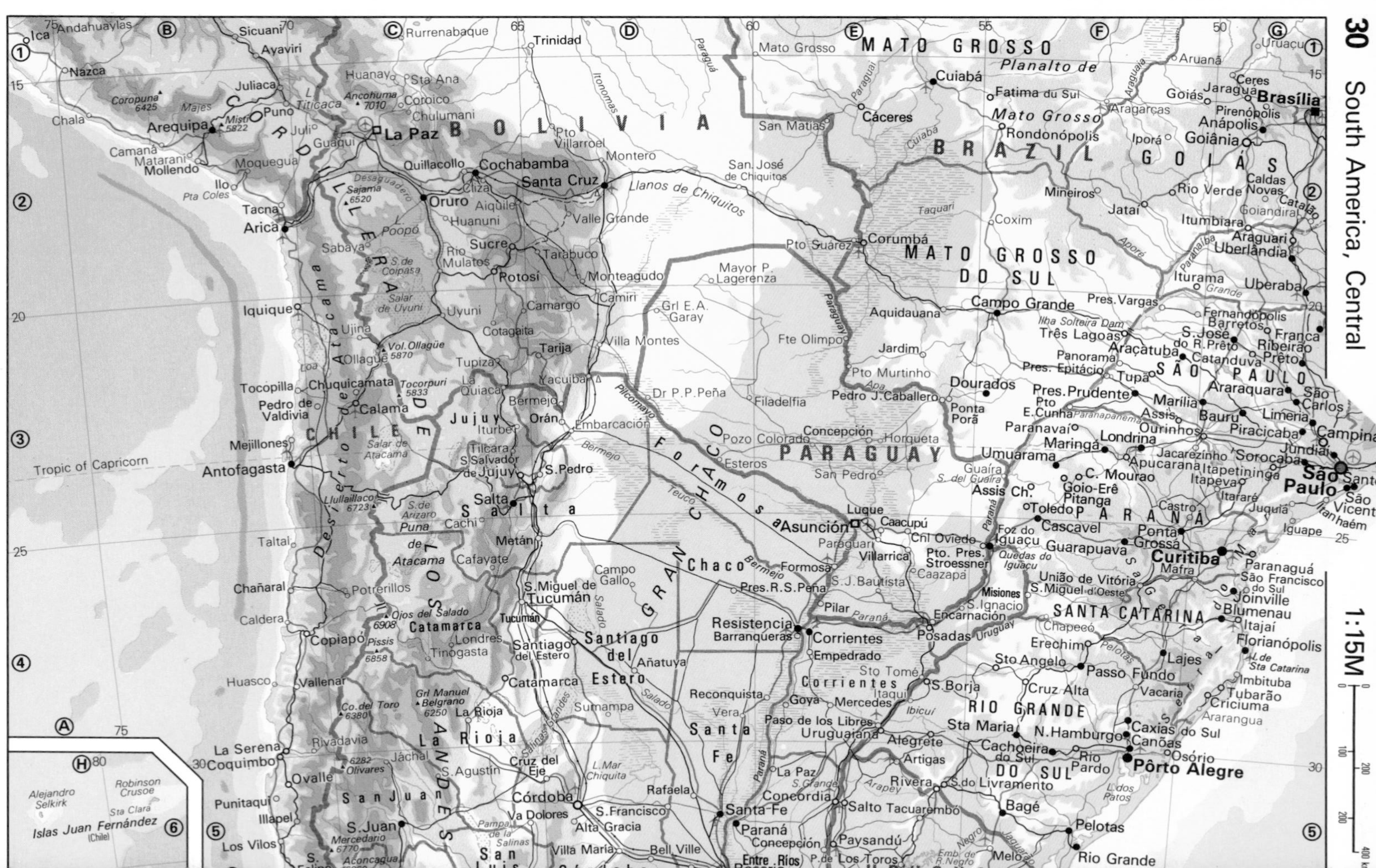
0 200 400 km
0 100 200
MATO GROSSO
Planalto de Mato Grosso
BRAZIL
GOIÁS
MATO GROSSO DO SUL
SÃO PAULO
PARANÁ
SANTA CATARINA
RIO GRANDE DO SUL
BOLIVIA
PARAGUAY
GRAN CHACO
CHILE
ANDES
Brasília
Goiânia
Anápolis
Uberlândia
Uberaba
Campinas
São Paulo
Santos
Curitiba
Florianópolis
Pôrto Alegre
Cuiabá
Cáceres
Corumbá
Campo Grande
Dourados
Londrina
Maringá
Asunción
Corrientes
Resistencia
Posadas
Encarnación
Santa Fe
Paraná
Córdoba
Santiago del Estero
S.Miguel de Tucumán
Salta
Jujuy
Catamarca
La Rioja
S.Juan
La Paz
Oruro
Cochabamba
Santa Cruz
Sucre
Potosí
Tarija
Trinidad
Arica
Iquique
Antofagasta
Calama
Copiapó
La Serena
Coquimbo
Arequipa
Puno
Tacna
Tropic of Capricorn
Desierto de Atacama
L. Titicaca
Llanos de Chiquitos
Salar de Uyuni
Islas Juan Fernández (Chile)
Robinson Crusoe
Alejandro Selkirk
Sta Clara

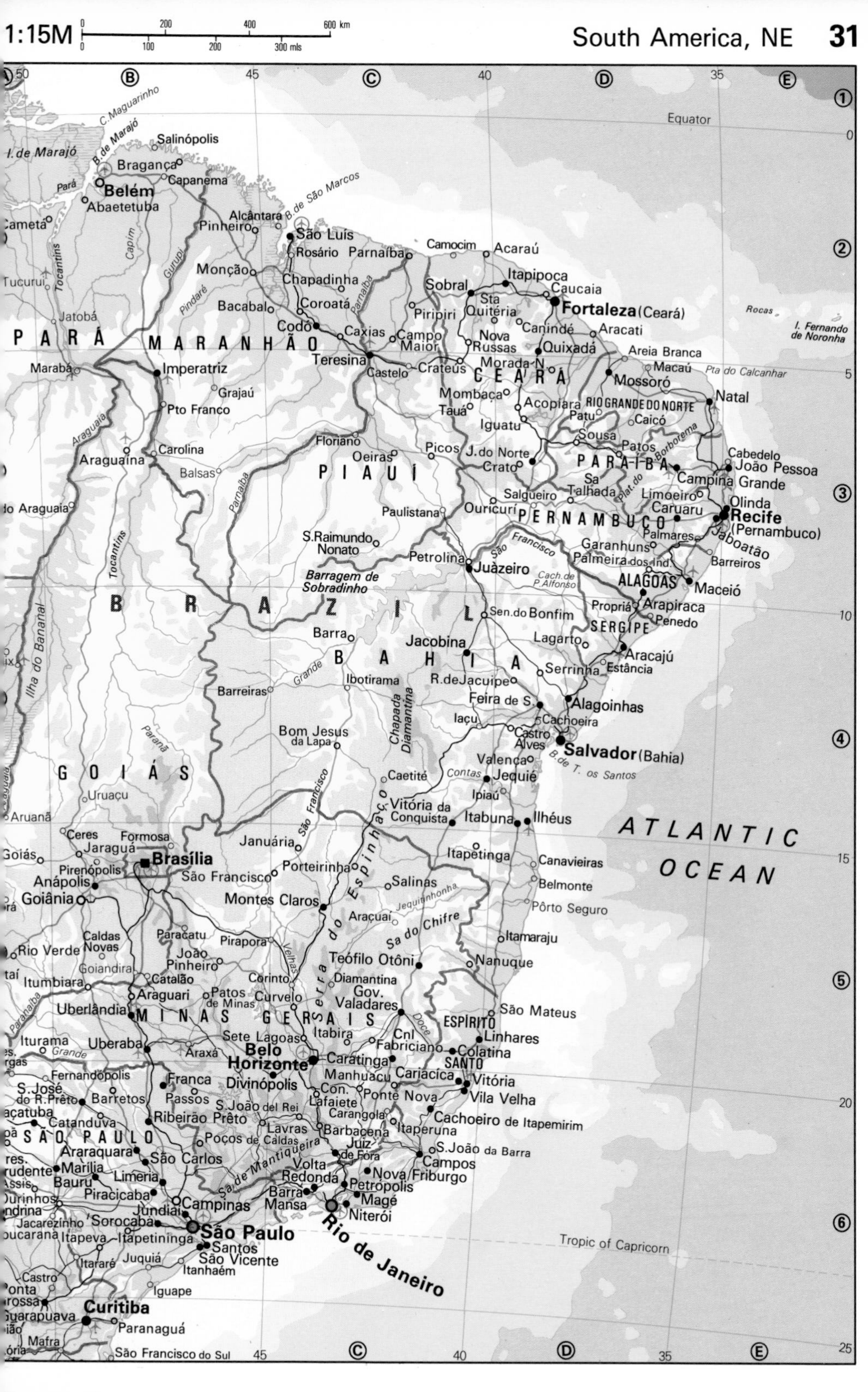

1:15M

200   400   600 km
100   200   300 mls

Equator

C. Maguarinho
I. de Marajó
B. de Marajó
Salinópolis
Bragança
Belém
Capanema
Abaetetuba
Cametá
Pinheiro
Pará
Alcântara
São Luís
Rosário
Monção
Chapadinha
Bacabal
Coroatá
Codó
Caxias
Campo Maior
Teresina
Castelo
Crateús
Morada N.
PARÁ
Marabá
MARANHÃO
Imperatriz
Grajaú
Pto Franco
Carolina
Araguaína
Balsas
Floriano
Oeiras
PIAUÍ
Picos
J. do Norte
Crato
BRAZIL
S.Raimundo Nonato
Petrolina
Juàzeiro
Barragem de Sobradinho
BAHIA
Barra
Jacobina
Ibotirama
R.de Jacuípe
Feira de S.
Iaçu
Castro Alves
Valença
Caetité
Contas
Jequié
Ipiaú
Itabuna
Ilhéus
Vitória da Conquista
Canavieiras
Belmonte
Pôrto Seguro
GOIÁS
Uruaçu
Aruanã
Ceres
Jaraguá
Formosa
Brasília
São Francisco
Porteirinha
Januária
Salinas
Araçuaí
Itamaraju
Nanuque
Goiás
Pirenópolis
Anápolis
Goiânia
Montes Claros
Teófilo Otôni
Sa do Chifre
Caldas Novas
Rio Verde
Itumbiara
Goiandira
Paracatu
João Pinheiro
Pirapora
Diamantina
Gov. Valadares
São Mateus
Catalão
Uberlândia
MINAS GERAIS
Patos de Minas
Curvelo
Itabira
Cnl Fabriciano
ESPÍRITO
Linhares
Colatina
SANTO
Iturama
Uberaba
Araguari
Araxá
Sete Lagoas
Carangola
Vitória
Vila Velha
Fernandópolis
Franca
Belo Horizonte
Manhuaçu
Cariacica
Cachoeiro de Itapemirim
S.José do R. Prêto
Barretos
Divinópolis
Con.
Ponte Nova
Itaperuna
S.João da Barra
SÃO PAULO
Catanduva
Ribeirão Prêto
Poços de Caldas
Lavras
Juiz de Fora
Campos
Araraquara
São Carlos
Limeira
Barbacena
Nova Friburgo
Bauru
Piracicaba
Jundiaí
Campinas
Volta Redonda
Petrópolis
Magé
Niterói
Sorocaba
São Paulo
Rio de Janeiro
Itapetininga
Santos
São Vicente
Itanhaém
Itapeva
Juquiá
Iguape
Itararé
Curitiba
Paranaguá
Mafra

CEARÁ
Fortaleza (Ceará)
Camocim
Acaraú
Itapipoca
Caucaia
Sobral
Sta Quitéria
Canindé
Aracati
Nova Russas
Quixadá
Mossoró
RIO GRANDE DO NORTE
Natal
Macau
Areia Branca
Pta do Calcanhar
Caicó
Patos
PARAÍBA
Campina Grande
João Pessoa
Cabedelo
Sousa
Ouricuri
PERNAMBUCO
Caruaru
Recife (Pernambuco)
Olinda
Jaboatão
Garanhuns
Palmeira dos Ind.
Palmares
Barreiros
Propriá
ALAGOAS
Maceió
Arapiraca
Penedo
SERGIPE
Lagarto
Estância
Aracajú
Sen.do Bonfim
Serrinha
Alagoinhas
Cachoeira
Salvador (Bahia)
B. de T. os Santos

Rocas
I. Fernando de Noronha

ATLANTIC OCEAN

Tropic of Capricorn
São Francisco do Sul

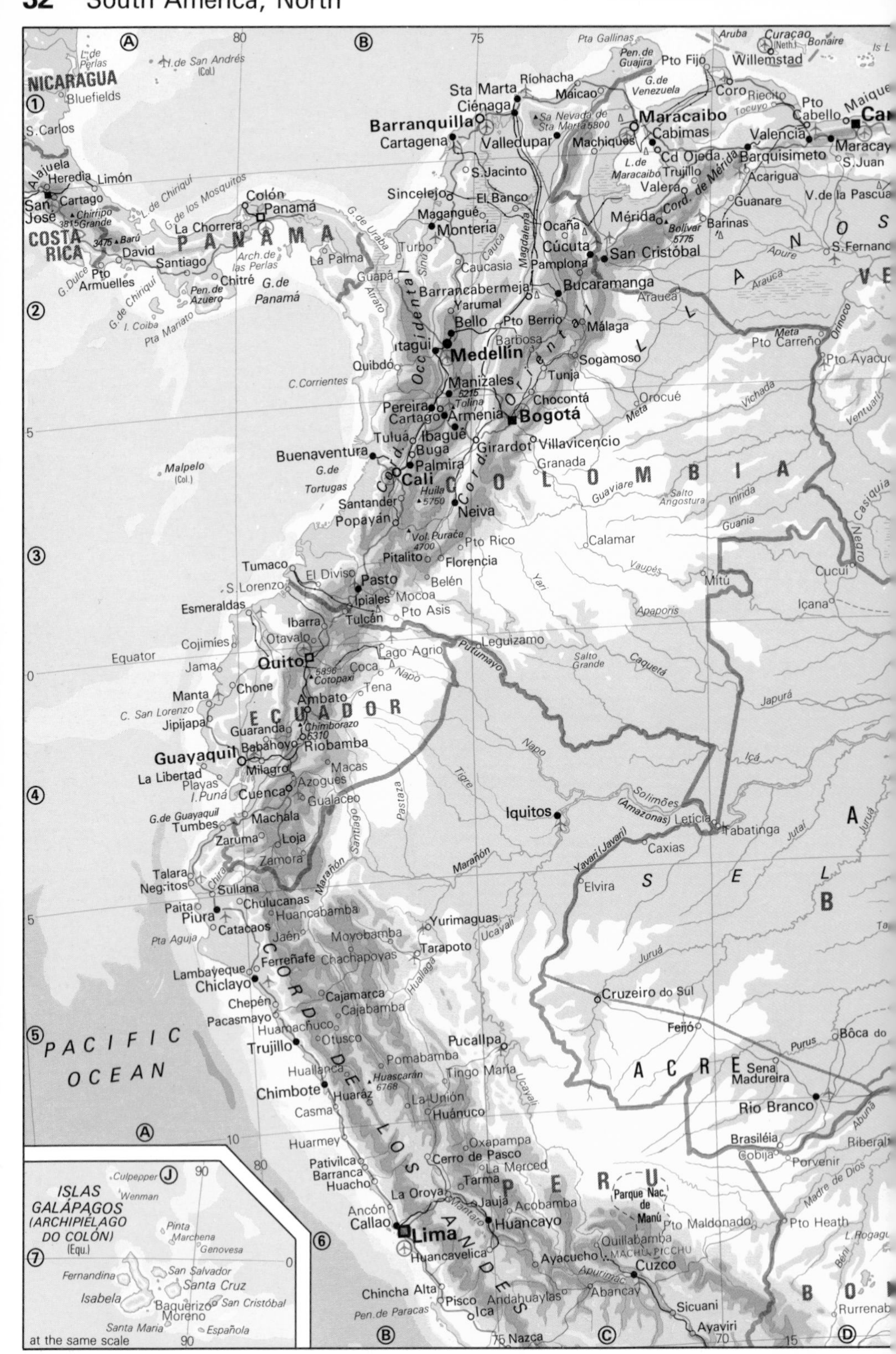
NICARAGUA
Bluefields
S.Carlos
L.de Perlas
I.de San Andrés (Col.)
Alajuela
Heredia
Limón
San José
Cartago
Chirripo Grande 3815
COSTA RICA
Barú 3475
David
Pto Armuelles
G.Dulce
L.de Chiriquí
G.de los Mosquitos
Colón
Panamá
La Chorrera
PANAMA
Santiago
Chitré
Pen.de Azuero
Arch.de las Perlas
G.de Panamá
G.de Chiriquí
I. Coiba
Pta Mariato
G.de Uraba
La Palma
Guapá
Atrato
Turbo
Sinú
Pta Gallinas
Pen.de Guajira
Aruba
Curaçao (Neth.)
Bonaire
Willemstad
Pto Fijo
Ríohacha
Sta Marta
Ciénaga
Maicao
G.de Venezuela
Coro
Riecito
Pto Cabello
Maiquetía
Caracas
Barranquilla
Cartagena
Sa Nevada de Sta Marta 5800
Valledupar
Maracaibo
Cabimas
Tocuyo
Valencia
Maracay
Machiques
L.de Maracaibo
Cd Ojeda
Barquisimeto
S.Juan
S.Jacinto
Trujillo
Acarigua
Valera
Cord. de Mérida
Guanare
V.de la Pascua
Sincelejo
El Banco
Magangué
Montería
Mérida
Bolívar 5775
Barinas
Ocaña
Cúcuta
San Cristóbal
Apure
S.Fernando
LLANOS
Caucasia
Cauca
Magdalena
Pamplona
Barrancabermeja
Bucaramanga
Arauca
Yarumal
Bello
Pto Berrio
Málaga
Meta
Pto Carreño
Orinoco
Pto Ayacucho
Itagui
Medellín
Barbosa
Sogamoso
Quibdó
Cord. Occidental
Cord. Oriental
Tunja
C.Corrientes
Manizales
5215 Tolina
Chocontá
Orocué
Vichada
Pereira
Cartago
Armenia
Bogotá
Ventuari
Tuluá
Ibagué
Buga
Girardot
Villavicencio
Buenaventura
G.de Tortugas
Palmira
Cali
Cord. Central
Granada
COLOMBIA
Malpelo (Col.)
Huila 5750
Neiva
Guaviare
Salto Angostura
Inírida
Casiquiare
Santander
Popayán
Guania
Negro
Vol. Puracé 4700
Pto Rico
Calamar
Pitalito
Florencia
Yarí
Vaupés
Mitú
Cucui
Tumaco
El Diviso
Pasto
Belén
S.Lorenzo
Esmeraldas
Ipiales
Mocoa
Içana
Ibarra
Tulcán
Pto Asis
Apaporis
Otavalo
Cojimíes
Leguizamo
Equator
Lago Agrio
Putumayo
Salto Grande
Caquetá
Jama
Quito
5896 Cotopaxi
Coca
Napo
Chone
Tena
Manta
Ambato
Japurá
C. San Lorenzo
ECUADOR
Jipijapa
Guaranda
Chimborazo 6310
Babahoyo
Riobamba
Guayaquil
Napo
Içá
La Libertad
Milagro
Macas
Tigre
Playas
Azogues
Pastaza
Solimões (Amazonas)
I.Puná
Cuenca
Gualaceo
Iquitos
Leticia
Tabatinga
G.de Guayaquil
Machala
Santiago
Tumbes
Yavari (Javari)
Jutaí
Juruá
Zaruma
Loja
Caxias
Zamora
Marañón
Talara
Negritos
Chira
Sullana
Elvira
SELVAS
BRAZIL
Paita
Chulucanas
Piura
Huancabamba
Yurimaguas
Catacaos
Ucayali
Pta Aguja
Jaén
Moyobamba
Tarapoto
Chachapoyas
Lambayeque
Ferreñafe
Huallaga
Juruá
Chiclayo
Cruzeiro do Sul
Chepén
Cajamarca
Cajabamba
Pacasmayo
Huamachuco
Feijó
PACIFIC OCEAN
Otusco
Pucallpa
Purus
Bôca do Acre
Trujillo
Pomabamba
Huallanca
Huascarán 6768
Tingo María
ACRE
Sena Madureira
Chimbote
Huaráz
La Unión
Rio Branco
Casma
Huánuco
Abunã
Huarmey
Oxapampa
Brasiléia
Riberalta
Pativilca
Barranca
Huacho
Cerro de Pasco
La Merced
Cobija
Porvenir
Tarma
Madre de Dios
CORD. DE LOS ANDES
PERU
Parque Nac. de Manú
La Oroya
Jauja
Acobamba
Ancón
Callao
Lima
Mantaro
Huancayo
Pto Maldonado
Pto Heath
L.Rogaguado
Beni
Quillabamba
MACHU PICCHU
Huancavelica
Ayacucho
Cuzco
Apurímac
Abancay
Chincha Alta
Pisco
Andahuaylas
Sicuani
BOLIVIA
Rurrenabaque
Pen.de Paracas
Ica
Ayaviri
Nazca
ISLAS GALÁPAGOS (ARCHIPIÉLAGO DO COLÓN) (Equ.)
Culpepper
Wenman
Pinta
Marchena
Genovesa
Fernandina
San Salvador
Santa Cruz
Isabela
Baquerizo Moreno
San Cristóbal
Santa María
Española
at the same scale
80
75
70
65
90
5
0
10
A
B
C
D
J
1
2
3
4
5
6
7

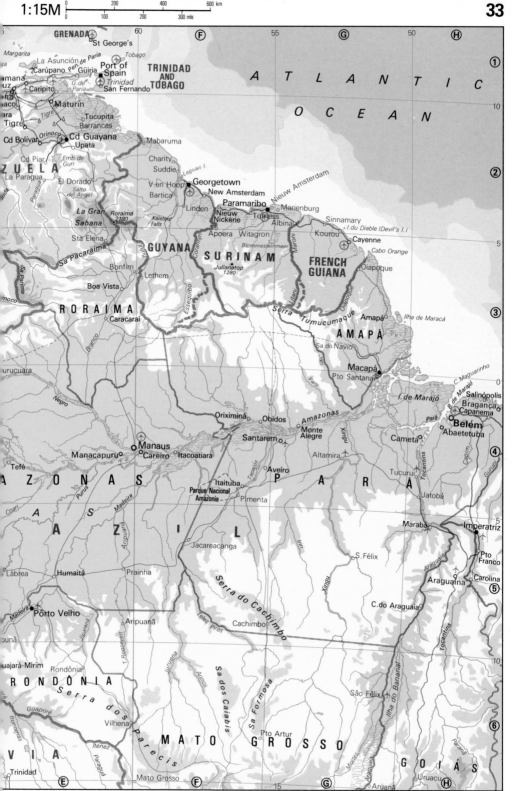

1:15M

0 200 400 600 km

0 100 200 300 mls

GRENADA
St George's

Margarita
La Asunción de Paria
Carúpano Pen. de Paria
Güiria
Tobago

TRINIDAD AND TOBAGO

mana
uz
RB
aco
Maturín
Tigre
Tigre
Tucupita
Barrancas

ara
Cd Bolívar
Orinoco
Cd Guayana
Upata

Caripito
G. de Paria
Trinidad
San Fernando
Port of Spain

ATLANTIC

OCEAN

60

F

55

G

50

H

1

10

Cd Piar
La Paragua
Emb. de Guri

ZUELA
El Dorado
Salto del Ángel

La Gran
Sabana
Roraima 2180

Sta Elena

Sa Pacaraima

Bonfim

Lethem

Boa Vista

RORAIMA

Caracaraí

Mabaruma

Charity
Suddie

V-en Hoop
Bartica

Georgetown
New Amsterdam
Paramaribo
Nieuw Nickerie
Apoera
Witagron

GUYANA

Kaieteur Falls

Essequibo

Corantijn

SURINAM

Julianatop 1280

Blommesteinmeer

Leguan I.

Nieuw Amsterdam

Linden

Tottness
Albina

Marienburg

Sinnamary

I. du Diable (Devil's I.)

Kourou

Cayenne

FRENCH GUIANA

Cabo Orange

Oiapoque

Serra Tumucumaque

Amapá

Ilha de Maracá

AMAPÁ

2

5

3

inoco

Negro

Tefé

Manacapuru

Manaus
Careiro
Itacoatiara

A Z O N A S

A
S

A
Z

I

Purus

Madeira

Coarí

Oriximiná

Obidos

Santarem

Tapajós

Aveíro

Itaituba

Parque Nacional
Amazónia

Pimenta

Amazonas

Monte Alegre

Altamira

P A R Á

Xingu

Jacareacanga

S. Félix

Sa do Navio

Jari

Paru

Macapá
Pto Santana

I. de Marajó

B. de Marajó

C. Maguarinho

0

Pará

Cametá

Salinópolis
Bragança
Capanema

Belém
Abaetetuba

Tocantins

Tucuruí

Jatobá

Marabá

Maraba

Imperatriz

C. Maguarinho

Guamá

Capim

4

5

Lábrea

Humaitá

Prainha

Aripuaná

Porto Velho

Madeira

Jiparaná

Aripuaná

RONDÔNIA

Guajará-Mirim

Rondônia

Serra dos Parecis

Vilhena

VIA

Trinidad

Guaporé

Iténez

Paraguá

Mato Grosso

MATO GROSSO

Serra do Cachimbo

Cachimbo

Teles Pires

Sa dos Caiabis

Juruena

Arinos

Sa Formosa

Pto Artur

São Félix

GROSSO

Xingu

Iriri

C. do Araguaia

Araguaína

Araguaia

Carolina

Pto Franco

Tocantins

Ilha do Bananal

Mortes

Araguaia

GOIÁS

Uruaçu

Aruanã

E

15

F

G

H

6

10

5

5

10

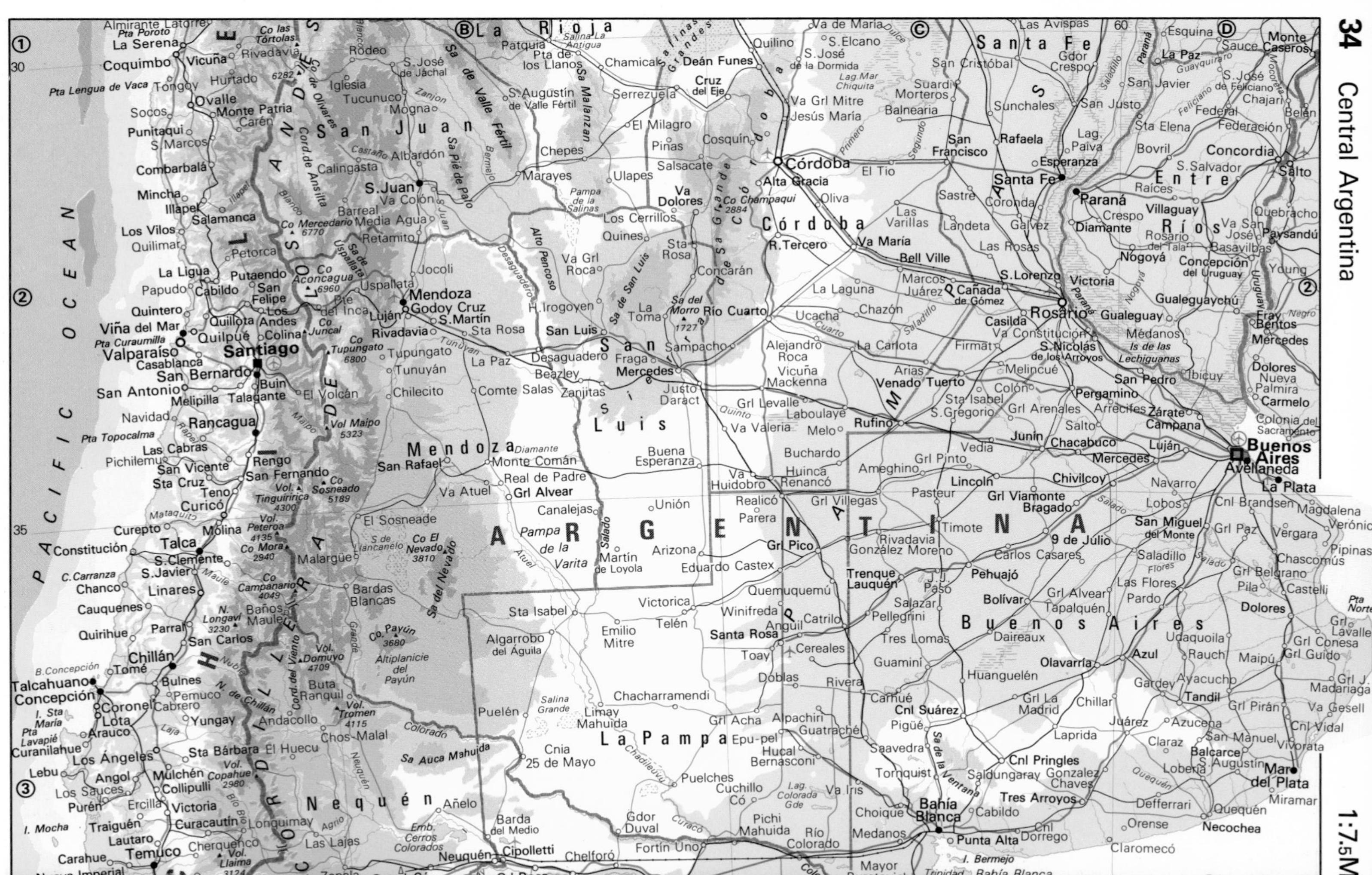
PACIFIC OCEAN
CHILE
CORDILLERA DE LOS ANDES
ARGENTINA
La Rioja
San Juan
Córdoba
Santa Fe
Entre Ríos
San Luis
Mendoza
La Pampa
Buenos Aires
Neuquén
Buenos Aires
La Plata
Rosario
Santa Fe
Paraná
Córdoba
Mendoza
San Juan
San Luis
Santiago
Valparaíso
Viña del Mar
Concepción
Talcahuano
Chillán
Talca
Rancagua
Temuco
Neuquén
Cipolletti
Santa Rosa
Bahía Blanca
Mar del Plata
Tandil
Olavarría
Azul
Río Cuarto
Villa María
Concordia
Salto
Paysandú
Gualeguaychú
San Rafael
Mercedes
Junín
Pergamino
Necochea
Tres Arroyos
Chivilcoy
Pehuajó
Trenque Lauquen
Rufino
Venado Tuerto

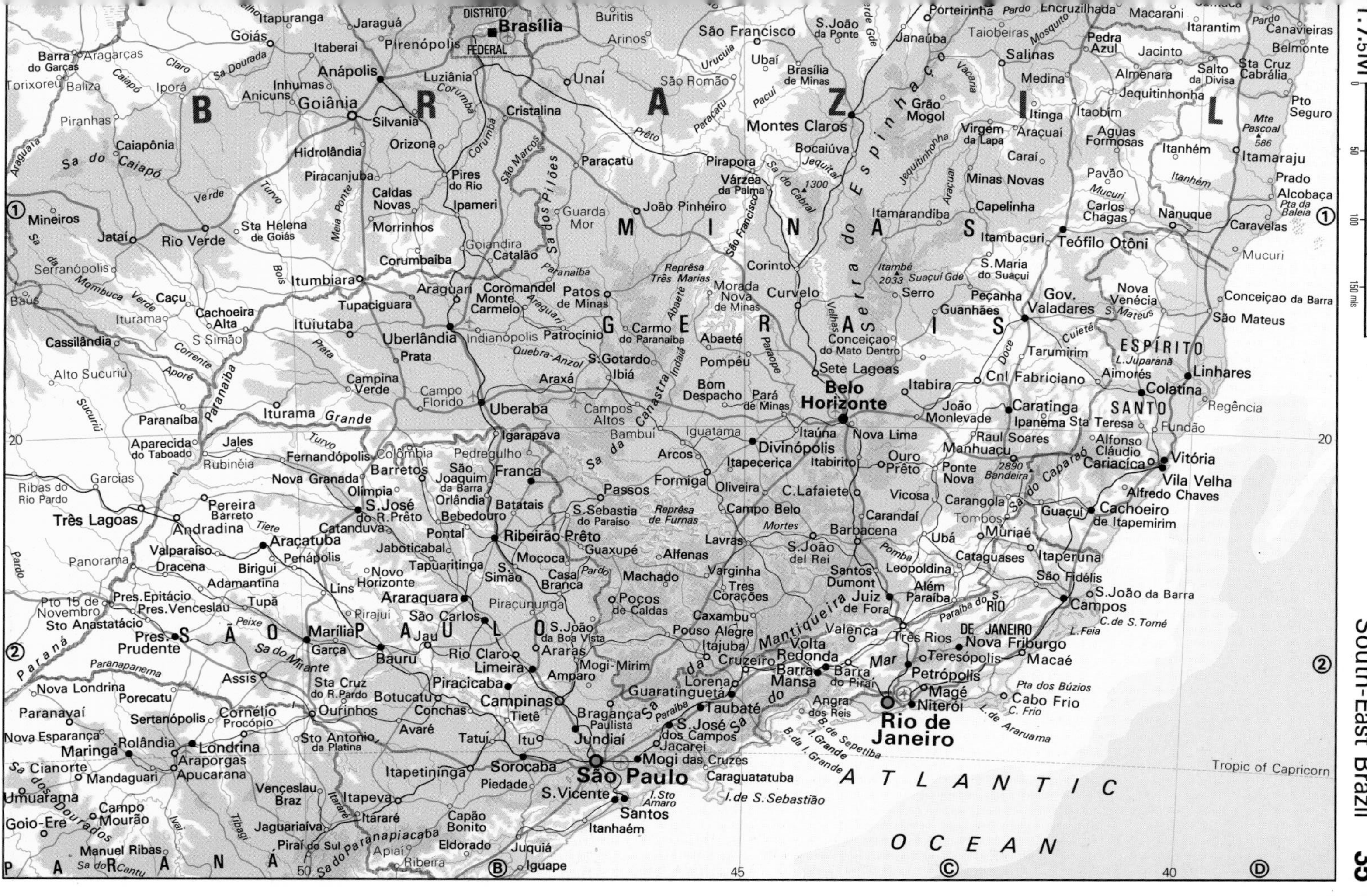
BRAZIL
MINAS GERAIS
SÃO PAULO
ESPÍRITO SANTO
RIO DE JANEIRO
PARANÁ
DISTRITO FEDERAL
ATLANTIC OCEAN
Tropic of Capricorn
Brasília
Goiânia
Anápolis
Belo Horizonte
Rio de Janeiro
São Paulo
Vitória
Vila Velha
Niterói
Campinas
Santos
Uberlândia
Uberaba
Ribeirão Prêto
Juiz de Fora
Montes Claros
Gov. Valadares
Teófilo Otôni
Londrina
Maringá
Campos
Sorocaba
Bauru
Serra do Espinhaço
Serra da Mantiqueira
Serra da Canastra
Paranaíba
São Francisco
Paraná
Tietê

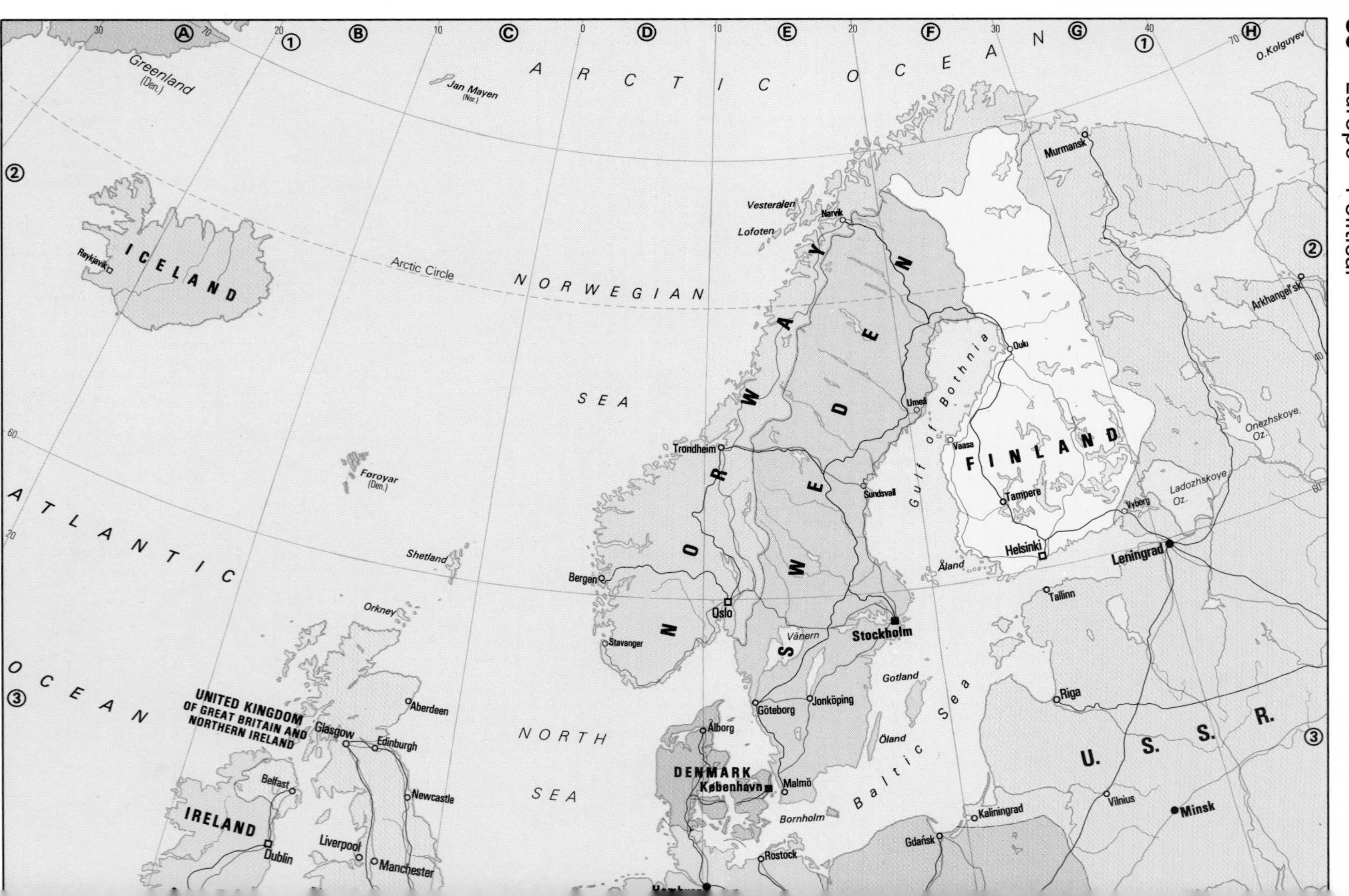
ARCTIC OCEAN
NORWEGIAN SEA
NORTH SEA
ATLANTIC OCEAN
Baltic Sea
Gulf of Bothnia
Arctic Circle
Greenland (Den.)
Jan Mayen (Nor.)
ICELAND
Reykjavík
Føroyar (Den.)
Shetland
Orkney
UNITED KINGDOM OF GREAT BRITAIN AND NORTHERN IRELAND
IRELAND
Aberdeen
Glasgow
Edinburgh
Newcastle
Belfast
Dublin
Liverpool
Manchester
NORWAY
Vesterålen
Lofoten
Narvik
Trondheim
Bergen
Stavanger
Oslo
SWEDEN
Umeå
Sundsvall
Stockholm
Vänern
Göteborg
Jönköping
Malmö
Gotland
Öland
Bornholm
DENMARK
Ålborg
København
FINLAND
Oulu
Vaasa
Tampere
Helsinki
Åland
Vyborg
U. S. S. R.
Murmansk
Arkhangel'sk
O.Kolguyev
Onezhskoye Oz.
Ladozhskoye Oz.
Leningrad
Tallinn
Riga
Vilnius
Minsk
Kaliningrad
Gdańsk
Rostock

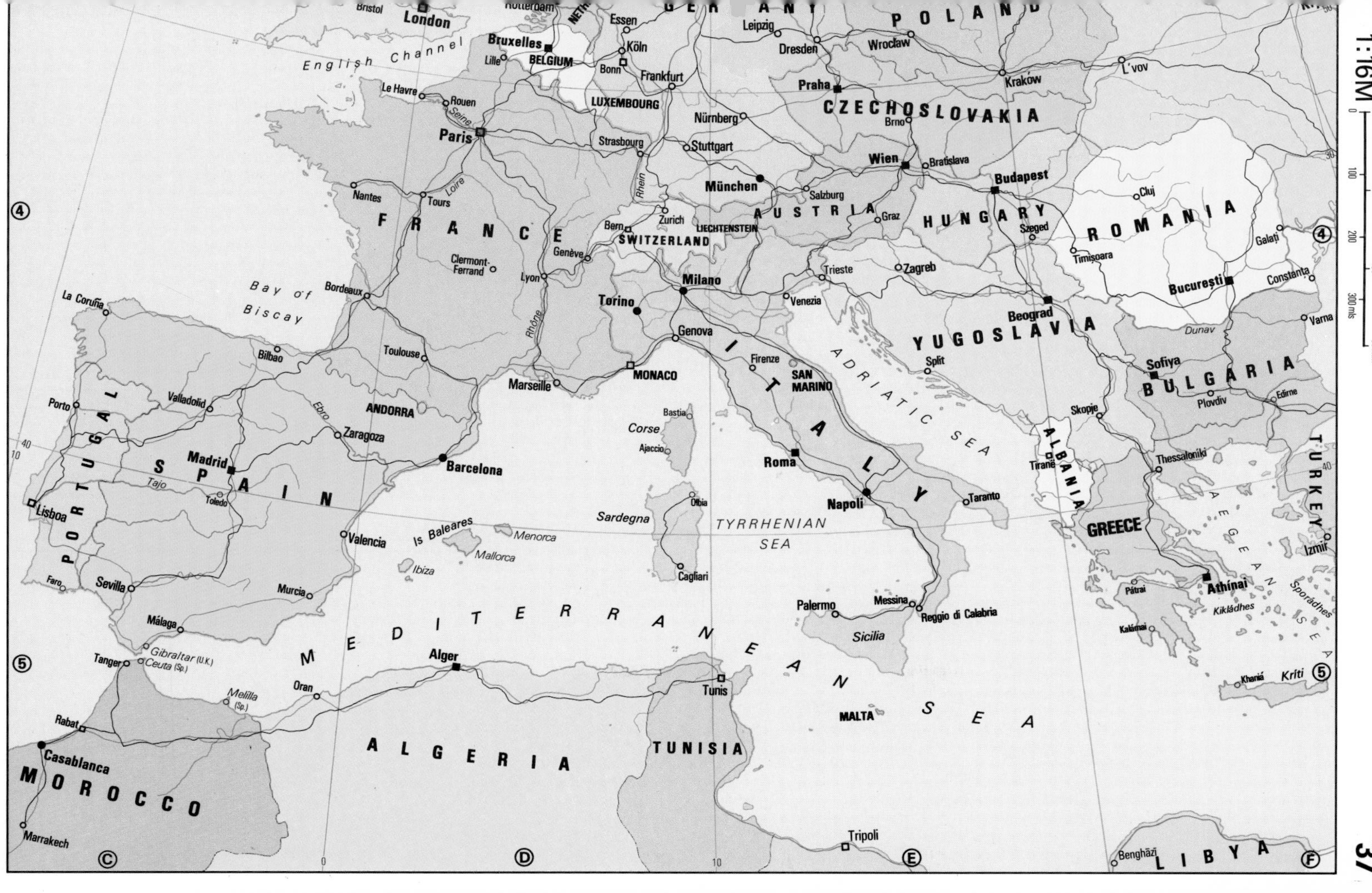
POLAND
CZECHOSLOVAKIA
HUNGARY
ROMANIA
BULGARIA
TURKEY
YUGOSLAVIA
ALBANIA
GREECE
AUSTRIA
SWITZERLAND
LIECHTENSTEIN
ITALY
SAN MARINO
MONACO
FRANCE
LUXEMBOURG
BELGIUM
ANDORRA
SPAIN
PORTUGAL
MOROCCO
ALGERIA
TUNISIA
LIBYA
MALTA
MEDITERRANEAN SEA
AEGEAN SEA
ADRIATIC SEA
TYRRHENIAN SEA
Bay of Biscay
English Channel
London
Bristol
Paris
Rouen
Le Havre
Seine
Loire
Tours
Nantes
Clermont-Ferrand
Lille
Bruxelles
Bonn
Köln
Essen
Frankfurt
Strasbourg
Rhein
Stuttgart
Nürnberg
München
Leipzig
Dresden
Praha
Wrocław
Kraków
L'vov
Brno
Wien
Bratislava
Budapest
Szeged
Salzburg
Graz
Zürich
Bern
Genève
Lyon
Rhône
Marseille
Milano
Torino
Genova
Venezia
Trieste
Zagreb
Beograd
Split
Skopje
Tiranë
Timişoara
Cluj
Bucureşti
Galaţi
Constanţa
Varna
Dunav
Sofiya
Plovdiv
Edirne
İzmir
Thessaloniki
Athínai
Pátrai
Kalámai
Kikládhes
Sporádhes
Khaniá
Kríti
Firenze
Roma
Napoli
Taranto
Reggio di Calabria
Messina
Palermo
Sicilia
Corse
Bastia
Ajaccio
Sardegna
Olbia
Cagliari
Tunis
Tripoli
Benghāzī
Toulouse
Bordeaux
Barcelona
Zaragoza
Ebro
Bilbao
Valladolid
Madrid
Toledo
Tajo
Valencia
Murcia
Málaga
Sevilla
Faro
Lisboa
Porto
La Coruña
Is Baleares
Mallorca
Menorca
Ibiza
Alger
Oran
Melilla (Sp.)
Gibraltar (U.K.)
Ceuta (Sp.)
Tanger
Rabat
Casablanca
Marrakech

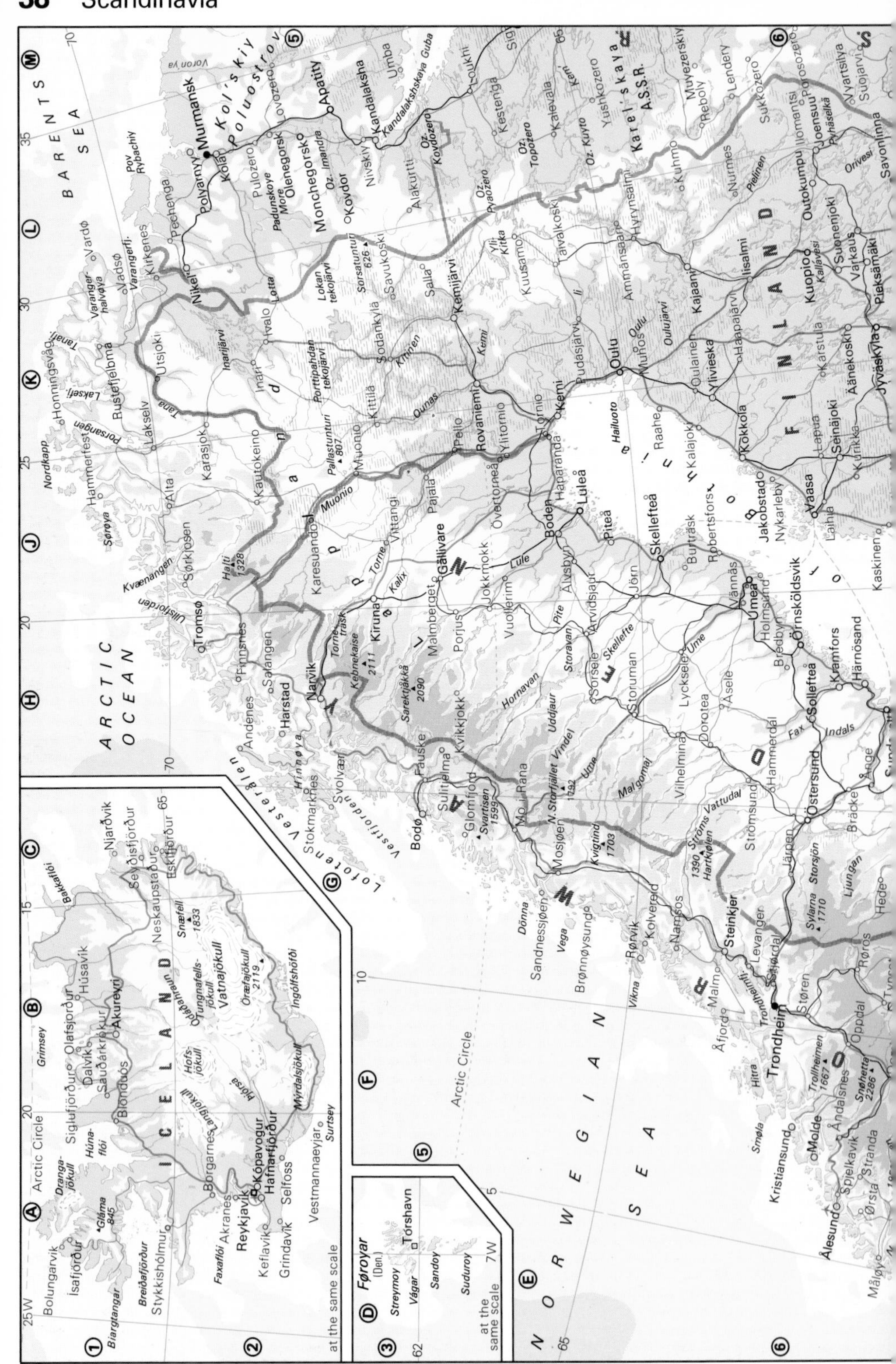
BARENTS SEA
ARCTIC OCEAN
NORWEGIAN SEA
Gulf of Bothnia
Lapland
FINLAND
SWEDEN
NORWAY
Kol'skiy Poluostrov
Karel'skaya A.S.S.R.
Murmansk
Kola
Polyarnyy
Apatity
Kandalaksha
Monchegorsk
Olenegorsk
Kovdor
Nikel
Kirkenes
Vadsø
Vardø
Varangerfj.
Hammerfest
Nordkapp
Honningsvåg
Lakselv
Karasjok
Kautokeino
Alta
Tromsø
Narvik
Harstad
Andenes
Bodø
Fauske
Mo i Rana
Mosjøen
Lofoten
Vesterålen
Vestfjorden
Kiruna
Gällivare
Jokkmokk
Luleå
Boden
Piteå
Skellefteå
Umeå
Örnsköldsvik
Härnösand
Kramfors
Sollefteå
Östersund
Storsjön
Steinkjer
Trondheim
Kristiansund
Molde
Ålesund
Rovaniemi
Kemi
Tornio
Haparanda
Oulu
Kajaani
Kuopio
Iisalmi
Kokkola
Jakobstad
Vaasa
Seinäjoki
Jyväskylä
Joensuu
Savonlinna
Kebnekaise 2111
Sarektjåkkå 2090
Halti 1328
Snøhetta 2286
Arctic Circle
ICELAND
Reykjavík
Akureyri
Húsavík
Ísafjörður
Vatnajökull
Hvannadalshnúkur
Hofsjökull
Langjökull
Mýrdalsjökull
Vestmannaeyjar
Surtsey
Færøyar (Den.)
Tórshavn
Streymoy
Vágar
Sandoy
Suðuroy
at the same scale

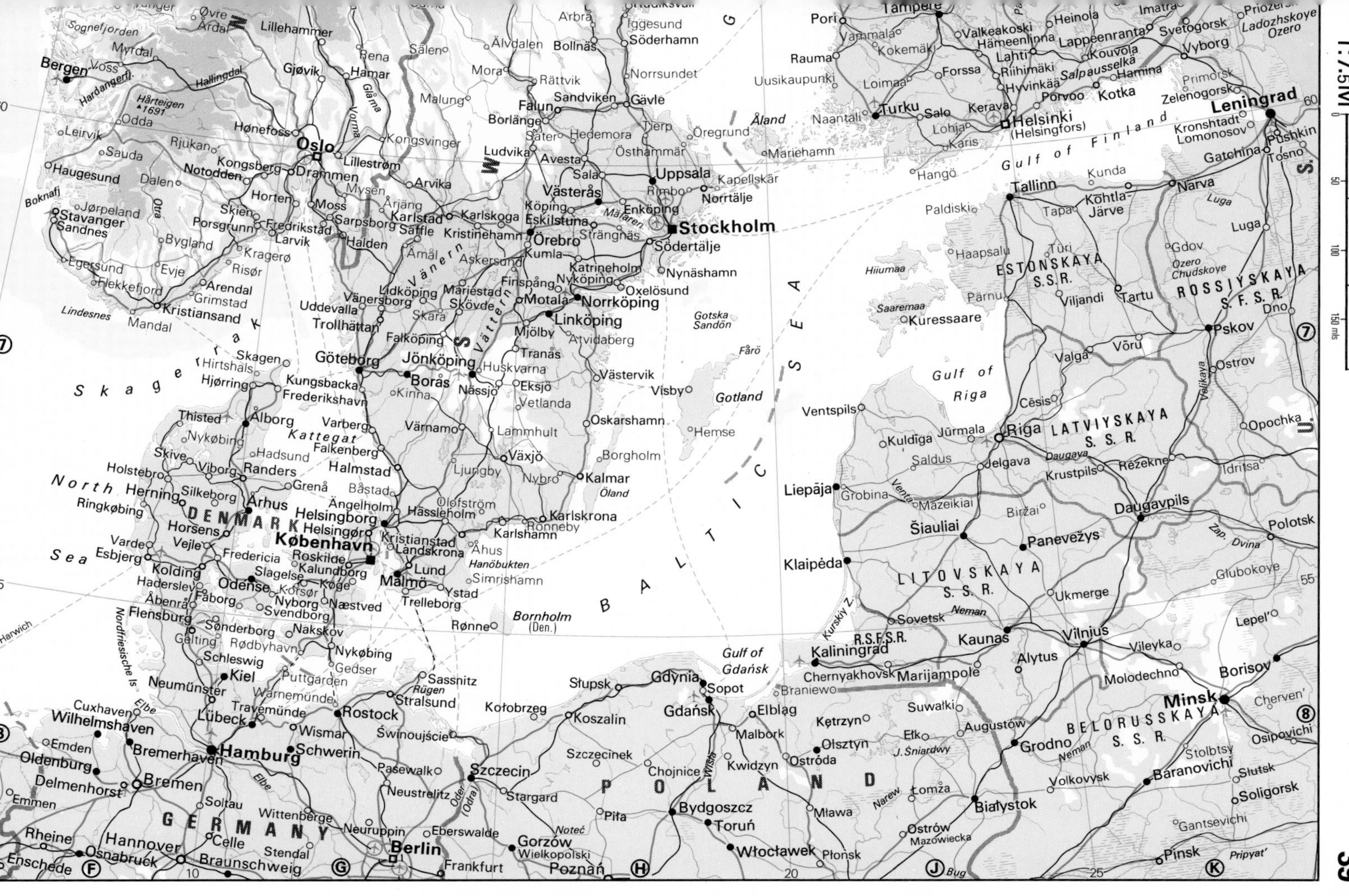
Leningrad
Helsinki (Helsingfors)
Tallinn
Riga
Vilnius
Minsk
Kaunas
Stockholm
Oslo
København
Göteborg
Hamburg
Berlin
Gdańsk
Gulf of Finland
Gulf of Riga
Gulf of Gdańsk
BALTIC SEA
North Sea
Skagerrak
Kattegat
ESTONSKAYA S.S.R.
LATVIYSKAYA S.S.R.
LITOVSKAYA S.S.R.
BELORUSSKAYA S.S.R.
ROSSIYSKAYA S.F.S.R.
R.S.F.S.R.
POLAND
GERMANY
DENMARK
Gotland
Öland
Bornholm (Den.)
Åland
Saaremaa
Hiiumaa
Turku
Tampere
Pori
Narva
Pskov
Tartu
Daugavpils
Šiauliai
Klaipėda
Liepāja
Kaliningrad
Białystok
Grodno
Uppsala
Västerås
Örebro
Norrköping
Linköping
Jönköping
Kalmar
Karlskrona
Malmö
Helsingborg
Århus
Ålborg
Odense
Kiel
Lübeck
Rostock
Szczecin
Bremen
Hannover
Bergen
Stavanger
Kristiansand
Gdynia
Bydgoszcz
Toruń
Poznań

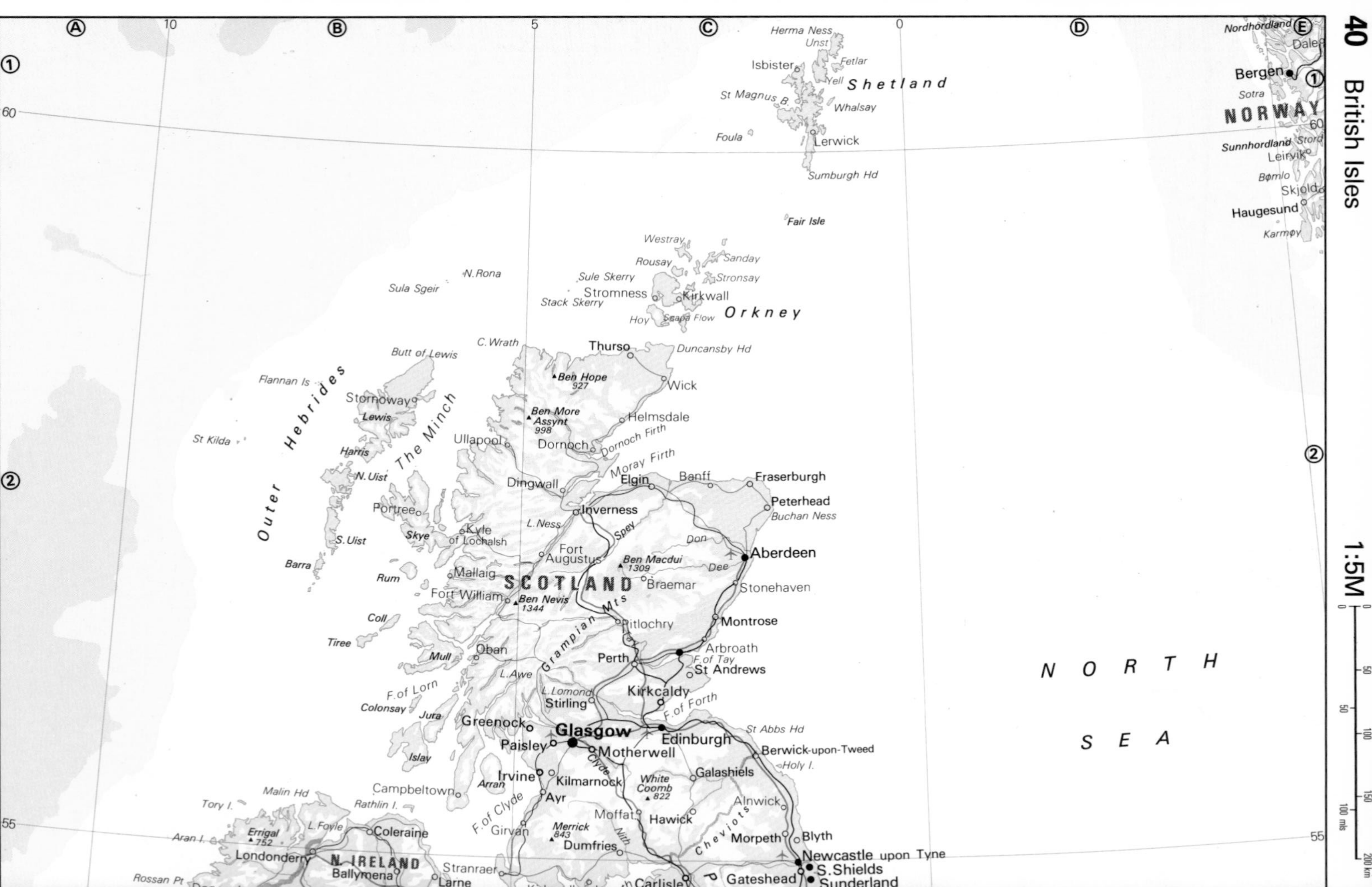

1:5M

0 50 100 150 200 km
0 50 100 mls

NORWAY
Nordhordland Dale
Bergen Sotra
Sunnhordland Stord
Leirvik
Bømlo Skjold
Haugesund
Karmøy

NORTH SEA

Shetland
Herma Ness
Unst
Fetlar
Isbister Yell Whalsay
St Magnus B.
Foula Lerwick
Sumburgh Hd
Fair Isle

Orkney
Westray Sanday
Rousay Stronsay
Sule Skerry Stromness Kirkwall
Stack Skerry Hoy Scapa Flow
Duncansby Hd

N. Rona
Sula Sgeir

Butt of Lewis
Flannan Is.
Stornoway
Lewis
Harris
N. Uist
Outer Hebrides
S. Uist
Barra
St Kilda

The Minch

C. Wrath
Ben Hope 927
Ben More Assynt 998
Ullapool
Thurso
Wick
Helmsdale
Dornoch Firth
Dingwall
Inverness
Moray Firth
L. Ness
Fort Augustus
Mallaig
Fort William
Ben Nevis 1344
Kyle of Lochalsh
Portree
Skye
Rum
Coll
Tiree
Mull
Oban
F. of Lorn
Colonsay
Jura
Islay
Campbeltown
Rathlin I.

SCOTLAND
Elgin
Banff
Spey
Ben Macdui 1309
Braemar
Dee
Don
Fraserburgh
Peterhead
Buchan Ness
Aberdeen
Stonehaven
Montrose
Arbroath
St Andrews
F. of Tay
Perth
Pitlochry
Tay
Grampian
Alve
L. Awe
L. Lomond
Stirling
Greenock
Paisley
Glasgow
Motherwell
Kilmarnock
Irvine
Ayr
Clyde
Arran
F. of Clyde
Girvan
Merrick 843
Stranraer
Larne

Kirkcaldy
F. of Forth
Edinburgh
St Abbs Hd
Berwick-upon-Tweed
Holy I.
Galashiels
Hawick
White Coomb 822
Moffat
Dumfries
Nith
Carlisle

Alnwick
Morpeth
Blyth
Newcastle upon Tyne
S. Shields
Gateshead Sunderland
Cheviot

N. IRELAND
Coleraine
Ballymena
Londonderry
L. Foyle
Malin Hd
Tory I.
Errigal 752
Aran I.
Rossan Pt.

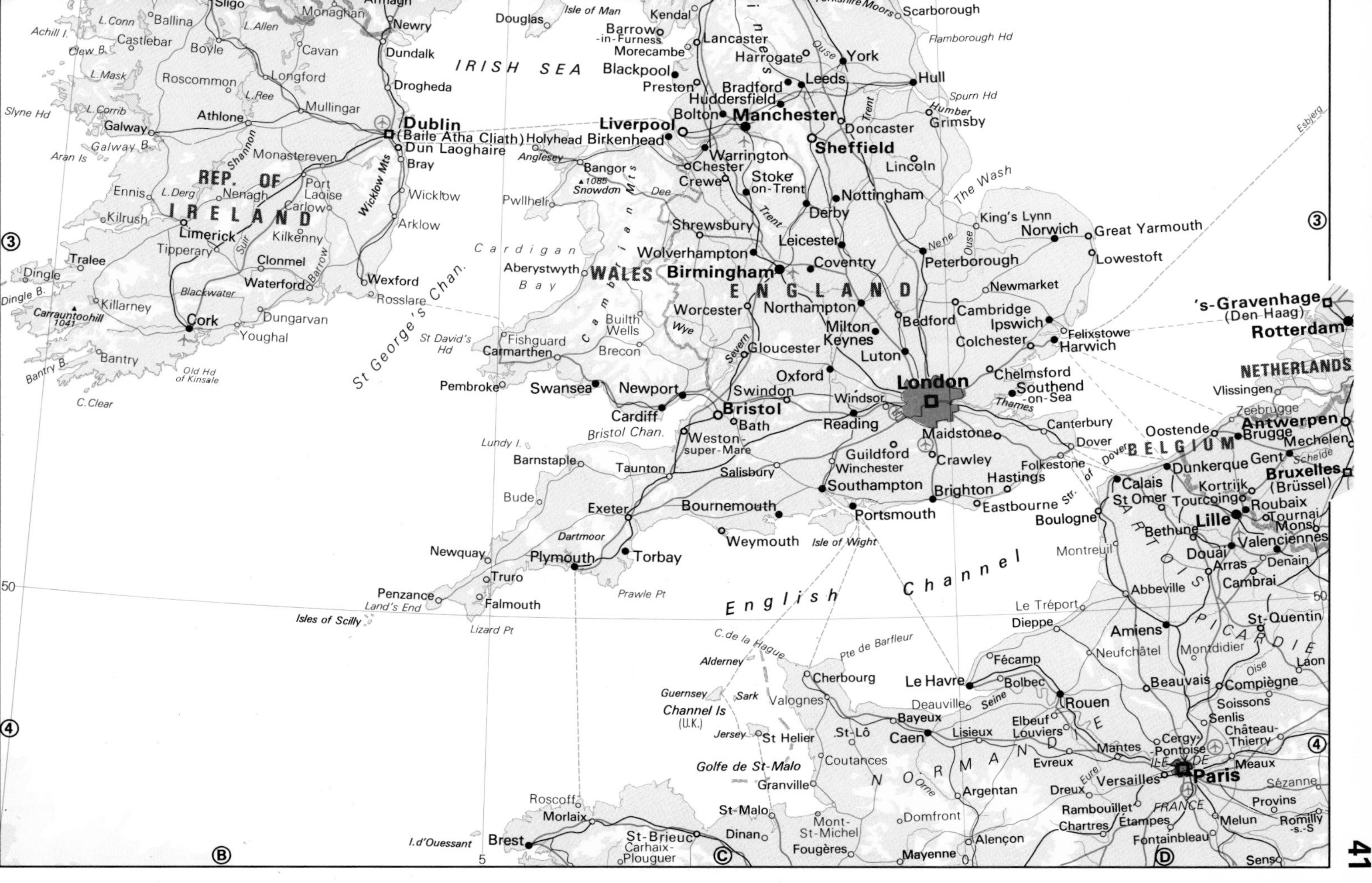

3
4
B
C
D
5
50
0
Sligo
Ballina
Castlebar
Boyle
Cavan
Monaghan
Armagh
Newry
Dundalk
Drogheda
Longford
Mullingar
Roscommon
Athlone
Galway
Dublin
(Baile Atha Cliath)
Dun Laoghaire
Bray
Wicklow
Arklow
Wexford
Rosslare
Monasterevan
Port Laoise
Carlow
Kilkenny
Nenagh
Ennis
Kilrush
Limerick
Tipperary
Clonmel
Waterford
Dungarvan
Youghal
Cork
Killarney
Tralee
Dingle
Bantry
REP. OF IRELAND
Wicklow Mts
Carrauntoohill
1041
C.Clear
Achill I.
Aran Is
Slyne Hd
IRISH SEA
Isle of Man
Douglas
Kendal
Barrow-in-Furness
Morecambe
Lancaster
Blackpool
Preston
Harrogate
York
Scarborough
Yorkshire Moors
Flamborough Hd
Hull
Spurn Hd
Grimsby
Leeds
Bradford
Huddersfield
Bolton
Manchester
Liverpool
Birkenhead
Holyhead
Anglesey
Bangor
Snowdon
Pwllheli
Warrington
Chester
Crewe
Stoke-on-Trent
Doncaster
Sheffield
Lincoln
Nottingham
Derby
The Wash
King's Lynn
Norwich
Great Yarmouth
Lowestoft
Shrewsbury
Leicester
Wolverhampton
Coventry
Peterborough
Birmingham
WALES
ENGLAND
Cardigan Bay
Aberystwyth
Newmarket
Cambridge
Ipswich
Felixstowe
Harwich
Colchester
Worcester
Northampton
Milton Keynes
Bedford
Luton
Builth Wells
Brecon
Fishguard
Carmarthen
St George's Chan.
St David's Hd
Gloucester
Oxford
Chelmsford
Southend-on-Sea
London
Pembroke
Swansea
Newport
Cardiff
Swindon
Windsor
Bristol
Bath
Reading
Bristol Chan.
Weston-super-Mare
Maidstone
Canterbury
Dover
Lundy I.
Barnstaple
Taunton
Salisbury
Guildford
Winchester
Crawley
Folkestone
Hastings
Southampton
Brighton
Eastbourne
Bude
Exeter
Bournemouth
Portsmouth
Dartmoor
Weymouth
Isle of Wight
Newquay
Plymouth
Torbay
Truro
Penzance
Land's End
Falmouth
Prawle Pt
Isles of Scilly
Lizard Pt
English Channel
'S-Gravenhage
(Den Haag)
Rotterdam
NETHERLANDS
Vlissingen
Zeebrugge
Oostende
Antwerpen
Brugge
Mechelen
BELGIUM
Gent
Bruxelles
(Brüssel)
Dunkerque
Calais
St Omer
Kortrijk
Tourcoing
Roubaix
Lille
Tournai
Mons
Boulogne
Bethune
Valenciennes
Douai
Arras
Denain
Cambrai
Montreuil
Abbeville
Le Tréport
Dieppe
Amiens
St-Quentin
PICARDIE
Neufchâtel
Montdidier
Laon
Fécamp
Le Havre
Bolbec
Rouen
Beauvais
Compiègne
Soissons
Senlis
Château-Thierry
C.de la Hague
Pte de Barfleur
Alderney
Cherbourg
Guernsey
Sark
Valognes
Channel Is
(U.K.)
Deauville
Bayeux
Jersey
St Helier
St-Lô
Caen
Lisieux
Elbeuf
Louviers
Mantes
Cergy-Pontoise
ILE DE FRANCE
Paris
Meaux
Golfe de St-Malo
Coutances
NORMANDIE
Evreux
Versailles
Sézanne
Granville
Argentan
Dreux
Provins
Roscoff
Morlaix
St-Malo
Mont-St-Michel
Domfront
Rambouillet
Chartres
Étampes
Melun
Romilly-s.-S
Brest
I.d'Ouessant
St-Brieuc
Carhaix-Plouguer
Dinan
Fougères
Alençon
Mayenne
Fontainebleau
Sens

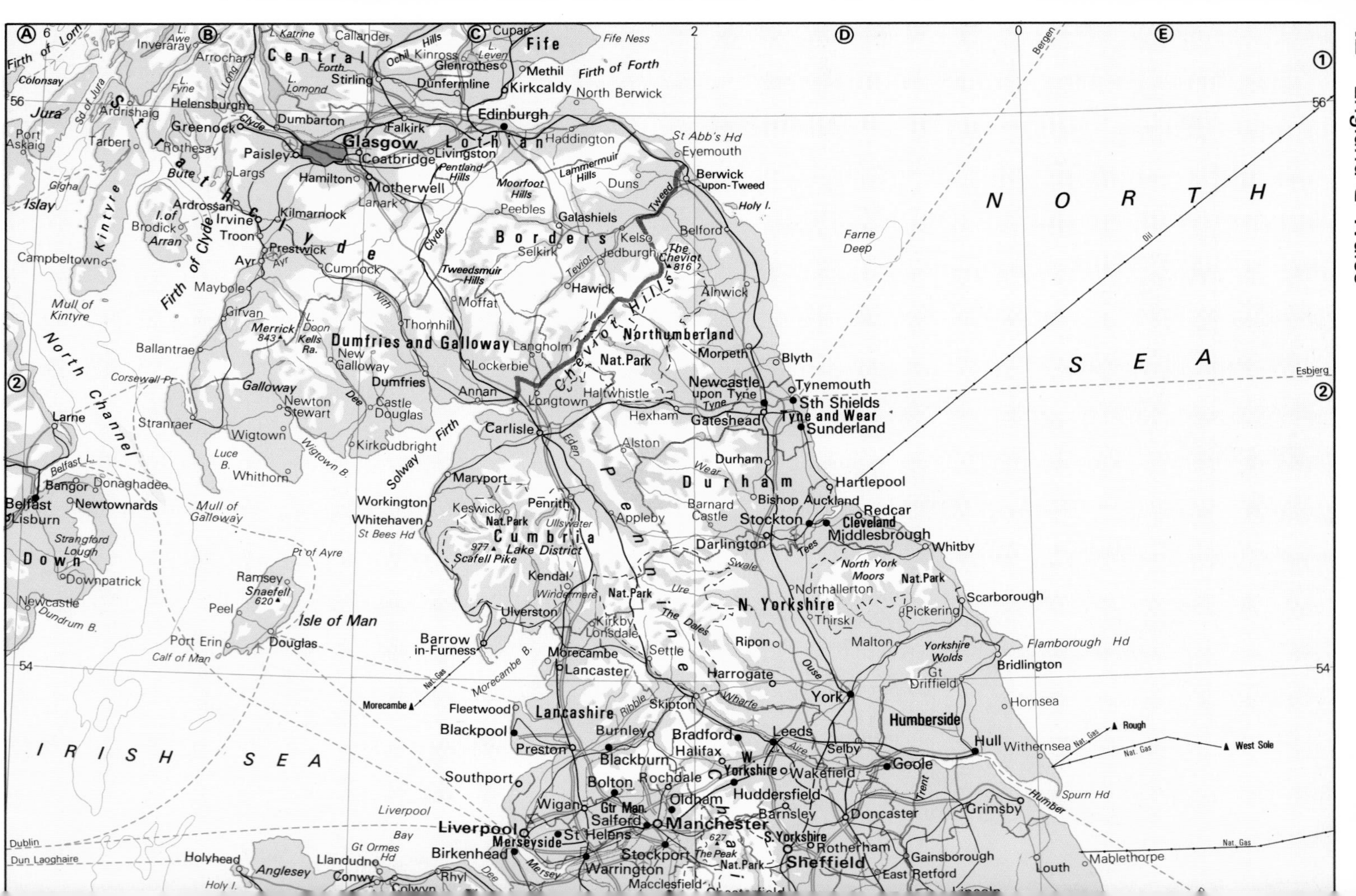
NORTH SEA
IRISH SEA
North Channel
Isle of Man
Firth of Forth
Firth of Clyde
Solway Firth
Liverpool Bay
Morecambe B.
Farne Deep
Flamborough Hd
Spurn Hd
Humber
Fife
Central
Lothian
Borders
Strathclyde
Dumfries and Galloway
Northumberland
Tyne and Wear
Durham
Cleveland
Cumbria
N. Yorkshire
Humberside
Lancashire
W. Yorkshire
S. Yorkshire
Gtr Man.
Merseyside
Down
Cheviot Hills
Pennine
Lake District
North York Moors
Yorkshire Wolds
The Dales
Nat. Park
Glasgow
Edinburgh
Newcastle upon Tyne
Sunderland
Sth Shields
Tynemouth
Gateshead
Middlesbrough
Hartlepool
Stockton
Darlington
Durham
York
Leeds
Bradford
Hull
Grimsby
Sheffield
Manchester
Liverpool
Birkenhead
Blackpool
Preston
Lancaster
Carlisle
Berwick upon-Tweed
Scarborough
Whitby
Bridlington
Goole
Doncaster
Wakefield
Huddersfield
Halifax
Harrogate
Ripon
Barrow in-Furness
Workington
Whitehaven
Kendal
Penrith
Belfast
Bangor
Newtownards
Larne
Douglas
Stranraer
Ayr
Kilmarnock
Paisley
Greenock
Dumfries
Holyhead
Anglesey
Rhyl
Conwy
Llandudno
Nat. Gas
Oil
Bergen
Esbjerg
West Sole
Rough
Morecambe

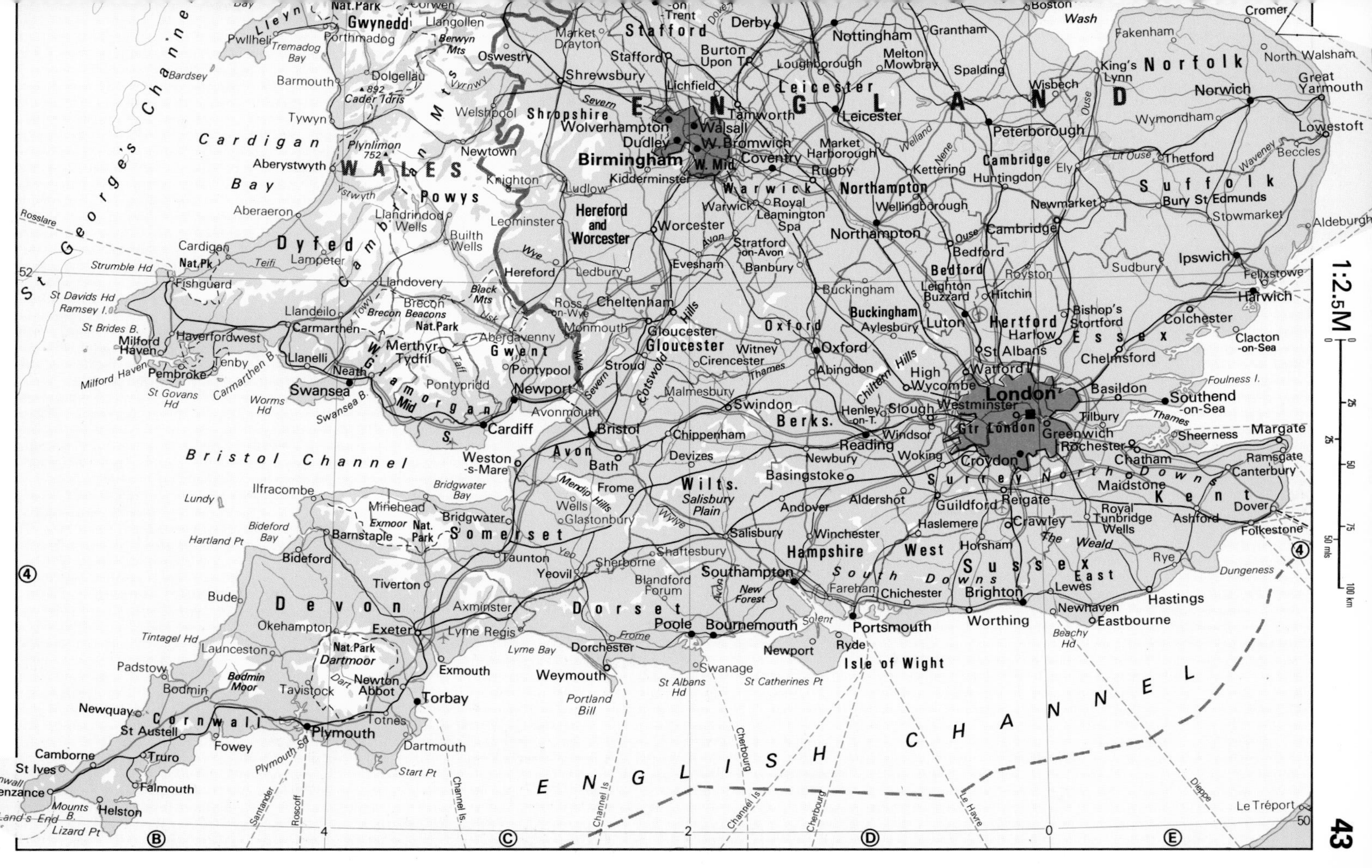
E N G L A N D
W A L E S
E N G L I S H C H A N N E L
Bristol Channel
Cardigan Bay
St George's Channel
Isle of Wight
London
Gtr London
Westminster
Birmingham
W. Mid.
Norfolk
Suffolk
Essex
Kent
Cambridge
Hertford
Bedford
Buckingham
Northampton
Leicester
Warwick
Stafford
Shropshire
Hereford and Worcester
Gloucester
Oxford
Berks.
Wilts.
Hampshire
Surrey
West Sussex
East Sussex
Dorset
Somerset
Avon
Devon
Cornwall
Dyfed
Powys
Gwynedd
Gwent
W. Glamorgan
Mid Glamorgan
S. Glamorgan
Norwich
Ipswich
Colchester
Chelmsford
Southend-on-Sea
Peterborough
Nottingham
Derby
Coventry
Wolverhampton
Reading
Southampton
Portsmouth
Bournemouth
Brighton
Bristol
Cardiff
Newport
Swansea
Exeter
Plymouth
Torbay
Penzance
Land's End
Lizard Pt
Dover
Folkestone
Canterbury
Hastings
Eastbourne
Salisbury
Weymouth
Dartmoor
Exmoor Nat. Park
Salisbury Plain
New Forest
Cotswold Hills
Chiltern Hills
Brecon Beacons Nat. Park
Le Havre
Dieppe
Le Tréport
Cherbourg
Channel Is.
Roscoff
Santander

0 25 50 75 100 km
0 25 50 mls

Shetland
Herma Ness
Unst
Yell
Fetlar
Whalsay
Muckle Roe
Brae
St Magnus Bay
Bressay
Lerwick
Hanstholm-Bergen
Grutness
Isbister
The Faither
Hillswick
Papa Stour
Scalloway
Fitful Hd
Sumburgh Hd
Fair Isle
Foula

Long Forties

NORTH SEA

Orkney
Papa Westray
N. Ronaldsay
Sanday
Stronsay
Eday
Shapinsay
Westray
Rousay
Kirkwall
Burray
S. Ronaldsay
Birsay
Mainland
Stromness
Hoy
Scapa Flow
Pentland Firth
Dunnet Hd
Eynemouth

Buchan Deep
Kinnairds Hd
Fraserburgh
Peterhead
Buchan Ness

Hoy
S. Ronaldsay
Burray
Pentland Firth
Dunnet Hd
Duncansby Hd
John o' Groats
Thurso
Wick
Lybster
Helmsdale
Brora
Dunrobin
Dornoch
Dornoch Firth
Tarbat Ness
Tain
Cromarty
Moray Firth
Lossiemouth
Elgin
Forres
Nairn
Banff
Keith
Dufftown
Huntly
Deveron
Inverurie
Aberdeen
Girdle Ness
Stonehaven
Montrose
Arbroath

Grampian
Grantown-on-Spey
Spey
Cairngorms
Ben Macdui 1310
Ballater
Braemar
Lochnagar 1155
Dee
Banchory
N. Esk
Brechin
Forfar
Sidlaw Hills
Dundee
St Andrews
Fife Ness
North Berwick
St Abb's Hd

Inverness
Loch Ness
Aviemore
Kingussie
Monadhliath Mts
Findhorn
Blair Atholl
Pitlochry
Aberfeldy
Tayside
Perth
Cupar
Fife
Methil
Kirkcaldy
Leven
Glenrothes
Kinross
Dunfermline
Firth of Forth
Edinburgh
Lothian
Haddington
Livingston
Falkirk
Glasgow

C. Wrath
Durness
Eriboll
Loch Eriboll
Kyle of Tongue
Ben Hope 927
Ben Loyal
Ben Kilbreck 961
Loch Shin
Lairg
L. Naver
Ben More Assynt 998
Ben Dearg 1081
Ben Wyvis 1045
Dingwall
Beauly
Strathpeffer
Alness
Black Isle
Garve

Lochinver
Eddrachillis Bay
Enard Bay
Ullapool
L. Broom
L. Maree
Gairloch
Loch Ewe
Greenstone Pt
Rubha Reidh
Loch Torridon
Applecross
Raasay
Ben Attow 1031
Fort Augustus
Loch Lochy
Ben Nevis 1344
Fort William
Loch Linnhe
Ballachulish

Butt of Lewis
Lewis
Stornoway
Loch Roag
Tarbert
Harris
North Uist
Benbecula
South Uist
Barra
Castlebay
Barra Hd

North Minch
Little Minch
The Minch
Rubha Hunish
Uig
Portree
Loch Snizort
Isle of Skye
Cuillin Hills
Loch Bracadale
Broadford
Kyle of Lochalsh
Kyleakin
Mallaig
Arisaig
Loch Morar
Loch Shiel
Eigg
Rum
Muck
Canna
Ardnamurchan Pt
Coll
Tiree
Tobermory
Staffa
Iona
Ulva
Mull
Firth of Lorn
Oban
Loch Etive
Loch Awe
Inveraray
Lochgilphead
Jura
Colonsay
Port Askaig

Morvern
Sound of Mull
Loch Linnhe
Loch Sunart

SCOTLAND
Highland
Central

Moffat
Ben Lawers 1214
L. Rannoch
L. Ericht
L. Tay
Loch Earn
Crieff
Killin
Crianlarich
Callander
Stirling
Dumbarton
Helensburgh
Greenock
Gourock
Rothesay
Arrochar
L. Lomond
L. Long
L. Fyne
Paisley

Beatrice

Oil

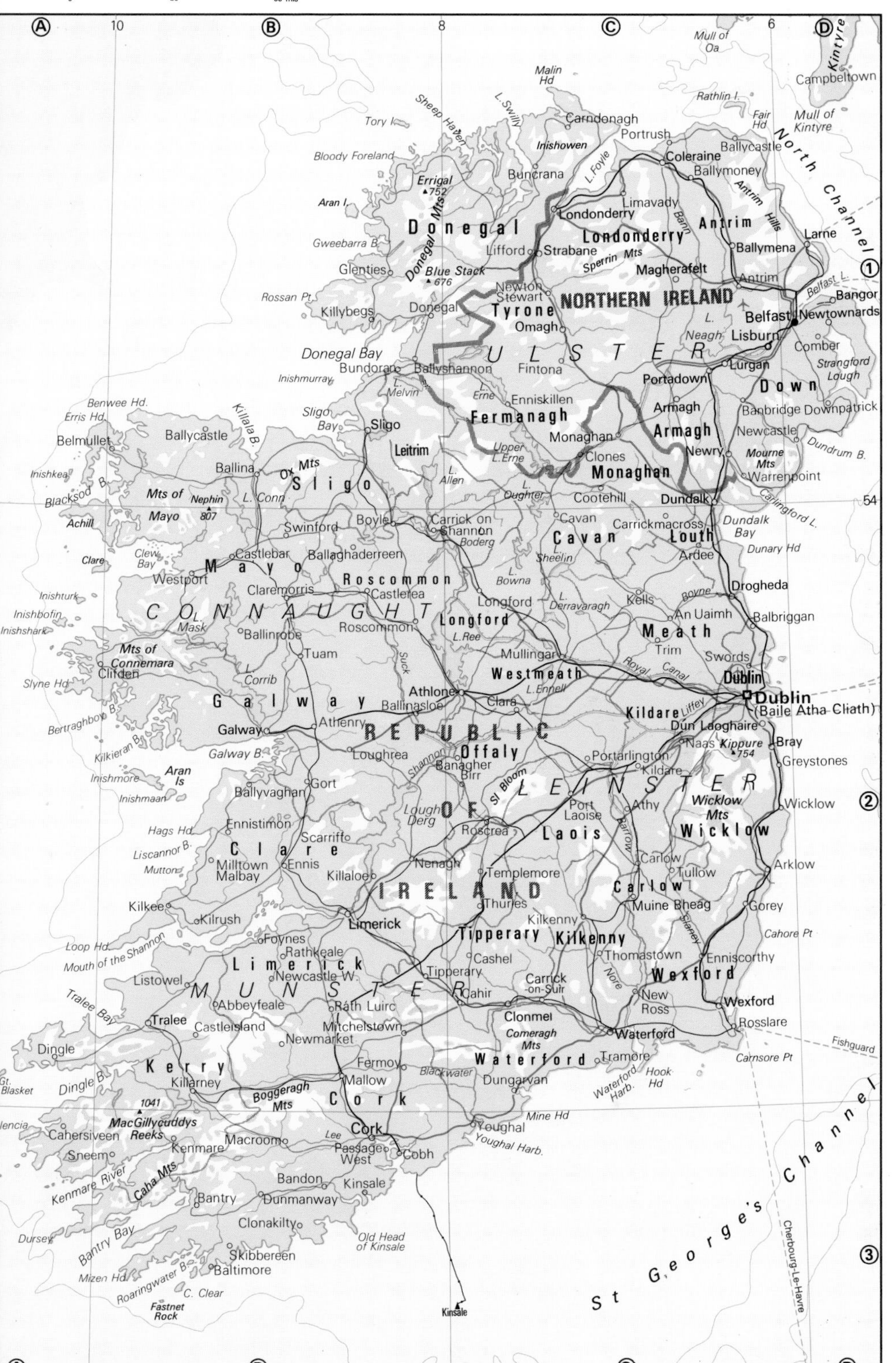
Malin Hd
L. Swilly
Sheep Haven
Tory I.
Carndonagh
Inishowen
Portrush
Rathlin I.
Fair Hd
Mull of Oa
Campbeltown
Kintyre
Mull of Kintyre
North Channel
Bloody Foreland
Buncrana
L. Foyle
Coleraine
Ballycastle
Ballymoney
Errigal 752
Aran I.
Londonderry
Limavady
Bann
Antrim
Antrim Hills
Larne
Donegal
Donegal Mts
Gweebarra B.
Lifford
Strabane
Londonderry
Ballymena
Sperrin Mts
Magherafelt
Glenties
Blue Stack 676
Newton Stewart
Antrim
Belfast L.
Bangor
Rossan Pt.
NORTHERN IRELAND
Killybegs
Donegal
Tyrone
Belfast
Newtownards
Omagh
L. Neagh
Lisburn
Comber
Donegal Bay
ULSTER
Strangford Lough
Bundoran
Ballyshannon
Fintona
Lurgan
Inishmurray
Portadown
Down
L. Melvin
L. Erne
Enniskillen
Benwee Hd.
Erris Hd.
Killala B.
Sligo Bay
Fermanagh
Armagh
Banbridge
Downpatrick
Belmullet
Ballycastle
Sligo
Monaghan
Armagh
Newcastle
Leitrim
Upper L. Erne
Clones
Newry
Mourne Mts
Dundrum B.
Inishkea
Ballina
Ox Mts
Monaghan
Warrenpoint
Blacksod B.
Sligo
L. Allen
Mts of Mayo
Nephin 807
L. Conn
L. Oughter
Cootehill
Dundalk
Carlingford L.
54
Achill
Boyle
Carrick on Shannon
Cavan
Carrickmacross
Dundalk Bay
Swinford
L. Boderg
Cavan
Louth
Clare
Clew Bay
Castlebar
Ballaghaderreen
L. Sheelin
Ardee
Dunany Hd
Westport
Mayo
Roscommon
Castlerea
L. Bowna
Inishturk
Claremorris
Boyne
Drogheda
Inishbofin
CONNAUGHT
Longford
L. Derravaragh
Kells
An Uaimh
Balbriggan
Inishshark
L. Mask
Roscommon
Longford
Ballinrobe
L.Ree
Meath
Trim
Mts of Connemara
Tuam
Suck
Mullingar
Swords
Clifden
Royal Canal
Slyne Hd
L. Corrib
Westmeath
Dublin
L. Ennell
Dublin
(Baile Atha Cliath)
Galway
Athlone
Clara
Kildare
Liffey
Bertraghboy B.
Ballinasloe
Dun Laoghaire
Galway
Athenry
REPUBLIC
Naas
Kippure 754
Bray
Kilkieran B.
Galway B.
Loughrea
Offaly
Portarlington
Greystones
Aran Is
Shannon
Banagher
Kildare
Inishmore
Birr
St Bloom
LEINSTER
Inishmaan
Ballyvaghan
Gort
Port Laoise
Athy
Wicklow Mts
Wicklow
Lough Derg
OF
Hags Hd
Ennistimon
Scarriff
Roscrea
Laois
Barrow
Wicklow
Liscannor B.
Clare
Mutton
Milltown Malbay
Ennis
Nenagh
Templemore
Carlow
Tullow
Arklow
Killaloe
IRELAND
Carlow
Muine Bheag
Kilkee
Thurles
Gorey
Kilrush
Limerick
Kilkenny
Slaney
Foynes
Tipperary
Kilkenny
Cahore Pt
Loop Hd
Mouth of the Shannon
Rathkeale
Cashel
Thomastown
Enniscorthy
Limerick
Newcastle W.
Tipperary
Nore
Wexford
Listowel
MUNSTER
Carrick -on-Suir
Tralee Bay
Abbeyfeale
Cahir
New Ross
Wexford
Rath Luirc
Tralee
Castleisland
Mitchelstown
Clonmel
Rosslare
Newmarket
Comeragh Mts
Waterford
Fishguard
Dingle
Fermoy
Waterford
Tramore
Carnsore Pt
Kerry
Blackwater
Hook Hd
Gt. Blasket
Dingle B.
Killarney
Mallow
Dungarvan
Waterford Harb.
Boggeragh Mts
Cork
1041
Mine Hd
Valencia
MacGillycuddys Reeks
Cork
Youghal
Cahersiveen
Kenmare
Macroom
Lee
Passage West
Youghal Harb.
Sneem
Cobh
St George's Channel
Kenmare River
Caha Mts
Bandon
Kinsale
Bantry
Dunmanway
Clonakilty
Bantry Bay
Dursey
Old Head of Kinsale
Cherbourg-Le-Havre
Skibbereen
Baltimore
Mizen Hd
Roaringwater B.
C. Clear
Fastnet Rock
Kinsale
A B C D
10 8 6
1 2 3

NORTH SEA

NETHERLANDS

BELGIUM

GERMANY

LUXEMBOURG

SWITZERLAND
AUSTRIA
ITALY
FRANCE
LIECHTENSTEIN
VORALBERG
TIROL
TRENTINO
VENETO
LOMBARDIA
PIEMONTE
VALLE D'AOSTA
FRANCHE COMTÉ
Bayerische Alpen
Kitzbüheler Alpen
Ötztal
Stubaier Alpen
Zillertaler Alpen
Lechtaler Alpen
Allgäu
Rhätikon
Silvretta
Engadin
Ortles
Alpi Retiche
Alpi Venoste
Dolomiti
Alpi Orobie
Berner Oberland
Glarner
Alpi Pennine
Alpes du Valais
Alpi Graie
Chablais
Bauges
Vanoise
Belledonne
Lago Maggiore
L. di Como
Lago di Garda
L. di Lugano
L. d'Orta
L. Léman (L. of Geneva)
L. de Neuchâtel
Zürich
Bern (Berne)
Basel (Basle)
Luzern (Lucerne)
Lausanne
Genève (Geneva)
Innsbruck
Bolzano (Bozen)
Trento
Verona
Vicenza
Padova (Padua)
Venezia (Venice)
Milano (Milan)
Torino (Turin)
Bergamo
Brescia
Novara
Alessandria
Piacenza
Parma
Modena
Bologna
Ferrara
Mantova (Mantua)
Cremona
Pavia
Como
Lecco
Lugano
Locarno
Bellinzona
Chur
St Gallen
St Moritz
Davos
Chamonix
Aosta
Annecy
Chambéry
Briançon
Besançon
Mt Blanc 4810
Matterhorn 4478
Mte Rosa 4556
Jungfrau 4158
Finsteraarhorn 4274
Gran Paradiso 4061
P. Bernina 4049
Ortles 3899
Marmolada 3342
Mt Viso 3841
St Gotthard P.
Simplon P.
Brenner 1371
Po
Adige
Rhein
Rhône
Inn
Ticino
Adda
Oglio

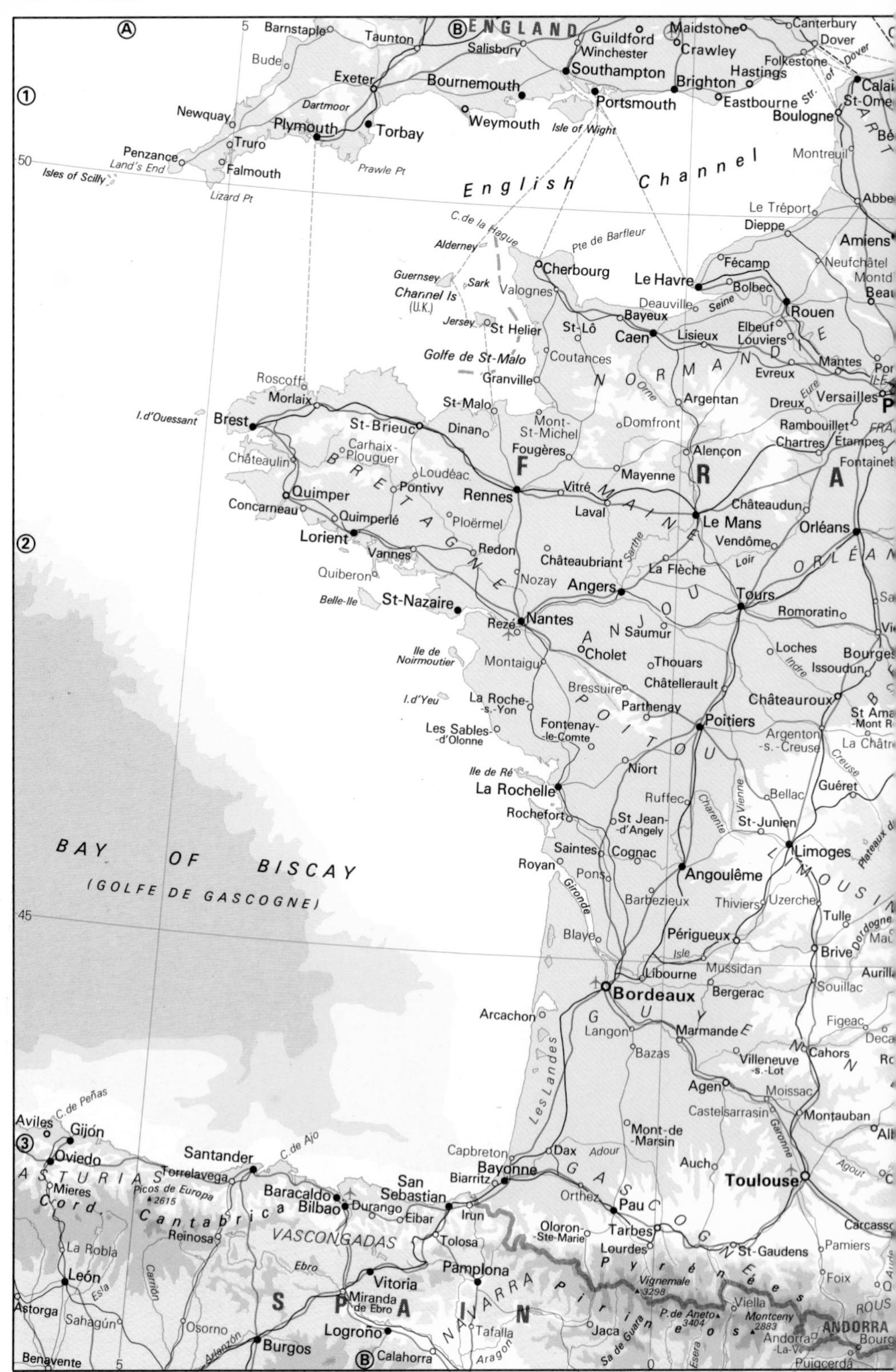

Barnstaple
Taunton
Bude
Newquay
Exeter
Plymouth
Torbay
Penzance
Truro
Falmouth
Land's End
Isles of Scilly
Lizard Pt
Prawle Pt
Dartmoor

ENGLAND
Salisbury
Guildford
Winchester
Bournemouth
Southampton
Crawley
Weymouth
Portsmouth
Isle of Wight
Brighton
Hastings
Eastbourne
Maidstone
Canterbury
Dover
Folkestone
Calais
St-Ome
Boulogne
Montreuil
Abbe
Le Tréport
Dieppe
Amiens
Neufchâtel
Montd
Bea

English Channel

C. de la Hague
Alderney
Guernsey
Channel Is
(U.K.)
Sark
St Helier
Jersey
Golfe de St-Malo
Granville
St-Malo
Dinan
Roscoff
Morlaix
Brest
I. d'Ouessant
St-Brieuc
Châteaulin
Carhaix-Plouguer
Loudéac
Quimper
Pontivy
Concarneau
Quimperlé
Ploërmel
Lorient
Vannes
Redon
Quiberon
Belle-Ile
St-Nazaire
Rezé
Nantes
Ile de Noirmoutier
Montaigu
I. d'Yeu
La Roche-s.-Yon
Les Sables-d'Olonne
Ile de Ré
La Rochelle
Rochefort
Cherbourg
Valognes
Pte de Barfleur
Le Havre
Fécamp
Bolbec
Deauville
Bayeux
St-Lô
Caen
Lisieux
Coutances
Mont-St-Michel
Fougères
Domfront
Argentan
Mayenne
Rennes
Vitré
Laval
Châteaubriant
Nozay
Angers
Saumur
Cholet
Thouars
Bressuire
Châtellerault
Parthenay
Fontenay-le-Comte
Niort
Poitiers
Argenton-s.-Creuse
Ruffec
St Jean-d'Angely
Saintes
Cognac
Royan
Pons
Barbezieux
Blaye
Blaye

Elbeuf
Louviers
Rouen
Mantes
Evreux
Dreux
Versailles
Rambouillet
Chartres
Étampes
Fontaine
Alençon
Châteaudun
Le Mans
Vendôme
Orléans
La Flèche
Tours
Romoratin
Loches
Bourges
Issoudun
Châteauroux
St Ama
Mont R
La Châtr
Creuse
Guéret
Bellac
St-Junien
Limoges
Uzerche
Thiviers
Tulle
Brive
Souillac
Aurill
Figeac
Deca
Cahors
Rc
Moissac
Montauban
All
Toulouse
Carcasso
Pamiers
St-Gaudens
Foix
ROUS
ANDORRA
Bourg

NORMANDIE
BRETAGNE
MAINE
ORLÉAN
POITOU
LIMOUSIN
GASCOGNE
Les Landes
Pyrénées

F R A N C E

BAY OF BISCAY
(GOLFE DE GASCOGNE)

Périgueux
Bergerac
Mussidan
Isle
Libourne
Bordeaux
Arcachon
Langon
Bazas
Marmande
Villeneuve-s.-Lot
Agen
Castelsarrasin
Capbreton
Dax
Adour
Mont-de-Marsin
Auch
Bayonne
Biarritz
Orthez
Pau
Tarbes
Lourdes
Oloron-Ste-Marie
Vignemale 3298
P. de Aneto 3404
Viella
Montceny 2883
Andorra-La-V
Puigcerdà

Aviles
Gijón
C. de Peñas
Oviedo
Mieres
La Robla
León
Astorga
Benavente
Sahagún
ASTURIAS
Cord.
Santander
Torrelavega
Reinosa
Picos de Europa 2615
Cantábrica
Baracaldo
Bilbao
Durango
Eibar
Irun
Tolosa
San Sebastian
VASCONGADAS
Carrion
Osorno
Ebro
Miranda de Ebro
Vitoria
Pamplona
Jaca
Sa de Guara
Esera
Sahagún
Burgos
Logroño
Calahorra
Tafalla
Aragon
NAVARRA
Esla
Astudillo
Pisuerga
C. de Ajo
 SPAIN

0 50 100 150 200 km
0 50 100 mils

① ② ③

Germany · **Hessen** · **Rheinland Pfalz** · **Saarland** · **Baden** · **Württemberg** · **Bayern** · **Switzerland** · **Austria**

Zeebrugge · Brugge · Gent · Bruxelles (Brüssel) · Roubaix · Tournai · Valenciennes · Denain · Maubeuge · Fourmies · St-Quentin · Charleville-Mézières · Laon · Compiègne · Reims · Epernay · Chalons-s.-M. · Sézanne · Troyes · Romilly-s.-S · Provins · Joigny · Auxerre · Avallon

Eindhoven · Antwerpen (Anvers) · Mechelen · Hasselt · Maastricht · Leuven · St-Truiden · Namur · Charleroi · Marche · Bastogne · Arlon · Longwy · Thionville · Sedan · Verdun · Metz · Sarreguemines · Sarrebourg · Nancy · St-Dizier · Chaumont · Langres · Dijon · Besançon · Montbéliard · Belfort · Vesoul

Mönchengladbach · Düsseldorf · Westfalen · Köln · Siegen · Aachen · Bonn · Bad Godesberg · Liège · Euskirchen · Andernach · Koblenz · Limburg · Bad Kreuznach · Bingen · Trier · Luxembourg · Saarlouis · Saarbrücken · Kaiserslautern · Pirmasens · Pforzheim · Rastatt

Erfurt · Jena · Eisenach · Gera · Zwickau · Bad Hersfeld · Alsfeld · Fulda · Coburg · Plauen · Hof · Cheb · Schweinfurt · Bamberg · Bayreuth · Weiden · Würzburg · Kitzingen · Erlangen · Fürth · Nürnberg · Amberg · Ansbach · Crailsheim · Parsberg · Regensburg · Donau · Ingolstadt

Marburg · Giessen · Frankfurt · Wiesbaden · Mainz · Offenbach · Darmstadt · Aschaffenburg · Worms · Mannheim · Heidelberg · Speyer · Heilbronn · Karlsruhe · Ludwigsburg · Stuttgart · Esslingen · Baden-Baden · Tübingen · Reutlingen · Offenburg · Freiburg · Mulhouse · Lörrach · Colmar · St-Dié · Strasbourg · Épinal

Ludwigshafen · Landshut · Dachau · Augsburg · Ulm · München · Starnberg · Rosenheim · Memmingen · Landsberg · Kempten · Bad Tölz · Kufstein · Garmisch-P. · Füssen · Friedrichshafen · Lindau · Dornbirn · Ravensburg · Biberach · Tuttlingen · Konstanz · Schaffhausen · Winterthur · St Gallen · Feldkirch · Bludenz · Innsbruck · Brenner 1370 · Landeck · Wildspitze 3774

Heidenheim · Donauwörth

Troyes · Bar-s-A. · Chaumont · Langres · Dôle · Beaune · Autun · Le Creusot · Chalon-s.-S. · Lons-l.-S. · Montceau-l.-M. · Mâcon · Bourg · Villefranche · Bellegarde · Genève · Annecy · Aix-l.-B. · Chambéry · Lyon · Villeurbanne · Vienne · Voiron · Grenoble

Dijon · Besançon · Biel · Neuchâtel · Pontarlier · Fribourg · Lausanne · Thun · Bern · Interlaken · Jungfrau 4158 · Luzern · Zug · Zürich · Basel · Olten · Zurich · St Gotthard 2112 · Schwyz · Arosa · Chur · St Moritz · Ortles 3899 · Bolzano · Merano · Brunico

Liechtenstein · Vaduz

Martigny · Col du Gd St Bernard 2469 · Matterhorn 4477 · Mt Blanc 4807 · Aosta · Brig · Simplon 2009 · Domodossola · L. di Como · Sondrio · Lecco · Lovère · Bergamo · L. di Garda · Vicenza · Rovereto · Bassano · Trento · Edolo · Marmolada 3342

Annecy · Albertville · Gran Paradiso 4061 · Ivrea · Biella · Varese · Como · Monza · Brescia · Verona · Mantova · Rovigo

Chambéry · Aix-l.-B. · Vienne · Voiron · Novara · Milano (Milan) · Lodi · Pavia · Cremona · Carpi · Ferrara · Modena · Bologna

St-Chamond · St-Étienne · Annonay · Romans-s.-I. · Bourg-d.-P. · Grenoble · Massif du Pelvoux · Briançon · Gap · Col du Mt Cenis 2803 · Susa · Torino (Turin) · Asti · Casale Monf. · Vercelli · Piacenza · Alessandria · Novi Ligure · Parma · Reggio n. E. · Bologna

Le Puy · Mt Mézenc 1754 · Valence · Mte Viso 3841 · Cuneo · Mondovi · Ovada · Alba · Appno Ligure · Genova (Genoa) · Rapallo · Savona · Carrara · Mte Cimone 2165

Aubenas · Montélimar · Nyons · Sisteron · Mt Pelat 3053 · Digne · C. de Tende 1870 · Savona · La Spezia · Massa · Viareggio · Lucca · Pistoia · Prato · Firenze (Florence)

Mende · Mt Aigoual 1565 · Alès · Bagnols-s.-Cèze · Orange · Carpentras · Cavaillon · Avignon · Nîmes · Arles · Salon-d.-P. · Aix-en-Provence · Aubagne · Marseille · Toulon · Hyères · Îles d'Hyères

Durance · Var · Castellane · Provence · Grasse · Draguignan · St Raphaël · St Tropez · Cannes · Monte Carlo · Monaco · San Remo · Imperia · Alassio · Nice · Côte d'Azur · Ligurian Sea · Pisa · Pontedera · Livorno · Cecina · Siena

Martigues · Golfe du Lion · Sète · Narbonne · Perpignan · C. de Creus

Cap Corse · G. de St Florent · Bastia · Elba · Piombino · Portoferraio · Pianosa · Grosseto · Montecristo · Giglio · Orbetello · Follonica

Calvi · Corse (Corsica) · Mt Cinto 2710 · C. Rosso · Ponte Lecca · Corte · Montechristo · Cateraggio · Ajaccio

Massif Central · Nord du Limousin · Loir · Allier · Saône · Doubs · Jura · Savoie · Dauphiné · Franche-Comté · Bourgogne · Nivernais · Champagne · Ardennes · Lorraine · Luxembourg · Picardie · Moselle · Rhein · Donau · Po · Adige · Taro · Stura · Verdon

Ⓓ Ⓔ

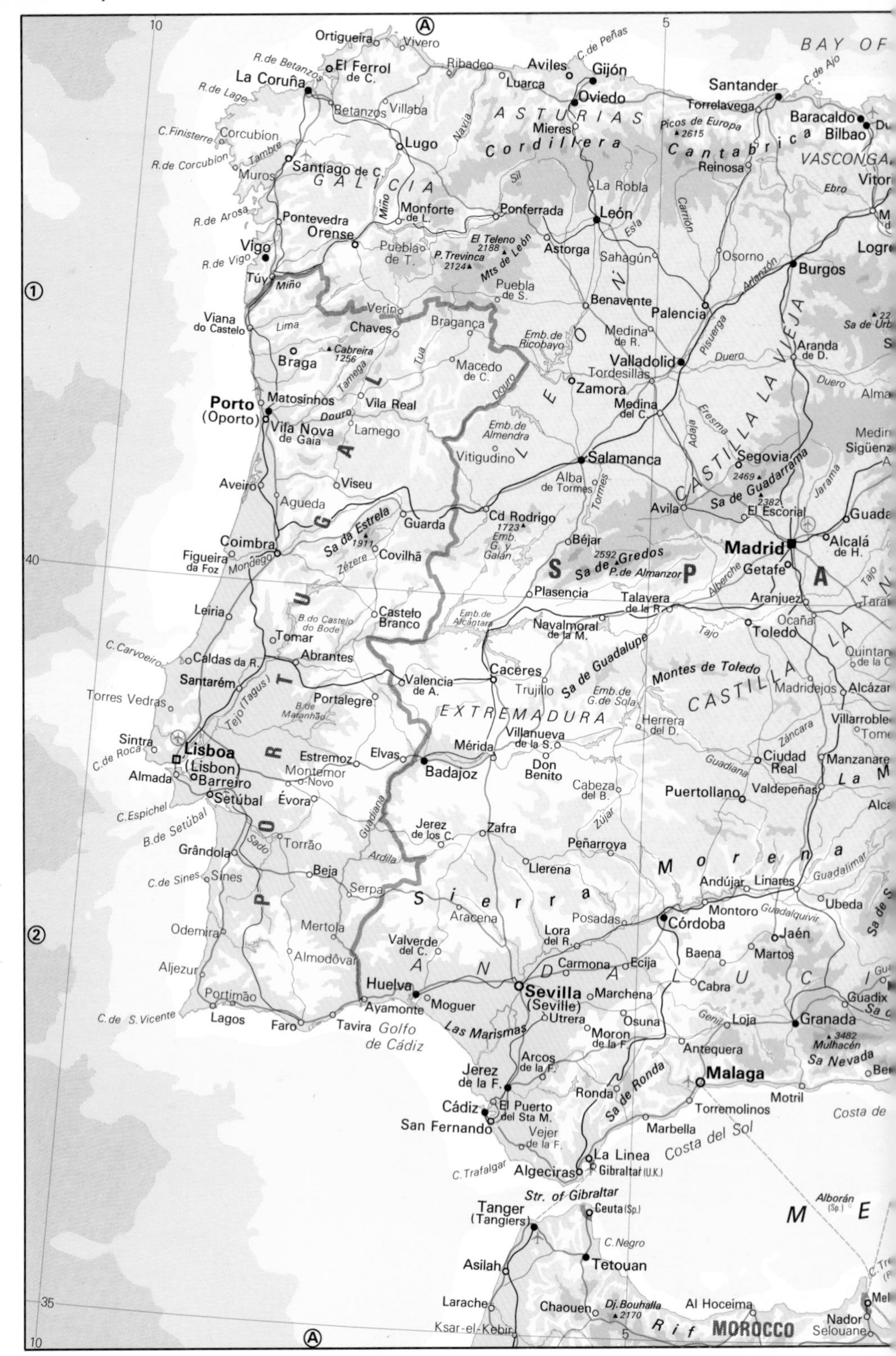
BAY OF
La Coruña
El Ferrol de C.
Ortigueira
Vivero
Ribadeo
Luarca
Aviles
Gijón
Oviedo
Mieres
Santander
Torrelavega
Baracaldo
Bilbao
Reinosa
ASTURIAS
Cordillera Cantabrica
Picos de Europa
VASCONGA
GALICIA
Santiago de C.
Lugo
Betanzos
Villaba
Corcubíon
Muros
Monforte de L.
Ponferrada
León
Astorga
La Robla
Pontevedra
Orense
Vigo
Túy
Miño
Sahagún
Osorno
Burgos
Logr
Vitori
Ebro
El Teleno 2188
P. Trevinca 2124
Mts de León
Puebla de S.
Puebla de T.
Benavente
Palencia
Verín
Chaves
Bragança
Viana do Castelo
Braga
Cabreira 1256
Macedo de C.
Medina de R.
Valladolid
Tordesillas
Zamora
Medina del C.
LEON
CASTILLA LA VIEJA
Aranda de D.
Duero
Douro
Porto (Oporto)
Matosinhos
Vila Nova de Gaia
Vila Real
Lamego
Emb. de Almendra
Vitigudino
Salamanca
Segovia
Sa de Guadarrama
2469
2382
El Escorial
Avila
Viseu
Aveiro
Agueda
Alba de Tormes
Cd Rodrigo
1723
Guarda
Sa da Estrela
1911
Covilhã
Coimbra
Figueira da Foz
Mondego
Béjar
Madrid
Alcalá de H.
Getafe
2592 Gredos
Sa de P. de Almanzor
SPAIN
PORTUGAL
Plasencia
Talavera de la R.
Aranjuez
Leiria
Castelo Branco
Tomar
Emb. de Alcántara
Navalmoral de la M.
Toledo
Ocaña
Tajo
C. Carvoeiro
Caldas da R.
Abrantes
Caceres
Sa de Guadalupe
Montes de Toledo
Santarém
Valencia de A.
Trujillo
Emb. de G. de Sola
CASTILLA LA NUEVA
Madridejos
Alcázar
Torres Vedras
Portalegre
Tejo (Tagus)
EXTREMADURA
Herrera del D.
Sintra
C. de Roca
Lisboa (Lisbon)
Almada
Barreiro
Mérida
Villanueva de la S.
Don Benito
Elvas
Estremoz
Badajoz
Montemor-o-Novo
Ciudad Real
Guadiana
Puertollano
Valdepeñas
Cabeza del B.
Setúbal
Évora
C. Espichel
B. de Setúbal
Jerez de los C.
Zafra
Peñarroya
Grândola
Torrão
Sado
Llerena
Sierra Morena
Andújar
Linares
Beja
C. de Sines
Sines
Serpa
Aracena
Posadas
Montoro
Guadalquivir
Córdoba
Ubeda
Jaén
Odemira
Mertola
Valverde del C.
Lora del R.
Baena
Martos
Aljezur
Almodôvar
ANDALUCIA
Carmona
Ecija
Huelva
Sevilla (Seville)
Marchena
Cabra
Guadix
Portimão
C. de S. Vicente
Lagos
Faro
Tavira
Ayamonte
Moguer
Golfo de Cádiz
Las Marismas
Utrera
Osuna
Loja
Granada
3482 Mulhacén
Sa Nevada
Moron de la F.
Antequera
Arcos de la F.
Jerez de la F.
Malaga
Ronda
Sa de Ronda
Cádiz
El Puerto del Sta M.
San Fernando
Torremolinos
Motril
Costa de
Vejer de la F.
Marbella
Costa del Sol
La Linea
C. Trafalgar
Algeciras
Gibraltar (U.K.)
Str. of Gibraltar
Tanger (Tangiers)
Ceuta (Sp.)
Alborán (Sp.)
C. Negro
Asilah
Tetouan
Larache
Chaouen
Dj. Bouhalla 2170
Al Hoceima
Rif
MOROCCO
Nador
Selouane
Ksar-el-Kebir
Mel
10
5
40
35
A
1
2

1:5M

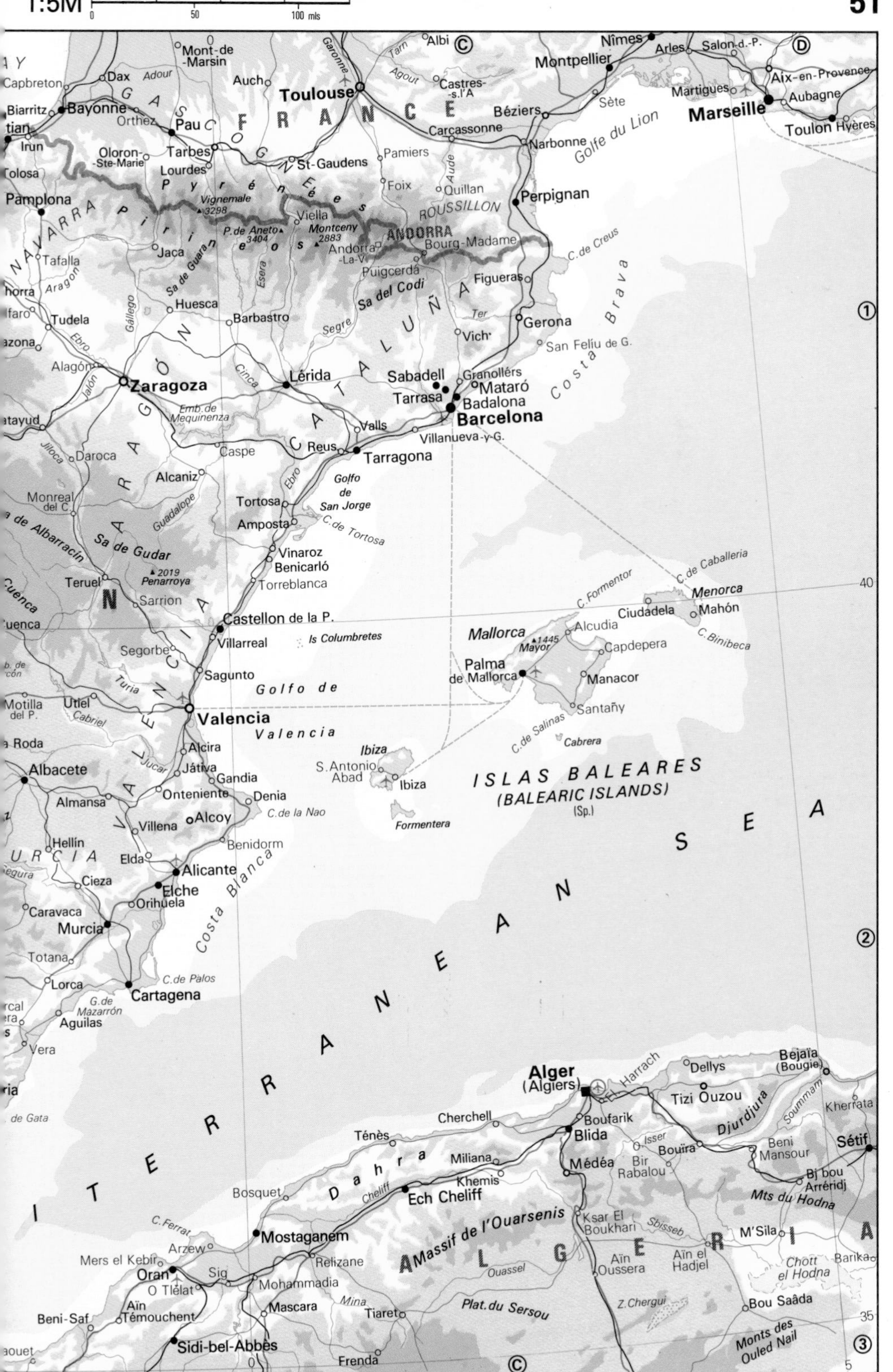

Albi © Nîmes Arles Salon-d.-P. ⑤

Castres-s.l'A Montpellier Martigues Aix-en-Provence

Mont-de-Marsin Auch Toulouse FRANCE Béziers Sète Aubagne

Capbreton Dax Adour Orthez Pau Tarbes St-Gaudens Pamiers Narbonne Golfe du Lion Marseille Toulon Hyères

Biarritz Bayonne Oloron-Ste-Marie Lourdes Pyrénées Foix Carcassonne

Irun Tolosa Pamplona NAVARRA Jaca Vignemale ▲3298 Viella Monteny ▲2883 ANDORRA Bourg-Madame Quillan Perpignan C. de Creus

Tafalla Aragón P. de Aneto ▲3404 Andorra-La-V. Puigcerdá ROUSSILLON Figueras Costa Brava

horra ifaro Tudela Huesca Barbastro Sa del Codi Ter Gerona San Feliu de G.

azona Alagón Ebro Segre Vich ①

atayud Zaragoza Emb. de Mequinenza Lérida CATALUÑA Sabadell Granollérs Mataró

Daroca Cinca Caspe Reus Tarrasa Badalona Costa Brava

Monreal del C. Alcañiz Guadalope Ebro Valls Barcelona Villanueva-y-G.

Sa de Gudar Tortosa Tarragona

de Albarracín Teruel ▲2019 Peñarroya Sarrión Amposta Golfo de San Jorge C. de Tortosa

uenca Cuenca Segorbe Vinaroz Benicarló Torreblanca C. de Caballeria Menorca

Villarreal Castellon de la P. Is Columbretes C. Formentor Ciudadela Mahón

b. de cón Segorbe Villarreal Sagunto ▲1445 Mayor Mallorca Alcudia Capdepera C. Binibeca

Motilla del P. Utiel Turia Golfo de Palma de Mallorca Manacor 40

Roda Cabriel VALENCIA Valencia Santañy C. de Salinas Cabrera

Albacete Alcira Játiva Gandia Ibiza S. Antonio Abad Ibiza ISLAS BALEARES (BALEARIC ISLANDS) (Sp.)

Almansa Onteniente Denia C. de la Nao Formentera

URCIA Hellín Villena Alcoy Benidorm

Elda Alicante Costa Blanca

Caravaca Cieza Elche Orihuela

Totana Murcia ②

Lorca C. de Palos MEDITERRANEAN SEA

Aguilas G. de Mazarrón Cartagena

Vera de Gata

Bejaïa (Bougie)

Dellys Kherrata

Alger (Algiers) Harrach Tizi Ouzou Sétif

Cherchell Boufarik Djurdjura Beni Mansour

Ténès Blida Isser Bouira Bj bou Arréridj

Miliana Médéa Bir Rabalou Mts du Hodna

Bosquet Khemis Ksar El Boukhari Sbisseb M'Sila

Ech Cheliff ALGERIA

C. Ferrat Cheliff Massif de l'Ouarsenis Aïn Oussera Aïn el Hadjel Chott el Hodna Barika

Mostaganem Relizane Ouassel

Mers el Kebir Arzew Sig Bou Saâda

Oran O Tlélat Mohammadia Mina Tiaret Plat. du Sersou Z. Chergui Monts des Ouled Nail

Beni-Saf Aïn Témouchent Mascara

ouet Sidi-bel-Abbès Frenda © 35 ③ 5

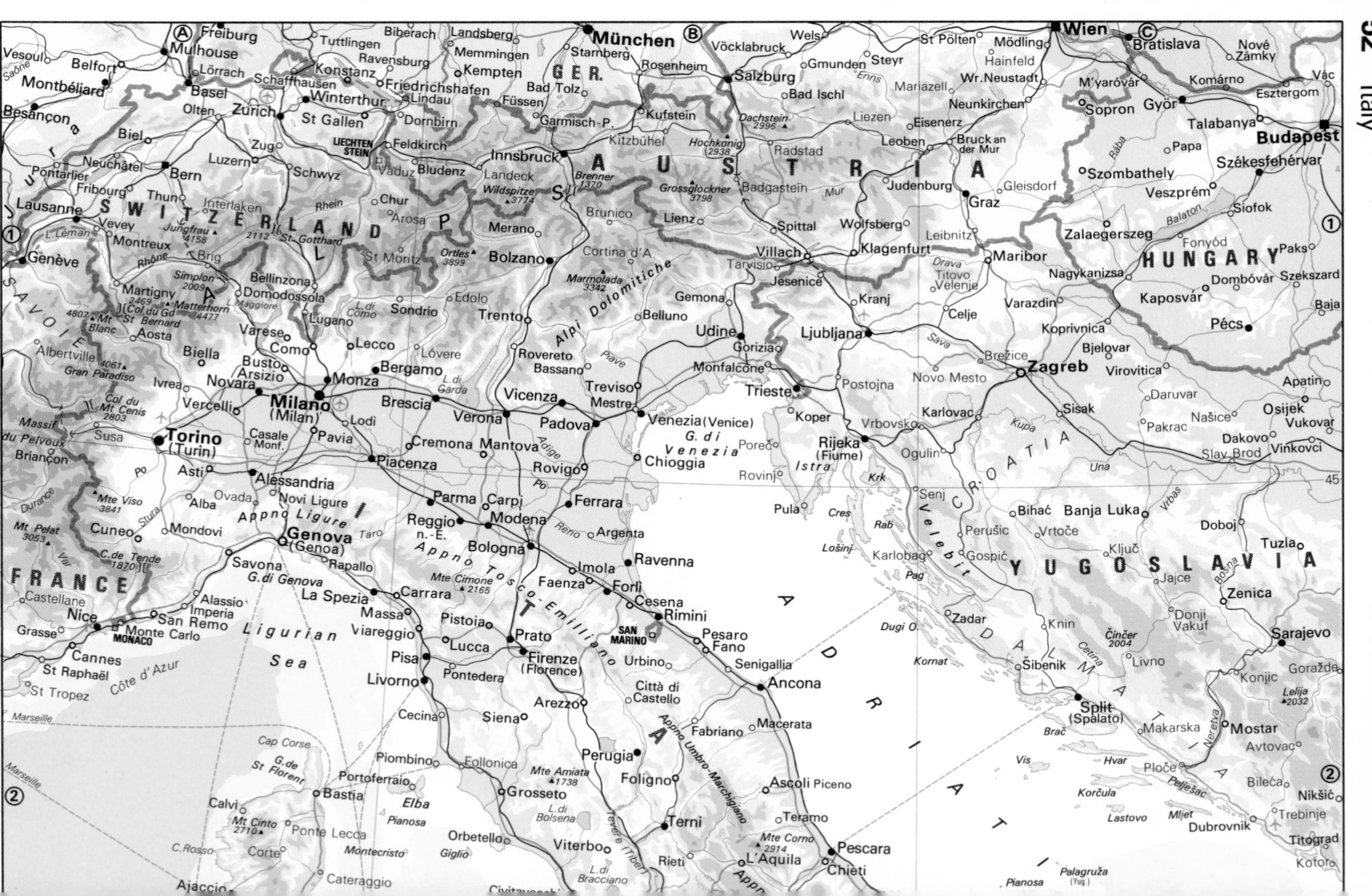

SWITZERLAND
AUSTRIA
HUNGARY
YUGOSLAVIA
FRANCE
GER.
SAN MARINO
MONACO
LIECHTENSTEIN
CROATIA
DALMATIA
ADRIATIC
Ligurian Sea
Appno Tosco-Emilliano
Appno Ligure
Alpi Dolomitiche
Appno Umbro-Marchigiano
München
Wien
Budapest
Bratislava
Zagreb
Sarajevo
Milano (Milan)
Torino (Turin)
Genova (Genoa)
Venezia (Venice)
Firenze (Florence)
Bologna
Verona
Trieste
Ljubljana
Rijeka (Fiume)
Split (Spalato)
Ancona
Pescara
Perugia
Pisa
Livorno
Nice
Cannes
Genève
Lausanne
Bern
Zürich
Basel
Innsbruck
Salzburg
Graz
Bolzano
Trento
Padova
Ferrara
Ravenna
Rimini
Parma
Modena
Brescia
Bergamo
Como
Lugano
Bastia
Ajaccio
Elba
G. di Venezia
G. di Genova
L. Maggiore
L. di Como
L. di Garda
Balaton
Mt Blanc 4807
Gran Paradiso 4061
Matterhorn 4477
Jungfrau 4158
Grossglockner 3798
Marmolada 3342
Mt Cinto 2710

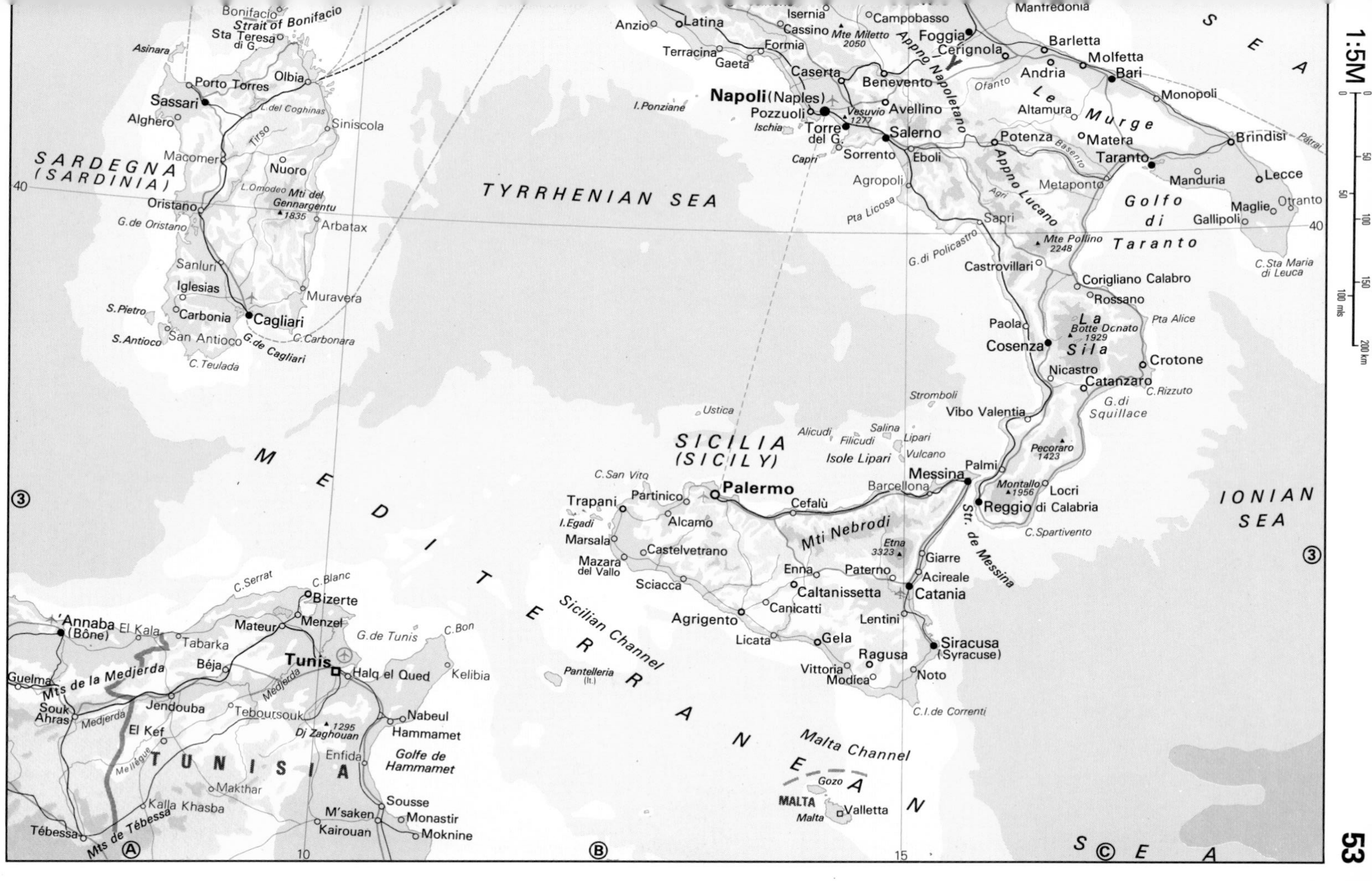
TYRRHENIAN SEA
IONIAN SEA
M E D I T E R R A N E A N S E A
SICILIA (SICILY)
SARDEGNA (SARDINIA)
TUNISIA
MALTA
Malta Channel
Sicilian Channel
Str. de Messina
Strait of Bonifacio
Golfo di Taranto
Le Murge
Appno Napoletano
Appno Lucano
La Sila
Mti Nebrodi
Isole Lipari
Napoli (Naples)
Palermo
Messina
Catania
Siracusa (Syracuse)
Reggio di Calabria
Cosenza
Catanzaro
Crotone
Taranto
Bari
Brindisi
Lecce
Foggia
Salerno
Cagliari
Sassari
Olbia
Nuoro
Oristano
Tunis
Bizerte
Sousse
Kairouan
'Annaba (Bône)
Trapani
Marsala
Agrigento
Caltanissetta
Enna
Ragusa
Gela
Etna 3323
Vesuvio 1277
Pantelleria (It.)
Ustica
Stromboli
Capri
Ischia
Gozo
Valletta

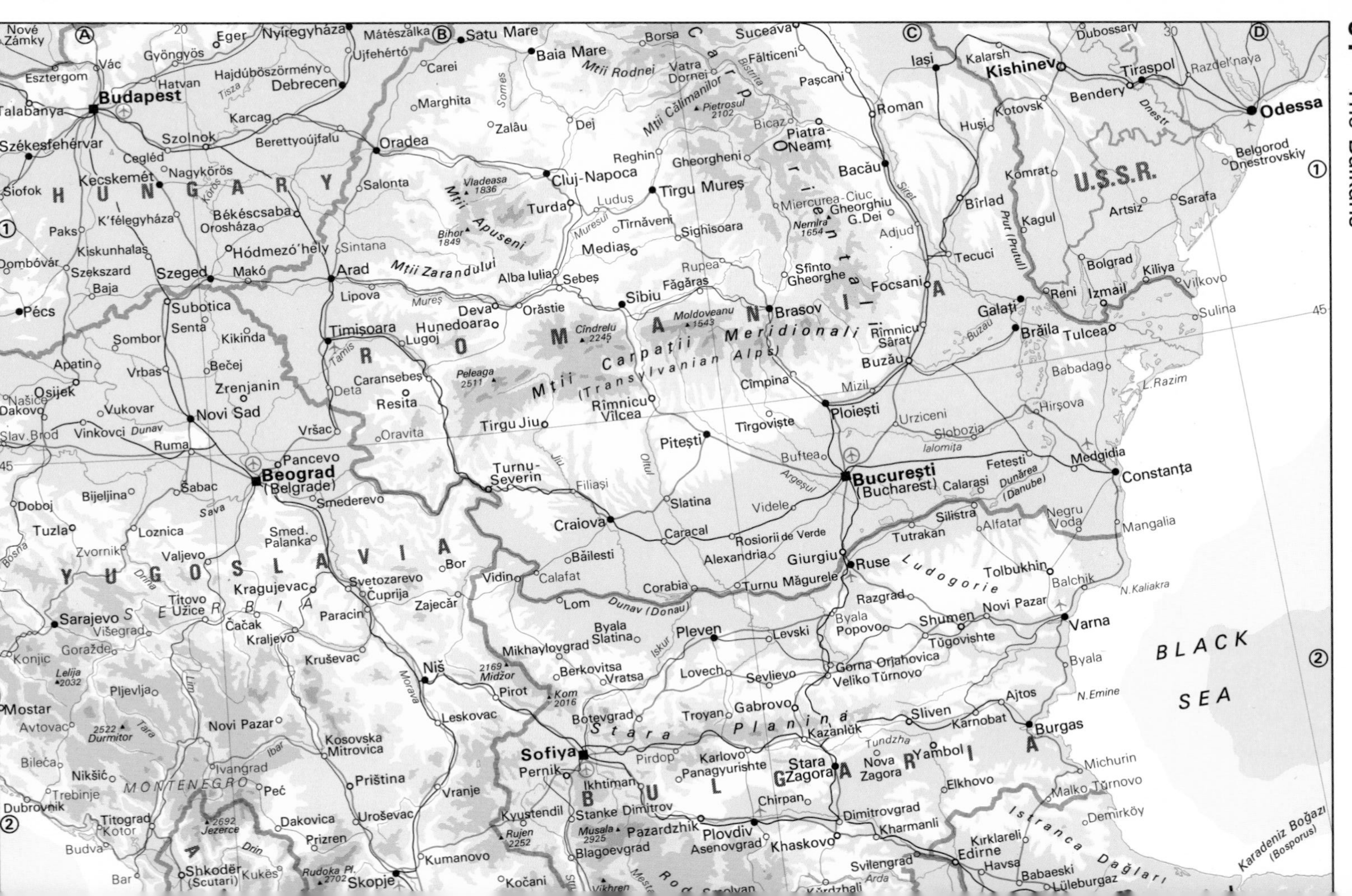
BLACK SEA
U.S.S.R.
HUNGARY
ROMANIA
YUGOSLAVIA
SERBIA
BULGARIA
MONTENEGRO
Odessa
Kishinev
Tiraspol
Bendery
Iaşi
Galaţi
Brăila
Tulcea
Izmail
Constanţa
Bucureşti (Bucharest)
Ploieşti
Brasov
Sibiu
Cluj-Napoca
Tîrgu Mureş
Timişoara
Arad
Oradea
Craiova
Piteşti
Budapest
Debrecen
Szeged
Kecskemét
Pécs
Beograd (Belgrade)
Novi Sad
Niš
Skopje
Sarajevo
Titograd
Sofiya
Plovdiv
Varna
Burgas
Ruse
Pleven
Stara Zagora
Edirne
Mţii Carpaţii Meridionali (Transylvanian Alps)
Stara Planina
Dunav (Donau)
Prut (Prutul)
Dnestr

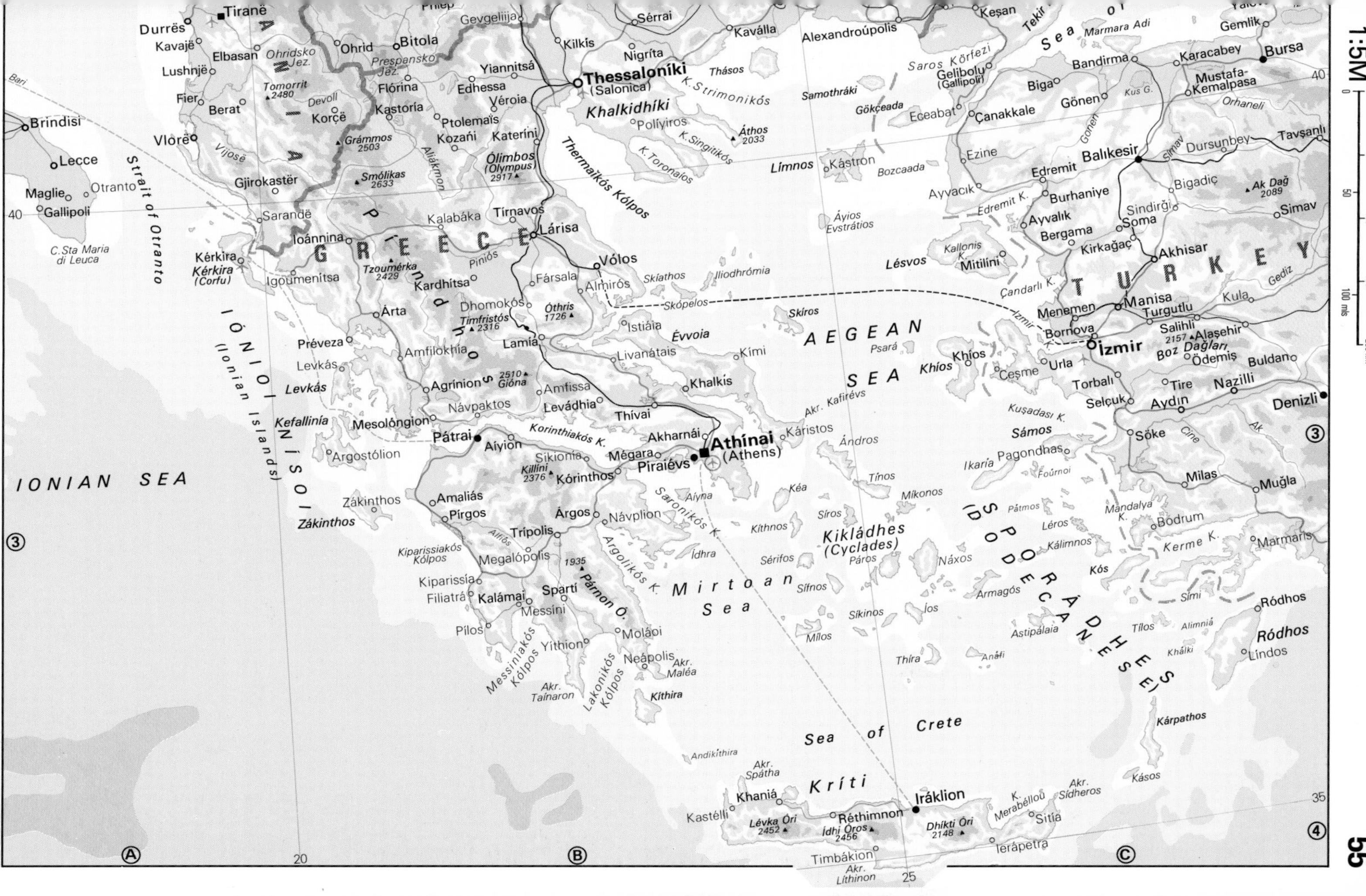

1:5M

0   50   100   150   200 km
0   50   100 mls

TURKEY

Bursa
Karacabey
Mustafa
Kemalpaşa
Gemlik
Tavşanlı
Simav
Ak Dağ 2089
Denizli ③
④
Muğla
Marmaris
Ródhos
Rhódos
Líndos

Sea of Marmara
Marmara Adı
Tekir
Bigadiç
 Orhaneli
 Gediz
Kula
Buldano
Ak.
Kerme K.
Kásos
Kárpathos

Kesan
Gelibolu
Gallipoli
Bandırma
Gönen
Balıkesir
Sındırğı
Soma
Akhisar
Salihli
Alaşehir
Ödemiş
Tire
Nazilli
Aydın
Söke
Simi
Astipálaia
Akr. Sídheros
Sitía
C

Saros Körfezi
Eceabat
Çanakkale
Edremit K.
Burhaniye
Bergama
Kırkağaç
Manisa
İzmir
Bornova
Urla
Selçuk
Söke
Kuşadası K.
Kálimnos
Léros
Pátmos
Kós
Kálimnos

Alexandroúpolis
Samothráki
Gökçeada
Bozcaada
Ezine
Ayvacık
Ayvalık
Mitilíni
Kalonís K.
Çandarlı K.
Çeşme
Khíos
Khíos
Sámos
Ikaría
Foúrnoi
(SPORADHES (DODECANESE)
Metalloú
25

Sea of Crete

Iráklion
Dhíkti Óri 2148
Réthimnon
Kríti
Khaniá
Lévka Óri 2452
Ídhi Óri 2456
Timbákion
Akr. Líthinon
Terápetra

Thásos
Kástron
Límnos
Ágios Evstrátios
Lésvos
Psará
AEGEAN SEA
Skíros
Andí
Thíra
Síkinos
Míloni
Sérifos
Akr. Kafiréus
Kíthnos
Kéa
Síros
Pátros
Náxos
Mikonos
Tínos
Ándros
Kikládhes (Cyclades)
Kýthira
Andikíthira
Akr. Spátha

Kaválla
Néa Zíkhni
Sérrai
Kilkís
Thessaloníki (Salonica)
Nigríta
Khalkidhikí
Polígiros
K. Toronaíos
K. Singitikós
Áthos 2033
K. Sithonía
Thermaïkós Kólpos
Vólos
Istiaía
Livanátais
Khalkís
Évvoia
Kími
Iliodhrómia
Skópelos
Skíathos
Alíveri

Flórina
Édhessa
Véroia
Kateríni
Kozáni
Ptolemaΐs
Olimbos (Olympus) 2917
Elassóna
Lárisa
Tírnavos
Ossa 1978
Volos
Almirós
Fársala
Dhomokós
Othris 1726
Lamía
Amfíssa
Thívai
Leivádhia
Athínai (Athens)
Piraiévs
Akharnaí
Mégara
Saronikós Kólpos
Áyina
Ídhra

Ohrid
Bitola
Préspansko jez.
Kastoria
Grámmos 2520
Smólikas 2633
Ioánnina
Métsovo
Tzoumérka 2429
Kalabáka
Kardhítsa
Árta
Agrínion
Amfilokhía
Timfristós 2315
Karpenísion
Návpaktos
Aíyion
Pátrai
Kórinthos
Sikióna
Korinthiakós K.
Kíllini
Trípolis
Mégalópolis
Párnon Ó. 1936
Sparti
Spárti

Durrës
Kavajë
Lushnjë
Fier
Berat
Vlorë
Gjirokastër
Sarandë
Igoumenítsa
Préveza
Levkás
Levkás
Mesolóngion
Argostólion
Kefallinía
Zákinthos
Zákinthos
Amaliás
Pírgos
Kiparissía
Kiparissiakós Kólpos
Filiatrá
Kalámai
Messíni
Pílos
Yíthion
Neápolis
Akr. Maléa
Kíthira
Akr. Taínaron
Messiniakós Kólpos
Lakonikós Kólpos
Molóoi

Tiranë
Elbasan
Ohridsko jez.
Tomorrit 2480
Devoll
Korçë
Vijosë

GREECE

ALBANIA

PÍNDHOS (mountains)

Íthaki

IÓNIOI NÍSOI (Ionian Islands)

IONIAN SEA

Mírtóan Sea

Argolikós Kólpos
Návplion
Árgos

Strait of Otranto

Brindisi
Lecce
Maglie
Gallipoli
C. Sta Maria di Leuca
Bari

③

Ⓑ

Ⓐ

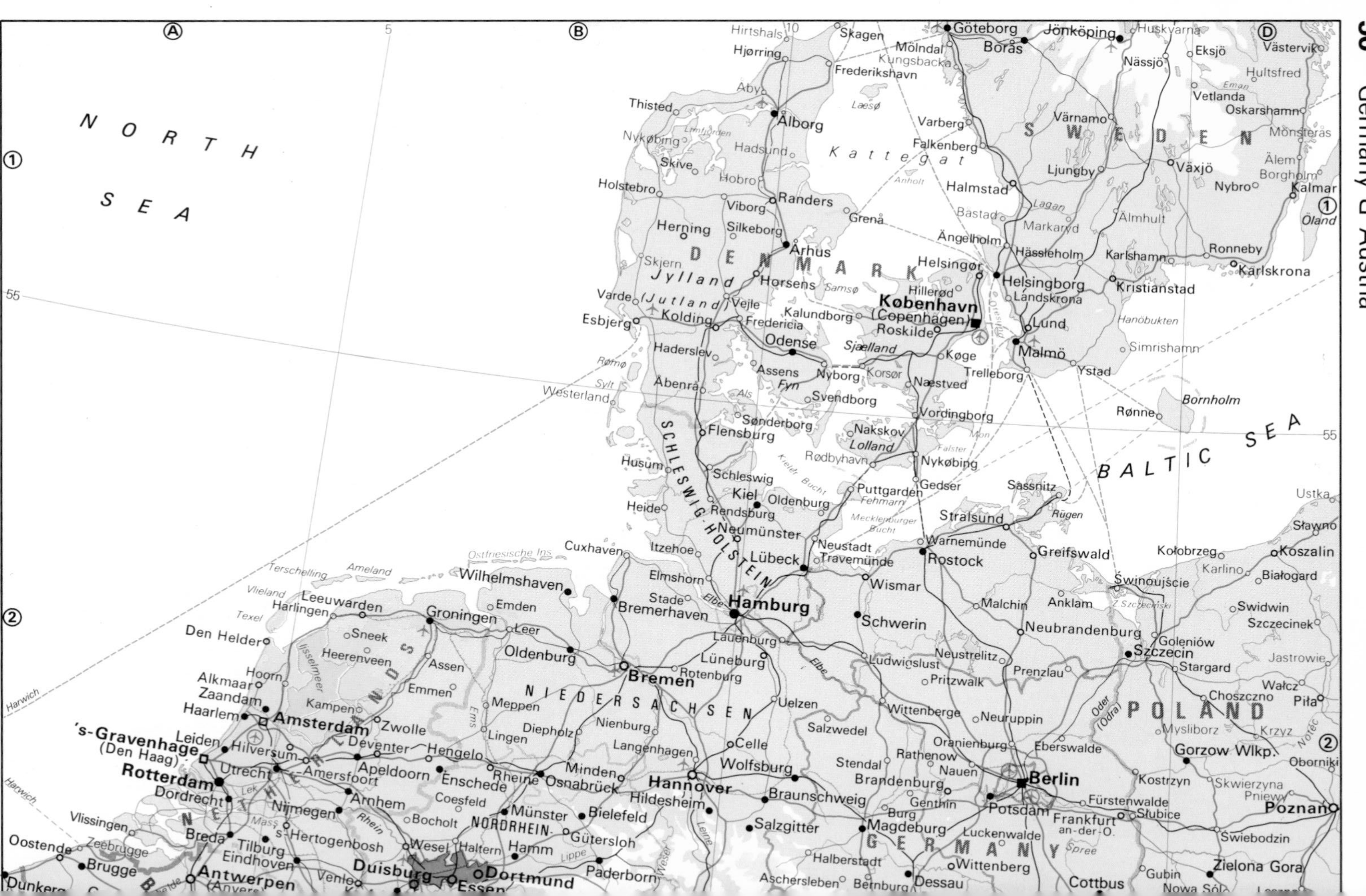
NORTH SEA
BALTIC SEA
SWEDEN
DENMARK
POLAND
GERMANY
NIEDERSACHSEN
NORDRHEIN-
SCHLESWIG-HOLSTEIN
Kattegat
Jylland (Jutland)
Sjælland
Fyn
Lolland
Falster
Møn
Bornholm
Rügen
Fehmarn
Öland
Als
Rømø
Sylt
Samsø
Læsø
Anholt
Ameland
Terschelling
Vlieland
Texel
Ostfriesische Ins.
Ijsselmeer
Öresund
Hanöbukten
Kieler Bucht
Mecklenburger Bucht
Elbe
Ems
Rhein
Weser
Leine
Oder (Odra)
Noteć
Spree
Lippe
Lagan
Eman
Maas
Lek
Göteborg
Borås
Jönköping
Huskvarna
Västervik
Eksjö
Hultsfred
Vetlanda
Oskarshamn
Mönsterås
Kalmar
Borgholm
Älem
Nybro
Växjö
Nässjö
Värnamo
Ljungby
Älmhult
Markaryd
Hässleholm
Karlshamn
Ronneby
Karlskrona
Kristianstad
Simrishamn
Ystad
Lund
Malmö
Trelleborg
Landskrona
Helsingborg
Ängelholm
Båstad
Halmstad
Falkenberg
Varberg
Kungsbacka
Mölndal
Skagen
Frederikshavn
Hirtshals
Hjørring
Ålborg
Aby
Thisted
Nykøbing
Skive
Hadsund
Randers
Grenå
Århus
Viborg
Hobro
Silkeborg
Herning
Holstebro
Skjern
Horsens
Vejle
Fredericia
Kolding
Varde
Esbjerg
Haderslev
Åbenrå
Sønderborg
Odense
Assens
Nyborg
Svendborg
Kalundborg
Korsør
Roskilde
København (Copenhagen)
Hillerød
Helsingør
Køge
Næstved
Vordingborg
Nykøbing
Nakskov
Rødbyhavn
Gedser
Rønne
Flensburg
Schleswig
Husum
Heide
Westerland
Kiel
Rendsburg
Neumünster
Itzehoe
Elmshorn
Lübeck
Oldenburg
Puttgarden
Neustadt
Travemünde
Hamburg
Cuxhaven
Stade
Bremerhaven
Bremen
Wilhelmshaven
Emden
Leer
Oldenburg
Rotenburg
Lüneburg
Lauenburg
Uelzen
Celle
Wolfsburg
Braunschweig
Salzgitter
Hannover
Hildesheim
Nienburg
Langenhagen
Minden
Bielefeld
Gütersloh
Paderborn
Osnabrück
Münster
Hamm
Dortmund
Essen
Duisburg
Wesel
Haltern
Bocholt
Coesfeld
Rheine
Lingen
Meppen
Diepholz
Wismar
Schwerin
Rostock
Warnemünde
Stralsund
Sassnitz
Greifswald
Anklam
Neubrandenburg
Malchin
Neustrelitz
Prenzlau
Ludwigslust
Pritzwalk
Wittenberge
Neuruppin
Oranienburg
Eberswalde
Berlin
Potsdam
Nauen
Rathenow
Brandenburg
Genthin
Burg
Magdeburg
Stendal
Salzwedel
Halberstadt
Aschersleben
Bernburg
Dessau
Wittenberg
Luckenwalde
Frankfurt an-der-O.
Fürstenwalde
Cottbus
Świnoujście
Szczecin
Goleniów
Stargard
Kołobrzeg
Karlino
Białogard
Koszalin
Sławno
Ustka
Swidwin
Szczecinek
Wałcz
Jastrowie
Piła
Choszczno
Mysliborz
Gorzow Wlkp.
Kostrzyn
Słubice
Krzyz
Skwierzyna
Pniewy
Oborniki
Poznań
Swiebodzin
Zielona Gora
Gubin
Nowa Sól
Groningen
Assen
Emmen
Leeuwarden
Harlingen
Sneek
Heerenveen
Zwolle
Kampen
Hengelo
Enschede
Deventer
Apeldoorn
Amersfoort
Arnhem
Nijmegen
Venlo
Den Helder
Hoorn
Alkmaar
Zaandam
Haarlem
Amsterdam
Hilversum
Utrecht
Leiden
's-Gravenhage (Den Haag)
Rotterdam
Dordrecht
Breda
Tilburg
's-Hertogenbosh
Eindhoven
Antwerpen
Brugge
Zeebrugge
Vlissingen
Oostende
Harwich

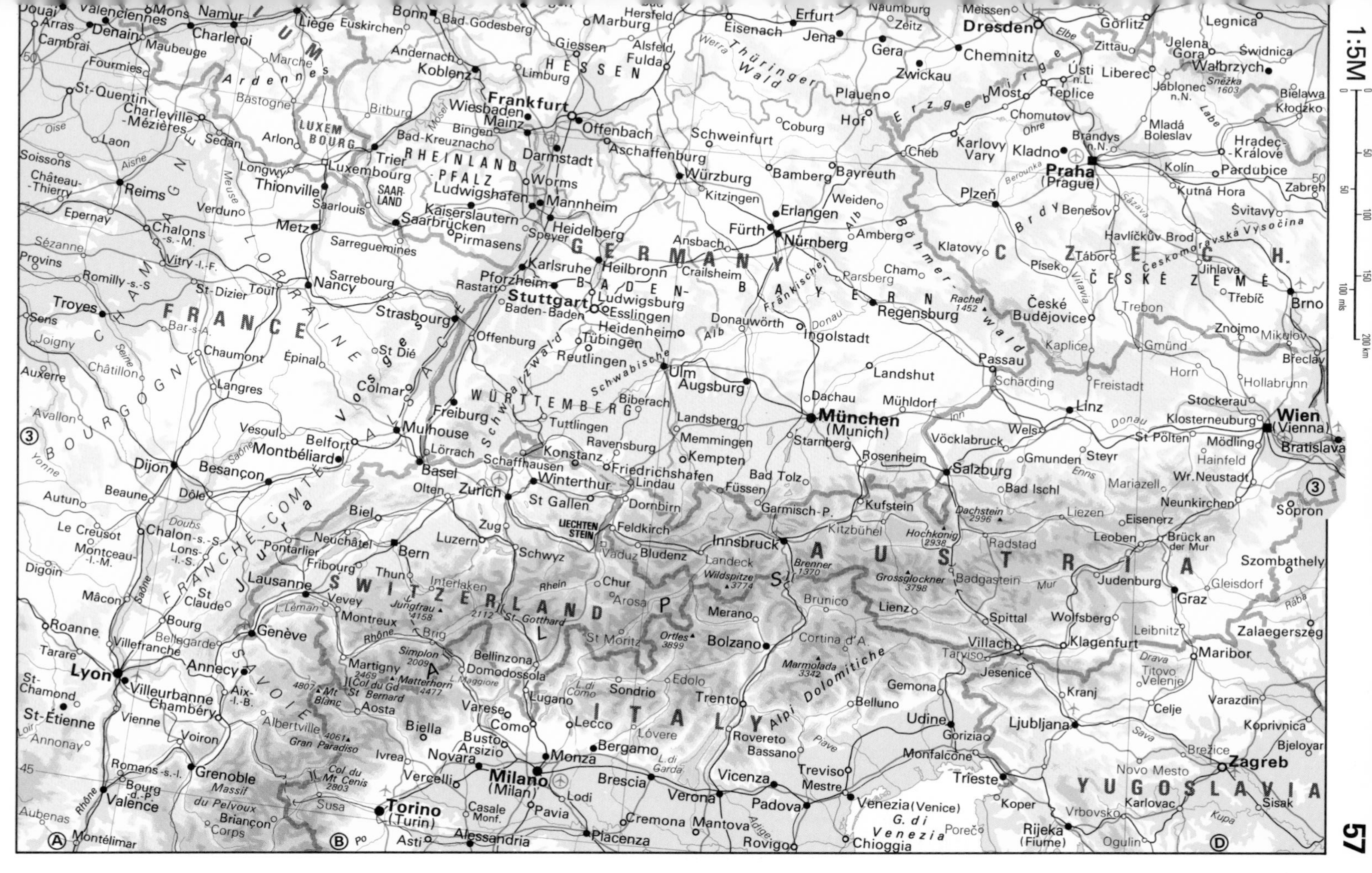
Dresden
Chemnitz
Zwickau
Gera
Jena
Erfurt
Eisenach
Plauen
Hof
Bayreuth
Bamberg
Coburg
Schweinfurt
Würzburg
Erlangen
Nürnberg
Fürth
Ansbach
Crailsheim
Regensburg
Ingolstadt
Donauwörth
Augsburg
Ulm
München
(Munich)
Dachau
Landshut
Mühldorf
Passau
Rosenheim
Kufstein
Garmisch-P.
Kempten
Memmingen
Landsberg
Füssen
Bad Tolz
Starnberg
Frankfurt
Wiesbaden
Mainz
Offenbach
Darmstadt
Aschaffenburg
Fulda
Marburg
Giessen
Koblenz
Bonn
Andernach
Mannheim
Heidelberg
Worms
Ludwigshafen
Kaiserslautern
Saarbrücken
Pirmasens
Trier
Karlsruhe
Heilbronn
Stuttgart
Ludwigsburg
Esslingen
Pforzheim
Baden-Baden
Rastatt
Tübingen
Reutlingen
Offenburg
Freiburg
Lörrach
Konstanz
Friedrichshafen
Ravensburg
Biberach
Tuttlingen
GERMANY
BAYERN
BADEN-WÜRTTEMBERG
HESSEN
RHEINLAND-PFALZ
SAARLAND
Thüringer Wald
Erzgebirge
Böhmer-wald
Schwarzwald
Schwäbische Alb
Fränkische Alb
Praha
(Prague)
Plzeň
Karlovy Vary
Kladno
Teplice
Ústí n.L.
Liberec
Most
Chomutov
Cheb
Klatovy
České Budějovice
Tábor
Písek
Jihlava
Brno
Pardubice
Hradec-Králové
Kolín
Kutná Hora
Mladá Boleslav
Třebíč
Znojmo
Břeclav
ČESKÉ ZEMĚ
CZECH.
Wien
(Vienna)
Bratislava
Linz
Wels
Steyr
Salzburg
Gmunden
Bad Ischl
Innsbruck
Landeck
Bludenz
Feldkirch
Dornbirn
Kitzbühel
Lienz
Villach
Spittal
Klagenfurt
Wolfsberg
Graz
Leoben
Judenburg
Bruck an der Mur
Wr.Neustadt
Mödling
St Pölten
Sopron
AUSTRIA
Grossglockner
3798
Hochkönig
2938
Dachstein
2996
Wildspitze
3774
Brenner
1370
Zurich
Basel
Bern
Luzern
Zug
Schwyz
Winterthur
St Gallen
Schaffhausen
Olten
Biel
Thun
Interlaken
Neuchâtel
Fribourg
Lausanne
Genève
Montreux
Vevey
Chur
Arosa
St Moritz
Bellinzona
Lugano
Martigny
Brig
Vaduz
LIECHTENSTEIN
SWITZERLAND
Jungfrau
4158
Matterhorn
4477
Simplon
2009
Col du Gd St Bernard
2469
St Gotthard
2112
Mt Blanc
4807
Gran Paradiso
4061
Col du Mt Cenis
2803
Milano
(Milan)
Torino
(Turin)
Monza
Bergamo
Brescia
Verona
Vicenza
Padova
Venezia (Venice)
Mestre
Treviso
Trento
Bolzano
Merano
Brunico
Cortina d'A.
Belluno
Udine
Gorizia
Trieste
Como
Lecco
Varese
Novara
Vercelli
Biella
Aosta
Ivrea
Asti
Alessandria
Pavia
Lodi
Cremona
Mantova
Placenza
Rovigo
Chioggia
Domodossola
Sondrio
Susa
ITALY
Alpi Dolomitiche
Marmolada
3342
Ortles
3899
Ljubljana
Maribor
Celje
Kranj
Zagreb
Rijeka
(Fiume)
Koper
Varazdin
YUGOSLAVIA
Lyon
Villeurbanne
St-Étienne
Grenoble
Chambéry
Annecy
Valence
Vienne
Roanne
Mâcon
Bourg
Chalon-s.-S.
Dijon
Besançon
Beaune
Dôle
Montbéliard
Belfort
Mulhouse
Colmar
Strasbourg
Nancy
Metz
Thionville
Épinal
Vesoul
Langres
Chaumont
Troyes
Reims
Chalons-s.-M.
Epernay
Soissons
Laon
St-Quentin
Charleville-Mézières
Sedan
Verdun
Toul
St-Dizier
Sens
Auxerre
Avallon
Autun
Le Creusot
Montceau-l.-M.
Luxembourg
LUXEMBOURG
Arlon
Liège
Namur
Charleroi
Mons
Valenciennes
Arras
Cambrai
Douai
Maubeuge
FRANCE
LORRAINE
BOURGOGNE
FRANCHE-COMTÉ
SAVOIE
CHAMPAGNE
Ardennes
Vosges
Jura

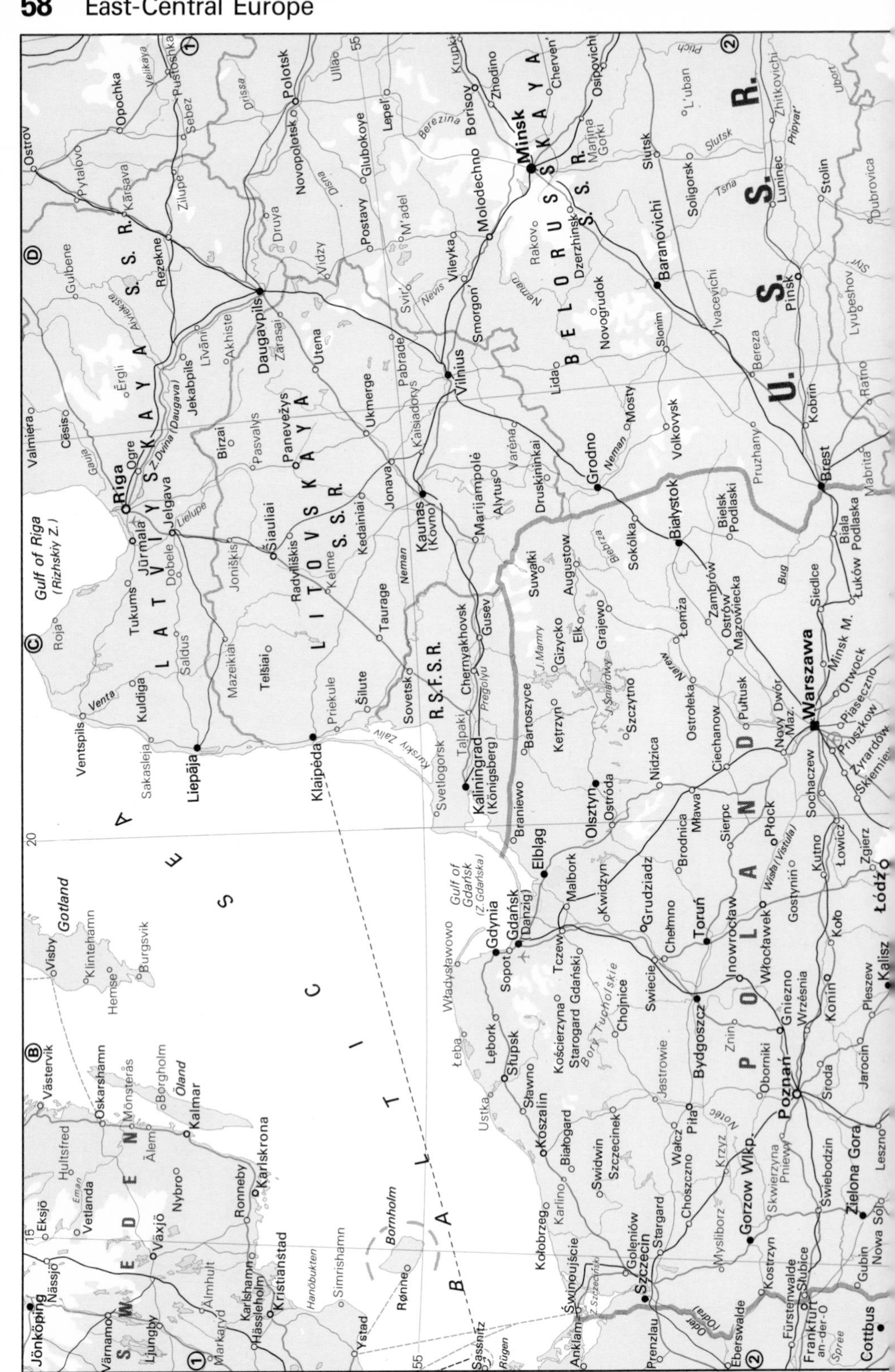

Gulf of Riga
(Rizhskiy Z.)
Gulf of Gdańsk
(Z. Gdańska)
Kurskiy Zaliv
Z. Szczecinski
B A L T I C S E A
S W E D E N
Gotland
Öland
Bornholm
Hanöbukten
Rügen
L A T V I Y S K A Y A S. S. R.
L I T O V S K A Y A S. S. R.
B E L O R U S S K A Y A S. S. R.
R.S.F.S.R.
U. S. S. R.
P O L A N D
Jönköping
Värnamo
Nässjö
Eksjö
Vetlanda
Hultsfred
Västervik
Oskarshamn
Mönsterås
Borgholm
Kalmar
Nybro
Ålem
Växjö
Ljungby
Markaryd
Älmhult
Hässleholm
Kristianstad
Karlshamn
Ronneby
Karlskrona
Ystad
Simrishamn
Rønne
Visby
Klintehamn
Hemse
Burgsvik
Sassnitz
Anklam
Świnoujście
Szczecin
Goleniów
Stargard
Kołobrzeg
Karlino
Białogard
Koszalin
Sławno
Słupsk
Ustka
Łeba
Lębork
Władysławowo
Gdynia
Sopot
Gdańsk
(Danzig)
Tczew
Starogard Gdański
Kościerzyna
Chojnice
Bory Tucholskie
Malbork
Elbląg
Braniewo
Kwidzyn
Grudziadz
Chełmno
Toruń
Bydgoszcz
Świecie
Inowrocław
Włocławek
Gniezno
Poznań
Gorzow Wlkp.
Piła
Wałcz
Choszczno
Myślibórz
Kostrzyn
Słubice
Frankfurt an-der-O
Fürstenwalde
Eberswalde
Prenzlau
Cottbus
Gubin
Zielona Gora
Nowa Sól
Świebodzin
Leszno
Kalisz
Łódź
Zgierz
Łowicz
Kutno
Płock
Sierpc
Mława
Ciechanów
Pułtusk
Nowy Dwór Maz.
Warszawa
Otwock
Piaseczno
Pruszków
Żyrardów
Skierniewice
Sochaczew
Mińsk M.
Siedlce
Łuków
Biała Podlaska
Brest
Białystok
Bielsk Podlaski
Łomża
Zambrów
Ostrów Mazowiecka
Ostrołęka
Szczytno
Olsztyn
Ostróda
Nidzica
Kętrzyn
Bartoszyce
Giżycko
Ełk
Grajewo
Augustów
Suwałki
Kaliningrad
(Königsberg)
Svetlogorsk
Chernyakhovsk
Gusev
Sovetsk
Klaipėda
Šilutė
Priekule
Taurage
Kelme
Radviliškis
Šiauliai
Joniškis
Panevėžys
Kėdainiai
Jonava
Kaunas
(Kovno)
Marijampolė
Alytus
Druskininkai
Varėna
Vilnius
Ukmerge
Utena
Zarasai
Daugavpils
Liepāja
Ventspils
Kuldiga
Saldus
Tukums
Jūrmala
Riga
Jelgava
Dobele
Ogre
Jēkabpils
Cēsis
Valmiera
Gulbene
Rezekne
Kārsava
Ostrov
Pytalovo
Opochka
Pustoshka
Sebez
Zilupe
Polotsk
Novopolotsk
Glubokoye
Postavy
Molodechno
Smorgon'
Vileyka
Lida
Grodno
Volkovysk
Mosty
Slonim
Novogrudok
Baranovichi
Dzerzhinsk
Minsk
Borisov
Zhodino
Lepel'
Slutsk
Soligorsk
Luninec
Pinsk
Kobrin
Stolin
Neman
Bug
Narew
Wisła (Vistula)
Oder (Odra)
Noteć
Spree
Pripyat'
Berezina
Z. Dvina (Daugava)
Venta
Lielupe

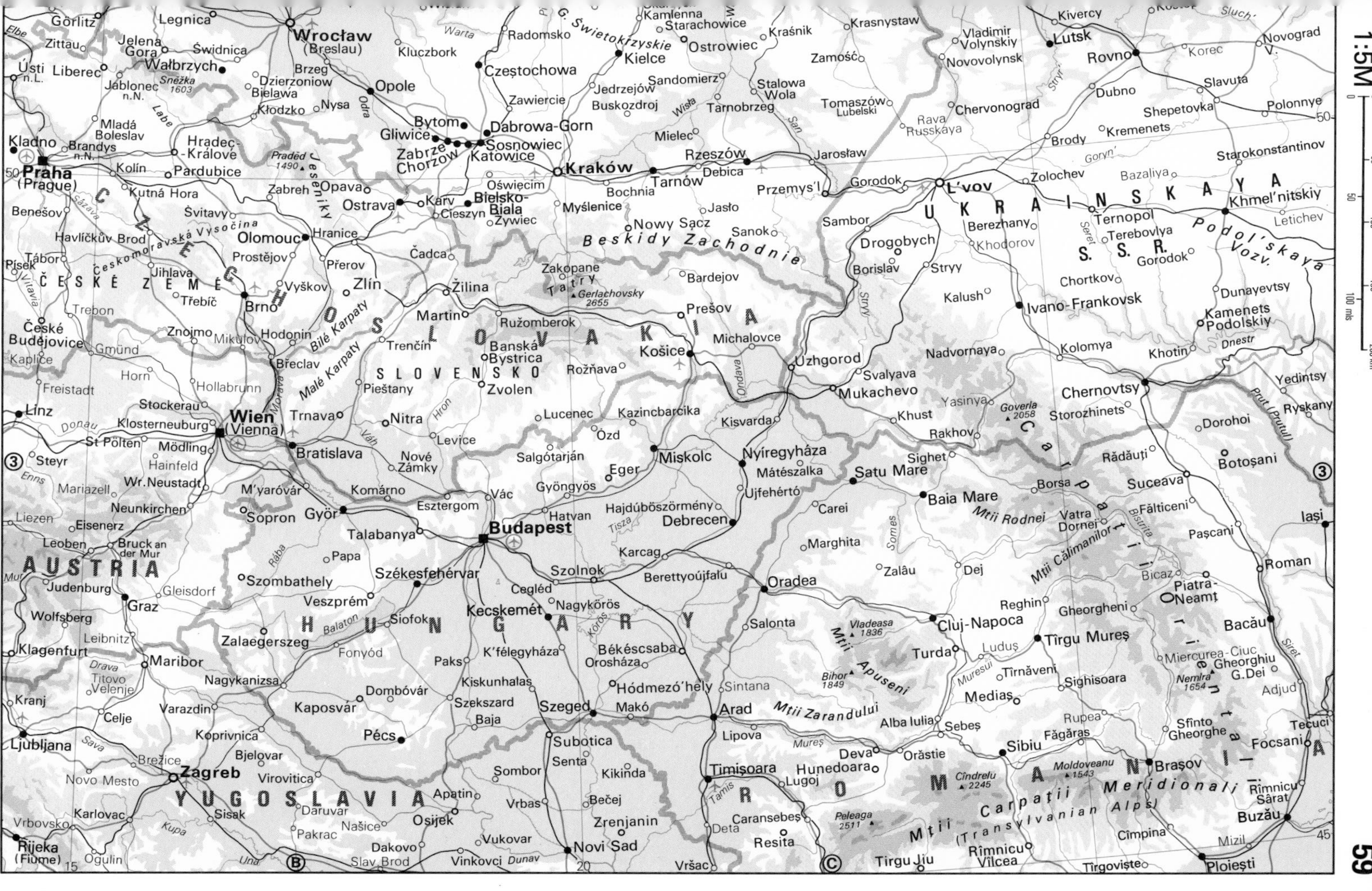

1:5M

50   100   150   200 km

50   100 mls

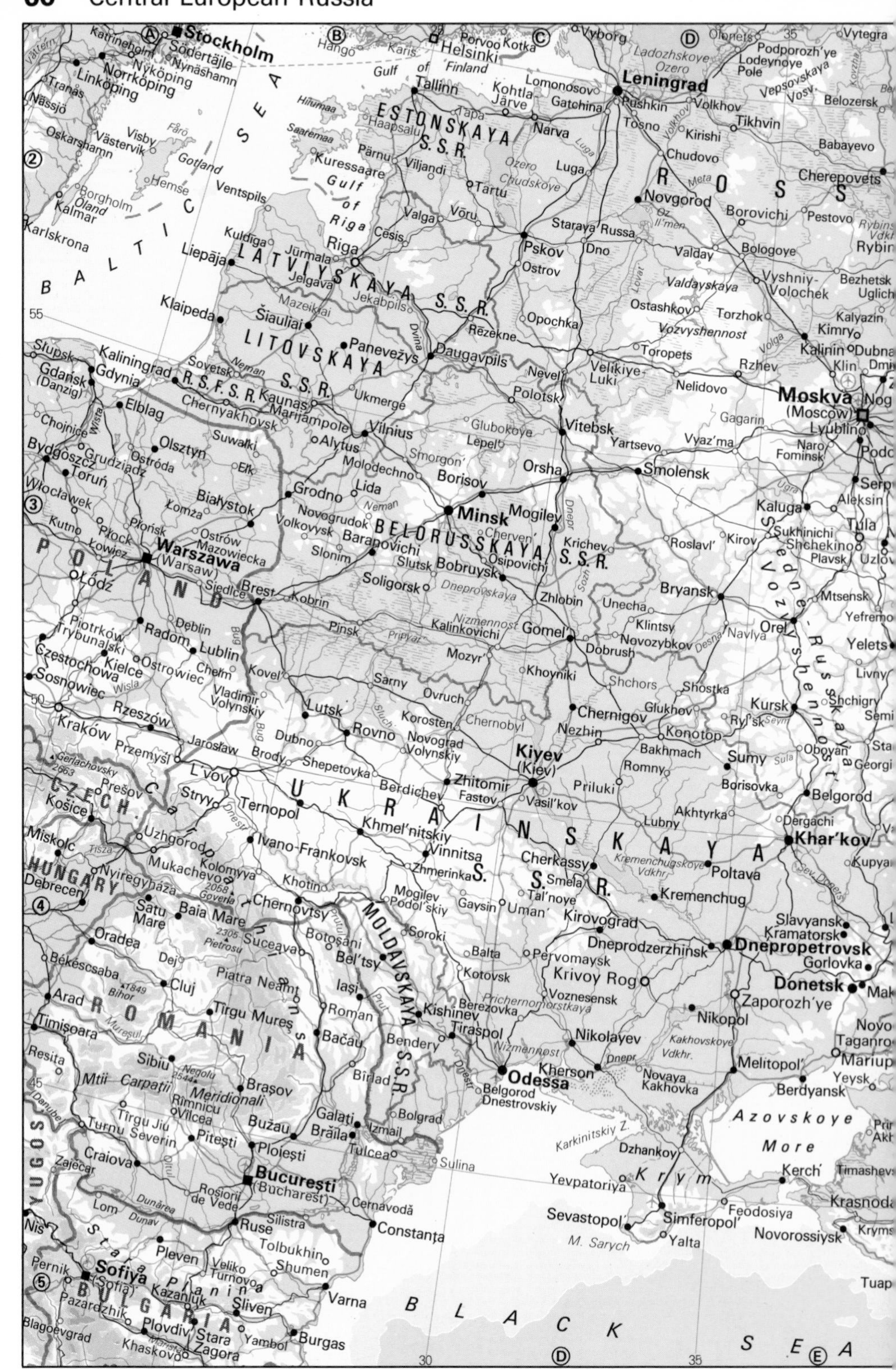
Stockholm
Södertälje
Nynäshamn
Nyköping
Norrköping
Linköping
Katrineholm
Vättern
Tranås
Nässjö
Västervik
Visby
Fårö
Gotland
Oskarshamn
Hemse
Borgholm
Öland
Kalmar
Karlskrona
B A L T I C S E A
Hangö
Karis
Helsinki
Porvoo
Kotka
Gulf of Finland
Vyborg
Ladozhskoye Ozero
Olonets
Podporozh'ye
Lodeynoye Pole
Vepsovskaya Vosv.
Vytegra
Belozersk
Leningrad
Lomonosov
Gatchina
Pushkin
Volkhov
Tosno
Kirishi
Tikhvin
Babayevo
Chudovo
Cherepovets
Tallinn
Kohtla-Järve
Hiiumaa
Tapa
Haapsalu
ESTONSKAYA S.S.R.
Narva
Saaremaa
Pärnu
Viljandi
Kuressaare
Luga
Ozero Chudskoye
Tartu
Gulf of Riga
Ventspils
Novgorod
Meta
Oz. Il'men
R O S S
Borovichi
Pestovo
Rybinsk
Valga
Võru
Staraya Russa
Kuldiga
Cēsis
Pskov
Dno
Valday
Bologoye
Riga
Jūrmala
Liepāja
LATVIYSKAYA S.S.R.
Jelgava
Jekabpils
Ostrov
Valdayskaya Vozvyshennost
Vyshniy-Volochek
Bezhetsk
Uglich
Klaipeda
Mazeikiai
Šiauliai
Rezekne
Opochka
Ostashkov
Torzhok
Kalyazin
Kimry
Dvina
Lovat
Volga
Kalinin
Dubna
Klin
55
Słupsk
Kaliningrad
Gdańsk (Danzig)
Gdynia
Sovetsk
Neman
R.S.F.S.R.
LITOVSKAYA S.S.R.
Panevežys
Daugavpils
Toropets
Nevel
Velikiye-Luki
Rzhev
Nelidovo
Kaunas
Ukmerge
Polotsk
Moskva (Moscow)
Chernyakhovsk
Marijampole
Elbląg
Vilnius
Glubokoye
Vitebsk
Gagarin
Lyublino
Chojnice
Wisła
Suwałki
Alytus
Lepel'
Yartsevo
Vyaz'ma
Naro Fominsk
Olsztyn
Smorgon'
Bydgoszcz
Grudziądz
Ostróda
Ełk
Molodechno
Orsha
Smolensk
Toruń
Borisov
Lida
Grodno
Włocławek
Białystok
Łomża
Minsk
Mogilev
Kaluga
Aleksin
Tula
Ugra
Novogrudok
Volkovysk
Dnepr
Kutno
Płock
Płońsk
Ostrów Mazowiecka
Baranovichi
BELORUSSKAYA S.S.R.
Cherven'
Krichev
Roslavl'
Kirov
Sukhinichi
Shchekino
Plavsk
POLAND
Łowicz
Warszawa (Warsaw)
Slonim
Slutsk
Bobruysk
Osipovichi
Srednerusskaya Vozvyshennost'
Łódź
Siedlce
Brest
Kobrin
Soligorsk
Dneprovskaya
Zhlobin
Sozh
Unecha
Bryansk
Mtsensk
Yefremov
Dęblin
Bug
Pinsk
Pripyat'
Kalinkovichi
Nizmennost'
Gomel'
Klintsy
Novozybkov
Desna
Navlya
Orel
Yelets
Piotrków Trybunalski
Radom
Lublin
Mozyr'
Dobrush
Częstochowa
Kielce
Ostrowiec
Chełm
Kovel'
Khoyniki
Livny
Sosnowiec
Sarny
Ovruch
Shchors
Shostka
50
Vladimir Volynskiy
Lutsk
Sluch
Korosten
Chernobyl
Chernigov
Glukhov
Kursk
Shchigry
Rzeszów
Kraków
Dubno
Rovno
Novograd Volynskiy
Nezhin
Konotop
Ryl'sk
Seym
Przemyśl
Jarosław
Brody
Kiyev (Kiev)
Bakhmach
Sumy
Oboyan'
Gerlachovsky 2663
Shepetovka
Romny
Sula
L'vov
Zhitomir
Priluki
Borisovka
Belgorod
Prešov
CZECH.
Stryy
Berdichev
Fastov
Vasil'kov
Košice
Ternopol
UKRAINSKAYA S.S.R.
Akhtyrka
Dergachi
Dnestr
Khmel'nitskiy
Lubny
Khar'kov
Miskolc
Tisza
Uzhgorod
Ivano-Frankovsk
Vinnitsa
Cherkassy
Kremenchugskoye Vdkhr.
Kupyansk
HUNGARY
Mukachevo
Kolomyya
Zhmerinka
Smela
Poltava
Sev. Donets
Debrecen
Nyiregyháza
Goverla 2058
Khotin
Mogilev Podol'skiy
Tal'noye
Uman'
Kremenchug
Satu Mare
Baia Mare
Chernovtsy
Gaysin
Kirovograd
Slavyansk
Kramatorsk
Prut
Soroki
MOLDAVSKAYA S.S.R.
Pietrosu 2305
Suceava
Botoşani
Dneprodzerzhinsk
Dnepropetrovsk
Oradea
Bel'tsy
Balta
Pervomaysk
Gorlovka
Dej
Krivoy Rog
Békéscsaba
Piatra Neamț
Iaşi
Kotovsk
Donetsk
Bihor 1849
Cluj
Voznesensk
Zaporozh'ye
Arad
Prichernomorskaya
Roman
Kishinev
Berezovka
ROMANIA
Tîrgu Mureş
Nikopol
Timişoara
Mureşul
Tiraspol
Nizmennost'
Bacău
Bendery
Nikolayev
Kakhovskoye Vdkhr.
Taganrog
Reşiţa
Sibiu
Negolu 2544
Novaya Kakhovka
Melitopol'
Mariupol'
Bîrlad
Kherson
Odessa
Yeysk
45
Mtii Carpaţii Meridionali
Braşov
Belgorod Dnestrovskiy
Berdyansk
Danube
Rîmnicu Vîlcea
Galaţi
Bolgrad
Tîrgu Jiu
Buzău
Brăila
Izmail
Azovskoye More
Turnu Severin
Piteşti
Karkinitskiy Z.
YUGOS.
Ploieşti
Tulcea
Dzhankoy
Craiova
Zaječar
Sulina
Bucureşti (Bucharest)
Krym
Kerch'
Timashevsk
Rosiorii de Vede
Yevpatoriya
Dunărea
Cernavodă
Krasnodar
Lom
Dunav
Feodosiya
Sevastopol'
Simferopol'
Niš
Silistra
Constanţa
Novorossiysk
Krymsk
Ruse
Yalta
M. Sarych
Pleven
Tolbukhin
Pernik
Veliko Turnovo
Shumen
Sofiya (Sofia)
Stara Planina
Kazanluk
Sliven
Varna
BULGARIA
Pazardzhik
Blagoevgrad
Plovdiv
Stara Zagora
Yambol
Burgas
Khaskovo
BLACK SEA
Tuapse
30
35

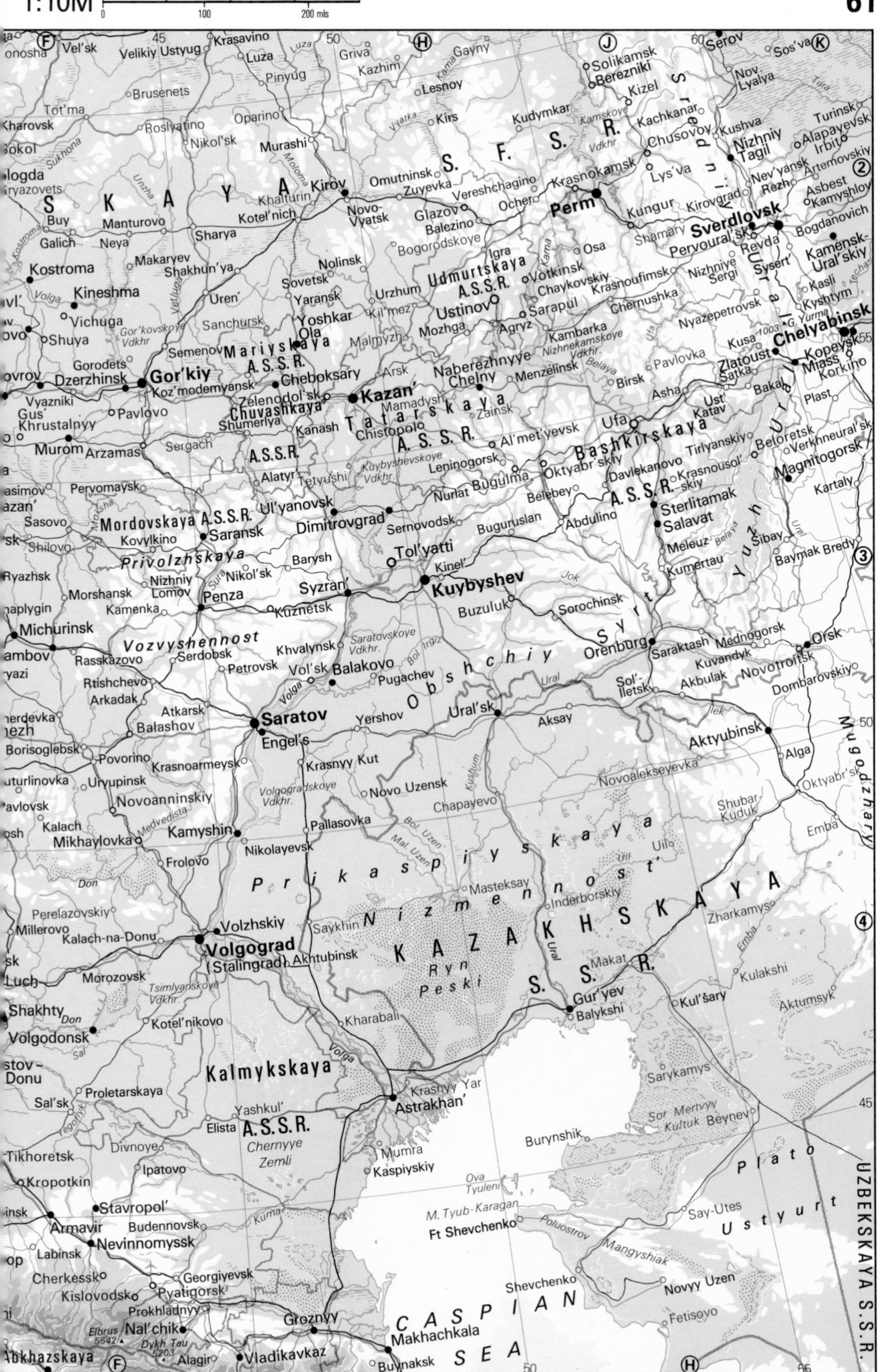

F   Vel'sk   Krasavino   Griva   H   Gayny   J   Solikamsk   Serov   K
onosha   Velikiy Ustyug   Luza   Kazhim   Berezniki   Nov.   Sos'va
Luza   Pinyug   Lesnoy   Kizel   Lyalya
Tot'ma   Brusenets   Oparino   Kudymkar   Kachkanar   Turinsk
kharovsk   Roslyatino   Kirs   Nikol'sk   Chusovoy   Nizhniy   Alapayevsk
Sokol   Nikol'sk   Murashi   Omutninsk   Krasnokamsk   Tagil   Nev'yansk
ogda   Buy   Manturovo   Kirov   Zuyevka   Vereshchagino   Ochero   **Perm**   Kungur   Kirovgrad   **Sverdlovsk**   Artemovskiy
ryazovets   Galich   Neya   Novo-   Glazov   Pervoural'sk   Revda   Kamyshlov
Kostroma   Makaryev   Vyatsk   Balezino   Bogorodskoye   Igra   Votkinsk   Chaykovskiy   Krasnoufimsk   Nizhniye   Sysert'   Kamensk-Ural'skiy
Kineshma   Shakhun'ya   **Udmurtskaya**   Sergi   Kasli
vl'   Vichuga   Uren'   Yaransk   Urzhum   Kil'mez   **A.S.S.R.**   Sarapul   Chernushka   Nyazepetrovsk   Kyshtym
ovo   Shuya   Semenov   Yoshkar   Malmyzh   Mozhga   Agryz   Kambarka   Birsk   Asha   **Chelyabinsk**
ovrov   Gorodets   Koz'modemyansk   Ola   **Mariyskaya**   Arsk   Naberezhnyye   Menzelinsk   Nizhnekamsk   Pavlovka   Zlatoust   Miass   Korkino
Dzerzhinsk   **Gor'kiy**   **A.S.S.R.**   Cheboksary   **Kazan'**   Chelny   Ust'   Bakal   Plast
Vyazniki   Zelenodol'sk   Mamadysh   Al'met'yevsk   Ufa   **Bashkirskaya**
Gus'   Khrustalnyy   **Chuvashskaya**   Kanash   Chistopol   Zainsk   Oktyabr'skiy   Davlekanovo   Krasnousol'-   **A.S.S.R.**
Murom   Arzamas   Sergach   Alatyr   **Tatarskaya**   Leningorsk   skiy   Magnitogorsk
asimov'   Peryomaysk   Tetyushi   Kuybyshevskoye   Nurlat   Bugulma   Belebey   Buguruslan   Abdulino   Sterlitamak   Kartaly
azan'   Sasovo   Ul'yanovsk   Vdkhr.   Salavat
sk   Shilovo   **Mordovskaya A.S.S.R.**   Dimitrovgrad   Sernovodsk   Meleuz   Baymak   Bredy
Ryazhsk   Kovylkino   Saransk   Barysh   **Privolzhskaya**   Tol'yatti   Kinel'   Kumertau   Sibay
aplygin   Nizhniy   Penza   Syzran'   Kuznetsk   **Kuybyshev**   Sorochinsk   Baymak   Bredy
Michurinsk   Lomov   Kamenka   **Vozvyshennost**   Buzuluk   Orenburg   Saraktash   Mednogorsk   Orsk
ambov   Rasskazovo   Serdobsk   Khvalynsk   Saratovskoye   Ural   Sol'-Iletsk   Kuvandyk   Novotroitsk
yazi   Rtishchevo   Petrovsk   Vol'sk   Balakovo   Pugachev   Akbulak   Dombarovskiy
erdevka   Arkadak   Atkarsk   Yershov   Ural'sk   Aksay   Aktyubinsk   Alga
Borisoglebsk   Balashov   **Saratov**   Yershov   Novoalekseyevka   Oktyabr'-skiy
uturlinovka   Povorino   Engel's   Krasnyy Kut   Shubar-
avlovsk   Uryupinsk   Krasnoarmeysk   Chapayevo   Kuduk   Emba
osh   Novoanninskiy   Novo Uzensk   Uilo
Mikhaylovka   Kamyshin   Volgogradskoye   Pallasovka
Kalach   Frolovo   Vdkhr.   Zharkamys
Perelazovskiy   Nikolayevsk   **Prikaspiyskaya**
Millerovo   Kalach-na-Donu   Volzhskiy   Masteksay   Inderborskiy   Kulakshi
Luch   Morozovsk   **Volgograd**   Saykhin   Akhtubinsk   **Nizmennost'**
Shakhty   Kotel'nikovo   **(Stalingrad)**   **KAZAKHSKAYA**   Makat   Aktumsyk
Volgodonsk   Tsimlyanskoye   Ryn   **S.S.R.**   Gur'yev   Kulsary
stov-   Vdkhr.   Peski   Balykshi   Sarykamys
Donu   Kharabali
Sal'sk   **Kalmykskaya**   Krasnyy Yar   Sor. Mertvyy
Tikhoretsk   Proletarskaya   Yashkul'   **A.S.S.R.**   Astrakhan'   Kultuk   Beynev   **Plato**
Kropotkin   Divnoye   Elista   Chernnyye   Burynshik   Say-Utes   **Ustyurt**
Ipatovo   Zemli   Mumra
Stavropol'   Budennovsk   Kaspiyskiy   Ova   M. Tyub-Karagan
Armavir   Nevinnomyssk   Georgiyevsk   Tyuleni   Poluostrov
Labinsk   Pyatigorsk   M. Tyub-Karagan   Shevchenko   Novyy Uzen
Cherkessko   Kislovodsk   Ft Shevchenko   Mangyshlak   Fetisovo
Prokhladnyy   Nal'chik   Grozny   **C A S P I A N**   **UZBEKSKAYA S.S.R.**
Elbrus   Dykh Tau   Alagir   Makhachkala
bkhazskaya   F   Vladikavkaz   Buynaksk   **S E A**   H

S   K   A   Y   A

S.   F.   S.   R.

K   a   m   a

U   r   a   l

Y   u   z   h   n   y   y

S   y   r   t

O   b   s   h   c   h   i   y

0 600 1200 1800
0 300 600 900mls

Bering Sea

INTERNATIONAL DATELINE

Kuril'skiye Ostrova

Petropavlovsk-Kamchatskiy

Sakhalin

Sea of Okhotsk

Magadan

Hokkaido

Tokyo
Osaka
Nagoya
Kyūshū
Shikoku
JAPAN
Sea of Japan

Sapporo
Vladivostok
Khabarovsk
Kita-Kyūshū

ARCTIC OCEAN

Severnaya Zemlya

Novosibirskiye Ostrova

ARCTIC CIRCLE

Yakutsk

Lena

Zemlya Frantsa Iosifa

Svalbard (Nor.)

Barents Sea

Nbr'sk

Yenisey

Vorkuta

Sergino

Nadym

Norway

SWEDEN

FINLAND

UNION OF SOVIET SOCIALIST REPUBLICS

Krasnoyarsk
Novosibirsk
Barnaul
Bratsk

Ulaanbaatar

MONGOLIA

INNER MONGOLIA

C H I N A

SINKIANG

Ürümqi

Alma Ata

Karaganda
Omsk
Chelyabinsk
Sverdlovsk

Tashkent

Aral Sea

Kabul
AFGHANISTAN
Herat
Mashhad
Ashkhabad
Kerman

Ob'

N.KOREA
Pyongyang
S.KOREA
Seoul
Pusan
Qingdao
Lüda
Yellow Sea
Shenyang
Harbin
Changchun
Beijing
Tianjin
Zhengzhou
Xi'an
Taiyuan
Lanzhou
Nanjing
Shanghai
Huang He

Murmansk
Arkhangel'sk

Leningrad
Helsinki
Stockholm
Oslo
Faerøerne (Den.)

Gor'kiy
Kazan'
Ufa
Kuybyshev
Saratov
Volgograd
Astrakhan
Caspian Sea

Moskva
Khar'kov
Donetsk
Rostov
Tbilisi
Baku
Yerevan
IRAN
Tehrān
Esfahān
Ābādān

Riga
Minsk
Kiyev
Dnepropetrovsk
Odessa
Black Sea
İstanbul
Ankara
TURKEY
Mosul
Baghdad
SAUDI ARABIA
KUWAIT
Al Başrah

København
Warszawa
POLAND
GERMANY
CZECHOSLOVAKIA
AUSTRIA
HUNGARY
ROMANIA
Bucureşti
BULGARIA
YUGOSLAVIA
CYPRUS
SYRIA
Damascus
Ḥalab
Adana
Trabzon
LEB.
Beirut
Jerusalem
ISRAEL
JOR.

Edinburgh
UNITED KINGDOM
DENMARK
NETH.
BEL.
LUX.
IRELAND
Dublin
London
Paris

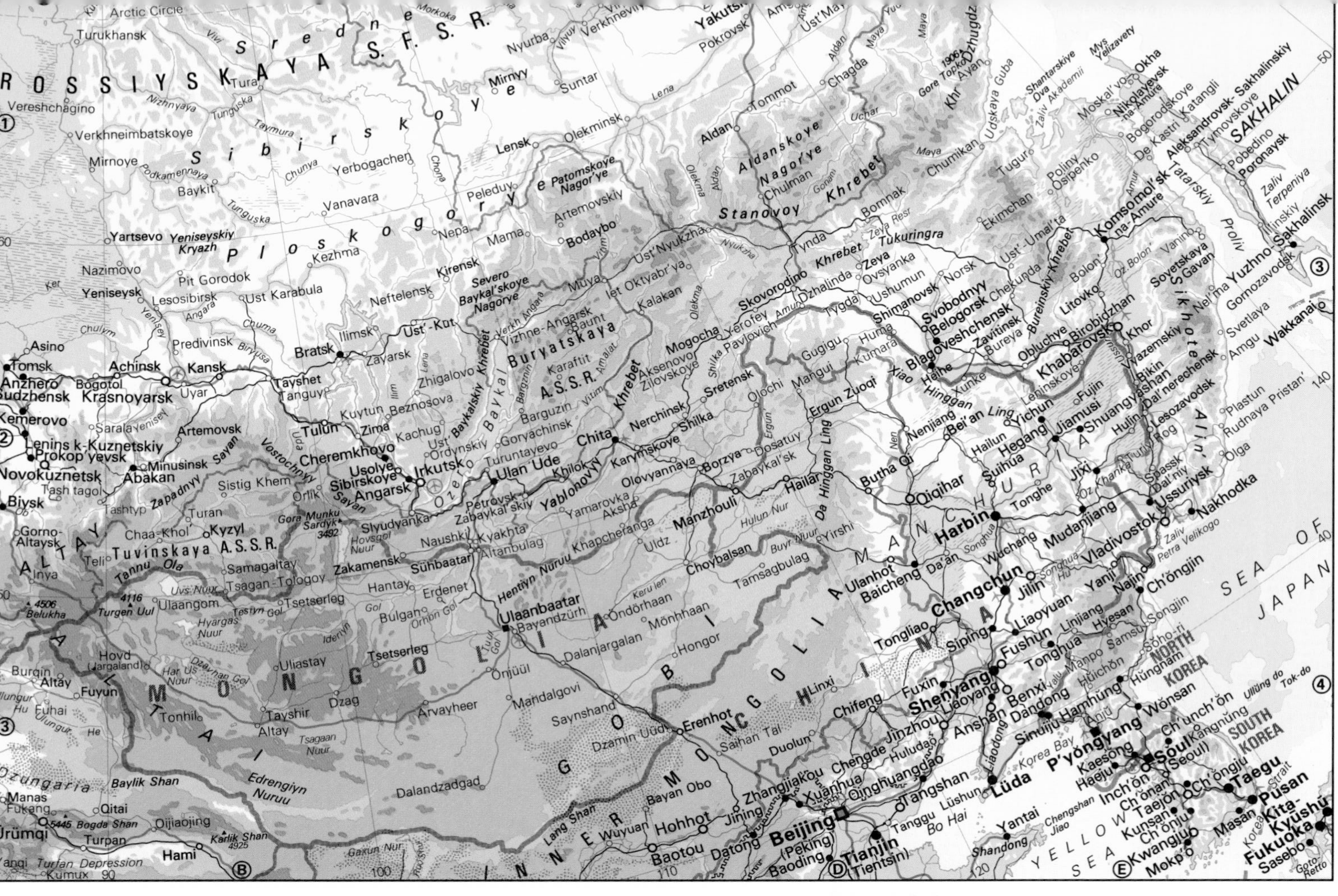
ROSSIYSKAYA S.F.S.R.
Sredne Sibirskoye Ploskogorye
SAKHALIN
SEA OF JAPAN
NORTH KOREA
SOUTH KOREA
YELLOW SEA
MONGOLIA
INNER MONGOLIA
MANCHURIA
GOBI
ALTAY
Buryatskaya A.S.S.R.
Tuvinskaya A.S.S.R.
Harbin
Changchun
Shenyang
Beijing (Peking)
Tianjin (Tientsin)
Vladivostok
Khabarovsk
Irkutsk
Ulan Ude
Chita
Ulaanbaatar
Krasnoyarsk
Novokuznetsk
Kemerovo
Bratsk
Blagoveshchensk
Komsomol'sk-na-Amure
Yuzhno-Sakhalinsk
P'yŏngyang
Soul (Seoul)
Pusan
Ürümqi
Arctic Circle

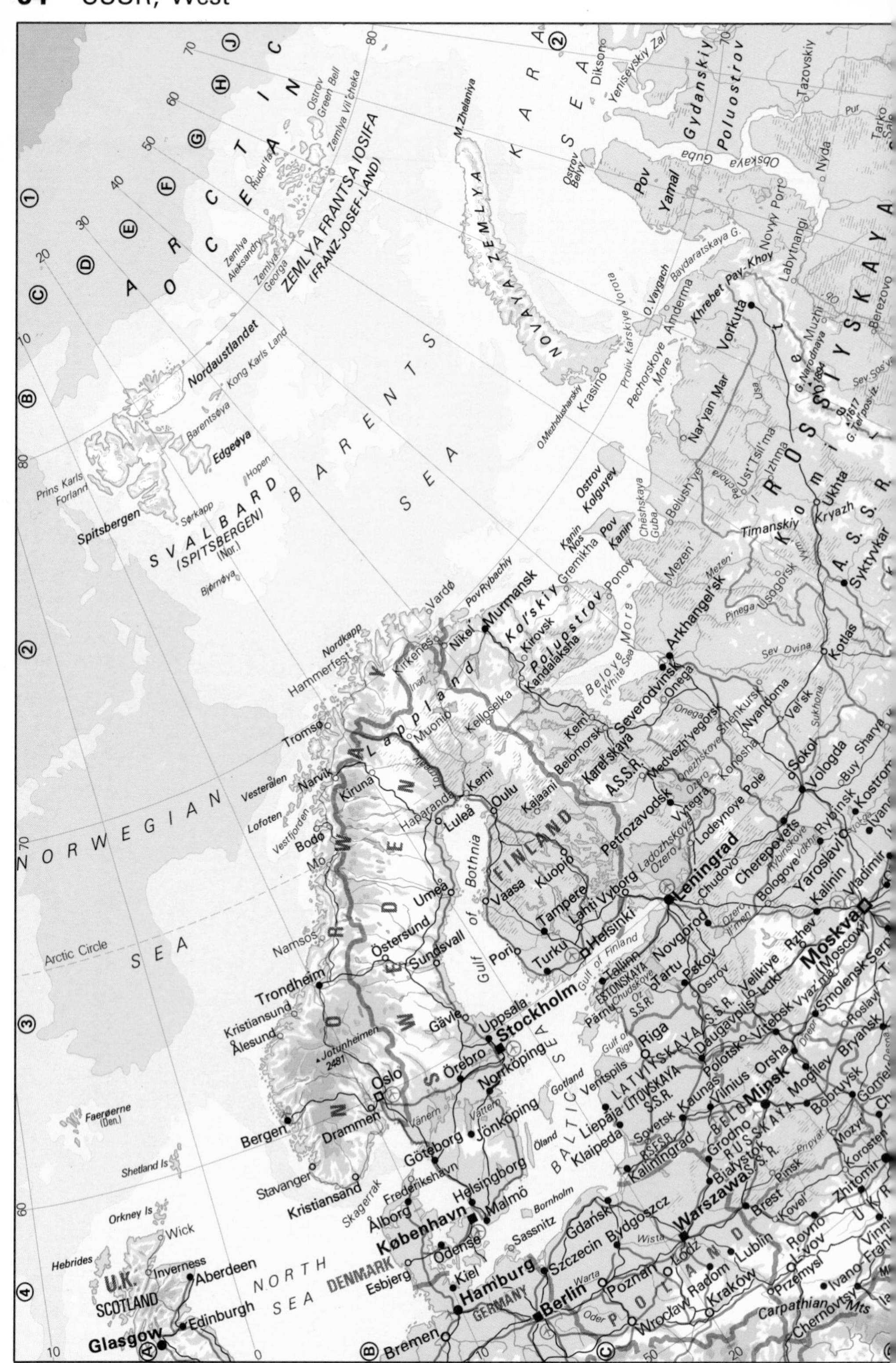
ARCTIC OCEAN
ZEMLYA FRANTSA IOSIFA
(FRANZ-JOSEF-LAND)
Ostrov Rudol'fa
Zemlya Aleksandry
Zemlya Georga
Ostrov Green Bell
Zemlya Vil'cheka
M.Zhelaniya
NOVAYA ZEMLYA
KARA SEA
Dikson
Yeniseyskiy Zal.
Gydanskiy Poluostrov
Ostrov Belyy
Pov Yamal
Obskaya Guba
Tazovskiy
Nyda
Pur
Novyy Port
Baydaratskaya G.
Labytnangi
O. Vaygach
Amderma
Khrebet Pay-Khoy
Vorkuta
Proliv Karskiye Vorota
Pechorskoye More
Nar'yan Mar
Usa
Pechora
Ust'Tsil'ma
Izhma
Ukhta
Kryazh
Timanskiy
KOMI A.S.S.R.
ROSSIYSKAYA
Syktyvkar
Kotlas
Sev Dvina
Vel'sk
Sukhona
Nordaustlandet
Kong Karls Land
Barentsøya
Edgeøya
Hopen
Prins Karls Forland
Spitsbergen
Sørkapp
SVALBARD
(SPITSBERGEN)
(Nor.)
Bjørnøya
BARENTS SEA
O.Mezhdusharskiy
Krasino
Ostrov Kolguyev
Kanin Nos
Pov Kanin
Chëshskaya Guba
Belush'ye
Mezen'
Mezen
Pinega
Usogorsk
Arkhangel'sk
Severodvinsk
Onega
Nyandoma
Shenkursk
Medvezh'yegorsk
Onezhskoye Ozero
Konosha
Sokol
Vologda
Sharya
Buy
Kostroma
Gremikha
Ponoy
Kol'skiy Poluostrov
Murmansk
Pov Rybachiy
Vardø
Nikel'
Kirkenes
Kirovsk
Kandalaksha
Beloye More (White Sea)
Kem'
Belomorsk
Karel'skaya A.S.S.R.
Petrozavodsk
Vytegra
Lodeynoye Pole
Ladozhskoye Ozero
Leningrad
Chudovo
Cherepovets
Rybinskoye Vdkhr
Rybinsk
Yaroslavl'
Bologoye
Kalinin
Vladimir
Novgorod
Ozero Il'men
Rzhev
Moskva (Moscow)
Nordkapp
Hammerfest
Inari
Lappland
Muonio
Kelloselka
Tromsø
Narvik
Kiruna
Vesterålen
Lofoten
Vestfjorden
Bodø
Mo
Haparanda
Kemi
Luleå
Oulu
Kajaani
FINLAND
Kuopio
Vaasa
Tampere
Lahti
Vyborg
Helsinki
Turku
Pori
Gulf of Bothnia
Gulf of Finland
Umeå
Östersund
Sundsvall
Namsos
Trondheim
Kristiansund
Ålesund
Jotunheimen
2481
NORWAY
SWEDEN
Gävle
Uppsala
Stockholm
Örebro
Norrköping
Oslo
Drammen
Bergen
Vänern
Vättern
Jönköping
Göteborg
Gotland
Öland
Stavanger
Kristiansand
Skagerrak
Frederikshavn
Helsingborg
Ålborg
Malmö
København
Bornholm
Odense
DENMARK
Esbjerg
Kiel
Hamburg
GERMANY
Bremen
Berlin
Sassnitz
Szczecin
Gdańsk
Bydgoszcz
Poznań
Warta
Oder
Wrocław
Łódź
Warszawa
Wisła
Radom
Kraków
Lublin
POLAND
Tallinn
ESTONSKAYA S.S.R.
Pärnu
Chudskoye Oz
Tartu
Pskov
Ostrov
Velikiye Luki
Gulf of Riga
Riga
Ventspils
LATVIYSKAYA S.S.R.
Daugavpils
Liepāja
LITOVSKAYA S.S.R.
Klaipeda
Sovetsk
Kaunas
Vilnius
Polotsk
Vitebsk
Orsha
Minsk
Mogilev
Smolensk
Vyaz'ma
Roslavl'
Bryansk
Gomel'
Bobruysk
Kaliningrad
RSFSR
Grodno
Białystok
BELORUSSKAYA S.S.R.
Brest
Pinsk
Pripyat'
Mozyr'
Korosten'
Kovel'
Rovno
Zhitomir
L'vov
Przemyśl
Ivano-Frankovsk
Chernovtsy
Carpathian Mts
Faerøerne (Den.)
Shetland Is
Orkney Is
Wick
Hebrides
Inverness
Aberdeen
U.K.
SCOTLAND
Edinburgh
Glasgow
NORTH SEA
NORWEGIAN SEA
Arctic Circle
BALTIC SEA

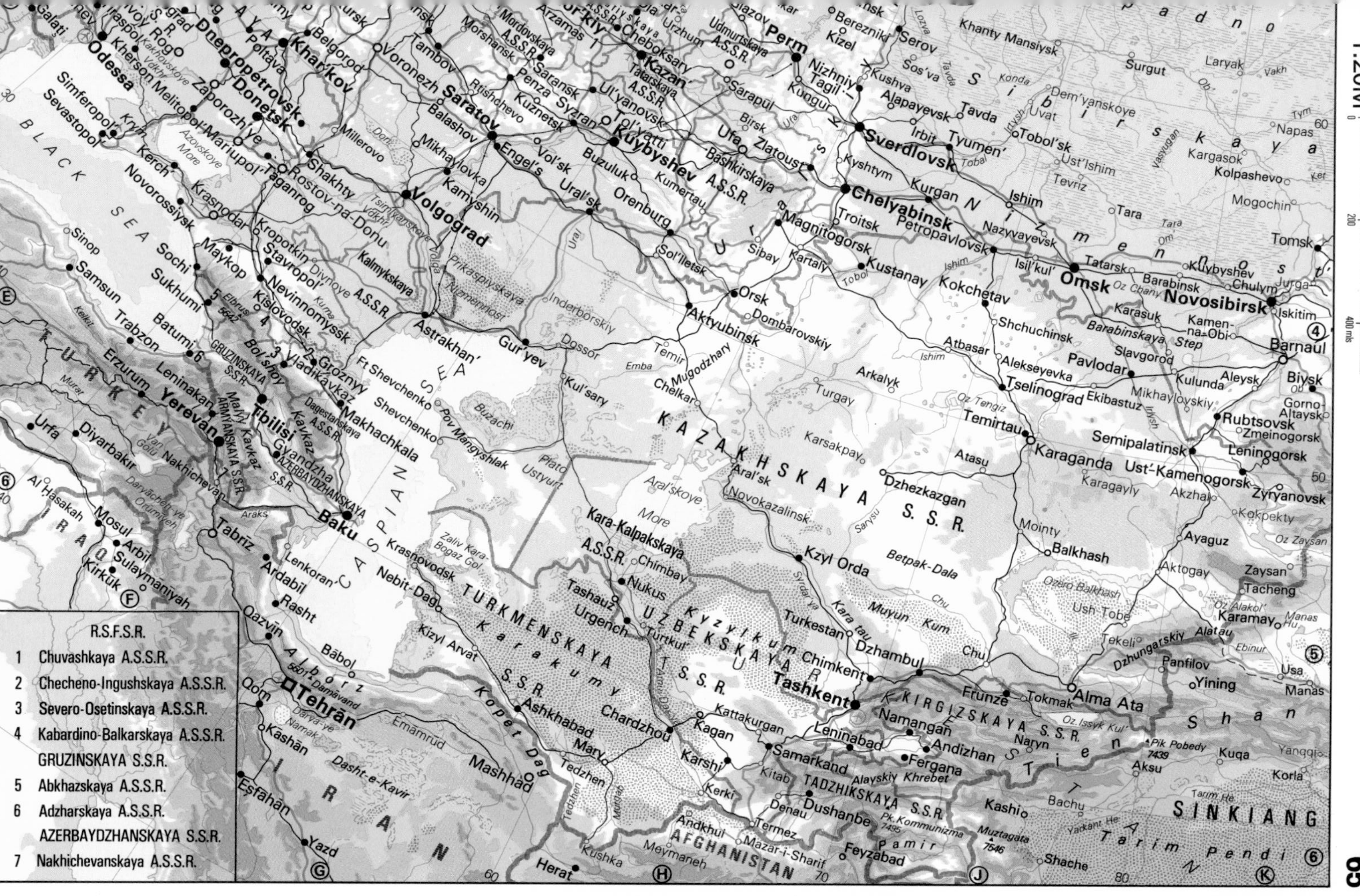

1:20M

200   400   600   800 km
200   400 mils

R.S.F.S.R.
1 Chuvashskaya A.S.S.R.
2 Checheno-Ingushskaya A.S.S.R.
3 Severo-Osetinskaya A.S.S.R.
4 Kabardino-Balkarskaya A.S.S.R.
   GRUZINSKAYA S.S.R.
5 Abkhazskaya A.S.S.R.
6 Adzharskaya A.S.S.R.
   AZERBAYDZHANSKAYA S.S.R.
7 Nakhichevanskaya A.S.S.R.

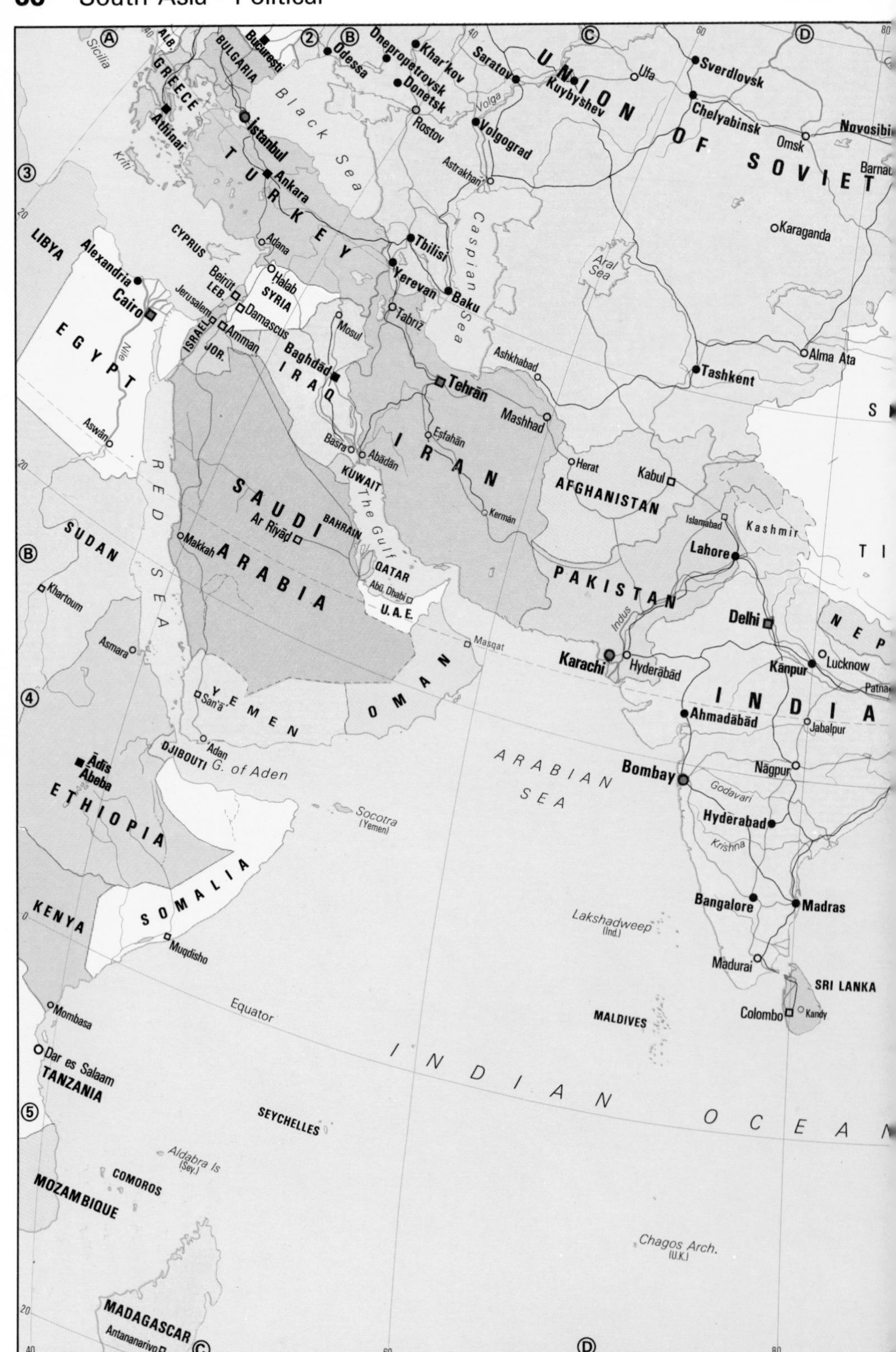
UNION OF SOVIET
TURKEY
IRAN
IRAQ
SAUDI ARABIA
EGYPT
LIBYA
SUDAN
ETHIOPIA
SOMALIA
KENYA
TANZANIA
MOZAMBIQUE
MADAGASCAR
AFGHANISTAN
PAKISTAN
INDIA
SRI LANKA
MALDIVES
SEYCHELLES
COMOROS
YEMEN
OMAN
U.A.E.
QATAR
BAHRAIN
KUWAIT
SYRIA
LEB.
ISRAEL
JOR.
CYPRUS
GREECE
BULGARIA
ALB.
DJIBOUTI
Black Sea
Caspian Sea
Aral Sea
RED SEA
The Gulf
G. of Aden
ARABIAN SEA
INDIAN OCEAN
Equator
Socotra (Yemen)
Lakshadweep (Ind.)
Chagos Arch. (U.K.)
Aldabra Is (Sey.)
Kashmir
Sicilia
Kriti
Nile
Volga
Indus
Godavari
Krishna
București
Odessa
Dnepropetrovsk
Khar'kov
Donetsk
Rostov
Saratov
Kuybyshev
Ufa
Sverdlovsk
Chelyabinsk
Omsk
Novosibi
Barnau
Volgograd
Astrakhan'
Karaganda
Alma Ata
Tashkent
Athínai
İstanbul
Ankara
Adana
Tbilisi
Yerevan
Baku
Tabrīz
Mosul
Halab
Beirūt
Damascus
Jerusalem
Amman
Alexandria
Cairo
Aswān
Baghdād
Tehrān
Ashkhabad
Mashhad
Esfahān
Basra
Abādān
Kermān
Herat
Kabul
Islamabad
Lahore
Delhi
Ar Riyāḍ
Makkah
Khartoum
Asmara
Abū Dhabi
Masqaṭ
Karachi
Hyderābād
Kānpur
Lucknow
Patna
Ahmadābād
Jabalpur
Nāgpur
Bombay
Hyderabad
Bangalore
Madras
Madurai
Colombo
Kandy
San'ā'
'Adan
Ādīs Ābeba
Muqdisho
Mombasa
Dar es Salaam
Antananarivo
NEP
TI
S

1:40M

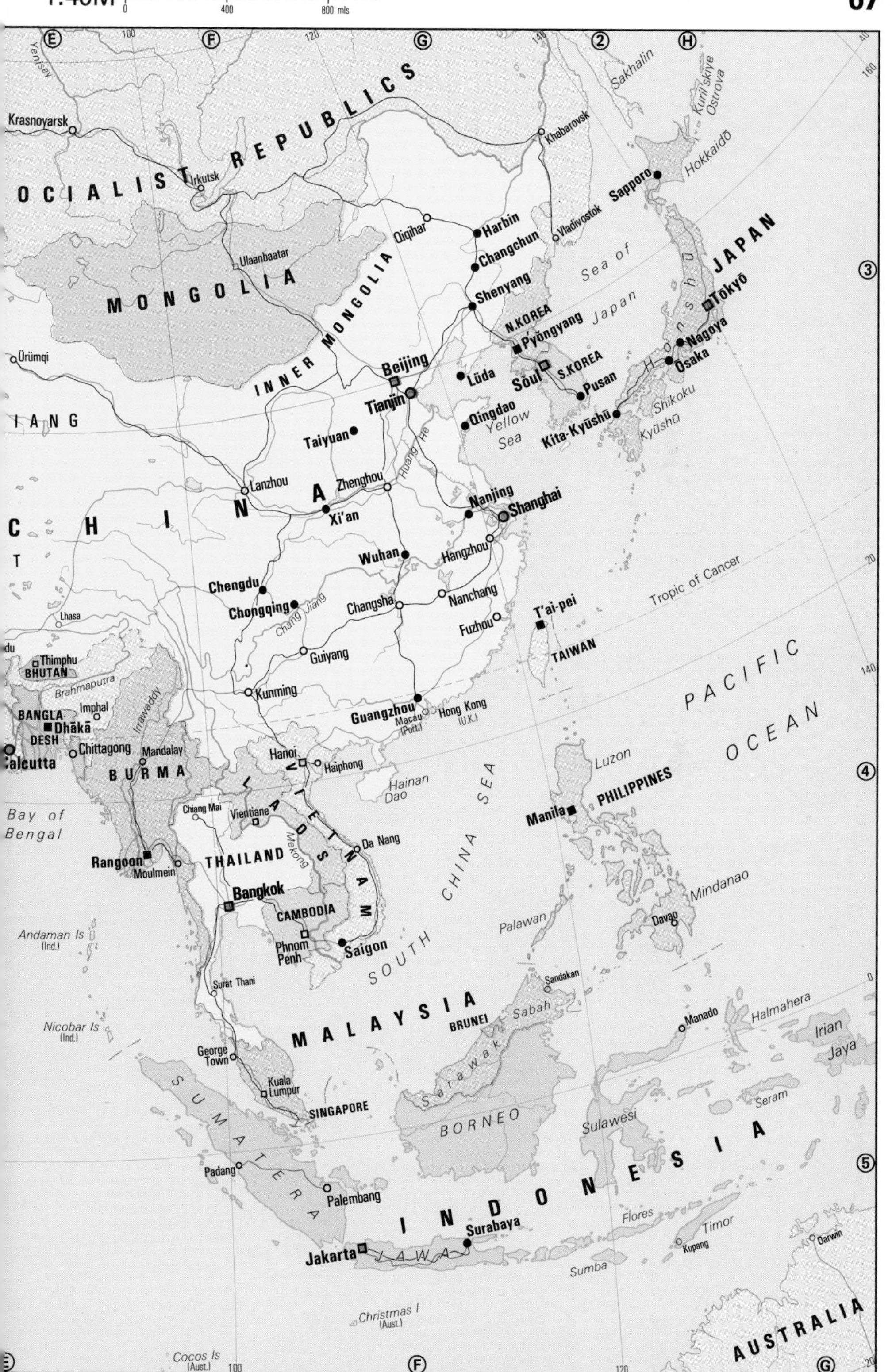

E F 120 G 140 ② H 160

Krasnoyarsk

Yenisey

O C I A L I S T   R E P U B L I C S

Irkutsk

Khabarovsk

Sakhalin

Kuril'skiye Ostrova

MONGOLIA

Ulaanbaatar

Qiqihar

Harbin

Changchun

Shenyang

Vladivostok

Sea of Japan

Sapporo

Hokkaidō

JAPAN

③

INNER MONGOLIA

Beijing

Tianjin

Taiyuan

N.KOREA

Pyŏngyang

Sŏul

S.KOREA

Lüda

Qingdao

Yellow Sea

Pusan

Kita-Kyūshū

Kyūshū

Shikoku

Honshū

Tōkyō

Nagoya

Ōsaka

IANG

Lanzhou

Zhenghou

Hoang He

C H I N A

Xi'an

Nanjing

Shanghai

Ürümqi

C

T

Lhasa

du

Thimphu

BHUTAN

Brahmaputra

BANGLA

DESH

Dhaka

Calcutta

Chittagong

Mandalay

B U R M A

Irrawaddy

Chengdu

Chongqing

Chang Jiang

Wuhan

Hangzhou

Changsha

Nanchang

Guiyang

Fuzhou

Kunming

Guangzhou

Macau (Port.)

Hong Kong (U.K.)

T'ai-pei

TAIWAN

Tropic of Cancer

20

140

PACIFIC

OCEAN

④

Bay of Bengal

Imphal

Chiang Mai

Hanoi

Haiphong

Hainan Dao

Luzon

Manila

PHILIPPINES

Rangoon

Moulmein

THAILAND

Vientiane

L A O S

V I E T N A M

Mekong

Da Nang

Mindanao

Davao

Andaman Is (Ind.)

Bangkok

CAMBODIA

Phnom Penh

Saigon

SOUTH CHINA SEA

Palawan

Sandakan

Nicobar Is (Ind.)

Surat Thani

M A L A Y S I A

BRUNEI

Sabah

Manado

Halmahera

Irian Jaya

Seram

George Town

Kuala Lumpur

SINGAPORE

S U M A T E R A

Sarawak

B O R N E O

Sulawesi

I N D O N E S I A

⑤

Padang

Palembang

Flores

Timor

Darwin

Jakarta

J A W A

Surabaya

Sumba

Kupang

Christmas I (Aust.)

Cocos Is (Aust.)

100 F 120 G 20

AUSTRALIA

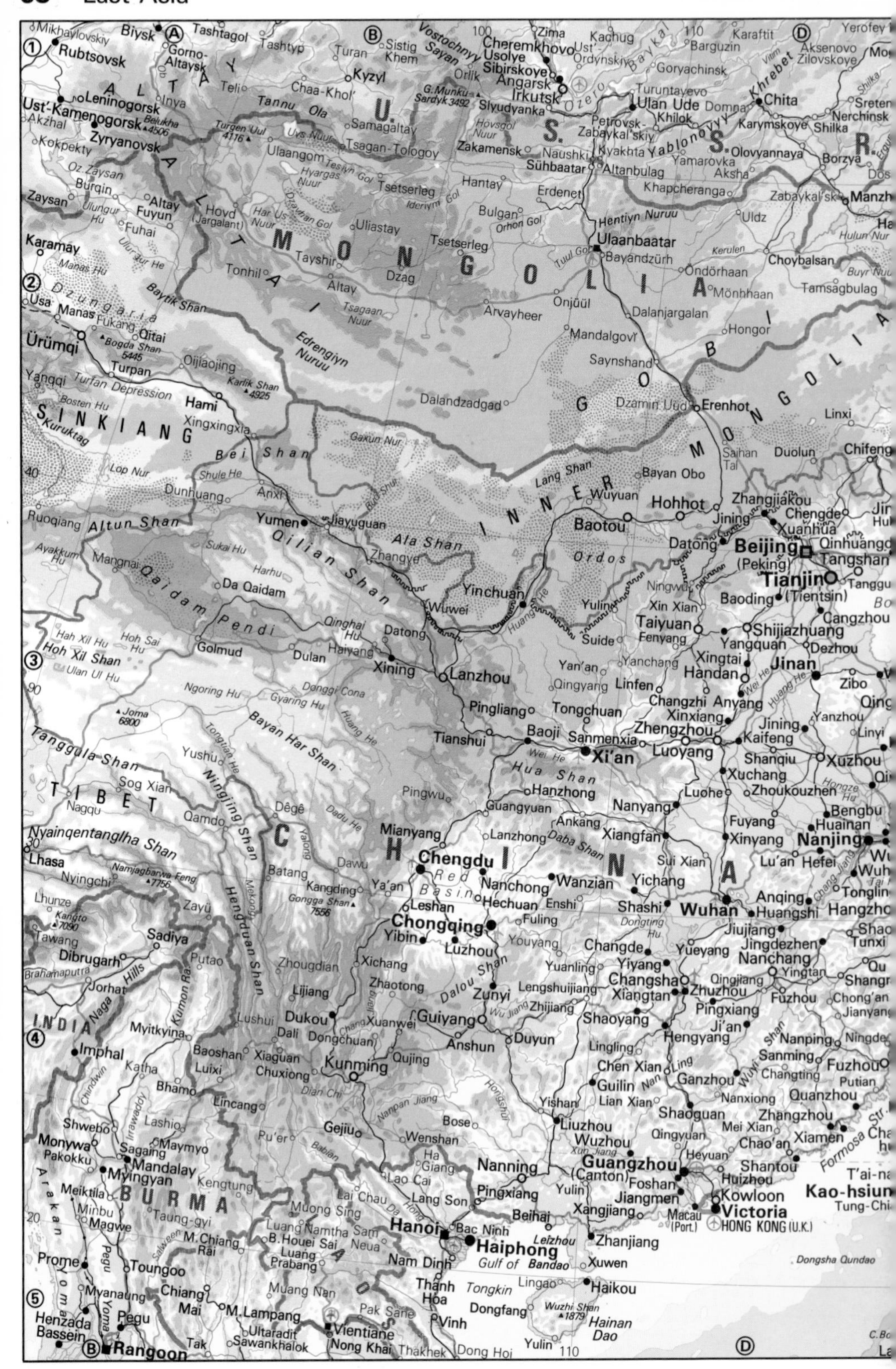

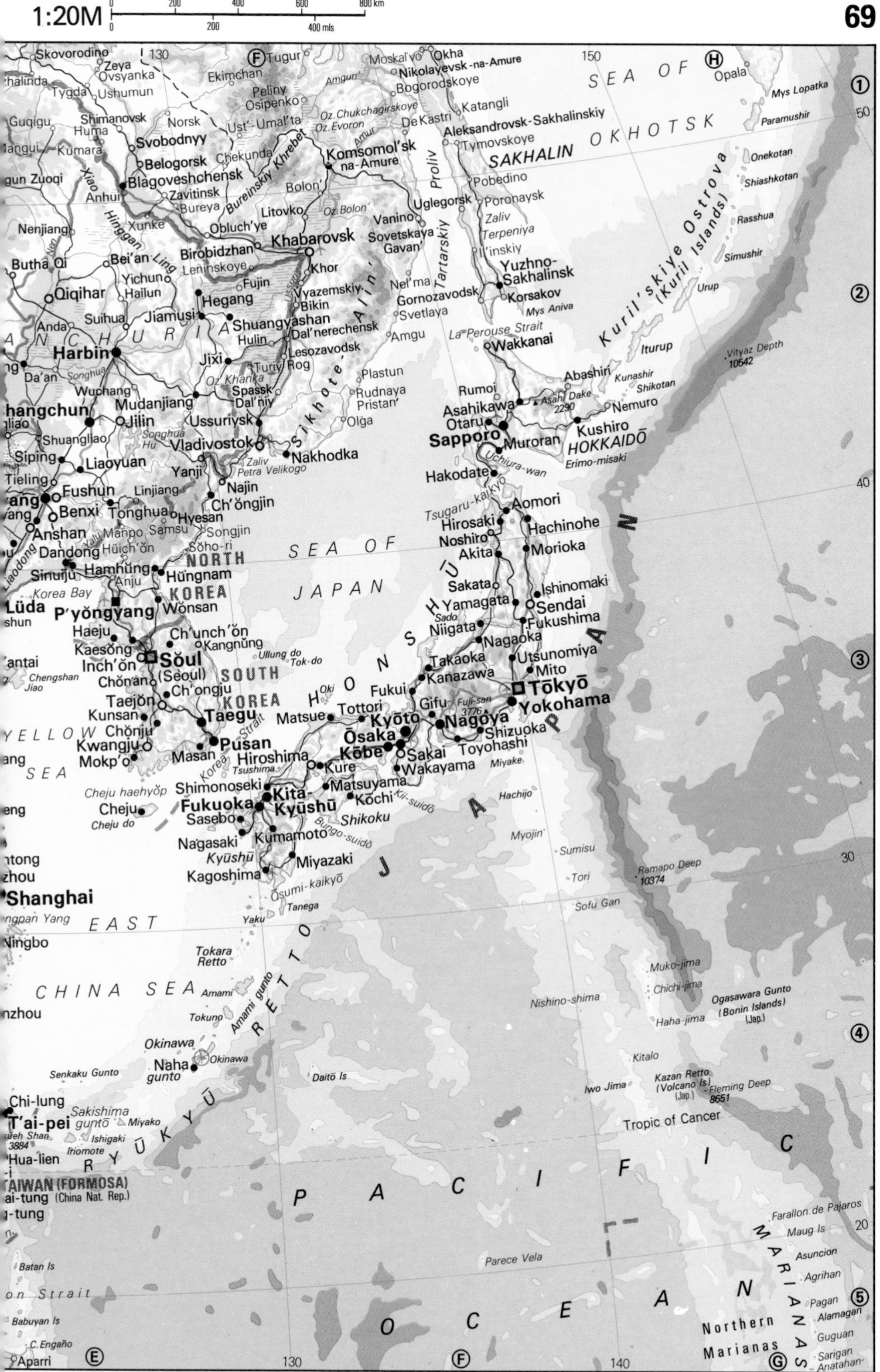

1:20M

200   400   600   800 km
200   400 mils

Skovorodino
Zeya
Tugur
Ekimchan
Moskal'vo   Okha
Nikolayevsk -na-Amure
Bogorodskoye

SEA OF

Mys Lopatka

130 ①
50

Shimanovsk
Ovsyanka
Ushumun
Pelny
Osipenko

Katangli

Paramushir

Guigu
Huma
Norsk
Ust'-Umal'ta
Oz. Chukchagirskoye
De Kastri
Tymovskoye

OKHOTSK

Onekotan

Shiashkotan

langui
Kumara
Svobodnyy
Belogorsk
Chekunda
Komsomol'sk
na-Amure
Aleksandrovsk-Sakhalinskiy

SAKHALIN

gun Zuogi
Anhui
Blagoveshchensk
Zavitinsk
Litovko
Pobedino

Rasshua

Nenjiang
Xunke
Bureya
Obluch'ye
Khor
Poronaysk

Kuril'skiye Ostrova

Simushir

Butha Qi
Bei'an
Birobidzhan
Leninskoye
Fujin
Yuzhno-
Sakhalinsk

(Kuril Islands)

Qiqihar
Hailun
Hegang
Nyazemskiy
Vanino
Korsakov

Urup

②
40

Anda
Suihua
Jiamusi
Shuangyashan
Dal'nerechensk
Mys Aniva

Vityaz Depth
10542

Harbin
Jixi
Hulin
Lesozavodsk
Svetlaya
Wakkanai

La Perouse Strait

hangchun
Mudanjiang
Spassk
Rudnaya
Pristan'
Rumoi
Abashiri
Kunashir
Nemuro

Jilin
Ussuriysk
Olga
Asahikawa
Asahi Dake
2290
Shikotan

Siping
Vladivostok
Nakhodka
Otaru
Kushiro

Liaoyuan
Yanji
Najin
Sapporo
Muroran
HOKKAIDŌ
Erimo-misaki

ang
Fushun
Linjiang
Ch'ŏngjin
Hakodate
Uchiura-wan

Benxi
Tonghua
Hyesan
Aomori
Tsugaru-kaikyo

Anshan
Manpo
Samsu
Songjin
Hirosaki
Hachinohe

Dandong
Huich'ŏn
Sŏho-ri
Noshiro
Morioka

NORTH
Hamhŭng
Akita

Sinuiju
Anju
KOREA
Hŭngnam
Sakata
Ishinomaki

Korea Bay
Wŏnsan
Yamagata
Sendai

Lüda
P'yŏngyang
Niigata
Fukushima

Haeju
Ch'unch'ŏn
Nagaoka

Kaesŏng
Kangnŭng
Takaoka
Utsunomiya

Inch'ŏn
Sŏul
(Seoul)
SOUTH
Kanazawa
Mito

Chŏnan
Ch'ŏngju
Fukui
Tōkyō

Taejŏn
KOREA
Gifu
Yokohama

Taegu
Matsue
Tottori
Kyōto
Nagoya
Shizuoka

Kunsan
Chŏnju
Osaka
Kōbe
Toyohashi

Mokp'o
Masan
Pusan
Hiroshima
Sakai
Wakayama

Cheju
Shimonoseki
Kure
Matsuyama

Fukuoka
Kita-
Kyūshū
Kōchi

Nagasaki
Sasebo
Kumamoto
Miyazaki

Kagoshima

Shanghai

Ningbo

Tokara
Retto

CHINA SEA

Amami gunto

Okinawa
Naha
gunto

Chi-lung
T'ai-pei

Hua-lien

TAIWAN (FORMOSA)

RYŪKYŪ

PACIFIC

OCEAN

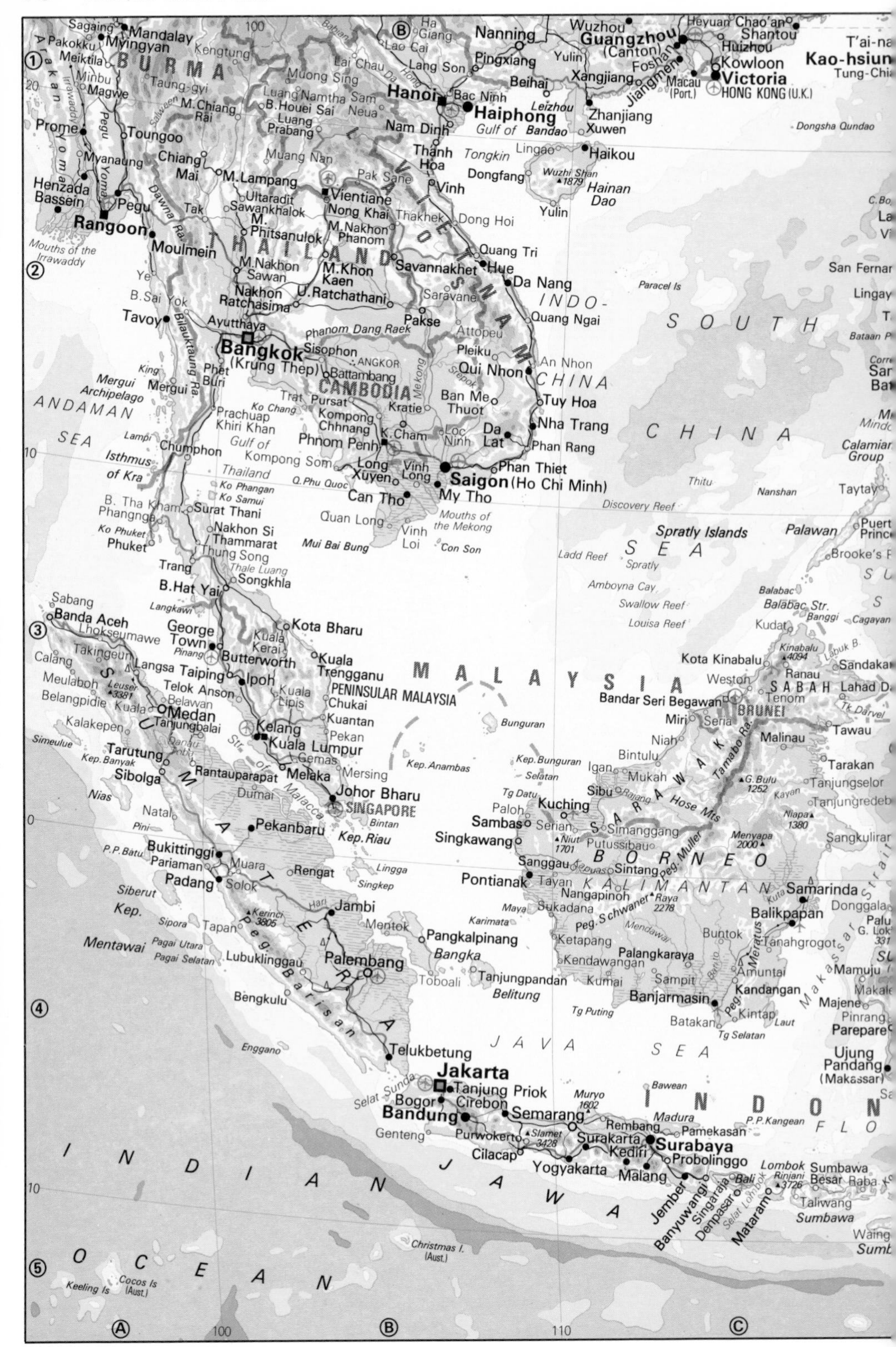
Sagaing
Mandalay
Pakokku
Myingyan
Meiktila
BURMA
Kengtung
Minbu
Magwe
Taung-gyi
Arakan Yoma
Irrawaddy
Pegu
Salween
M. Chiang Rai
Prome
Toungoo
Myanaung
Yoma
Henzada
Bassein
Pegu
Rangoon
Mouths of the Irrawaddy
Chiang Mai
M. Lampang
Tak
Dawna Ra.
Uttaradit
Sawankhalok
M. Phitsanulok
Moulmein
THAILAND
M. Nakhon Sawan
Ye
Nakhon Ratchasima
B. Sai Yok
Tavoy
Bilauktaung Ra.
Ayutthaya
Bangkok
(Krung Thep)
Phet Buri
King
Mergui
Mergui Archipelago
ANDAMAN
SEA
Lampi
Prachuap Khiri Khan
Chumphon
Isthmus of Kra
Gulf of Thailand
Ko Phangan
Ko Samui
B. Tha Kham
Phangnga
Surat Thani
Ko Phuket
Phuket
Nakhon Si Thammarat
Thung Song
Trang
Thale Luang
Songkhla
B. Hat Yai
Langkawi
Sabang
Banda Aceh
Lhokseumawe
Takingeun
Calang
Meulaboh
Leuser 3381
Belangpidie
Kuala
Langsa
Belawan
Medan
Tanjungbalai
Kalakepen
Simeulue
Tarutung
Kep. Banyak
Sibolga
Danau Toba
Rantauparapat
Nias
Natal
Pini
P.P. Batu
Bukittinggi
Pariaman
Padang
Muara
Solok
Siberut
Kep. Mentawai
Sipora
Pagai Utara
Pagai Selatan
Tapan
Kerinci 3805
Peg. Barisan
Bengkulu
Enggano
Lubuklinggau
SUMATERA
George Town
Pinang
Butterworth
Taiping
Ipoh
Telok Anson
Kuala Kerai
Kota Bharu
Kuala Trengganu
Kuala Lipis
PENINSULAR MALAYSIA
Chukai
Kuantan
Pekan
Kelang
Kuala Lumpur
Gemas
Melaka
Mersing
Str. of Malacca
Dumai
Johor Bharu
SINGAPORE
Bintan
Kep. Riau
Pekanbaru
Rengat
Lingga
Singkep
Hari
Jambi
Mentok
Pangkalpinang
Bangka
Palembang
Toboali
Tanjungpandan
Belitung
Telukbetung
Selat Sunda
Jakarta
Tanjung Priok
Bogor
Cirebon
Bandung
Genteng
Semarang
Muryo 1602
Purwokerto
Slamet 3428
Cilacap
Yogyakarta
Surakarta
Rembang
Madura
Pamekasan
Surabaya
Kediri
Malang
Probolinggo
Jember
Banyuwangi
Singaraja
Denpasar
Bali
Selat Lombok
Mataram
Lombok
Rinjani 3726
Sumbawa Besar
Raba
Taliwang
Sumbawa
Waing
P.P. Kangean
Bawean
JAWA
JAVA SEA
INDON
FLO
INDIAN OCEAN
Christmas I. (Aust.)
Cocos Is (Aust.)
Keeling Is
Ha Giang
Lao Cai
Lai Chau
Lang Son
Muong Sing
Luang Namtha
Sam Neua
B. Houei Sai
Luang Prabang
Hanoi
Bac Ninh
Haiphong
Nam Dinh
Thanh Hoa
Vinh
Muang Nan
Pak Sane
Vientiane
Nong Khai
Thakhek
M. Nakhon Phanom
Dong Hoi
LAOS
VIETNAM
Quang Tri
Hue
Savannakhet
M. Khon Kaen
Da Nang
U. Ratchathani
Saravane
Pakse
Attopeu
Quang Ngai
Phanom Dang Raek
Sisophon
ANGKOR
Battambang
CAMBODIA
Mekong
Srepok
Pleiku
Qui Nhon
An Nhon
Trat
Pursat
Ko Chang
Kompong Chhnang
Kratie
Ban Me Thuot
Tuy Hoa
K. Cham
Loc Ninh
Da Lat
Nha Trang
Phnom Penh
Phan Rang
Kompong Som
Long Xuyen
Vinh Long
Saigon (Ho Chi Minh)
Phan Thiet
Q. Phu Quoc
Can Tho
My Tho
Quan Long
Mouths of the Mekong
Vinh Loi
Mui Bai Bung
Con Son
Nanning
Pingxiang
Beihai
Wuzhou
Yulin
Guangzhou
(Canton)
Foshan
Jiangmen
Xangjiang
Macau (Port.)
Heyuan
Chao'an
Shantou
Huizhou
Kowloon
Victoria
HONG KONG (U.K.)
T'ai-na
Kao-hsiun
Tung-Chi
Leizhou
Zhanjiang
Xuwen
Gulf of Tongkin
Bandao
Lingao
Haikou
Dongfang
Wuzhi Shan 1879
Hainan Dao
Yulin
Dongsha Qundao
Paracel Is
INDO-CHINA
SOUTH CHINA SEA
Thitu
Nanshan
Discovery Reef
Spratly Islands
Ladd Reef
Spratly
Amboyna Cay
Swallow Reef
Louisa Reef
San Fernar
Lingay
Bataan
Taytay
Calamian Group
Palawan
Puerto Princesa
Brooke's P
Balabac
Balabac Str.
Banggi
Cagayan
Kudat
Kota Kinabalu
Kinabalu 4094
Labuk B.
Sandakan
Ranau
Weston
SABAH
Lahad Datu
Tenom
Bandar Seri Begawan
BRUNEI
Tk. Darvel
Miri
Seria
Niah
Malinau
Tawau
Bintulu
Tarakan
Mukah
Tamabo Ra.
Igan
SARAWAK
G. Bulu 1252
Kayan
Tanjungselor
Tanjungredeb
Sibu
Rajang
Hose Mts
Niapa 1380
MALAYSIA
Bunguran
Kep. Anambas
Kep. Bunguran Selatan
Tg Datu
Paloh
Kuching
Sambas
Serian
Simanggang
Niut 1701
Putussibau
Menyapa 2000
Sangkulirang
Singkawang
BORNEO
Peg. Muller
Sanggau
Kapuas
Sintang
Pontianak
Tayan
KALIMANTAN
Kuta
Samarinda
Nangapinoh
Peg. Schwaner
Raya 2278
Sukadana
Maya
Karimata
Balikpapan
Donggala
Palu
Mendawai
Ketapang
Buntok
Peg. Meratus
Tanahgrogot
Kendawangan
Palangkaraya
Barito
Amuntai
Mamuju
Sampit
Kumai
Kandangan
Makale
Banjarmasin
Majene
Tg Puting
Kintap
Pinrang
Batakan
Laut
Parepare
Tg Selatan
Ujung Pandang (Makassar)
Makassar Strait
100
110
10
0
A
B
C
1
2
3
4
5

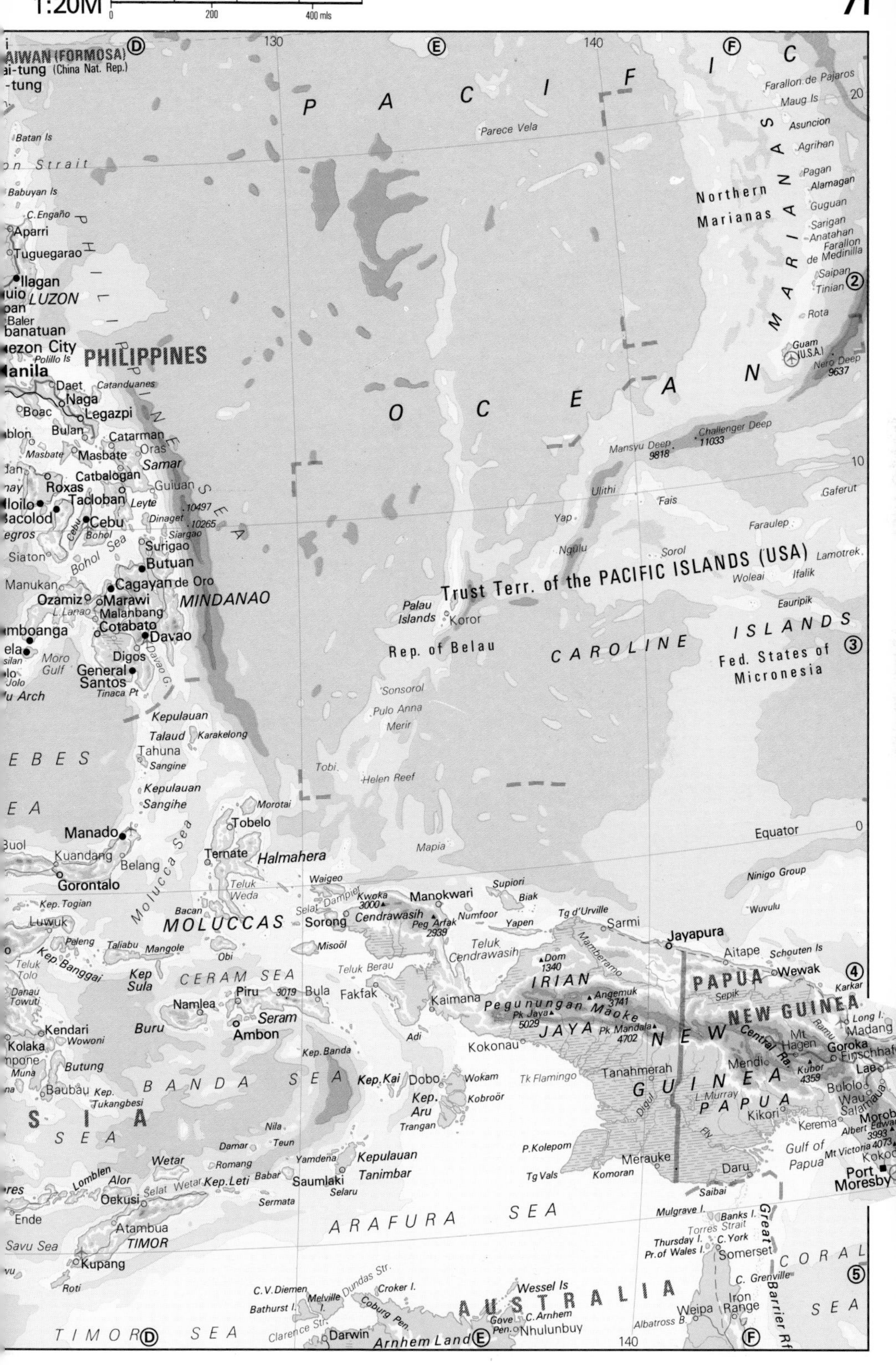

1:20M

200 400 600 800 km
200 400 mils

TAIWAN (FORMOSA) **D** (China Nat. Rep.)
-tung
-tung

Batan Is

Babuyan Is

C. Engaño
Aparri
Tuguegarao

Ilagan
LUZON
-pan
Baler
banatuan
ezon City
PHILIPPINES
Manila
Polillo Is
Daet Catanduanes
Naga
Legazpi
Boac
Bulan
blon
Catarman
Masbate
Masbate
Oras
Samar
lan
Catbalogan
nay
Roxas
Guiuan
Iloilo
Tacloban Leyte
acolod
Cebu
Dinagat 10497
egros
Bohol
Siargao 10265
Siaton
Bohol Sea
Surigao
Manukan
Butuan
Ozamiz
Cagayan de Oro
L. Lanao
Marawi
MINDANAO
mboanga
Malanbang
Cotabato
ela
Digos
Davao
silan
Moro
General
lo
Gulf
Santos
Jolo
Tinaca Pt.
u Arch

CELEBES
SEA
uol
Manado
Kuandang
Belang
Gorontalo
Kep. Togian
Luwuk
Paleng
Taliabu
Mangole
Kep. Banggai
Obi
Danau
Tolo
Towuti
Kendari
Wowoni
Kolaka
Butung
mpone
Muna
na
Baubau Kep.
Tukangbesi
S I A
S E A

C. Engaño

Parece Vela

P A C I F I C

O C E A N

Mansyu Deep 9818

Ulithi

Yap

Ngulu

Sorol

Palau
Islands

Trust Terr. of the PACIFIC ISLANDS (USA)

Koror
Rep. of Belau

C A R O L I N E

Sonsorol

Pulo Anna
Merir

Tobi

Helen Reef

Kepulauan
Talaud
Karakelong
Tahuna
Sangine

Kepulauan
Sangihe
Morotai
Tobelo

Ternate
Halmahera

Mapia

Waigeo

Teluk
Weda

Bacan
Kwoka
3000
Dampier
Selat
MOLUCCAS
Sorong
Cendrawasih
Misool
Teluk Berau
Fakfak
CERAM SEA
Kep.
Sula
Piru 3079
Bula
Namlea
Seram
Ambon
Buru
Kep. Banda

B A N D A
S E A
Kep. Kai
Dobo
Kep.
Aru
Kobroör
Trangan

Nila
Teun
Damar
Yamdena
Romang
Kepulauan
Tanimbar
Wetar
Babar
Saumlaki
Selat Wetar
Kep. Leti
Selaru
Oekusi
Sermata

res
Lomblen
Alor
TIMOR
Ende
Atambua
A R A F U R A
S E A

Savu Sea
Kupang
Roti

T I M O R
D
S E A

Farallon de Pajaros
Maug Is
20
Asuncion
Agrihan
Pagan
Alamagan
Northern
Guguan
Marianas
Sarigan
Anatahan
Farallon
de Medinilla
Saipan
Tinian
Rota

M A R I A N A S

Guam
(U.S.A.)
Nero Deep
9637

Challenger Deep
11033

10

Fais
Gaferut

Faraulep

Faraulep
Lamotrek
Woleai
Ifalik
Eauripik

I S L A N D S

Fed. States of
Micronesia

Equator 0

Ninigo Group

Wuvulu

Supiori
Biak
Manokwari
Numfoor
Peg. Arfak
2939
Yapen
Tg d'Urville
Sarmi
Teluk
Cendrawasih
Mamberamo
Jayapura
Aitape
Schouten Is
Karkar
Dom
1340
IRIN
PAPUA
Wewak
Sepik
NEW GUINEA
Long I.
Madang
Angemuk
3741
JAYA
Pegunungan Maoke
Pk Mandala
4702
Central Ra.
Mt
Hagen
Goroka
Finschhafe
Kaimana
Pk Jaya
5029
Kubor
4359
Lae
Adi
Bulolo
Kokonau
Mendi
Wau
Salamaua
Kikori
Kerema
Morobe
GUINEA
Mt Victoria 4073
Tk Flamingo
L. Murray
Kokoda
Wokam
Tanahmerah
Digul
PAPUA
Daru
Port
Gulf of
Moresby
Papua
Saibai
P. Kolepom
Merauke
Komoran
Tg Vals
Mulgrave I.
Banks I.
Thursday I.
C. York
Torres Strait
Pr. of Wales I.
Somerset
C O R A L
C. Grenville
S E A
C.V. Diemen
Croker I.
Melville I.
Dundas Str.
Wessel Is
Bathurst I.
Coburg Pen.
C. Arnhem
Nhulunbuy
Iron
Clarence Str.
AUSTRALIA
Weipa
Range
Darwin
Arnhem Land
E
C. Arnhem
Albatross B.
Albatross B.
140
Arnhem Pen.

130
E
140
F

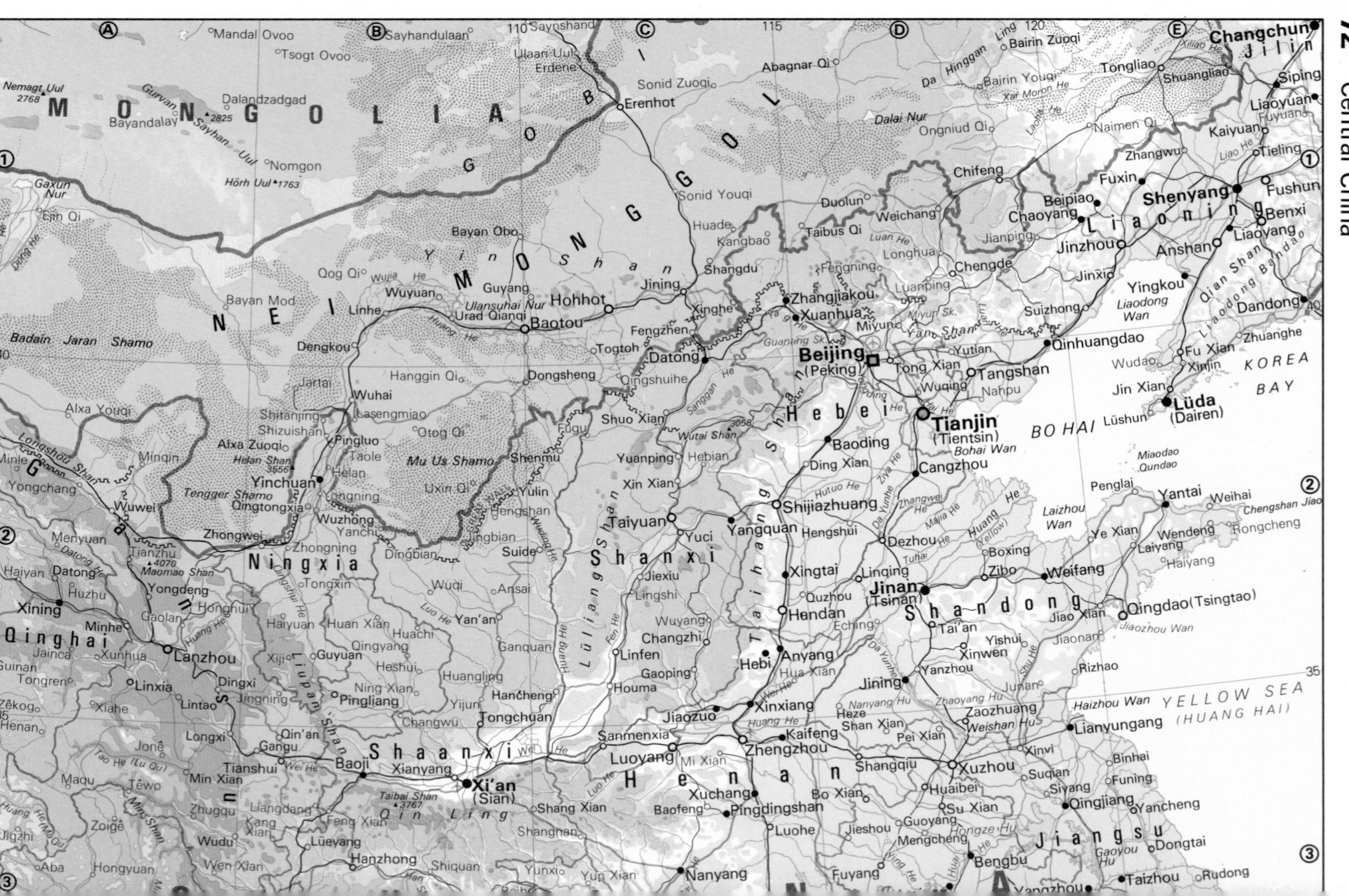
MONGOLIA
NEI MONGGOL
GOBI
Ningxia
Qinghai
Gansu
Shaanxi
Shanxi
Henan
Hebei
Shandong
Liaoning
Jilin
Jiangsu
BO HAI
KOREA BAY
YELLOW SEA
(HUANG HAI)
Bohai Wan
Laizhou Wan
Liaodong Wan
Haizhou Wan
Jiaozhou Wan
Beijing
(Peking)
Tianjin
(Tientsin)
Shenyang
Changchun
Lüda
(Dairen)
Qingdao (Tsingtao)
Jinan
(Tsinan)
Zhengzhou
Xi'an
(Sian)
Lanzhou
Yinchuan
Xining
Taiyuan
Hohhot
Baotou
Shijiazhuang
Datong
Luoyang
Kaifeng
Xuzhou
Dandong
Anshan
Fushun
Benxi
Fuxin
Jinzhou
Yingkou
Qinhuangdao
Tangshan
Zhangjiakou
Chengde
Chifeng
Baoding
Handan
Anyang
Xinxiang
Weifang
Zibo
Yantai
Weihai
Lianyungang
Bengbu
Nanyang
Pingdingshan
Baoji
Tianshui
Wuhai
Erenhot
Huang He
Mu Us Shamo
Tengger Shamo
Badain Jaran Shamo
Yin Shan
Lüliang Shan
Taihang Shan
Qin Ling
Liupan Shan
Helan Shan
Min Shan
Dalai Nur
Gaxun Nur
Taibai Shan
3767

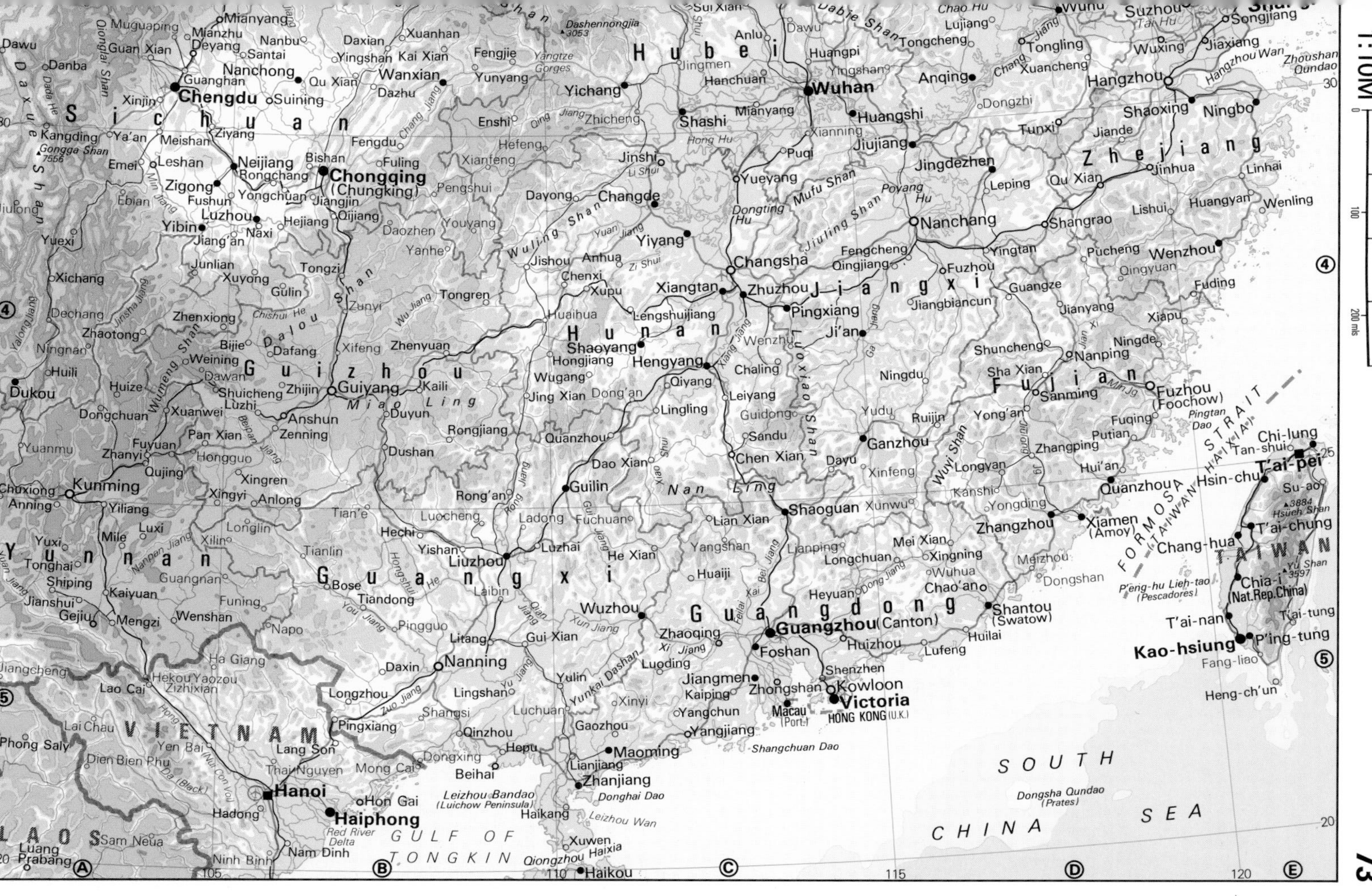

1:10M

0 100 200 300 400 km
0 100 200 mls

SOUTH CHINA SEA

GULF OF TONGKIN

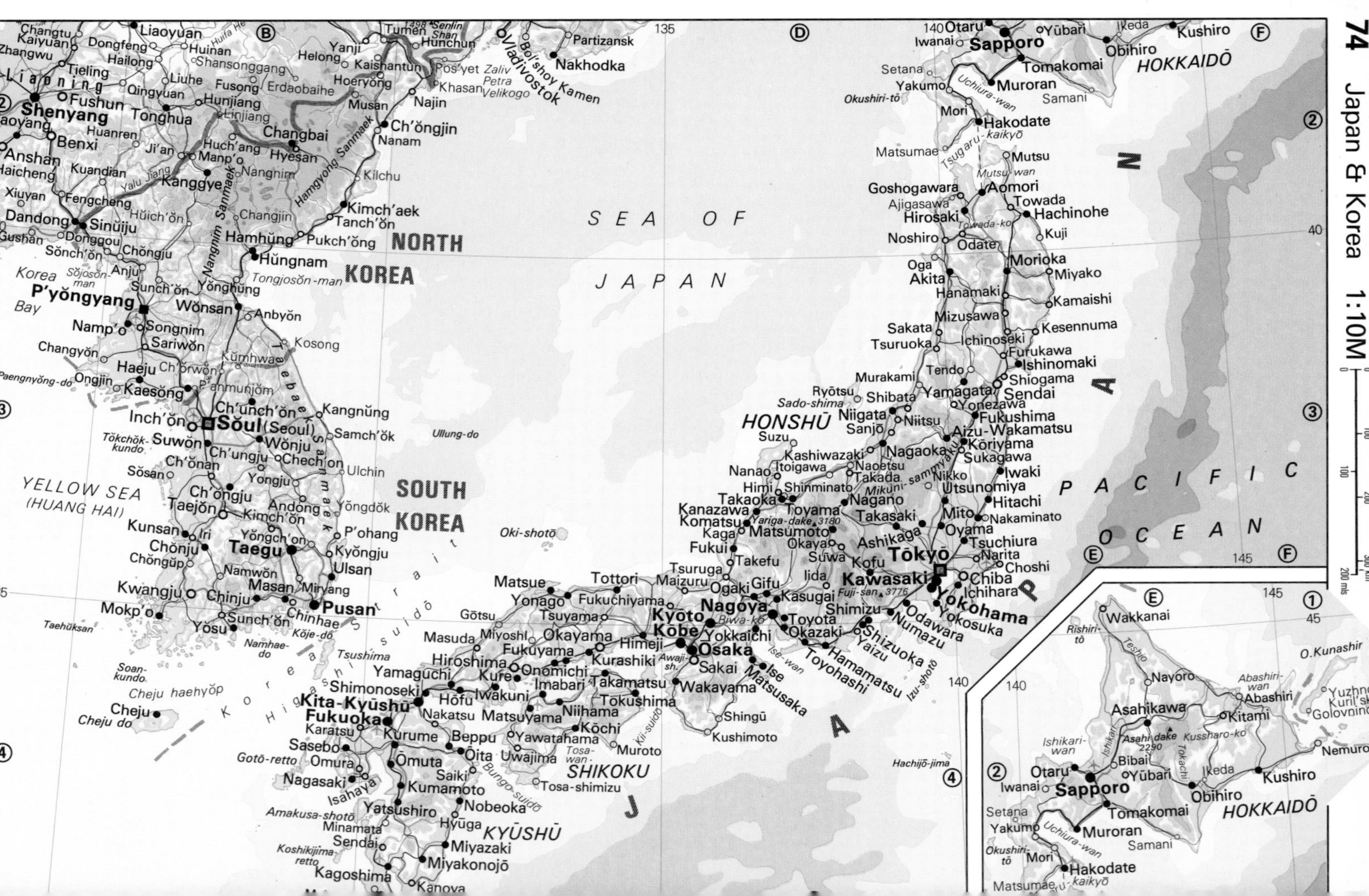
0 100 200 300 km
0 100 200 mls
SEA OF JAPAN
PACIFIC OCEAN
YELLOW SEA (HUANG HAI)
NORTH KOREA
SOUTH KOREA
JAPAN
HONSHŪ
SHIKOKU
KYŪSHŪ
HOKKAIDŌ
Korea Bay
Korea Strait
Tōkyō
Yokohama
Kawasaki
Nagoya
Ōsaka
Kyōto
Kōbe
Sapporo
Sendai
Hiroshima
Fukuoka
Kita-Kyūshū
Sŏul (Seoul)
P'yŏngyang
Pusan
Taegu
Inch'ŏn
Vladivostok
Nakhodka
Partizansk
Shenyang
Fushun
Dandong
Sado-shima
Oki-shotō
Ullung-do
Cheju do
Tsushima
Okushiri-tō
Rishiri-tō
Hachijō-jima
Izu-shotō
Kii-suidō
Bungo-suidō
Gotō-retto
Koshikijima-retto
Amakusa-shotō
Fuji-san 3776
Yariga-dake 3180
Asahi dake 2290
Biwa-ko
Towada-ko
Kussharo-ko
Tsugaru-kaikyō
Uchiura-wan
Ishikari-wan
Abashiri-wan
Mutsu-wan
Ise-wan
O.Kunashir
Yuzhno-Kuril'sk
Golovnino
Nemuro
Kushiro
Obihiro
Asahikawa
Wakkanai
Hakodate
Muroran
Otaru
Aomori
Hachinohe
Morioka
Akita
Niigata
Kanazawa
Shizuoka
Hamamatsu
Wakayama
Okayama
Matsuyama
Kōchi
Nagasaki
Kumamoto
Kagoshima
Miyazaki
Ōita
Kwangju
Taejŏn
Ulsan
Wŏnsan
Hamhŭng
Hŭngnam
Ch'ŏngjin
Kimch'aek
Sinŭiju
Namp'o
Kaesŏng
Hamgyong Sanmaek
Nangnim Sanmaek
Taebaek Sanmaek
Tongjosŏn-man
Paengnyŏng-do
Taehŭksan
Cheju haehyŏp
Mikuni-sammyaku
135
140
145
35
40
45

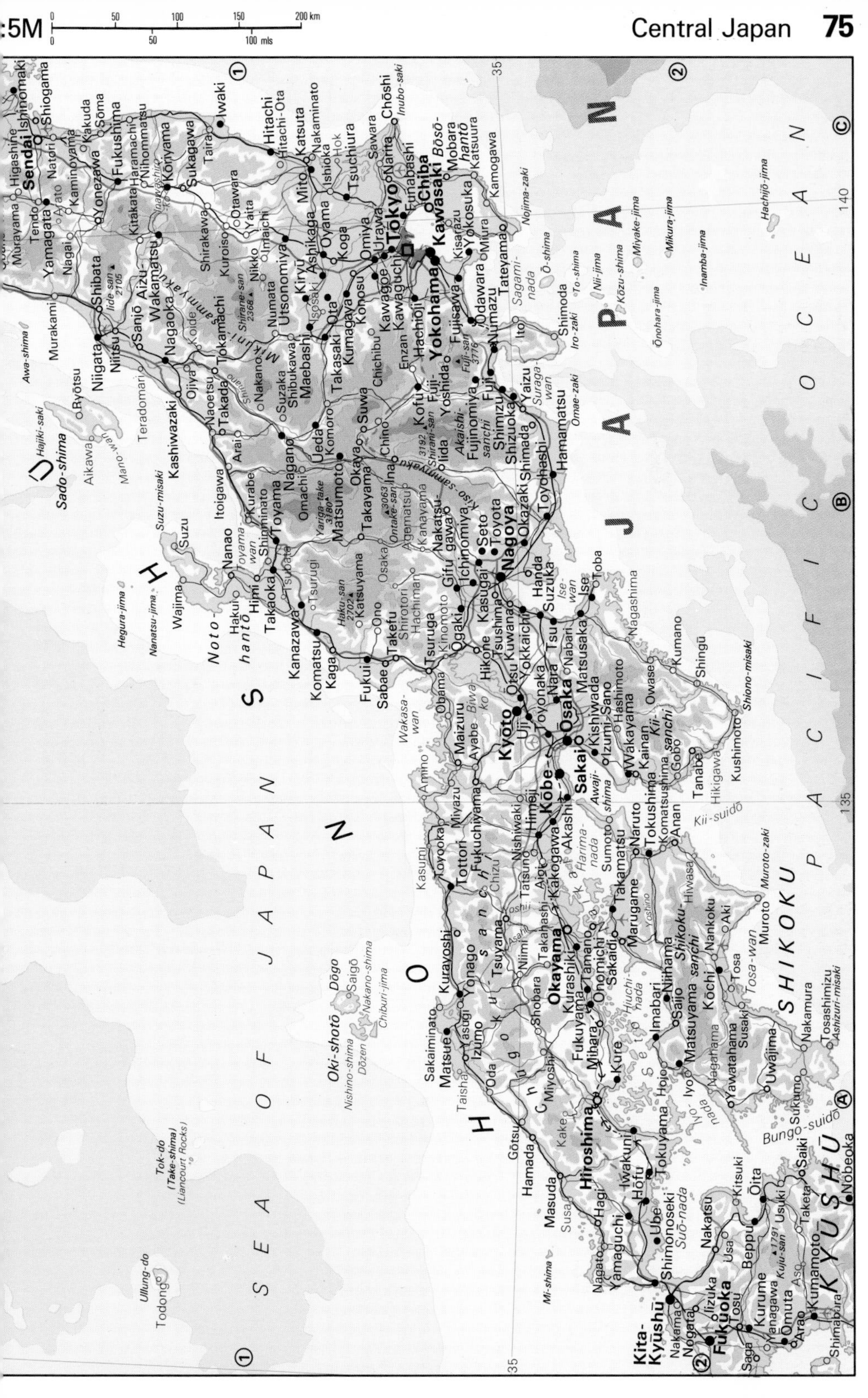

:5M

0 50 100 150 200 km
0   50   100 mls

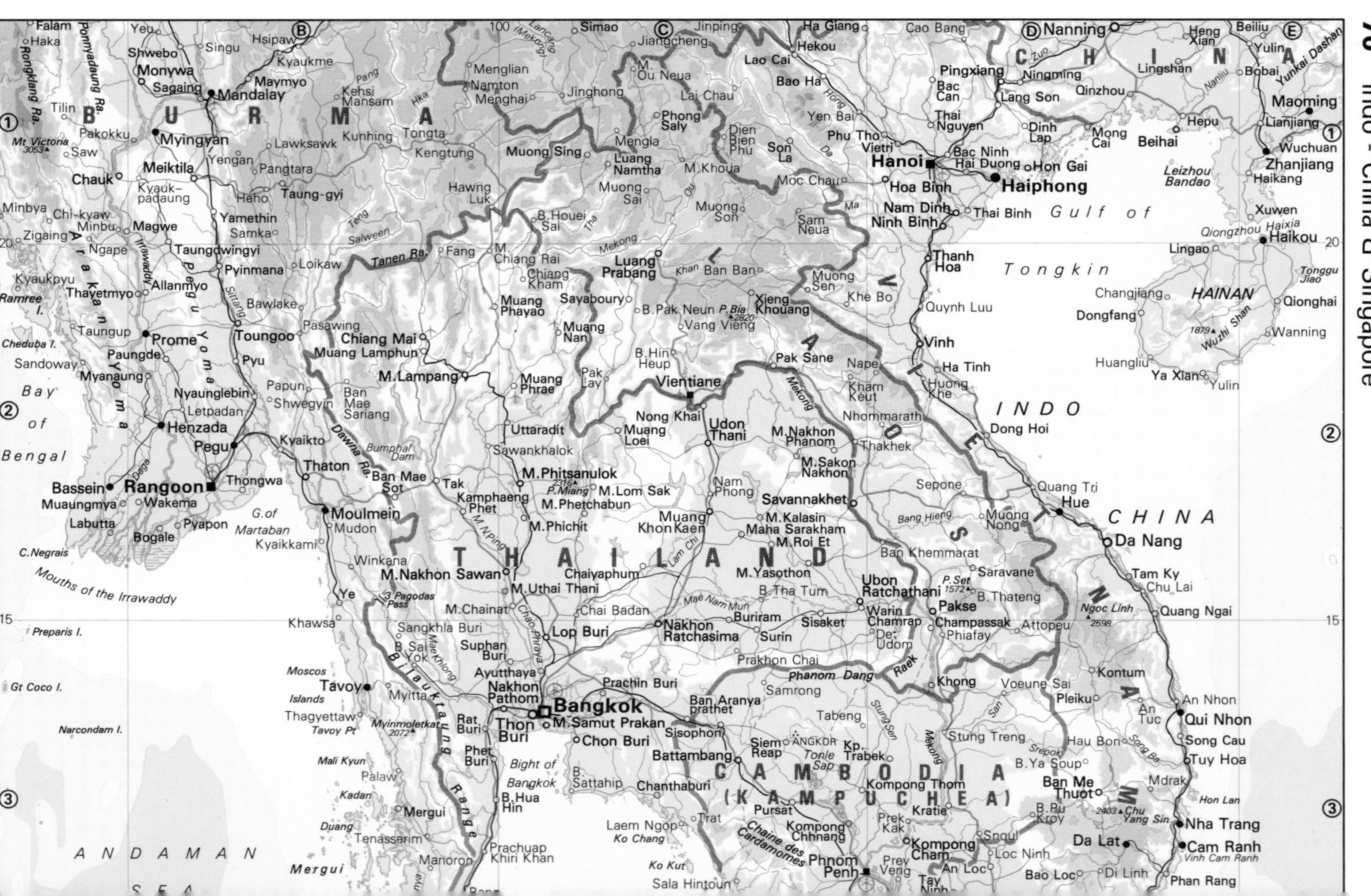

BURMA
CHINA
LAOS
VIETNAM
THAILAND
CAMBODIA (KAMPUCHEA)
HAINAN
Gulf of Tongkin
INDO CHINA
Bay of Bengal
G. of Martaban
ANDAMAN SEA
Mergui
Bight of Bangkok
Mouths of the Irrawaddy
Nanning
Beihai
Haikou
Zhanjiang
Maoming
Hanoi
Haiphong
Hon Gai
Nam Dinh
Thanh Hoa
Vinh
Dong Hoi
Hue
Da Nang
Quang Ngai
Qui Nhon
Nha Trang
Cam Ranh
Da Lat
Ban Me Thuot
Kontum
Pleiku
Vientiane
Luang Prabang
Xieng Khouang
Savannakhet
Pakse
Udon Thani
Ubon Ratchathani
Nakhon Ratchasima
Bangkok
Thon Buri
Phnom Penh
Kompong Cham
Battambang
Siem Reap
Chiang Mai
M. Lampang
Mandalay
Myingyan
Meiktila
Toungoo
Pegu
Rangoon
Bassein
Henzada
Prome
Moulmein
Tavoy
Mergui
Mekong
Irrawaddy
Pegu Yoma
Arakan Yoma
Bilauktaung Range
Tanen Ra.
Dawna Ra.

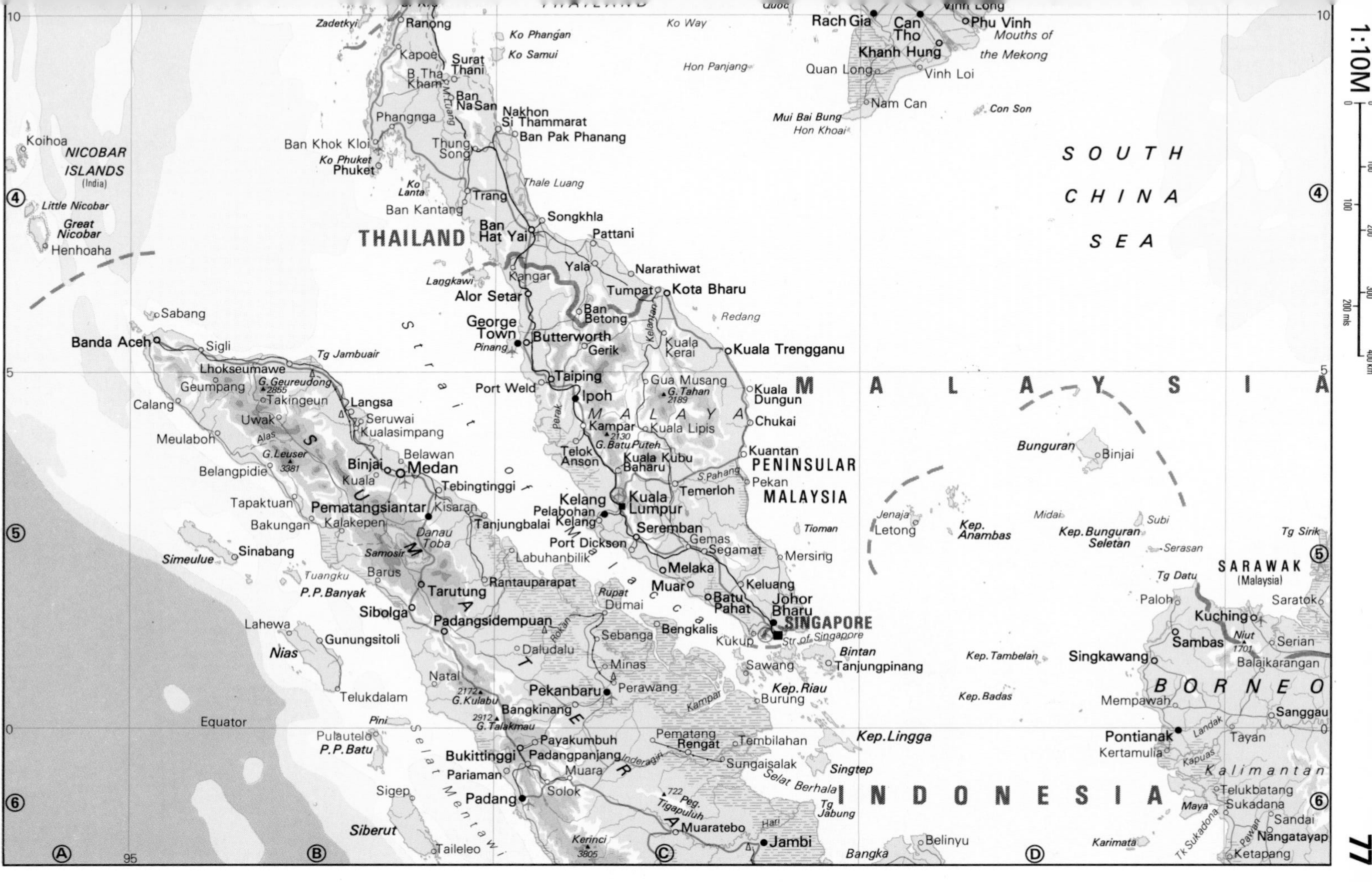
SOUTH CHINA SEA
THAILAND
MALAYSIA
PENINSULAR MALAYSIA
MALAYA
SARAWAK
(Malaysia)
BORNEO
Kalimantan
INDONESIA
SUMATERA
Strait of Malacca
NICOBAR ISLANDS
(India)
Koihoa
Little Nicobar
Great Nicobar
Henhoaha
Sabang
Banda Aceh
Sigli
Lhokseumawe
Geumpang
G. Geureudong
2855
Takingeun
Calang
Uwak
Meulaboh
Alas
G. Leuser
3381
Belangpidie
Tapaktuan
Bakungan
Simeulue
Sinabang
Tg Jambuair
Langsa
Seruwai
Kualasimpang
Belawan
Binjai
Medan
Kuala
Tebingtinggi
Pematangsiantar
Kisaran
Kalakepen
Danau Toba
Samosir
Tanjungbalai
Labuhanbilik
Barus
Tuangku
P.P. Banyak
Rantauparapat
Tarutung
Sibolga
Padangsidempuan
Lahewa
Gunungsitoli
Nias
Daludalu
Rokan
Minas
Natal
2172
G. Kulabu
Telukdalam
Pekanbaru
Perawang
Equator
Pini
2912
G. Talakmau
Bangkinang
Pulautelo
P.P. Batu
Payakumbuh
Bukittinggi
Padangpanjang
Muara
Pariaman
Selat Mentawai
Sigep
Padang
Solok
Siberut
Taileleo
Kerinci
3805
Pematang
Rengat
Inderagiri
Tembilahan
Sungaisalak
Selat Berhala
722
Peg. Tigapuluh
Muaratebo
Hari
Jambi
Tg Jabung
Zadetkyi
Ranong
Kapoe
Ko Phangan
Ko Samui
Surat Thani
B. Tha Kham
M. Luang
Ban Na San
Phangnga
Nakhon Si Thammarat
Ban Pak Phanang
Ban Khok Kloi
Thung Song
Ko Phuket
Phuket
Thale Luang
Ko Lanta
Trang
Ban Kantang
Songkhla
Ban Hat Yai
Pattani
Yala
Narathiwat
Langkawi
Kangar
Alor Setar
Tumpat
Kota Bharu
Ban Betong
Redang
George Town
Pinang
Butterworth
Kelantan
Kuala Kerai
Kuala Trengganu
Gerik
Taiping
Port Weld
Gua Musang
G. Tahan
2189
Kuala Dungun
Ipoh
Perak
Kampar
2130
G. Batu Puteh
Kuala Lipis
Chukai
Telok Anson
Kuala Kubu Baharu
Kuantan
S. Pahang
Pekan
Kelang
Kuala Lumpur
Temerloh
Pelabohan Kelang
Seremban
Port Dickson
Gemas
Segamat
Tioman
Mersing
Melaka
Muar
Keluang
Rupat
Dumai
Batu Pahat
Johor Bharu
SINGAPORE
Sebanga
Bengkalis
Kukup
Str. of Singapore
Bintan
Tanjungpinang
Sawang
Kep. Riau
Burung
Kampar
Kep. Lingga
Singtep
Bangka
Belinyu
Ko Way
Hon Panjang
Rach Gia
Can Tho
Khanh Hung
Vinh Long
Phu Vinh
Mouths of the Mekong
Quan Long
Vinh Loi
Nam Can
Mui Bai Bung
Hon Khoai
Con Son
Bunguran
Binjai
Jenaja
Letong
Kep. Anambas
Midai
Kep. Bunguran Seletan
Subi
Serasan
Tg Sirik
Tg Datu
Paloh
Saratok
Kuching
Sambas
Niut
1701
Serian
Kep. Tambelan
Singkawang
Balaikarangan
Kep. Badas
Mempawah
Sanggau
Pontianak
Landak
Tayan
Kertamulia
Kapuas
Telukbatang
Maya
Sukadana
Tk. Sukadana
Sandai
Pawan
Karimata
Nangatayap
Ketapang
10
5
0
95
A
B
C
D
4
5
6

1:10M

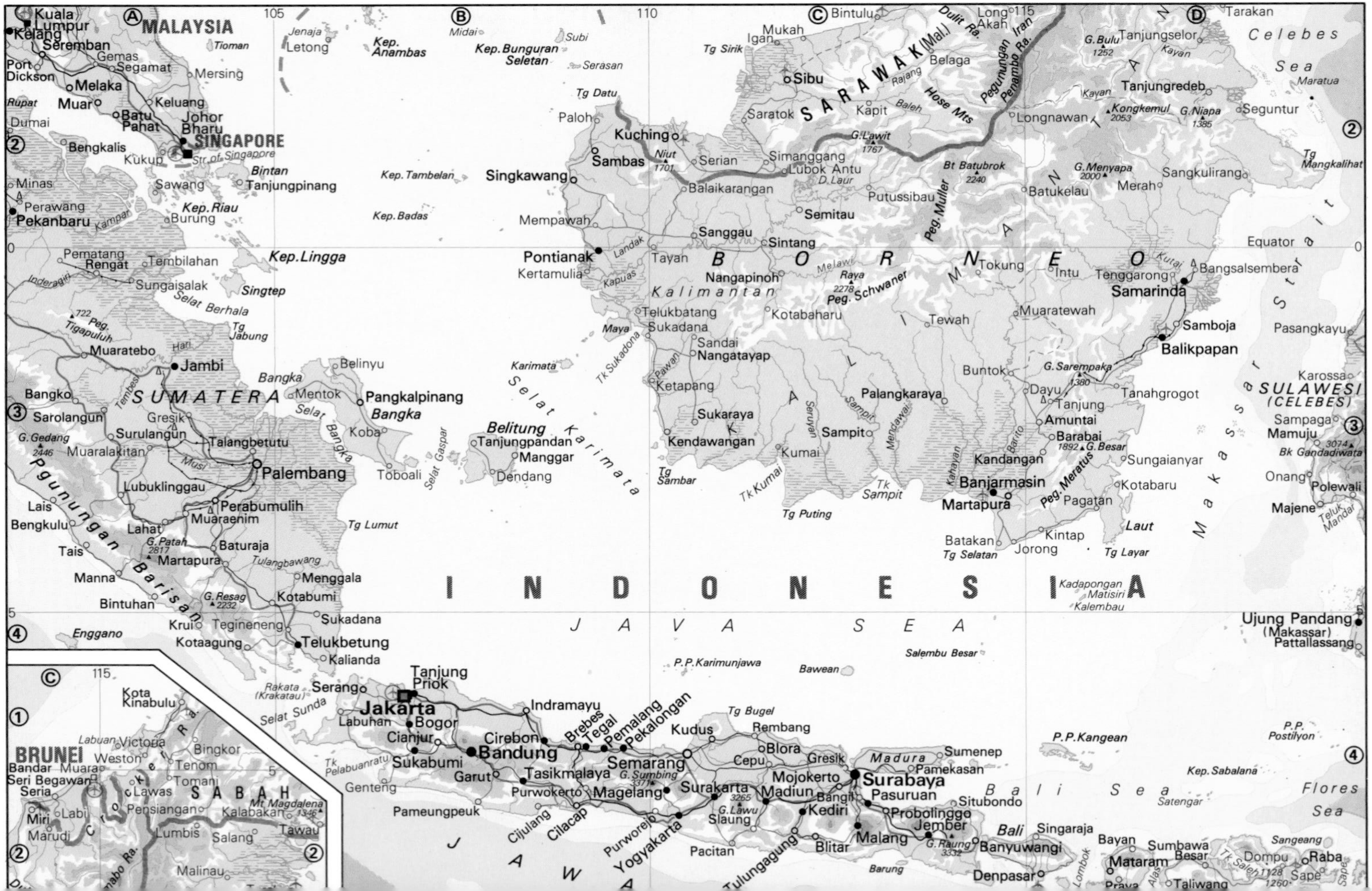
MALAYSIA
Kuala Lumpur
Kelang
Seremban
Port Dickson
Melaka
Muar
Batu Pahat
Johor Bharu
SINGAPORE
Str. of Singapore
Tioman
Mersing
Kep. Anambas
Kep. Bunguran Seletan
Kep. Tambelan
Kep. Badas
Kep. Riau
Bintan
Tanjungpinang
Kep. Lingga
Singtep
Selat Berhala
Pekanbaru
Jambi
SUMATERA
Palembang
Pangkalpinang
Bangka
Selat Bangka
Belitung
Tanjungpandan
Selat Karimata
Selat Gaspar
Pgunungan Barisan
Bengkulu
Telukbetung
Enggano
Selat Sunda
Rakata (Krakatau)
Kuching
Sambas
Singkawang
Pontianak
SARAWAK (Mal.)
Sibu
Bintulu
Hose Mts
Dulit Ra.
Pegunungan Iran
Penambo Ra.
BORNEO
Kalimantan
Peg. Schwaner
Peg. Muller
Palangkaraya
Banjarmasin
Martapura
Balikpapan
Samarinda
Tarakan
Celebes Sea
Makassar Strait
Equator
SULAWESI (CELEBES)
Ujung Pandang (Makassar)
INDONESIA
JAVA SEA
Jakarta
Tanjung Priok
Bogor
Bandung
Cirebon
Semarang
Surakarta
Yogyakarta
Surabaya
Malang
Madura
JAWA
Bali
Denpasar
Bali Sea
Flores Sea
Lombok
Mataram
Sumbawa
BRUNEI
Bandar Seri Begawan
SABAH
Kota Kinabalu

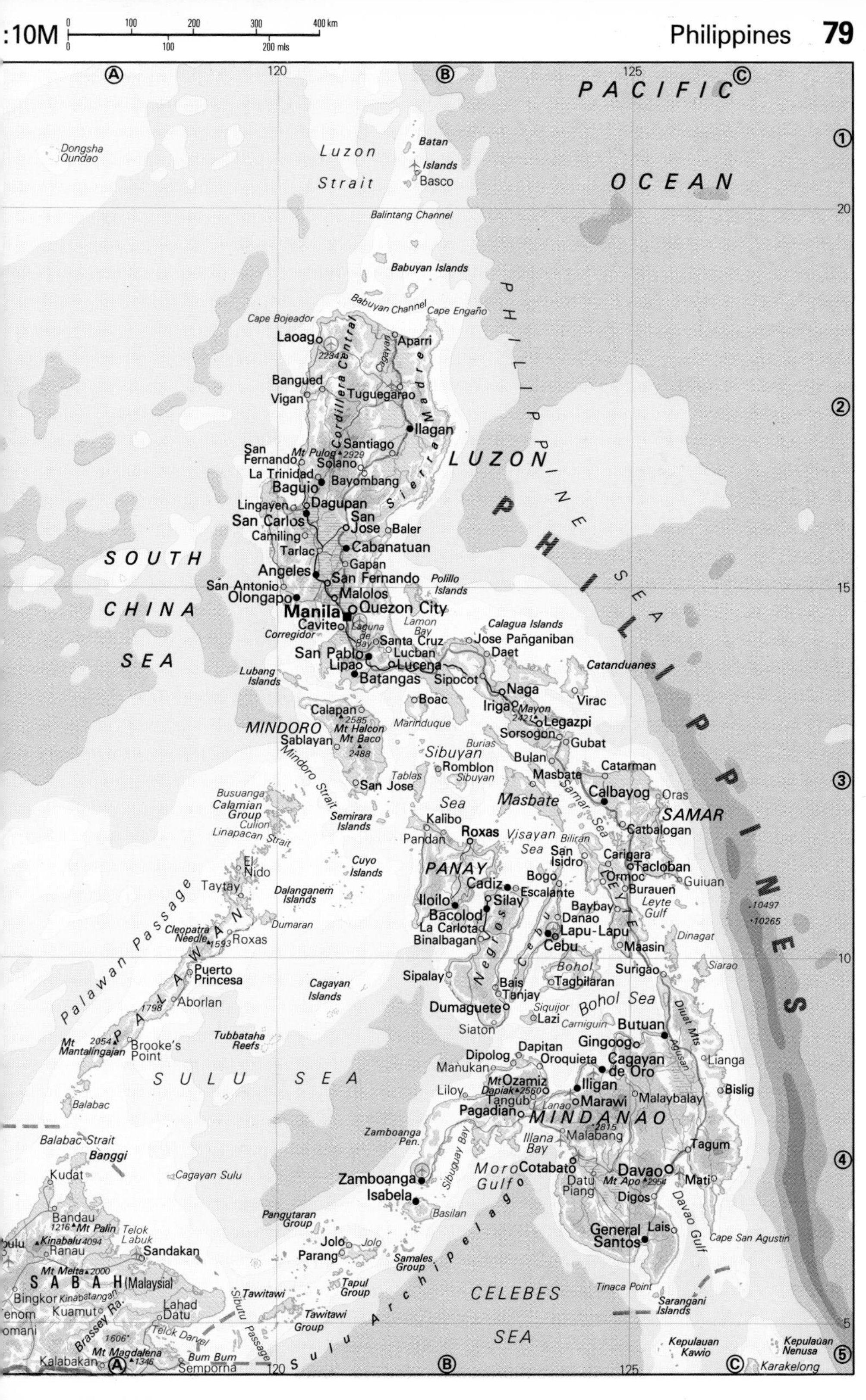

:10M

0 100 200 300 400 km
0 100 200 mils

A | 120 | B | 125 | C

PACIFIC

① *Dongsha*
Qundao

OCEAN

Luzon
Strait
Batan
Islands Basco
Balintang Channel
20

Babuyan Islands

Babuyan Channel *Cape Engaño*
② Cape Bojeador
Laoag ○ ● Aparri
2234
Bangued ● Tuguegarao
Vigan ● ● Ilagan
San ● Santiago
Fernando ○ ● Solano
La Trinidad ● *Mt Pulog 2929*
Baguio ● ● Bayombong
Lingayen ○ Dagupan ○
San Carlos ● San ○ Baler
Camiling ○ Jose
Tarlac ○ ● Cabanatuan
Angeles ● ● Gapan
San Antonio ● San Fernando *Polillo*
Olongapo ○ Malolos *Islands*
Manila ● Quezon City
Cavite ○ *Lamon*
Corregidor ○ *Laguna* *Bay*
San Pablo ● Santa Cruz ● *Calagua Islands*
Lipao ○ Lucban ● Jose Pañganiban
Batangas ● ● Daet
Boac ● Sipocot ○ *Catanduanes*
Calapan ○ ● Naga
2585 Iriga ○ ● Virac
Sablayan ○ *Mt Halcon* *Mayon*
Mt Baco *Marinduque* *2421* Legazpi
2488 Sorsogon ●
Busuanga San Jose ● *Sibuyan* Bulan ● Gubat
Calamian *Romblon* *Burias* Catarman
Group *Tablas* *Sibuyan* Masbate ● Oras
Culion *Sea* **Masbate** Calbayog ○
Linapacan Strait Kalibo ○ *Samar* **SAMAR**
El *Semirara* Roxas ● *Sea* Catbalogan ○
Nido ○ *Islands* Pandan ○ San Bilican
Cuyo *Visayan* Isidro ○ Carigara ○ Tacloban
Taytay ○ *Islands* **PANAY** *Sea* Bogo ● Ormoc ○ Burauen
Dalanganem Cadiz ○ Escalante ○ Baybay ● Guiuan
Islands Iloilo ○ Silay ○ Danao ● *Leyte* •10497
Dumaran Bacolod ● Lapu-Lapu ● *Gulf* •10265
Cleopatra La Carlota ○ Cebu ● *Dinagat*
Needle *1593* Binalbagan ○ Maasin ○
Roxas ● Sipalay ○ *Bohol* Surigao ●
Puerto Bais ○ Tagbilaran ○ *Siargao*
Princesa ● Tanjay ○ *Bohol Sea*
Aborlan ○ Dumaguete ○ *Siquijor* Butuan ●
Cagayan Siaton ○ Lazi ○ *Camiguin* Gingoog ●
Islands Dapitan ● Oroquieta ○ Cagayan *Diwot Mts*
Dipolog ○ *Mt Ozamiz 2560* de Oro ● Lianga
Manukan ○ *Dapiak* Iligan ● Bislig
Mt *2054* Tangub ○ *Lanao* Malaybalay ○
Mantalingajan Liloy ○ Pagadian ○ Marawi ●
Brooke's *2815*
Point **MINDANAO**
SULU SEA *Zamboanga* Malabang ○ Tagum ●
Pen. *Illana* Malabang
Balabac *Bay* Cotabato ● Davao ●
Zamboanga ● Datu *Mt Apo 2954* Mati ●
Balabac Strait Isabela ● Piang ● Digos ●
Banggi *Basilan* General Lais ● *Davao Gulf*
Kudat ● Jolo ○ *Jolo* Santos ● *Cape San Agustin*
1216 *Mt Palin* Parang ○ *Samales*
Bandau *Group*
Kinabalu *4094* *Tapul* CELEBES
SABAH (Malaysia) *Group* *Tinaca Point*
Sandakan ● *Tawitwi* *Sarangani*
Mt Melia 2000 *Group* SEA *Islands*
Kuamut ● *1606* *Mt Magdalena 1345* *Kepulauan*
Kalabakan ● *Bum Bum* 120 *Kawio*
Semporna A *Sulu* B 125 C Karakelong

Cordillera Central
Sierra Madre
PHILIPPINE SEA
SOUTH
CHINA
SEA
MINDORO
Mindoro Strait
Lubang
Islands
Palawan Passage
PALAWAN
NEGROS
CEBU
LEYTE

① ② ③ ④ ⑤
15
10

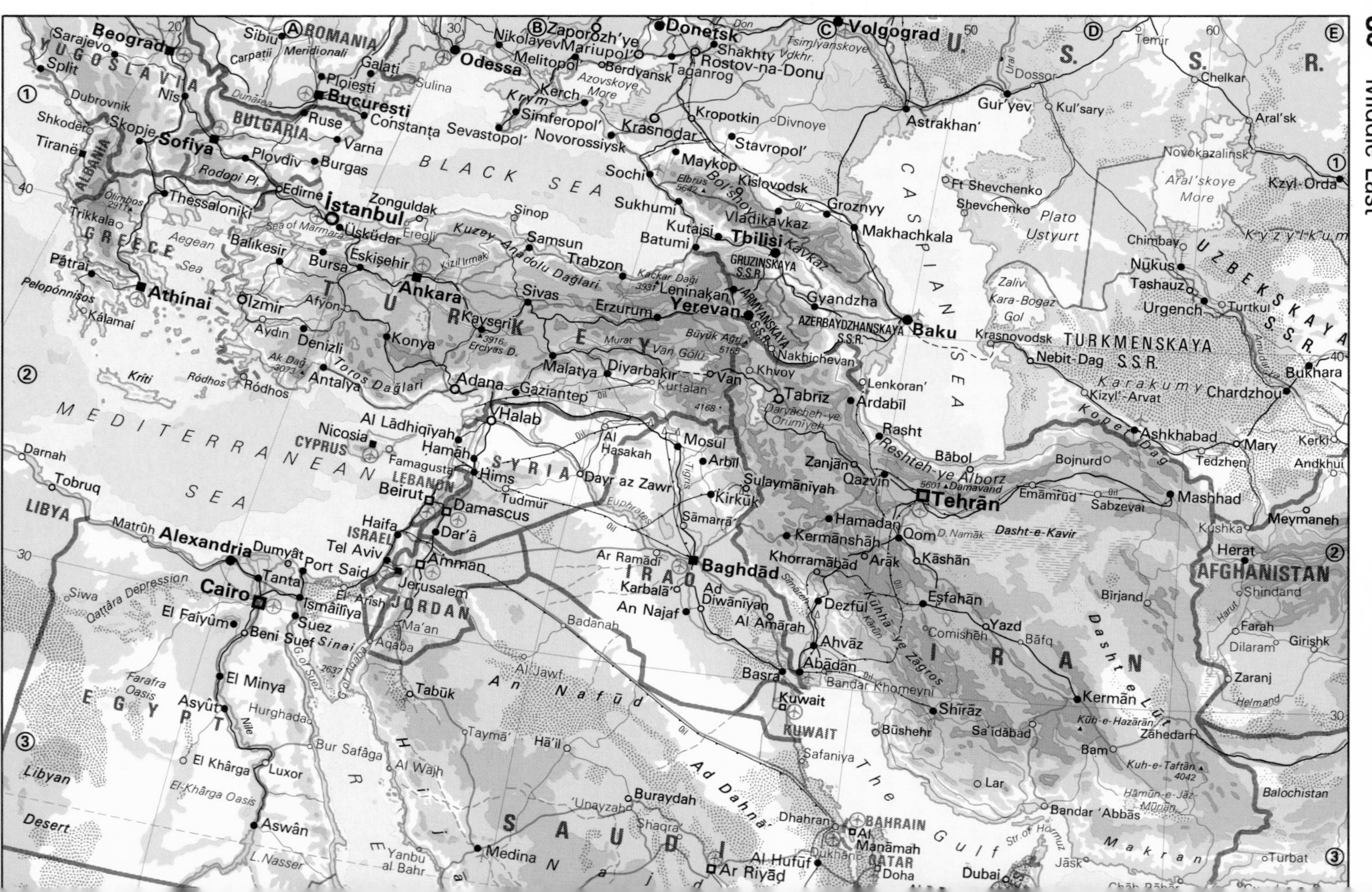
CASPIAN SEA
BLACK SEA
MEDITERRANEAN SEA
The Gulf
Aral'skoye More
U. S. S. R.
UZBEKSKAYA S.S.R.
TURKMENSKAYA S.S.R.
AZERBAYDZHANSKAYA S.S.R.
ARMYANSKAYA S.S.R.
GRUZINSKAYA S.S.R.
AFGHANISTAN
IRAN
IRAQ
SYRIA
TURKEY
JORDAN
ISRAEL
LEBANON
CYPRUS
KUWAIT
BAHRAIN
QATAR
SAUDI
EGYPT
LIBYA
GREECE
BULGARIA
ROMANIA
YUGOSLAVIA
ALBANIA
Tehrān
Baghdād
Baku
Tbilisi
Yerevan
Ankara
İstanbul
Damascus
Beirut
Amman
Jerusalem
Cairo
Alexandria
Athínai
Sofiya
Bucureşti
Beograd
Volgograd
Donetsk
Odessa
Kuwait
Ar Riyāḑ
Mashhad
Eşfahān
Shīrāz
Kermān
Herat
Basra
Mosul
Halab
Nicosia
Tabrīz
Ashkhabad
Bukhara
Dasht-e Lūt
Dasht-e-Kavir
Kūhhā-ye Zāgros
Reshteh-ye Alborz
Karakumy
Kyzylkum
Ad Dahnā
An Nafūd
Libyan Desert
Nile
Tigris
Euphrates
Volga

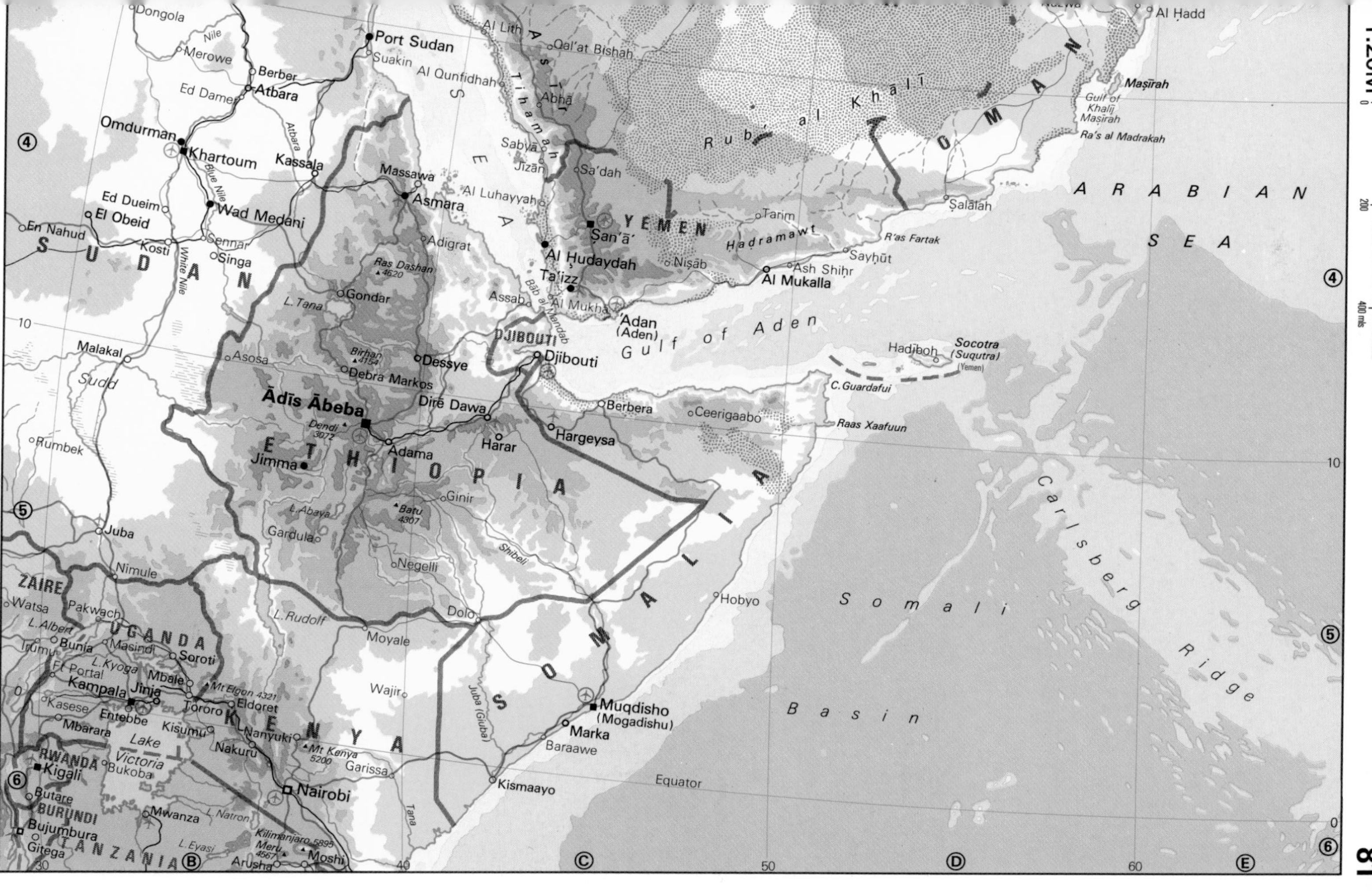

1:20M

200   400   600   800 km

200   400 mils

④   10   ⑤   0 ⑥

Y Al Hadd

Ⓔ   60

Gulf of
Khalij
Masirah   Masīrah

Ra's al Madrakah

A R A B I A N   S E A

N
A
M
O

Carlsberg   Ridge   Ⓓ

Salālah

al   Khali   Ras Fartak

Socotra
(Suqutra)
(Yemen)

Somali

B a s i n

Rub'   Sayḥūt

Hadiboh

C. Guardafui   50

Ḥaḍramawt   Raas Xaafuun

Ash Shihr
Al Mukalla   Hobyo

Nisāb   Ceerigaabo   Equator

Adan
(Aden)   Berbera   Muqdisho
(Mogadishu)   Ⓒ

YEMEN   Al Mukha   Marka

Şan'ā'   Hargeysa   Baraawe

Al Hudaydah   Djibouti

Ta'izz   DJIBOUTI   Harar   Kismaayo

Sa'dah   Bāb al Mandab   Dirē Dawa   Juba (Giuba)

Abhā   Assab   Ginir

Al Lith   Jīzān   Desyē   Adama   Batu   Dolo

A   Al Luhayyah   Negelli

S   Tihamah   Sablah   Ras Dashan   Bebra Markos   Moyale

I   Adigrat   4620

R   Massawa   Gondar   E T H I O P I A   Wajir   Tana

Port Sudan   Asmara   Brihan   Mt Kenya   Nairobi

Suakin Al Qunfidhah   L. Tana   Ādīs Ābeba   5200

Dongola   Kassala   Dendi   Jimma   L Abaya   Garissa

Merowe   Atbara   3072   Gardulo   K E N Y A   Moshi

Berber   Asosa   L. Rudolf   Mt Elgon   Kilimanjaro   Merk

Ed Damer   Atbara   Singa   Eldoret   4321   5200   4565

Khartoum   Wad Medani   Kitale   Nakuru   Arusha

Omdurman   Blue Nile   Soroti   Mt Eboi

Gedaref   Tororo   Kisumu   Mwanza

White Nile   Kaabong   Mbale   L Eyasi

Kosti   U G A N D A   L. Victoria

Ed Dueim   Juba   L.Kyoga   Kampala   Jinja   Bukoba   T A N Z A N I A   Ⓑ

El Obeid   Nimule   Masindi   Entebbe

S U D A N   Pakwach   L. Albert   Bunia   RWANDA

Ed Nahud   Malakal   Bor   ZAIRE   Kigali

Sobat   Rumbek   Watsa   Goma   BURUNDI   Girega

④   10   ⑤   0   ⑥

Bujumbura   Bukavu

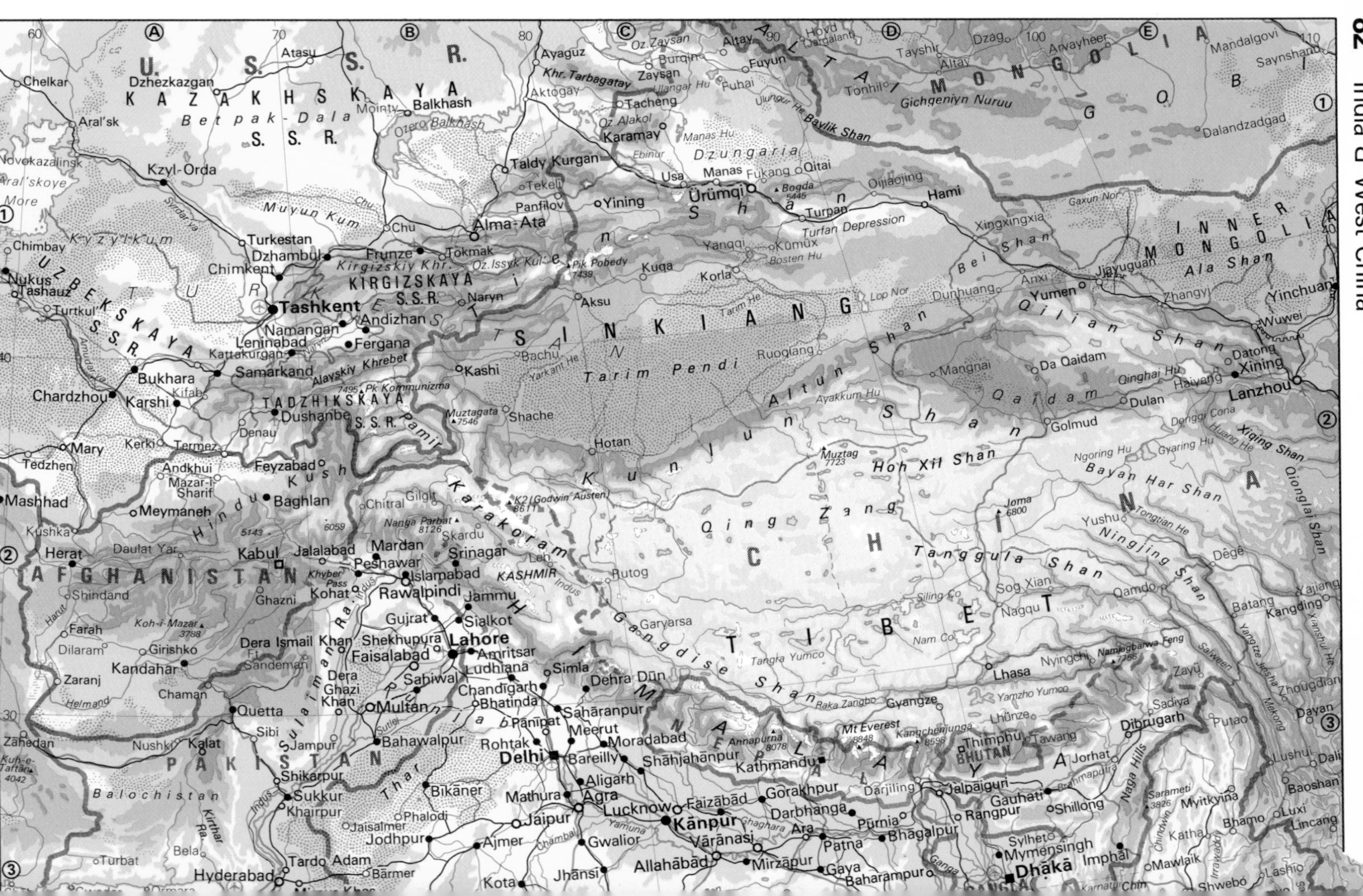
U. S. S. R.
KAZAKHSKAYA S. S. R.
UZBEKSKAYA S. S. R.
KIRGIZSKAYA S.S.R.
TADZHIKSKAYA S.S.R.
AFGHANISTAN
PAKISTAN
INDIA
NEPAL
BHUTAN
MONGOLIA
INNER MONGOLIA
CHINA
TIBET
SINKIANG
KASHMIR
Himalaya
Karakoram
Hindu Kush
Pamir
Kunlun Shan
Tian Shan
Altun Shan
Qilian Shan
Tanggula Shan
Gangdise Shan
Ningjing Shan
Bayan Har Shan
Hoh Xil Shan
Bei Shan
Ala Shan
Qionglai Shan
Xiqing Shan
Gobi
Tarim Pendi
Qaidam
Turfan Depression
Dzungaria
Thar
Balochistan
Kyzyl Kum
Muyun Kum
Betpak Dala
Ozero Balkhash
Aral'skoye More
Lop Nor
Qinghai Hu
Mt Everest 8848
K2 (Godwin Austen) 8611
Nanga Parbat 8126
Kangchenjunga 8598
Annapurna 8078
Muztagata 7546
Muztag 7723
Pik Pobedy 7439
Pik Kommunizma 7495
Bogda 5445
Indus
Ganga
Brahmaputra
Yangtze
Mekong
Salween
Huang He
Amudarya
Syrdarya
Tashkent
Alma-Ata
Frunze
Dushanbe
Samarkand
Bukhara
Kabul
Kandahar
Herat
Mashhad
Quetta
Peshawar
Rawalpindi
Islamabad
Lahore
Multan
Hyderabad
Srinagar
Delhi
Agra
Lucknow
Kanpur
Allahabad
Varanasi
Patna
Kathmandu
Thimphu
Dhaka
Lhasa
Kashi
Hotan
Aksu
Yining
Ürümqi
Turpan
Hami
Korla
Lanzhou
Xining
Golmud
Yumen
Jiayuguan
Wuwei
Yinchuan
Dunhuang
Karamay

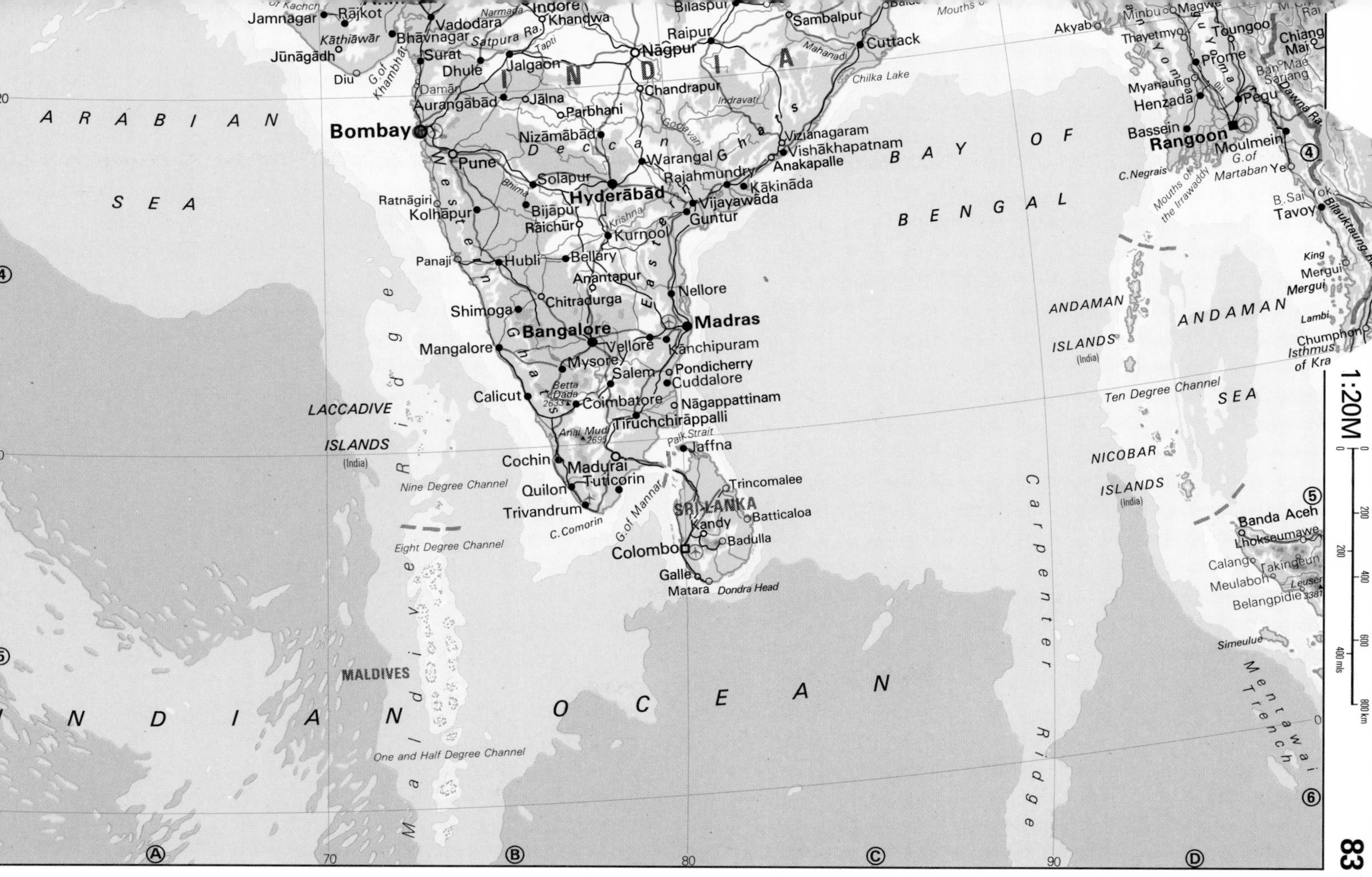
ARABIAN SEA
BAY OF BENGAL
ANDAMAN SEA
INDIAN OCEAN
Carpenter Ridge
Mentawai Trench
LACCADIVE ISLANDS (India)
MALDIVES
ANDAMAN ISLANDS (India)
NICOBAR ISLANDS (India)
SRI LANKA
Bombay
Madras
Bangalore
Hyderābād
Rangoon
Colombo
Ten Degree Channel
Nine Degree Channel
Eight Degree Channel
One and Half Degree Channel
Palk Strait
G. of Mannar
C. Comorin
Isthmus of Kra
Jamnagar
Rājkot
Jūnāgadh
Diu
Bhāvnagar
Surat
Vadodara
Dhule
Jalgaon
Aurangābād
Pune
Solapur
Nāgpur
Raipur
Cuttack
Sambalpur
Vishākhapatnam
Vizianagaram
Kākināda
Rajahmundry
Vijayawāda
Guntur
Warangal
Nellore
Kurnool
Bellary
Hubli
Panaji
Mangalore
Shimoga
Mysore
Calicut
Cochin
Quilon
Trivandrum
Madurai
Tuticorin
Tiruchchirāppalli
Coimbatore
Salem
Vellore
Kānchipuram
Pondicherry
Cuddalore
Nāgappattinam
Jaffna
Trincomalee
Batticaloa
Kandy
Badulla
Galle
Matara
Dondra Head
Akyab
Bassein
Henzada
Prome
Pegu
Moulmein
Tavoy
Mergui
Chumphon
Banda Aceh
Lhokseumawe
Simeulue

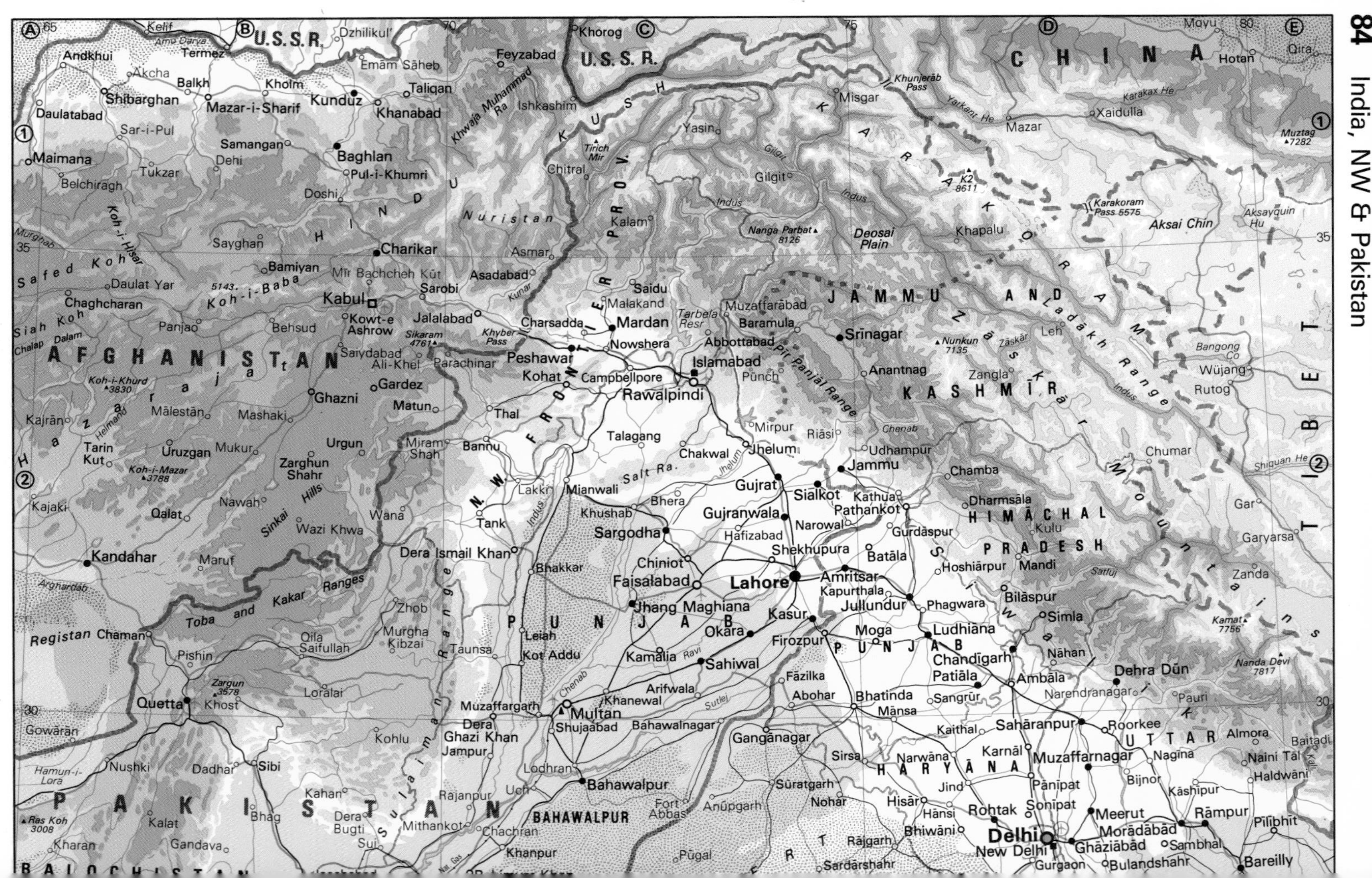
CHINA
U.S.S.R.
AFGHANISTAN
PAKISTAN
JAMMU AND KASHMĪR
HIMĀCHAL PRADESH
PUNJAB
HARYĀNA
UTTAR
N.W. FRONTIER PROV.
BAHAWALPUR
BALOCHISTAN
KARAKORAM
HINDU KUSH
TIBET
Ladākh Range
Pir Panjal Range
Salt Ra.
Toba and Kakar Ranges
Sulaiman Range
Koh-i-Baba
Nuristan
Aksai Chin
Deosai Plain
Registan
Kabul
Islamabad
Rawalpindi
Peshawar
Lahore
Delhi
New Delhi
Srīnagar
Jammu
Amritsar
Faisalabad
Multan
Quetta
Kandahar
Ghazni
Jalalabad
Mazar-i-Sharif
Kunduz
Baghlan
Charikar
Gilgit
Leh
Simla
Chandīgarh
Ludhiana
Jullundur
Sialkot
Gujranwala
Gujrat
Jhelum
Sargodha
Sahiwal
Okara
Bahawalpur
Dera Ismail Khan
Dera Ghazi Khan
Meerut
Morādābād
Bareilly
Rāmpur
Dehra Dūn
Ambāla
Patiāla
Rohtak
Hisār
Bhatinda
Firozpur
Kasur
Muzaffarābād
Abbottabad
Mardan
Kohat
Bannu
Sibi
Hotan
K2 8611
Nanga Parbat 8126
Nanda Devi 7817
Kamat 7756
Tirich Mir
Khyber Pass
Karakoram Pass 5575
Indus
Chenab
Jhelum
Ravi
Sutlej

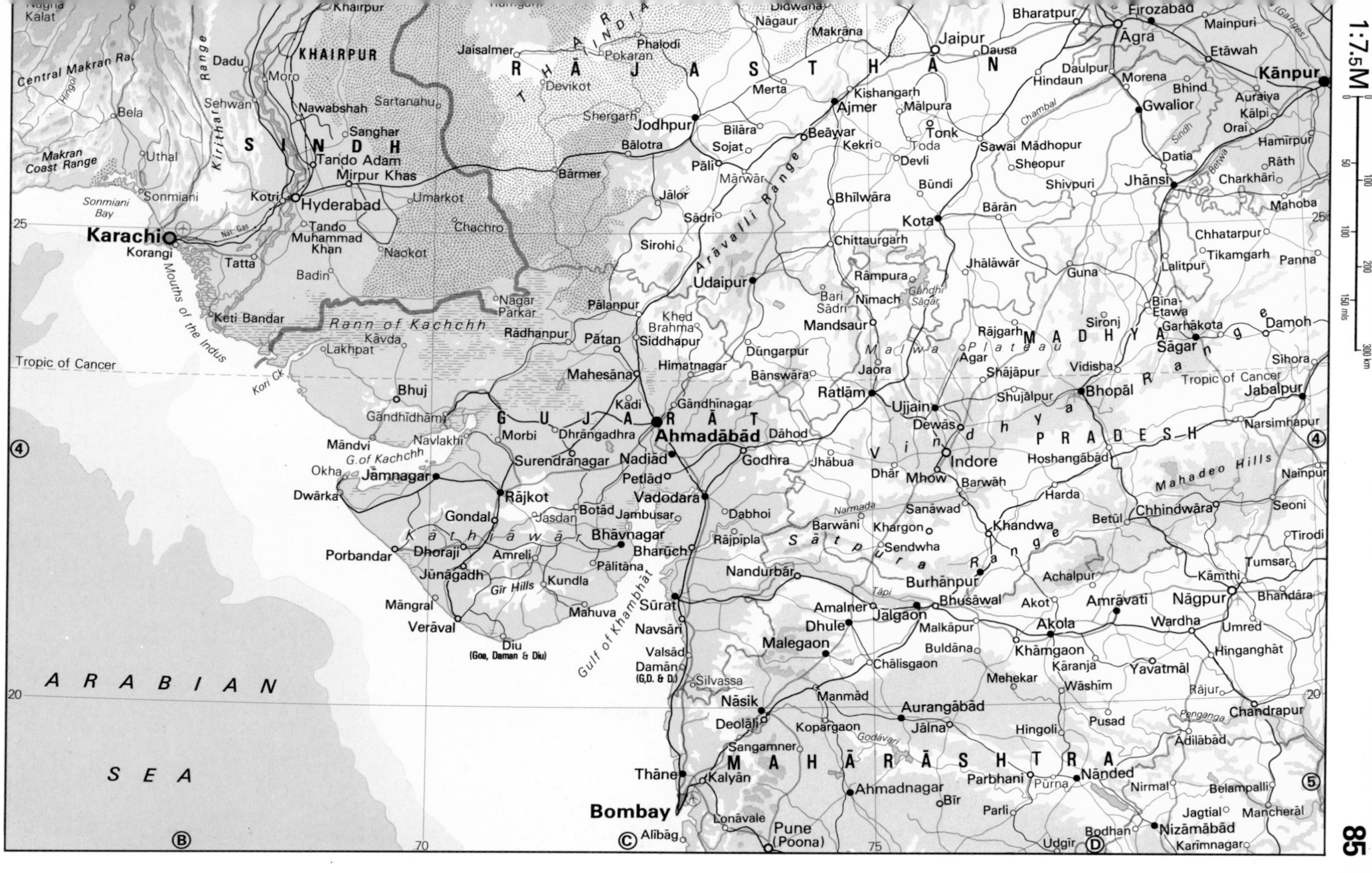
Kalat
Central Makran Ra.
Hingol
Bela
Makran Coast Range
Uthal
Sonmiani
Sonmiani Bay
Kirthar Range
Dadu
Moro
Sehwan
KHAIRPUR
Khairpur
Nawabshah
Sartanahu
Sanghar
SINDH
Tando Adam
Mirpur Khas
Kotri
Hyderabad
Umarkot
Tando Muhammad Khan
Chachro
Naokot
Karachi
Korangi
Tatta
Badin
Mouths of the Indus
Keti Bandar
Nagar Parkar
Rann of Kachchh
Kāvda
Lakhpat
Tropic of Cancer
Kori Ck
Bhuj
Gāndhīdhām
Māndvi
Navlakhi
G. of Kachchh
Okha
Jāmnagar
Dwārka
Rājkot
Morbi
Gondal
Jasdan
Kāthiāwār
Porbandar
Dhorāji
Amreli
Jūnāgadh
Gīr Hills
Kundla
Māngral
Verāval
Mahuva
Diu (Goa, Daman & Diu)
ARABIAN SEA
Jaisalmer
Phalodi
Pokaran
Devikot
THAR
INDIA
RĀJASTHĀN
Shergarh
Jodhpur
Bālotra
Bārmer
Nāgaur
Didwāna
Makrāna
Merta
Bilāra
Sojat
Pāli
Mārwār
Jālor
Sādri
Sirohi
Arāvalli Range
Udaipur
Pālanpur
Khed Brahma
Rādhanpur
Pātan
Siddhapur
Himatnagar
Mahesāna
Kādi
Gāndhīnagar
GUJARĀT
Dhrāngadhra
Ahmadābād
Surendranagar
Nadiād
Petlād
Vadodara
Botād
Jambusar
Bhāvnagar
Bharūch
Pālitāna
Gulf of Khambhāt
Sūrat
Navsāri
Valsād
Damān (G.D. & D.)
Silvassa
Dāhod
Godhra
Dabhoi
Rājpipla
Nandurbār
Jaipur
Dausa
Kishangarh
Ajmer
Mālpura
Beāwar
Tonk
Kekri
Toda
Devli
Bhīlwāra
Būndi
Chittaurgarh
Kota
Rāmpura
Gāndhi Sāgar
Bari Sādri
Nimach
Mandsaur
Dūngarpur
Bānswāra
Mālwa Plateau
Jaora
Ratlām
Ujjain
Dewās
Jhābua
Dhār
Mhow
Indore
Vindhya Range
Barwāh
Narmada
Sanāwad
Barwāni
Khargon
Sendhwa
Sātpura Range
Khandwa
Burhānpur
Tāpi
Bhusāwal
Amalner
Jalgaon
Dhule
Malkāpur
Malegaon
Buldāna
Chālisgaon
Nāsik
Manmād
Deolāli
Kopargaon
Godāvari
Sangamner
Aurangābād
Jālna
MAHĀRĀSHTRA
Thāne
Kalyān
Bombay
Lonāvale
Pune (Poona)
Alībāg
Ahmadnagar
Bīr
Parbhani
Pūrna
Parli
Udgīr
Bharatpur
Hindaun
Daulpur
Firozabad
Āgra
Morena
Gwalior
Bhind
Mainpuri
Etāwah
Kānpur
Auraiya
Kālpi
Orai
Hamīrpur
Chambal
Sindh
Betwa
Sawai Mādhopur
Sheopur
Shivpuri
Datia
Jhānsi
Rāth
Charkhāri
Mahoba
Bārān
Jhālāwār
Guna
Chhatarpur
Tikamgarh
Panna
Lalitpur
Bina-Etawa
Sironj
Garhākota
Damoh
Rājgarh
MADHYA PRADESH
Sāgar Range
Agar
Vidisha
Sihora
Shājāpur
Shujālpur
Bhopāl
Tropic of Cancer
Jabalpur
Narsimhapur
Hoshangābād
Mahadeo Hills
Nainpur
Harda
Betūl
Chhindwāra
Seoni
Tirodi
Tumsar
Achalpur
Kāmthi
Akot
Amrāvati
Nāgpur
Bhandāra
Akola
Wardha
Umred
Khāmgaon
Kāranja
Yavatmāl
Hinganghāt
Mehekar
Wāshīm
Rājur
Hingoli
Pusad
Penganga
Chandrapur
Ādilābād
Nānded
Nirmal
Belampalli
Jagtial
Mancherāl
Bodhan
Nizāmābād
Karīmnagar
25
20
70
75
4
5
B
C
D

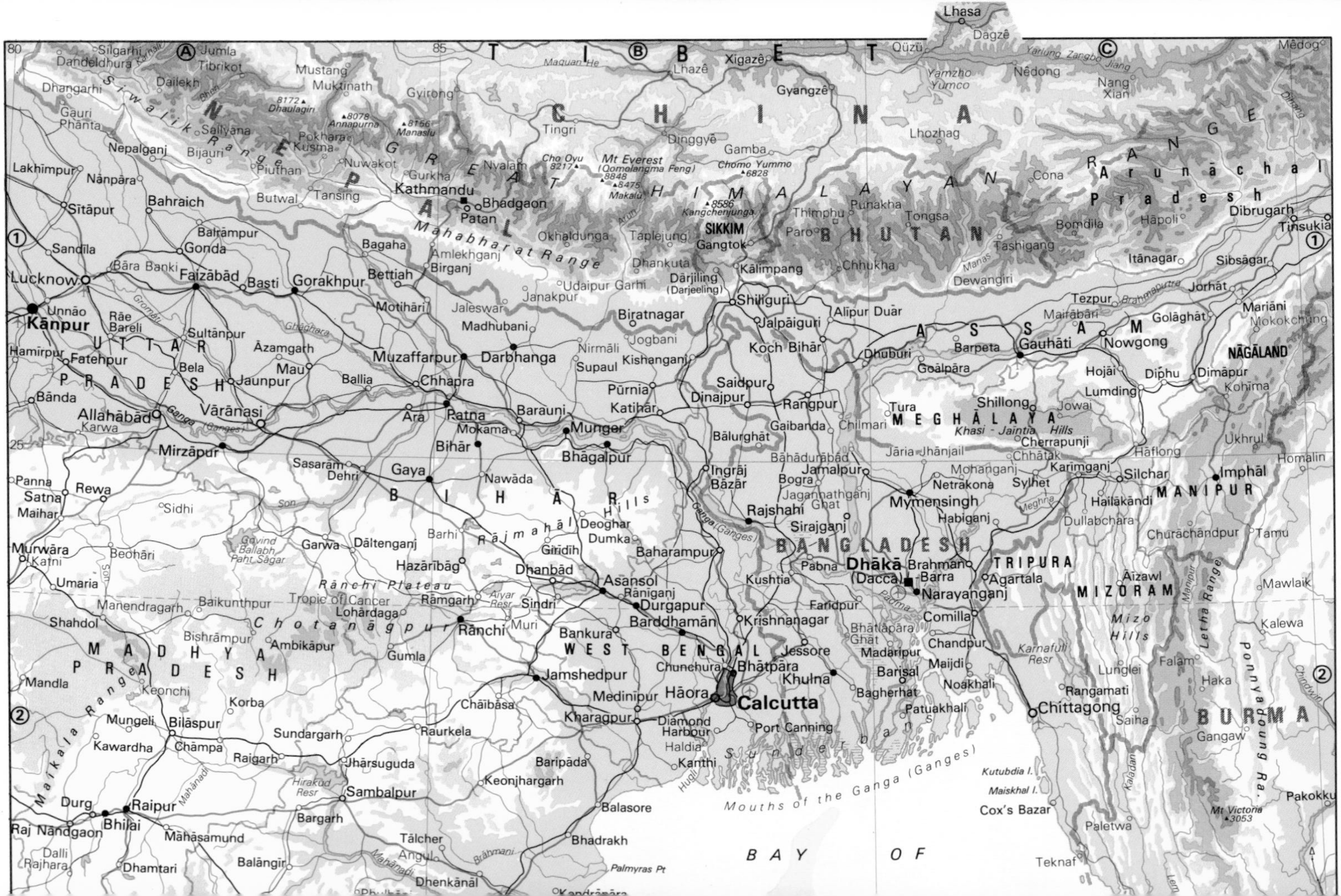
T I B E T
C H I N A
N E P A L
G R E A T H I M A L A Y A N R A N G E
B H U T A N
SIKKIM
A r u n ā c h a l P r a d e s h
A S S A M
NĀGĀLAND
MANIPUR
M E G H Ā L A Y A
TRIPURA
MIZORAM
B A N G L A D E S H
WEST BENGAL
B I H Ā R
U T T A R P R A D E S H
M A D H Y A P R A D E S H
B U R M A
B A Y O F
Lhasa
Dagzê
Qüxü
Xigazê
Gyangzê
Lhazê
Tingri
Dinggyê
Gamba
Lhozhag
Nêdong
Nang Xian
Mêdog
Yamzho Yumco
Yarlung Zangbo Jiang
Maquan He
Mt Everest (Qomolangma Feng) 8848
Makalu 8475
Cho Oyu 8217
Kangchenjunga 8586
Chomo Yummo 6828
Dhaulagiri 8172
Annapurna 8078
Manaslu 8156
Siwalik Range
Mahabharat Range
Kathmandu
Bhadgaon
Patan
Pokhara
Kusma
Mustang
Muktinath
Jumla
Tibrikot
Dailekh
Silgarhi
Dandeldhura
Dhangarhi
Nepalganj
Bijauri
Sallyana
Piuthan
Nuwakot
Gurkha
Nyalam
Gyirong
Butwal
Tansing
Okhaldunga
Taplejung
Dhankuta
Udaipur Garhi
Biratnagar
Janakpur
Birganj
Amlekhganj
Gangtok
Dārjiling (Darjeeling)
Kālimpang
Thimphu
Paro
Punakha
Tongsa
Chhukha
Tashigang
Dewangiri
Bomdila
Hāpoli
Itānagar
Cona
Dibrugarh
Tinsukia
Sibsāgar
Jorhāt
Mariāni
Mokokchung
Golāghāt
Tezpur
Brahmaputra
Mairābāri
Gauhāti
Nowgong
Barpeta
Goālpāra
Dhuburi
Alīpur Duār
Shilīguri
Jalpāiguri
Koch Bihār
Hojāi
Diphu
Dimāpur
Kohīma
Lumding
Shillong
Jowai
Khasi - Jaintia Hills
Cherrapunji
Tura
Chilmari
Hāflong
Ukhrul
Imphāl
Homalin
Silchar
Karimganj
Hailākāndi
Sylhet
Chhātak
Jāria Jhānjail
Mohanganj
Netrakona
Mymensingh
Jamalpur
Bogra
Jagannathganj Ghat
Sirajganj
Rajshahi
Rangpur
Saidpur
Dinajpur
Gaibanda
Bālurghāt
Bāhādurābād
Ingrāj Bāzār
Pabna
Dhākā (Dacca)
Brahman Barra
Narayanganj
Habiganj
Agartala
Comilla
Chandpur
Faridpur
Kushtia
Krishnanagar
Jessore
Bhātlāpāra Ghat
Madaripur
Barisal
Maijdi
Noakhali
Khulna
Bagherhat
Patuakhali
Bhātpāra
Calcutta
Hāora
Chunchura
Port Canning
Diamond Harbour
Haldia
Kanthi
Sunderbans
Mouths of the Ganga (Ganges)
Hugli
Padma
Meghna
Karnafuli Resr
Chittagong
Rangamati
Cox's Bazar
Kutubdia I.
Maiskhal I.
Teknaf
Paletwa
Lunglei
Saiha
Āīzawl
Mizo Hills
Dullabchara
Churāchāndpur
Tamu
Mawlaik
Kalewa
Falam
Haka
Gangaw
Letha Range
Ponnyadoung Ra.
Mt Victoria 3053
Pakokku
Chindwin
Kaladan
Manipur
Lucknow
Kānpur
Unnāo
Lakhīmpur
Nānpāra
Sītāpur
Bahraich
Sandīla
Balrāmpur
Gonda
Bāra Banki
Faizābād
Basti
Gorakhpur
Rāe Bareli
Sultānpur
Āzamgarh
Mau
Jaunpur
Bela
Fatehpur
Hamīrpur
Bānda
Allahābād
Karwa
Vārānasi
Mirzāpur
Ganga (Ganges)
Gomati
Ghāghara
Bagaha
Bettiah
Motihāri
Jaleswar
Madhubani
Darbhanga
Muzaffarpur
Chhapra
Ballia
Ara
Patna
Mokama
Barauni
Munger
Bhāgalpur
Bihār
Nirmāli
Jogbani
Supaul
Kishanganj
Pūrnia
Katihār
Gaya
Sasarām
Dehri
Nawāda
Rājmahāl Hills
Deoghar
Dumka
Giridih
Barhi
Hazāribāg
Dāltenganj
Garwa
Dhanbād
Asansol
Rāniganj
Durgapur
Barddhamān
Baharampur
Bankura
Sindri
Muri
Rāmgarh
Aiyar Resr
Rānchi
Rānchi Plateau
Lohārdaga
Chotanāgpur
Tropic of Cancer
Gumla
Jamshedpur
Chāībāsa
Medinipur
Kharagpur
Raurkela
Sundargarh
Jhārsuguda
Sambalpur
Hirakud Resr
Baripāda
Keonjhargarh
Balasore
Bhadrakh
Tālcher
Angul
Dhenkānāl
Brāhmani
Mahānadi
Palmyras Pt
Bargarh
Balāngir
Raigarh
Champa
Korba
Bilāspur
Mungeli
Kawardha
Raipur
Bhilai
Durg
Raj Nāndgaon
Dalli Rajhara
Dhamtari
Mahāsamund
Keonchi
Mandla
Maikala Range
Bishrāmpur
Ambikāpur
Manendragarh
Baikunthpur
Shahdol
Umaria
Katni
Murwāra
Beohāri
Maihar
Satna
Panna
Rewa
Sidhi
Son
Govind Ballabh Pant Sāgar

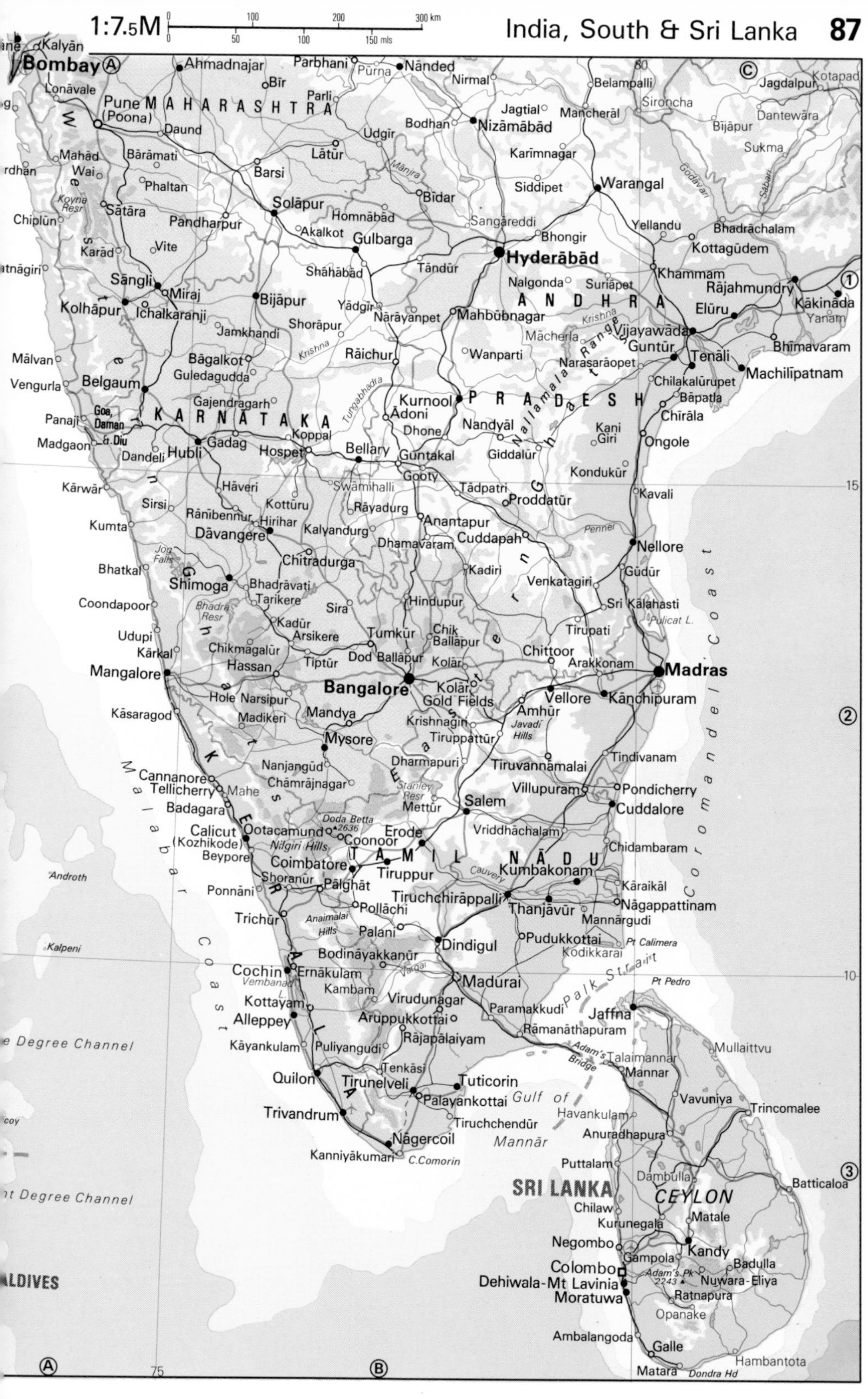

Kalyān
Bombay
A
C
80
Ahmadnajar
Parbhani
Pūrna
Nānded
Nirmal
Belampalli
Jagdalpur
Kotapad
Lonāvale
Bīr
Parli
Sironcha
Pune
(Poona)
MAHARASHTRA
Jagtial
Mancherāl
Dantewāra
Daund
Udgīr
Bodhan
Nizāmābād
Bījāpur
Sukma
Mahād
Bārāmati
Lātūr
Karīmnagar
Wai
Barsi
Mānjra
Godāvari
Sabari
Phaltan
Siddipet
Warangal
Koyna Resr
Sātāra
Solāpur
Bīdar
Chiplūn
Pandharpur
Homnābād
Sangāreddi
Yellandu
Bhadrāchalam
Akalkot
Gulbarga
Bhongir
Karād
Vite
Kottagūdem
Hyderābād
Tāndūr
Shāhābād
Khammam
Sāngli
Miraj
Nalgonda
Suriāpet
Rājahmundry
1
Kolhāpur
Ichalkaranji
Bījāpur
Yādgīr
ANDHRA
Kākināda
Nārāyanpet
Mahbūbnagar
Elūru
Yanam
Jamkhandi
Shorāpur
Krishna
Māchcherla
Vijayawāda
Guntūr
Bhīmavaram
Mālvan
Bāgalkot
Rāichur
Wanparti
Narasarāopet
Tenāli
Guledagudda
Machilīpatnam
Vengurla
Belgaum
Tungabhadra
Chilakalūrupet
Gajendragarh
Kurnool
PRADESH
Bāpatla
Panaji
Goa, Daman & Diu
KARNATAKA
Ādoni
Nallamala Range
Chīrāla
Dhone
Nandyāl
Madgaon
Gadag
Koppal
Kani Giri
Ongole
Dandeli
Hubli
Hospet
Bellary
Guntakal
Giddalūr
Kondukūr
Kārwār
Gooty
15
Hāveri
Swāmihalli
Tādpatri
Kavali
Sirsi
Kottūru
Proddatūr
Rānibennur
Hirihar
Rāyadurg
Anantapur
Kumta
Dāvangere
Kalyandurg
Penner
Dhamavaram
Cuddapah
Nellore
Jog Falls
Chitradurga
Bhatkal
Kadiri
Gūdūr
Shimoga
Bhadrāvati
Venkatagiri
Tarikere
Coondapoor
Bhadra Resr
Sira
Hindupur
Sri Kālahasti
Kadūr
Pulicat L.
Udupi
Arsikere
Tumkūr
Chik Ballāpur
Tirupati
Kārkal
Chikmagalūr
Chittoor
Dod Ballāpur
Mangalore
Tiptūr
Hassan
Kolār
Arakkonam
Madras
Bangalore
Kolār Gold Fields
Vellore
Kānchipuram
Hole Narsipur
Kāsaragod
Mandya
Āmhūr
Madikeri
2
Krishnagiri
Javadi Hills
Mysore
Tiruppattūr
Tindivanam
Dharmapuri
Tiruvannāmalai
Nanjangūd
Cannanore
Chāmrājnagar
Pondicherry
Tellicherry
Mahe
Stanley Resr
Villupuram
Mettūr
Salem
Badagara
Cuddalore
Doda Betta 2636
Calicut
(Kozhikode)
Ootacamund
Coonoor
Erode
Vriddhāchalam
Nilgiri Hills
TAMIL NADU
Chidambaram
Beypore
Coimbatore
Tiruppur
Cauvery
Kumbakonam
Androth
Shoranūr
Pālghāt
Kāraikāl
Ponnāni
Tiruchchirāppalli
Thanjāvūr
Nāgappattinam
Pollāchi
Mannārgudi
Trichūr
Anaimalai Hills
Palani
Pudukkottai
Dindigul
Pt Calimera
Kalpeni
Kodikkarai
Bodināyakkanūr
Palk Strait
Cochin
Ernākulam
Vaigai
10
Vembanad L.
Madurai
Pt Pedro
Kambam
Kottayam
Virudunagar
Paramakkudi
Jaffna
Alleppey
Aruppukkottai
Rāmanāthapuram
Rājapālaiyam
Degree Channel
Kāyankulam
Puliyangudi
Adam's Bridge
Talaimannar
Mullaittvu
Tenkāsi
Mannar
Quilon
Tirunelveli
Tuticorin
Palayankottai
Gulf of Mannār
Vavuniya
Trincomalee
Trivandrum
Havankulam
Tiruchchendūr
Anuradhapura
Nāgercoil
Kanniyākumari
C.Comorin
Puttalam
3
Dambulla
Batticaloa
SRI LANKA
CEYLON
Degree Channel
Chilaw
Kurunegala
Matale
Negombo
Kandy
Gampola
Colombo
Badulla
Adam's Pk 2243
Dehiwala-Mt Lavinia
Nuwara-Eliya
Moratuwa
Ratnapura
LDIVES
Opanake
Ambalangoda
Galle
Hambantota
A
75
B
Matara
Dondra Hd
Malabar Coast
Western Ghats
Coromandel Coast
Eastern Ghats
KERALA

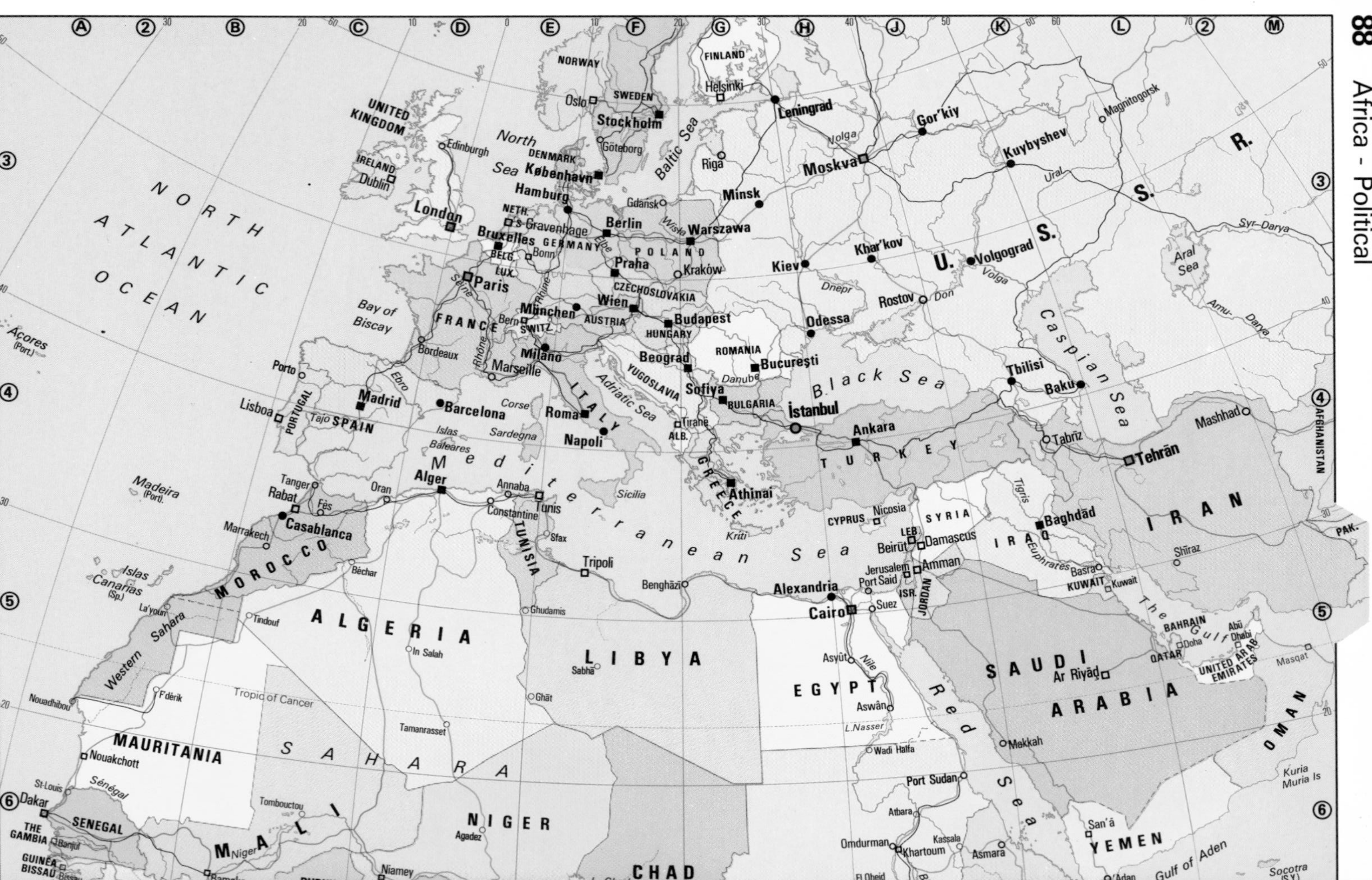

88

AFGHANISTAN

R.

S.

U. S.

Syr-Darya

Amu-Darya

Aral Sea

Caspian Sea

Magnitogorsk

Kuybyshev

Gor'kiy

Leningrad

Volgograd

Moskva

Kharkov

Rostov

Kiev

Odessa

Minsk

Warszawa

Kraków

FINLAND

Helsinki

Riga

Baltic Sea

SWEDEN

Stockholm

Göteborg

NORWAY

Oslo

København

DENMARK

Hamburg

'S-Gravenhage

NETH.

Bruxelles

BEL.

Lux.

Berlin

GERMANY

Praha

CZECHOSLOVAKIA

Wien

AUSTRIA

Budapest

HUNGARY

Beograd

YUGOSLAVIA

ROMANIA

Bucureşti

BULGARIA

Sofiya

ALB.

GREECE

Athinai

Istanbul

Ankara

TURKEY

Mashhad

Tehrän

Baku

Tbilisi

Tabriz

Shiraz

IRAN

OMAN

Masqat

Kuria Muria Is.

Socotra (S.Y.)

Gulf of Aden

Abu Dhabi

UNITED EMIRATES

QATAR

Doha

BAHRAIN

Al Dhahr

KUWAIT

Ar Riyad

SAUDI ARABIA

Makkah

Asmara

Kassala

Khartoum

Omdurman

El Obeid

Atbara

Port Sudan

Wadi Halfa

San'ä

YEMEN

Red Sea

The Gulf

Baghdad

IRAQ

Basra

Euphrates

Tigris

SYRIA

Damascus

Beirut

LEB.

Amman

JORDAN

Nicosia

CYPRUS

Jerusalem

ISR.

Port Said

Suez

Alexandria

Cairo

Asyüt

Nile

Aswan

L. Nasser

EGYPT

LIBYA

Benghazi

Tripoli

Sabha

Ghat

Ghadames

Sfax

Tunis

TUNISIA

Annaba

Constantine

Black Sea

Dnepr

Danube

Mediterranean Sea

Sicilia

Kriti

Adriatic Sea

ITALY

Roma

Napoli

Milano

Marseille

FRANCE

Corse

Sardegna

Bordeaux

Paris

Seine

Rhône

München

SWITZ.

Bern

Zürich

Rhine

Garonne

Loire

London

UNITED KINGDOM

IRELAND

Dublin

Edinburgh

NORTH ATLANTIC OCEAN

Bay of Biscay

Ebro

Madrid

Barcelona

SPAIN

Islas Baleares

PORTUGAL

Lisboa

Porto

Madeira (Port.)

Islas Canarias (Sp.)

Açores (Port.)

Oran

Alger

ALGERIA

MOROCCO

Casablanca

Rabat

Fès

Tanger

Marrakech

Bechar

In Salah

Tindouf

Reggan

Tamanrasset

Agadez

NIGER

CHAD

L. Chad

SAHARA

Tropic of Cancer

MALI

Niger

Timbouktou

Niamey

MAURITANIA

Nouakchott

Western Sahara

La Ayoun

Nouadhibou

St-Louis

SENEGAL

Dakar

THE GAMBIA

GUINEA-BISSAU

Bissau

Sénégal

Banjul

BURKINA

Bamako

North Sea

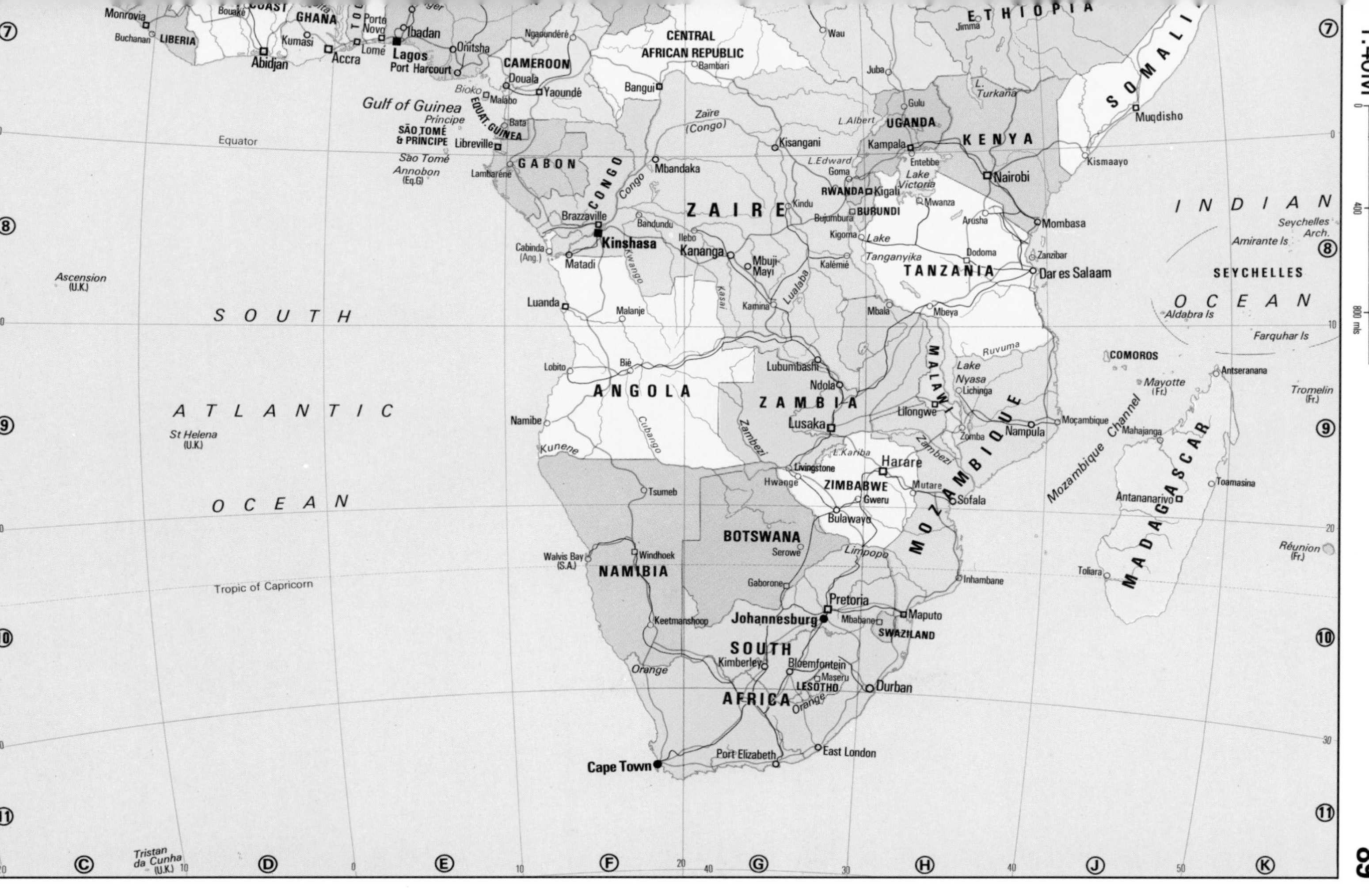

1:40M

0 400 800 1200 1600 km
0 400 800 mils

U.S.S.R.

Karakum

Caspian Sea

Baku

Tehrān

Mashhad

Neyshābūr

Ashkhabad

Bezmein

Tedzhen

Dushak

Sarākhs

Farīmān

Torbat-e Jām

Ghurīān

Avaz

Dasht-e Naomid

Daryāchen-ye Sīstān

Zābol

Joveyn

Lash-e Joveyn

Chestme 2-vy

Bakhardok

Kaakhka

Kūh-e-Hazār Masjed

Shirvān

Qūchān

Bojnūrd

Hokmābād

Sabzevār

Sharīfābād

Torbat-e Heydarīyeh

Kāshmar

Jūymand

Qāyen

Ferdow

Birjand

Khosf

Sarbīsheh

Nehbandān

Shāh Kūh 2729

Kizyl Arvat

Bakhardok

Bakhardok

Moraveh Tappeh

Dasht

Jajarm

Kāhak

Mayamey

Bjärmand

Turān

Nāy Band

Khvor

Tabas

Deyhuk

Bejestān

Bāfq

Khrebet Kopet Dag

Kazandzhik

Nebit-Dag

Kum-Dag

573

Sharlauk

Mādau

Bugdayli

Kizyl-Atrek

Gonbad-e Kāvūs

Gorgān

Dāmghan

Emāmrūd

Torūd

Kūh Dūreh

Kevir-i-Namak

Posht-e Badam

Dasht-e Kavir

Dasht-e Lut

Rāvar

L U T

Gasan Kuli

Bandar-e Torkoman

Behshahr

Ghaem Shahr

Sārī

Bābol

Āmol

Now Shahr

Qāleh-ye Darvand 5607

Alborz Mts

Reshteh (Elburz) ye

Damāvand

Semnān

Āhūvān

Lāsjerd

Garmsar

Jandaq

Anārak

Na'īn

'Aqdā

Yazd

Sīāh Kūh 4074

Mehrīz

Khārānaq

Kharānaq

Nadūshan

Ardekān

Ābādeh

Yazd-e Khvāst

Semīrom

Turkmenskiy Zaliv

Krasnovodsk

Krasnovodskiy Zal.

Cheleken

O.Ogurchinskiy

Rāmsar

Lāhījān

Bandar Anzalī

Rasht

Herowābād

Gorgān

Daryācheh-ye Namak

Varāmīn

Qom

Kāshān

Delījān

Maḥallāt

Golpāyegān

Khvānsār

Najafābād

Eṣfahān

Shahr Kord

Borūjen

Lordegān

Zagros

Kūh-e Karkas

Ardestān

Kūhpāyeh

Murchen Khvort

Qomisheh (Shahrezā)

Chengordan

Dārān

Aligūdarz

Khorramābād

Borūjerd

Mountains

Kuhha ye Zagros

Zard Kuh 4548

Masjed Soleymān

Dezfūl

Ahvāz

Kabir Kuh

Rāmhormoz

Karkheh

Dehlorān

Al 'Amārah

Al Kūt

Tigris (Dijlah)

Al Hayy (Al Gharbi)

Ash Shaṭrah

Qal'at Sāliḥ

'Alī al Gharbī

Ar Rifā'ī

 Aṣ Saḥrā

An Nāṣirīyah

Al Qurnah

Qom

Sāveh

Rāherd

Nāhāvand

Malāyer

Arāk

Kangāvar

Hamadān

Kermānshāh

Bīsotūn

Qorveh

Sanandaj

Alīābād

Dezh Shāhpūr

Dzh.

Saqqez

Mahābād

Baneh

Sardasht

Sulaymānīyah

Ḥalabja

Ravānsar

Qaṣr-e Shīrīn

Shāhābād

Īlām

Mehrān

Smaireh

Lur-i

Dīwala

Az Zubair

Shāhīn Dezh

Kīrk Bulag D. 3707

Bījār

Bijar

Takestān

Zanjān

Mīāneh

Qazvīn

Karaj

Abhar

Razan

Row'ān

Qeydār

Zarand

Takestān

Rūdbār

Zanjān

Kūh-e

Oshnavīyeh

Tabrīz

Marand

Ahar

Sarāb

Mīāndowāb

Marāgheh

Ardabīl

Astara

Hashtpar

Lenkoran'

Masally

Sal'yany

Kazi Magomed

Agdam

Goris

Kapydzhik 3906

Nakhichevan'

Julfa

Kūh-e Sahand 3770

Hashtrūd

Sar Dasht

Naqadeh

Daryācheh-ye Urumīyeh

Māku

Kara Dag

Qareh

Dzhebrail

Ōz. Sevan

Kamo

Kirpili

Nebit-Dag

Kazandzhik

Hashtrpar

Alyat

Sal'yany

Āstārā

Lārī

Shīmi 3621

Gīdzhān

Nakhichevan'

The Gulf
Gulf of Oman
Strait of Hormuz
Trucial Coast
KUWAIT
Kuwait
BAHRAIN
Manāmah
QATAR
Doha
U. A. E.
Abū Dhabi
Dubai
Sharjah
Ajman
Umm al Qaiwain
Ras al Khaimah
Fujairah
OMAN
Masqaṭ (Muscat)
Maṭraḥ
Ṣūr
MUSCAT
SAUDI ARABIA
Ar Riyāḍ (Riyadh)
Ad Dammam
Al Hufūf
Al Mubarraz
Dhahran
Al Qaṭīf
Al Jubayl
Ra's Tannūrah
Al Hasa
Ad Dahnā'
Al Jāfūrah
Ar Rub' al Khālī
Tropic of Cancer
Shiraz
Bandar 'Abbās
Būshehr
Chāh Bahār
Zāhedān
Bam
Lārestān
Qeshm
Musandam Pen. (Oman)
Al Ḥajar al Gharbī
Al Ḥajar ash Sharqī
J. Akhḍar 3018
Kūh-e Jebāl Barez
Kūh-e Taftān 4042
Kūh-e Bazmān 3489
Kūh-e Lāleh Zār 4374
Ramlat Al Wahībah
Umm as Samīm
Sabkhat Maṭṭī
Al Liwā'
Bdy under dispute
Ra's al Ḥadd

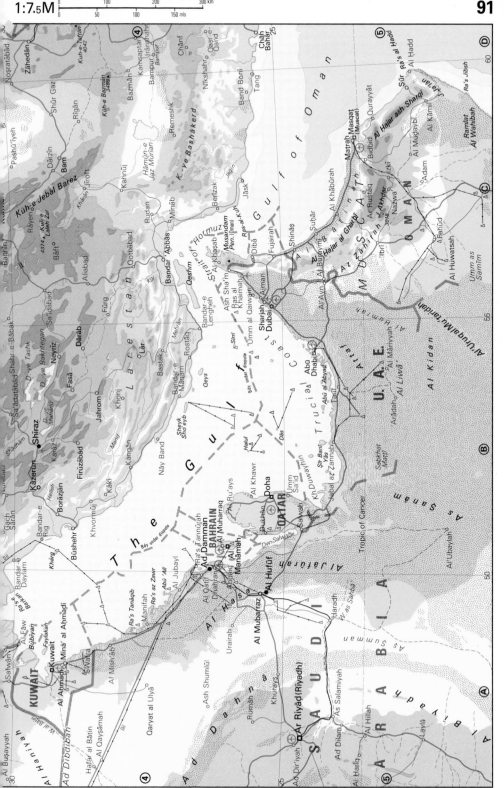

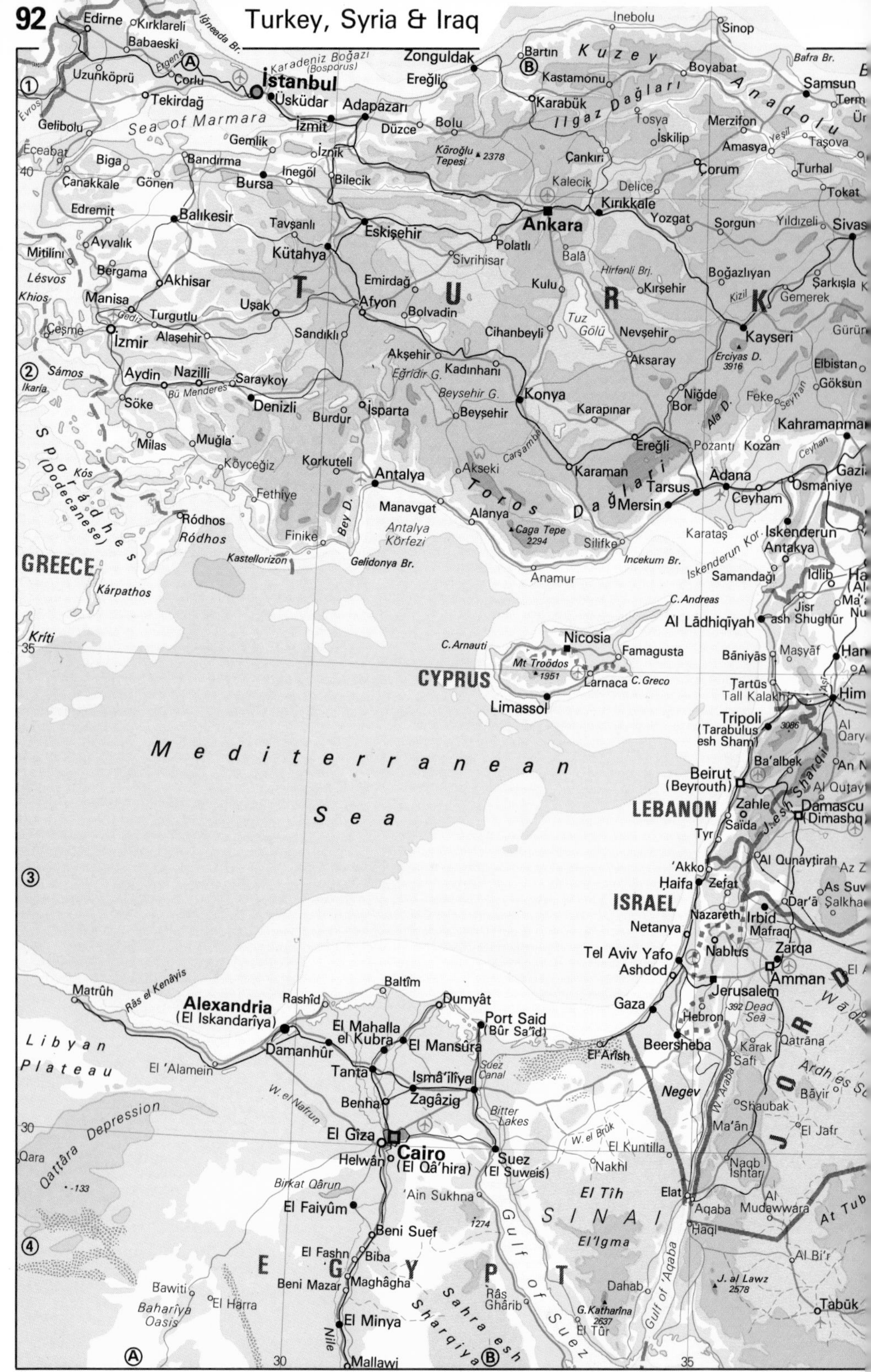

Edirne Kırklareli
Babaeski
İğneada Br.
Uzunköprü Çorlu (A)
Tekirdağ
İstanbul
Üsküdar Adapazarı
İzmit
İznik
Gemlik
Bandırma İnegöl
Gönen Bursa
Çanakkale
Edremit
Biga

Inebolu
Sinop
Zonguldak Bartın Kuzey
Ereğli (B) Kastamonu Boyabat Bafra Br.
Karabük Ilgaz Dağları Samsun
Tosya İskilip Merzifon Taşova
Çankırı Kalecik Delice Çorum Turhal
Kırıkkale Yozgat Sorgun Yıldızeli Sivas

Sea of Marmara

Karadeniz Boğazı
(Bosporus)

Düzce Bolu
Köroğlu
Tepesi ▲ 2378

Kuzey Anadolu

Amasya
Tokat

Balıkesir
Tavşanlı Eskişehir
Kütahya
Emirdağ
Afyon
Uşak
Bolvadin

Ankara
Polatlı
Sivrihisar Balâ
Kulu
Cihanbeyli
Akşehir Kadınhanı
İsparta Beyşehir G.
Burdur Beyşehir
Kırşehir Boğazlıyan
Nevşehir
Aksaray
Tuz
Gölü Niğde
Bor

Kayseri
Erciyas D.
3916
Elbistan
Feke Göksun

GREECE

Denizli
Saraykoy
Aydın Nazilli
Söke Bü Menderes
Milas Muğla
Köyceğiz Korkuteli
Fethiye
Finike

Konya Karapınar
Ereğli Pozantı Kozan
Karaman Adana
Akseki Tarsus Ceyhan
Alanya Totos Dağları Mersin Osmaniye
Caga Tepe Silifke Karataş İskenderun
2294 Antakya
İncekum Br. Samandağı Idlib

Mediterranean
Sea

Nicosia
CYPRUS Famagusta
Mt Troödos Larnaca C. Greco
1951
Limassol

Al Lādhiqīyah
Jisr
ash Shughūr Māʾ
Bāniyās Maşyāf Ham
Tartūs Tall Kalakh
Tripoli Hims
(Tarabulus Al
esh Sham) Baʿalbek
Beirut
(Beyrouth)
LEBANON Zahle Damascu
Saïda Dimashq
Tyr

ISRAEL
Haifa Zefat
Nazareth Irbid
Netanya Mafraq
Tel Aviv Yafo Nablus Zarqa
Ashdod Amman
Gaza Jerusalem
Hebron Dead Sea
Beersheba
El ʿArîsh Negev

Libyan
Plateau

Matrûh Râs el Kenâyis
Alexandria
(El Iskandarîya) Rashîd
Baltîm
Dumyât
El Mahalla Port Said
Damanhûr el Kubra (Bûr Saʿîd)
El Mansûra
Tanta Ismâʿilîya
Benha Zagâzig
El Gîza
Cairo Suez
Helwân (El Qâhira) (El Suweis)
ʿAin Sukhna
El Faiyûm
Beni Suef
El Fashn Biba
Beni Mazar Maghâgha
El Harra
Bawiti Baharîya Oasis
El Minya
Mallawi

EGYPT
SINAI
Elat Aqaba
Dahab
G. Katharîna 2637
El Tûr

JORDAN

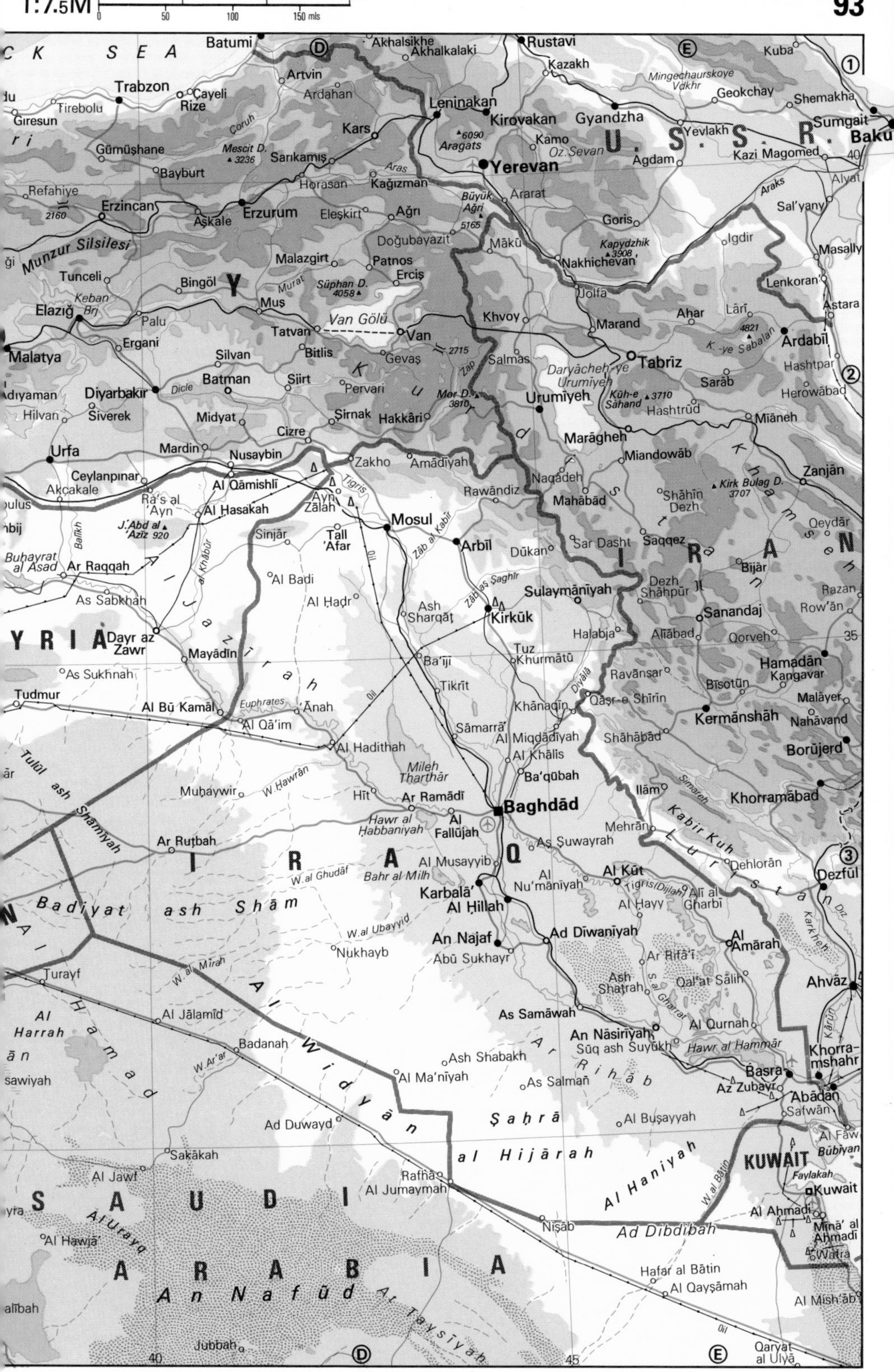

1:7.5M

0 100 200 300 km
0 50 100 150 mls

CK SEA

Batumi

Akhalsikhe
Akhalkalaki
Rustavi
Kazakh
Kuba

Artvin
Ardahan
Leninakan
Kirovakan
Gyandzha
Geokchay
Shemakha

Trabzon
Çayeli
Rize
Kars
6090 ▲
Aragats
Kamo
Oz.Sevan
Yevlakh
U . S . S . R
Sumgait
Baku

Çoruh

Tirebolu
Giresun
Gümüşhane
Mescit D.
▲ 3236
Sarıkamış
Kamo
Agdam
Kazi Magomed
40

Refahiye
2160
Bayburt
Horasan
Kağızman
Ararat
Goris
Kapydzhik
3908 ▲
Igdir
Sal'yany
Alyat

Erzincan
Aşkale
Erzurum
Eleşkirt
Ağrı
Doğubayazıt
Büyük
Ağrı
5165
Māku
Nakhichevan
Igdir
Masally

Tunceli
Bingöl
Malazgirt
Patnos
Erciş
Süphan D.
4058 ▲
Jolfa
Marand
Ahar
Lārī
4821 ▲
K. ye Sabalan
Ardabīl
Lenkoran
Astara

Elazığ
Keban
Brj
Palu
Ergani
Muş
Murat
Tatvan
Van Gölü
Van
2715
Khvoy
Marand
Hashtpar
Herowābād

Malatya
Silvan
Bitlis
Gevaş
Zab
Mor D.
3810
Salmas
Daryâcheh-ye
Urumiyeh
Tabriz
Sarāb
Miāneh

ıdıyaman
Hilvan
Diyarbakır
Dicle
Batman
Siirt
Pervari
Şırnak
Hakkāri
Urumīyeh
Kūh-e
Sahand
▲ 3710
Hashtrūd

Urfa
Siverek
Midyat
Cizre
Marāgheh
Miandowāb
Zanjān

Akçakale
Ceylanpınar
Mardin
Nusaybin
Zakho
Amādiyah
Naqadeh
Mahābād
Kirk Bulag D.
3707

Ra's al
'Ayn
Al Qāmishlī
Ayn
Zālah
Rawāndiz
Shāhīn
Dezh
Qeydār

J. Abd al
'Aziz 920
Al Hasakah
Sinjār
Tall
'Afar
Mosul
Arbīl
Dūkan
Sar Dasht
Saqqez
Bijār
Razan
Row'ān
35

Buhayrat
al Asad
Ar Raqqah
Al Badi
Al Hadr
Zāb al Kabīr
Sulaymāniyah
Dezh
Shāhpūr
Aliābad
Sanandaj
Qorveh

As Sabkhah
Zāb as Şaghīr
Ash
Sharqāt
Kirkūk
Halabja
Hamadān
Kangavar

Y R I A
Dayr az
Zawr
Mayādin
J a z i r a h
Ba'ıjī
Tuz
Khurmātū
Diyala
Ravānsar
Bisotūn
Malāyer

As Sukhnah
Sinjār
Tikrīt
Khānaqīn
Qaşr-e Shīrīn
Kermānshāh
Nahāvand

Tudmur
Al Bū Kamāl
Euphrates
Ānah
Al Qā'im
Al Hadithah
Sāmarrā'
Al Miqdādiyah
Shāhābād
Borūjerd

J.
Mileh
Tharthār
Al Khālis
Ba'qūbah
Īlām
Khorramābād

Muhaywir
W. Hawrān
Hīt
Ar Ramādī
Baghdād
Mehrān
Kabir
Kuh

Ar Rutbah
Hawr al
Habbaniyah
Al
Fallūjah
As Suwayrah
Dehlorān
Dezfūl

I R A Q
Al Musayyib
Bahr al Milh
Nu'māniyah
Al Kūt
Tigris/Dijlah
Alī al
Gharbī
Dez
Ahvāz

Turayf
Al Ghudāf
Karbalā'
Al Hillah
Ad Dīwāniyah
Ar Hayy
Al
Amārah
Khorramshahr

Al Jālamīd
Nukhayb
An Najaf
Abū Sukhayr
Ar Rifā'ī
Qal'at Sālih

N A
Badanah
Al Ma'nīyah
As Samāwah
Ash
Shatrah
Al Qurnah
Basra
Abādan

Al
Harrah
An Nāsiriyah
Sūq ash Suyūkh
Hawr al Hammār
Az Zubayr
Al Fāw
Bübiyan

Al Jawf
Al Duwayd
Ash Shabakh
As Salmān
Ar
Rihāb
Al Buşayyah
KUWAIT
Faylakah

Rafha
Al Jumaymah
Nişāb
Ad Dibdibah
Al Ahmadi
Minā' al
Ahmadi
Şafwān

S A U D I
Hafar al Bātin
Al Qayşamah
Al Mish'āb

A R A B I A
A n   N a f ū d
Jubbah
Qaryat
al Ulyā

0 25 50 75 100 k
0 25 50 mls

CYPRUS

Paleokhorio Larnaca 34 C.Greco
Lefkara Larnaca Bay
Zyyi C.Kiti
Limassol
Akrotiri Bay
C.Gata

M E D I T E R R A N E A N

S E A

Ţarţūs Kafrūn Bashūr
An Arwad Duraykīsh Nasirah Tall Bīsa
Şafitā Qal'at al Hisn
Ḥamīdīyah Tall Kalakh (KRAK-DES (CHEVALIERS) Hi
Kleia Kebīr Qoubayat Shins Al Qusayr
El Mīna Halba
El Hermel
Tripoli Zghorta Jūsī
(Tarābulus esh Shām) Qornet es His
Batroun Amioune Saouda Laboue
Bcharre 3086
Jubail Kartaba Deir el Dayr 'Aṭī
BYBLOS Ṟhazīr Ahma 2659
LEBANON Bikfaya Ba'albek An Nat
Jounieh 2628 Yabrūd
Baie de St Georges
Beirut Bikfaya
(Beyrouth) Baabda Zahle Rayak
Aley Al Ma'lūla
Az. Qutayfah
Damour Zabdāni 1910
Beit ed Dine 'Ayn al Fījah Dur
Saïda Machgharab At Dūma Adhr
(Sidon) Jezzine Rachaya Barādā Damascu
Qatana (Dimashq)
Ḥāşbaiya J.ash Shaykh
Lītāni (Mt Hermon) Al Kiswah A'waj
Marjayoun Dayr 'Alī
Tyr Q.Shemona Baniyas Burāq
(Tyre, Sour) Jouai'ya Mas'adah SYRIA
CEASE FIRE Ghabāghib Mismīyat
Enn Nāqoūra LINES 1974 Al Qunayṭirah
Bennt Yesud Aş Sanamayn Khabab
Jbail HamaKala Al Lajāh 863
Nahariya 1208 Khushnīyah Shac
Ma'alot Har Meron Nawā Izra'
'Akko Tarshīhā Zefat Shahbā
(Acre) Rama (Safad) Tiberias Jaba
B.of Haifa Q.Yam (Yam Kinneret) Shaykh Miskīn
Haifa Q.Shefar'am (Sea of Galilee) Ṭasīl
(Hefa) Q. Fiq Ma'agan As Suwayda
'Atlit Ata Tiberias Dar'a
Mt Nazareth Irbid
Carmel Afula Ramtha
Zikhron Ya'aqov Deir Abu Husn Buşrā
MEGIDDO Sa'id J. Um ed ash S
ARMAGEDDON Beyt Dara Şalk
Pardes Hanna Jenin Shean Ajlūn 1247 Tisīya
Hadera Qabatiya Jarash
Netanya Tulkarm Tubas Es Samra
Sabastiya Zarqa Er Rummān
ISRAEL Nablus Suweilih Qa
Herzliyya Kefar Sava Salt Marka Khanna
Petah Tiqwa Amman
Ramat Gan Yarqon Ba'al Hazor Karama
Tel Aviv 1016 Wadi es Sir Sahab
Yafo (Jaffa) Holon Ramallah Na'ur
Rishon le Zion Lod Jericho Jiza
Rehovot Ramla (Arīhā) Qasr el Kharana
Ashdod Latrun Jerusalem (El Quds) Mādabā Jebel
Beit Jala (Yerushalayim) Mudeisisat
Bethlehem Dab'a Wad ath
Qiryat (Bayt Lahm)
Ashqelon Gat Bet
Guvrin Hebron En Gedi Dhībān Khan ez Zabīb
Gaza Sederot (El Khalil) Mazra
Gaza Strip Dura Yatta Rabba
Khan Yunis Edh El Lisān Qatrāna
Rafah Dhahiriya Mazra
Ofaqim Beersheba MEZADA Rabba
Zeelim (Be'er Sheva) Qa'el Hafira
Râs Burūn Be'er Nevatim Arad
Sabkhet Sheva
el Bardawil HALUZA Sedom
El 'Arīsh Revivim Dimona MAMSHIT Manzil
Yeroham Safi Mazār
Qeziot Oron J.Ed Dabab Tafila Ḥāsā
SHIVTA Zin Qa'el Jinz
AVEDAT W. el Ghor 1356 Rashādīya Jurf ed Darāwīsh
G.Libni El Quseima N e g e v Hazev Danā 1641 Jebel
463 Eln J.el Atā'ita
G.Maghāra 892 Mizpe Yahav Nijil 1082
735 G.Hallal Ramon Shaubak
1305 Uneisa
E G Y P T Har Ramon
Bîr Gifgâfa Bîr Hasana Har Saggi Har Hakippa Jum Şuwwāna
1006 467

JORDA

A 34 36 C

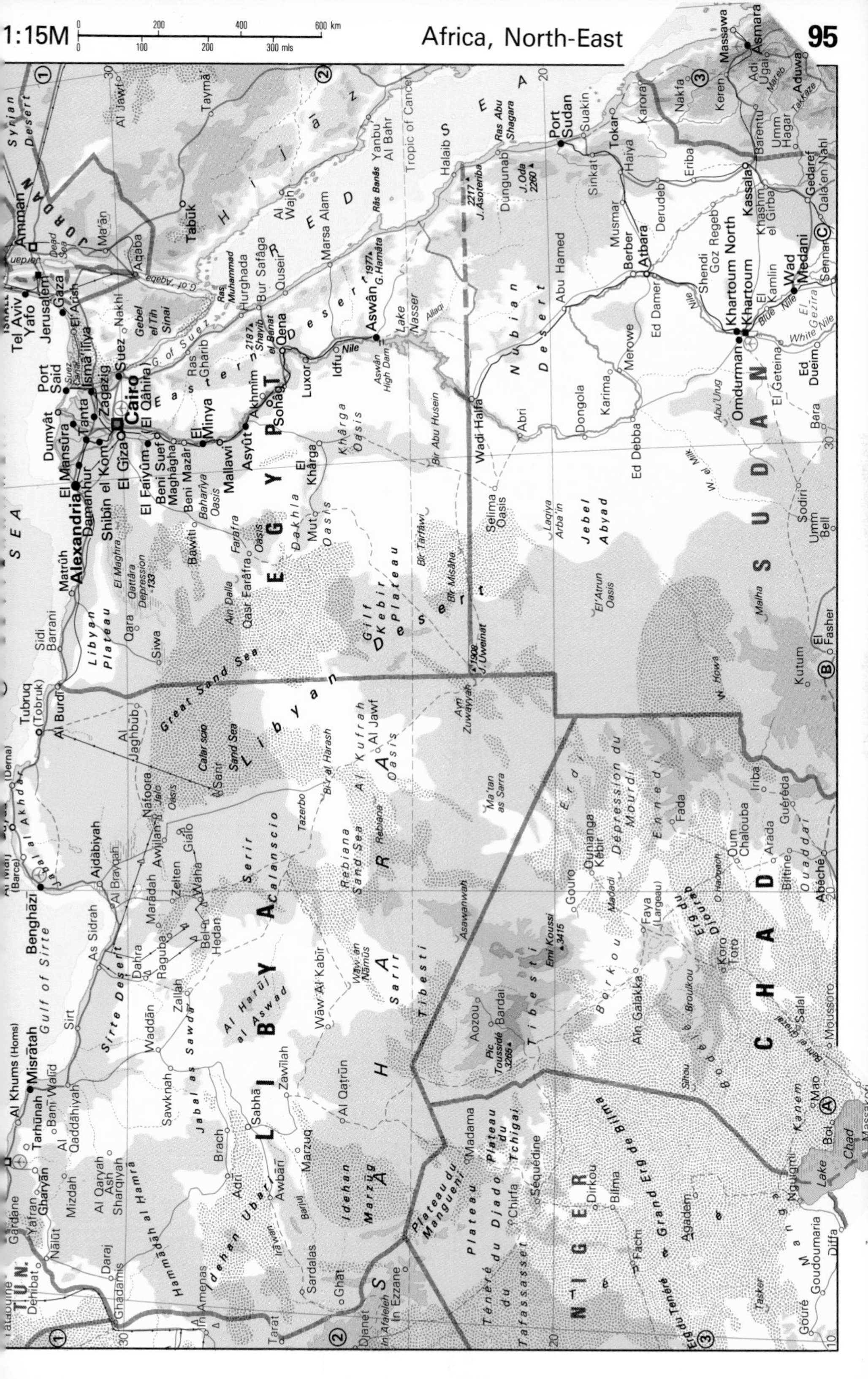

200 · 400 · 600 km
100 · 200 · 300 mls

1

2

3

Africa, North-East

95

A

B

C

Massawa
Asmara
Adi Ugali
Aduwa
Keren
Nakfa
Kassala
Wad Medani
Khartoum
Omdurman
Port Sudan
Berber
Atbara

SUDAN

EGYPT

LIBYA

Cairo
El Qâhira
Alexandria
El Gîza
Suez
Port Said
Ismâ'ilîya
Aswân
Luxor
Qena

CHAD

NIGER

TUN.

Benghazi
Misrâtah
Sabhā

Amman
Jerusalem
Tel Aviv
Yafo
Gaza

Libyan Desert

Nubian Desert

Great Sand Sea

Tibesti

SEA

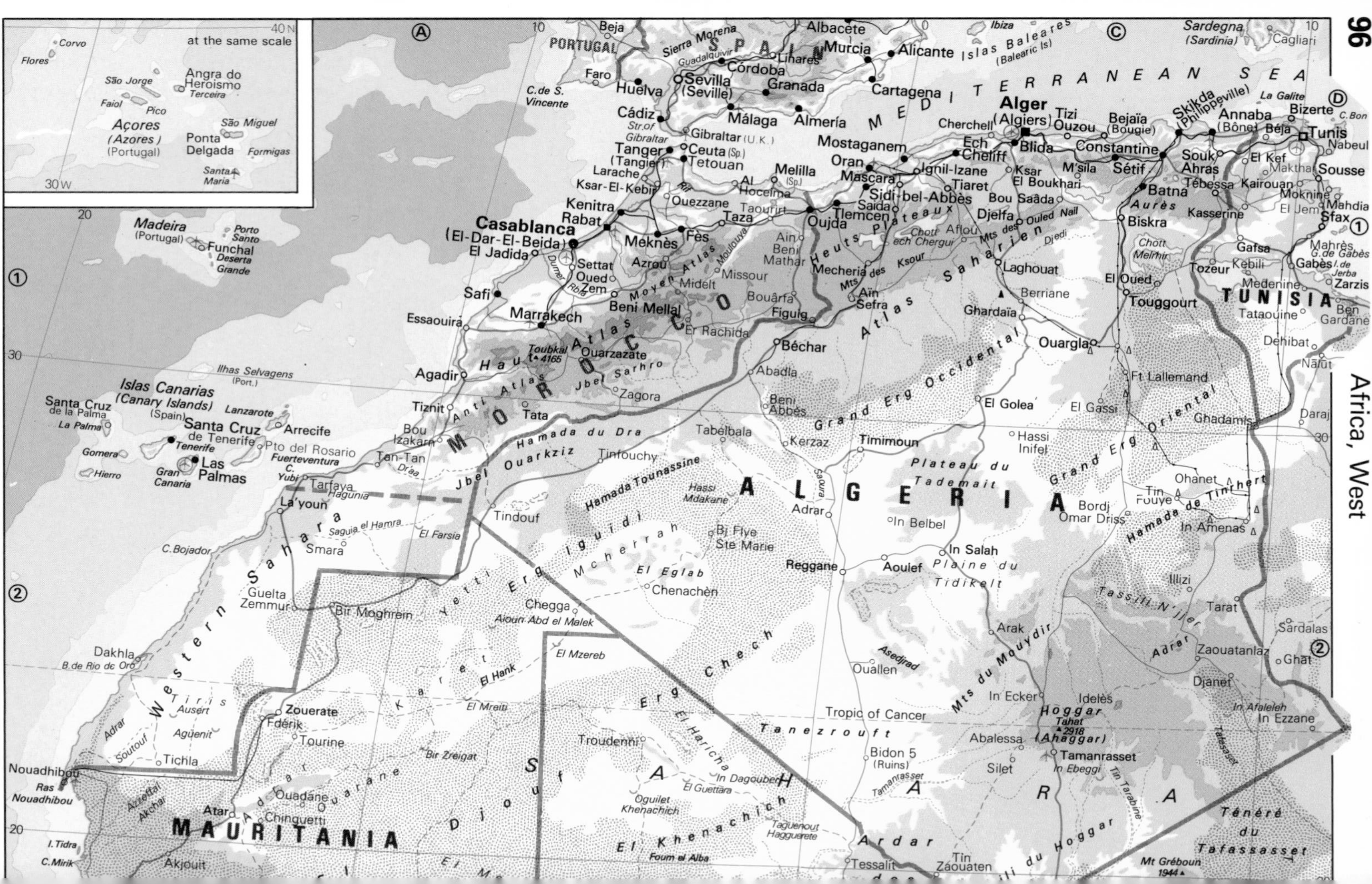

MEDITERRANEAN SEA
SPAIN
PORTUGAL
MOROCCO
ALGERIA
TUNISIA
Western Sahara
MAURITANIA
Islas Canarias (Canary Islands) (Spain)
Madeira (Portugal)
Açores (Azores) (Portugal)
at the same scale
Alger (Algiers)
Tunis
Casablanca (El-Dar-El-Beida)
Rabat
Marrakech
Fès
Meknès
Oran
Constantine
Tanger (Tangier)
Gibraltar (U.K.)
Sevilla (Seville)
Granada
Málaga
Alicante
Cartagena
Murcia
Ouargla
Tamanrasset
In Salah
Béchar
Tindouf
Agadir
Nouadhibou
Zouerate
Atar
Tropic of Cancer
Grand Erg Occidental
Grand Erg Oriental
Hoggar (Ahaggar)
Tanezrouft
Erg Chech
Haut Atlas
Anti Atlas
Atlas Saharien
Tassili N'Ajjer

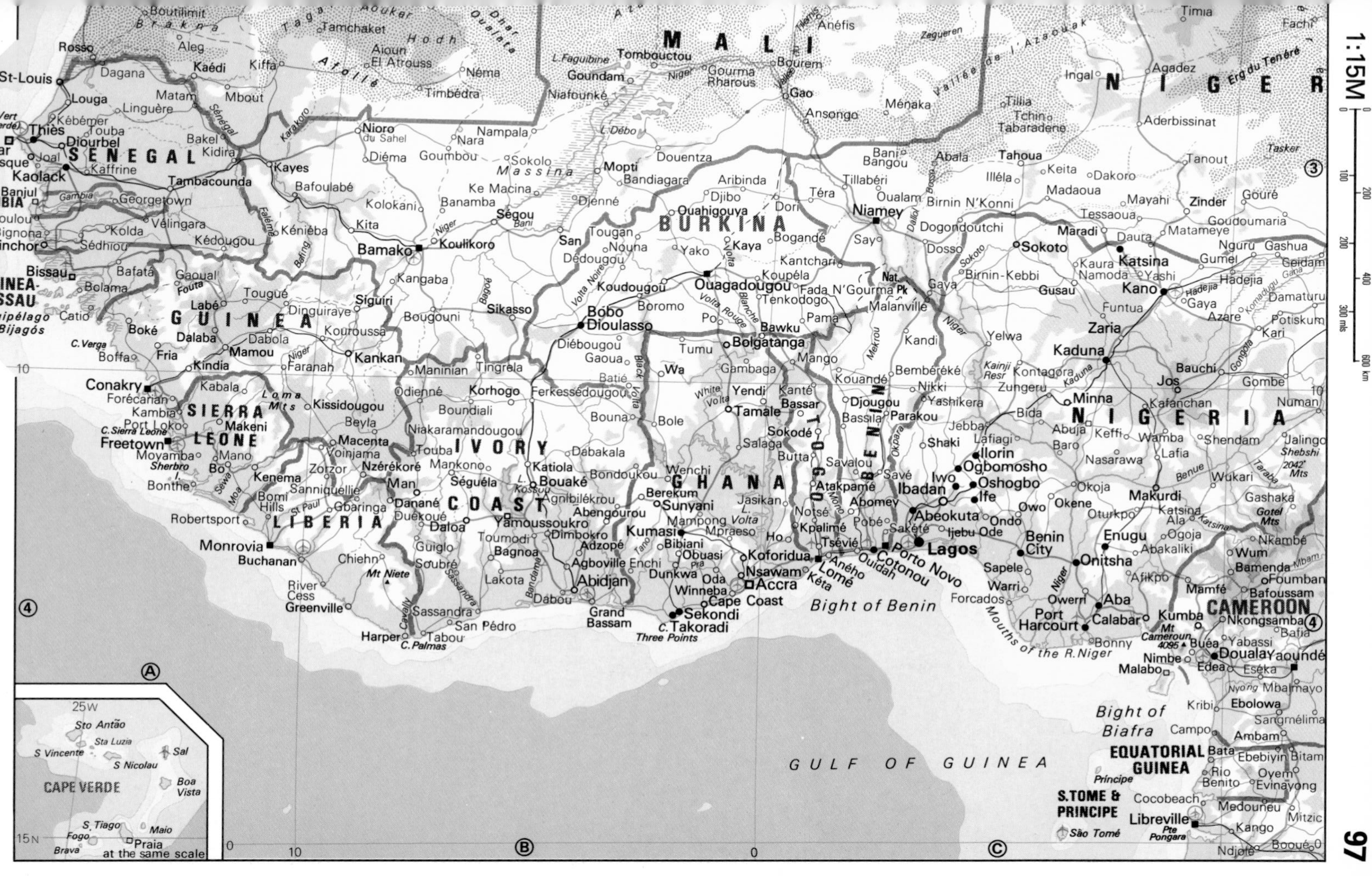
MALI
NIGER
NIGERIA
BURKINA
GHANA
TOGO
BENIN
IVORY COAST
LIBERIA
SIERRA LEONE
GUINEA
GUINEA-BISSAU
SENEGAL
CAMEROON
EQUATORIAL GUINEA
S.TOME & PRINCIPE
CAPE VERDE
GULF OF GUINEA
Bight of Benin
Bight of Biafra
Mouths of the R.Niger
Niamey
Ouagadougou
Bamako
Lagos
Accra
Lomé
Porto Novo
Cotonou
Abidjan
Yamoussoukro
Monrovia
Freetown
Conakry
Bissau
Yaoundé
Douala
Malabo
Libreville
São Tomé
Praia
Kano
Kaduna
Zaria
Ibadan
Enugu
Onitsha
Benin City
Port Harcourt
Calabar
Kumasi
Tamale
Sekondi
C.Takoradi
Cape Coast
Bouaké
Bobo Dioulasso
Tombouctou
Gao
Mopti
Ségou
Kankan
Kayes
Kaolack
St-Louis
Thiès
Sokoto
Katsina
Zinder
Maradi
Bolgatanga
Koudougou
Ouahigouya
Korhogo
Man
Daloa
Kenema
Harper
at the same scale

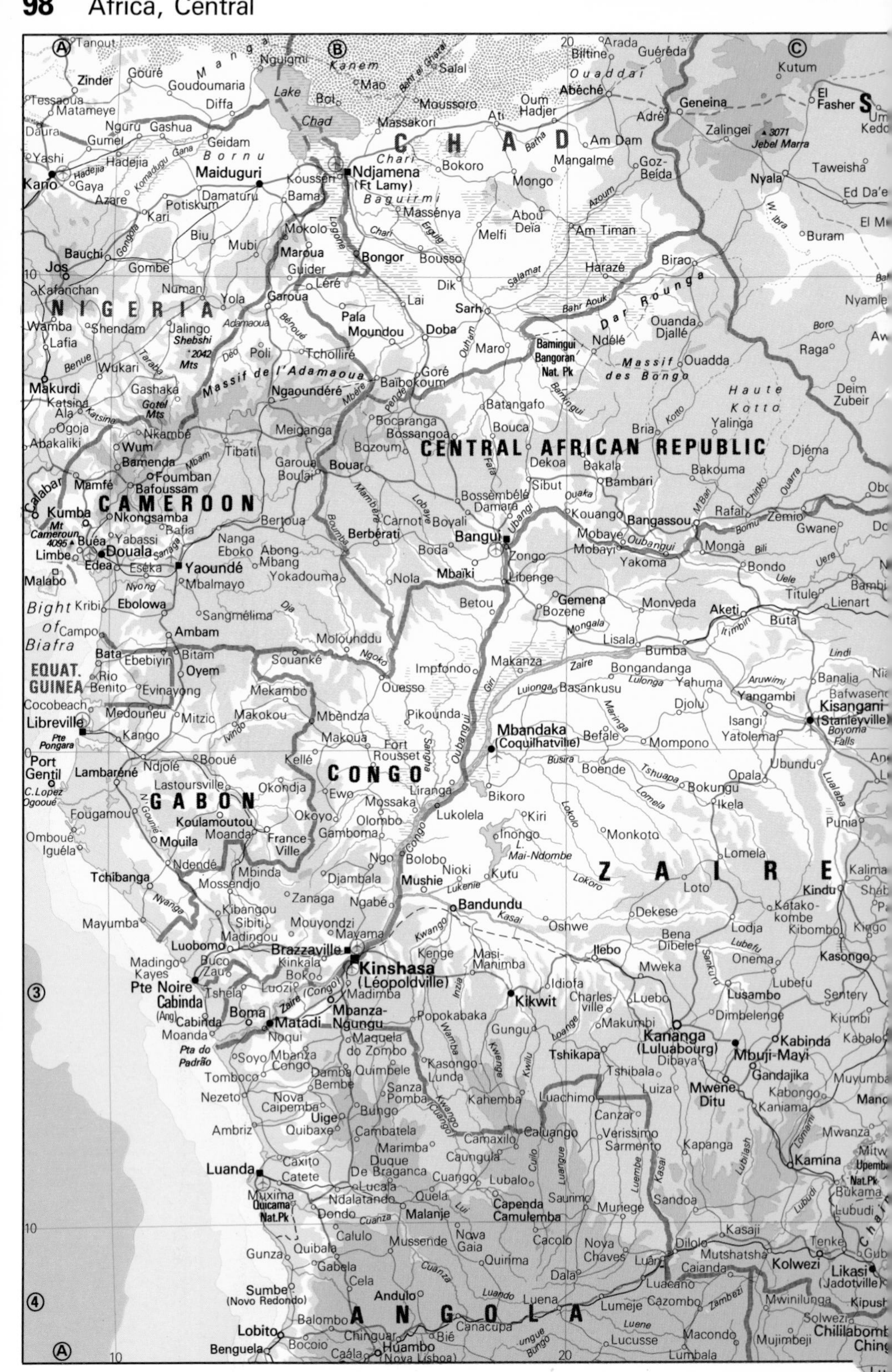

A
B
C
Tanout
Zinder
Gouré
Goudoumaria
Manga
Nguigmi
Kanem
Salal
Mao
Bahr el Ghazal
Lake Chad
Bol
Moussoro
Massakori
Biltine
Arada
Guéréda
Ouaddai
Abéché
Oum Hadjer
Ati
Adré
Geneina
Kutum
El Fasher
Zalingei
3071 Jebel Marra
Tessaoua
Matameye
Daura
Diffa
Nguru
Gashua
Gumel
Geidam
Bornu
Yashi
Hadejia
Kano
Gaya
Azare
Potiskum
Damaturu
Kari
Maiduguri
Koussen
Ndjamena
(Ft Lamy)
Bama
Chari
Baguirmi
Massénya
Bokoro
Mongo
CHAD
Am Dam
Mangalmé
Goz-Beída
Batha
Nyala
Taweisha
Ed Da'e
El M
Buram
Biu
Mubi
Mokolo
Maroua
Guider
Bongor
Bousso
Logone
Erguig
Melfi
Abou Deïa
Azoum
Am Timan
Bauchi
Jos
Gombe
Numan
Yola
Garoua
Léré
Lai
Dik
Salamat
Haraze
Birao
Kafanchan
NIGERIA
Wamba
Shendam
Jalingo
Shebshi
2042 Mts
Pala
Moundou
Doba
Sarh
Bahr Aouk
Dar Rounga
Ouanda Djallé
Ndélé
Nyamle
Lafia
Benue
Wukari
Poli
Tcholliré
Maro
Bamingui Bangoran Nat. Pk
Massif des Bongo
Ouadda
Raga
Makurdi
Katsina
Ala
Gashaka
Gotel Mts
Massif de l'Adamaoua
Ngaoundéré
Baïbokoum
Goré
Batangafo
Haute Kotto
Deim Zubeir
Ogoja
Abakaliki
Nkambé
Wum
Meiganga
Bocaranga
Bossangoa
Bouca
Bria
Yalinga
Bamenda
Tibati
Bozoum
CENTRAL AFRICAN REPUBLIC
Djéma
Foumban
Garoua Boulai
Bouar
Dekoa
Bakala
Bakouma
Calabar
Mamfé
Bafoussam
Sibut
Bambari
CAMEROON
Bossembélé
Damara
Kumba
Nkongsamba
Bafia
Bertoua
Carnot
Boyali
Kouango
Bangassou
Rafai
Zemio
Gwane
Mt Cameroun 4095
Buéa
Yabassi
Berbérati
Bangui
Mobaye
Mobayi
Monga
Bili
Limbe
Douala
Edea
Eséka
Yaoundé
Nanga Eboko
Abong Mbang
Boda
Zongo
Yakoma
Bondo
Malabo
Nyong
Mbalmayo
Yokadouma
Nola
Mbaïki
Libenge
Titule
Bambi
Bight of Biafra
Kribi
Ebolowa
Campo
Sangmélima
Dja
Betou
Gemena
Bozene
Monveda
Aketi
Buta
Lienart
Ambam
Moloundou
Mongala
Lisala
Bumba
Itimbiri
Bata
Ebebiyin
Bitam
Souanké
Ngoko
EQUAT. GUINEA
Rio Benito
Oyem
Evinayong
Impfondo
Makanza
Zaire
Bongandanga
Lulonga
Yahuma
Aruwimi
Banalia
Mekambo
Ouesso
Basankusu
Bafwasende
Cocobeach
Libreville
Medouneu
Mitzic
Makokou
Mbendza
Pikounda
Yangambi
Kisangani
(Stanleyville)
Boyoma Falls
Pte Pongara
Kango
Makoua
Fort Rousset
Sangha
Mbandaka
(Coquilhatville)
Befale
Mompono
Isangi
Yatolema
Port Gentil
Lambaréné
Ndjolé
Booué
Kellé
CONGO
Oubangui
Busira
Boende
Tshuapa
Bokungu
Opala
Ubundu
C. Lopez
Ogooué
Lastoursville
GABON
Okondja
Ewo
Liranga
Bikoro
Lomela
Ikela
Lualaba
Fougamou
Koulamoutou
Mossaka
Okoyo
Olombo
Lukolela
Kiri
Lokolo
Punia
Omboué
Iguéla
Mouila
Moanda
Franceville
Gamboma
Inongo
L. Mai-Ndombe
Monkoto
Lomela
ZAIRE
Kalima
Tchibanga
Ndendé
Mbinda
Mossendjo
Ngo
Djambala
Bolobo
Nioki
Mushie
Kutu
Lokoro
Loto
Kindu
Nyanga
Zanaga
Ngabé
Lukenie
Bandundu
Kasai
Dekese
Katako-kombe
Mayumba
Kibangou
Sibiti
Madingou
Mouyondzi
Mayama
Kwango
Oshwe
Bena Dibele
Lodja
Kibombo
Luobomo
Brazzaville
Kinshasa
(Léopoldville)
Kenge
Masi-Manimba
Ilebo
Lubefu
Onema
Kasongo
Madingo Kayes
Buco Zau
Kinkala
Boko
Mweka
Sankuru
Pte Noire
Cabinda
(Ang)
Tshela
Luozi
Zaire (Congo)
Madimba
Inzia
Kikwit
Idiofa
Charlesville
Luebo
Lusambo
Lubefu
Sentery
Boma
Matadi
Mbanza-Ngungu
Popokabaka
Gungu
Loange
Makumbi
Kananga
(Luluabourg)
Dimbelenge
Kiumbi
Moanda
Pta do Padrão
Noqui
Maquela do Zombo
Wamba
Kwenge
Kwilu
Tshikapa
Dibaya
Mbuji-Mayi
Kabinda
Kabalo
Soyo
Mbanza Congo
Kasongo-Lunda
Tshibala
Gandajika
Tomboco
Damba
Quimbele
Bembe
Luiza
Mwene-Ditu
Nezeto
Nova Caipemba
Sanza Pomba
Kwango (Cuango)
Kahemba
Luachimo
Kabongo
Kaniama
Uige
Bungo
Canzar
Ambriz
Quibaxe
Cambatela
Camaxilo
Caluango
Verissimo Sarmento
Kapanga
Mwanza
Marimba
Caungula
Lomami
Kamina
Luanda
Caxito
Catete
Duque de Braganca
Cuango
Lubalo
Cuilo
Luangue
Luembe
Kasai
Lubilash
Muxima
Quicama Nat. Pk
Lucala
Ndalatando
Quela
Capenda Camulemba
Saurimo
Muriege
Sandoa
Upemba Nat. Pk
Bukama
Lubudi
Dondo
Cuanza
Malanje
Lui
Kasaji
Calulo
Mussende
Nova Gaia
Cacolo
Nova Chaves
Dilolo
Mutshatsha
Tenke
Gunza
Quibala
Quirima
Luau
Caianda
Kolwezi
Likasi
(Jadotville)
Gabela
Cela
Dala
Luacano
Sumbe
(Novo Redondo)
Andulo
Luando
Luena
Lumeje
Cazombo
Zambezi
Mwinilunga
Kipush
Balombo
ANGOLA
Canacupa
Luena
Solwezi
Lobito
Chinguar
Bié
Lucusse
Macondo
Chililabomb
Benguela
Bocoio
Caála
Huambo
(Nova Lisboa)
Lumbala
Mujimbeji
Ching
10
20
3
4

200 km
100
200 mls

SUDAN

El Geteina
El Obeid
Ed Dueim
Bara
El Gezira
Sennar
Singa
Kassala
Khashm al Girba
Barentu
Umm Hagar
Adi Ugri
Keren
Massawa
Asmara
40

Wad Medani
Gedaref
Qala'en Nahl
El Hawata
Gallabat
Gondar
Dabat
Ras Dashan 4620
Sokota 3657
Aduwa
Adigrat
Makale
Matsa Fatma
Edd
Ta'izz
Al Mukha (Mocha)
Shaykh Uthman
Adan (Aden)

El Obeid
Kosti
El Jebelein
Renk
Er Rahad
Umm Ruwaba
Dilling
Nuba Mts
Rashad
Kadugli
Kaka
Paloich
Kodok

Dunkur
Debra Tabor
Bahar Dar
Dangila
Belfodio
Asosa
Dembidollo
Nejo
Lekemti
Soddo
Gore
Jimma
Abera
Mizan Teferi
Maji

ETHIOPIA

Adis Abeba
Dendi 3298
Awash
Adama
Aselle
Shashamanna
Goba
Ginir
Yirga Alem
Mendebo Mts
Gughe 4200
Arba Minch
Gardula
Negelli

Tandaho
Waldia
Dessye
4000 Abuye Meda
Debra Markos
Fiche
Debra Birhan
Dirē Dawa
Harar
Golocha
Ahmar Mts

Assab
Obock
Tadjoura
Dikhil
Zeila
DJIBOUTI
Djibouti
Biyo Kaboba
Berbera
Burco
Hargeysa
Caynabo
Laas Caanood
Damot
Awarem
Dagabur
Warder
Galadi
Gaalkacyo
Sinadogo
Ceelbuur

Gulf of Aden
Str. of Bab al Mandeb
Ras Khanzira
Karin
Guban
Haud
Ogaden

Nasir
Malakal
Fangak
Bentiu
Meshra Er Req
Ayod
Abwong
Duk Faiwil
Shambe
Rumbek
Yirol
Bor
Tali Post
Amadi
Mongalla
Juba
Torit
Laylo
Kapoeta
Lokitaung
Mizan
Nimule

Sudd
Bahr el Ghazal

UGANDA
Gulu
Lira
Soroti
Mbale
Tororo
Kampala
Jinja
Entebbe
Masaka
Kisumu
Kisii
Kakamega

KENYA
Kitale
Eldoret
Isiolo
Nanyuki
Nyeri
Nakuru
Nairobi
Kajiado
Machakos
Thika
Embu
Mt Kenya 5200
Garissa
Wajir
Mado Gashi
Marsabit
Moyale
Mega
Buna
El Goran
Belet Uen
Mandera
Dolo
Luuq
Baydhabo
Xuddur
Buur Hakaba
Baardheere
Afmadu
Jilib
Giamame
Kismaayo

Lake Turkana
Mt Kulal 2293
Mt Nyiru 2805
Lokichokio

SOMALIA
Buulo Barde
Tiyeglow
Meregh
Dirri
Wanle Weyne
Jowhar
Afgooye
Uarsciek
Markad
Muqdisho (Mugadisho)
Baraawe

RWANDA
Kigali
BURUNDI
Gitega
Bukoba
Musoma

Lake Victoria

TANZANIA
Mwanza
Shinyanga
Tabora
Dodoma
Arusha
Moshi
Kilimanjaro 5895
Meru 4565
Singida
Manyoni
Mpwapwa
Morogoro
Dar es Salaam
Zanzibar
Bagamoyo
Tanga
Mombasa
Kwale
Malindi
Kilifi
Voi
Tsavo Nat. Pk
Masai Steppe
Lushoto
Pangani
Pemba I.
Mafia I.
Mbeya
Iringa
Ifakara
Mahenge
Mohoro
Kilwa Kivinje
Kilwa Kisiwani
Lindi
Mtwara
Nachingwea
Masasi
Tunduru
Songea
Newala
Mbamba Bay
Nkhata Bay
Liwale

Equator

SEYCHELLES
Aldabra Is
Assumption
Is Glorieuses
Mayotte (Fr.)
Dzaoudzi
COMOROS
Moroni
Grande Comore
Mutsamudu
Anjouan
Mohéli

Laas Qoray
Ceerigaabo
Qardho
Laas Caanood Damot
Gaalkacyo
El Hamurre
Dabaro
Hobyo
Eyl
Bender Beyla
Ras Xaafuun
Alula
Candala
Boosaaso
Hordiyo
C. Guardafui
Carcar Mts
Nugaal

SOMALIA
at the same scale

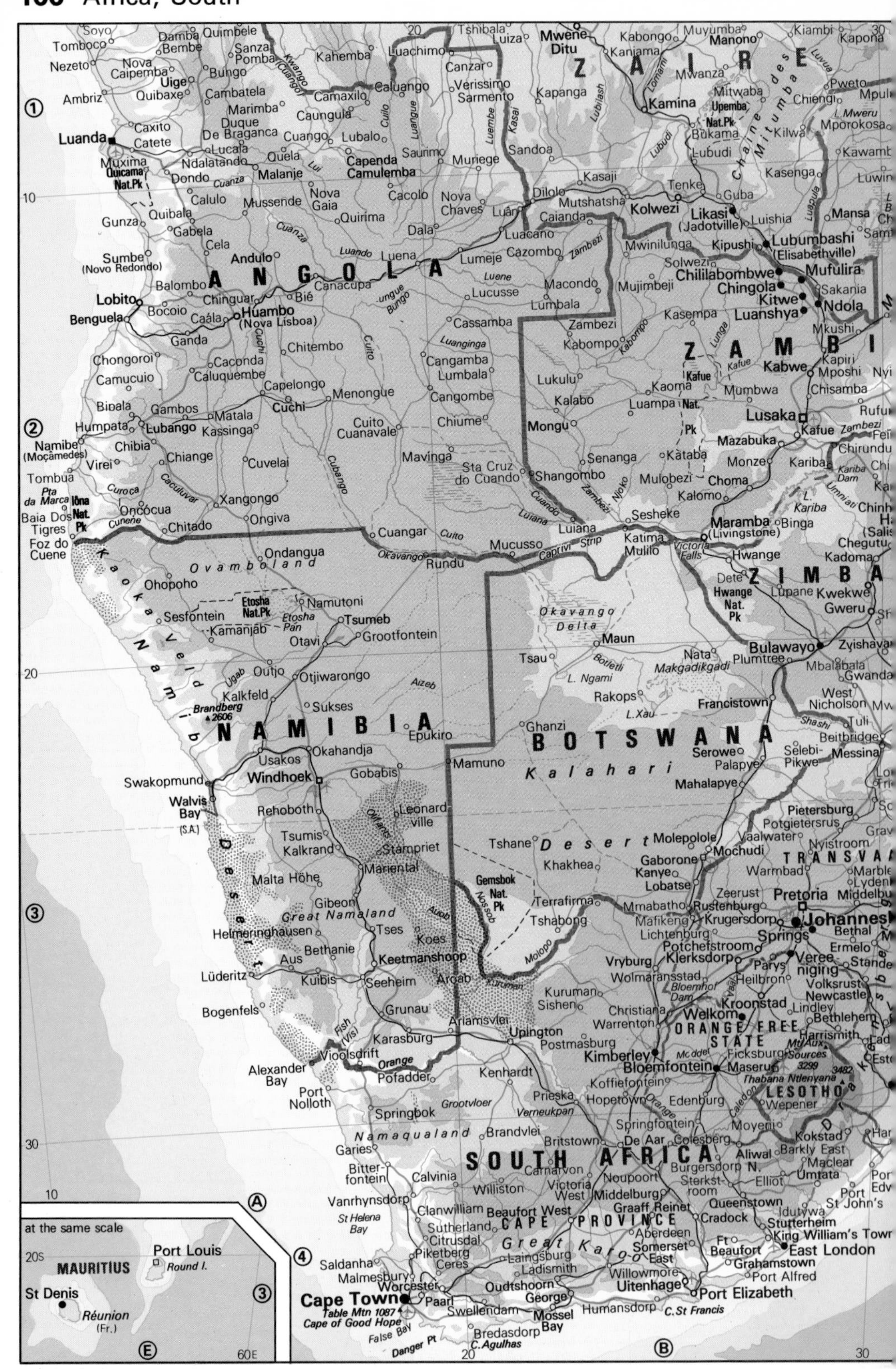
ANGOLA
ZAIRE
ZAMBIA
NAMIBIA
BOTSWANA
ZIMBABWE
SOUTH AFRICA
CAPE PROVINCE
ORANGE FREE STATE
TRANSVAAL
LESOTHO
MAURITIUS
Luanda
Lobito
Benguela
Huambo (Nova Lisboa)
Lubango
Namibe (Moçâmedes)
Windhoek
Walvis Bay (S.A.)
Swakopmund
Lüderitz
Keetmanshoop
Lusaka
Kafue
Livingstone
Bulawayo
Francistown
Gaborone
Pretoria
Kimberley
Bloemfontein
Cape Town
Port Elizabeth
East London
Kalahari Desert
Namib Desert
Okavango Delta
Makgadikgadi
Great Karoo
Namaqualand
Great Namaland
Caprivi Strip
Orange
Zambezi
Cape of Good Hope
C. Agulhas
Table Mtn 1087
Port Louis
St Denis
Réunion (Fr.)
Round I.
at the same scale

①

SEYCHELLES

Providence
Aldabra Is
Assumption
Cosmoledo Is
Farquhar Is

L. Rukwa
Ruaha Nat.Pk.
Sumbawanga
Mikumi
Kliindonni
Kisiju
Mafia I.
Iringa
Ifakara
Chunya
Sao Hill
Mahenge
Kilwa Kivinje
Mohoro
Mbeya
Rungwe *2959
Njombe
Liwale
Kilwa Kisiwani
Tukuyu
Karonga
Manda
Nachingwea
Lindi
Mtwara
Isoka
Chilumba
Songea
Masasi
C.Delgado
Rumphi
Mbamba Bay
Tunduru
Newala
Palma
Mueda
Mocímboa da Praia

Moroni
Grande Comore
COMOROS
Mutsamudu
Anjouan
Mohéli
Dzaoudzi
Mayotte (Fr.)

Cap d'Ambre
C. St Sébastien
Antseranana
Mgne d'Ambre *1478
Ambilobe
Nosy Bé
Vohimarina
Ambanja
Massif du Tsaratanana *2876
Sambava

Lupilichi
Mecula
Macomia
Ilbo
Metangula
Marrupa
Montepuez
Pemba
Lichinga
Maúa
Namuno
Namapa
Mecufi
Mandimba
Memba
Mecuburi
Nacala
Meconta
Moçambique

Analalava
Antsohihy
Antalaha
Befandriana
Maroantsetra

MADAGASCAR
(MALAGASY REP.)

Nampula
Mahajanga (Majunga)
Marovoay
Mampikony
Mananara
C.Masoala
B.Antongila
Nosy Boraha
Ambodifototra
Fenoarivo

Tsaratanana
Ivongo
Soanierana
Atsinanana

Besalampy
Morafenobe
Ankazobe
Anjozorobe
Toamasina (Tamatave)
Vohibinany

Maintirano
Nosy Barren
Tsiroanomandidy
Moramanga
Antananarivo (Tananarive)

Miandrivazo
Betafo
Antsirabe
Mahanoro

Morondava
Manabo
Atofinandrahana
Nosy Varika

Malaimbandy
Ambositra
Ambosho
Ambohimahasoa

Mania
Mangoky
Fianarantsoa
Ifanadiana
Mananjary

Morombe
C.St Vincent
Ambalavao
Manakara

Ankazoabo
Ihosy
Ivohibe

Sakaraha
Betroka
Farafangana
Vangaindrano

Toliara
Midongy Atsimo
Tropic of Capricorn

B.de St Augustin
Isoanala

Ampanihy
Amboasary
Taolañaro
Beloha
Ambovombe
Tsihombe
C. Ste Marie

②

③

Mozambique Channel

Juan de Nova (Fr.)
Bassas da India (Fr.)
Europa (Fr.)

L.Malawi (L.Nyasa)

Lilongwe
Zomba
Blantyre
Limbe
Teteo
Chikwawa
Mocuba
Quelimane
Sofala (Beira)

Nova Mambone
Bartolomeu Dias
I.Bazaruto
Vilanculos
Pta de Barra Falsa

Massinga
Morrumbene
Inhambane
Inharrime
Quissico

Xai Xai
Manhica
Maputo (Lourenço Marques)

Bela Vista

Swartruggens
Rustenburg
Brits
Middelburg
Waterval
Barberton
Marracuene
Maputo

Mafikeng
Koster
Krugersdorp
Pretoria
Witbank
Belfast
Komati
Namaacha
Matola

Lichtenburg
Randfontein
Johannesburg
Carolina
Mbabane
Bela Vista

Carletonville
Heidelberg
Springs
Leslie
Breyten
Ermelo
SWAZILAND
Manzini
Stegi

Potchefstroom
Evaton
Sasolburg
Bethal
Amsterdam
Usutu

Klerksdorp
Vereeniging
Standerton
Morgenzon
Piet Retief

Vaal Dam
Villiers
Amersfoort
Nhlangano
Lavumisa

Ottosdal
Parys
Frankfort
Volksrust
Paulpietersburg
Pongola
Sibayi L.

Schweizer Reneke
Viljoenskroon
Heilbron
Vrede
Utrecht
Mkuzi

B'tswana
Kroonstad
Odendaalsrus
Petrus Steyn
Warden
Newcastle
Vryheid
Nongoma
L.St Lucia

Christiana
Hoopstad
Welkom
Lindley
Bethlehem
Glencoe
Dundee
Mtubatuba

Warrenton
Bultfontein
Virginia
Ventersburg
Reitz
Harrismith
Ladysmith
Melmoth

Boshof
Theunissen
Winburg
Senekal
Colenso
Empangeni

ORANGE FREE STATE
Dealesville
Brandfort
Ficksburg
Ladybrand
Weenen
Eshowe
Richard's Bay

Kimberley
B'tswana
Teyateyaneng
Estcourt
Greytown
Gingindlovu

Petrusburg
Bloemfontein
Maseru
Mokhotlong
Mooi River
New Hanover
Stanger

Koffiefontein
Dewetsdorp
LESOTHO
Howick
Tongaat
Verulam

Hopetown
Edenburg
Wepener
Mafeteng
Underberg
Richmond
Pietermaritzburg
Donnybrook
Durban

NATAL

1:7.5M

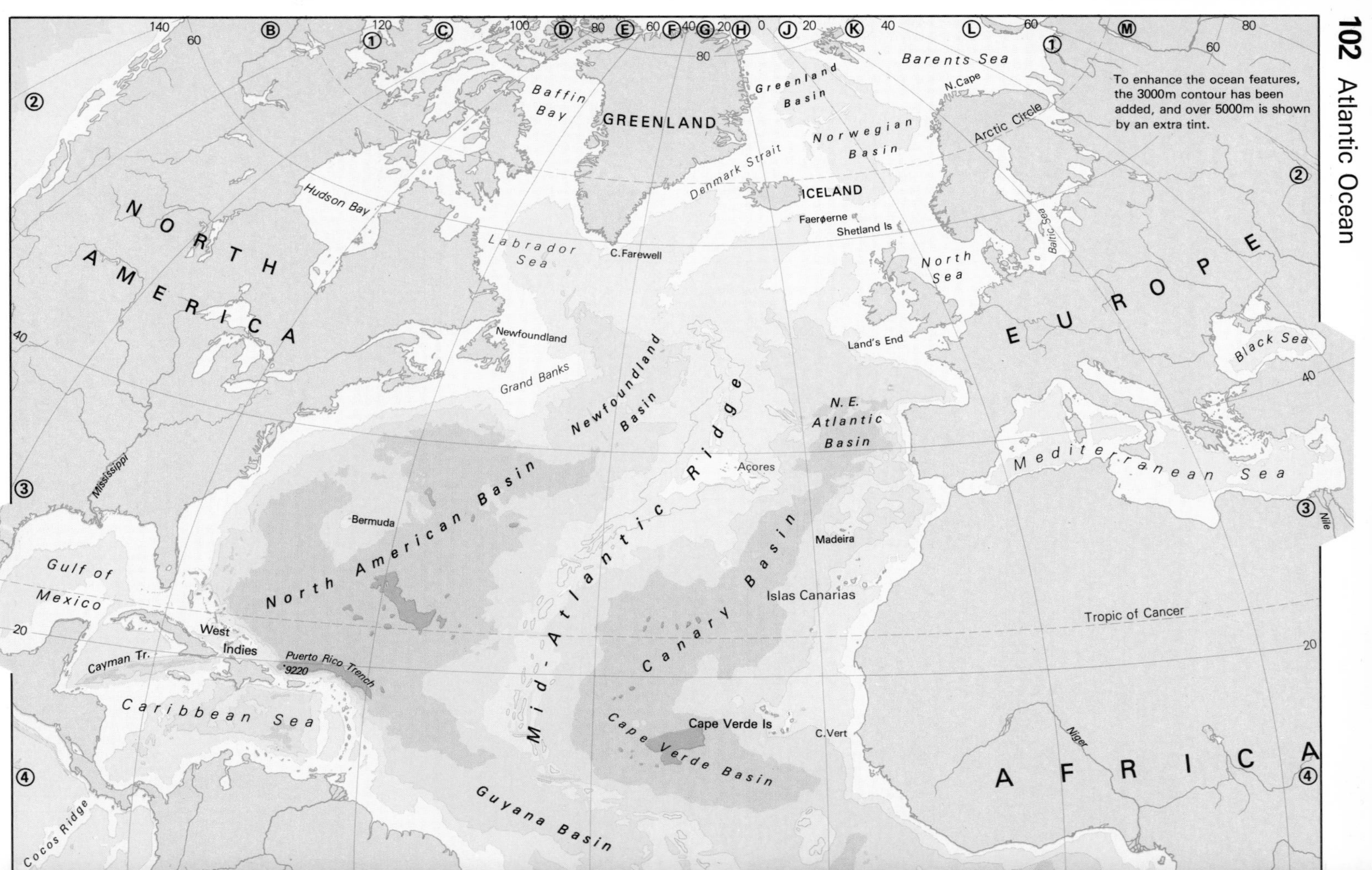

To enhance the ocean features, the 3000m contour has been added, and over 5000m is shown by an extra tint.

EUROPE

AFRICA

NORTH AMERICA

GREENLAND

ICELAND

Barents Sea

Black Sea

Mediterranean Sea

Nile

Niger

Tropic of Cancer

N.Cape

Arctic Circle

North Sea

Baltic Sea

Norwegian Basin

Greenland Basin

Denmark Strait

Baffin Bay

Labrador Sea

Faeroerne

Shetland Is

Land's End

N.E. Atlantic Basin

Madeira

Islas Canarias

C.Vert

Açores

Cape Verde Is

Canary Basin

Cape Verde Basin

Mid-Atlantic Ridge

Newfoundland Basin

Newfoundland

Grand Banks

C.Farewell

Hudson Bay

Bermuda

North American Basin

Guyana Basin

Puerto Rico Trench

9220

West Indies

Caribbean Sea

Cayman Tr.

Gulf of Mexico

Mississippi

Cocos Ridge

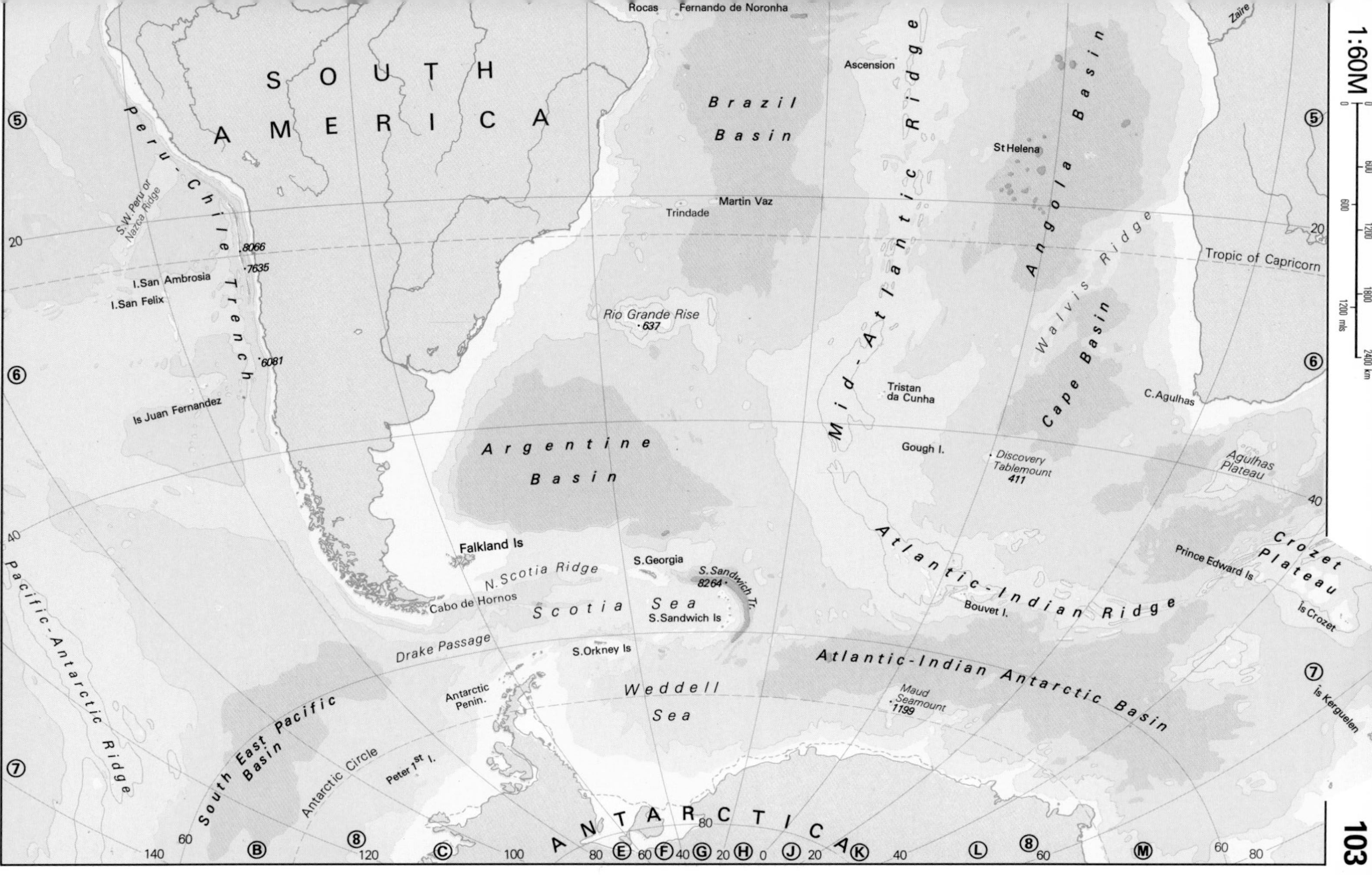

1:60M

| 0 | 600 | 1200 | 1800 | 2400 km |
| 0 | | 600 | | 1200 mls |

Crozet Plateau

Agulhas Plateau

Prince Edward Is

Is Crozet

Is Kerguelen

Tropic of Capricorn

C.Agulhas

Angola Basin

Cape Basin

Walvis Ridge

Discovery Tablemount 411

Atlantic-Indian Ridge

Bouvet I.

Atlantic-Indian Antarctic Basin

Maud Seamount 1199

St Helena

Mid-Atlantic Ridge

Tristan da Cunha

Gough I.

Ascension

Zaïre

Brazil Basin

Fernando de Noronha

Martim Vaz

Trindade

Rio Grande Rise 637

S.Sandwich Tr. 8264

S.Georgia

S.Sandwich Is

Weddell Sea

A N T A R C T I C A

Rocas

Argentine Basin

N.Scotia Ridge

Scotia Sea

S.Orkney Is

S O U T H

Falkland Is

Cabo de Hornos

Drake Passage

Antarctic Penin.

A M E R I C A

Peter I.

Peru-Chile Trench

8066

7635

6081

S.W. Peru or Nazca ridge

I.San Ambrosia

I.San Felix

Is Juan Fernandez

Antarctic Circle

South East Pacific Basin

Pacific-Antarctic Ridge

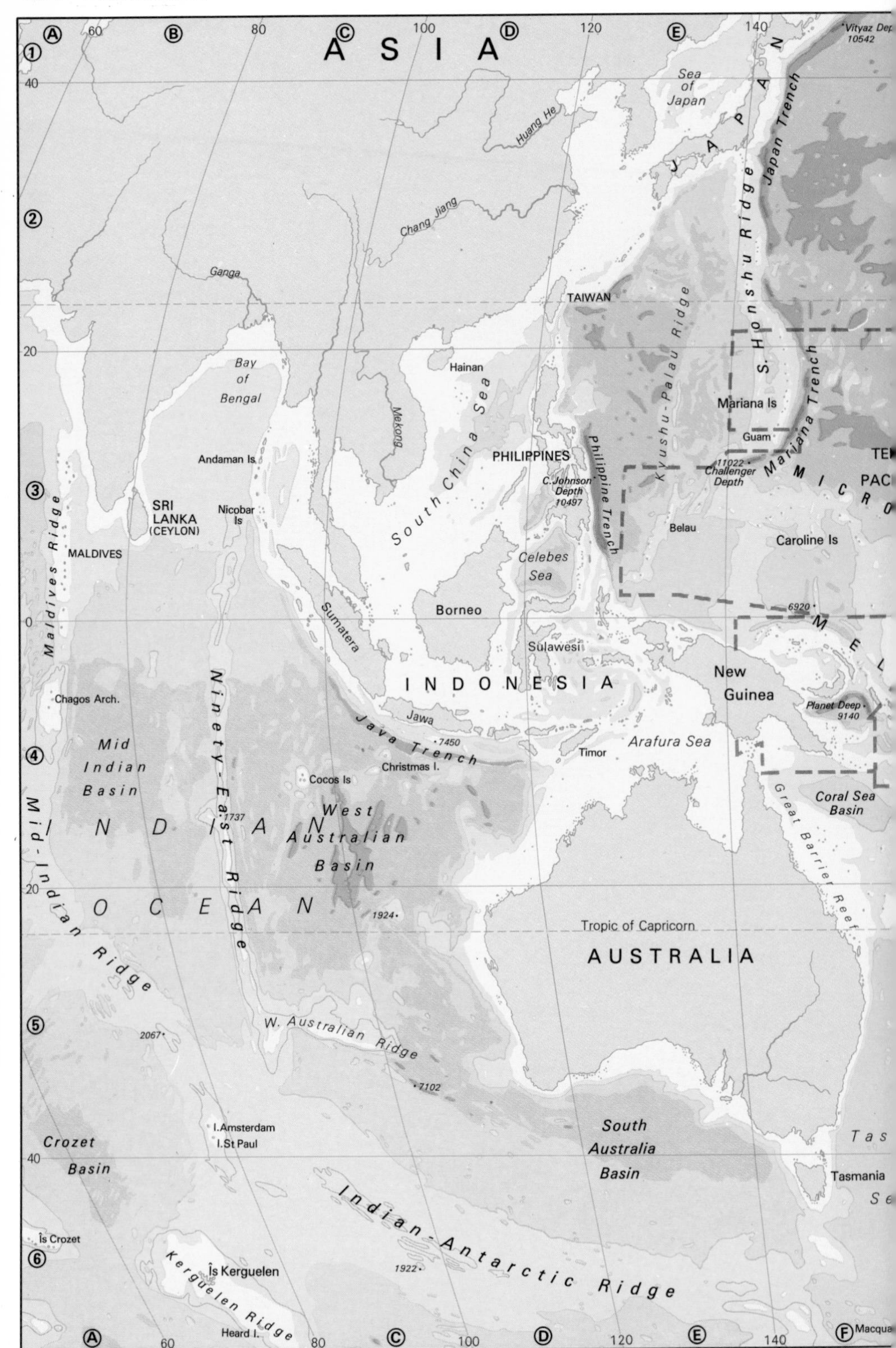

A S I A

Vityaz Dep.
10542

Sea of Japan

J A P A N

Japan Trench

Huang He

Chang Jiang

Ganga

S. Honshu Ridge

TAIWAN

Bay
of
Bengal

Hainan

Mariana Is

Kyushu-Palau Ridge

Mariana Trench

Guam

Andaman Is

South China Sea

PHILIPPINES

C. Johnson
Depth
10497

11022
Challenger
Depth

TE

PAC

MICRO

SRI
LANKA
(CEYLON)

Nicobar
Is

Mekong

Belau

Caroline Is

Maldives Ridge

MALDIVES

Celebes
Sea

Philippine Trench

Sumatera

Borneo

Sulawesi

Chagos Arch.

Ninety-East Ridge

Mid
Indian
Basin

I N D O N E S I A

New
Guinea

Planet Deep
9140

6920

M E L

Jawa

Java Trench

Timor

Arafura Sea

7450

Christmas I.

Mid-Indian Ridge

I N D I A N

Cocos Is

West
Australian
Basin

1737

O C E A N

1924

Tropic of Capricorn

Great Barrier Reef

Coral Sea
Basin

A U S T R A L I A

W. Australian Ridge

2067

7102

I. Amsterdam
I. St Paul

South
Australia
Basin

Tas

Crozet
Basin

Tasmania

S e

40

Ìs Crozet

Kerguelen Ridge

Ìs Kerguelen

Indian-Antarctic Ridge

1922

Heard I.

Macqua

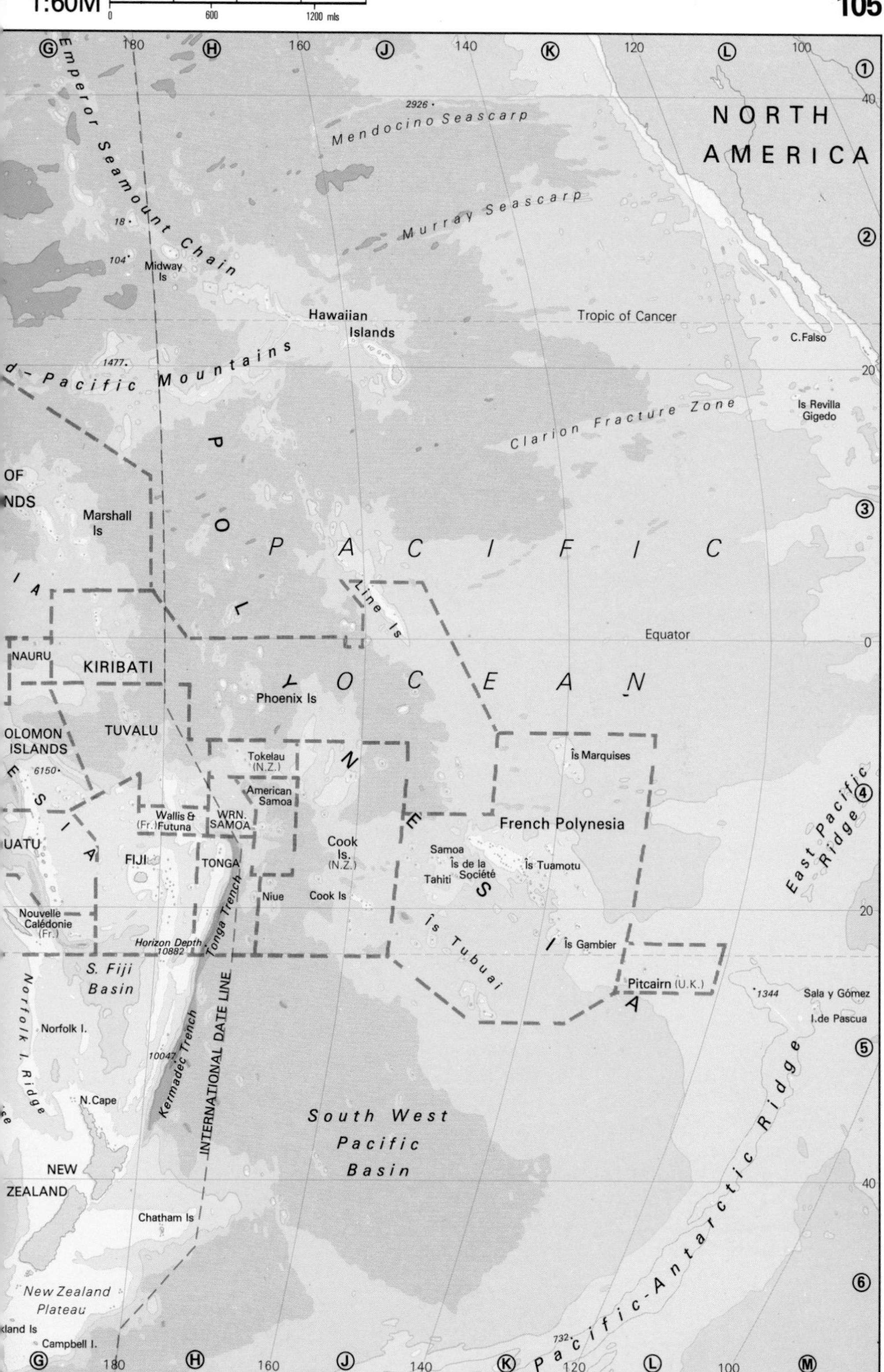

0   600   1200   1800   2400 km
0   600   1200 mls

G   180   H   160   J   140   K   120   L   100

① 40

**N O R T H
A M E R I C A**

Emperor Seamount Chain

2926·

Mendocino Seascarp

②

Murray Seascarp

18·

104·   Midway
         Is

Hawaiian
Islands   Tropic of Cancer   C.Falso

20

1477·

d – Pacific Mountains   Is Revilla
                                                         Gigedo

OF   Clarion Fracture Zone
NDS   Marshall
           Is   ③

P A C I F I C   C

IA

NAURU   Equator   0

KIRIBATI   L

TUVALU   O   Phoenix Is   Îs Marquises

OLOMON   ④
ISLANDS   6150·   Tokelau   French Polynesia
E   (N.Z.)   N
S   Wallis &   American
A   Wallis &   (Fr.)Futuna Samoa   Samoa
UATU   WRN.SAMOA   Îs de la   Îs Tuamotu
     FIJI   TONGA   Cook   Tahiti Société
                      Is.
Nouvelle   (N.Z.)   East Pacific Ridge
Calédonie   FIJI   TONGA   Niue   Cook Is   Îs Gambier
(Fr.)   20
           Horizon Depth·   Îs Tubuai
S. Fiji   10882   Pitcairn (U.K.)   ·1344   Sala y Gómez
Basin   I.de Pascua
Norfolk I Ridge
           Norfolk I.   ⑤
10047
NEW   N.Cape   South West
ZEALAND   Pacific
                        Basin   40
           Chatham Is
New Zealand
Plateau   Pacific-Antarctic Ridge
kland Is
    Campbell I.   732·   ⑥

G   180   H   160   J   140   K   120   L   100   M

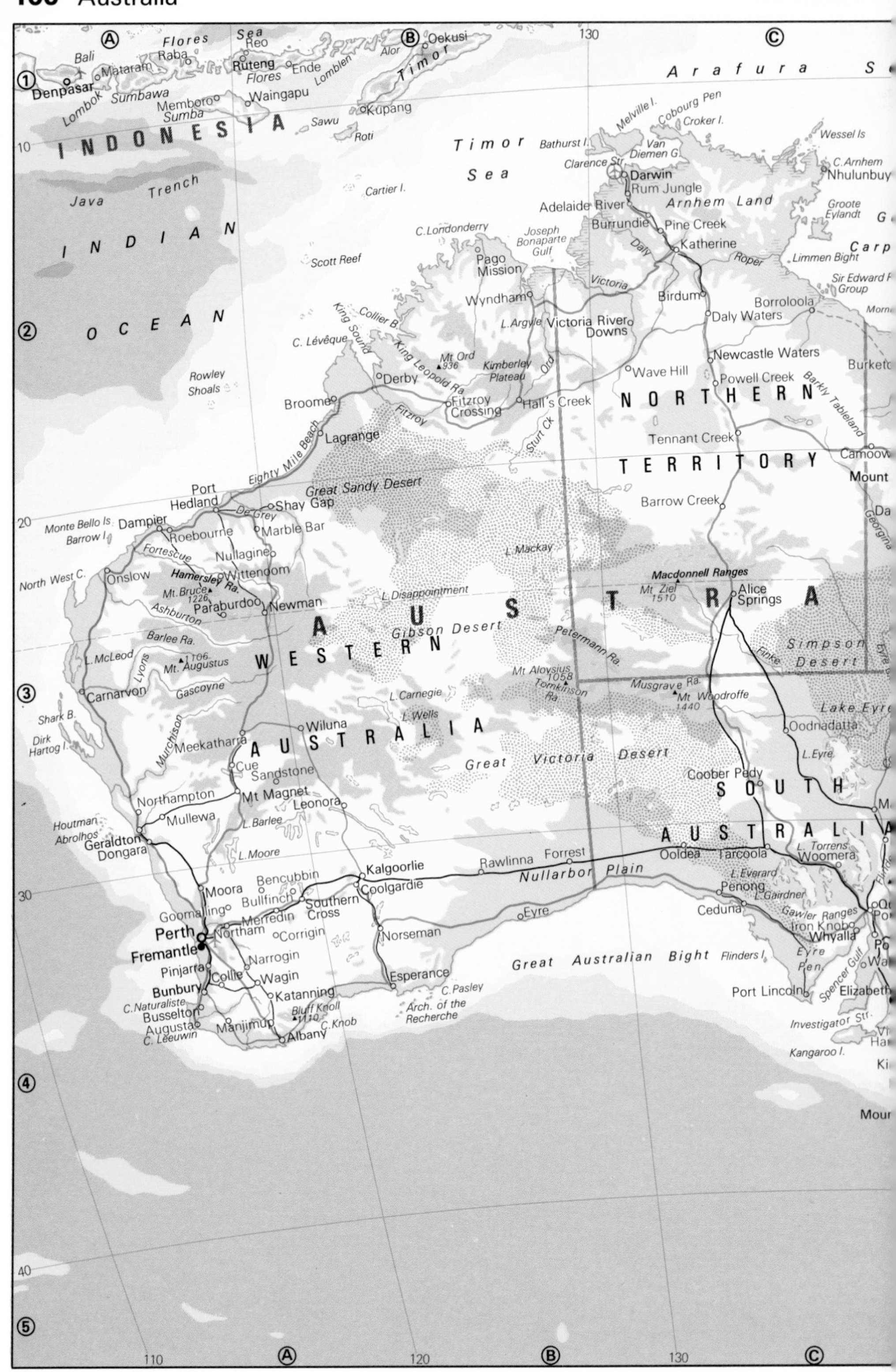

Flores Sea
Bali
Denpasar
Mataram
Lombok
Sumbawa
Memboro
Sumba
INDONESIA
Raba
Ruteng
Flores
Ende
Lomblen
Alor
Waingapu
Sawu
Roti
Kupang
Reo
Oekusi
Timor
Arafura Sea

Java Trench
Cartier I.
INDIAN
OCEAN
Scott Reef

Rowley
Shoals

Melville I.
Cobourg Pen
Croker I.
Bathurst I.
Van Diemen G.
Clarence Str.
Darwin
Rum Jungle
Adelaide River
Burrundie
Pine Creek
Katherine
Roper
Daly
Victoria
Birdum
Wyndham
L.Argyle
Victoria River Downs
Daly Waters
Borroloola
Wessel Is
C. Arnhem
Nhulunbuy
Groote
Eylandt
Limmen Bight
Sir Edward
Group

C.Londonderry
Joseph
Bonaparte
Gulf
Pago
Mission
C.Lévêque
King Sound
Mt Ord
936
Kimberley
Plateau
Qld
Wave Hill
Powell Creek
Newcastle Waters
Barkly Tableland
Burket
NORTHERN
Derby
Fitzroy Crossing
Hall's Creek
TERRITORY
Camoow
Mount
Da
Georgi

Broome
Fitzroy
Sturt Ck
Tennant Creek
Eighty Mile Beach
Lagrange
Great Sandy Desert
Barrow Creek

Port Hedland
De Grey
Shay Gap
Marble Bar
L. Mackay
Macdonnell Ranges
Mt Ziel
1510
Alice
Springs
Simpson
Desert

Monte Bello Is
Barrow I
Dampier
Roebourne
Nullagine
Fortescue
Hamersley Ra.
Wittenoom
Onslow
Mt.Bruce
1226
Ashburton
Paraburdoo
Newman
L.Disappointment
Gibson Desert
WESTERN
Petermann Ra.
Mt Aloysius
1058
Tomkinson
Ra.
Finke
Musgrave Ra.
Mt Woodroffe
1440
Lake Eyre
Oodnadatta
L.Eyre

North West C.
Barlee Ra.
L.McLeod
Mt. Augustus
1106
Lyons
Carnarvon
Gascoyne
Murchison
Shark B.
Dirk Hartog I.
AUSTRALIA
L.Carnegie
L.Wells
Great
Victoria
Desert
Coober Pedy
SOUTH
M

Wiluna
Meekatharra
Cue
Sandstone
Mt Magnet
Leonora
L.Barlee
AUSTRALIA
L.Everard
Penong
L.Gairdner
Tarcoola
Woomera
L.Torrens

Northampton
Mullewa
L.Moore
Kalgoorlie
Rawlinna
Forrest
Nullarbor Plain
Ooldea
Ceduna
Gawler Ranges
Iron Knobs
Po
Elizabeth
Wa
P

Houtman
Abrolhos
Geraldton
Dongara
Moora
Bencubbin
Bullfinch
Coolgardie
Eyre
Penong
Gawler Ranges
Iron Knobs

Goomalling
Bullfinch
Merredin
Southern
Cross
Norseman
Great Australian Bight
Flinders I.
Port Lincoln
Eyre
Pen.
Spencer Gulf
Perth
Fremantle
Northam
Corrigin
Pinjarra
Narrogin
Collie
Wagin
Bunbury
Katanning
C.Naturaliste
Busselton
Augusta
C. Leeuwin
Manjimup
Bluff Knoll
1110
C. Knob
Albany
Esperance
C. Pasley
Arch. of the
Recherche
Investigator Str.
Kangaroo I.

Mour

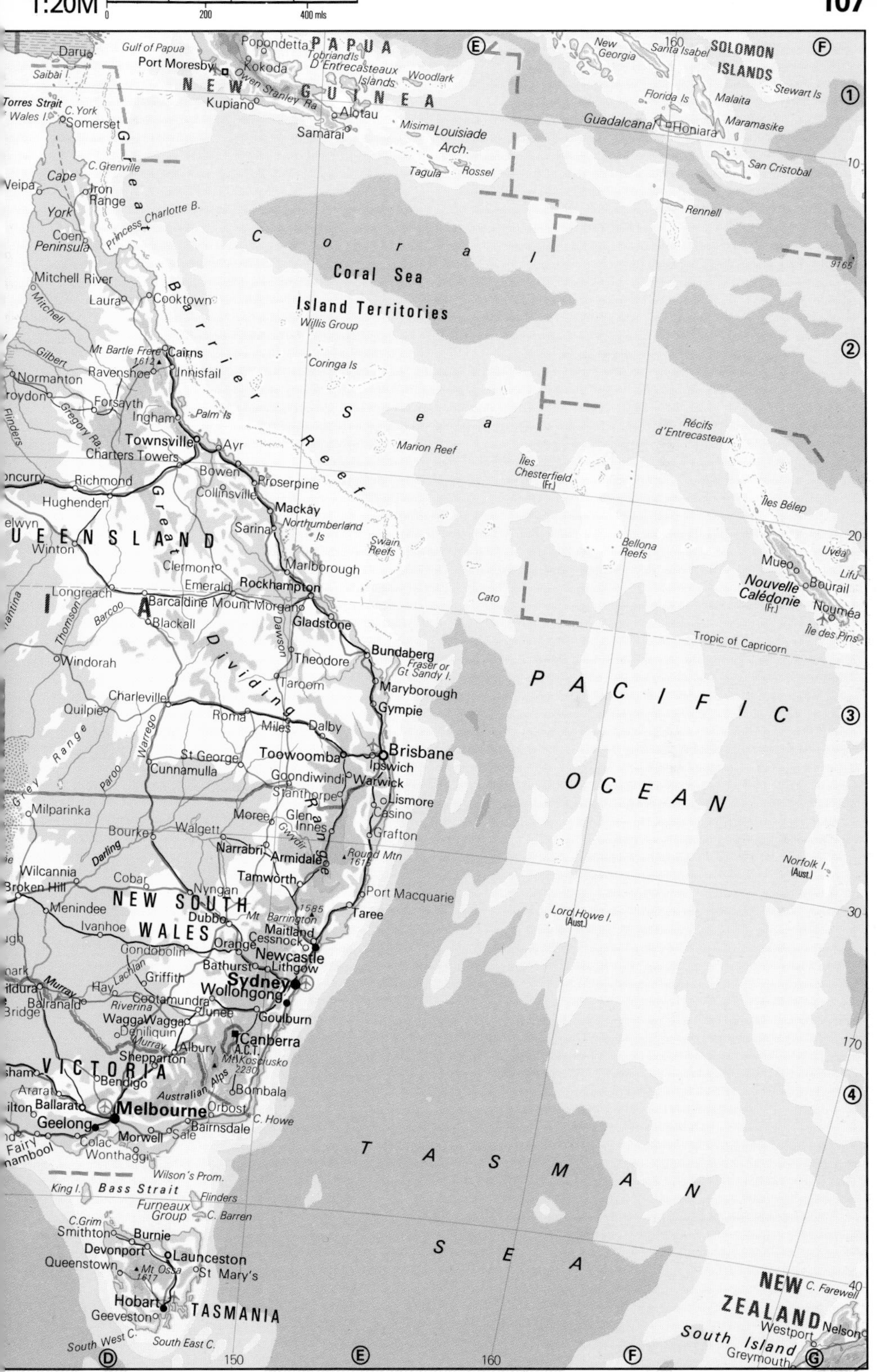

200 400 600 800 km
200 400 mls

PAPUA NEW GUINEA

Gulf of Papua
Popondetta
Port Moresby
Rokoda
Tobriand Is.
D'Entrecasteaux
Islands
Woodlark

SOLOMON ISLANDS

New Georgia
Santa Isabel
160
Florida Is
Malaita
Stewart Is
Maramasike

①

Daru
Saibai I.
Kupiano
Alotau

Torres Strait
Wales I.
C. York
Somerset

Open Stanley Ra.
Samarai
Misima
Louisiade
Arch.
Tagula
Rossel

Guadalcanal
Honiara
San Cristobal

10

Veipa
Cape
York
Iron
Range
C. Grenville

Coen
Peninsula
Princess Charlotte B.

Rennell

9165

Mitchell River
Laura
Cooktown

**Coral Sea
Island Territories**
Willis Group

②

Normanton
roydon
Mt Bartle Frere
1612
Cairns
Ravenshoe
Innisfail

Coringa Is

Récifs
d'Entrecasteaux

Îles Bélep

Gilbert
Mitchell
Forsayth
Ingham
Palm Is

S e a

oncurry
Richmond
Townsville
Charters Towers
Ayr
Bowen
Proserpine
Collinsville

Marion Reef

Îles
Chesterfield
(Fr.)

Bellona
Reefs

Uvéa
Muéo
Lifu
Bourail
Nouvelle
Calédonie
(Fr.)
Nouméa
Île des Pins

20

Hughenden

QUEENSLAND
Winton

Mackay
Northumberland
Is
Sarina
Marlborough

Swain
Reefs

elwyn
Longreach
Clermont
Emerald
Rockhampton
Barcaldine
Mount Morgan
Blackall
Gladstone

Cato

Tropic of Capricorn

PACIFIC

③

Windorah
Charleville
Quilpie
Theodore
Taroom
Bundaberg
Fraser or
Gt Sandy I.
Maryborough
Gympie

OCEAN

Roma
Miles
Dalby
Toowoomba
St George
Cunnamulla
Goondiwindi
Stanthorpe
Brisbane
Ipswich
Warwick

Milparinka
Bourke
Walgett
Moree
Glen
Innes
Lismore
Casino
Grafton

Norfolk I.
(Aust.)

30

Wilcannia
Cobar
Nyngan
Narrabri
Armidale
Round Mtn
1615
Tamworth

Port Macquarie

Lord Howe I.
(Aust.)

Broken Hill
Menindee
Ivanhoe
Dubbo
Mt Barrington
1585
Taree

170

**NEW SOUTH
WALES**

Gondobolin
Orange
Lithgow
Maitland
Cessnock
Newcastle

VICTORIA

Sydney
Wollongong
Goulburn

Canberra
A.C.T.

④

Melbourne

TASMAN

Hobart
TASMANIA

SEA

**NEW
ZEALAND**
C. Farewell
Westport
Nelson
South Island
Greymouth

40

150
⑤
160
⑥
⑦

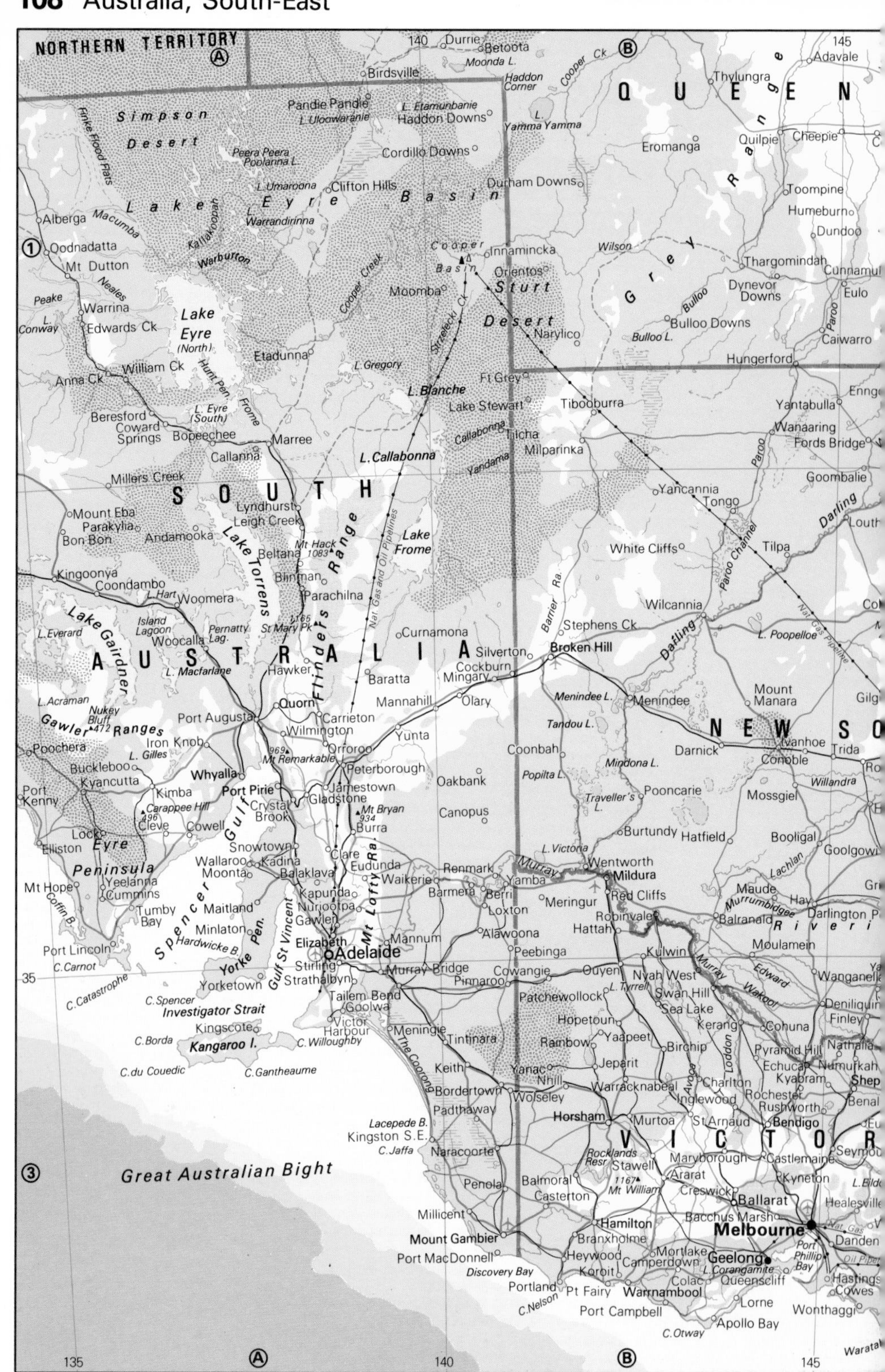

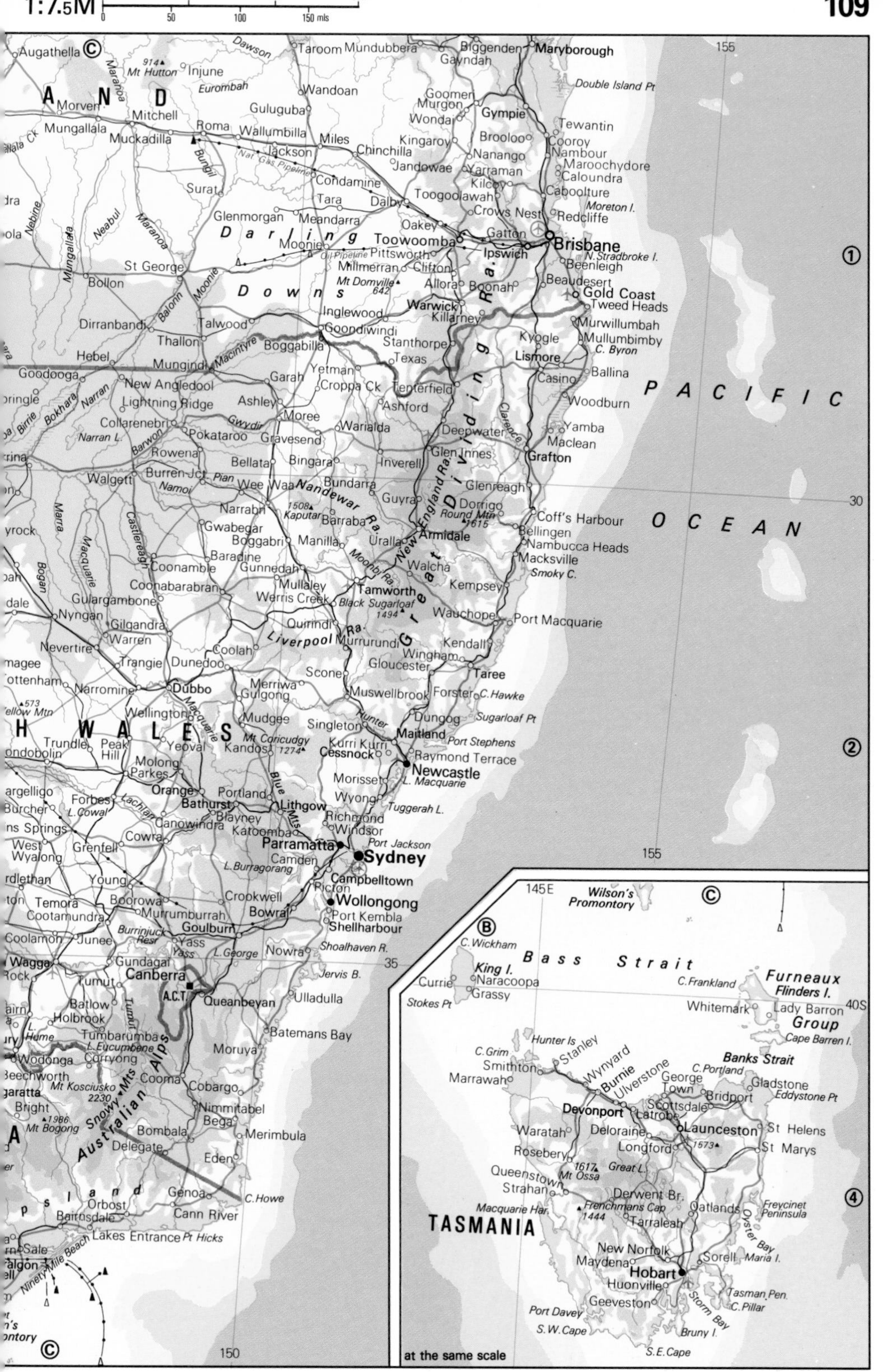

100 200 300 km
50 100 150 mls

Augathella C
914 ▲ Mt Hutton Injune
Dawson
Taroom Mundubbera
Biggenden **Maryborough**
Gayndah
Double Island Pt

A N D
Morven Mitchell
Eurombah
Wandoan
Goomeri
Murgon **Gympie**
Wondai Brooloo
Tewantin
Cooroy
155

Mungallala
Muckadilla Roma Wallumbilla
Nat Gas Pipeline Miles Chinchilla
Kingaroy Nanango
Jandowae Yarraman
Kilcoy
Nambour
Maroochydore
Caloundra

Jackson
Condamine
Surat Tara Dalby
Toogoolawah
Caboolture
Moreton I.
Redcliffe

Glenmorgan Meandarra
Oakey Crows Nest
Gatton
N. Stradbroke I.
①

Darling
Toowoomba
Moonie Pittsworth **Ipswich**
Brisbane
Beenleigh

St George
Clifton
Millmerran
Mt Domville 642 ▲ Allora
Beaudesert
Gold Coast

Bollon
Downs
Talwood **Warwick** Inglewood
Killarney
Tweed Heads
Murwillumbah

Dirranbandi
Thallon
Goondiwindi
Stanthorpe
Kyogle
Mullumbimby
C. Byron

Hebel Mungindi Boggabilla
Garah Yetman
Texas Tenterfield
Lismore Ballina
Casino

Goodooga
New Angledool
Ashley Croppa Ck
Deepwater
Woodburn
P A C I F I C

Lightning Ridge
Pokataroo Moree Warialda
Glen Innes
Yamba
Maclean

Collarenebri
Narran L.
Gwydir
Bellata Bingara
Glencreagh
Grafton

Rowena
Wee Waa Nandewar
Bundarra
Guyra
Dorrigo
30

Walgett Burren Jct. Pian
Narrabri
1508 ▲ Kaputar
Barraba
Round Mtn
1615 ▲
Coff's Harbour
O C E A N

Namoi
Gwabegar
Boggabri Manilla
Uralla **Armidale**
Bellingen
Nambucca Heads

Baradine
Gunnedah
Walcha
Macksville
Smoky C.

Coonamble
Mullaley
Werris Creek Black Sugarloaf 1494 ▲
Tamworth
Kempsey

Coonabarabran
Quirindi
Wauchope
Port Macquarie

Nyngan Gilgandra
Coolah
Murrurundi
Kendall

Warren
Liverpool Ra.
Scone
Wingham

H W A L E S
Trangie Dunedoo
Merriwa
Gloucester
Taree

Narromine **Dubbo**
Gulgong Muswellbrook
Forster
C. Hawke

Wellington
Mudgee
Singleton
Dungog
Sugarloaf Pt

Mt Canobolas 1274 ▲
Kandos
Maitland Port Stephens

Molong
Yeoval
Kurri Kurri
Cessnock
Raymond Terrace

Parkes **Orange**
Portland
Newcastle
②

Forbes Bathurst
Lithgow
L. Macquarie

Grenfell Canowindra
Blayney Katoomba
Morisset Wyong
Tuggerah L.

Cowra
Windsor
Richmond
Port Jackson

Young
Parramatta
Camden
● **Sydney**
155

Boorowa
Cootamundra Murrumburrah
Picton
Campbelltown
● **Wollongong**

Junee
Burrinjuck Res.
Goulburn
Port Kembla
Shellharbour

Coolamon
Yass
L. George
Nowra
Shoalhaven R.
35

Wagga
Gundagai
Canberra
Jervis B.

Tumut
A.C.T
Queanbeyan
Ulladulla

Batlow Holbrook
Tumbarumba
Home
Batemans Bay

Corryong
L. Eucumbene
Cooma Cobargo
Moruya

Beechworth
Mt Kosciusko 2230 ▲
Nimmitabel
Bega Merimbula

Bright
1986 ▲ Mt Bogong
Australian Alps
Bombala
Delegate
Eden

A
Snowy Mts
Genoa
C. Howe

I s l a n d
Orbost
Cann River

Bairnsdale
Lakes Entrance
Pt Hicks

Sale
Ninety Mile Beach
C

150

145E Wilson's Promontory C

B
C. Wickham
B a s s   S t r a i t
C. Frankland

King I. Naracoopa
Furneaux
Flinders I.

Currie
Grassy
Whitemark Lady Barron
40S

Stokes Pt
Cape Barren I.
Group

C. Grim
Hunter Is Stanley
Banks Strait

Smithton
Wynyard
George Town
C. Portland
Gladstone

Marrawah
Burnie
Ulverstone
Scottsdale
Eddystone Pt

Waratah
Devonport Latrobe
Launceston
St Helens

Deloraine
Longford
1573 ▲
St Marys

Rosebery
Great L.

Queenstown 1617 ▲ Mt Ossa
Derwent Br.
Oatlands
Freycinet

Strahan
Frenchmans Cap 1444 ▲
Tarraleah
Peninsula

Macquarie Har.
Oyster Bay
④

TASMANIA
New Norfolk
Sorell
Maria I.

Maydena
Hobart
Tasman Pen.

Huonville
Geeveston
C. Pillar

Port Davey
Bruny I.
S.W. Cape
Storm Bay

at the same scale
S.E. Cape

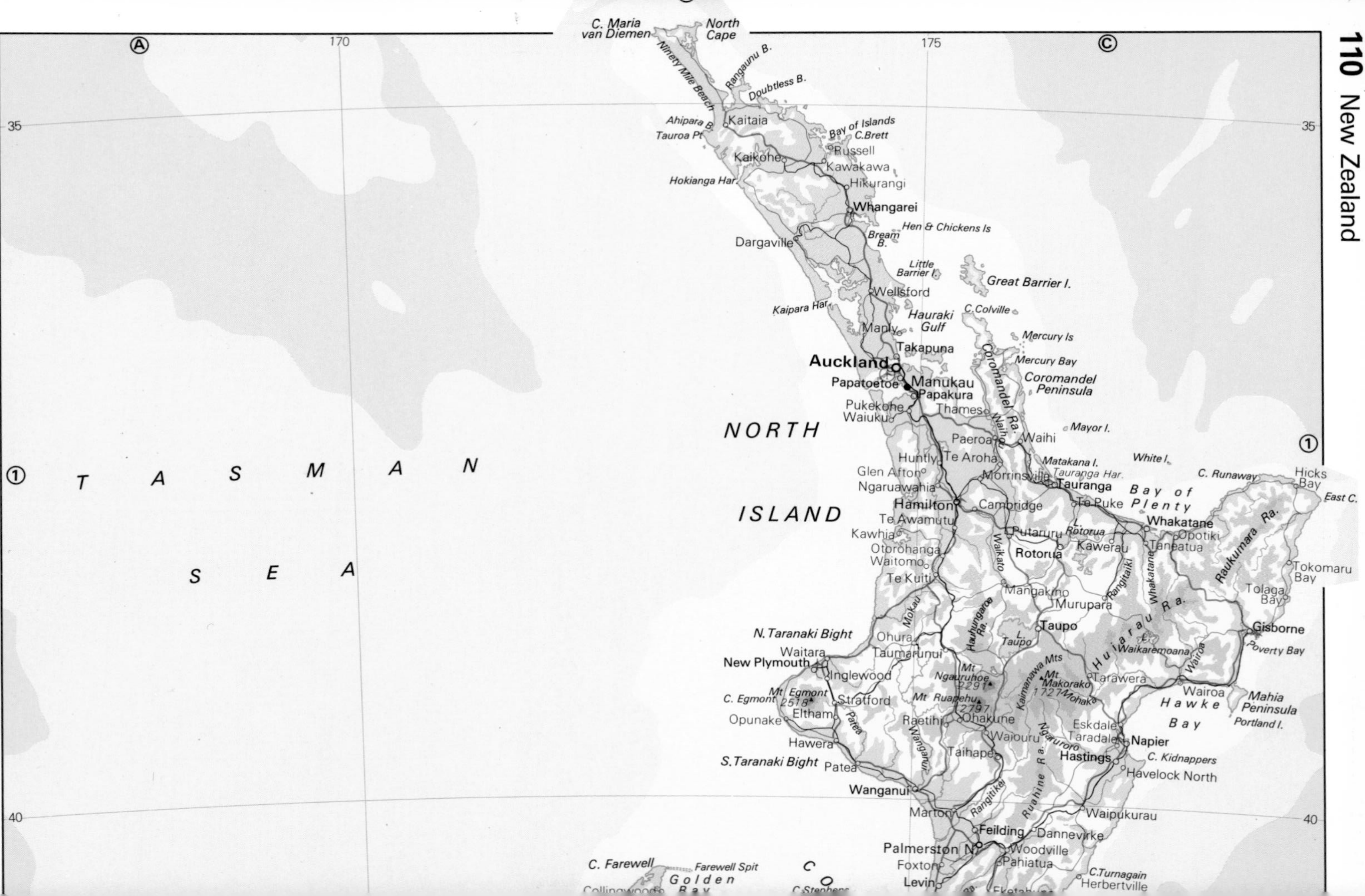
TASMAN SEA
NORTH ISLAND
C. Maria van Diemen
North Cape
Ninety Mile Beach
Rangaunu B.
Doubtless B.
Kaitaia
Ahipara B.
Tauroa Pt
Kaikohe
Hokianga Har.
Bay of Islands
C.Brett
Russell
Kawakawa
Hikurangi
Whangarei
Bream B.
Hen & Chickens Is
Dargaville
Kaipara Har.
Wellsford
Little Barrier I.
Great Barrier I.
Hauraki Gulf
Manly
Takapuna
Auckland
Manukau
Papatoetoe
Papakura
Pukekohe
Waiuku
C. Colville
Coromandel Ra.
Coromandel Peninsula
Mercury Is
Mercury Bay
Thames
Paeroa
Waihi
Mayor I.
Te Aroha
Huntly
Glen Afton
Ngaruawahia
Hamilton
Te Awamutu
Cambridge
Morrinsville
Matakana I.
Tauranga Har.
Tauranga
Te Puke
Bay of Plenty
White I.
Whakatane
Opotiki
Taneatua
C. Runaway
Raukumara Ra.
Hicks Bay
East C.
Tokomaru Bay
Tolaga Bay
Gisborne
Poverty Bay
Mahia Peninsula
Portland I.
Wairoa
Hawke Bay
C. Kidnappers
Napier
Hastings
Havelock North
Taradale
Eskdale
Tarawera
Waipukurau
Dannevirke
Woodville
Pahiatua
C.Turnagain
Herbertville
Rotorua
L. Rotorua
Kawerau
Putaruru
Murupara
Mangakino
Taupo
L. Taupo
Waikato
Rangitaiki
Whakatane
Waikaremoana
Huiarau Ra.
Kaimanawa Mts
Mt. Makorako 1727
Mohaka
Ngaruroro
Ruahine Ra.
Rangitikei
Hauhungaroa Ra.
Mokau
Te Kuiti
Otorohanga
Waitomo
Kawhia
Ohura
Taumarunui
Mt Ngauruhoe 2291
Mt Ruapehu 2797
Ohakune
Raetihi
Waiouru
Taihape
Wanganui
Marton
Feilding
Palmerston N.
Foxton
Levin
N. Taranaki Bight
Waitara
New Plymouth
Inglewood
Stratford
Mt Egmont 2518
C. Egmont
Eltham
Opunake
Hawera
Patea
S. Taranaki Bight
C. Farewell
Farewell Spit
Golden Bay
A
C
1
35
170
175
40

1:5M

0 50 100 150 200 km
0 50 100 mls

② ③

P A C I F I C   O C E A N

45

175

ⓒ

ⓑ

ⓐ

170

45

SOUTH

ISLAND

S   O   U   T   H   E   R   N   A   L   P   S

Wellington
Lower Hutt
Martinborough
Mt. Ross 963
C. Palliser
Palliser Bay
C. Campbell
Blenheim
Wairau
Mt. Tapuaenuku 2885
Kaikoura Ra.
Kaikoura
Kaikoura Pen.
Richmond
Richmond Ra.
Wairau
Mt. Rintoul
Nelson
1828
Motueka
Mt. Owen
L. Rotoiti
L. Rotoroa
Murchison
Spenser Mts.
Mt. Travers 2338
Lewis Pass
Hanmer Springs
Cheviot
Waiau
Waipara
Culverden
Hurunui
Victoria Ra.
Seddonville
Karamea Bight
Westport
C. Foulwind
Buller
Brunner
L. Sumner
Arthurs Pass
Waimakariri
Rangiora
Pegasus Bay
Banks Peninsula
Lyttelton
Christchurch
Akaroa
Kaiapoi
Reefton
Runanga
Greymouth
Grey
Hokitika
Ross
Abut Hd
Franz Josef Gd
Mt. Cook 3764
Mt. Sefton 3157
L. Coleridge
Rakaia
Ashburton
Methven
Rangitata
Geraldine
L. Tekapo
L. Pukaki
Fairlie
Mt. Tasman
The Hermitage
Temuka
Timaru
Waimate
Canterbury Bight
Lincoln
L. Ellesmere
Banks Peninsula
Waitaki
Kurow
L. Benmore
L. Aviemore
Omarama
Oamaru
Hampden
Palmerston
Waikouaiti
Port Chalmers
Otago Peninsula
Dunedin
Mosgiel
Taieri
Ranfurly
Hawkdun Ra.
Jackson Hd
Cascade Pt
Awarua Pt
Mt. Aspiring 3027
Young Ra.
Haast
Paringa
2194
Wanaka
L. Wanaka
L. Hawea
Cromwell
Clyde
Alexandra
Roxburgh
Heriot
Clutha
Balclutha
Kaitangata
Milton
Lawrence
Milford Sd
George Sd
Mt. Pyramid 2326
Homer Tunnel
Te Anau
L. Te Anau
Queenstown
Arrowtown
Wakatipu
Kingston
Lumsden
Riversdale
Gore
Mataura
Owaka
Secretary I.
Doubtful Sd
Caswell Sd
Manapouri
L. Manapouri
Mt. Ward 2118
Fiordland Nat. Park
Cameron Mts
Breaksea Sd
Resolution I.
Dusky Sd
Puysegur Pt
Solander I.
Te Waewae Bay
Tuatapere
Ohai
Otautau
Winton
Wallacetown
Riverton
Invercargill
Bluff
Foveaux Strait
Oreti
Codfish I.
Oban
Mt. Allen 730
Stewart Island
Paterson Inlet
Shelter Pt
Port Pegasus

1:40M

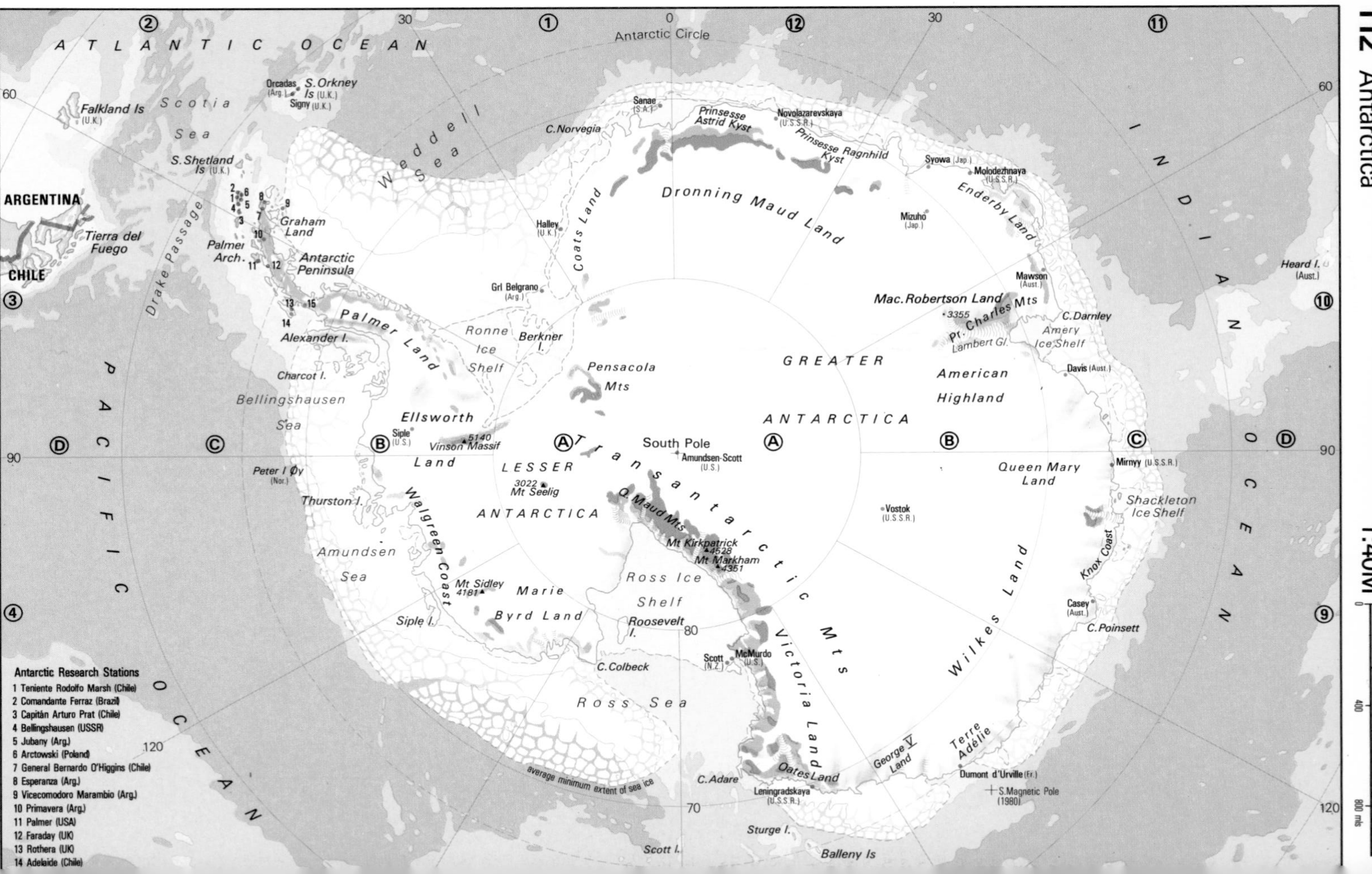
0 400 800 1200 1600
0 400 800 mls
INDIAN OCEAN
ATLANTIC OCEAN
PACIFIC OCEAN
Heard I. (Aust.)
Shackleton Ice Shelf
Mirnyy (U.S.S.R.)
C. Poinsett
Knox Coast
Casey (Aust.)
Davis (Aust.)
C. Darnley
Amery Ice Shelf
Mawson (Aust.)
Enderby Land
Molodezhnaya (U.S.S.R.)
Syowa (Jap.)
Mizuho (Jap.)
Mac. Robertson Land
3355
Prince Charles Mts
Lambert Gl.
American Highland
Queen Mary Land
Wilkes Land
Terre Adélie
Dumont d'Urville (Fr.)
S. Magnetic Pole (1980)
Vostok (U.S.S.R.)
George V Land
Balleny Is
GREATER ANTARCTICA
Prinsesse Ragnhild Kyst
Novolazarevskaya (U.S.S.R.)
Prinsesse Astrid Kyst
Dronning Maud Land
Transantarctic Mts
Victoria Land
Oates Land
Leningradskaya (U.S.S.R.)
Sturge I.
McMurdo (U.S.)
Mt Kirkpatrick 4528
Mt Markham 4351
South Pole
Amundsen-Scott (U.S.)
Scott (N.Z.)
C. Adare
Antarctic Circle
Sanae (S.Af.)
Q. Maud Mts
Ross Ice Shelf
Roosevelt I.
Scott I.
Pensacola Mts
Coats Land
C. Norvegia
Halley (U.K.)
Grl Belgrano (Arg.)
Berkner I.
LESSER ANTARCTICA
3022 Mt Seelig
C. Colbeck
Ross Sea
average minimum extent of sea ice
Weddell Sea
Ronne Ice Shelf
5140 Vinson Massif
Ellsworth Land
Marie Byrd Land
Mt Sidley 4181
Walgreen Coast
Siple I.
Siple (U.S.)
Palmer Land
Amundsen Sea
Thurston I.
S. Orkney Is (U.K.)
Orcadas (Arg.)
Signy (U.K.)
Graham Land
Antarctic Peninsula
Alexander I.
Charcot I.
Bellingshausen Sea
Peter I Øy (Nor.)
S. Shetland Is (U.K.)
Palmer Arch.
Scotia Sea
Drake Passage
Falkland Is (U.K.)
Tierra del Fuego
ARGENTINA
CHILE
Antarctic Research Stations
1 Teniente Rodolfo Marsh (Chile)
2 Comandante Ferraz (Brazil)
3 Capitán Arturo Prat (Chile)
4 Bellingshausen (USSR)
5 Jubany (Arg.)
6 Arctowski (Poland)
7 General Bernardo O'Higgins (Chile)
8 Esperanza (Arg.)
9 Vicecomodoro Marambio (Arg.)
10 Primavera (Arg.)
11 Palmer (USA)
12 Faraday (UK)
13 Rothera (UK)
14 Adelaide (Chile)

Index

In the index, the first number refers to the page, and the following letter and number to the section of the map in which the index entry can be found. For example, 48C2 **Paris** means that Paris can be found on page 48 where column C and row 2 meet.

Abbreviations used in the index

fghan	Afghanistan	Germ	Germany	Phil	Philippines	Arch	Archipelago
lb	Albania	Hung	Hungary	Pol	Poland	B	Bay
lg	Algeria	Ind	Indonesia	Port	Portugal	C	Cape
nt	Antarctica	Irish Rep	Ireland	Rom	Romania	Chan	Channel
rg	Argentina	Leb	Lebanon	S Arabia	Saudi Arabia	Gl	Glacier
ust	Australia	Lib	Liberia	Scot	Scotland	I(s)	Island(s)
ang	Bangladesh	Liech	Liechtenstein	Sen	Senegal	Lg	Lagoon
elg	Belgium	Lux	Luxembourg	S Africa	South Africa	L	Lake
ol	Bolivia	Madag	Madagascar	Switz	Switzerland	Mt(s)	Mountain(s)
ulg	Bulgaria	Malay	Malaysia	Tanz	Tanzania	O	Ocean
urk	Burkina	Maur	Mauritania	Thai	Thailand	P	Pass
amb	Cambodia	Mor	Morocco	Turk	Turkey	Pen	Peninsula
an	Canada	Mozam	Mozambique		Union of	Plat	Plateau
AR	Central African Republic	Neth	Netherlands		Soviet Socialist	Pt	Point
zech	Czechoslovakia	NZ	New Zealand	USSR	Republics	Res	Reservoir
en	Denmark	Nic	Nicaragaua		United States	R	River
om Rep	Dominican Republic	N Ire	Northern Ireland	USA	of America	S	Sea
Sal	El Salvador	Nig	Nigeria	Urug	Uruguay	Sd	Sound
ng	England	Nor	Norway	Ven	Venezuela	Str	Strait
q Guinea	Equatorial Guinea	Pak	Pakistan	Viet	Vietnam	V	Valley
th	Ethiopia	PNG	Papua New Guinea	Yugos	Yugoslavia		
in	Finland	Par	Paraguay	Zim	Zimbabwe		

96C2 **Adrar** *Mts* Alg
96A2 **Adrar Soutouf** Region, Mor
98C1 **Adré** Chad
95A2 **Adri** Libya
47E2 **Adria** Italy
14B2 **Adrian** Michigan, USA
52B2 **Adriatic S** Italy/Yugos
99D1 **Aduwa** Eth
97B4 **Adzopé** Ivory Coast
55B3 **Aegean** *S* Greece
80E2 **Afghanistan** Republic, Asia
99E2 **Afgooye** Somalia
97C4 **Afikpo** Nig
38G6 **Åfjord** Nor
96C1 **Aflou** Alg
99E2 **Afmadu** Somalia
97A3 **Afollé** Region, Maur
94B2 **Afula** Israel
92B2 **Afyon** Turk
95A3 **Agadem** Niger
97C3 **Agadez** Niger
96B1 **Agadir** Mor
85D4 **Agar** India
86C2 **Agartala** India
20B1 **Agassiz** Can
97B4 **Agboville** Ivory Coast
93E1 **Agdam** USSR
75B1 **Agematsu** Japan
48C3 **Agen** France
90A3 **Agha Jārī** Iran
96A2 **Aghwinit** *Well* Mor
47D2 **Agno** *R* Italy
47E1 **Agordo** Italy
48C3 **Agout** *R* France
85D3 **Āgra** India
93D2 **Ağri** Turk
53C2 **Agri** *R* Italy
53B3 **Agrigento** Italy
55B3 **Agrínion** Greece
34A3 **Agrio** *R* Chile
53B2 **Agropoli** Italy
61H2 **Agryz** USSR
6E3 **Agto** Greenland
27D3 **Aguadilla** Puerto Rico
24B1 **Agua Prieta** Mexico
24B2 **Aguascalientes** Mexico
23A1 **Aguascalientes** State, Mexico
35C1 **Aguas Formosas** Brazil
50A1 **Agueda** Port
96C3 **Aguelhok** Mali
50B2 **Aguilas** Spain
23A2 **Aguililla** Mexico
100B4 **Agulhas,C** S Africa
79C4 **Agusan** *R* Phil
Ahaggar = Hoggar
93E2 **Ahar** Iran
110B1 **Ahipara B** NZ
85C4 **Ahmadābād** India
87A1 **Ahmadnagar** India
99E2 **Ahmar** *Mts* Eth
46D1 **Ahr** *R* Germany
46D1 **Ahrgebirge** Region, Germany
23A1 **Ahuacatlán** Mexico
23A1 **Ahualulco** Mexico
39G7 **Åhus** Sweden
90B2 **Āhuvān** Iran
90A3 **Ahvāz** Iran
26A4 **Aiajuela** Costa Rica
47B1 **Aigle** Switz
47B2 **Aiguille d'Arves** *Mt* France
47B2 **Aiguille de la Grand Sassière** *Mt* France
75B1 **Aikawa** Japan
17B1 **Aiken** USA
73A5 **Ailao Shan** *Upland* China
35C1 **Aimorés** Brazil
96B1 **Ain Beni Mathar** Mor
95B2 **Ain Dalla** *Well* Egypt
51C2 **Aïn el Hadjel** Alg
95A3 **Aïn Galakka** Chad
96B1 **Aïn Sefra** Alg
92B4 **'Ain Sukhna** Egypt
75A2 **Aioi** Japan
96B2 **Aioun Abd el Malek** *Well* Maur
97B3 **Aïoun El Atrouss** Maur
30C2 **Aiquile** Bol
97C3 **Aïr** *Desert Region* Niger
13E2 **Airdrie** Can
46B1 **Aire** France
42D3 **Aire** *R* Eng
46C2 **Aire** *R* France
6C3 **Airforce I** Can
47C1 **Airolo** Switz
4E3 **Aishihik** Can
12G2 **Aishihik L** Can
46B2 **Aisne** Department, France
49C2 **Aisne** *R* France
71F4 **Aitape** PNG
58D1 **Aiviekste** *R* USSR
72B2 **Aixa Zuogi** China
49D3 **Aix-en-Provence** France
47A2 **Aix-les-Bains** France
86B2 **Aiyar Res** India
55B3 **Aíyion** Greece
55B3 **Aíyna** *I* Greece
86C2 **Āīzawl** India
100A3 **Aizeb** *R* Namibia
74E3 **Aizu-Wakamatsu** Japan
52A2 **Ajaccio** Corse
23B2 **Ajalpan** Mexico
95B1 **Ajdabiyah** Libya
74E2 **Ajigasawa** Japan
94B2 **Ajlūn** Jordan
91C4 **Ajman** UAE
85C3 **Ajmer** India
9B3 **Ajo** USA
23A2 **Ajuchitan** Mexico
55C3 **Ak** *R* Turk
75B1 **Akaishi-sanchi** *Mts* Japan
87B1 **Akalkot** India
111B2 **Akaroa** NZ
75A2 **Akashi** Japan
61J3 **Akbulak** USSR
93C2 **Akçakale** Turk
96A2 **Akchar** *Watercourse* Maur
55C3 **Akdağ** *Mt* Turk
98C2 **Aketi** Zaïre
93D1 **Akhalkalaki** USSR
93D1 **Akhalsikhe** USSR
55B3 **Akharnái** Greece
12D3 **Akhiok** USA
92A2 **Akhisar** Turk
58D1 **Akhiste** USSR
95C2 **Akhmîm** Egypt
61G4 **Akhtubinsk** USSR
60D4 **Akhtyrka** USSR
75A2 **Aki** Japan
7B4 **Akimiski I** Can
74E3 **Akita** Japan
96A3 **Akjoujt** Maur
94B2 **'Akko** Israel
4E3 **Aklavik** USA
97B3 **Aklé Aouana** *Desert Region* Maur
99D2 **Akobo** Sudan
99D2 **Akobo** *R* Sudan
84B1 **Akoha** Afghan
85D4 **Akola** India
85D4 **Akot** India
6D3 **Akpatok I** Can
55B3 **Ákra Kafirévs** *C* Greece
55B3 **Ákra Maléa** *C* Greece
38A2 **Akranes** Iceland
55C3 **Ákra Sídheros** *C* Greece
55B3 **Ákra Spátha** *C* Greece
55B3 **Ákra Taínaron** *C* Greece
10B2 **Akron** USA
94A1 **Akrotiri B** Cyprus
84D1 **Aksai Chin** *Mts* China
92B2 **Aksaray** Turk
61H3 **Aksay** USSR
84D1 **Aksayquin Hu** *L* China
92B2 **Akşehir** Turk
92B2 **Akseki** Turk
63D2 **Aksenovo Zilovskoye** USSR
68D1 **Aksha** USSR
82C1 **Aksu** China
65J5 **Aktogay** USSR
61J4 **Aktumsyk** USSR
65G4 **Aktyubinsk** USSR
38B1 **Akureyri** Iceland
65K5 **Akzhal** USSR
11B3 **Alabama** State, USA
11B3 **Alabama** *R* USA
17A1 **Alabaster** USA
92C2 **Ala Dağlari** *Mts* Tur
61F5 **Alagir** USSR
47B2 **Alagna** Italy
31D3 **Alagoas** State, Brazil
31D4 **Alagoinhas** Brazil
51B1 **Alagón** Spain
93E4 **Al Ahmadi** Kuwait
25D3 **Alajuela** Costa Rica
12B2 **Alakanuk** USA
38L5 **Alakurtti** USSR
93E3 **Al Amārah** Iraq
21A2 **Alameda** USA
23B1 **Alamo** Mexico
9C3 **Alamogordo** USA
9C3 **Alamosa** USA
39H6 **Åland** *I* Fin
92B2 **Alanya** Turk
17B1 **Alapaha** *R* USA
65H4 **Alapayevsk** USSR
92A2 **Alaşehir** Turk
68C3 **Ala Shan** *Mts* China
4C3 **Alaska** State, USA
4D4 **Alaska,G of** USA
12C3 **Alaska Pen** USA
4C3 **Alaska Range** *Mts* USA
52A2 **Alassio** Italy
12D1 **Alatna** *R* USA
61G3 **Alatyr** USSR
108B2 **Alawoona** Aust
91C5 **Al'Ayn** UAE
82B2 **Alayskiy Khrebet** *Mts* USSR
49D3 **Alba** Italy
92C2 **Al Bāb** Syria
51B2 **Albacete** Spain
50A1 **Alba de Tormes** Spain
93D2 **Al Badi** Iraq
54B1 **Alba Iulia** Rom
54A2 **Albania** Republic, Europe
106A4 **Albany** Aust
17B1 **Albany** Georgia, USA
15D2 **Albany** New York, USA
8A2 **Albany** Oregon, USA
7B4 **Albany** *R* Can
34B2 **Albardón** Arg
91C5 **Al Batinah** Region, Oman
71F5 **Albatross B** Aust
95B1 **Al Baydā** Libya
11C3 **Albemarle Sd** USA
50B1 **Alberche** *R* Spain
108A1 **Alberga** Aust
46B1 **Albert** France
5G4 **Alberta** Province, Can
99D2 **Albert,L** Uganda/Zaïre
10A2 **Albert Lea** USA
99D2 **Albert Nile** *R* Uganda
49D2 **Albertville** France
48C3 **Albi** France
18B1 **Albia** USA
33G2 **Albina** Suriname
14B2 **Albion** Michigan, USA
15C2 **Albion** New York, USA
92C4 **Al Bi'r** S Arabia
91A5 **Al Biyadh** Region, S Arabia
50B2 **Alborán** *I* Spain
39G7 **Ålborg** Den
95A1 **Al Brayqah** Libya
93D3 **Al Bū Kamāl** Syria
47C1 **Albula** *R* Switz
9C3 **Albuquerque** USA
91C5 **Al Buraymi** Oman
95B1 **Al Burdī** Libya
107D4 **Albury** Aust
93E3 **Al Buşayyah** Iraq
50B1 **Alcalá de Henares** Spain
53B3 **Alcamo** Italy
51B1 **Alcaniz** Spain
31C2 **Alcântara** Brazil
50B2 **Alcaraz** Spain
50B2 **Alcázar de San Juan** Spain
51B2 **Alcira** Spain
35D1 **Alcobaça** Brazil
50B1 **Alcolea de Pinar** Spain
51B2 **Alcoy** Spain
51C2 **Alcudia** Spain
89J8 **Aldabra** *Is* Indian O
63E2 **Aldan** USSR
63E2 **Aldanskoye Nagor'ye** *Upland* USSR
43E3 **Aldeburgh** Eng
48B2 **Alderney** *I* UK
43D4 **Aldershot** Eng
97A3 **Aleg** Maur
30E4 **Alegrete** Brazil
34C2 **Alejandro Roca** Arg
30H6 **Alejandro Selkirk** *I* Chile
63G2 **Aleksandrovsk Sakhalinskiy** USSR
65J4 **Alekseyevka** USSR
60E3 **Aleksin** USSR
58B1 **Älem** Sweden
35C2 **Além Paraíba** Brazil
49C2 **Alençon** France
21C4 **Alenuihaha Chan** Hawaiian Is
Aleppo = Ḩalab
6D1 **Alert** Can
49C3 **Alès** France
52A2 **Alessandria** Italy
64B3 **Ålesund** Nor
12C3 **Aleutian Range** *Mts* USA
4E4 **Alexander Arch** USA
100A3 **Alexander Bay** S Africa
17A1 **Alexander City** USA
112C3 **Alexander I** Ant
111A3 **Alexandra** NZ
29G8 **Alexandra,C** South Georgia
6C2 **Alexandra Fjord** Can
95B1 **Alexandria** Egypt
11A3 **Alexandria** Louisiana, USA
10A2 **Alexandria** Minnesota, USA
10C3 **Alexandria** Virginia, USA
55C2 **Alexandroúpolis** Greece
13C2 **Alexis Creek** Can
94B2 **Aley** Leb
65K4 **Aleysk** USSR
93D3 **Al Fallūjah** Iraq
51B1 **Alfaro** Spain
54C2 **Alfatar** Bulg
93E3 **Al Fāw** Iraq
35B2 **Alfensas** Brazil
55B3 **Alfiós** *R* Greece
47D2 **Alfonsine** Italy
35C2 **Alfonzo Cláudio** Brazil
35C2 **Alfredo Chaves** Brazil
61J4 **Alga** USSR
34B3 **Algarrobo del Águila** Arg
50A2 **Algeciras** Spain
96C1 **Alger** Alg
96B2 **Algeria** Republic, Africa
53A2 **Alghero** Sardegna

Algiers = Alger
15C1 **Algonquin Park** Can
91C5 **Al Hadd** Oman
93D3 **Al Hadithah** Iraq
92C3 **Al Hadithah** S Arabia
93D2 **Al Haḍr** Iraq
91C5 **Al Hajar al Gharbī** *Mts* Oman
91C5 **Al Hajar ash Sharqī** *Mts* Oman
93C3 **Al Hamad** *Desert Region* Jordan/ S Arabia
93E4 **Al Haniyah** *Desert Region* Iraq
91A5 **Al Hariq** S Arabia
93C3 **Al Harrah** *Desert Region* S Arabia
95A2 **Al Harūj al Aswad** *Upland* Libya
91A4 **Al Hasa** *Region,* S Arabia
93D2 **Al Hasakah** Syria
93C4 **Al Hawja'** S Arabia
93E3 **Al Hayy** Iraq
94C2 **Al Hijānah** Syria
93D3 **Al Hillah** Iraq
91A5 **Al Hillah** S Arabia
96B1 **Al Hoceima** Mor
91A4 **Al Hufūf** S Arabia
91B5 **Al Humrah** *Region,* UAE
91C5 **Al Huwatsah** Oman
90A2 **Alīābad** Iran
91C4 **Aliabad** Iran
55B2 **Aliákmon** *R* Greece
93E3 **Alī al Gharbī** Iraq
87A1 **Alībāg** India
51B2 **Alicante** Spain
9D4 **Alice** USA
106C3 **Alice Springs** Aust
53B3 **Alicudi** *I* Italy
84D3 **Aligarh** India
90A3 **Aligūdarz** Iran
84B2 **Ali-Khel** Afghan
55C2 **Alimniá** *I* Greece
86B1 **Alīpur Duār** India
14B2 **Aliquippa** USA
22B2 **Alisal** USA
93C3 **Al' Īsawiyah** S Arabia
100B4 **Aliwal North** S Africa
95B2 **Al Jaghbūb** Libya
93D3 **Al Jālamīd** S Arabia
95B2 **Al Jawf** Libya
93C4 **Al Jawf** S Arabia
93D2 **Al Jazīrah** *Desert Region* Syria/Iraq
50A2 **Aljezur** Port
91A4 **Al Jubayl** S Arabia
91C5 **Al Kāmil** Oman
93D2 **Al Khābūr** *R* Syria
91C5 **Al Khābūrah** Oman
93D3 **Al Khālis** Iraq
91C4 **Al Khasab** Oman
91B4 **Al Khawr** Qatar
95A1 **Al Khums** Libya
91B5 **Al Kidan** *Region,* S Arabia
94C2 **Al Kiswah** Syria
56A2 **Alkmaar** Neth
95B2 **Al Kufrah Oasis** Libya
93E3 **Al Kūt** Iraq
92C2 **Al Lādhiqīyah** Syria
86A1 **Allahābād** India
94C2 **Al Lajāh** *Mt* Syria
12D1 **Allakaket** USA
76B2 **Allanmyo** Burma
95C2 **'Allaqi** *Watercourse* Egypt
17B1 **Allatoona** *L* USA
15C2 **Allegheny** *R* USA
10C3 **Allegheny Mts** USA
17B1 **Allendale** USA
111A3 **Allen,Mt** NZ
15C2 **Allentown** USA
87B3 **Alleppey** India
49C2 **Aller** *R* France
47D1 **Allgäu** *Mts* Germany

8C2 **Alliance** USA
81C3 **Al Līth** S Arabia
91B5 **Al Liwā** *Region,* UAE
109D1 **Allora** Aust
14B2 **Alma** Michigan, USA
82B1 **Alma Ata** USSR
50A2 **Almada** Port
Al Madīnah = Medina
71F2 **Almagan** *I* Pacific O
91B4 **Al Manāmah** Bahrain
93D3 **Al Ma'nīyah** Iraq
21A1 **Almanor,L** USA
51B2 **Almansa** Spain
13B1 **Alma Peak** *Mt* Can
91B5 **Al Māriyyah** UAE
95B1 **Al Marj** Libya
50B1 **Almazán** Spain
35C1 **Almenara** Brazil
50B2 **Almeria** Spain
61H3 **Al'met'yevsk** USSR
56C1 **Älmhult** Sweden
93E3 **Al Miqdādīyah** Iraq
112C3 **Almirante Brown** *Base* Ant
34A1 **Almirante Latorre** Chile
55B3 **Almirós** Greece
91A4 **Al Mish'āb** S Arabia
50A2 **Almodôvar** Port
84D3 **Almora** India
91A4 **Al Mubarraz** S Arabia
92C4 **Al Mudawwara** Jordan
91C5 **Al Mudaybi** Oman
91B4 **Al Muharraq** Bahrain
81C4 **Al Mukallā** Yemen
81C4 **Al Mukhā** Yemen
93D3 **Al Musayyib** Iraq
44B3 **Alness** Scot
93E3 **Al Nu'mānīyah** Iraq
42D2 **Alnwick** Eng
71D4 **Alor** *I* Indon
77C4 **Alor Setar** Malay
Alost = Aalst
107E2 **Alotau** PNG
106B3 **Aloysius,Mt** Aust
34C3 **Alpachiri** Arg
14B1 **Alpena** USA
47B2 **Alpes du Valais** *Mts* Switz
52B1 **Alpi Dolomitiche** *Mts* Italy
47B2 **Alpi Graie** *Mts* Italy
9C3 **Alpine** Texas, USA
47C1 **Alpi Orobie** *Mts* Italy
47B2 **Alpi Pennine** *Mts* Italy
47C1 **Alpi Retiche** *Mts* Switz
47D1 **Alpi Venoste** *Mts* Italy
52A1 **Alps** *Mts* Europe
95A1 **Al Qaddāhīyah** Libya
94C1 **Al Qadmūs** Syria
93D3 **Al Qā'im** Iraq
93C4 **Al Qalībah** S Arabia
93D2 **Al Qāmishlī** Syria
95A1 **Al Qaryah Ash Sharqiyah** Libya
92C3 **Al Qaryatayn** Syria
91A4 **Al Qatif** S Arabia
95A2 **Al Qatrūn** Libya
91A4 **Al Qaysāmah** S Arabia
94C2 **Al Quatayfah** Syria
92C3 **Al Qunayṭirah** Syria
81C4 **Al Qunfidhah** S Arabia
93E3 **Al Qurnah** Iraq
94C1 **Al Quṣayr** Syria
92C3 **Al Qutayfah** Syria
56B1 **Als** *I* Den
49D2 **Alsace** *Region,* France
57B2 **Alsfeld** Germany
42C2 **Alston** Eng
38J5 **Alta** Nor
29D2 **Alta Gracia** Arg
27D5 **Altagracia de Orituco** Ven
68A2 **Altai** *Mts* Mongolia
17B1 **Altamaha** *R* USA

33G4 **Altamira** Brazil
23B1 **Altamira** Mexico
53C2 **Altamura** Italy
68C1 **Altanbulag** Mongolia
71F4 **Altape** PNG
24B2 **Altata** Mexico
63A3 **Altay** China
63B3 **Altay** Mongolia
63A2 **Altay** *Mts* USSR
47C1 **Altdorf** Switz
46D1 **Altenkirchen** Germany
34B3 **Altiplanicie del Payún** *Plat* Arg
47B1 **Altkirch** France
101C2 **Alto Molócue** Mozam
10A3 **Alton** USA
15C2 **Altoona** USA
34B2 **Alto Pencoso** *Mts* Arg
35A1 **Alto Sucuriú** Brazil
23B2 **Altotonga** Mexico
23A2 **Altoyac de Alvarez** Mexico
82C2 **Altun Shan** *Mts* China
20B2 **Alturas** USA
9D3 **Altus** USA
91B5 **Al'Ubaylah** S Arabia
99F1 **Alula** Somalia
93C4 **Al Urayq** *Desert Region* S Arabia
91B5 **Al'Uruq al Mu'taridah** *Region,* S Arabia
9D2 **Alva** USA
23B2 **Alvarado** Mexico
19A3 **Alvarado** USA
39G6 **Älvdalen** Sweden
19A4 **Alvin** USA
38J5 **Alvsbyn** Sweden
80B3 **Al Wajh** S Arabia
85D3 **Alwar** India
93D3 **Al Widyān** *Desert Region* Iraq/ S Arabia
72A2 **Alxa Yougi** China
93E2 **Alyat** USSR
39J8 **Alytus** USSR
46E2 **Alzey** Germany
23B2 **Amacuzac** *R* Mexico
99D2 **Amadi** Sudan
93D2 **Am ādīyah** Iraq
6C3 **Amadjuak** *L* Can
74B4 **Amakusa-shotō** *I* Japan
39G7 **Åmål** Sweden
63D2 **Amalat** *R* USSR
55B3 **Amaliás** Greece
85D4 **Amalner** India
69E4 **Amami** *I* Japan
69E4 **Amami gunto** *Arch* Japan
100C4 **Amanzimtoti** S Africa
33G3 **Amapá** Brazil
33G3 **Amapá** State, Brazil
9C3 **Amarillo** USA
60E5 **Amasya** Turk
23A1 **Amatitan** Mexico
Amazonas = Solimões
32D4 **Amazonas** State, Brazil
28C3 **Amazonas** *R* Brazil
84D2 **Ambāla** India
87C3 **Ambalangoda** Sri Lanka
101D3 **Ambalavao** Madag
98B2 **Ambam** Cam
101D2 **Ambanja** Madag
1C7 **Ambarchik** USSR
32B4 **Ambato** Ecuador
101D2 **Ambato-Boeny** Madag
101D2 **Ambatolampy** Madag
101D2 **Ambatondrazaka** Madag
57C3 **Amberg** Germany
25D3 **Ambergris Cay** *I* Belize
86A2 **Ambikāpur** India
101D2 **Ambilobe** Madag
101D3 **Amboasary** Madag
101D2 **Ambodifototra** Madag

101D3 **Ambohimahasoa** Madag
71D4 **Ambon** Indon
101D3 **Ambositra** Madag
101D3 **Ambovombe** Madag
98B3 **Ambriz** Angola
98C1 **Am Dam** Chad
64H3 **Amderma** USSR
24B2 **Ameca** Mexico
23B2 **Amecacameca** Mexico
34C2 **Ameghino** Arg
56B2 **Ameland** *I* Neth
16C2 **Amenia** USA
112B10 **American Highland** *Upland* Ant
105H4 **American Samoa** *Is* Pacific O
17B1 **Americus** USA
101G1 **Amersfoort** S Africa
112C10 **Amery Ice Shelf** Ant
55B3 **Amfilokhía** Greece
55B3 **Amfissa** Greece
63F1 **Amga** USSR
63F1 **Amgal** *R* USSR
69F2 **Amgu** USSR
69F1 **Amgun'** *R* USSR
99D1 **Amhara** *Region* Eth
7D5 **Amherst** Can
16C1 **Amherst** Massachusetts, USA
87B2 **Amhūr** India
48C2 **Amiens** France
75B1 **Amino** Japan
94B1 **Amioune** Leb
89K8 **Amirante Is** Indian O
86B1 **Amlekhgan** Nepal
92C3 **Amman** Jordan
38K6 **Ämmänsaario** Fin
56B2 **Ammersfoort** Neth
80E1 **Amoda'ya** *R* USSR
90B2 **Amol** Iran
55C3 **Amorgós** *I* Greece
7C5 **Amos** Can
Amoy = Xiamen
101D3 **Ampanihy** Madag
35B2 **Amparo** Brazil
51C1 **Amposta** Spain
85D4 **Amrāvati** India
85C4 **Amreli** India
84C2 **Amritsar** India
56A2 **Amsterdam** Neth
101H1 **Amsterdam** S Africa
15D2 **Amsterdam** USA
98C1 **Am Timan** Chad
88L3 **Amu Darya** *R* USSR
6A2 **Amund Ringes I** Can
4F2 **Amundsen G** Can
112B4 **Amundsen S** Ant
112A **Amundsen-Scott** *Base* Ant
78D3 **Amuntai** Indon
63E2 **Amur** *R* USSR
33E2 **Anaco** Ven
8B2 **Anaconda** USA
20B1 **Anacortes** USA
55C3 **Anáfi** *I* Greece
93D3 **'Anah** Iraq
21B3 **Anaheim** USA
87B2 **Anaimalai Hills** India
83C4 **Anakapalle** India
12E1 **Anaktuvuk P** USA
101D2 **Analalaya** Madag
92B2 **Anamur** Turk
75A2 **Anan** Japan
87B2 **Anantapur** India
84D2 **Anantnag** India
31B5 **Anápolis** Brazil
90C3 **Anār** Iran
90B3 **Anārak** Iran
71F2 **Anatahan** *I* Pacific O
30D4 **Añatuya** Arg
74B3 **Anbyŏn** N Korea
22C4 **Ancapa Is** USA
4D3 **Anchorage** USA
30C2 **Ancohuma** *Mt* Bol
32B6 **Ancón** Peru
52B2 **Ancona** Italy
16C1 **Ancram** USA

46B2 **Argenteuil** France	23A1 **Arriaga** Mexico	91C4 **Ash Sha'm** UAE	11B3 **Atlanta** Georgia, USA
28C7 **Argentina** Republic, S America	93E3 **Ar Rifā't** Iraq	93D2 **Ash Sharqāt** Iraq	14B2 **Atlanta** Michigan, USA
103F7 **Argentine Basin** Atlantic O	93E3 **Ar Rihāb** *Desert Region* Iraq	93E3 **Ash Shatrah** Iraq	18A1 **Atlantic** USA
48C2 **Argenton-sur-Creuse** France	91A5 **Ar Riyāḍ** S Arabia	81C4 **Ash Shihr** Yemen	10C3 **Atlantic City** USA
54C2 **Argeş** *R* Rom	44B3 **Arrochar** Scot	91A4 **Ash Shumlul** S Arabia	16B2 **Atlantic Highlands** USA
84B2 **Arghardab** *R* Afghan	111A2 **Arrowtown** NZ	14B2 **Ashtabula** USA	103H8 **Atlantic Indian Basin** Atlantic O
55B3 **Argolikós Kólpos** *G* Greece	23B1 **Arroyo Seco** Mexico	7D4 **Ashuanipi L** Can	103H7 **Atlantic Indian Ridge** Atlantic O
46C2 **Argonne** Region, France	91B4 **Ar Ru'ays** Qatar	92C3 **'Aşī** *R* Syria	96C1 **Atlas Saharien** *Mts* Alg
55B3 **Árgos** Greece	91C5 **Ar Rustaq** Oman	47D2 **Asiago** Italy	4E4 **Atlin** Can
55B3 **Argostólion** Greece	93D3 **Ar Rutbah** Iraq	53A2 **Asinara** *I* Medit S	4E4 **Atlin L** Can
22B3 **Arguello,Pt** USA	47D2 **Arsiero** Italy	65K4 **Asino** USSR	94B2 **'Atlit** Israel
106B2 **Argyle,L** Aust	49D2 **Arsizio** Italy	93D2 **Aşkale** Turk	23B2 **Atlixco** Mexico
56C1 **Århus** Den	61G2 **Arsk** USSR	39G7 **Askersund** Sweden	11B3 **Atmore** USA
100A3 **Ariamsvlei** Namibia	55B3 **Árta** Greece	84C1 **Asmar** Afghan	101D3 **Atofinandrahana** Madag
34C2 **Arias** Arg	23A2 **Arteaga** Mexico	95C3 **Asmara** Eth	
97B3 **Aribinda** Burkina	63B2 **Artemovsk** USSR	75A2 **Aso** Japan	12D3 **Atognak I** USA
30B2 **Arica** Chile	63D2 **Artemovskiy** USSR	99D1 **Asosa** Eth	19A3 **Atoka** USA
84C2 **Arifwala** Pak	9C3 **Artesia** USA	111A2 **Aspiring,Mt** NZ	23A1 **Atotonilco** Mexico
Arihā = Jericho	111B2 **Arthurs P** NZ	99E1 **Assab** Eth	23B2 **Atoyac** *R* Mexico
27L1 **Arima** Trinidad	6B2 **Artic Bay** Can	93C2 **As Sabkhah** Syria	32B2 **Atrato** *R* Colombia
35B1 **Arinos** Brazil	29E2 **Artigas** Urug	91A5 **As Salamiyah** S Arabia	91B5 **Attaf** Region, UAE
33F6 **Arinos** *R* Brazil	4H3 **Artillery L** Can	92C2 **As Salamīyah** Syria	81C3 **At Tā'if** S Arabia
23A2 **Ario de Rosales** Mexico	48C1 **Artois** Region, France	93D3 **As Salmān** Iraq	94C2 **At Tall** Syria
27L1 **Aripo,Mt** Trinidad	112C2 **Arturo Prat** *Base* Ant	86C1 **Assam** State, India	17A1 **Attalla** USA
33E5 **Aripuana** Brazil	93D1 **Artvin** Turk	93E3 **As Samāwah** Iraq	7B4 **Attauapiskat** Can
33E5 **Aripuaná** *R* Brazil	99D2 **Aru** Zaïre	91B5 **As Şanām** Region, S Arabia	7B4 **Attauapiskat** *R* Can
44B3 **Arisaig** Scot	33G6 **Aruanã** Brazil	94C2 **As Sanamayn** Syria	93D3 **At Taysīyah** *Desert Region* S Arabia
87B2 **Ariskere** India	27C4 **Aruba** *I* Caribbean S	56B2 **Assen** Neth	14A2 **Attica** Indiana, USA
13B2 **Aristazabal I** Can	86B1 **Arun** *R* Nepal	56B1 **Assens** Den	46C2 **Attigny** France
34B3 **Arizona** Arg	86C1 **Arunāchal Pradesh** Union Territory, India	95A1 **As Sidrah** Libya	15D2 **Attleboro** Massachusetts, USA
9B3 **Arizona** State, USA	87B3 **Aruppukkottai** India	5H5 **Assiniboia** Can	76D3 **Attopeu** Laos
39G7 **Ärjäng** Sweden	99D3 **Arusha** Tanz	5G4 **Assiniboine,Mt** Can	92C4 **At Tubayq** *Upland* S Arabia
61F3 **Arkadak** USSR	98C2 **Aruwimi** *R* Zaïre	30F3 **Assis** Brazil	34B3 **Atuel** *R* Arg
19B3 **Arkadelphia** USA	68C2 **Arvayheer** Mongolia	93C3 **As Sukhnah** Syria	39H7 **Atvidaberg** Sweden
65H4 **Arkalya** USSR	47B2 **Arve** *R* France	91A5 **As Summan** Region, S Arabia	22B2 **Atwater** USA
11A3 **Arkansas** State, USA	7C5 **Arvida** Can	99E3 **Assumption** *I* Seychelles	49D3 **Aubagne** France
11A3 **Arkansas** *R* USA	38H5 **Arvidsjaur** Sweden	92C3 **As Suwaydā'** Syria	46C2 **Aube** Department, France
18A2 **Arkansas City** USA	39G7 **Arvika** Sweden	93D3 **As Suwayrah** Iraq	49C3 **Aubenas** France
64F3 **Arkhangel'sk** USSR	21B2 **Arvin** USA	93E2 **Astara** USSR	17A1 **Auburn** Alabama, USA
41B3 **Arklow** Irish Rep	94B1 **Arwad** *I* Syria	52A2 **Asti** Italy	21A2 **Auburn** California, USA
50B1 **Arlanzón** *R* Spain	61F2 **Arzamas** USSR	55C3 **Astipálaia** *I* Greece	14A2 **Auburn** Indiana, USA
47D1 **Arlberg P** Austria	84C2 **Asadabad** Afghan	50A1 **Astorga** Spain	18A1 **Auburn** Nebraska, USA
49C3 **Arles** France	75A2 **Asahi** *R* Japan	8A2 **Astoria** USA	15C2 **Auburn** New York, USA
19A3 **Arlington** Texas, USA	74E2 **Asahi dake** *Mt* Japan	61G4 **Astrakhan'** USSR	20B1 **Auburn** Washington, USA
15C3 **Arlington** Virginia, USA	74E2 **Asahikawa** Japan	50A1 **Asturias** Region, Spain	48C3 **Auch** France
20B1 **Arlington** Washington, USA	86B2 **Asansol** India	30E4 **Asunción** Par	110B1 **Auckland** NZ
97C3 **Arlit** Niger	95A2 **Asawanwah** *Well* Libya	99D2 **Aswa** *R* Uganda	105G6 **Auckland Is** NZ
57B3 **Arlon** Belg	61K2 **Asbest** USSR	80B3 **Aswân** Egypt	48C3 **Aude** *R* France
Armageddon= **Megiddo**	15D2 **Asbury Park** USA	95C2 **Aswân High Dam** Egypt	7B4 **Auden** Can
45C1 **Armagh** County, N Ire	103H5 **Ascension** *I* Atlantic O	95C2 **Asyût** Egypt	47B1 **Audincourt** France
45C1 **Armagh** N Ire	57B3 **Aschaffenburg** Germany	92C3 **As Zilaf** Syria	109C1 **Augathella** Aust
61F5 **Armavir** USSR	56C2 **Aschersleben** Germany	97C4 **Atakpamé** Togo	57C3 **Augsburg** Germany
23A2 **Armena** Mexico	52B2 **Ascoli Piceno** Italy	71D4 **Atambua** Indon	106A4 **Augusta** Aust
32B3 **Armenia** Colombia	47C1 **Ascona** Switz	6E3 **Atangmik** Greenland	11B3 **Augusta** Georgia, USA
107E4 **Armidale** Aust	96C2 **Asedjirad** *Upland* Alg	96A2 **Atar** Maur	18A2 **Augusta** Kansas, USA
13D2 **Armstrong** Can	38H6 **Åsele** Sweden	65J5 **Atasu** USSR	10D2 **Augusta** Maine, USA
65F5 **Armyanskaya SSR** Republic, USSR	99D2 **Aselle** Eth	95C3 **Atbara** Sudan	12D3 **Augustine I** USA
7C3 **Arnaud** *R* Can	54B2 **Asenovgrad** Bulg	65H4 **Atbasar** USSR	58C2 **Augustow** Pol
92B2 **Arnauti** *C* Cyprus	46C2 **Asfeld** France	11A4 **Atchafalaya B** USA	106A3 **Augustus,Mt** Aust
56B2 **Arnhem** Neth	61J2 **Asha** USSR	10A3 **Atchison** USA	46A2 **Aumale** France
106C2 **Arnhem,C** Aust	17B1 **Ashburn** USA	16B3 **Atco** USA	85D3 **Auraiya** India
106C2 **Arnhem Land** Aust	111B2 **Ashburton** NZ	23A1 **Atenguillo** Mexico	85D5 **Aurangābād** India
22B1 **Arnold** USA	106A3 **Ashburton** *R* Aust	52B2 **Atessa** Italy	96C1 **Aurès** *Mts* Alg
15C1 **Arnprior** Can	92B3 **Ashdod** Israel	46B1 **Ath** Belg	48C3 **Aurillac** France
46E1 **Arnsberg** Germany	19B3 **Ashdown** USA	13E2 **Athabasca** Can	8C3 **Aurora** Colorado, USA
100A3 **Aroab** Namibia	11B3 **Asheville** USA	5G4 **Athabasca** *R* Can	10B2 **Aurora** Illinois, USA
47C2 **Arona** Italy	109D1 **Ashford** Aust	5H4 **Athabasca L** Can	14B3 **Aurora** Indiana, USA
12B2 **Aropuk L** USA	43E4 **Ashford** Eng	45B2 **Athenry** Irish Rep	18B2 **Aurora** Mississippi, USA
52A1 **Arosa** Switz	74D3 **Ashikaga** Japan	**Athens** = **Athínai**	
97A3 **Arquipélago dos Bijagós** *Arch* Guinea-Bissau	75A2 **Ashizuri-misaki** *Pt* Japan	11B3 **Athens** Georgia, USA	100A3 **Aus** Namibia
93D3 **Ar Ramādī** Iraq	65G6 **Ashkhabad** USSR	14B3 **Athens** Ohio, USA	14B2 **Au Sable** USA
42B2 **Arran** *I* Scot	10B3 **Ashland** Kentucky, USA	19A3 **Athens** Texas, USA	10A2 **Austin** Minnesota, USA
93C2 **Ar Raqqah** Syria	18A1 **Ashland** Nebraska, USA	55B3 **Athínai** Greece	
49C1 **Arras** France	14B2 **Ashland** Ohio, USA	41B3 **Athlone** Irish Rep	
96A2 **Arrecife** Canary Is	8A2 **Ashland** Oregon, USA	16C1 **Athol** USA	
34C2 **Arrecifes** Arg	109C1 **Ashley** Aust	55B2 **Áthos** *Mt* Greece	
	16B2 **Ashokan Res** USA	45C2 **Athy** Irish Rep	
	94B3 **Ashqelon** Israel	98B1 **Ati** Chad	
	93D3 **Ash Shabakh** Iraq	7A5 **Atikoken** Can	
		61F3 **Atkarsk** USSR	
		18B2 **Atkins** USA	
		23B2 **Atlacomulco** Mexico	

21B2 **Austin** Nevada, USA
9D3 **Austin** Texas, USA
107D4 **Australian Alps** *Mts* Aust
37E4 **Austria** Federal Republic, Europe
46A1 **Authie** *R* France
24B3 **Autlán** Mexico
49C2 **Autun** France
49C2 **Auvergne** Region, France
49C2 **Auxerre** France
46B1 **Auxi-le-Châteaux** France
49C2 **Avallon** France
22C4 **Avalon** USA
7E5 **Avalon Pen** Can
35B2 **Avaré** Brazil
90D3 **Avaz** Iran
94B3 **Avedat** *Hist Site* Israel
33F4 **Aveíro** Brazil
50A1 **Aveiro** Port
29E2 **Avellaneda** Arg
53B2 **Avellino** Italy
46B1 **Avesnes-sur-Helpe** France
39H6 **Avesta** Sweden
52B2 **Avezzano** Italy
44C3 **Aviemore** Scot
111B2 **Aviemore,L** NZ
47B2 **Avigliana** Italy
49C3 **Avignon** France
50B1 **Avila** Spain
50A1 **Aviles** Spain
47D1 **Avisio** *R* Italy
108B3 **Avoca** *R* Aust
43C4 **Avon** County, Eng
43D4 **Avon** *R* Dorset, Eng
43D3 **Avon** *R* Warwick, Eng
43C4 **Avonmouth** Wales
17B2 **Avon Park** USA
46B2 **Avre** *R* France
54A2 **Avtovac** Yugos
94C2 **A'waj** *R* Syria
74D4 **Awaji-shima** *B* Japan
99E2 **Awarem** Eth
111A2 **Awarua Pt** NZ
99E2 **Awash** Eth
99E2 **Awash** *R* Eth
75B1 **Awa-shima** *I* Japan
111B2 **Awatere** *R* NZ
95A2 **Awbārī** Libya
98C2 **Aweil** Sudan
95B2 **Awjilan** Libya
96A2 **Awserd** *Well* Mor
6A2 **Axel Heiburg I** Can
43C4 **Axminster** Eng
75B1 **Ayabe** Japan
29E3 **Ayacucho** Arg
32C6 **Ayacucho** Peru
65K5 **Ayaguz** USSR
82C2 **Ayakkum Hu** *L* China
50A2 **Ayamonte** Spain
63F2 **Ayan** USSR
32C6 **Ayauiri** Peru
92A2 **Aydin** Turk
55C3 **Áyios Evstrátios** *I* Greece
43D4 **Aylesbury** Eng
13D2 **Aylmer,Mt** Can
94C2 **'Ayn al Fijah** Syria
93D2 **Ayn Zālah** Iraq
95B2 **Ayn Zuwayyah** *Well* Libya
99D2 **Ayod** Sudan
107D2 **Ayr** Aust
42B2 **Ayr** Scot
42B2 **Ayr** *R* Scot
42B2 **Ayre,Pt of** Eng
54C2 **Aytos** Bulg
76C3 **Aytthaya** Thai
23A1 **Ayutla** Mexico
55C3 **Ayvacik** Turk
55C3 **Ayvalik** Turk
86A1 **Āzamgarh** India
97B3 **Azaouad** *Desert Region* Mali
97D3 **Azare** Nig
92C2 **A'Zāz** Syria

Azbine = Aïr
96A2 **Azzeffal** *R* Maur
65F5 **Azerbaydzhanskaya SSR** Republic, USSR
32B4 **Azogues** Ecuador
Azores = Açores
98C1 **Azoum** *R* Chad
60E4 **Azovskoye More** *S* USSR
96B1 **Azrou** Mor
34D3 **Azucena** Arg
32A2 **Azuero,Pen de** Panama
29E3 **Azúl** Arg
94C2 **Az-Zabdānī** Syria
91C5 **Az Zāhirah** *Mts* Oman
93E3 **Az Zubayr** Iraq

B

94B2 **Ba'abda** Leb
92C3 **Ba'albek** Leb
94B3 **Ba'al Hazor** *Mt* Israel
99E2 **Baardheere** Somalia
54C2 **Babadag** Rom
92A1 **Babaeski** Turk
32B4 **Babahoyo** Ecuador
81C4 **Bāb al Mandab** *Str* Djibouti/Yemen
71D4 **Babar** *I* Indon
99D3 **Babati** Tanz
60E2 **Babayevo** USSR
14B2 **Baberton** USA
13B1 **Babine** *R* Can
5F4 **Babine L** Can
90B2 **Bābol** Iran
79B2 **Babuyan Chan** Phil
79B2 **Babuyan Is** Phil
31C2 **Bacabal** Brazil
71D4 **Bacan** *I* Indon
60C4 **Bačau** Rom
76D1 **Bac Can** Viet
108B3 **Bacchus Marsh** Aust
82B2 **Bachu** China
4J3 **Back** *R* Can
12J2 **Backbone Ranges** *Mts* Can
76D1 **Bac Ninh** Viet
79B3 **Bacolod** Phil
79B3 **Baco,Mt** Phil
87B2 **Badagara** India
72A1 **Badain Jaran Shamo** *Desert* China
50A2 **Badajoz** Spain
51C1 **Badalona** Spain
93D3 **Badanah** S Arabia
46D2 **Bad Bergzabern** Germany
46D1 **Bad Ems** Germany
47C1 **Baden** Switz
57B3 **Baden-Baden** Germany
57B3 **Baden-Württemberg** State, Germany
57C3 **Badgastein** Austria
22C2 **Badger** USA
57B2 **Bad-Godesberg** Germany
57B2 **Bad Hersfeld** Germany
46D1 **Bad Honnef** Germany
85B4 **Badin** Pak
52B1 **Bad Ischl** Austria
93C3 **Badiyat ash Sham** *Desert Region* Jordan/Iraq
57B3 **Bad-Kreuznach** Germany
46D1 **Bad Nevenahr-Ahrweiler** Germany
47C1 **Bad Ragaz** Switz
57C3 **Bad Tolz** Germany
87C3 **Badulla** Sri Lanka
50B2 **Baena** Spain
97A3 **Bafatá** Guinea-Bissau
4H2 **Baffin** *Region* Can
6C2 **Baffin B** Greenland/Can
6C2 **Baffin I** Can
98B2 **Bafia** Cam
97A3 **Bafing** *R* Mali

97A3 **Bafoulabé** Mali
98B2 **Bafoussam** Cam
90C3 **Bāfq** Iran
60E5 **Bafra Burun** *Pt* Turk
91C4 **Bāft** Iran
98C2 **Bafwasende** Zaïre
86A1 **Bagaha** India
87B1 **Bāgalkot** India
99D3 **Bagamoyo** Tanz
29F2 **Bagé** Brazil
93D3 **Baghdād** Iraq
86B2 **Bagherhat** Bang
91C3 **Bāghīn** Iran
84B1 **Baghlan** Afghan
49C3 **Bagnols-sur-Cèze** France
97B3 **Bagoé** *R* Mali
79B2 **Baguio** Phil
86B1 **Bāhādurābād** India
11C4 **Bahamas,The** *Is* Caribbean S
86B2 **Baharampur** India
99D1 **Bahar Dar** Eth
92A4 **Bahariya Oasis** Egypt
84C3 **Bahawalpur** Pak
84C3 **Bahawalpur** Province, Pak
85C3 **Bahawathagar** Pak
Bahia = Salvador
31C4 **Bahia** State, Brazil
29D3 **Bahía Blanca** Arg
29D3 **Bahía Blanca** *B* Arg
34A3 **Bahía Concepción** *B* Chile
35C2 **Bahia da Ilha Grande** *B* Brazil
24B2 **Bahia de Banderas** *B* Mexico
24C2 **Bahia de Campeche** *B* Mexico
25D3 **Bahia de la Ascension** *B* Mexico
24B3 **Bahia de Petacalco** *B* Mexico
96A2 **Bahia de Rio de Oro** *B* Mor
35C2 **Bahia de Sepetiba** *B* Brazil
29C6 **Bahía Grande** *B* Arg
9B4 **Bahía Kino** Mexico
24A2 **Bahía Magdalena** *B* Mexico
24A2 **Bahia Sebastia Vizcaino** *B* Mexico
86A1 **Bahraich** India
80D3 **Bahrain** Sheikdom, Arabian Pen
93D3 **Bahr al Milh** *L* Iraq
98C2 **Bahr Aouk** *R* Chad/CAR
Bahrat Lut = Dead S
98C2 **Bahr el Arab** *Watercourse* Sudan
99D2 **Bahr el Ghazal** *R* Sudan
98B1 **Bahr el Ghazal** *Watercourse* Chad
101H1 **Baia de Maputo** *B* Mozam
31B2 **Baia de Marajó** *B* Brazil
101D2 **Baiá de Pemba** *B* Mozam
31C2 **Baia de São Marcos** *B* Brazil
50A2 **Baia de Setúbal** *B* Port
31D4 **Baia de Todos os Santos** *B* Brazil
100A2 **Baia dos Tigres** Angola
60B4 **Baia Mare** Rom
98B2 **Baïbokoum** Chad
69E2 **Baicheng** China
101E2 **Baie Antongila** *B* Madag
7D5 **Baie-Comeau** Can
101D2 **Baie de Bombetoka** *B* Madag
101D2 **Baie de Mahajamba** *B* Madag

101D3 **Baie de St Augustin** *B* Madag
94B2 **Baie de St Georges** *B* Leb
10D2 **Baie des Chaleurs** *B* Can
7C4 **Baie-du-Poste** Can
72B3 **Baihe** China
72C3 **Bai He** *R* China
93D3 **Ba'ījī** Iraq
86A2 **Baikunthpur** India
Baile Atha Cliath = Dublin
54B2 **Băilesti** Rom
46B1 **Bailleul** France
72A3 **Baima** China
17B1 **Bainbridge** USA
12B2 **Baird Inlet** USA
4B3 **Baird Mts** USA
72D1 **Bairin Youqi** China
72D1 **Bairin Zuoqi** China
107D4 **Bairnsdale** Aust
79B4 **Bais** Phil
54A1 **Baja** Hung
9B3 **Baja California** State, Mexico
24A1 **Baja California** *Pen* Mexico
61J2 **Bakal** USSR
98C2 **Bakala** CAR
97A3 **Bakel** Sen
8C2 **Baker** Montana, USA
8B2 **Baker** Oregon, USA
6A3 **Baker Foreland** *Pt* Can
4J3 **Baker L** Can
4J3 **Baker Lake** Can
8A2 **Baker,Mt** USA
9B3 **Bakersfield** USA
90C2 **Bakharden** USSR
90C2 **Bakhardok** USSR
60D3 **Bakhmach** USSR
38C1 **Bakkaflói** *B* Iceland
99D2 **Bako** Eth
98C2 **Bakouma** CAR
65F5 **Baku** USSR
92B2 **Balâ** Turk
79A4 **Balabac** *I* Phil
70C3 **Balabac** *Str* Malay
78C2 **Balaikarangan** Indon
108A2 **Balaklava** Aust
61G3 **Balakovo** USSR
86A2 **Balāngir** India
61F3 **Balashov** USSR
86B2 **Balasore** India
80A3 **Balât** Egypt
52C1 **Balaton** *L* Hung
45C2 **Balbriggan** Irish Rep
29E3 **Balcarce** Arg
54C2 **Balchik** Bulg
111B3 **Balclutha** NZ
18B2 **Bald Knob** USA
17B1 **Baldwin** USA
9C3 **Baldy Peak** *Mt* USA
Balearic Is = Islas Baleares
78C2 **Baleh** *R* Malay
79B2 **Baler** Phil
61H2 **Balezino** USSR
106A1 **Bali** *I* Indon
92A2 **Balıkesir** Turk
93C2 **Balīkh** *R* Syria
78D3 **Balikpapan** Indon
79B2 **Balintang Chan** Phil
78C4 **Bali S** Indon
35A1 **Baliza** Brazil
84B1 **Balkh** Afghan
65J5 **Balkhash** USSR
44B3 **Ballachulish** Scot
45B2 **Ballaghaderreen** Irish Rep
42B2 **Ballantrae** Scot
4G2 **Ballantyne Str** Can
87B2 **Ballapur** India
107D4 **Ballarat** Aust
44C3 **Ballater** Scot
112C7 **Balleny Is** Ant
86A1 **Ballia** India

Bata

109D1 **Ballina** Aust
41B3 **Ballina** Irish Rep
45B2 **Ballinasloe** Irish Rep
45B2 **Ballinrobe** Irish Rep
45B1 **Ballycastle** Irish Rep
45C1 **Ballycastle** N Ire
45C1 **Ballymena** N Ire
45C1 **Ballymoney** N Ire
45B1 **Ballyshannon**
　　　Irish Rep
45B2 **Ballyvaghan** Irish Rep
108B3 **Balmoral** Aust
34C2 **Balnearia** Arg
84B3 **Balochistan** Region,
　　　Pak
100A2 **Balombo** Angola
109C1 **Balonn** R Aust
85C3 **Balotra** India
86A1 **Balrāmpur** India
107D4 **Balranald** Aust
31B3 **Balsas** Brazil
23B2 **Balsas** Mexico
24B3 **Balsas** R Mexico
60C4 **Balta** USSR
39H7 **Baltic S** N Europe
92B3 **Baltīm** Egypt
45B3 **Baltimore** Irish Rep
10C3 **Baltimore** USA
86B1 **Bālurghāt** India
61H4 **Balykshi** USSR
91C4 **Bam** Iran
98B1 **Bama** Nig
97B3 **Bamako** Mali
98C2 **Bambari** CAR
17B1 **Bamberg** USA
57C3 **Bamberg** Germany
98C2 **Bambili** Zaïre
35B2 **Bambui** Brazil
98B2 **Bamenda** Cam
13C3 **Bamfield** Can
98B2 **Bamingui** R CAR
98B2 **Bamingui Bangoran**
　　　National Park CAR
84B2 **Bamiyan** Afghan
91D4 **Bampur** Iran
91D4 **Bampur** R Iran
98C2 **Banalia** Zaïre
97B3 **Banamba** Mali
76C3 **Ban Aranyaprathet**
　　　Thai
76C2 **Ban Ban** Laos
77C4 **Ban Betong** Thai
45C1 **Banbridge** N Ire
43D3 **Banbury** Eng
44C3 **Banchory** Scot
25D3 **Banco Chinchorro** Is
　　　Mexico
15C1 **Bancroft** Can
86A1 **Bānda** India
70A3 **Banda Aceh** Indon
97B4 **Bandama** R Ivory
　　　Coast
91C4 **Bandar Abbās** Iran
90A2 **Bandar Anzalī** Iran
91B4 **Bandar-e Daylam** Iran
91B4 **Bandar-e Lengheh**
　　　Iran
91B4 **Bandar-e Māqām** Iran
91B4 **Bandar-e Rig** Iran
90B2 **Bandar-e Torkoman**
　　　Iran
91A3 **Bandar Khomeynī** Iran
78C2 **Bandar Seri Begawan**
　　　Brunei
71D4 **Banda S** Indon
91C4 **Band Bonī** Iran
35C2 **Bandeira** Mt Brazil
97B3 **Bandiagara** Mali
60C5 **Bandirma** Turk
45B3 **Bandon** Irish Rep
98B3 **Bandundu** Zaïre
78B4 **Bandung** Indon
25E2 **Banes** Cuba
13D2 **Banff** Can
44C3 **Banff** Scot
5G4 **Banff** R Can
13D2 **Banff Nat Pk** Can
87B2 **Bangalore** India

98C2 **Bangassou** CAR
70C3 **Banggi** I Malay
76D2 **Bang Hieng** R Laos
78B3 **Bangka** I Indon
78A3 **Bangko** Indon
76C3 **Bangkok** Thai
82C3 **Bangladesh** Republic,
　　　Asia
84D2 **Bangong Co** L China
10D2 **Bangor** Maine, USA
45D1 **Bangor** N Ire
16B2 **Bangor** Pennsylvania,
　　　USA
42B3 **Bangor** Wales
78D3 **Bangsalsembera**
　　　Indon
76B3 **Bang Saphan Yai** Thai
79B2 **Bangued** Phil
98B2 **Bangui** CAR
100C2 **Bangweulu** L Zambia
77C4 **Ban Hat Yai** Thai
76C2 **Ban Hin Heup** Laos
76C1 **Ban Houei Sai** Laos
76B3 **Ban Hua Hin** Thai
97B3 **Bani** R Mali
97C3 **Bani Bangou** Niger
95A1 **Banī Walīd** Libya
92C2 **Bāniyās** Syria
94B2 **Baniyas** Syria
52C2 **Banja Luka** Yugos
78C3 **Banjarmasin** Indon
97A3 **Banjul** The Gambia
77B4 **Ban Kantang** Thai
76D2 **Ban Khemmarat** Laos
77B4 **Ban Khok Kloi** Thai
71F5 **Banks I** Aust
5E4 **Banks I** British
　　　Columbia, Can
4F2 **Banks I** Northwest
　　　Territories, Can
20C1 **Banks L** USA
111B2 **Banks Pen** NZ
109C4 **Banks Str** Aust
86B2 **Bankura** India
76B2 **Ban Mae Sariang** Thai
76B2 **Ban Mae Sot** Thai
76D3 **Ban Me Thuot** Viet
45C1 **Bann** R N Ire
77B4 **Ban Na San** Thai
84C2 **Bannu** Pak
34A3 **Baños Maule** Chile
76C2 **Ban Pak Neun** Laos
77C4 **Ban Pak Phanang** Thai
76D3 **Ban Ru Kroy** Camb
76B3 **Ban Sai Yok** Thai
76C3 **Ban Sattahip** Thai
59B3 **Banská Bystrica** Czech
85C4 **Bānswāra** India
77B4 **Ban Tha Kham** Thai
76D2 **Ban Thateng** Laos
76C2 **Ban Tha Tum** Thai
41B3 **Bantry** Irish Rep
41A3 **Bantry** B Irish Rep
76D3 **Ban Ya Soup** Viet
78C4 **Banyuwangi** Indon
72C3 **Baofeng** China
76C1 **Bao Ha** Viet
72B3 **Baoji** China
76D3 **Bao Loc** Viet
68B4 **Baoshan** China
72C1 **Baotou** China
87C1 **Bāpatla** India
46B1 **Bapaume** France
93D3 **Ba'Qūbah** Iraq
32J7 **Baquerizo Morena**
　　　Ecuador
54A2 **Bar** Yugos
99D1 **Bara** Sudan
99E2 **Baraawe** Somalia
78D3 **Barabai** Indon
86A1 **Bāra Banki** India
65J4 **Barabinsk** USSR
65J4 **Barabinskaya Step**
　　　Steppe USSR
50B1 **Baracaldo** Spain
26C2 **Baracoa** Cuba
94C2 **Baradá** R Syria
109C2 **Baradine** Aust

87A1 **Bārāmati** India
84C2 **Baramula** Pak
85D3 **Bārān** India
79B3 **Barangas** Phil
4E4 **Baranof I** USA
60C3 **Baranovichi** USSR
108A2 **Baratta** Aust
86B1 **Barauni** India
31C6 **Barbacena** Brazil
27F4 **Barbados** I
　　　Caribbean S
51C1 **Barbastro** Spain
101H1 **Barberton** S Africa
48B2 **Barbezieux** France
32C2 **Barbòsa** Colombia
27E3 **Barbuda** I
　　　Caribbean S
107D3 **Barcaldine** Aust
　　　Barce = Al Marj
53C3 **Barcellona** Italy
51C1 **Barcelona** Spain
33E1 **Barcelona** Ven
107D3 **Barcoo** R Aust
34B3 **Barda del Medio** Arg
95A2 **Bardai** Chad
29C3 **Bardas Blancas** Arg
86B2 **Barddhamān** India
59C3 **Bardejov** Czech
47C2 **Bardi** Italy
47B2 **Bardonecchia** Italy
43B3 **Bardsey** I Wales
84D3 **Bareilly** India
64D2 **Barentsøya** I
　　　Barents S
64E2 **Barents S** USSR
95C3 **Barentu** Eth
86A2 **Bargarh** India
47B2 **Barge** Italy
63D2 **Barguzin** USSR
63D2 **Barguzin** R USSR
86B2 **Barhi** India
53C2 **Bari** Italy
51D2 **Barika** Alg
32C2 **Barinas** Ven
86B2 **Baripāda** India
85C4 **Bari Sādri** India
86C2 **Barisal** Bang
78C3 **Barito** R Indon
95A2 **Barjuj** *Watercourse*
　　　Libya
73A3 **Barkam** China
18C2 **Barkley,L** USA
13B3 **Barkley Sd** Can
100B4 **Barkly East** S Africa
106C2 **Barkly Tableland** Mts
　　　Aust
46C2 **Bar-le-Duc** France
106A3 **Barlee,L** Aust
106A3 **Barlee Range** Mts
　　　Aust
53C2 **Barletta** Italy
85C3 **Barmer** India
108B2 **Barmera** Aust
43B3 **Barmouth** Wales
42D2 **Barnard Castle** Eng
65K4 **Barnaul** USSR
16B3 **Barnegat** USA
16B3 **Barnegat B** USA
6C2 **Barnes Icecap** Can
17B1 **Barnesville** Georgia,
　　　USA
14B3 **Barnesville** Ohio, USA
42D3 **Barnsley** Eng
43B4 **Barnstaple** Eng
97C4 **Baro** Nig
86C1 **Barpeta** India
32D1 **Barquisimeto** Ven
31C4 **Barra** Brazil
44A3 **Barra** I Scot
109D2 **Barraba** Aust
23A2 **Barra de Navidad**
　　　Mexico
35C2 **Barra de Piraí** Brazil
35A1 **Barra do Garças** Brazil
50A2 **Barragem do Castelo**
　　　do Bode Res Port
50A2 **Barragem do**
　　　Maranhão Port

44A3 **Barra Head** Pt Scot
31C6 **Barra Mansa** Brazil
32B6 **Barranca** Peru
32C2 **Barrancabermeja**
　　　Colombia
33E2 **Barrancas** Ven
30E4 **Barranqueras** Arg
32C1 **Barranquilla** Colombia
44A3 **Barra,Sound of** Chan
　　　Scot
16C1 **Barre** USA
34B2 **Barreal** Arg
31C4 **Barreiras** Brazil
50A2 **Barreiro** Port
31D3 **Barreiros** Brazil
107D5 **Barren,C** Aust
12D3 **Barren Is** USA
31B6 **Barretos** Brazil
13E2 **Barrhead** Can
14C2 **Barrie** Can
13C2 **Barrière** Can
108B2 **Barrier Range** Mts
　　　Aust
107E4 **Barrington,Mt** Aust
27N2 **Barrouaillie** St Vincent
4C2 **Barrow** USA
45C2 **Barrow** R Irish Rep
106C3 **Barrow Creek** Aust
106A3 **Barrow I** Aust
42C2 **Barrow-in-Furness**
　　　Eng
4C2 **Barrow,Pt** USA
6A2 **Barrow Str** Can
15C1 **Barry's Bay** Can
87B1 **Barsi** India
9B3 **Barstow** USA
49C2 **Bar-sur-Aube** France
33F2 **Bartica** Guyana
92B1 **Bartın** Turk
107D2 **Bartle Frere,Mt** Aust
9D3 **Bartlesville** USA
101C3 **Bartolomeu Dias**
　　　Mozam
58C2 **Bartoszyce** Pol
78C4 **Barung** I Indon
85D4 **Barwāh** India
85C4 **Barwāni** India
109C1 **Barwon** R Aust
61G3 **Barysh** USSR
98B2 **Basankusu** Zaïre
34D2 **Basavilbas** Arg
79B1 **Basco** Phil
52A1 **Basel** Switz
53C2 **Basento** R Italy
13E2 **Bashaw** Can
79B1 **Bashi Chan** Phil
61H3 **Bashkirskaya ASSR**
　　　Republic, USSR
79B4 **Basilan** I Phil
43E4 **Basildon** Eng
43D4 **Basingstoke** Eng
8B2 **Basin Region** USA
93E3 **Basra** Iraq
46D2 **Bas-Rhin** Department,
　　　France
76D3 **Bassac** R Camb
13E2 **Bassano** Can
52B1 **Bassano** Italy
47D2 **Bassano del Grappa**
　　　Italy
97C4 **Bassari** Togo
101C3 **Bassas da India** I
　　　Mozam Chan
76A2 **Bassein** Burma
27E3 **Basse Terre**
　　　Guadeloupe
97C4 **Bassila** Benin
22C2 **Bass Lake** USA
107D4 **Bass Str** Aust
39G7 **Båstad** Sweden
91B4 **Bastak** Iran
86A1 **Basti** India
52A2 **Bastia** Corse
57B3 **Bastogne** Belg
19B3 **Bastrop** Louisiana,
　　　USA
19A3 **Bastrop** Texas, USA
98A2 **Bata** Eq Guinea

Batakan

78C3 **Batakan** Indon
84D2 **Batala** India
68B3 **Batang** China
98B2 **Batangafo** CAR
79B1 **Batan Is** Phil
35B2 **Batatais** Brazil
15C2 **Batavia** USA
109D3 **Batemans Bay** Aust
17B1 **Batesburg** USA
18B2 **Batesville** Arkansas, USA
19C3 **Batesville** Mississippi, USA
43C4 **Bath** Eng
15C2 **Bath** New York, USA
98B1 **Batha** *R* Chad
107D4 **Bathurst** Aust
7D5 **Bathurst** Can
4F2 **Bathurst,C** Can
106C2 **Bathurst I** Aust
4H2 **Bathurst I** Can
4H3 **Bathurst Inlet** *B* Can
97B3 **Batié** Burkina
90B3 **Bātlāq-e-Gavkhūnī** *Salt Flat* Iran
109C3 **Batlow** Aust
93D2 **Batman** Turk
96C1 **Batna** Alg
11A3 **Baton Rouge** USA
94B1 **Batroun** Leb
76C3 **Battambang** Camb
87C3 **Batticaloa** Sri Lanka
13F2 **Battle** *R* Can
10B2 **Battle Creek** USA
7E4 **Battle Harbour** Can
20C2 **Battle Mountain** USA
78D2 **Batukelau** Indon
65F5 **Batumi** USSR
77C5 **Batu Pahat** Malay
78A3 **Baturaja** Indon
94B2 **Bat Yam** Israel
71D4 **Baubau** Indon
97C3 **Bauchi** Nig
47B2 **Bauges** *Mts* France
7E4 **Bauld,C** Can
47B1 **Baumes-les-Dames** France
63D2 **Baunt** USSR
31B6 **Bauru** Brazil
35A1 **Baus** Brazil
57C2 **Bautzen** Germany
78C4 **Baween** *I* Indon
95B2 **Bawiti** Egypt
97B3 **Bawku** Ghana
76B2 **Bawlake** Burma
108A2 **Bawlen** Aust
17B1 **Baxley** USA
25E2 **Bayamo** Cuba
78D4 **Bayan** Indon
72A1 **Bayandalay** Mongolia
68C2 **Bayandzürh** Mongolia
68B3 **Bayan Har Shan** *Mts* China
72A1 **Bayan Mod** China
72B1 **Bayan Obo** China
47A2 **Bayard** *P* France
12J3 **Bayard,Mt** Can
79B3 **Baybay** Phil
93D1 **Bayburt** Turk
10B2 **Bay City** Michigan, USA
19A4 **Bay City** Texas, USA
92B2 **Bay Dağlari** Turk
64H3 **Baydaratskaya Guba** *B* USSR
99E2 **Baydhabo** Somalia
48B2 **Bayeux** France
47D1 **Bayerische Alpen** *Mts* Germany
57C3 **Bayern** State, Germany
92C3 **Bāyir** Jordan
68C1 **Baykalskiy Khrebet** *Mts* USSR
63B1 **Baykit** USSR
63B3 **Baylik Shan** *Mts* China/Mongolia
61J3 **Baymak** USSR

79B2 **Bayombong** Phil
48B3 **Bayonne** France
57C3 **Bayreuth** Germany
19C3 **Bay St Louis** USA
15D2 **Bay Shore** USA
15C1 **Bays,L of** Can
68A2 **Baytik Shan** *Mts* China
Bayt Lahm=Bethlehem
19B4 **Baytown** USA
50B2 **Baza** Spain
59D3 **Bazaliya** USSR
48B3 **Bazas** France
73B3 **Bazhong** China
91D4 **Bazmān** Iran
94C1 **Bcharre** Leb
16B3 **Beach Haven** USA
43E4 **Beachy Head** Eng
16C2 **Beacon** USA
101D2 **Bealanana** Madag
18B1 **Beardstown** USA
Bear I = Bjørnøya
22B1 **Bear Valley** USA
8D2 **Beatrice** USA
44C2 **Beatrice** *Oilfield* N Sea
13C1 **Beatton** *R* Can
5F4 **Beatton River** Can
29E6 **Beauchene Is** Falkland Is
109D1 **Beaudesert** Aust
1B5 **Beaufort S** Can
100B4 **Beaufort West** S Africa
15D1 **Beauharnois** Can
44B3 **Beauly** Scot
21B3 **Beaumont** California, USA
11A3 **Beaumont** Texas, USA
49C2 **Beaune** France
48C2 **Beauvais** France
13F1 **Beauval** Can
12E1 **Beaver** Alaska, USA
13F2 **Beaver** *R* Saskatchewan, Can
4D3 **Beaver Creek** Can
12E1 **Beaver Creek** USA
18C2 **Beaver Dam** Kentucky, USA
13E2 **Beaverhill L** Can
14A1 **Beaver I** USA
18B2 **Beaver L** USA
13D1 **Beaverlodge** Can
85C3 **Beawar** India
34B2 **Beazley** Arg
35B2 **Bebedouro** Brazil
43E3 **Beccles** Eng
54B1 **Bečej** Yugos
96B1 **Béchar** Alg
12C3 **Becharof L** USA
11B3 **Beckley** USA
43D3 **Bedford** County, Eng
43D3 **Bedford** Eng
14A3 **Bedford** Indiana, USA
27M2 **Bedford Pt** Grenada
4D2 **Beechey** Pt USA
109C3 **Beechworth** Aust
109D1 **Beenleigh** Aust
92B3 **Beersheba** Israel
Beèr Sheva = Beersheba
94B3 **Beér Sheva** *R* Israel
9D4 **Beeville** USA
98C2 **Befale** Zaïre
101D2 **Befandriana** Madag
109C3 **Bega** Aust
91B3 **Behbehān** Iran
12H3 **Behm Canal** *Sd* USA
90B2 **Behshahr** Iran
84B2 **Behsud** Afghan
69E2 **Bei'an** China
73B5 **Beihai** China
72D2 **Beijing** China
76E1 **Beiliu** China
73B4 **Beipan Jiang** *R* China
72E1 **Beipiao** China
Beira = Sofala
92C3 **Beirut** Leb

68B2 **Bei Shan** *Mts* China
94B2 **Beit ed Dīne** Leb
94B3 **Beit Jala** Israel
50A2 **Beja** Port
96C1 **Beja** Tunisia
96C1 **Bejaïa** Alg
50A1 **Béjar** Spain
90C3 **Bejestān** Iran
59C3 **Békéscsaba** Hung
101D3 **Bekily** Madag
86A1 **Bela** India
85B3 **Bela** Pak
78C2 **Belaga** Malay
16A3 **Bel Air** USA
87B1 **Belamoalli** India
71D3 **Belang** Indon
70A3 **Belangpidie** Indon
71E3 **Belau** Republic, Pacific O
104E3 **Belau** *I* Pacific O
101C3 **Bela Vista** Mozam
70A3 **Belawan** Indon
61J2 **Belaya** *R* USSR
6A2 **Belcher Chan** Can
7C4 **Belcher Is** Can
84B1 **Belchiragh** Afghan
61H3 **Belebey** USSR
31B2 **Belém** Brazil
32B3 **Belén** Colombia
34D2 **Belén** Urug
9C3 **Belen** USA
99E2 **Belet Uen** Somalia
45D1 **Belfast** N Ire
101H1 **Belfast** S Africa
45D1 **Belfast Lough** *Estuary* N Ire
99D1 **Belfodio** Eth
42D2 **Belford** Eng
49D2 **Belfort** France
87A1 **Belgaum** India
56A2 **Belgium** Kingdom, N W Europe
60E3 **Belgorod** USSR
60D4 **Belgorod Dnestrovskiy** USSR
Belgrade = Beograd
95A2 **Bel Hedan** Libya
78B3 **Belinyu** Indon
78B3 **Belitung** *I* Indon
25D3 **Belize** Belize
25D3 **Belize** Republic, Cent America
48C2 **Bellac** France
5F4 **Bella Coola** Can
47C2 **Bellagio** Italy
19A4 **Bellaire** USA
47C1 **Bellano** Italy
87B1 **Bellary** India
109C1 **Bellata** Aust
47B2 **Belledonne** *Mts* France
8C2 **Belle Fourche** USA
49D2 **Bellegarde** France
17B2 **Belle Glade** USA
7E4 **Belle I** Can
48B2 **Belle-Ile** *I* France
7E4 **Belle Isle,Str of** Can
7C5 **Belleville** Can
18A2 **Belleville** Kansas, USA
20B1 **Bellevue** Washington, USA
109D2 **Bellingen** Aust
8A2 **Bellingham** USA
112C2 **Bellingshausen** *Base* Ant
112C3 **Bellingshausen S** Ant
52A1 **Bellinzona** Switz
32B2 **Bello** Colombia
107E3 **Bellona Reefs** Nouvelle Calédonie
22B1 **Bellota** USA
15D2 **Bellows Falls** USA
6B3 **Bell Pen** Can
52B1 **Belluno** Italy
29D2 **Bell Ville** Arg
31D5 **Belmonte** Brazil
25D3 **Belmopan** Belize
45B1 **Belmullet** Irish Rep

69E1 **Belogorsk** USSR
101D3 **Beloha** Madag
31C5 **Belo Horizonte** Brazil
10B2 **Beloit** Wisconsin, USA
64E3 **Belomorsk** USSR
61J3 **Beloretsk** USSR
60C3 **Belorusskaya SSR** Republic, USSR
101D2 **Belo-Tsiribihina** Madag
64E3 **Beloye More** *S* USSR
60E1 **Beloye Ozero** *L* USSR
60E1 **Belozersk** USSR
14B3 **Belpre** USA
108A2 **Beltana** Aust
19A3 **Belton** USA
59D3 **Bel'tsy** USSR
16B2 **Belvidere** New Jersey, USA
98B3 **Bembe** Angola
97C3 **Bembéréke** Benin
10A2 **Bemidji** USA
39G6 **Bena** Nor
98C3 **Bena Dibele** Zaïre
108C3 **Benalla** Aust
44B3 **Ben Attow** *Mt* Scot
50A1 **Benavente** Spain
44A3 **Benbecula** *I* Scot
106A4 **Bencubbin** Aust
8A2 **Bend** USA
44B3 **Ben Dearg** *Mt* Scot
99F2 **Bender Beyla** Somalia
60C4 **Bendery** USSR
107D4 **Bendigo** Aust
57C3 **Benešov** Czech
53B2 **Benevento** Italy
83C4 **Bengal,B of** Asia
96D1 **Ben Gardane** Tunisia
72D3 **Bengbu** China
95B1 **Benghāzī** Libya
78A2 **Bengkalis** Indon
78A3 **Bengkulu** Indon
100A2 **Benguela** Angola
92B3 **Benha** Egypt
44B2 **Ben Hope** *Mt* Scot
99C2 **Beni** Zaïre
32D6 **Béni** *R* Bol
96B1 **Beni Abbes** Alg
51C1 **Benicarló** Spain
7A5 **Benidji** USA
51B2 **Benidorm** Spain
51C2 **Beni Mansour** Alg
95C2 **Beni Mazar** Egypt
96B1 **Beni Mellal** Mor
97C4 **Benin** Republic, Africa
97C4 **Benin City** Nig
95C2 **Beni Suef** Egypt
44B2 **Ben Kilbreck** *Mt* Scot
44B3 **Ben Lawers** *Mt* UK
109C4 **Ben Lomond** *Mt* Aust
44C3 **Ben Macdui** *Mt* Scot
44B2 **Ben More Assynt** *Mt* Scot
111B2 **Benmore,L** NZ
44B3 **Ben Nevis** *Mt* Scot
15D2 **Bennington** USA
94B2 **Bennt Jbail** Leb
98B2 **Bénoué** *R* Cam
9B3 **Benson** Arizona, USA
99C2 **Bentiu** Sudan
19B3 **Benton** Arkansas, USA
18C2 **Benton** Kentucky, USA
14A2 **Benton Harbor** USA
97C4 **Benue** *R* Nig
45B1 **Benwee Hd** *C* Irish Rep
44B3 **Ben Wyvis** *Mt* Scot
72E1 **Benxi** China
54B2 **Beograd** Yugos
86A2 **Beohari** India
74C4 **Beppu** Japan
55A2 **Berat** Alb
95C3 **Berber** Sudan
99E1 **Berbera** Somalia
98B2 **Berbérati** CAR
46A1 **Berck** France

Blakely

17B1 **Blakely** USA
108A1 **Blanche,L** Aust
34A2 **Blanco** R Arg
34B1 **Blanco** R Arg
8A2 **Blanco,C** USA
7E4 **Blanc Sablon** Can
43C4 **Blandford Forum** Eng
46A2 **Blangy-sur-Bresle**
France
46B1 **Blankenberge** Belg
101C2 **Blantyre** Malawi
48B2 **Blaye** France
109C2 **Blayney** Aust
111B2 **Blenheim** NZ
96C1 **Blida** Alg
14B1 **Blind River** Can
108A2 **Blinman** Aust
78C4 **Blitar** Indon
15D2 **Block I** USA
16D2 **Block Island Sd** USA
101G1 **Bloemfontein** S Africa
101G1 **Bloemhof** S Africa
101G1 **Bloemhof Dam** Res
S Africa
33F3 **Blommesteinmeer** L
Surinam
38A1 **Blonduós** Iceland
45B1 **Bloody Foreland** C
Irish Rep
14A3 **Bloomfield** Indiana,
USA
18B1 **Bloomfield** Iowa, USA
10B2 **Bloomington** Illinois,
USA
14A3 **Bloomington** Indiana,
USA
16A2 **Bloomsburg** USA
78C4 **Blora** Indon
6H3 **Blosseville Kyst** Mts
Greenland
57B3 **Bludenz** Austria
11B3 **Bluefield** USA
32A1 **Bluefields** Nic
26B3 **Blue Mountain Peak**
Mt Jamaica
16A2 **Blue Mt** USA
109D2 **Blue Mts** Aust
27J1 **Blue Mts** Jamaica
8A2 **Blue Mts** USA
Blue Nile = Bahr el
Azraq
99D1 **Blue Nile** R Sudan
4G3 **Bluenose L** Can
11B3 **Blue Ridge Mts** USA
13D2 **Blue River** Can
45B1 **Blue Stack** Mt
Irish Rep
111A3 **Bluff** NZ
106A4 **Bluff Knoll** Mt Aust
30G4 **Blumenau** Brazil
49D2 **Blundez** Austria
20B2 **Bly** USA
12E3 **Blying Sd** USA
42D2 **Blyth** Eng
9B3 **Blythe** USA
11B3 **Blytheville** USA
97A4 **Bo** Sierra Leone
79B3 **Boac** Phil
72D2 **Boading** China
14B2 **Boardman** USA
63C3 **Boatou** China
33E3 **Boa Vista** Brazil
97A4 **Boa Vista** I Cape
Verde
76E1 **Bobai** China
47C2 **Bóbbio** Italy
97B3 **Bobo Dioulasso**
Burkina
60C3 **Bobruysk** USSR
17B2 **Boca Chica Key** I USA
32D5 **Bôca do Acre** Brazil
35C1 **Bocaiúva** Brazil
98B2 **Bocaranga** CAR
17B2 **Boca Raton** USA
59C3 **Bochnia** Pol
56B2 **Bocholt** Germany
46D1 **Bochum** Germany
100A2 **Bocoio** Angola

98B2 **Boda** CAR
63D2 **Bodaybo** USSR
21A2 **Bodega Head** Pt USA
95A3 **Bodélé** Region Chad
38J5 **Boden** Sweden
47C1 **Bodensee** L Switz/
Germany
87B1 **Bodhan** India
87B2 **Bodināyakkanūr** India
43B4 **Bodmin** Eng
43B4 **Bodmin Moor** Upland
Eng
38G5 **Bodø** Nor
63G2 **Bodorodskoye** USSR
55C3 **Bodrum** Turk
98C3 **Boende** Zaïre
97A3 **Boffa** Guinea
76B2 **Bogale** Burma
19C3 **Bogalusa** USA
109C2 **Bogan** R Aust
97B3 **Bogandé** Burkina
6H3 **Bogarnes** Iceland
92C2 **Boğazlıyan** Turk
61K2 **Bogdanovich** USSR
68A2 **Bogda Shan** Mt China
100A3 **Bogenfels** Namibia
109D1 **Boggabilla** Aust
109C2 **Boggabri** Aust
45B2 **Boggeragh Mts**
Irish Rep
79B3 **Bogo** Phil
109C3 **Bogong,Mt** Aust
78B4 **Bogor** Indon
61H2 **Bogorodskoye** USSR
32C3 **Bogotá** Colombia
63A2 **Bogotol** USSR
86B2 **Bogra** Bang
72D2 **Bo Hai** B China
46B2 **Bohain-en-Vermandois**
France
72D2 **Bohai Wan** B China
57C3 **Böhmer-Wald** Upland
Germany
79B4 **Bohol** I Phil
79B4 **Bohol S** Phil
35A1 **Bois** R Brazil
14B1 **Bois Blanc I** USA
8B2 **Boise** USA
96A2 **Bojador,C** Mor
79B2 **Bojeador,C** Phil
90C2 **Bojnürd** Iran
97A3 **Boké** Guinea
109C1 **Bokhara** R Aust
39F7 **Boknafjord** Inlet Nor
98B3 **Boko** Congo
76C3 **Bokor** Camb
98C3 **Bokungu** Zaïre
98B1 **Bol** Chad
97A3 **Bolama** Guinea-Bissau
23A1 **Bolaños** Mexico
23A1 **Bolanos** R Mexico
48C2 **Bolbec** France
97B4 **Bole** Ghana
59B2 **Boleslawiec** Pol
97B3 **Bolgatanga** Ghana
60C4 **Bolgrad** USSR
34C3 **Bolívar** Arg
18B2 **Bolivar** Missouri, USA
18C2 **Bolivar** Tennessee,
USA
30C2 **Bolivia** Republic,
S America
38H6 **Bollnas** Sweden
109C1 **Bollon** Aust
32C2 **Bollvar** Mt Ven
52B2 **Bologna** Italy
60D2 **Bologoye** USSR
69F2 **Bolon** USSR
61G3 **Bol'shoy Irgiz** R USSR
74C2 **Bol'shoy Kamen**
USSR
65F5 **Bol'shoy Kavkaz** Mts
USSR
61G4 **Bol'shoy Uzen** R
USSR
9C4 **Bolson de Mapimi**
Desert Mexico
43C3 **Bolton** Eng

92B1 **Bolu** Turk
38A1 **Bolungarvik** Iceland
92B2 **Bolvadin** Turk
52B1 **Bolzano** Italy
98B3 **Boma** Zaïre
107D4 **Bombala** Aust
87A1 **Bombay** India
99D2 **Bombo** Uganda
35B1 **Bom Despacho** Brazil
86C1 **Bomdila** India
97A4 **Bomi Hills** Lib
31C4 **Bom Jesus da Lapa**
Brazil
63E2 **Bomnak** USSR
99C2 **Bomokandi** R Zaïre
98C2 **Bomu** R CAR/Zaïre
27D4 **Bonaire** I Caribbean S
12F2 **Bona,Mt** USA
25D3 **Bonanza** Nic
7E5 **Bonavista** Can
108A2 **Bon Bon** Aust
98C2 **Bondo** Zaïre
97B4 **Bondoukou** Ivory Coast
Bône = 'Annaba
33E3 **Bonfim** Guyana
98C2 **Bongandanga** Zaïre
98B1 **Bongor** Chad
19A3 **Bonham** USA
53A2 **Bonifacio** Corse
52A2 **Bonifacio,Str of** Chan
Medit S
Bonin Is = Ogasawara
Gunto
17B2 **Bonita Springs** USA
57B2 **Bonn** Germany
20C1 **Bonners Ferry** USA
12H1 **Bonnet Plume** R Can
13E2 **Bonnyville** Can
97A4 **Bonthe** Sierra Leone
99E1 **Booaaso** Somalia
108B2 **Booligal** Aust
109D1 **Boonah** Aust
15C2 **Boonville** USA
109C2 **Boorowa** Aust
6A2 **Boothia,G of** Can
6A2 **Boothia Pen** Can
98B3 **Booué** Gabon
108A1 **Bopeechee** Aust
99D2 **Bor** Sudan
92B2 **Bor** Turk
54B2 **Bor** Yugos
8B2 **Borah Peak** Mt USA
39G7 **Borås** Sweden
91B4 **Borãzjän** Iran
108A3 **Borda,C** Aust
48B3 **Bordeaux** France
4G2 **Borden I** Can
6B2 **Borden Pen** Can
16B2 **Bordentown** USA
42C2 **Borders** Region, Scot
108B3 **Bordertown** Aust
96C2 **Bordi Omar Dris** Alg
8D1 **Borens River** Can
38A2 **Borgarnes** Iceland
9C3 **Borger** USA
39H7 **Borgholm** Sweden
47C2 **Borgosia** Italy
47D1 **Borgo Valsugana** Italy
59C3 **Borislav** USSR
61F3 **Borisoglebsk** USSR
60C3 **Borisov** USSR
60E3 **Borisovka** USSR
95A3 **Borkou** Region Chad
39H6 **Borlänge** Sweden
47C2 **Bormida** Italy
47D1 **Bormio** Italy
67F5 **Borneo** I Malay/Indon
39H7 **Bornholm** I Den
55C3 **Bornova** Turk
98C2 **Boro** R Sudan
97B3 **Boromo** Burkina
60D2 **Borovichi** USSR
106C2 **Borroloola** Aust
54B1 **Borsa** Rom
90A3 **Borüjed** Iran
90B3 **Borüjen** Iran
58B2 **Bory Tucholskie**
Region, Pol

63D2 **Borzya** USSR
54A1 **Bosanki Brod** Yugos
73B5 **Bose** China
101G1 **Boshof** S Africa
54A2 **Bosna** R Yugos
75C1 **Bösö-hantö** B Japan
Bosporus = Karadeniz
Boğazi
51C2 **Bosquet** Alg
98B2 **Bossangoa** CAR
98B2 **Bossèmbélé** CAR
19B3 **Bossier City** USA
65K5 **Bosten Hu** L China
43D3 **Boston** Eng
10C2 **Boston** USA
11A3 **Boston Mts** USA
85C4 **Botād** India
54B2 **Botevgrad** Bulg
101G1 **Bothaville** S Africa
64C3 **Bothnia,G of** Sweden/
Fin
100B3 **Botletli** R Botswana
60C4 **Botosani** Rom
100B3 **Botswana** Republic,
Africa
53C3 **Botte Donato** Mt Italy
46D1 **Bottrop** Germany
35B2 **Botucatu** Brazil
7E5 **Botwood** Can
89D7 **Bouaké** Ivory Coast
98B2 **Bouar** CAR
96B1 **Bouârfa** Mor
98B2 **Bouca** CAR
51C2 **Boufarik** Alg
Bougie = Bejaïa
97B3 **Bougouni** Mali
46C2 **Bouillon** France
96B2 **Bou Izakarn** Mor
46D2 **Boulay-Moselle**
France
8C2 **Boulder** Colorado,
USA
9B3 **Boulder City** USA
22A2 **Boulder Creek** USA
48C1 **Boulogne** France
98B2 **Boumba** R CAR
97B4 **Bouna** Ivory Coast
8B3 **Boundary Peak** Mt
USA
97B4 **Boundiali** Ivory Coast
107F3 **Bourail** Nouvelle
Calédonie
97B3 **Bourem** Mali
49D2 **Bourg** France
49D2 **Bourg de Péage**
France
48C2 **Bourges** France
48C3 **Bourg-Madame**
France
49C2 **Bourgogne** Region,
France
47B2 **Bourg-St-Maurice**
France
108C2 **Bourke** Aust
43D4 **Bournemouth** Eng
96C1 **Bou Saâda** Alg
98B1 **Bousso** Chad
97A3 **Boutilmit** Maur
103J7 **Bouvet I** Atlantic O
34D2 **Bovril** Arg
13E2 **Bow** R Can
107D2 **Bowen** Aust
19A3 **Bowie** Texas, USA
13E2 **Bow Island** Can
11B3 **Bowling Green**
Kentucky, USA
18B2 **Bowling Green**
Missouri, USA
14B2 **Bowling Green** Ohio,
USA
15C3 **Bowling Green**
Virginia, USA
15C2 **Bowmanville** Can
109D2 **Bowral** Aust
13C2 **Bowron** R Can
72D3 **Bo Xian** China
72D2 **Boxing** China
92B1 **Boyabat** Turk

98B2 **Boyali** CAR	56A2 **Breda** Neth	48C2 **Brive** France	7E5 **Buchans** Can
5J4 **Boyd** Can	100B4 **Bredasdorp** S Africa	59B3 **Brno** Czech	34C2 **Buchardo** Arg
16B2 **Boyertown** USA	38H6 **Bredbyn** Sweden	17B1 **Broad** *R* USA	**Bucharest = Bucureşti**
13E2 **Boyle** Can	61J3 **Bredy** USSR	7C4 **Broadback** *R* Can	47C1 **Buchs** Switz
41B3 **Boyle** Irish Rep	15C2 **Breezewood** USA	44A2 **Broad Bay** *Inlet* Scot	43D3 **Buckingham** Eng
45C2 **Boyne** *R* Irish Rep	47C1 **Bregenz** Austria	44B3 **Broadford** Scot	12B1 **Buckland** USA
17B2 **Boynoton Beach** USA	47C1 **Bregenzer Ache** *R*	5H4 **Brochet** Can	12B1 **Buckland** *R* USA
98C2 **Boyoma Falls** Zaïre	Austria	4G2 **Brock I** Can	108A2 **Buckleboo** Aust
55C3 **Bozca Ada** *I* Turk	38A1 **Breiðafjörður** *B*	15C2 **Brockport** USA	98B3 **Buco Zau** Congo
55C3 **Boz Dağlari** *Mts* Turk	Iceland	16D1 **Brockton** USA	54C2 **Bucureşti** Rom
8B2 **Bozeman** USA	47C2 **Brembo** *R* Italy	15C2 **Brockville** Can	59B3 **Budapest** Hung
Bozen = Bolzano	17A1 **Bremen** USA	6B2 **Brodeur Pen** Can	84D3 **Budaun** India
98B2 **Bozene** Zaïre	56B2 **Bremen** Germany	42B2 **Brodick** Scot	43B4 **Bude** Eng
98B2 **Bozoum** CAR	56B2 **Bremerhaven**	58B2 **Brodnica** Pol	19B3 **Bude** USA
47B2 **Bra** Italy	Germany	60C3 **Brody** USSR	61F5 **Budennovsk** USSR
52C2 **Brač** *I* Yugos	20B1 **Bremerton** USA	19B3 **Broken Bow**	54A2 **Budva** Yugos
15C1 **Bracebridge** Can	19A3 **Brenham** USA	Oklahoma, USA	98A2 **Buéa** Cam
95A2 **Brach** Libya	57C3 **Brenner** *P* Austria/	19B3 **Broken Bow L** USA	22B3 **Buellton** USA
38H6 **Bräcke** Sweden	Italy	107D4 **Broken Hill** Aust	34B2 **Buena Esperanza** Arg
17B2 **Bradenton** USA	47D2 **Breno** Italy	47C2 **Broni** Italy	32B3 **Buenaventura**
42D3 **Bradford** Eng	47D2 **Brenta** *R* Italy	38G5 **Brønnøysund** Nor	Colombia
44E1 **Brae** Scot	22B2 **Brentwood** USA	16C2 **Bronx** *Borough,* New	23A2 **Buenavista** Mexico
44C3 **Braemar** Scot	52B1 **Brescia** Italy	York, USA	29E2 **Buenos Aires** Arg
50A1 **Braga** Port	**Breslau = Wrocław**	79A4 **Brooke's Point** Phil	29D3 **Buenos Aires** State,
34C3 **Bragado** Arg	47D1 **Bressanone** Italy	18B2 **Brookfield** Missouri,	Arg
50A1 **Bragana** Port	44E1 **Bressay** *I* Scot	USA	18B2 **Buffalo** Mississipi,
31B2 **Bragança** Brazil	48B2 **Bressuire** France	11A3 **Brookhaven** USA	USA
35B2 **Bragança Paulista**	48B2 **Brest** France	20B2 **Brookings** Oregon,	10C2 **Buffalo** New York,
Brazil	58C2 **Brest** USSR	USA	USA
86C2 **Brahman-Baria** Bang	48B2 **Bretagne** *Region,*	8D2 **Brookings** South	8C2 **Buffalo** South Dakota,
86B2 **Brāhmani** *R* India	France	Dakota, USA	USA
86C1 **Brahmaputra** *R* India	46B2 **Breteuil** France	16D1 **Brookline** USA	19A3 **Buffalo** Texas, USA
7E5 **Braie Verte** Can	16B2 **Breton Woods** USA	16C2 **Brooklyn** *Borough,*	8C2 **Buffalo** Wyoming,
60C4 **Brăila** Rom	110B1 **Brett,C** NZ	New York, USA	USA
10A2 **Brainerd** USA	109C1 **Brewarrina** Aust	5G4 **Brooks** Can	101H1 **Buffalo** *R* S Africa
97A3 **Brakna** Region, Maur	16C2 **Brewster** New York,	12C3 **Brooks,L** USA	13E2 **Buffalo L** Alberta, Can
5F4 **Bralorne** Can	USA	12A1 **Brooks Mt** USA	5G3 **Buffalo L** Northwest
14C2 **Brampton** Can	20C1 **Brewster** Washington,	4C3 **Brooks Range** *Mts*	Territories, Can
33E3 **Branco** *R* Brazil	USA	USA	5H4 **Buffalo Narrows** Can
100A3 **Brandberg** *Mt*	101G1 **Breyten** S Africa	17B2 **Brooksville** USA	17B1 **Buford** USA
Namibia	52C1 **Brežice** Yugos	109D1 **Brooloo** Aust	54C2 **Buftea** Rom
56C2 **Brandenburg**	98C2 **Bria** CAR	106B2 **Broome** Aust	59C2 **Bug** *R* Pol/USSR
Germany	49D3 **Briancon** France	44C2 **Brora** Scot	32B3 **Buga** Colombia
56C2 **Brandenburg** State,	49C2 **Briare** France	20B2 **Brothers** USA	90B2 **Bugdayli** USSR
Germany	21B2 **Bridgeport** California,	95A3 **Broulkou** Chad	61H3 **Bugulma** USSR
101G1 **Brandfort** S Africa	USA	13E3 **Browning** USA	61H3 **Buguruslan** USSR
8D2 **Brandon** Can	15D2 **Bridgeport**	9D4 **Brownsville** USA	93C2 **Buhayrat al Asad** *Res*
100B4 **Brandvlei** S Africa	Connecticut, USA	9D3 **Brownwood** USA	Syria
57C2 **Brandys nad Lebem**	19A3 **Bridgeport** Texas,	46B1 **Bruay-en-Artois**	41C3 **Builth Wells** Wales
Czech	USA	France	34A2 **Buin** Chile
58B2 **Braniewo** Pol	22C1 **Bridgeport Res** USA	106A3 **Bruce,Mt** Aust	99C3 **Bujumbura** Burundi
10B2 **Brantford** Can	16B3 **Bridgeton** USA	14B1 **Bruce Pen** Can	98C3 **Bukama** Zaïre
108B3 **Branxholme** Aust	27F4 **Bridgetown** Barbados	59B3 **Brück an der Mur**	99C3 **Bukavu** Zaïre
7D5 **Bras d'Or L** Can	7D5 **Bridgewater** Can	Austria	80E2 **Bukhara** USSR
35C1 **Brasila de Minas** Brazil	16D2 **Bridgewater** USA	**Bruges = Brugge**	78C2 **Bukit Batubrok** *Mt*
32D6 **Brasiléia** Brazil	43C4 **Bridgwater** Eng	46B1 **Brugge** Belg	Indon
31B5 **Brasilia** Brazil	43C4 **Bridgwater B** Eng	46D1 **Brühl** Germany	70B4 **Bukittinggi** Indon
54C1 **Brasov** Rom	42D2 **Bridlington** Eng	78C2 **Brunei** Sultanate,	99D3 **Bukoba** Tanz
78D1 **Brassay Range** *Mts*	109C4 **Bridport** Aust	S E Asia	78D3 **Buku Gandadiwata** *Mt*
Malay	47B1 **Brienzer See** *L* Switz	52B1 **Brunico** Italy	Indon
59B3 **Bratislava** Czech	46C2 **Briey** France	111B2 **Brunner,L** NZ	71E4 **Bula** Indon
63C2 **Bratsk** USSR	52A1 **Brig** Switz	11B3 **Brunswick** Georgia,	79B3 **Bulan** Phil
15D2 **Brattleboro** USA	8B2 **Brigham City** USA	USA	84D3 **Bulandshahr** India
56C2 **Braunschweig**	109C3 **Bright** Aust	18B2 **Brunswick**	100B3 **Bulawayo** Zim
Germany	43D4 **Brighton** Eng	Mississippi, USA	55C3 **Buldan** Turk
97A4 **Brava** *I* Cape Verde	46E1 **Brilon** Germany	29B6 **Brunswick,Pen de**	85D4 **Buldāna** India
9B3 **Brawley** USA	55A2 **Brindisi** Italy	Chile	68C2 **Bulgan** Mongolia
45C2 **Bray** Irish Rep	19B3 **Brinkley** USA	109C4 **Bruny I** Aust	54B2 **Bulgaria**
6C3 **Bray I** Can	107E3 **Brisbane** Aust	61F1 **Brusenets** USSR	Republic, Europe
13D2 **Brazeau** *R* Can	15D2 **Bristol** Connecticut,	26A3 **Brus Laguna**	47B1 **Bulle** Switz
13D2 **Brazeau,Mt** Can	USA	Honduras	111B2 **Buller** *R* NZ
28D4 **Brazil** Republic,	43C4 **Bristol** Eng	**Brüssel = Bruxelles**	109C3 **Buller,Mt** Aust
S America	15D2 **Bristol** Pennsylvania,	56A2 **Bruxelles** Belg	106A4 **Bullfinch** Aust
103G5 **Brazil Basin** Atlantic O	USA	9D3 **Bryan** USA	108B1 **Bulloo** *R* Aust
9D3 **Brazos** *R* USA	16D2 **Bristol** Rhode Island,	108A2 **Bryan,Mt** Aust	108B1 **Bulloo Downs** Aust
98B3 **Brazzaville** Congo	USA	60D3 **Bryansk** USSR	108B1 **Bulloo L** Aust
57C3 **Brdy** *Upland* Czech	11B3 **Bristol** Tennessee,	19B3 **Bryant** USA	18B2 **Bull Shoals Res** USA
111A3 **Breaksea Sd** NZ	USA	59B2 **Brzeg** Pol	34A3 **Bulnes** Chile
110B1 **Bream B** NZ	12B3 **Bristol B** USA	93E4 **Būbīyan** *I* Kuwait/Iraq	71F4 **Bulolo** PNG
78B4 **Brebes** Indon	43B4 **Bristol Chan** Eng/	99D3 **Bubu** *R* Tanz	101G1 **Bultfontein** S Africa
44C3 **Brechin** Scot	Wales	32C2 **Bucaramanga**	98C2 **Bumba** Zaïre
46C1 **Brecht** Belg	4D3 **British** *Mts* USA	Colombia	76B2 **Bumphal Dam** Thai
59B3 **Břeclav** Czech	5F4 **British Columbia**	44D3 **Buchan** *Oilfield* N Sea	99D2 **Buna** Kenya
43C4 **Brecon** Wales	Province, Can	97A4 **Buchanan** Lib	106A4 **Bunbury** Aust
43C4 **Brecon Beacons** *Mts*	6B1 **British Empire Range**	44D3 **Buchan Deep** N Sea	45C1 **Buncrana** Irish Rep
Wales	*Mts* Can	6C2 **Buchan G** Can	107E3 **Bundaberg** Aust
43B3 **Brecon Beacons Nat**	101G1 **Brits** S Africa	40C2 **Buchan Ness** *Pen*	109D2 **Bundarra** Aust
Pk Wales	100B4 **Britstown** S Africa	Scot	85D3 **Būndi** India

25E2 **Camagüey,Arch de** *Is*
Cuba
30B2 **Camaná** Peru
30C3 **Camargo** Bol
22C3 **Camarillo** USA
29C4 **Camarones** Arg
20B1 **Camas** USA
98B3 **Camaxilo** Angola
98B3 **Cambatela** Angola
76C3 **Cambodia** Republic,
S E Asia
43B4 **Camborne** Eng
49C1 **Cambrai** France
43C3 **Cambrian Mts** Wales
14B2 **Cambridge** Can
43D3 **Cambridge** County,
Eng
43E3 **Cambridge** Eng
27H1 **Cambridge** Jamaica
15C3 **Cambridge** Maryland,
USA
15D2 **Cambridge**
Massachussets, USA
110C1 **Cambridge** NZ
14B2 **Cambridge** Ohio, USA
4H3 **Cambridge Bay** Can
60E5 **Cam Burun** *Pt* Turk
11A3 **Camden** Arkansas,
USA
109D2 **Camden** Aust
15D3 **Camden** New Jersey,
USA
17B1 **Camden** South
Carolina, USA
18B2 **Cameron** Missouri,
USA
19A3 **Cameron** Texas, USA
4H2 **Cameron** I Can
111A3 **Cameron Mts** NZ
98A2 **Cameroon** Federal
Republic, Africa
98A2 **Cameroun** *Mt* Cam
31B2 **Cametá** Brazil
79B4 **Camiguin** I Phil
79B2 **Camiling** Phil
17B1 **Camilla** USA
22B1 **Camino** USA
30D3 **Camiri** Bol
31C2 **Camocim** Brazil
106C2 **Camooweal** Aust
34D2 **Campana** Arg
29A5 **Campana** I Chile
13B2 **Campania** I Can
111B2 **Campbell,C** NZ
13B2 **Campbell I** Can
105G6 **Campbell I** NZ
4E3 **Campbell,Mt** Can
84C2 **Campbellpore** Pak
5F5 **Campbell River** Can
7D5 **Campbellton** Can
109D2 **Campbelltown** Aust
42B2 **Campbeltown** Scot
25C3 **Campeche** Mexico
108B3 **Camperdown** Aust
31D3 **Campina Grande**
Brazil
31B6 **Campinas** Brazil
35B1 **Campina Verde** Brazil
98A2 **Campo** Cam
53B2 **Campobasso** Italy
35B2 **Campo Belo** Brazil
35B1 **Campo Florido** Brazil
30D4 **Campo Gallo** Arg
30F3 **Campo Grande** Brazil
31C2 **Campo Maior** Brazil
30F3 **Campo Mourão** Brazil
35C2 **Campos** Brazil
35B1 **Campos Altos** Brazil
47D1 **Campo Tures** Italy
76D3 **Cam Ranh** Viet
5G4 **Camrose** Can
100A2 **Camucuio** Angola
27K1 **Canaan** Tobago
16C1 **Canaan** USA
100A2 **Canacupa** Angola
2F3 **Canada** Dominion,
N America
29D2 **Cañada de Gomez** Arg

9C3 **Canadian** *R* USA
60C5 **Canakkale** Turk
34B3 **Canalejas** Arg
13D2 **Canal Flats** Can
24A1 **Cananea** Mexico
102G3 **Canary Basin** Atlantic O
Canary Is = Islas
Canarias
23A2 **Canas** Mexico
24B2 **Canatlán** Mexico
11B4 **Canaveral,C** USA
31D5 **Canavieiras** Brazil
107D4 **Canberra** Aust
20B2 **Canby** California, USA
99F1 **Candala** Somalia
55C3 **Çandarli Körfezi** *B*
Turk
16C2 **Candlewood,L** USA
29E2 **Canelones** Urug
18A2 **Caney** USA
100A2 **Cangamba** Angola
100B2 **Cangombe** Angola
72D2 **Cangzhou** China
7D4 **Caniapiscau** *R* Can
7D4 **Caniapiscau,L** Can
53B3 **Canicatti** Italy
31D2 **Canindé** Brazil
92B1 **Çankırı** Turk
13D2 **Canmore** Can
44A3 **Canna** I Scot
87B2 **Cannanore** India
49D3 **Cannes** France
109C3 **Cann River** Aust
30F4 **Canõas** Brazil
13F1 **Canoe L** Can
9C3 **Canon City** USA
108B2 **Canopus** Aust
5H4 **Canora** Can
109C2 **Canowindra** Aust
45C2 **Cansore Pt** Irish Rep
43E4 **Canterbury** Eng
111B2 **Canterbury Bight** *B* NZ
111B2 **Canterbury Plains** NZ
77D4 **Can Tho** Viet
Canton = Guangzhou
19C3 **Canton** Mississippi,
USA
18B1 **Canton** Missouri, USA
10B2 **Canton** Ohio, USA
12E2 **Cantwell** USA
20C2 **Canyon City** USA
12J2 **Canyon Range** *Mts*
Can
20B2 **Canyonville** USA
98C3 **Canzar** Angola
76D1 **Cao Bang** Viet
31B2 **Capanema** Brazil
35B2 **Capão Bonito** Brazil
48B3 **Capbreton** France
24B2 **Cap Corrientes** *C*
Mexico
52A2 **Cap Corse** *C* Corse
101D2 **Cap d'Ambre** *C* Madag
48B2 **Cap de la Hague** *C*
France
15D1 **Cap-de-la-Madeleine**
Can
6C3 **Cap de Nouvelle-France**
C Can
51C2 **Capdepera** Spain
23A2 **Cap de Tancitiario** *C*
Mexico
109C4 **Cape Barren I** Aust
103J6 **Cape Basin** Atlantic O
7E5 **Cape Breton I** Can
97B4 **Cape Coast** Ghana
15D2 **Cape Cod B** USA
6C3 **Cape Dorset** Can
17C1 **Cape Fear** *R* USA
18C2 **Cape Girardeau** USA
6B3 **Cape Henrietta Maria**
Cape Horn = Cabo de
Hornos
104E3 **Cape Johnston Depth**
Pacific O
35C1 **Capelinha** Brazil
4B3 **Cape Lisburne** USA

100A2 **Capelongo** Angola
15D3 **Cape May** USA
5F5 **Cape Mendocino** USA
98B3 **Capenda Camulemba**
Angola
4F2 **Cape Perry** Can
100B4 **Cape Province**
S Africa
7A4 **Cape Tatnam** Can
100A4 **Cape Town** S Africa
102G4 **Cape Verde** *Is*
Atlantic O
102G4 **Cape Verde Basin**
Atlantic O
12F3 **Cape Yakataga** USA
107D2 **Cape York Pen** Aust
46A1 **Cap Gris Nez** *C*
France
26C3 **Cap-Haitien** Haiti
31B2 **Capim** *R* Brazil
27P2 **Cap Moule à Chique** *C*
St Lucia
53C3 **Capo Isola de Correnti**
C Italy
53C3 **Capo Rizzuto** *C* Italy
55A3 **Capo Santa Maria di**
Leuca *C* Italy
53B3 **Capo San Vito** Italy
53C3 **Capo Spartivento** *C*
Italy
27P2 **Cap Pt** St Lucia
53B2 **Capri** I Italy
100B2 **Caprivi Strip** Region,
Namibia
52A2 **Cap Rosso** *C* Corse
102H4 **Cap Vert** *C* Sen
32C4 **Caquetá** *R* Colombia
54B2 **Caracal** Rom
33E3 **Caracaraí** Brazil
32D1 **Caracas** Ven
35B2 **Caraguatatuba** Brazil
29B3 **Carahue** Chile
35C1 **Caraí** Brazil
35C2 **Carandaí** Brazil
31C6 **Carangola** Brazil
54B1 **Caransebeş** Rom
108A2 **Carappee Hill** *Mt* Aust
26A3 **Caratasca** Honduras
35C1 **Caratinga** Brazil
51B2 **Caravaca** Spain
35D1 **Caravelas** Brazil
18C2 **Carbondale** Illinois,
USA
53A3 **Carbonia** Sardegna
7E5 **Carborear** Can
5G4 **Carcaion** Can
99E1 **Carcar Mts** Somalia
48C3 **Carcassonne** France
4E3 **Carcross** Can
23B2 **Cardel** Mexico
25D2 **Cardenas** Cuba
23B1 **Cárdenas** Mexico
43C4 **Cardiff** Wales
43B3 **Cardigan** Wales
43B3 **Cardigan B** Wales
13E2 **Cardston** Can
54B1 **Carei** Rom
33F4 **Careiro** Brazil
34A2 **Carén** Chile
14B2 **Carey** USA
48B2 **Carhaix-Plouguer**
France
29D3 **Carhué** Arg
31C6 **Cariacica** Brazil
5J4 **Caribou** Can
5G4 **Caribou Mts** Alberta,
Can
5F4 **Caribou Mts** British
Columbia, Can
79B3 **Carigara** Phil
46C2 **Carignan** France
33E1 **Caripito** Ven
15C1 **Carleton Place** Can
101G1 **Carletonville** S Africa
18C2 **Carlinville** USA
42C2 **Carlisle** Eng
15C2 **Carlisle** USA
34C3 **Carlos** Arg

35C1 **Carlos Chagas** Brazil
45C2 **Carlow** County,
Irish Rep
45C2 **Carlow** Irish Rep
21B3 **Carlsbad** California,
USA
9C3 **Carlsbad** New Mexico,
USA
5H5 **Carlyle** Can
12G2 **Carmacks** Can
47B2 **Carmagnola** Italy
43B4 **Carmarthen** Wales
43B4 **Carmarthen B** Wales
22B2 **Carmel** California,
USA
16C2 **Carmel** New York,
USA
94B2 **Carmel,Mt** Israel
34D2 **Carmelo** Urug
22B2 **Carmel Valley** USA
9B4 **Carmen** I Mexico
29D4 **Carmen de Patagones**
Arg
18C2 **Carmi** USA
21A2 **Carmichael** USA
35B1 **Carmo do Paranaiba**
Brazil
50A2 **Carmona** Spain
106A3 **Carnarvon** Aust
100B4 **Carnarvon** S Africa
35D1 **Carncacá** Brazil
45C1 **Carndonagh** Irish Rep
106B3 **Carnegi,L** Aust
98B2 **Carnot** CAR
108A2 **Carnot,C** Aust
17B2 **Carol City** USA
31B3 **Carolina** Brazil
101H1 **Carolina** S Africa
17C1 **Carolina Beach** USA
104F3 **Caroline Is** Pacific O
60B4 **Carpathians** *Mts*
E Europe
59D3 **Carpatii Orientali** *Mts*
Rom
106C2 **Carpentaria,G of** Aust
83C5 **Carpenter Ridge**
Indian O
49D3 **Carpentras** France
52B2 **Carpi** Italy
22C3 **Carpinteria** USA
17B2 **Carrabelle** USA
52B2 **Carrara** Italy
41B3 **Carrauntoohill** *Mt*
Irish Rep
45C2 **Carrickmacross**
Irish Rep
45B2 **Carrick on Shannon**
Irish Rep
45C2 **Carrick-on-Suir**
Irish Rep
108A2 **Carrieton** Aust
8D2 **Carrington** USA
50B1 **Carrión** *R* Spain
10A2 **Carroll** USA
17A1 **Carrollton** Georgia,
USA
14A3 **Carrollton** Kentucky,
USA
18B2 **Carrollton** Missouri,
USA
18C2 **Carruthersville** USA
60E5 **Carsamba** Turk
92B2 **Carsamba** *R* Turk
8B3 **Carson City** USA
14B2 **Carsonville** USA
26B4 **Cartagena** Colombia
51B2 **Cartagena** Spain
32B3 **Cartago** Colombia
25D4 **Cartago** Costa Rica
111C2 **Carterton** NZ
18B2 **Carthage** Missouri,
USA
15C2 **Carthage** New York,
USA
19B3 **Carthage** Texas, USA
106B2 **Cartier I** Timor S
7E4 **Cartwright** Can
31D3 **Caruaru** Brazil

33E1 **Carúpano** Ven
46B1 **Carvin** France
34A2 **Casablanca** Chile
96B1 **Casablanca** Mor
35B2 **Casa Branca** Brazil
9B3 **Casa Grande** USA
52A1 **Casale Monferrato** Italy
47D2 **Casalmaggiore** Italy
34C3 **Casares** Arg
13C3 **Cascade Mts** Can/USA
111A2 **Cascade Pt** NZ
8A2 **Cascade Range** *Mts* USA
30F3 **Cascavel** Brazil
53B2 **Caserta** Italy
112C9 **Casey** *Base* Ant
45C2 **Cashel** Irish Rep
34C2 **Casilda** Arg
107E3 **Casino** Aust
32B5 **Casma** Peru
51B1 **Caspe** Spain
8C2 **Casper** USA
65G6 **Caspian S** USSR
14C3 **Cass** USA
100B2 **Cassamba** Angola
46B1 **Cassel** France
12J3 **Cassiar** Can
4E3 **Cassiar Mts** Can
35A1 **Cassilândia** Brazil
53B2 **Cassino** Italy
22C3 **Castaic** USA
34B2 **Castaño** *R* Arg
47D2 **Castelfranco** Italy
49D3 **Castellane** France
34D3 **Castelli** Arg
51B2 **Castellon de la Plana** Spain
31C3 **Castelo** Brazil
50A2 **Castelo Branco** Port
48C3 **Castelsarrasin** France
53B3 **Castelvetrano** Italy
108B3 **Casterton** Aust
50B2 **Castilla La Nueva** Region, Spain
50B1 **Castilla La Vieja** Region, Spain
41B3 **Castlebar** Irish Rep
44A3 **Castlebay** Scot
42C2 **Castle Douglas** Scot
20C1 **Castlegar** Can
45B2 **Castleisland** Irish Rep
108B3 **Castlemain** Aust
45B2 **Castlerea** Irish Rep
109C2 **Castlereagh** Aust
48C3 **Castres-sur-l'Agout** France
27E4 **Castries** St Lucia
29B4 **Castro** Arg
30F3 **Castro** Brazil
31D4 **Castro Alves** Brazil
53C3 **Castrovillari** Italy
22B2 **Castroville** USA
111A2 **Caswell Sd** NZ
25E2 **Cat** *I* The Bahamas
79B3 **Catabalogan** Phil
32A5 **Catacaos** Peru
35C2 **Cataguases** Brazil
19B3 **Catahoula L** USA
35B1 **Catalão** Brazil
51C1 **Cataluña** Region, Spain
30C4 **Catamarca** Arg
30C4 **Catamarca** State, Arg
101C2 **Catandica** Mozam
79B3 **Catanduanes** *I* Phil
31B6 **Catanduva** Brazil
53C3 **Catania** Italy
53C3 **Catanzaro** Italy
79B3 **Catarman** Phil
108A2 **Catastrophe,C** Aust
26C5 **Catatumbo** *R* Ven
16A2 **Catawissa** USA
23B2 **Catemaco** Mexico
49D3 **Cater** Corse
52A2 **Cateraggio** Corse
98B3 **Catete** Angola
97A3 **Catio** Guinea-Bissau
7A4 **Cat Lake** Can
13D3 **Catlegar** Can

107E3 **Cato** *I* Aust
25D2 **Catoche,C** Mexico
16A3 **Catoctin Mt** USA
15C3 **Catonsville** USA
34C3 **Catrilo** Arg
15D2 **Catskill** USA
15D2 **Catskill Mts** USA
32C2 **Cauca** *R* Colombia
31D2 **Caucaia** Brazil
32B2 **Caucasia** Colombia
Caucasus = Bol'shoy Kavkaz
46B1 **Caudry** France
98B3 **Caungula** Angola
29B3 **Cauquenes** Chile
87B2 **Cauvery** *R* India
49D3 **Cavaillon** France
47D1 **Cavalese** italy
97B4 **Cavally** *R* Lib
45C2 **Cavan** County, Irish Rep
45C2 **Cavan** Irish Rep
79B3 **Cavite** Phil
31C2 **Caxias** Brazil
32C4 **Caxias** Brazil
30F4 **Caxias do Sul** Brazil
98B3 **Caxito** Angola
17B1 **Cayce** USA
93D1 **Çayeli** Turk
33G3 **Cayenne** French Guiana
46A1 **Cayeux-sur-Mer** France
25E3 **Cayman Brac** *I* Caribbean S
26A3 **Cayman Is** Caribbean S
26A3 **Cayman Trench** Caribbean S
99E2 **Caynabo** Somalia
25E2 **Cayo Romana** *I* Cuba
25D3 **Cayos Miskitos** *Is* Nic
26A2 **Cay Sal** *I* Caribbean S
100B2 **Cazombo** Angola
Ceará = Fortaleza
31C3 **Ceara** State, Brazil
79B3 **Cebu** Phil
79B3 **Cebu** *I* Phil
16B3 **Cecilton** USA
52B2 **Cecina** Italy
8B3 **Cedar City** USA
19A3 **Cedar Creek Res** USA
5J4 **Cedar L** Can
10A2 **Cedar Rapids** USA
17A1 **Cedartown** USA
24A2 **Cedros** *I* Mexico
106C4 **Ceduna** Aust
99E2 **Ceelbuur** Somalia
99E1 **Ceerigaabo** Somalia
53B3 **Cefalù** Italy
59B3 **Cegléd** Hung
100A2 **Cela** Angola
24B2 **Celaya** Mexico
Celebes = Sulawesi
70C3 **Celebes S** S E Asia
14B2 **Celina** USA
52C1 **Celje** Yugos
56C2 **Celle** Germany
71E4 **Cendrawasih** *Pen* Indon
47C2 **Ceno** *R* Italy
19B3 **Center** USA
16C2 **Center Moriches** USA
17A1 **Center Point** USA
47D2 **Cento** Italy
44B3 **Central** Region, Scot
98B2 **Central African Republic** Africa
16D2 **Central Falls** USA
18C2 **Centralia** Illinois, USA
8A2 **Centralia** Washington, USA
20B2 **Central Point** USA
71F4 **Central Range** *Mts* PNG
16A3 **Centreville** Maryland, USA
78C4 **Cepu** Indon

Ceram = Seram
71D4 **Ceram Sea** Indon
34C3 **Cereales** Arg
31B5 **Ceres** Brazil
100A4 **Ceres** S Africa
22B2 **Ceres** USA
48C2 **Cergy-Pontoise** France
53C2 **Cerignola** Italy
60C5 **Cernavodă** Rom
9C4 **Cerralvo** *I* Mexico
23A1 **Cerritos** Mexico
34B2 **Cerro Aconcagua** *Mt* Arg
23B1 **Cerro Azul** Mexico
34A3 **Cerro Campanario** *Mt* Chile
34C2 **Cerro Champaqui** *Mt* Arg
23A2 **Cerro Cuachaia** *Mt* Mexico
23B1 **Cerro de Astillero** Mexico
34B2 **Cerro de Olivares** *Mt* Arg
32B6 **Cerro de Pasco** Peru
27D3 **Cerro de Punta** *Mt* Puerto Rico
23A2 **Cerro El Cantado** *Mt* Mexico
34B3 **Cerro El Nevado** *Mt* Arg
23A2 **Cerro Grande** *Mts* Mexico
34A2 **Cerro Juncal** *Mt* Arg/ Chile
23A1 **Cerro la Ardilla** *Mts* Mexico
34B1 **Cerro las Tortolas** *Mt* Chile
23A2 **Cerro Laurel** *Mt* Mexico
34A2 **Cerro Mercedario** *Mt* Arg
34A3 **Cerro Mora** *Mt* Chile
27C4 **Cerron** *Mt* Ven
34B3 **Cerro Payún** *Mt* Arg
23B2 **Cerro Penón del Rosario** *Mt* Mexico
34B2 **Cerro Sosneado** *Mt* Arg
23A2 **Cerro Teotepec** *Mt* Mexico
34B2 **Cerro Tupungato** *Mt* Arg
23B2 **Cerro Yucuyacau** *Mt* Mexico
47C2 **Cervo** *R* Italy
52B2 **Cesena** Italy
60B2 **Cēsis** USSR
57C3 **České Budějovice** Czech
57C3 **České Země** Region, Czech
59B3 **Českomoravská Vysočina** *U* Czech
55C3 **Çeşme** Turk
107E4 **Cessnock** Aust
52C2 **Cetina** *R* Yugos
96B1 **Ceuta** N W Africa
92C2 **Ceyham** Turk
92C2 **Ceyhan** *R* Turk
93C2 **Ceylanpınar** Turk
Ceylon = Sri Lanka
63B2 **Chaa-Khol** USSR
48C2 **Chaâteaudun** France
47B1 **Chablais** Region, France
34C2 **Chacabuco** Arg
32B5 **Chachapoyas** Peru
34B3 **Chacharramendi** Arg
84C3 **Chachran** Pak
30D4 **Chaco** State, Arg
98B1 **Chad** Republic, Africa
98B1 **Chad** *L* C Africa
34B3 **Chadileuvu** *R* Arg
8C2 **Chadron** USA
18C2 **Chaffee** USA
85A3 **Chagai** Pak
63F2 **Chagda** USSR

84B2 **Chaghcharan** Afghan
104B4 **Chagos Arch** Indian O
27L1 **Chaguanas** Trinidad
91D4 **Chāh Bahār** Iran
76C2 **Chai Badan** Thai
86B2 **Chāībāsa** India
76C3 **Chaine des Cardamomes** *Mts* Camb
98C4 **Chaine des Mitumba** *Mts* Zaïre
76C2 **Chaiyaphum** Thai
34D2 **Chajari** Arg
84C2 **Chakwal** Pak
30B2 **Chala** Peru
100C2 **Chalabesa** Zambia
84A2 **Chalap Dalam** *Mts* Afghan
73C4 **Chaling** China
85C4 **Chālisgaon** India
12F1 **Chalkyitsik** USA
46C2 **Challerange** France
46C2 **Châlons sur Marne** France
49C2 **Chalon sur Saône** France
57C3 **Cham** Germany
84B2 **Chaman** Pak
84D2 **Chamba** India
85D3 **Chambal** *R* India
15C3 **Chambersburg** USA
49D2 **Chambéry** France
46B2 **Chambly** France
85A3 **Chambor Kalat** Pak
90B3 **Chamgordan** Iran
34B2 **Chamical** Arg
47B2 **Chamonix** France
86A2 **Champa** India
49C2 **Champagne** Region, France
101G1 **Champagne Castle** *Mt* Lesotho
47A1 **Champagnole** France
10B2 **Champaign** USA
76D3 **Champassak** Laos
10C2 **Champlain,L** USA
87B2 **Chāmrājnagar** India
30B4 **Chañaral** Chile
34A3 **Chanco** Chile
4D3 **Chandalar** USA
4D3 **Chandalar** *R* USA
84D2 **Chandīgarh** India
86C2 **Chandpur** Bang
85D5 **Chandrapur** India
91D4 **Chānf** Iran
101C2 **Changara** Mozam
74B2 **Changbai** China
69E2 **Changchun** China
73C4 **Changde** China
68E4 **Chang-hua** Taiwan
76D2 **Changjiang** China
73D3 **Chang Jiang** *R* China
74B2 **Changjin** N Korea
73C4 **Changsha** China
72E3 **Changshu** China
74A2 **Changtu** China
72B2 **Changwu** China
74B3 **Changyŏn** N Korea
72C2 **Changzhi** China
73E3 **Changzhou** China
48B2 **Channel Is** UK
9B3 **Channel Is** USA
7E5 **Channel Port-aux-Basques** Can
76C3 **Chanthaburi** Thai
46B2 **Chantilly** France
18A2 **Chanute** USA
73D5 **Chaoàn** China
73D5 **Chao'an** China
73D3 **Chao Hu** *L* China
76C3 **Chao Phraya** *R* Thai
72E1 **Chaoyang** China
31C1 **Chapada Diamantina** *Mts* Brazil
31C2 **Chapadinha** Brazil
23A1 **Chapala** Mexico
23A1 **Chapala,Lac de** *L* Mexico

61H3	**Chapayevo** USSR
30F4	**Chapecó** Brazil
27H1	**Chapeltown** Jamaica
7B5	**Chapleau** Can
61E3	**Chaplygin** USSR
112C3	**Charcot I** Ant
80E2	**Chardzhou** USSR
48C2	**Charente** *R* France
98B1	**Chari** *R* Chad
98B1	**Chari Baguirmi** Region, Chad
84B1	**Charikar** Afghan
18B1	**Chariton** *R* USA
33F2	**Charity** Guyana
85D3	**Charkhāri** India
46C1	**Charleroi** Belg
18C2	**Charleston** Illinois, USA
18C2	**Charleston** Missouri, USA
11C3	**Charleston** S Carolina, USA
10B3	**Charleston** W Virginia, USA
98C3	**Charlesville** Zaïre
107D3	**Charleville** Aust
49C2	**Charleville-Mézières** France
14A1	**Charlevoix** USA
14B2	**Charlotte** Michigan, USA
11B3	**Charlotte** N Carolina, USA
17B2	**Charlotte Harbor** *B* USA
10C3	**Charlottesville** USA
7D5	**Charlottetown** Can
27K1	**Charlotteville** Tobago
108B3	**Charlton** Aust
10C1	**Charlton I** Can
84C2	**Charsadda** Pak
107D3	**Charters Towers** Aust
48C2	**Chartres** France
29E3	**Chascomús** Arg
13D2	**Chase** Can
48B2	**Châteaubriant** France
48C2	**Châteaudun** France
48B2	**Châteaulin** France
48C2	**Châteauroux** France
46D2	**Château-Salins** France
49C2	**Cháteau-Thierry** France
46C1	**Châtelet** Belg
48C2	**Châtellerault** France
43E4	**Chatham** Eng
7D5	**Chatham** New Brunswick, Can
16C1	**Chatham** New York, USA
14B2	**Chatham** Ontario, Can
13A2	**Chatham Sd** Can
12H3	**Chatham Str** USA
49C2	**Châtillon** France
47B2	**Châtillon** Italy
16B3	**Chatsworth** USA
17B1	**Chattahoochee** USA
17A1	**Chattahoochee** *R* USA
11B3	**Chattanooga** USA
76A1	**Chauk** Burma
49D2	**Chaumont** France
46B2	**Chauny** France
77D3	**Chau Phu** Viet
50A1	**Chaves** Port
50B2	**Chazaouet** Alg
34C2	**Chazón** Arg
32C2	**Chcontá** Colombia
57C2	**Cheb** Czech
65F4	**Cheboksary** USSR
10B2	**Cheboygan** USA
74B3	**Chech'on** S Korea
85C3	**Chechro** Pak
18A2	**Checotah** USA
76A2	**Cheduba I** Burma
108B1	**Cheepie** Aust
96B2	**Chegga** Maur
100C2	**Chegutu** Zim
20B1	**Chehalis** USA
74B4	**Cheju** S Korea
74B4	**Cheju do** *I* S Korea
74B4	**Cheju-haehyŏp** *Str* S Korea
63F2	**Chekunda** USSR
20B1	**Chelan,L** USA
90B2	**Cheleken** USSR
34B3	**Chelforo** Arg
80D1	**Chelkar** USSR
59C2	**Chelm** Pol
58B2	**Chelmno** Pol
43E4	**Chelmsford** Eng
43C4	**Cheltenham** Eng
65H4	**Chelyabinsk** USSR
101C2	**Chemba** Mozam
57C2	**Chemnitz** Germany
84D2	**Chenab** *R* India/Pak
96B2	**Chenachane** Alg
20C1	**Cheney** USA
18A2	**Cheney Res** USA
72D1	**Chengda** China
73A3	**Chengdu** China
72E2	**Chengshan Jiao** *Pt* China
73C4	**Chenxi** China
73C4	**Chen Xian** China
73D3	**Cheo Xian** China
32B5	**Chepén** Peru
34B2	**Chepes** Arg
48C2	**Cher** *R* France
23A2	**Cheran** Mexico
17C1	**Cheraw** USA
48B2	**Cherbourg** France
96C1	**Cherchell** Alg
63C2	**Cheremkhovo** USSR
60E2	**Cherepovets** USSR
60D4	**Cherkassy** USSR
61F5	**Cherkessk** USSR
60D3	**Chernigov** USSR
60D2	**Chernobyl** USSR
60C4	**Chernovtsy** USSR
61J2	**Chernushka** USSR
60B3	**Chernyakhovsk** USSR
61G4	**Chernyye Zemli** Region, USSR
18A2	**Cherokees,L o'the** USA
34A3	**Cherquenco** Chile
86C1	**Cherrapunji** India
60C3	**Cherven'** USSR
59C2	**Chervonograd** USSR
10C3	**Chesapeake** *B* USA
42C3	**Cheshire** County, Eng
16C1	**Cheshire** USA
64F3	**Chëshskaya Guba** *B* USSR
21A1	**Chester** California, USA
42C3	**Chester** Eng
18C2	**Chester** Illinois, USA
16C1	**Chester** Massachusets, USA
15C3	**Chester** Pennsylvania, USA
17B1	**Chester** S Carolina, USA
16A3	**Chester** *R* USA
42D3	**Chesterfield** Eng
6A3	**Chesterfield Inlet** Can
16A3	**Chestertown** USA
25D3	**Chetumal** Mexico
13C1	**Chetwynd** Can
12A2	**Chevak** USA
111B2	**Cheviot** NZ
40C2	**Cheviots** *Hills* Eng/Scot
13D3	**Chewelah** USA
8C2	**Cheyenne** USA
86A1	**Chhapra** India
86C1	**Chhātak** Bang
85D4	**Chhatarpur** India
85D4	**Chhindwāra** India
86B1	**Chhuka** Bhutan
73E5	**Chia'I** Taiwan
100A2	**Chiange** Angola
76C2	**Chiang Kham** Thai
76B2	**Chiang Mai** Thai
47C1	**Chiavenna** Italy
74E3	**Chiba** Japan
100A2	**Chibia** Angola
7C4	**Chibougamou** Can
75A1	**Chiburi-jima** *I* Japan
101C3	**Chibuto** Mozam
10B2	**Chicago** USA
14A2	**Chicago Heights** USA
12G3	**Chichagof I** USA
43D4	**Chichester** Eng
75B1	**Chichibu** Japan
69G4	**Chichi-jima** *I* Japan
11B3	**Chickamauga L** USA
19C3	**Chickasawhay** *R* USA
9D3	**Chickasha** USA
12F2	**Chicken** USA
32A5	**Chiclayo** Peru
8A3	**Chico** USA
29C4	**Chico** *R* Arg
101C2	**Chicoa** Mozam
15D2	**Chicopee** USA
7C5	**Chicoutimi** Can
101C3	**Chicualacuala** Mozam
87B2	**Chidambaram** India
6D3	**Chidley,C** Can
17B2	**Chiefland** USA
99C3	**Chiengi** Zambia
47B2	**Chieri** Italy
46C2	**Chiers** *R* France
47C1	**Chiesa** Italy
47D2	**Chiese** *R* Italy
52B2	**Chieti** Italy
72D1	**Chifeng** China
12C3	**Chiginigak,Mt** USA
4C3	**Chigmit Mts** USA
23B2	**Chignahuapán** Mexico
12C3	**Chignik** USA
24B2	**Chihuahua** Mexico
87B2	**Chik Ballāpur** India
87B2	**Chikmagalūr** India
12C2	**Chikuminuk L** USA
101C2	**Chikwawa** Malawi
76A1	**Chi-kyaw** Burma
87C1	**Chilakalūrupet** India
23B2	**Chilapa** Mexico
87B3	**Chilaw** Sri Lanka
28B6	**Chile** Republic
34B2	**Chilecito** Mendoza, Arg
100B2	**Chililabombwe** Zambia
86B2	**Chilka** *L* India
13C2	**Chilko** *R* Can
5F4	**Chilko L** Can
13C2	**Chilkotin** *R* Can
34A3	**Chillán** Chile
34D3	**Chillar** Arg
18B2	**Chillicothe** Missouri, USA
14B3	**Chillicothe** Ohio, USA
13C3	**Chilliwack** Can
86B1	**Chilmari** India
101C2	**Chilongozi** Zambia
20B2	**Chiloquin** USA
24C3	**Chilpancingo** Mexico
43D4	**Chiltern Hills** *Upland* Eng
14A2	**Chilton** USA
101C2	**Chilumba** Malawi
69E4	**Chi-lung** Taiwan
101C2	**Chilwa** *L* Malawi
100C2	**Chimanimani** Zim
46C1	**Chimay** Belg
65G5	**Chimbay** USSR
32B4	**Chimborazo** *Mt* Ecuador
32B5	**Chimbote** Peru
65H5	**Chimkent** USSR
101C2	**Chimoio** Mozam
67E3	**China** Republic, Asia
	China National Republic = Taiwan
25D3	**Chinandega** Nic
32B6	**Chincha Alta** Peru
109D1	**Chinchilla** Aust
101C2	**Chinde** Mozam
86C2	**Chindwin** *R* Burma
100B2	**Chingola** Zambia
100A2	**Chinguar** Angola
96A2	**Chinguetti** Maur
74B3	**Chinhae** S Korea
100C2	**Chinhoyi** Zim
12D3	**Chiniak,C** USA
84C2	**Chiniot** Pak
74B3	**Chinju** S Korea
98C2	**Chinko** *R* CAR
75B1	**Chino** Japan
101C2	**Chinsali** Zambia
52B1	**Chioggia** Italy
101C2	**Chipata** Zambia
101C3	**Chipinge** Zim
87A1	**Chiplūn** India
43C4	**Chippenham** Eng
10A2	**Chippewa Falls** USA
32A4	**Chira** *R* Peru
87C1	**Chīrāla** India
101C3	**Chiredzi** Zim
95A2	**Chirfa** Niger
32A2	**Chiriqui** *Mt* Panama
54C2	**Chirpan** Bulg
32A2	**Chirrípo Grande** *Mt* Costa Rica
100B2	**Chirundu** Zim
100B2	**Chisamba** Zambia
73B4	**Chishui He** *R* China
47B2	**Chisone** *R* Italy
68D1	**Chita** USSR
100A2	**Chitado** Angola
100A2	**Chitembo** Angola
12F2	**Chitina** USA
12F2	**Chitina** *R* USA
87B2	**Chitradurga** India
84C1	**Chitral** Pak
32A2	**Chitré** Panama
86C2	**Chittagong** Bang
85C4	**Chittaurgarh** India
87B2	**Chittoor** India
100B2	**Chiume** Angola
47D1	**Chiusa** Italy
47B2	**Chivasso** Italy
29D2	**Chivilcoy** Arg
100C2	**Chivu** Zim
75A1	**Chizu** Japan
29C3	**Choele Choel** Arg
34C3	**Choique** Arg
24B2	**Choix** Mexico
58B2	**Chojnice** Pol
99D1	**Choke** *Mts* Eth
48B2	**Cholet** France
23B2	**Cholula** Mexico
100B2	**Choma** Zambia
86B1	**Chomo Yummo** *Mt* China/India
57C2	**Chomutov** Czech
63C1	**Chona** *R* USSR
74B3	**Ch'ŏnan** S Korea
76C3	**Chon Buri** Thai
32A4	**Chone** Ecuador
74B2	**Ch'ŏngjin** N Korea
74B3	**Chŏngju** S Korea
74B3	**Ch'ŏngju** S Korea
100A2	**Chongoroi** Angola
73B4	**Chongqing** China
74B3	**Chŏngŭp** S Korea
74B3	**Chŏnju** S Korea
86B1	**Chooyu** *Mt* China/Nepal
59D3	**Chortkov** USSR
74B3	**Ch'ŏrwŏn** N Korea
59B2	**Chorzow** Pol
74E3	**Choshi** Japan
34A3	**Chos-Malal** Arg
58B2	**Choszczno** Pol
86A2	**Chotanāgpur** Region, India
96C1	**Chott Melrhir** Alg
22B2	**Chowchilla** USA
63D3	**Choybalsan** Mongolia
6A3	**Chrantrey Inlet** *B* Can
61H2	**Chraykovskiy** USSR
111B2	**Christchurch** NZ
101G1	**Christiana** S Africa
6D2	**Christian,C** USA
12H3	**Christian Sd** USA
6E3	**Christianshab** Greenland
104D4	**Christmas I** Indian O

Covington

90B3	**Daryācheh-ye Namak** *Salt Flat* Iran
90D3	**Daryacheh-ye-Sistan** *Salt L* Iran/Afghan
91B4	**Daryācheh-ye Tashk** *L* Iran
80C2	**Daryācheh-ye Orūmīyeh** *L* Iran
91C4	**Dārzīn** Iran
91B4	**Das** *I* UAE
73C3	**Dashennonglia** *Mt* China
90C2	**Dasht** Iran
90B3	**Dasht-e-Kavir** *Salt Desert* Iran
90C3	**Dasht-e Lut** *Salt Desert* Iran
90D3	**Dasht-e Naomid** *Desert Region* Iran
85D3	**Datia** India
72A2	**Datong** China
72C1	**Datong** China
72A2	**Datong He** *R* China
79B4	**Datu Piang** Phil
39K7	**Daugava** *R* USSR
60C2	**Daugavpils** USSR
6D1	**Dauguard Jensen Land** Greenland
84A1	**Daulatabad** Afghan
85D3	**Daulpur** India
46D1	**Daun** Germany
87A1	**Daund** India
5H4	**Dauphin** Can
16A2	**Dauphin** USA
49D2	**Dauphiné** *Region,* France
97C3	**Daura** Nig
85D3	**Dausa** India
87B2	**Dāvangere** India
79C4	**Davao** Phil
79C4	**Davao G** Phil
22A2	**Davenport** California, USA
10A2	**Davenport** Iowa, USA
32A2	**David** Panama
4D3	**Davidson Mts** USA
21A2	**Davis** USA
112C10	**Davis** *Base* Ant
7D4	**Davis Inlet** Can
6E3	**Davis Str** Greenland/Can
61J3	**Davlekanovo** USSR
47C1	**Davos** Switz
99E2	**Dawa** *R* Eth
73A4	**Dawan** China
84B2	**Dawat Yar** Afghan
91B4	**Dawḥat Salwah** *B* Qatar/S Arabia
76B2	**Dawna Range** *Mts* Burma
4E3	**Dawson** Can
17B1	**Dawson** Georgia, USA
107D3	**Dawson** *R* Aust
5F4	**Dawson Creek** Can
13D2	**Dawson,Mt** Can
12G2	**Dawson Range** *Mts* Can
73A3	**Dawu** China
73C3	**Dawu** China
48B3	**Dax** France
73B3	**Daxian** China
73B5	**Daxin** China
73A3	**Daxue Shan** *Mts* China
73C4	**Dayong** China
94C2	**Dayr'Ali** Syria
94C1	**Dayr'Atīyah** Syria
93D2	**Dayr az Zawr** Syria
10B3	**Dayton** Ohio, USA
19B4	**Dayton** Texas, USA
20C1	**Dayton** Washington, USA
11B4	**Daytona Beach** USA
73C4	**Dayu** China
78D3	**Dayu** Indon
72D2	**Da Yunhe** *R* China
20C2	**Dayville** USA
73B3	**Dazhu** China
100B4	**De Aar** S Africa
26C2	**Deadman's Cay** The Bahamas
92C3	**Dead S** Israel/Jordan
46A1	**Deal** Eng
101G1	**Dealesville** S Africa
13B2	**Dean** *R* Can
13B2	**Dean Chan** Can
34C2	**Deán Funes** Arg
14B2	**Dearborn** USA
4F3	**Dease Arm** *B* Can
4E4	**Dease Lake** Can
9B3	**Death V** USA
48C2	**Deauville** France
97B4	**Debakala** Ivory Coast
12B2	**Debauch Mt** USA
27L1	**Débé** Trinidad
59C2	**Debica** Pol
58C2	**Deblin** Pol
97B3	**Débo,L** Mali
99D2	**Debra Birhan** Eth
99D1	**Debra Markos** Eth
99D1	**Debra Tabor** Eth
59C3	**Debrecen** Hung
11B3	**Decatur** Alabama, USA
17B1	**Decatur** Georgia, USA
10B3	**Decatur** Illinois, USA
14B2	**Decatur** Indiana, USA
48C3	**Decazeville** France
73A4	**Dechang** China
97B3	**Dédougou** Burkina
101C2	**Dedza** Malawi
42B2	**Dee** *R* Dumfries and Galloway, Scot
42C3	**Dee** *R* Eng/Wales
44C3	**Dee** *R* Grampian, Scot
15C1	**Deep River** Can
16C2	**Deep River** USA
109D1	**Deepwater** Aust
7E5	**Deer Lake** Can
8B2	**Deer Lodge** USA
34D3	**Defferrari** Arg
17A1	**De Funiak Springs** USA
68B3	**Dêgê** China
106A3	**De Grey** *R* Aust
91B3	**Deh Bid** Iran
84B1	**Dehi** Afghan
96D1	**Dehibat** Tunisia
87B3	**Dehiwala-Mt Lavinia** Sri Lanka
90A3	**Dehlorān** Iran
84D2	**Dehra Dūn** India
86A2	**Dehri** India
98C2	**Deim Zubeir** Sudan
94B2	**Deir Abu Sa'id** Jordan
94C1	**Deir el Ahmar** Leb
60B4	**Dej** Rom
19B3	**De Kalb** Texas, USA
63G2	**De Kastri** USSR
98C3	**Dekese** Zaïre
98B2	**Dekoa** CAR
106B1	**Dekusi** Indon
9B3	**Delano** USA
10C3	**Delaware** State, USA
14B2	**Delaware** USA
15C2	**Delaware** *R* USA
10C3	**Delaware B** USA
109C3	**Delegate** Aust
47B1	**Delemont** Switz
101D2	**Delgado** *C* Mozam
84D3	**Delhi** India
15D2	**Delhi** New York, USA
92B1	**Delice** Turk
24B2	**Delicias** Mexico
90B3	**Delījān** Iran
47B1	**Delle** France
22D4	**Del Mar** USA
39F8	**Delmenhorst** Germany
4B3	**De Long** *Mts* USA
109C4	**Deloraine** Aust
5H5	**Deloraine** Can
17B2	**Delray Beach** USA
9C4	**Del Rio** USA
8B3	**Delta** USA
12E2	**Delta** *R* USA
12E2	**Delta Junction** USA
99D2	**Dembidollo** Eth
46C1	**Demer** *R* Belg
9C3	**Deming** USA
54C2	**Demirköy** Turk
49C1	**Denain** France
82A2	**Denau** USSR
42C3	**Denbigh** Wales
12B2	**Denbigh,C** USA
78B3	**Dendang** Indon
46C1	**Dendermond** Belg
99D2	**Dendi** *Mt* Eth
46B1	**Dèndre** *R* Belg
72B1	**Dengkou** China
72C3	**Deng Xian** China
	Den Haag = **'s-Gravenhage**
27H1	**Denham,Mt** Jamaica
56A2	**Den Helder** Neth
51C2	**Denia** Spain
107D4	**Deniliquin** Aust
20C2	**Denio** USA
9D3	**Denison** Texas, USA
12D3	**Denison,Mt** USA
92A2	**Denizli** Turk
39F7	**Denmark** *Kingdom, Europe*
1C1	**Denmark Str** Greenland/Iceland
27P2	**Dennery** St Lucia
78D4	**Denpasar** Indon
16B3	**Denton** Maryland, USA
9D3	**Denton** Texas, USA
107E1	**D'Entrecasteaux Is** PNG
47B1	**Dents du Midi** *Mt* Switz
8C3	**Denver** USA
98B2	**Déo** *R* Cam
86B2	**Deoghar** India
85C5	**Deolāli** India
84D1	**Deosai Plain** India
95B3	**Dépression du Mourdi** Chad
19B3	**De Queen** USA
84C3	**Dera** Pak
84B3	**Dera Bugti** Pak
84C2	**Dera Ismail Khan** Pak
106B2	**Derby** Aust
16C2	**Derby** Connecticut, USA
43D3	**Derby** County, Eng
43D3	**Derby** Eng
18A2	**Derby** Kansas, USA
60E3	**Dergachi** USSR
19B3	**De Ridder** USA
	Derna = Darnah
95C3	**Derudeb** Sudan
109C4	**Derwent Bridge** Aust
34B2	**Desaguadero** Arg
34B2	**Desaguadero** *R* Arg
30C2	**Désaguadero** *R* Bol
21B3	**Descanso** Mexico
20B2	**Deschutes** *R* USA
29C5	**Deseado** Arg
29C5	**Deseado** *R* Arg
47D2	**Desenzano** Italy
96A1	**Deserta Grande** *I* Medeira
30C4	**Desierto de Atacama** *Desert* Chile
18B2	**Desloge** USA
10A2	**Des Moines** Iowa, USA
60D3	**Desna** *R* USSR
29B6	**Desolación** *I* Chile
14A2	**Des Plaines** USA
56C2	**Dessau** Germany
99D1	**Dessye** Eth
12G2	**Destruction Bay** Can
46A1	**Desvres** France
54B1	**Deta** Rom
100B2	**Dete** Zim
10B2	**Detroit** USA
76D3	**Det Udom** Thai
54B1	**Deva** Rom
56B2	**Deventer** Neth
44C3	**Deveron** *R* Scot
85C3	**Devikot** India
22C2	**Devil Postpile Nat Mon** USA
22C1	**Devils Gate** *P* USA
	Devil's Island = Isla du Diable
8D2	**Devils Lake** USA
12H3	**Devils Paw** *Mt* Can
43D4	**Devizes** Eng
85D3	**Devli** India
55B2	**Devoll** *R* Alb
43B4	**Devon** County, Eng
6A2	**Devon I** Can
107D5	**Devonport** Aust
86C1	**Dewangiri** Bhutan
85D4	**Dewās** India
101G1	**Dewetsdorp** S Africa
11B3	**Dewey Res** USA
19B3	**De Witt** USA
18C2	**Dexter** Missouri, USA
73A3	**Deyang** China
90C3	**Deyhuk** Iran
90A3	**Dezfūl** Iran
72D2	**Dezhou** China
90A2	**Dezh Shāhpūr** Iran
91B4	**Dhahran** S Arabia
86C2	**Dhākā** Bang
87B2	**Dhamavaram** India
86A2	**Dhamtari** India
86B2	**Dhanbād** India
86A1	**Dhangarhi** Nepal
86B1	**Dhankuta** Nepal
85D4	**Dhār** India
87B2	**Dharmapuri** India
84D2	**Dharmsāla** India
97B3	**Dhar Oualata** *Desert Region* Maur
86A1	**Dhaulagiri** *Mt* Nepal
86B2	**Dhenkānāi** India
94B3	**Dhibah** Jordan
55C3	**Dhíkti Óri** *Mt* Greece
55C3	**Dhodhekánisos** *Is* Greece
55B3	**Dhomokós** Greece
87B1	**Dhone** India
85C4	**Dhoraji** India
85C4	**Dhrāngadhra** India
86B1	**Dhuburi** India
85C4	**Dhule** India
22B2	**Diablo,Mt** USA
21A2	**Diablo Range** *Mts* USA
34C2	**Diamante** Arg
34B2	**Diamante** *R* Arg
31C5	**Diamantina** Brazil
107D3	**Diamantina** *R* Aust
86B2	**Diamond Harbours** India
22B1	**Diamond Springs** USA
91C4	**Dibā** UAE
98C3	**Dibaya** Zaïre
86C1	**Dibrugarh** India
8C2	**Dickinson** USA
1B10	**Dickson** USSR
15C2	**Dickson City** USA
93D2	**Dicle** *R* Turk
13E2	**Didsbury** Can
85C3	**Dīdwāna** India
97B3	**Diebougou** Burkina
46D2	**Diekirch** Lux
97B3	**Diéma** Mali
76C1	**Dien Bien Phu** Viet
56B2	**Diepholz** Germany
48C2	**Dieppe** France
46C1	**Diest** Belg
46D2	**Dieuze** France
7D5	**Digby** Can
49D3	**Digne** France
49C2	**Digoin** France
79C4	**Digos** Phil
71E4	**Digul** *R* Indon
86C1	**Dihang** *R* India
	Dijlah = Tigris
49C2	**Dijon** France
98B2	**Dik** Chad
99E1	**Dikhil** Djibouti
46B1	**Diksmuide** Belg
82A2	**Dilaram** Afghan
76D3	**Di Linh** Viet

Dillenburg

20

46E1 **Dillenburg** Germany
99C1 **Dilling** Sudan
12C3 **Dillingham** USA
8B2 **Dillon** USA
16A2 **Dillsburg** USA
100B2 **Dilolo** Zaïre
　　　Dimashq = Damascus
98C3 **Dimbelenge** Zaïre
97B4 **Dimbokro** Ivory Coast
54C2 **Dimitrovgrad** Bulg
61G3 **Dimitrovgrad** USSR
94B3 **Dimona** Israel
86C1 **Dimpāpur** India
79C3 **Dinagat** I Phil
86B1 **Dinajpur** India
48B2 **Dinan** France
46C1 **Dinant** Belg
92B2 **Dinar** Turk
99D1 **Dinder** R Sudan
87B2 **Dindigul** India
72B2 **Dingbian** China
86B1 **Dinggyê** China
41A3 **Dingle** Irish Rep
41A3 **Dingle** B Irish Rep
97A3 **Dinguiraye** Guinea
44B3 **Dingwall** Scot
72A2 **Dingxi** China
72D2 **Ding Xian** China
76D1 **Dinh Lap** Viet
22C2 **Dinuba** USA
97A3 **Diouloulou** Sen
86C1 **Diphu** India
99E2 **Dirē Dawa** Eth
106A3 **Dirk Hartog** I Aust
95A3 **Dirkou** Niger
109C1 **Dirranbandi** Aust
99E2 **Dirri** Somalia
29G8 **Disappointment,C**
　　　South Georgia
20B1 **Disappointment,C** USA
106B3 **Disappointment,L** Aust
108B3 **Discovery B** Aust
103J7 **Discovery Tablemount**
　　　Atlantic O
47C1 **Disentis Muster** Switz
6E3 **Disko** Greenland
6E3 **Disko Bugt** B Greenland
6E3 **Diskorjord** Greenland
58D1 **Disna** R USSR
35B1 **Distrito Federal** Federal
　　　District, Brazil
85C4 **Diu** India
79C4 **Diuat Mts** Phil
31C6 **Divinópolis** Brazil
61F4 **Divnoye** USSR
93C2 **Divriği** Turk
22B1 **Dixon** California, USA
5E4 **Dixon Entrance** Sd Can/
　　　USA
13D1 **Dixonville** Can
93E3 **Diyālā** R Iraq
65F6 **Diyarbakir** Turk
90A3 **Diz** R Iran
98B2 **Dja** R Cam
96C1 **Djadi** R Alg
95A2 **Djado,Plat du** Niger
98B3 **Djambala** Congo
96C2 **Djanet** Alg
50A2 **Djebel Bouhalla** Mt Mor
96C1 **Djelfa** Alg
98C2 **Djéma** CAR
97B3 **Djenné** Mali
97B3 **Djibo** Burkina
99E1 **Djibouti** Djibouti
99E1 **Djibouti** Republic, E
　　　Africa
98C2 **Djolu** Zaïre
97C4 **Djougou** Benin
99D2 **Djugu** Zaïre
38C2 **Djúpivogur** Iceland
51C2 **Djurdjura** Mts Alg
60E2 **Dmitrov** USSR
60D4 **Dnepr** R USSR
60D4 **Dneprodzerzhinsk** USSR
60E4 **Dnepropetrovsk** USSR
60C3 **Dneprovskaya**
　　　Nizmennost' Region,
　　　USSR

60B4 **Dnestr** R USSR
60D2 **Dno** USSR
98B2 **Doba** Chad
58C1 **Dobele** USSR
34C3 **Doblas** Arg
71E4 **Dobo** Indon
54A2 **Doboj** Yugos
54B2 **Dobreta-Turnu-Severin**
　　　Rom
60D3 **Dobrush** USSR
31C5 **Doce** R Brazil
30D3 **Doctor R P Peña** Arg
87B2 **Dod** India
87B2 **Doda Betta** Mt India
　　　Dodecanese =
　　　Sporádhes
9C3 **Dodge City** USA
99D3 **Dodoma** Tanz
75A1 **Dōgo** I Japan
97C3 **Dogondoutchi** Niger
93D2 **Doğubayazit** Turk
91B4 **Doha** Qatar
7C5 **Dolbeau** Can
49D2 **Dôle** France
43C3 **Dolgellau** Wales
99E2 **Dolo** Eth
47D1 **Dolomitche** Mts Italy
29E3 **Dolores** Arg
34D2 **Dolores** Urug
23A1 **Dolores Hidalgo**
　　　Mexico
4G3 **Dolphin and Union Str**
　　　Can
29E6 **Dolphin,C** Falkland Is
71E4 **Dom** Mt Indon
65G4 **Dombarovskiy** USSR
38F6 **Dombas** Nor
46D2 **Dombasle-sur-Meurthe**
　　　France
54A1 **Dombóvár** Hung
48B2 **Domfront** France
27E3 **Dominica** I
　　　Caribbean S
27C3 **Dominican Republic**
　　　Caribbean S
6C3 **Dominion,C** Can
7E4 **Domino** Can
68D1 **Domna** USSR
52A1 **Domodossola** Italy
78D4 **Dompu** Indon
29B3 **Domuyo** Mt Arg
109D1 **Domville,Mt** Aust
65H4 **Dom-yanskoya** USSR
44C3 **Don** R Scot
61F4 **Don** R USSR
45C1 **Donaghadee** N Ire
57C3 **Donau** R Germany
57C3 **Donauwörth** Germany
50A2 **Don Benito** Spain
42D3 **Doncaster** Eng
98B3 **Dondo** Angola
101C2 **Dondo** Mozam
87C3 **Dondra Head** C
　　　Sri Lanka
45B1 **Donegal** County,
　　　Irish Rep
40B3 **Donegal** Irish Rep
40B3 **Donegal B** Irish Rep
45B1 **Donegal Mts** Irish Rep
60E4 **Donetsk** USSR
73C4 **Dong'an** China
106A3 **Dongara** Aust
73A4 **Dongchuan** China
76D2 **Dongfang** China
74B2 **Dongfeng** China
70C4 **Donggala** Indon
68B3 **Donggi Cona** L China
74A3 **Donggou** China
73C5 **Donghai Dao** I China
72A1 **Dong He** R China
76D2 **Dong Hoi** Viet
73C5 **Dong Jiang** R China
95C3 **Dongola** Sudan
73D5 **Dongshan** China
68D4 **Dongsha Qundao** I
　　　China
72C2 **Dongsheng** China
72E3 **Dongtai** China

73C4 **Dongting Hu** L China
73B5 **Dongxing** China
73D3 **Dongzhi** China
18B2 **Doniphan** USA
52C2 **Donji Vakuf** Yugos
38G5 **Dönna** I Nor
21A2 **Donner** P USA
46D2 **Donnersberg** Mt
　　　Germany
101G1 **Donnybrook** S Africa
22B2 **Don Pedro Res** USA
12D1 **Doonerak,Mt** USA
79B4 **Dopolong** Phil
73A3 **Do Qu** R China
47B2 **Dora Baltea** R Italy
49D2 **Dorbirn** Austria
43C4 **Dorchester** Eng
6C3 **Dorchester,C** Can
48C2 **Dordogne** R France
56A2 **Dordrecht** Neth
13F2 **Doré** L Can
13F2 **Doré Lake** Can
97B3 **Dori** Burkina
46B2 **Dormans** France
57B3 **Dornbirn** Austria
44B3 **Dornoch** Scot
44B3 **Dornoch Firth** Estuary
　　　Scot
38H6 **Dorotea** Sweden
109D2 **Dorrigo** Aust
20B2 **Dorris** USA
43C4 **Dorset** County, Eng
46D1 **Dorsten** Germany
56B2 **Dortmund** Germany
98C2 **Doruma** Zaïre
63D2 **Dosatuy** USSR
84B1 **Doshi** Afghan
22B2 **Dos Palos** USA
97C3 **Dosso** Niger
65G5 **Dossor** USSR
11B3 **Dothan** USA
49C1 **Douai** France
98A2 **Douala** Cam
109D1 **Double Island Pt** Aust
49D2 **Doubs** R France
111A3 **Doubtful Sd** NZ
97B3 **Douentza** Mali
9C3 **Douglas** Arizona, USA
42B2 **Douglas** Eng
17B1 **Douglas** Georgia, USA
8C2 **Douglas** Wyoming,
　　　USA
12A1 **Douglas,C** USA
13B2 **Douglas Chan** Can
12D3 **Douglas,Mt** USA
46B1 **Doullens** France
45C1 **Doun** County, N Ire
30F3 **Dourados** Brazil
50A1 **Douro** R Port
15C3 **Dover** Delaware, USA
43E4 **Dover** Eng
15D2 **Dover** New
　　　Hampshire, USA
16B2 **Dover** New Jersey,
　　　USA
14B2 **Dover** Ohio, USA
43D3 **Dover** R Eng
41D3 **Dover,Str of** UK/
　　　France
16B3 **Downington** USA
42B2 **Downpatrick** N Ire
13C2 **Downton,Mt** Can
16B2 **Doylestown** USA
75A1 **Dōzen** I Japan
96A2 **Dr'aa** R Mor
35A2 **Dracena** Brazil
16D1 **Dracut** USA
49D3 **Draguignan** France
101C3 **Drakensberg** Mts
　　　S Africa
101G1 **Drakensberg** Mt
　　　S Africa
103E7 **Drake Pass** Pacific/
　　　Atlantic O
55B2 **Dráma** Greece
39G7 **Drammen** Nor
38A1 **Drangajökull** Iceland
52C1 **Drava** R Yugos

13D2 **Drayton Valley** Can
49C2 **Dreaux** France
57C2 **Dresden** Germany
48C2 **Dreux** France
20C2 **Drewsey** USA
54B2 **Drin** R Alb
54A2 **Drina** R Yugos
58D1 **Drissa** R USSR
45C2 **Drogheda** Irish Rep
59C3 **Drogobych** USSR
112B12 **Dronning Maud Land**
　　　Region, Ant
30D3 **Dr P.P. Pená** Par
5G4 **Drumheller** Can
14B1 **Drummond I** USA
15D1 **Drummondville** Can
58C2 **Druskininksi** USSR
12G3 **Dry B** USA
7A5 **Dryden** Can
27H1 **Dry Harbour Mts**
　　　Jamaica
76B3 **Duang** I Burma
91C4 **Dubai** UAE
5H3 **Dubawnt** R Can
4H3 **Dubawnt L** Can
107D4 **Dubbo** Aust
45C2 **Dublin** County,
　　　Irish Rep
45C2 **Dublin** Irish Rep
17B1 **Dublin** USA
60E2 **Dubna** USSR
60C3 **Dubno** USSR
15C2 **Du Bois** USA
13B2 **Dubose,Mt** Can
58D2 **Dubrovica** USSR
54A2 **Dubrovnik** Yugos
10A2 **Dubuque** USA
46D2 **Dudelange** Lux
1C10 **Dudinka** USSR
43C3 **Dudley** Eng
97B4 **Duekoué** Ivory Coast
50B1 **Duero** R Spain
44C3 **Dufftown** Scot
52B2 **Dugi Otok** I Yugos
56B2 **Duisburg** Germany
93E3 **Dūkan** Iraq
99D2 **Duk Faiwil** Sudan
91B4 **Dukhān** Qatar
73A4 **Dukou** China
68B3 **Dulan** China
34C2 **Dulce** R Arg
78C2 **Dulit Range** Mts
　　　Malay
86C2 **Dullabchara** India
10A2 **Duluth** USA
94C2 **Dūmā** Syria
78A2 **Dumai** Indon
79A3 **Dumaran** I Phil
9C3 **Dumas** USA
94C2 **Dumayr** Syria
42B2 **Dumbarton** Scot
42C2 **Dumfries** Scot
42B2 **Dumfries and**
　　　Galloway Region,
　　　Scot
86B2 **Dumka** India
15C1 **Dumoine,L** Can
112C8 **Dumont d'Urville** Base
　　　Ant
95C1 **Dumyat** Egypt
54C2 **Dunărea** R Rom
45C2 **Dunary Head** Pt
　　　Irish Rep
54B2 **Dunav** R Bulg
59D3 **Dunayevtsy** USSR
13C3 **Duncan** Can
16A2 **Duncannon** USA
44C2 **Duncansby Head** Pt
　　　Scot
45C1 **Dundalk** Irish Rep
16A3 **Dundalk** USA
45C2 **Dundalk B** Irish Rep
6D2 **Dundas** Greenland
4G2 **Dundas Pen** Can
71E5 **Dundas Str** Aust
101H1 **Dundee** S Africa
44C3 **Dundee** Scot
108B1 **Dundoo** Aust

42B2 **Dundrum** *B* N Ire
111B3 **Dunedin** NZ
17B2 **Dunedin** USA
109C2 **Dunedoo** Aust
44C3 **Dunfermline** Scot
85C4 **Dungarpur** India
45C2 **Dungarvan** Irish Rep
43E4 **Dungeness** Eng
109D2 **Dungog** Aust
99C2 **Dungu** Zaïre
95C2 **Dungunab** Sudan
68B2 **Dunhuang** China
46B1 **Dunkerque** France
10C2 **Dunkirk** USA
99D1 **Dunkur** Eth
97B4 **Dunkwa** Ghana
41B3 **Dun Laoghaire** Irish Rep
45B3 **Dunmanway** Irish Rep
26B1 **Dunmore Town** The Bahamas
44C2 **Dunnet Head** *Pt* Scot
42C2 **Duns** Scot
20B2 **Dunsmuir** USA
111A2 **Dunstan Mts** NZ
46C2 **Dun-sur-Meuse** France
72D1 **Duolun** China
98B3 **Duque de Braganca** Angola
18C2 **Du Quoin** USA
94B3 **Dura** Israel
49D3 **Durance** *R* France
24B2 **Durango** Mexico
50B1 **Durango** Spain
9C3 **Durango** USA
29E2 **Durano** Urug
9D3 **Durant** USA
94C1 **Duraykīsh** Syria
101H1 **Durban** S Africa
46D1 **Duren** Germany
86A2 **Durg** India
86B2 **Durgapur** India
42D2 **Durham** County, Eng
42D2 **Durham** Eng
11C3 **Durham** N Carolina, USA
16D1 **Durham** New Hampshire, USA
108B1 **Durham Downs** Aust
54A2 **Durmitor** *Mt* Yugos
44B2 **Durness** Scot
55A2 **Durrës** Alb
108B1 **Durrie** Aust
45A3 **Dursey** *I* Irish Rep
55C3 **Dursunbey** Turk
110B2 **D'Urville I** NZ
90D2 **Dushak** USSR
73B4 **Dushan** China
82A2 **Dushanbe** USSR
111A3 **Dusky Sd** NZ
56B2 **Düsseldorf** Germany
73B4 **Duyun** China
92B1 **Düzce** Turk
60C2 **Dvina** *R* USSR
85B4 **Dwārka** India
6D3 **Dyer,C** Can
11B3 **Dyersburg** USA
43B3 **Dyfed** County, Wales
61F5 **Dykh Tau Dağlari** *Mt* USSR
108B1 **Dynevor Downs** Aust
68B2 **Dzag** Mongolia
63C3 **Dzamin Uüd** USSR
101D2 **Dzaoudzi** Mayotte
68C2 **Dzarnïn Uüd** Mongolia
68B2 **Dzavhan Gol** *R* Mongolia
80E1 **Dzehezkazgan** USSR
61F2 **Dzerzhinsk** USSR
63E2 **Dzhalinda** USSR
65J5 **Dzhambul** USSR
60D4 **Dzhankoy** USSR
65H4 **Dzhezkazgan** USSR
84B1 **Dzhilikul'** USSR
65J5 **Dzhungarskiy Alatau** *Mts* USSR
59B2 **Dzierzoniow** Pol
82C1 **Dzungaria** Basin, China

E

7B4 **Eabamet L** Can
12F2 **Eagle** Alaska, USA
20B2 **Eagle L** California, USA
19A3 **Eagle Mountain L** USA
9C4 **Eagle Pass** USA
4E3 **Eagle Plain** Can
12E2 **Eagle River** USA
21B2 **Earlimart** USA
17B1 **Easley** USA
15C2 **East Aurora** USA
43E4 **Eastbourne** Eng
14A2 **East Chicago** USA
69E3 **East China Sea** China/ Japan
83B4 **Eastern Ghats** *Mts* India
29E6 **East Falkland** *I* Falkland Is
12E1 **East Fork** *R* USA
21B2 **Eastgate** USA
16C1 **Easthampton** USA
16C2 **East Hampton** USA
14A2 **East Lake** USA
14B2 **East Liverpool** USA
100B4 **East London** S Africa
7C4 **Eastmain** Can
7C4 **Eastmain** *R* Can
17B1 **Eastman** USA
15C3 **Easton** Maryland, USA
15C2 **Easton** Pennsylvania, USA
16B2 **East Orange** USA
105L4 **East Pacific Ridge** Pacific O
17B1 **East Point** USA
42D3 **East Retford** Eng
11A3 **East St Louis** USA
1B7 **East Siberian S** USSR
43E4 **East Sussex** County, Eng
17B1 **Eatonton** USA
10A2 **Eau Claire** USA
71F3 **Eauripik** *I* Pacific O
23B1 **Ebano** Mexico
98B2 **Ebebiyin** Eq Guinea
56C2 **Eberswalde** Germany
73A4 **Ebian** China
65K5 **Ebinur** *L* China
53C2 **Eboli** Italy
98B2 **Ebolowa** Cam
51B1 **Ebro** *R* Spain
92A1 **Eceabat** Turk
96C1 **Ech Cheliff** Alg
72D2 **Eching** China
20C1 **Echo** USA
4G3 **Echo Bay** Can
46D2 **Echternach** Lux
108B3 **Echuca** Aust
50A2 **Ecija** Spain
6B2 **Eclipse Sd** Can
32B4 **Ecuador** Republic, S America
44C2 **Eday** *I* Scot
99E1 **Edd** Eth
98C1 **Ed Da'ein** Sudan
95C3 **Ed Damer** Sudan
95C3 **Ed Debba** Sudan
44B2 **Eddrachillis** *B* Scot
99D1 **Ed Dueim** Sudan
109C4 **Eddystone Pt** Aust
98A2 **Edea** Cam
109C3 **Eden** Aust
42C2 **Eden** *R* Eng
101G1 **Edenburg** S Africa
111A3 **Edendale** NZ
46E2 **Edenkoben** Germany
46E1 **Eder** *R* Germany
6D3 **Edgell I** Can
64D2 **Edgeøya** *I* Barents S
16A3 **Edgewood** USA
94B3 **Edh Dhahiriya** Israel
55B2 **Edhessa** Greece
44C3 **Edinburgh** Scot
60C5 **Edirne** Turk
17B1 **Edisto** *R* USA
13D2 **Edith Cavell,Mt** Can
20B1 **Edmonds** USA
5G4 **Edmonton** Can
7D5 **Edmundston** Can
19A4 **Edna** USA
12H3 **Edna Bay** USA
52B1 **Edolo** Italy
94B3 **Edom** Region, Jordan
92A2 **Edremit** Turk
55C3 **Edremit Körfezi** *B* Turk
68B2 **Edrengiyn Nuruu** *Mts* Mongolia
5G4 **Edson** Can
34C3 **Eduardo Castex** Arg
12J2 **Eduni,Mt** Can
108B3 **Edward** *R* Aust
99C3 **Edward,L** Uganda\Zaïre
108A1 **Edwards Creek** Aust
9C3 **Edwards Plat** USA
18C2 **Edwardsville** USA
12H3 **Edziza,Mt** Can
12B2 **Eek** USA
46B1 **Eeklo** Belg
10B3 **Effingham** USA
6E3 **Egedesminde** Greenland
12C3 **Egegik** USA
59C3 **Eger** Hung
39F7 **Egersund** Nor
16B3 **Egg Harbor City** USA
4G2 **Eglinton I** Can
110B1 **Egmont,C** NZ
110B1 **Egmont,Mt** NZ
92B2 **Eğridir Gölü** *L* Turk
95B2 **Egypt** Republic, Africa
50B1 **Eibar** Spain
49C2 **Eibeuf** France
46D1 **Eifel** Region, Germany
44A3 **Eigg** *I* Scot
83B5 **Eight Degree Chan** Indian O
106B2 **Eighty Mile Beach** Aust
108C3 **Eildon,L** Aust
56B2 **Eindhoven** Neth
47C1 **Einsiedeln** Switz
94B3 **Ein Yahav** Israel
57C2 **Eisenach** Germany
57C3 **Eisenerz** Austria
46D1 **Eitorf** Germany
72A1 **Ejin qi** China
23B2 **Ejutla** Mexico
110C2 **Eketahuna** NZ
65J4 **Ekibastuz** USSR
63F2 **Ekimchan** USSR
92B3 **Ek Mahalla el Kubra** Egypt
39H7 **Eksjo** Sweden
10B1 **Ekwen** *R* Can
92A3 **El'Alamein** Egypt
92B3 **El'Arîsh** Egypt
92B4 **Elat** Israel
95B3 **El'Atrun Oasis** Sudan
93C2 **Elazig** Turk
92C3 **El Azraq** Jordan
52B2 **Elba** *I* Italy
95C2 **El Balyana** Egypt
32C2 **El Banco** Colombia
55B2 **Elbasan** Alb
27D5 **El Baúl** Ven
57C2 **Elbe** *R* Germany
94C1 **El Bega'a** *R* Leb
14A2 **Elberta** USA
8C3 **Elbert,Mt** USA
17B1 **Elberton** USA
92C2 **Elbistan** Turk
58B2 **Elblag** Pol
29B4 **El Bolson** Arg
61F5 **Elbrus** *Mt* USSR
Elburz Mts = Reshteh-ye Alborz
21B3 **El Cajon** USA
19A4 **El Campo** USA
51B2 **Elche** Spain
51B2 **Elda** Spain
32B3 **El Diviso** Colombia
96B2 **El Djouf** *Desert Region* Maur
18B2 **Eldon** USA
11A3 **El Dorado** Arkansas, USA
35B2 **Eldorado** Brazil
9D3 **El Dorado** Kansas, USA
24B2 **El Dorado** Mexico
33E2 **El Dorado** Ven
99D2 **Eldoret** Kenya
22C1 **Eleanor,L** USA
96B2 **El Eglab** Region, Alg
50B1 **El Escorial** Spain
93D2 **Eleşkirt** Turk
11C4 **Eleuthera** *I* The Bahamas
92B4 **El Faiyûm** Egypt
96B2 **El Farsia** *Well* Mor
98C1 **El Fasher** Sudan
92B4 **El Fashn** Egypt
50A1 **El Ferrol del Caudillo** Spain
99C1 **El Fula** Sudan
96C1 **El Gassi** Alg
99D1 **El Geteina** Sudan
99D1 **El Gezīra** Region, Sudan
94B3 **El Ghor** *V* Israel/ Jordan
10B2 **Elgin** Illinois, USA
44C3 **Elgin** Scot
92B3 **El Gîza** Egypt
96C1 **El Golea** Alg
99D2 **Elgon,Mt** Uganda/ Kenya
99E2 **El Goran** Eth
23A2 **El Grullo** Mexico
96B2 **El Guettara** *Well* Mali
99E2 **El Hamurre** Somalia
96B2 **El Haricha** *Desert Region* Mali
92A4 **El Harra** Egypt
51C2 **El Harrach** Alg
99D1 **El Hawata** Sudan
23B1 **El Higo** Mexico
34A3 **El Huecu** Arg
92B4 **El'Igma** *Desert Region* Egypt
12B2 **Elim** USA
4H2 **Elira,C** Can
Elisabethville = Lubumbashi
39K6 **Elisenvaara** Fin
El Iskandarîya = Alexandria
61F4 **Elista** USSR
106C4 **Elizabeth** Aust
15D2 **Elizabeth** USA
11C3 **Elizabeth City** USA
17C1 **Elizabethtown** N Carolina, USA
16A2 **Elizabethtown** Pennsylvania, USA
96B1 **El Jadida** Mor
92C3 **El Jafr** Jordan
99D1 **El Jebelein** Sudan
96D1 **El Jem** Tunisia
58C2 **Elk** Pol
16B3 **Elk** *R* Maryland, USA
14B3 **Elk** *R* W Virginia, USA
95C3 **El Kamlin** Sudan
22B1 **Elk Grove** USA
El Khalil = Hebron
80B3 **El Khârga** Egypt
80B3 **El-Khârga Oasis** Egypt
14A2 **Elkhart** USA
96B2 **El Khenachich** *Desert Region* Mali
54C2 **Elkhovo** Bulg
14C3 **Elkins** USA
8B2 **Elko** USA
16B3 **Elkton** USA
92B3 **El Kuntilla** Egypt
99C1 **El Lagowa** Sudan
4H2 **Ellef Ringnes I** Can
8A2 **Ellensburg** USA

16B2 **Ellenville** USA
6B2 **Ellesmere I** Can
111B2 **Ellesmere,L** NZ
16A3 **Ellicott City** USA
100B4 **Elliot** S Africa
7B5 **Elliot Lake** Can
94B3 **El Lisan** *Pen* Jordan
112B3 **Ellsworth Land** *Region* Ant
95B1 **El Maghra** *L* Egypt
92B3 **El Mansûra** Egypt
16B3 **Elmer** USA
96B3 **El Merelé** *Desert Region* Maur
34B2 **El Milagro** Arg
94B1 **El Mīna** Leb
92B4 **El Minya** Egypt
22B1 **Elmira** California, USA
10C2 **Elmira** New York, USA
96B2 **El Mreitl** *Well* Maur
56B2 **Elmshorn** Germany
98C1 **El Muglad** Sudan
96B2 **El Mzereb** *Well* Mali
79A3 **El Nido** Phil
99D1 **El Obeid** Sudan
23A2 **El Oro** Mexico
96C1 **El Oued** Alg
9C3 **El Paso** USA
21A2 **El Porta** USA
22C2 **El Portal** USA
50A2 **El Puerto del Sta Maria** Spain
El Qâhira = Cairo
El Quds = Jerusalem
94B3 **El Quseima** Egypt
9D3 **El Reno** USA
4E3 **Elsa** Can
25D3 **El Salvador** Republic, Cent America
22D4 **Elsinore L** USA
34B3 **El Sosneade** Arg
57C2 **Elsterwerde** Germany
El Suweis = Suez
50A1 **El Teleno** *Mt* Spain
110B1 **Eltham** NZ
33E2 **El Tigre** Ven
92B4 **El Tîh** *Desert Region* Egypt
34C2 **El Tio** Arg
20C1 **Eltopia** USA
92B4 **El Tûr** Egypt
87C1 **Elūru** India
50A2 **Elvas** Port
32C5 **Elvira** Brazil
34A2 **El Volcán** Chile
14A2 **Elwood** USA
43E3 **Ely** Eng
10A2 **Ely** Minnesota, USA
8B3 **Ely** Nevada, USA
14B2 **Elyria** USA
90B2 **Emāmrūd** Iran
84B1 **Emām Sāheb** Afghan
58B1 **Eman** *R* Sweden
61J4 **Emba** USSR
61J4 **Emba** *R* USSR
29C3 **Embalse Cerros Colorados** *L* Arg
51B2 **Embalse de Alarcón** *Res* Spain
50A2 **Embalse de Alcántarà** *Res* Spain
50A1 **Embalse de Almendra** *Res* Spain
50A2 **Embalse de Garcia de Sola** *Res* Spain
33E2 **Embalse de Guri** *L* Ven
51B1 **Embalse de Mequinenza** *Res* Spain
50A1 **Embalse de Ricobayo** *Res* Spain
29E2 **Embalse de Rio Negro** *Res* Urug
29C3 **Embalse El Chocón** *L* Arg
29C4 **Embalse Florentine Ameghino** *L* Arg
50A1 **Embalse Gabriel y Galan** *Res* Spain
30D3 **Embarcación** Arg
5G4 **Embarras Portage** Can
47B2 **Embrun** France
99D3 **Embu** Kenya
56B2 **Emden** Germany
73A4 **Emei** China
107D3 **Emerald** Aust
7D4 **Emeri** Can
5J5 **Emerson** Can
21B1 **Emigrant P** USA
95A3 **Emi Koussi** *Mt* Chad
34B3 **Emilo Mitre** Arg
92B2 **Emirdağ** Turk
16B2 **Emmaus** USA
56B2 **Emmen** Neth
20C2 **Emmett** USA
16A3 **Emmitsburg** USA
12B2 **Emmonak** USA
9C4 **Emory Peak** *Mt* USA
24A2 **Empalme** Mexico
101H1 **Empangeni** S Africa
30E4 **Empedrado** Arg
105G1 **Emperor Seamount Chain** Pacific O
18A2 **Emporia** Kansas, USA
56B2 **Ems** *R* Germany
44B2 **Enard** *B* Scot
23A1 **Encarnacion** Mexico
30E4 **Encarnación** Par
97B4 **Enchi** Ghana
22D4 **Encinitas** USA
35C1 **Encruzilhada** Brazil
106B1 **Ende** Indon
13D2 **Enderby** Can
112C11 **Enderby Land** Region, Ant
15C2 **Endicott** USA
12D1 **Endicott Mts** USA
47D1 **Engadin** *Mts* Switz
79B2 **Engaño,C** Phil
94B3 **En Gedi** Israel
47C1 **Engelberg** Switz
61G3 **Engel's** USSR
78A4 **Enggano** *I* Indon
41C3 **England** Country, UK
7E4 **Englee** Can
41C3 **English Channel** Eng/ France
97B3 **Enji** *Well* Maur
39H7 **Enkoping** Sweden
53B3 **Enna** Italy
99C1 **En Nahud** Sudan
95B3 **Ennedi** *Region* Chad
109C1 **Enngonia** Aust
41B3 **Ennis** Irish Rep
19A3 **Ennis** Texas, USA
45C2 **Enniscorthy** Irish Rep
45C1 **Enniskillen** N Ire
45B2 **Ennistimon** Irish Rep
94B2 **Enn Nâqoûra** Leb
57C3 **Enns** *R* Austria
39F8 **Enschede** Neth
24A1 **Ensenada** Mexico
73B3 **Enshi** China
99D2 **Entebbe** Uganda
17A1 **Enterprise** Alabama, USA
20C1 **Enterprise** Oregon, USA
97C4 **Enugu** Nig
75B1 **Enzan** Japan
49C2 **Epernay** France
16A2 **Ephrata** Pennsylvania, USA
20C1 **Ephrata** Washington, USA
49D2 **Épinal** France
46A2 **Epte** *R* France
100A3 **Epukiro** Namibia
34C3 **Epu pel** Arg
90B3 **Eqlid** Iran
89D7 **Equator**
98A2 **Equatorial Guinea** Republic, Africa
47C2 **Erba** Italy
46D2 **Erbeskopf** *Mt* Germany
34A3 **Ercilla** Chile
93D2 **Erciş** Turk
92C2 **Erciyas Daglari** *Mt* Turk
74B2 **Erdaobaihe** China
72C1 **Erdene** Mongolia
68C2 **Erdenet** Mongolia
95B3 **Erdi** *Region* Chad
30F4 **Erechim** Brazil
92B1 **Ereğlī** Turk
92B2 **Ereğli** Turk
68D2 **Erenhot** China
50B1 **Eresma** *R* Spain
46D1 **Erft** *R* Germany
57C2 **Erfurt** Germany
93C2 **Ergani** Turk
96B2 **Erg Chech** *Desert Region* Alg
95A3 **Erg du Djourab** *Desert* Chad
97D3 **Erg Du Ténéré** *Desert Region* Niger
92A1 **Ergene** *R* Turk
96B2 **Erg Iguidi** *Region* Alg
58D1 **Ērgli** USSR
98B1 **Erguig** *R* Chad
63D2 **Ergun'** USSR
68D1 **Ergun** *R* USSR
63E2 **Ergun Zuoqi** China
95C3 **Eriba** Sudan
10C2 **Erie** USA
10B2 **Erie,L** Can/USA
42B2 **Erin Port** Eng
44A3 **Eriskay** *I* Scot
46D1 **Erkelenz** Germany
57C3 **Erlangen** Germany
19B3 **Erling,L** USA
101G1 **Ermelo** S Africa
87B3 **Ernākulam** India
87B2 **Erode** India
108B1 **Eromanga** Aust
96B1 **Er Rachidia** Mor
99D1 **Er Rahad** Sudan
101C2 **Errego** Mozam
40B2 **Errigal** *Mt* Irish Rep
41A3 **Erris Head** *Pt* Irish Rep
99D1 **Er Roseires** Sudan
94B2 **Er Rummān** Jordan
57C2 **Erzgebirge** *Upland* Germany
93C2 **Erzincan** Turk
65F6 **Erzurum** Turk
48C3 **Esara** *R* Spain
56B1 **Esbjerg** Den
9C4 **Escalón** Mexico
10B2 **Escanaba** USA
25C3 **Escárcega** Mexico
46C2 **Esch** Lux
21B3 **Escondido** USA
24B2 **Escuinapa** Mexico
25C3 **Escuintla** Guatemala
98B2 **Eséka** Cam
51C1 **Esera** *R* Spain
90B3 **Eşfahān** Iran
101H1 **Eshowe** S Africa
110C1 **Eskdale** NZ
38C1 **Eskifjörður** Iceland
39H7 **Eskilstuna** Sweden
4E3 **Eskimo L** Can
7A3 **Eskimo Point** Can
92B2 **Eskisehir** Turk
50A1 **Esla** *R* Spain
29A5 **Esmeralda** *I* Chile
32B3 **Esmeraldas** Ecuador
26B2 **Esmerelda** Cuba
49C3 **Espalion** France
14B1 **Espanola** Can
32J7 **Española** *I* Ecuador
106B4 **Esperance** Aust
34C2 **Esperanza** Arg
112C2 **Esperanza** *Base* Ant
35C1 **Espírito Santo** State, Brazil
101C3 **Espungabera** Mozam
29B4 **Esquel** Arg
20B1 **Esquimalt** Can
34D2 **Esquina** Arg
94C2 **Es Samra** Jordan
96B1 **Essaourira** Mor
96A2 **Es Semara** Mor
56B2 **Essen** Germany
33F3 **Essequibo** *R* Guyana
43E4 **Essex** County, Eng
14B2 **Essexville** USA
57B3 **Esslingen** Germany
46B2 **Essonne** France
31D4 **Estância** Brazil
101G1 **Estcourt** S Africa
47D2 **Este** Italy
46B2 **Esternay** France
30D3 **Esteros** Par
5H5 **Estevan** Can
17B1 **Estill** USA
60B2 **Estonskaya SSR** Republic, USSR
29B6 **Estrecho de Magallanes** *Str* Chile
50A2 **Estremoz** Port
59B3 **Esztergom** Hung
108A1 **Etadunna** Aust
46C2 **Etam** France
48C2 **Etampes** France
108A1 **Etamunbanie,L** Aust
46A1 **Etaples** France
85D3 **Etāwah** India
99D2 **Ethiopia** Republic, Africa
23B2 **Etla** Mexico
53B3 **Etna** *Mt* Italy
12H3 **Etolin I** USA
12A2 **Etolin Str** USA
6C2 **Eton** Can
100A2 **Etosha Nat Pk** Namibia
100A2 **Etosha Pan** *Salt L* Namibia
17B1 **Etowah** *R* USA
46D2 **Ettelbruck** Lux
109C2 **Euabalong** Aust
14B2 **Euclid** USA
109C3 **Eucumbene,L** Aust
108A2 **Eudunda** Aust
19A2 **Eufala L** USA
17A1 **Eufaula** USA
8A2 **Eugene** USA
108C1 **Eulo** Aust
19B3 **Eunice** Louisiana, USA
46D1 **Eupen** Germany
93D3 **Euphrates** *R* Iraq
19C3 **Eupora** USA
48C2 **Eure** *R* France
20B2 **Eureka** California, USA
6B1 **Eureka** Can
8B3 **Eureka** Nevada, USA
6B2 **Eureka** *Sd* Can
108C3 **Euroa** Aust
109C1 **Eurombah** *R* Aust
101D3 **Europa** *I* Mozam Chan
57B2 **Euskirchen** Germany
13B2 **Eutsuk L** Can
13D2 **Evansburg** Can
6B1 **Evans,C** Can
7C4 **Evans,L** Can
6B3 **Evans Str** Can
14A2 **Evanston** Illinois, USA
8B2 **Evanston** Wyoming, USA
11B3 **Evansville** Indiana, USA
101G1 **Evaton** S Africa
106C4 **Everard,L** Aust
82C3 **Everest,Mt** China/ Nepal
8A2 **Everett** Washington, USA
16C1 **Everett,Mt** USA
11B4 **Everglades,The** *Swamp* USA
43D3 **Evesham** Eng
98B2 **Evinayong** Eq Guinea
39F7 **Evje** Nor
47B1 **Evolène** Switz
50A2 **Évora** Port
48C2 **Évreux** France
55B3 **Évvoia** *I* Greece
98B3 **Ewo** Congo

12D2 **Foraker,Mt** USA
46D2 **Forbach** France
109C2 **Forbes** Aust
97C4 **Forcados** Nig
38F6 **Forde** Nor
108C1 **Fords Bridge** Aust
19B3 **Fordyce** USA
97A4 **Forécariah** Guinea
6G3 **Forel,Mt** Greenland
14B2 **Forest** Can
17B1 **Forest Park** USA
22A1 **Forestville** USA
44C3 **Forfar** Scot
46A2 **Forges-les-Eaux** France
20B1 **Forks** USA
52B2 **Forlì** Italy
51C2 **Formentera** *I* Spain
53B2 **Formia** Italy
96A1 **Formigas** *I* Açores
Formosa = Taiwan
30E4 **Formosa** Arg
31B5 **Formosa** Brazil
30D3 **Formosa** State, Arg
73D5 **Formosa Str** Taiwan/ China
47D2 **Fornovo di Taro** Italy
38D3 **Føroyar** *Is* N Atlantic O
44C3 **Forres** Scot
106B4 **Forrest** Aust
11A3 **Forrest City** USA
107D2 **Forsayth** Aust
39J6 **Forssa** Fin
109D2 **Forster** Aust
18B2 **Forsyth** Missouri, USA
84C3 **Fort Abbas** Pak
7B4 **Fort Albany** Can
31D2 **Fortaleza** Brazil
44B3 **Fort Augustus** Scot
100B4 **Fort Beaufort** S Africa
21A2 **Fort Bragg** USA
8C2 **Fort Collins** USA
15C1 **Fort Coulogne** Can
27E4 **Fort de France** Martinique
17A1 **Fort Deposit** USA
10A2 **Fort Dodge** USA
106A3 **Fortescue** *R* Aust
7A5 **Fort Frances** Can
4F3 **Fort Franklin** Can
7C4 **Fort George** Can
4F3 **Fort Good Hope** Can
108B1 **Fort Grey** Aust
44B3 **Forth** *R* Scot
7B4 **Fort Hope** Can
34B3 **Fortin Uno** Arg
4F3 **Fort Laird** Can
96C1 **Fort Lallemand** Alg
Fort Lamy = Ndjamena
11B4 **Fort Lauderdale** USA
4F3 **Fort Liard** Can
5G4 **Fort Mackay** Can
5G5 **Fort Macleod** Can
5G4 **Fort McMurray** Can
4E3 **Fort McPherson** Can
18B2 **Fort Madison** USA
8C2 **Fort Morgan** USA
11B4 **Fort Myers** USA
5F4 **Fort Nelson** Can
4F3 **Fort Norman** Can
17A1 **Fort Payne** USA
8C2 **Fort Peck Res** USA
11B4 **Fort Pierce** USA
4G3 **Fort Providence** Can
5G3 **Fort Resolution** Can
98B3 **Fort Rousset** Congo
7C4 **Fort Rupert** Can
5F4 **Fort St James** Can
13C1 **Fort St John** Can
13E2 **Fort Saskatchewan** Can
18B2 **Fort Scott** USA
4E3 **Fort Selkirk** Can
7B4 **Fort Severn** Can
61H5 **Fort Shevchenko** USSR
4F3 **Fort Simpson** Can
5G3 **Fort Smith** Can
4G3 **Fort Smith** Region, Can
11A3 **Fort Smith** USA
9C3 **Fort Stockton** USA
20B2 **Fortuna** California, USA
5G4 **Fort Vermillion** Can
17A1 **Fort Walton Beach** USA
10B2 **Fort Wayne** USA
44B3 **Fort William** Scot
9D3 **Fort Worth** USA
12F2 **Fortymile** *R* USA
12E1 **Fort Yukon** USA
73C5 **Foshan** China
47B2 **Fossano** Italy
12G3 **Foster,Mt** USA
98B3 **Fougamou** Gabon
48B2 **Fougères** France
44D1 **Foula** *I* Scot
43E4 **Foulness I** Eng
111B2 **Foulwind,C** NZ
98B2 **Foumban** Cam
49C1 **Fourmies** France
55C3 **Foúrnoi** *I* Greece
97A3 **Fouta Djallon** *Mts* Guinea
111B3 **Foveaux** *Str* NZ
43B4 **Fowey** Eng
13D2 **Fox Creek** Can
6B3 **Foxe Basin** *G* Can
6B3 **Foxe Chan** Can
6C3 **Foxe Pen** Can
110C2 **Foxton** NZ
13F2 **Fox Valley** Can
45B2 **Foynes** Irish Rep
100A2 **Foz do Cuene** Angola
30F4 **Foz do Iquaçu** Brazil
16A2 **Frackville** USA
34B2 **Fraga** Arg
16D1 **Framingham** USA
31B6 **Franca** Brazil
49C2 **France** Republic, Europe
10A2 **Frances** Can
12J2 **Frances** *R* Can
98B3 **France Ville** Gabon
49D2 **Franche Comté** Region, France
100B3 **Francistown** Botswana
13B2 **Francois L** Can
14A2 **Frankfort** Indiana, USA
11B3 **Frankfort** Kentucky, USA
101G1 **Frankfort** S Africa
57B2 **Frankfurt** Germany
46E1 **Frankfurt am Main** Germany
56C2 **Frankfurt-an-der-Oder** Germany
57C3 **Fränkischer Alb** *Upland* Germany
14A3 **Franklin** Indiana, USA
19B4 **Franklin** Louisiana, USA
16D1 **Franklin** Massachusetts, USA
16B2 **Franklin** New Jersey, USA
14C2 **Franklin** Pennsylvania, USA
4F2 **Franklin B** Can
20C1 **Franklin D Roosevelt** *L* USA
4F3 **Franklin Mts** Can
4J2 **Franklin Str** Can
64D5 **Frankovsk** USSR
111B2 **Franz Josef Glacier** NZ
Franz-Joseph-Land = Zemlya Frantsa Iosifa
5F5 **Fraser** *R* Can
44C3 **Fraserburgh** Scot
107E3 **Fraser I** Aust
13B2 **Fraser L** Can
47B1 **Frasne** France
47C1 **Frauenfield** Switz
34D2 **Fray Bentos** Urug
40C2 **Frazerburgh** Scot
16B3 **Frederica** USA
56B1 **Fredericia** Den
15C3 **Frederick** Maryland, USA
15C3 **Fredericksburg** Virginia, USA
12H3 **Frederick Sd** USA
18B2 **Fredericktown** USA
7D5 **Fredericton** Can
6E3 **Frederikshab** Greenland
39G7 **Frederikshavn** Den
15C2 **Fredonia** USA
39G7 **Fredrikstad** Nor
16B2 **Freehold** USA
26B1 **Freeport** The Bahamas
19A4 **Freeport** Texas, USA
97A4 **Freetown** Sierra Leone
57B3 **Freiburg** Germany
57C3 **Freistadt** Austria
106A4 **Fremantle** Aust
22B2 **Fremont** California, USA
18A1 **Fremont** Nebraska, USA
14B2 **Fremont** Ohio, USA
33G3 **French Guiana** Dependency, S America
109C4 **Frenchmans Cap** *Mt* Aust
105J4 **French Polynesia** *Is* Pacific O
24B2 **Fresnillo** Mexico
8B3 **Fresno** USA
22C2 **Fresno** *R* USA
47A1 **Fretigney** France
46B1 **Frévent** France
109C4 **Freycinet Pen** Aust
97A3 **Fria** Guinea
22C2 **Friant** USA
22C2 **Friant Dam** USA
52A1 **Fribourg** Switz
57B3 **Friedrichshafen** Germany
6D3 **Frobisher B** Can
6D3 **Frobisher Bay** Can
5H4 **Frobisher L** Can
61F4 **Frolovo** USSR
43C4 **Frome** Eng
108A1 **Frome** *R* Aust
43C4 **Frome** *R* Eng
106C4 **Frome,L** Aust
25C3 **Frontera** Mexico
15C3 **Front Royal** USA
53B2 **Frosinone** Italy
82B1 **Frunze** USSR
73C5 **Fuchuan** China
73E4 **Fuding** China
24B2 **Fuerte** *R* Mexico
30E3 **Fuerte Olimpo** Par
96A2 **Fuerteventura** *I* Canary Is
72C2 **Fugu** China
68A2 **Fuhai** China
91C4 **Fujairah** UAE
75B1 **Fuji** Japan
73D4 **Fujian** Province, China
69F2 **Fujin** China
75B1 **Fujinomiya** Japan
74D3 **Fuji-san** *Mt* Japan
75B1 **Fujisawa** Japan
75B1 **Fuji-Yoshida** Japan
63A3 **Fukang** China
74C3 **Fukuchiyima** Japan
74D3 **Fukui** Japan
74C4 **Fukuoka** Japan
74E3 **Fukushima** Japan
74C4 **Fukuyama** Japan
57B2 **Fulda** Germany
57B2 **Fulda** *R* Germany
73B4 **Fuling** China
27L1 **Fullarton** Trinidad
22D4 **Fullerton** USA
18C2 **Fulton** Kentucky, USA
15C2 **Fulton** New York, USA
46C1 **Fumay** France
75C1 **Funabashi** Japan
96A1 **Funchal** Medeira
35C1 **Fundão** Brazil
7D5 **Fundy,B of** Can
101C3 **Funhalouro** Mozam
72D3 **Funing** China
73B5 **Funing** China
97C3 **Funtua** Nig
73D4 **Fuqing** China
101C2 **Furancungo** Mozam
91C4 **Fūrg** Iran
47C1 **Furka** *P* Switz
107D5 **Furneaux Group** *Is* Aust
56C2 **Fürstenwalde** Germany
57C3 **Fürth** Germany
74D3 **Furukawa** Japan
6B3 **Fury and Hecla St** Can
74A2 **Fushun** Liaoning, China
73A4 **Fushun** Sichuan, China
74B2 **Fusong** China
57C3 **Füssen** Germany
72E2 **Fu Xian** China
72E1 **Fuxin** China
72D3 **Fuyang** China
72E1 **Fuyuan** Liaoning, China
73A4 **Fuyuan** Yunnan, China
68A2 **Fuyun** China
73D4 **Fuzhou** China
56C1 **Fyn** *I* Den

G

99E2 **Gaalkacyo** Somalia
21B2 **Gabbs** USA
100A2 **Gabela** Angola
96D1 **Gabe's** Tunisia
22B2 **Gabilan Range** *Mts* USA
98B3 **Gabon** Republic, Africa
100B3 **Gaborone** Botswana
54C2 **Gabrovo** Bulg
91B3 **Gach Sārān** Iran
17A1 **Gadsden** Alabama, USA
10A1 **Gads L** Can
53B2 **Gaeta** Italy
71F3 **Gaferut** *I* Pacific O
96C1 **Gafsa** Tunisia
60D2 **Gagarin** USSR
97B4 **Gagnoa** Ivory Coast
7D4 **Gagnon** Can
61F5 **Gagra** USSR
86B1 **Gaibanda** India
29C4 **Gaimán** Arg
17B2 **Gainesville** Florida, USA
17B1 **Gainesville** Georgia, USA
19A3 **Gainesville** Texas, USA
42D3 **Gainsborough** Eng
108A2 **Gairdner,L** Aust
44B3 **Gairloch** Scot
16A3 **Gaithersburg** USA
87B1 **Gajendragarh** India
73D4 **Ga Jiang** *R* China
99E2 **Galadi** Eth
99D3 **Galana** *R* Kenya
103D5 **Galapagos Is** Pacific O
42C2 **Galashiels** Scot
54C1 **Galaţi** Rom
4C3 **Galena** Alaska, USA
18B2 **Galena** Kansas, USA
27L1 **Galeota Pt** Trinidad
27L1 **Galera Pt** Trinidad
10A2 **Galesburg** USA
15C2 **Galeton** USA
61F2 **Galich** USSR
50A1 **Galicia** Region, Spain
Galilee,S of = Tiberias,L
27J1 **Galina Pt** Jamaica
99D1 **Gallabat** Sudan
47C2 **Gallarate** Italy

87B2	**Hirihar** India
74E2	**Hirosaki** Japan
74C4	**Hiroshima** Japan
46C2	**Hirson** France
54C2	**Hirşova** Rom
56B1	**Hirtshals** Den
84D3	**Hisār** India
26C3	**Hispaniola** *I*
	Caribbean S
94C1	**Hisyah** Syria
93D3	**Hīt** Iraq
74E3	**Hitachi** Japan
75C1	**Hitachi-Ota** Japan
43D4	**Hitchin** Eng
38F6	**Hitra** *I* Nor
75A4	**Hiuchi-nada** *B* Japan
75A2	**Hiwasa** Japan
56B1	**Hjørring** Den
76B1	**Hka** *R* Burma
97C4	**Ho** Ghana
76D1	**Hoa Binh** Viet
76D3	**Hoa Da** Viet
109C4	**Hobart** Aust
9C3	**Hobbs** USA
56B1	**Hobro** Den
13C2	**Hobson L** Can
99E2	**Hobyo** Somalia
	Ho Chi Minh = Saigon
57C3	**Hochkonig** *Mt* Austria
54B1	**Hódmező'hely** Hung
59B3	**Hodonin** Czech
74B2	**Hoeryong** N Korea
57C2	**Hof** Germany
38B2	**Hofsjökull** *Mts*
	Iceland
74C4	**Hōfu** Japan
96C2	**Hoggar** *Upland* Alg
46D1	**Hohe Acht** *Mt*
	Germany
72C1	**Hohhot** China
6J3	**Höhn** Iceland
68B3	**Hoh Sai Hu** *L* China
82C2	**Hoh Xil Shan** *Mts*
	China
99D2	**Hoima** Uganda
86C1	**Hojāi** India
75A2	**Hojo** Japan
110B1	**Hokianga Harbour** *B*
	NZ
111B2	**Hokitika** NZ
74E2	**Hokkaidō** Japan
90C2	**Hokmābād** Iran
109C3	**Holbrook** Aust
9B3	**Holbrook** USA
19A2	**Holdenville** USA
87B2	**Hole Narsipur** India
27R3	**Holetown** Barbados
26B2	**Holguín** Cuba
111B2	**Holitika** NZ
12C2	**Holitna** *R* USA
59B3	**Hollabrunn** Austria
14A2	**Holland** USA
22B2	**Hollister** USA
19C3	**Holly Springs** USA
22C3	**Hollywood** California,
	USA
17B2	**Hollywood** Florida,
	USA
4G2	**Holman Island** Can
38J6	**Holmsund** Sweden
94B2	**Holon** Israel
56B1	**Holstebro** Den
6E3	**Holsteinborg**
	Greenland
14B2	**Holt** USA
18A2	**Holton** USA
12C2	**Holy Cross** USA
42B3	**Holyhead** Wales
42D2	**Holy I** Eng
43B3	**Holy I** Wales
16C1	**Holyoke**
	Massachusetts, USA
86C2	**Homalin** Burma
6D3	**Home B** Can
12D3	**Homer** Alaska, USA
19B3	**Homer** Louisiana,
	USA
111A2	**Homer Tunnel** NZ

17B1	**Homerville** USA
17B2	**Homestead** USA
17A1	**Homewood** USA
87B1	**Homnābād** India
101C3	**Homoine** Mozam
25D3	**Hondo** *R* Mexico
25D3	**Honduras** Republic,
	Cent America
25D3	**Honduras,G of**
	Honduras
39G6	**Hønefoss** Nor
15C2	**Honesdale** USA
21A1	**Honey L** USA
76C1	**Hong** *R* Viet
76D1	**Hon Gai** Viet
73A4	**Hongguo** China
73C4	**Hong Hu** *L* China
72B2	**Honghui** China
73C4	**Hongjiang** China
73C5	**Hong Kong** Colony,
	S E Asia
68D2	**Hongor** Mongolia
73B5	**Hongshui He** *R* China
72A3	**Hongyuan** China
72D3	**Hongze Hu** *L* China
107E1	**Honiara** Solomon Is
77C4	**Hon Khoai** *I* Camb
76D3	**Hon Lan** *I* Viet
38K4	**Honnigsvåg** Nor
21C4	**Honolulu** Hawaiian Is
77C4	**Hon Panjang** *I* Viet
74D3	**Honshu** *I* Japan
20B1	**Hood,Mt** USA
20B1	**Hood River** USA
45C2	**Hook Head** *C*
	Irish Rep
12G3	**Hoonah** USA
12A2	**Hooper Bay** USA
101G1	**Hoopstad** S Africa
56A2	**Hoorn** Neth
9B3	**Hoover Dam** USA
12E2	**Hope** Alaska, USA
19B3	**Hope** Arkansas, USA
13C3	**Hope** Can
7D4	**Hopedale** Can
64D2	**Hopen** *I* Barents S
6D3	**Hopes Advance,C** Can
108B3	**Hopetoun** Aust
100B3	**Hopetown** S Africa
18C2	**Hopkinsville** USA
20B1	**Hoquiam** USA
93D1	**Horasan** Turk
99F1	**Hordiyo** Somalia
47C1	**Horgen** Switz
105H5	**Horizon Depth**
	Pacific O
91C4	**Hormuz,Str of** Oman/
	Iran
59B3	**Horn** Austria
6H3	**Horn** *C* Iceland
38H5	**Hornavan** *L* Sweden
19B3	**Hornbeck** USA
20B2	**Hornbrook** USA
111B2	**Hornby** NZ
7B5	**Hornepayne** Can
4F3	**Horn Mts** Can
42D3	**Hornsea** Eng
72B1	**Horn Uul** *Mt*
	Mongolia
30E3	**Horqueta** Par
15C2	**Horseheads** USA
56C1	**Horsens** Den
20B1	**Horseshoe Bay** Can
108B3	**Horsham** Aust
43D4	**Horsham** Eng
39G7	**Horten** Nor
4F3	**Horton** *R* Can
78C2	**Hose Mts** Malay
85D4	**Hoshangābād** India
84D2	**Hoshiārpur** India
87B1	**Hospet** India
29C7	**Hoste** *I* Chile
82B2	**Hotan** China
19B3	**Hot Springs** Arkansas,
	USA
8C2	**Hot Springs** S. Dakota,
	USA
4G3	**Hottah** Can

46A2	**Houdan** France
72C2	**Houma** China
19B4	**Houma** USA
16C2	**Housatonic** *R* USA
13B2	**Houston** Can
19C3	**Houston** Mississippi,
	USA
19A4	**Houston** Texas, USA
106A3	**Houtman** *Is* Aust
68B2	**Hovd** Mongolia
68C1	**Hövsgol Nuur** *L*
	Mongolia
14A2	**Howard City** USA
12C1	**Howard P** USA
109C3	**Howe,C** Aust
101H1	**Howick** S Africa
44C2	**Hoy** *I* Scot
39F6	**Høyanger** Nor
59B2	**Hradeç-Králové** Czech
59B3	**Hranice** Czech
59B3	**Hron** *R* Czech
73E5	**Hsin-chu** Taiwan
73E5	**Hsüeh Shan** *Mt*
	Taiwan
72B2	**Huachi** China
32B6	**Huacho** Peru
72C1	**Huade** China
72D1	**Huaibei** China
72D3	**Huaibin** China
72D3	**Huai He** *R* China
73C4	**Huaihua** China
73C5	**Huaiji** China
72D3	**Huainan** China
69E4	**Hua-lien** Taiwan
32B5	**Huallaga** *R* Peru
32B5	**Huallanca** Peru
32B5	**Huamachuco** Peru
100A2	**Huambo** Angola
30C2	**Huanay** Bol
32B5	**Huancabamba** Peru
32B6	**Huancavelica** Peru
32B6	**Huancayo** Peru
73D3	**Huangchuan** China
	Huang Hai = Yellow S
72D2	**Huang He** *R* China
72B2	**Huangling** China
76D2	**Huangliu** China
73C3	**Huangpi** China
73D3	**Huangshi** China
34C3	**Huanguelén** Arg
73E4	**Huangyan** China
74B2	**Huanren** China
32B5	**Huánuco** Peru
30C2	**Huanuni** Bol
72B2	**Huan Xian** China
32B5	**Huaráz** Peru
32B6	**Huarmey** Peru
32B5	**Huascarán** *Mt* Peru
30B4	**Huasco** Chile
23B2	**Huatusco** Mexico
23B1	**Huauchinango** Mexico
23B2	**Huautla** Mexico
72C2	**Hua Xian** China
24B2	**Huayapan** *R* Mexico
73C3	**Hubei** Province, China
87B1	**Hubli** India
34C3	**Hucal** Arg
74B2	**Huch'ang** N Korea
42D3	**Huddersfield** Eng
39H6	**Hudiksvall** Sweden
17B2	**Hudson** Florida, USA
14B2	**Hudson** Michigan,
	USA
16C1	**Hudson** New York,
	USA
16C1	**Hudson** *R* USA
7B4	**Hudson B** Can
5H4	**Hudson Bay** Can
13C1	**Hudson's Hope** Can
6C3	**Hudson Str** Can
76D2	**Hue** Viet
23B1	**Huejutla** Mexico
50A2	**Huelva** Spain
23A2	**Hueramo** Mexico
51B2	**Húercal Overa** Spain
51B1	**Huesca** Spain
23B2	**Huexotla** *Hist Site*
	Mexico

107D3	**Hughenden** Aust
12D1	**Hughes** USA
86B2	**Hugli** *R* India
19A3	**Hugo** USA
73D4	**Hui'an** China
110C1	**Huiarau Range** *Mts*
	NZ
74B2	**Huich'ŏn** N Korea
74B2	**Huifa He** *R* China
32B3	**Huila** *Mt* Colombia
73D5	**Huilai** China
73A4	**Huili** China
74B2	**Huinan** China
34C2	**Huinca Renancó** Arg
25C3	**Huixtla** Mexico
73A4	**Huize** China
73C5	**Huizhou** China
23B2	**Hujuápan de Léon**
	Mexico
69F2	**Hulin** China
15C1	**Hull** Can
42D3	**Hull** Eng
58B1	**Hultsfred** Sweden
63D3	**Hulun Nur** *L* China
69E1	**Huma** China
33E5	**Humaita** Brazil
100B4	**Humansdorp** S Africa
42D3	**Humber** *R* Eng
42D3	**Humberside** County,
	Eng
5H4	**Humboldt** Can
20C2	**Humboldt** *R* USA
20B2	**Humboldt B** USA
6D2	**Humboldt Gletscher**
	Gl Greenland
21B2	**Humboldt L** USA
108C1	**Humeburn** Aust
109C3	**Hume,L** Aust
100A2	**Humpata** Angola
22C2	**Humphreys** USA
38A1	**Húnaflói** *B* Iceland
73C4	**Hunan** Province,
	China
74C2	**Hunchun** China
13C2	**Hundred Mile House**
	Can
54B1	**Hunedoara** Rom
59B3	**Hungary**
	Republic, Europe
108B1	**Hungerford** Aust
74B3	**Hüngnam** N Korea
74B2	**Hunjiang** China
46D2	**Hunsrück** Mts,
	Germany
109D2	**Hunter** *R* Aust
13B2	**Hunter I** Can
109C4	**Hunter Is** Aust
12D2	**Hunter,Mt** USA
14A3	**Huntingburg** USA
43D3	**Huntingdon** Eng
14A2	**Huntingdon** Indiana,
	USA
14B3	**Huntington** W
	Virginia, USA
22C4	**Huntington Beach**
	USA
22C4	**Huntington L** USA
110C1	**Huntly** NZ
44C3	**Huntly** Scot
12J2	**Hunt,Mt** Can
108A1	**Hunt Pen** Aust
17A1	**Huntsville** Alabama,
	USA
15C1	**Huntsville** Can
19A3	**Huntsville** Texas, USA
76D2	**Huong Khe** Viet
71F4	**Huon Peninsula** *Pen*
	PNG
109C4	**Huonville** Aust
14B1	**Hurd,C** Can
80B3	**Hurghada** Egypt
8D2	**Huron** S Dakota, USA
14B1	**Huron,L** Can/USA
34A2	**Hurtado** Chile
111B2	**Hurunui** *R* NZ
38B1	**Husavik** Iceland
54C1	**Huşi** Rom
39G7	**Huskvarna** Sweden

12C1	**Huslia** USA
94B2	**Husn** Jordan
56B2	**Husum** Germany
109C1	**Hutton,Mt** Aust
72D2	**Hutuo He** *R* China
46C1	**Huy** Belg
72A2	**Huzhu** China
52C2	**Hvar** *I* Yugos
100B2	**Hwange** Zim
100B2	**Hwange Nat Pk** Zim
15D2	**Hyannis** USA
68B2	**Hyaryas Nuur** *L* Mongolia
5E4	**Hydaburg** Can
16C2	**Hyde Park** USA
87B1	**Hyderābād** India
85B3	**Hyderabad** Pak
49D3	**Hyères** France
12J2	**Hyland** *R* Can
8B2	**Hyndman Peak** *Mt* USA
38K6	**Hyrynsalmi** Fin
13D1	**Hythe** Can
74C4	**Hyūga** Japan
39J6	**Hyvikää** Fin

I

31C4	**Iaçu** Brazil
54C2	**Ialomiţa** *R* Rom
54C1	**Iaşi** Rom
97C4	**Ibadan** Nig
32B3	**Ibagué** Colombia
54B2	**Ibar** *R* Yugos
32B3	**Ibarra** Ecuador
35B1	**Ibiá** Brazil
30E4	**Ibicuí** *R* Brazil
34D2	**Ibicuy** Arg
51C2	**Ibiza** Spain
51C2	**Ibiza** *I* Spain
101D2	**Ibo** Mozam
31C4	**Ibotirama** Brazil
91C5	**'Ibrī** Oman
32B6	**Ica** Peru
32D4	**Icá** *R* Brazil
32D3	**Icana** Brazil
38A1	**Iceland** Republic, N Atlantic O
13C2	**Ice Mt** Can
87A1	**Ichalkaranji** India
74E3	**Ichihara** Japan
75B1	**Ichinomiya** Japan
74E3	**Ichinoseki** Japan
12F3	**Icy B** USA
4B2	**Icy C** USA
63B2	**Ida** *R* USSR
19B3	**Idabell** USA
8B2	**Idaho Falls** USA
20B2	**Idanha** USA
46D2	**Idar Oberstein** Germany
95A2	**Idehan Marzūg** *Desert* Libya
95A2	**Idehan Ubari** *Desert* Libya
96C2	**Idelés** Alg
68B2	**Iderlym Gol** *R* Mongolia
95C2	**Idfu** Egypt
55B3	**Ídhi Óros** *Mt* Greece
55B3	**Ídhra** *I* Greece
98B3	**Idiofa** Zaïre
12C2	**Iditarod** *R* USA
92C2	**Idlib** Syria
39K7	**Idritsa** USSR
100B4	**Idutywa** S Africa
55C3	**Ierápetra** Greece
46B1	**Ieper** Belg
99D3	**Ifakara** Tanz
71F3	**Ifalik** *I* Pacific O
101D3	**Ifanadiana** Madag
97C4	**Ife** Nig
97C3	**Iférouane** Niger
78C2	**Igan** Malay
35B2	**Igaranava** Brazil
93E2	**Igdir** Iran
39H6	**Iggesund** Sweden

34B2	**Iglesia** Arg
53A3	**Iglesias** Sardegna
6B3	**Igloolik** Can
10A2	**Ignace** Can
55B3	**Igoumenítsa** Greece
61H2	**Igra** USSR
23B2	**Iguala** Mexico
31B6	**Iguape** Brazil
35B2	**Iguape** Brazil
35B2	**Iguatama** Brazil
31D3	**Iguatu** Brazil
98A3	**Iguéla** Gabon
101D3	**Ihosy** Madag
74D3	**Iida** Japan
75B1	**Iide-san** *Mt* Japan
38K6	**Iisalmi** Fin
75A2	**Iizuka** Japan
97C4	**Ijebu Ode** Nig
56B2	**Ijsselmeer** *S* Neth
55C3	**Ikaría** *I* Greece
74E2	**Ikeda** Japan
98C3	**Ikela** Zaïre
54B2	**Ikhtiman** Bulg
12D3	**Ikolik,C** USA
101D2	**Ikopa** *R* Madag
79B2	**Ilagan** Phil
90A3	**Ilām** Iran
47C1	**Ilanz** Switz
13F1	**Île à la Crosse** Can
13F1	**Île à la Crosse,L** Can
89G8	**Ilebo** Zaïre
96D1	**Île de Jerba** *I* Tunisia
48B2	**Île de Noirmoutier** *I* France
48B2	**Île de Ré** *I* France
107F3	**Île des Pins** *I* Nouvelle Calédonie
48A2	**Île d'Ouessant** *I* France
48B2	**Île d'Yeu** *I* France
61J3	**Ilek** *R* USSR
107F2	**Îles Bélèp** Nouvelle Calédonie
107E2	**Îs Chesterfield** Nouvelle Calédonie
49D3	**Iles d'Hyères** *Is* France
43B4	**Ilfracombe** Eng
92B1	**Ilgaz Dağlari** *Mts* Turk
101C3	**Ilha Bazaruto** *I* Mozam
33G3	**Ilha De Maracá** *I* Brazil
33G4	**Ilha de Marajó** *I* Brazil
35B2	**Ilha de São Sebastião** *I* Brazil
33G6	**Ilha do Bananal** *Region* Brazil
35C2	**Ilha Grande** *I* Brazil
35B2	**Ilha Santo Amaro** *I* Brazil
96A1	**Ilhas Selvegens** *I* Atlantic O
31D4	**Ilhéus** Brazil
12C3	**Iliamna L** USA
12D2	**Iliamna V** USA
79B4	**Iligan** Phil
63G3	**Il'inskiy** USSR
55B3	**Iliodhrómia** *I* Greece
79B4	**Illana B** Phil
34A2	**Illapel** Chile
34A2	**Illapel** *R* Chile
97C3	**Illéla** Niger
47D1	**Iller** *R* Germany
4C4	**Illiamna L** USA
10A2	**Illinois** State, USA
18B2	**Illinois** *R* USA
96C2	**Illizi** Alg
30B2	**Ilo** Peru
79B3	**Iloilo** Phil
38L6	**Ilomantsi** Fin
97C4	**Ilorin** Nig
75A2	**Imabari** Japan
75B1	**Imalchi** Japan
60C1	**Imatra** Fin
30G4	**Imbituba** Brazil
99E2	**Imi** Eth
20C2	**Imlay** USA
47D1	**Immenstadt** Germany

52B2	**Imola** Italy
31B3	**Imperatriz** Brazil
52A2	**Imperia** Italy
98B2	**Impfondo** Congo
86C2	**Imphāl** India
47D1	**Imst** Austria
12B1	**Imuruk L** USA
75B1	**Ina** Japan
96C2	**In Afahleleh** *Well* Alg
75B2	**Inamba-jima** *I* Japan
96C2	**In Amenas** Alg
38K5	**Inari** Fin
38K5	**Inarijärvi** *L* Fin
75C1	**Inawashiro-ko** *L* Japan
96C2	**In Belbel** Alg
60E5	**Ince Burun** *Pt* Turk
92B2	**Incekum Burun** *Pt* Turk
74B3	**Inch'ōn** S Korea
96B2	**In Dagouber** *Well* Mali
35B1	**Indaia** *R* Brazil
38H6	**Indals** *R* Sweden
21B2	**Independence** California, USA
18A2	**Independence** Kansas, USA
18B2	**Independence** Missouri, USA
78A3	**Inderagiri** *R* Indon
61H4	**Inderborskly** USSR
83B3	**India** Federal Republic, Asia
14A2	**Indiana** State, USA
15C2	**Indiana** USA
104C6	**Indian-Antarctic Ridge** Indian O
14A3	**Indianapolis** USA
	Indian Desert = Thar Desert
7E4	**Indian Harbour** Can
104B4	**Indian** O
18B1	**Indianola** Iowa, USA
19B3	**Indianola** Mississippi, USA
35B1	**Indianópolis** Brazil
76D2	**Indo China** Region, S E Asia
70C4	**Indonesia** Republic, S E Asia
85D4	**Indore** India
78B4	**Indramayu** Indon
48C2	**Indre** *R* France
85B3	**Indus** *R* Pak
60D5	**Inebdu** Turk
96C2	**In Ebeggi** *Well* Alg
96C2	**In Ecker** Alg
92A1	**Inegöl** Turk
96D2	**In Ezzane** Alg
97C3	**Ingal** Niger
14B2	**Ingersoll** Can
107D2	**Ingham** Aust
6D2	**Inglefield Land** *Region* Can
110B1	**Inglewood** NZ
109D1	**Inglewood** Queensland, Aust
22C4	**Inglewood** USA
108B3	**Inglewood** Victoria, Aust
38B2	**Ingólfshöfði** *I* Iceland
57C3	**Ingolstadt** Germany
86B2	**Ingrãj Bāzār** India
96C3	**In-Guezzam** *Well* Alg
101C3	**Inhambane** Mozam
101C3	**Inharrime** Mozam
35B1	**Inhumas** Brazil
32D3	**Inírida** *R* Colombia
45A2	**Inishbofin** *I* Irish Rep
45A1	**Inishkea** *I* Irish Rep
45B2	**Inishmaan** *I* Irish Rep
45B2	**Inishmore** *I* Irish Rep
45B1	**Inishmurray** *I* Irish Rep
45C1	**Inishowen** District, Irish Rep
45A2	**Inishshark** *I* Irish Rep

45A2	**Inishturk** *I* Irish Rep
109C1	**Injune** Aust
12H3	**Inklin** Can
12H3	**Inklin** *R* Can
12C1	**Inland L** USA
47D1	**Inn** *R* Austria
108B1	**Innamincka** Aust
68C2	**Inner Mongolia** Autonomous Region, China
107D2	**Innisfail** Aust
12C2	**Innoko** *R* USA
57C3	**Innsbruck** Austria
98B3	**Inongo** Zaïre
58B2	**Inowrocław** Pol
96C2	**In Salah** Alg
47B1	**Interlaken** Switz
24C3	**Intexpec** Mexico
47C2	**Intra** Italy
78D3	**Intu** Indon
75C1	**Inubo-saki** *C* Japan
7C4	**Inukjuac** Can
4E3	**Inuvik** Can
4F3	**Inuvik** *Region* Can
44B3	**Inveraray** Scot
111A3	**Invercargill** NZ
109D1	**Inverell** Aust
13D2	**Invermere** Can
44B3	**Inverness** Scot
44C3	**Inverurie** Scot
108A3	**Investigator Str** Aust
68A1	**Inya** USSR
101C2	**Inyanga** Zim
21B2	**Inyokern** USA
98B3	**Inzia** *R* Zaïre
55B3	**Ioánnina** Greece
18A2	**Iola** USA
44A3	**Iona** *I* Scot
100A2	**Iôna Nat Pk** Angola
20C1	**Ione** USA
	Ionian Is = Ioníoi Nísoi
55A3	**Ionian S** Italy/Greece
55B3	**Ioníoi Nísoi** *Is* Greece
55C3	**Íos** *I* Greece
10A2	**Iowa** *R* USA
10A2	**Iowa City** USA
35B1	**Ipameri** Brazil
35C1	**Ipanema** Brazil
61F4	**Ipatovo** USSR
32B3	**Ipiales** Colombia
77C5	**Ipoh** Malay
30F2	**Iporá** Brazil
55C2	**Ipsala** Turk
109D1	**Ipswich** Aust
43E3	**Ipswich** Eng
16D1	**Ipswich** USA
30B3	**Iquique** Chile
32C4	**Iquitos** Peru
55C3	**Iráklion** Greece
80D2	**Iran** Republic, S W Asia
91D4	**Irānshahr** Iran
23A1	**Irapuato** Mexico
93D3	**Iraq** Republic, S W Asia
95A2	**Irā Wan** *Watercourse* Libya
94B2	**Irbid** Jordan
61K2	**Irbit** USSR
36C3	**Ireland** Republic, NW Europe
33F3	**Ireng** *R* Guyana
74B3	**Iri** S Korea
71E4	**Irian Jaya** Province, Indon
95B3	**Iriba** Chad
79B3	**Iriga** Phil
99D3	**Iringa** Tanz
69E4	**Iriomote** *I* Japan
33G5	**Iriri** *R* Brazil
42B3	**Irish S** Eng/Irish Rep
12D1	**Irkillik** *R* USA
63C2	**Irkutsk** USSR
65J4	**Irlysh** USSR
108A2	**Iron Knob** Aust
14A1	**Iron Mountain** USA
107D2	**Iron Range** Aust
14A1	**Iron River** USA

63D3 **Kerulen** *R* Mongolia
96B2 **Kerzaz** Alg
55C2 **Keşan** Turk
74E3 **Kesennuma** Japan
38L5 **Kestenga** USSR
42C2 **Keswick** Eng
65K4 **Ket** *R* USSR
97C4 **Kéta** Ghana
78C3 **Ketapang** Indon
5E4 **Ketchikan** USA
97C3 **Ketia** Niger
85B4 **Keti Bandar** Pak
58C2 **Ketrzyn** Pol
43D3 **Kettering** Eng
14B3 **Kettering** USA
20C1 **Kettle** *R* Can
20C1 **Kettle River Range** *Mts* USA
7C3 **Kettlestone B** Can
90C3 **Kevir-i Namak** *Salt Flat* Iran
14A2 **Kewaunee** USA
14B1 **Key Harbour** Can
17B2 **Key Largo** USA
11B4 **Key West** USA
63C2 **Kezhma** USSR
54A1 **K'félegháza** Hung
12B2 **Kgun L** USA
94C2 **Khabab** Syria
62H3 **Khabarovsk** USSR
85B3 **Khairpur** Pak
85B3 **Khairpur** Region, Pak
100B3 **Khakhea** Botswana
55C3 **Khálki** *I* Greece
55B2 **Khalkidhíki** *Pen* Greece
55B3 **Khalkís** Greece
61G2 **Khalturin** USSR
85C4 **Khambhāt,G of** India
85D4 **Khāmgaon** India
76C2 **Kham Keut** Laos
87C1 **Khammam** India
90A2 **Khamseh** *Mts* Iran
76C2 **Khan** *R* Laos
84B1 **Khanabad** Afghan
93E3 **Khānaqīn** Iraq
85D4 **Khandwa** India
84C2 **Khanewal** Pak
94C3 **Khan ez Zabib** Jordan
77D4 **Khanh Hung** Viet
55B3 **Khaniá** Greece
84C3 **Khanpur** Pak
65H3 **Khanty-Mansiysk** USSR
94B3 **Khan Yunis** Egypt
84D1 **Khapalu** India
68C2 **Khapcheranga** USSR
61G4 **Kharabali** USSR
86B2 **Kharagpur** India
91C4 **Khāran** Iran
84B3 **Kharan** Pak
90B3 **Kharānaq** Iran
91B4 **Khārg** *Is* Iran
95C2 **Khârga Oasis** Egypt
85D4 **Khargon** India
60E4 **Khar'kov** USSR
54C2 **Kharmanli** Bulg
61F2 **Kharovsk** USSR
95C3 **Khartoum** Sudan
95C3 **Khartoum North** Sudan
74C2 **Khasan** USSR
95C3 **Khashm el Girba** Sudan
86C1 **Khasi-Jaīntīa Hills** India
54C2 **Khaskovo** Bulg
1B9 **Khatanga** USSR
76B3 **Khawsa** Burma
76C2 **Khe Bo** Viet
85C4 **Khed Brahma** India
51C2 **Khemis** Alg
51D2 **Kherrata** Alg
60D4 **Kherson** USSR
63D2 **Khilok** USSR
55C3 **Khíos** Greece
55C3 **Khíos** *I* Greece
60C4 **Khmel'nitskiy** USSR
59C3 **Khodorov** USSR
84B1 **Kholm** Afghan
76D3 **Khong** Laos
91B4 **Khonj** Iran
69F2 **Khor** USSR
91A3 **Khoramshahr** Iran
91B5 **Khōr Duwayhin** *B* UAE
84C1 **Khorog** USSR
90A3 **Khorramābad** Iran
90C3 **Khosf** Iran
84B2 **Khost** Pak
60C4 **Khotin** USSR
12C2 **Khotol** *Mt* USA
60C3 **Khoyniku** USSR
63F2 **Khrebet Dzhugdzhur** *Mts* USSR
90C2 **Khrebet Kopet Dag** *Mts* USSR
64H3 **Khrebet Pay-khoy** *Mts* USSR
82C1 **Khrebet Tarbagatay** *Mts* USSR
63E2 **Khrebet Tukuringra** *Mts* USSR
86B2 **Khulna** Bang
84D1 **Khunjerab** *P* China/India
90B3 **Khunsar** Iran
91A4 **Khurays** S Arabia
86B2 **Khurda** India
84D3 **Khurja** India
84C2 **Khushab** Pak
94B2 **Khushnīyah** Syria
59C3 **Khust** USSR
99C1 **Khuwei** Sudan
85B3 **Khuzdar** Pak
90D3 **Khvāf** Iran
61G3 **Khvalynsk** USSR
90C3 **Khvor** Iran
91B4 **Khvormūj** Iran
93D2 **Khvoy** Iran
84C1 **Khwaja Muhammad** *Mts* Afghan
84C2 **Khyber P** Afghan/Pak
99C3 **Kiambi** Zaïre
19A3 **Kiamichi** *R* USA
12B1 **Kiana** USA
98B3 **Kibangou** Congo
99D3 **Kibaya** Tanz
98C3 **Kibombo** Zaïre
99D3 **Kibondo** Tanz
99D3 **Kibungu** Rwanda
55B2 **Kičevo** Yugos
5G4 **Kicking Horse P** Can
97C3 **Kidal** Mali
43C3 **Kidderminster** Eng
97A3 **Kidira** Sen
110C1 **Kidnappers,C** NZ
56C2 **Kiel** Germany
59C2 **Kielce** Pol
56C2 **Kieler Bucht** *B* Germany
Kiev = Kiyev
80E2 **Kifab** USSR
97A3 **Kiffa** Maur
89H8 **Kigali** Rwanda
12A2 **Kigluaik Mts** USA
99C3 **Kigoma** Tanz
75B2 **Kii-sanchi** *Mts* Japan
74C4 **Kii-suido** *B* Japan
54B1 **Kikinda** Yugos
55B3 **Kikládhes** *Is* Greece
71F4 **Kikori** PNG
98B3 **Kikwit** Zaïre
21C4 **Kilauea Crater** *Mt* Hawaiian Is
4C3 **Kilbuck Mts** USA
74B2 **Kilchu** N Korea
109D1 **Kilcoy** Aust
45C2 **Kildare** County, Irish Rep
45C2 **Kildare** Irish Rep
19B3 **Kilgore** USA
99D3 **Kilifi** Kenya
99D3 **Kilimanjaro** *Mt* Tanz
99D3 **Kilindoni** Tanz
92C2 **Kilis** Turk
45B2 **Kilkee** Irish Rep
45C2 **Kilkenny** County, Irish Rep
45C2 **Kilkenny** Irish Rep
45B2 **Kilkieran B** Irish Rep
55B2 **Kilkís** Greece
45B1 **Killala B** Irish Rep
45B2 **Killaloe** Irish Rep
109D1 **Killarney** Aust
41B3 **Killarney** Irish Rep
19A3 **Killeen** USA
12D1 **Killik** *R* USA
44B3 **Killin** Scot
55B3 **Killíni** *Mt* Greece
45B1 **Killybegs** Irish Rep
42B2 **Kilmarnock** Scot
61H2 **Kil'mez** USSR
99D3 **Kilosa** Tanz
41B3 **Kilrush** Irish Rep
99C3 **Kilwa** Zaïre
99D3 **Kilwa Kisiwani** Tanz
99D3 **Kilwa Kivinje** Tanz
108A2 **Kimba** Aust
12F2 **Kimball,Mt** USA
13D3 **Kimberley** Can
101F1 **Kimberley** S Africa
106B2 **Kimberley Plat** Aust
74B2 **Kimch'aek** N Korea
74B3 **Kimch'ŏn** S Korea
55B3 **Kími** Greece
60E2 **Kimry** USSR
70C3 **Kinabalu** *Mt* Malay
78D1 **Kinabatangan** *R* Malay
14B2 **Kincardine** Can
13B1 **Kincolith** Can
19B3 **Kinder** USA
13F2 **Kindersley** Can
97A3 **Kindia** Guinea
98C3 **Kindu** Zaïre
61H3 **Kinel'** USSR
61F2 **Kineshma** USSR
109D1 **Kingaroy** Aust
21A2 **King City** USA
5F4 **Kingcome Inlet** Can
7C4 **King George Is** Can
107D4 **King I** Aust
13B2 **King I** Can
106B2 **King Leopold Range** *Mts* Aust
9B3 **Kingman** USA
98C3 **Kingombe** Zaïre
108A2 **Kingoonya** Aust
22C2 **Kingsburg** USA
21B2 **Kings Canyon Nat Pk** USA
108A3 **Kingscote** Aust
106B2 **King Sd** Aust
14A1 **Kingsford** USA
17B1 **Kingsland** USA
43E3 **King's Lynn** Eng
16C2 **Kings Park** USA
8B2 **Kings Peak** *Mt* USA
107C4 **Kingston** Aust
7C5 **Kingston** Can
25E3 **Kingston** Jamaica
15D2 **Kingston** New York, USA
111A3 **Kingston** NZ
27E4 **Kingstown** St Vincent
9D4 **Kingsville** USA
44B3 **Kingussie** Scot
4J3 **King William I** Can
100B4 **King William's Town** S Africa
98B3 **Kinkala** Congo
39G7 **Kinna** Sweden
44D3 **Kinnairds Head** *Pt* Scot
75B1 **Kinomoto** Japan
44C3 **Kinross** Scot
45B3 **Kinsale** Irish Rep
98B3 **Kinshasa** Zaïre
78D3 **Kintap** Indon
42B2 **Kintyre** *Pen* Scot
13D1 **Kinuso** Can
99D2 **Kinyeti** *Mt* Sudan
55B3 **Kiparissía** Greece
55B3 **Kiparissiakós Kólpos** *G* Greece
15C1 **Kipawa,L** Can
99D3 **Kipili** Tanz
12B3 **Kipnuk** USA
45C2 **Kippure** *Mt* Irish Rep
100B2 **Kipushi** Zaïre
63C2 **Kirensk** USSR
65J5 **Kirgizskaya SSR** Republic, USSR
82B1 **Kirgizskiy Khrebet** *Mts* USSR
98B3 **Kiri** Zaïre
105G4 **Kiribati** *Is* Pacific O
92B2 **Kırıkkale** Turk
60D2 **Kirishi** USSR
85B3 **Kirithar Range** *Mts* Pak
55C3 **Kirkağaç** Turk
90A2 **Kirk Bulāg Dāgh** *Mt* Iran
42C2 **Kirkby** Eng
44C3 **Kirkcaldy** Scot
42B2 **Kirkcudbright** Scot
38K5 **Kirkenes** Nor
7B5 **Kirkland Lake** Can
112A **Kirkpatrick,Mt** Ant
10A2 **Kirksville** USA
93D2 **Kirkūk** Iraq
44C2 **Kirkwall** Scot
18B2 **Kirkwood** USA
60D3 **Kirov** USSR
61G2 **Kirov** USSR
93D1 **Kirovakan** USSR
61J2 **Kirovgrad** USSR
60D4 **Kirovograd** USSR
61H2 **Kirs** USSR
92B2 **Kirşehir** Turk
56C2 **Kiruna** Sweden
75B1 **Kiryū** Japan
98C2 **Kisangani** Zaïre
75B1 **Kisarazu** Japan
86B1 **Kishanganj** India
85C3 **Kishangarh** India
60C4 **Kishinev** USSR
75B2 **Kishiwada** Japan
99D3 **Kisii** Kenya
99D3 **Kisiju** Tanz
59B3 **Kiskunhalas** Hung
65F5 **Kislovodsk** USSR
99E3 **Kismaayo** Somalia
75B1 **Kiso-sammyaku** *Mts* Japan
97A4 **Kissidougou** Guinea
17B2 **Kissimmee,L** USA
99D3 **Kisumu** Kenya
59C3 **Kisvárda** Hung
97B3 **Kita** Mali
65H6 **Kitab** USSR
75C1 **Kitakata** Japan
74C4 **Kita-Kyūshū** Japan
99D2 **Kitale** Kenya
69G4 **Kitalo** *I* Japan
74E2 **Kitami** Japan
7B5 **Kitchener** Can
99D2 **Kitgum** Uganda
55B3 **Kíthira** *I* Greece
55B3 **Kíthnos** *I* Greece
94A1 **Kiti,C** Cyprus
4H3 **Kitikmeot** *Region* Can
5F4 **Kitimat** Can
38K5 **Kitnen** *R* Fin
75A2 **Kitsuki** Japan
15C2 **Kittanning** USA
38J5 **Kittilä** Fin
99D3 **Kitunda** Tanz
13B1 **Kitwanga** Can
100B2 **Kitwe** Zambia
57C3 **Kitzbühel** Austria
47E1 **Kitzbühler Alpen** *Mts* Austria
57C3 **Kitzingen** Germany
98C3 **Kiumbi** Zaïre
12B1 **Kivalina** USA
59D2 **Kivercy** USSR
99C3 **Kivu,L** Zaïre/Rwanda
4B3 **Kiwalik** USA
60D3 **Kiyev** USSR

61J2	Kizel USSR
92C2	Kizil *R* Turk
80D2	Kizyl-Arvat USSR
90B2	Kizyl-Atrek USSR
57C2	Kladno Czech
57C3	Klagenfurt Austria
60B2	Klaipéda USSR
8A2	Klamath USA
20B2	Klamath *R* USA
8A2	Klamath Falls USA
20B2	Klamath Mts USA
57C3	Klatovy Czech
12H3	Klawak USA
94B1	Kleiat Leb
101G1	Klerksdorp S Africa
60E2	Klin USSR
58B1	Klintehamn Sweden
60D3	Klintsy USSR
52C2	Ključ Yugos
59B2	Kłodzko Pol
12G2	Klondike *R* Can/USA
4D3	Klondike Plat Can/ USA
59B3	Klosterneuburg Austria
12G2	Kluane *R* Can
12G2	Kluane L Can
12G2	Kluane Nat Pk Can
59B2	Kluczbork Pol
12G3	Klukwan USA
12E2	Klutina L USA
12E2	Knight I USA
43C3	Knighton Wales
52C2	Knin Yugos
106A4	Knob,C Aust
46B1	Knokke-Heist Belg
112C9	Knox Coast Ant
11B3	Knoxville Tennessee, USA
6H3	Knud Rasmussens Land *Region* Greenland
78B3	Koba Indon
6F3	Kobbermirebugt Greenland
74D4	Kobe Japan
56C1	København Den
57B2	Koblenz Germany
60B3	Kobrin USSR
71E4	Kobroör I Indon
12C1	Kobuk *R* USA
54B2	Kočani Yugos
76C3	Ko Chang I Thai
86B1	Koch Bihär India
47D1	Kochel Germany
6C3	Koch I Can
74C4	Köchi Japan
12D3	Kodiak USA
12D3	Kodiak I USA
87B2	Kodikkarai India
99D2	Kodok Sudan
100A3	Koes Namibia
101G1	Koffiefontein S Africa
97B4	Koforidua Ghana
74D3	Köfu Japan
75B1	Koga Japan
39G7	Køge Den
84C2	Kohat Pak
84B2	Koh-i-Baba *Mts* Afghan
84B1	Koh-i-Hisar *Mts* Afghan
84B2	Koh-i-Khurd *Mt* Afghan
86C1	Kohima India
84B1	Koh-i-Mazar *Mt* Afghan
84B3	Kohlu Pak
60C2	Kohtla Järve USSR
75B1	Koide Japan
12F2	Koidern Can
77A4	Koihoa *Is* Nicobar Is
74B4	Kŏje-do I S Korea
65H4	Kokchetav USSR
39J6	Kokemaki *L* Fin
38J6	Kokkola Fin
107D1	Kokoda PNG
14A2	Kokomo USA

71E4	Kokonau Indon
65K5	Kokpekty USSR
7D4	Koksoak *R* Can
100B4	Kokstad S Africa
76C3	Ko Kut I Thai
38L5	Kola USSR
71D4	Kolaka Indon
77B4	Ko Lanta I Thai
87B2	Kolär India
87B2	Kolär Gold Fields India
97A3	Kolda Sen
39F7	Kolding Den
87A1	Kolhäpur India
12C3	Koligk USA
59B2	Kolín Czech
57B2	Köln Germany
58B2	Kolo Pol
58B2	Kolobrzeg Pol
97B3	Kolokani Mali
60E2	Kolomna USSR
60C4	Kolomyya USSR
65K4	Kolpashevo USSR
68A2	Kolpekty USSR
55C3	Kólpos Merabéllou *B* Greece
55B2	Kólpos Singitikós *G* Greece
55B2	Kólpos Strimonikós *G* Greece
55B2	Kólpos Toronaíos *G* Greece
38L5	Kol'skiy Poluostrov *Pen* USSR
38G6	Kolvereid Nor
100B2	Kolwezi Zaïre
1C7	Kolyma *R* USSR
54B2	Kom *Mt* Bulg/Yugos
99D2	Koma Eth
97D3	Komaduga Gana *R* Nig
59B3	Komárno Czech
101H1	Komati *R* S Africa
74D3	Komatsu Japan
75A2	Komatsushima Japan
64G3	Komi A.S.S.R. Republic, USSR
70C4	Komodo I Indon
71E4	Komoran I Indon
75B1	Komoro Japan
55C2	Komotiní Greece
76D3	Kompong Cham Camb
76C3	Kompong Chhnang *Mts* Camb
77C3	Kompong Som Camb
76C3	Kompong Thom Camb
76D3	Kompong Trabek Camb
63F2	Komsomol'sk na Amure USSR
65H4	Konda *R* USSR
99D3	Kondoa Tanz
87B1	Kondukür India
6G3	Kong Christian IX Land *Region* Greenland
6F3	Kong Frederik VI Kyst *Mts* Greenland
64C2	Kong Karls Land *Is* Barents S
78D2	Kongkemul *Mt* Indon
98C3	Kongolo Zaïre
39F7	Kongsberg Den
39G6	Kongsvinger Nor
	Königsberg = Kaliningrad
58B2	Konin Pol
54A2	Konjic Yugos
61F1	Konosha USSR
75B1	Konosu Japan
60D3	Konotop USSR
63B2	Konsk USSR
59C2	Końskie Pol
49D2	Konstanz Germany
97C3	Kontagora Nig
76D3	Kontum Viet
92B2	Konya Turk
13D3	Kootenay *R* Can
85C5	Kopargaon India
6J3	Kópasker Iceland
38A2	Kópavogur Iceland

52B1	Koper Yugos
80D2	Kopet Dag *Mts* Iran/ USSR
61K2	Kopeysk USSR
77C4	Ko Phangan I Thai
77B4	Ko Phuket I Thai
39H7	Köping Sweden
87B1	Koppal India
52C1	Koprivnica Yugos
85B4	Korangi Pak
87C1	Koraput India
86A2	Korba India
57B2	Korbach Germany
4B3	Korbuk *R* USA
55B2	Korçë Alb
52C2	Korčula I Yugos
72E2	Korea B China/Korea
74B4	Korea Str S Korea/ Japan
59D2	Korec USSR
92B1	Körglu Tepesi *Mt* Turk
97B4	Korhogo Ivory Coast
85B4	Kori Creek India
55B3	Korinthiakós Kólpos *G* Greece
55B2	Kórinthos Greece
74E3	Köriyama Japan
61K3	Korkino USSR
92B2	Korkuteli Turk
82C1	Korla China
52C2	Kornat I Yugos
60D5	Köroğlu Tepesi *Mt* Turk
99D3	Korogwe Tanz
108B3	Koroit Aust
71E3	Koror Palau Is, Pacific O
59C3	Körös *R* Hung
60C3	Korosten USSR
95A3	Koro Toro Chad
12B3	Korovin I USA
69G2	Korsakov USSR
39G7	Korsør Den
46B1	Kortrijk Belg
55C3	Kós I Greece
77C4	Ko Samui I Thai
58B2	Koscierzyna Pol
107D4	Kosciusko *Mt* Aust
12H3	Kosciusko I USA
74B4	Koshikijima-retto I Japan
59C3	Košice Czech
74B3	Kosong N Korea
97B4	Kossou *L* Ivory Coast
101G1	Koster S Africa
99D1	Kosti Sudan
59D2	Kostopol' USSR
61F2	Kostroma USSR
56C2	Kostrzyn Pol
39H8	Koszalin Pol
85D3	Kota India
78A4	Kotaagung Indon
78C3	Kotabaharu Indon
78D3	Kotabaru Indon
77C4	Kota Bharu Malay
78A3	Kotabum Indon
84C2	Kot Addu Pak
78D1	Kota Kinabulu Malay
87C1	Kotapad India
61G2	Kotel'nich USSR
61F4	Kotel'nikovo USSR
39K6	Kotka Fin
64F3	Kotlas USSR
12B2	Kotlik USA
54A2	Kotor Yugos
60C4	Kotovsk USSR
85B3	Kotri Pak
87C1	Kottagüdem India
87B3	Kottayam India
98C2	Kotto *R* CAR
87B2	Kottüru India
12B1	Kotzebue USA
4B3	Kotzebue Sd USA
97C3	Kouande Benin
98C2	Kouango CAR
97B3	Koudougou Burkina
98B3	Koulamoutou Gabon

97B3	Koulikoro Mali
97B3	Koupéla Burkina
33G2	Kourou French Guiana
97B3	Kouroussa Guinea
98B1	Kousséri Cam
39K6	Kouvola Fin
60B3	Kovel USSR
	Kovno = Kaunas
61F2	Kovrov USSR
61F3	Kovylkino USSR
60E1	Kovzha *R* USSR
77C4	Ko Way I Thai
73C5	Kowloon Hong Kong
84B2	Kowt-e-Ashrow Afghan
92A2	Köyceğğiz Turk
38L5	Koydor USSR
87A1	Koyna Res India
12B2	Koyuk USA
12B1	Koyuk *R* USA
12C2	Koyukuk USA
12C1	Koyukuk *R* USA
92C2	Kozan Turk
55B2	Kozańi Greece
	Kozhikode = Calicut
61G2	Koz'modemyansk USSR
61F2	Koztroma USSR
75B2	Kōzu-shima I Japan
39F7	Kragerø Nor
54B2	Kragujevac Yugos
77B3	Kra,Isthmus of Burma/ Malay
	Krakatau = Rakata
94C1	Krak des Chevaliers *Hist Site* Syria
59B2	Kraków Pol
54B2	Kraljevo Yugos
60E4	Kramatorsk USSR
38H6	Kramfors Sweden
52B1	Kranj Yugos
61F4	Krapotkin USSR
61G1	Krasavino USSR
61J2	Krashnokamsk USSR
64G2	Krasino USSR
59C2	Kraśnik Pol
61G3	Krasnoarmeysk USSR
60E5	Krasnodar USSR
61K2	Krasnotur'insk USSR
61J2	Krasnoufimsk USSR
61J3	Krasnousol'-skiy USSR
65G3	Krasnovishersk USSR
65G5	Krasnovodsk USSR
63B2	Krasnoyarsk USSR
59C2	Krasnystaw Pol
61G3	Krasnyy Kut USSR
60E4	Krasnyy Luch USSR
61G4	Krasnyy Yar USSR
76D3	Kratie Camb
6E2	Kraulshavn Greenland
56B2	Krefeld Germany
60D4	Kremenchug USSR
60D4	Kremenchugskoye Vodokhranilische *Res* USSR
59D2	Kremenets USSR
98A2	Kribi Cam
60D3	Krichev USSR
47E1	Krimml Austria
87B1	Krishna *R* India
87B2	Krishnagiri India
86B2	Krishnangar India
39F7	Kristiansand Nor
39G7	Kristianstad Sweden
64B3	Kristiansund Nor
39G7	Kristinehamn Sweden
38J6	Kristiinankaupunki Fin
55B3	Kríti I Greece
60D4	Krivoy Rog USSR
52B1	Krk I Yugos
6G3	Kronpris Frederik Bjerge *Mts* Greenland
39K7	Kronshtadt USSR
101G1	Kroonstad S Africa
65F5	Kropotkin USSR
101G1	Krugersdorp S Africa

Lorraine

49D2 **Lorraine** *Region*
France
9C3 **Los Alamos** USA
34A2 **Los Andes** Chile
29B3 **Los Angeles** Chile
9B3 **Los Angeles** USA
21A2 **Los Banos** USA
34B2 **Los Cerrillos** Arg
21A2 **Los Gatos** USA
52B2 **Lošinj** *I* Yugos
29B3 **Los Lagos** Chile
24B2 **Los Mochis** Mexico
22B3 **Los Olivos** USA
34A3 **Los Sauces** Chile
44C3 **Lossiemouth** Scot
27E4 **Los Testigos** *Is* Ven
29B2 **Los Vilos** Chile
48C3 **Lot** *R* France
34A3 **Lota** Chile
42C2 **Lothian** Region, Scot
99D2 **Lotikipi Plain** Sudan/
Kenya
98C3 **Loto** Zaïre
47B1 **Lötschberg Tunnel**
Switz
38K5 **Lotta** *R* Fin/USSR
48B2 **Loudéac** France
97A3 **Louga** Sen
41B3 **Lough Allen** *L*
Irish Rep
45C2 **Lough Boderg** *L*
Irish Rep
43D3 **Loughborough** Eng
45C2 **Lough Bowna** *L*
Irish Rep
45C1 **Lough Carlingford** *L*
N Ire
41B3 **Lough Conn** *L*
Irish Rep
41B3 **Lough Corrib** *L*
Irish Rep
41B3 **Lough Derg** *L* Irish Rep
45C2 **Lough Derravaragh** *L*
Irish Rep
4H2 **Loughead I** Can
45C2 **Lough Ennell** *L*
Irish Rep
41B3 **Lough Erne** *L* N Ire
40B2 **Lough Foyle** *Estuary*
N Ire/Irish Rep
40B3 **Lough Neagh** *L* N Ire
45C1 **Lough Oughter** *L*
Irish Rep
45B2 **Loughrea** Irish Rep
45C2 **Lough Ree** *L* Irish Rep
45C2 **Lough Sheelin** *L*
Irish Rep
42B2 **Lough Strangford** *L*
Irish Rep
45C1 **Lough Swilly** *Estuary*
Irish Rep
14B3 **Louisa** USA
70C3 **Louisa Reef** *I* S E Asia
12E2 **Louise,L** USA
107E2 **Louisiade Arch**
Solomon Is
11A3 **Louisiana** State, USA
17B1 **Louisville** Georgia,
USA
11B3 **Louisville** Kentucky,
USA
38L5 **Loukhi** USSR
48B3 **Lourdes** France
108C2 **Louth** Aust
45C2 **Louth** County,
Irish Rep
42D3 **Louth** Eng
Louvain = Leuven
48C2 **Louviers** France
60D2 **Lovat** *R* USSR
54B2 **Lovech** Bulg
21B1 **Lovelock** USA
52B1 **Lóvere** Italy
9C3 **Lovington** USA
38L5 **Lovozero** USSR
6B3 **Low,C** Can
10C2 **Lowell** Massachusetts,
USA

20B2 **Lowell** Oregon, USA
16D1 **Lowell** USA
111B2 **Lower Hutt** NZ
7C4 **Lower Seal,L** Can
43E3 **Lowestoft** Eng
58B2 **Łowicz** Pol
108B2 **Loxton** Aust
5F4 **Loyd George,Mt** Can
54A2 **Loznica** Yugos
23A2 **Loz Reyes** Mexico
65H3 **Lozva** *R* USSR
100B2 **Luacano** Angola
98C3 **Luachimo** Angola
98C3 **Lualaba** *R* Zaïre
100B2 **Luampa** Zambia
100B2 **Luân** Angola
73D3 **Lu'an** China
98B3 **Luanda** Angola
100A2 **Luando** *R* Angola
100B2 **Luanginga** *R* Angola
76C1 **Luang Namtha** Laos
76C2 **Luang Prabang** Laos
98B3 **Luangue** *R* Angola
100C2 **Luangwa** *R* Zambia
72D1 **Luan He** *R* China
72D1 **Luanping** China
100B2 **Luanshya** Zambia
100B2 **Luapula** *R* Zaïre
50A1 **Luarca** Spain
98B3 **Lubalo** Angola
58D2 **L'uban** USSR
79B3 **Lubang Is** Phil
100A2 **Lubango** Angola
9C3 **Lubbock** USA
56C2 **Lübeck** Germany
98C3 **Lubefu** Zaïre
98C3 **Lubefu** *R* Zaïre
99C3 **Lubero** Zaïre
98C3 **Lubilash** *R* Zaïre
59C2 **Lublin** Pol
60D3 **Lubny** USSR
78C2 **Lubok Antu** Malay
98C3 **Lubudi** Zaïre
98C3 **Lubudi** *R* Zaïre
78A3 **Lubuklinggau** Indon
100B2 **Lubumbashi** Zaïre
98C3 **Lubutu** Zaïre
79B3 **Lucban** Phil
52B2 **Lucca** Italy
42B2 **Luce** *B* Scot
19C3 **Lucedale** USA
79B3 **Lucena** Phil
59B3 **Lucenec** Czech
Lucerne = Luzern
73C5 **Luchuan** China
56C2 **Luckenwalde**
Germany
101F1 **Luckhoff** S Africa
86A1 **Lucknow** India
100B2 **Lucusse** Angola
72E2 **Lüda** China
46D1 **Lüdenscheid** Germany
100A3 **Lüderitz** Namibia
84D2 **Ludhiana** India
14A2 **Ludington** USA
43C3 **Ludlow** Eng
54C2 **Ludogorie** *Upland*
Bulg
17B1 **Ludowici** USA
54B1 **Luduş** Rom
39H6 **Ludvika** Sweden
57B3 **Ludwigsburg**
Germany
57B3 **Ludwigshafen**
Germany
56C2 **Ludwigslust** Germany
98C3 **Luebo** Zaïre
98C3 **Luema** *R* Zaïre
98C3 **Luembe** *R* Angola
100A2 **Luena** Angola
100B2 **Luene** *R* Angola
72B3 **Lüeyang** China
73D5 **Lufeng** China
11A3 **Lufkin** USA
60C2 **Luga** USSR
60C2 **Luga** *R* USSR
52A1 **Lugano** Switz
60E4 **Lugansk** USSR

101C2 **Lugela** Mozam
101C2 **Lugenda** *R* Mozam
50A1 **Lugo** Spain
54B1 **Lugoj** Rom
72A3 **Luhuo** China
98B3 **Lui** *R* Angola
100B2 **Luiana** Angola
100B2 **Luiana** *R* Angola
Luichow Peninsula =
Leizhou Bandao
47C2 **Luino** Italy
98B2 **Luionga** *R* Zaïre
72B2 **Luipan Shan** *Upland*
China
100B2 **Luishia** Zaïre
68B4 **Luixi** China
98C3 **Luiza** Zaïre
34B2 **Luján** Arg
34D2 **Luján** Arg
73D3 **Lujiang** China
98B3 **Lukenie** *R* Zaïre
64E4 **Luki** USSR
98B3 **Lukolela** Zaïre
58C2 **Luków** Pol
98C3 **Lukuga** *R* Zaïre
100B2 **Lukulu** Zambia
38J5 **Lule** *R* Sweden
38J5 **Luleå** Sweden
54C2 **Lüleburgaz** Turk
72C2 **Lüliang Shan** *Mts*
China
19A4 **Luling** USA
98C2 **Lulonga** *R* Zaïre
Luluabourg = Kananga
100B2 **Lumbala** Angola
11C3 **Lumberton** USA
78D1 **Lumbis** Indon
86C1 **Lumding** India
100B2 **Lumeje** Angola
111A3 **Lumsden** NZ
39G7 **Lund** Sweden
101C2 **Lundazi** Zambia
100C3 **Lundi** *R* Zim
43B4 **Lundy** *I* Eng
56C2 **Lüneburg** Germany
46D2 **Lunéville** France
100B2 **Lunga** *R* Zambia
86C2 **Lunglei** India
100A2 **Lungue Bungo** *R*
Angola
58D2 **Luninec** USSR
98B3 **Luobomo** Congo
73B5 **Luocheng** China
73C5 **Luoding** China
72C3 **Luohe** China
72C3 **Luo He** *R* Henan,
China
72B2 **Luo He** *R* Shaanxi,
China
73C4 **Luoxiao Shan** *Hills*
China
72C3 **Luoyang** China
98B3 **Luozi** Zaïre
100B2 **Lupane** Zim
101C2 **Lupilichi** Mozam
Lu Qu = Tao He
30E4 **Luque** Par
45C1 **Lurgan** N Ire
101C2 **Lurio** *R* Mozam
90A3 **Luristan** Region, Iran
100B2 **Lusaka** Zambia
98C3 **Lusambo** Zaïre
55A2 **Lushnjë** Alb
99D3 **Lushoto** Tanz
68B4 **Lushui** China
72E2 **Lüshun** China
43D4 **Luton** Eng
60C3 **Lutsk** USSR
99E2 **Luuq** Somalia
99C3 **Luvua** *R* Zaïre
99D3 **Luwegu** *R* Tanz
100C2 **Luwingu** Zambia
71D4 **Luwuk** Indon
46D2 **Luxembourg** Grand
Duchy, N W Europe
49D2 **Luxembourg** Lux
73A5 **Luxi** China
95C2 **Luxor** Egypt

61G1 **Luza** USSR
61G1 **Luza** *R* USSR
52A1 **Luzern** Switz
73B5 **Luzhai** China
73B4 **Luzhi** China
73B4 **Luzhou** China
35B1 **Luziânia** Brazil
79B2 **Luzon** *I* Phil
79B1 **Luzon Str** Phil
59C3 **L'vov** USSR
44C2 **Lybster** Scot
38H6 **Lycksele** Sweden
100B3 **Lydenburg** S Africa
8B3 **Lyell,Mt** USA
16A2 **Lykens** USA
43C4 **Lyme B** Eng
43C4 **Lyme Regis** Eng
11C3 **Lynchburg** USA
108A2 **Lyndhurst** Aust
15D2 **Lynn** USA
12G3 **Lynn Canal** *Sd* USA
17A1 **Lynn Haven** USA
5H4 **Lynn Lake** Can
5H3 **Lynx L** Can
49C2 **Lyon** France
12G3 **Lyon Canal** *Sd* USA
17B1 **Lyons** Georgia, USA
106A3 **Lyons** *R* Aust
47B2 **Lys** *R* Italy
61J2 **Lys'va** USSR
111B2 **Lyttelton** NZ
13C2 **Lytton** Can
22A1 **Lytton** USA
58D2 **Lyubeshov** USSR
60E2 **Lyublino** USSR

M

76C1 **Ma** *R* Viet
94B2 **Ma'agan** Jordan
94B2 **Ma'alot Tarshīha**
Israel
92C3 **Ma'an** Jordan
73D3 **Ma'anshan** China
92C2 **Ma'arrat an Nu'mān**
Syria
46C1 **Maas** *R* Neth
46C1 **Maaseik** Belg
79B3 **Maasin** Phil
57B2 **Maastricht** Belg
101C3 **Mabalane** Mozam
33F2 **Mabaruma** Guyana
42E3 **Mablethorpe** Eng
101C3 **Mabote** Mozam
58C2 **Mabrita** USSR
35C2 **Macaé** Brazil
58D2 **M'adel** USSR
9D3 **McAlester** USA
9D4 **McAllen** USA
101C2 **Macaloge** Mozam
33G3 **Macapá** Brazil
35C1 **Macarani** Brazil
32B4 **Macas** Ecuador
31D3 **Macaú** Brazil
73C5 **Macau** Dependency,
China
13C2 **McBride** Can
12F2 **McCarthy** USA
13A2 **McCauley I** Can
42C3 **Macclesfield** Eng
6B1 **McClintock B** Can
4H2 **McClintock Chan** Can
16A2 **McClure** USA
22B2 **McClure,L** USA
4G2 **McClure Str** Can
19B3 **McComb** USA
8C2 **McCook** USA
6C2 **Macculloch,C** Can
13C1 **McCusker,Mt** Can
4F4 **McDame** Can
20C2 **McDermitt** USA
13E2 **Macdonald** *R* Can
106C3 **Macdonnell Ranges**
Mts Aust
50A1 **Macedo de Cavaleiros**
Port
31D3 **Maceió** Brazil

97B4 **Macenta** Guinea
52B2 **Macerata** Italy
108A2 **Macfarlane,L** Aust
19B3 **McGehee** USA
45B3 **MacGillycuddys Reeks** *Mts* Irish Rep
4C3 **McGrath** USA
35B2 **Machado** Brazil
101C3 **Machaíla** Mozam
99D3 **Machakos** Kenya
32B4 **Machala** Ecuador
101C3 **Machaze** Mozam
87B1 **Mācherla** India
94B2 **Machgharab** Leb
87C1 **Machilípatnam** India
32C1 **Machiques** Ven
32C6 **Machu-Picchu** *Hist Site* Peru
101C3 **Macia** Mozam
109C1 **MacIntyre** *R* Aust
107D3 **Mackay** Aust
106B3 **Mackay,L** Aust
14C2 **McKeesport** USA
13C1 **Mackenzie** Can
4F3 **Mackenzie** *R* Can
4E3 **Mackenzie B** Can
4G2 **Mackenzie King I** Can
4E3 **Mackenzie Mts** Can
14B1 **Mackinac,Str of** USA
14B1 **Mackinaw City** USA
12D2 **McKinley,Mt** USA
19A3 **McKinney** USA
6C2 **Mackinson Inlet** *B* Can
109D2 **Macksville** Aust
20B2 **Mclaoughlin,Mt** USA
109D1 **Maclean** Aust
100B4 **Maclear** S Africa
5G4 **McLennan** Can
13D2 **McLeod** *R* Can
4G3 **McLeod B** Can
106A3 **McLeod,L** Aust
13C1 **McLeod Lake** Can
4E3 **Macmillan** *R* Can
12H2 **Macmillan P** Can
20B1 **McMinnville** Oregon, USA
112B7 **McMurdo** *Base* Ant
13D2 **McNaughton L** Can
18B1 **Macomb** USA
53A2 **Macomer** Sardegna
101C2 **Macomia** Mozam
49C2 **Mâcon** France
11B3 **Macon** Georgia, USA
18B2 **Macon** Missouri, USA
100B2 **Macondo** Angola
18A2 **McPherson** USA
104F6 **Macquarie** *Is* Aust
109C2 **Macquarie** *R* Aust
109C4 **Macquarie Harbour** *B* Aust
109D2 **Macquarie,L** Aust
17B1 **McRae** USA
112B11 **Mac. Robertson Land** *Region,* Ant
45B3 **Macroom** Irish Rep
4G3 **McTavish Arm** *B* Can
108A1 **Macumba** *R* Aust
47C2 **Macunaga** Italy
4F3 **McVicar Arm** *B* Can
94B3 **Mādabā** Jordan
95A3 **Madadi** *Well* Chad
89J10 **Madagascar** *I* Indian O
95A2 **Madama** Niger
71F4 **Madang** PNG
97C3 **Madaoua** Niger
86C2 **Madaripur** Bang
90B2 **Madau** USSR
15C1 **Madawaska** *R* Can
96A1 **Madeira** *I* Atlantic O
33E5 **Madeira** *R* Brazil
24B2 **Madera** Mexico
21A2 **Madera** USA
87A1 **Madgaon** India
86B1 **Madhubani** India
86A2 **Madhya Pradesh** *State,* India

87B2 **Madikeri** India
98B3 **Madimba** Zaïre
98B3 **Madingo Kayes** Congo
98B3 **Madingou** Congo
10B3 **Madison** Indiana, USA
10B2 **Madison** Wisconsin, USA
18C2 **Madisonville** Kentucky, USA
19A3 **Madisonville** Texas, USA
78C4 **Madiun** Indon
99D2 **Mado Gashi** Kenya
47D1 **Madonna di Campiglio** Italy
87C2 **Madras** India
20B2 **Madras** USA
29A6 **Madre de Dios** *I* Chile
32D6 **Madre de Dios** *R* Bol
50B1 **Madrid** Spain
50B2 **Madridejos** Spain
78C4 **Madura** *I* Indon
87B3 **Madurai** India
75B1 **Maebashi** Japan
76B3 **Mae Khlong** *R* Thai
77B4 **Mae Nam Lunang** *R* Thai
76C2 **Mae Nam Mun** *R* Thai
76B2 **Mae Nam Ping** *R* Thai
101D2 **Maevatanana** Madag
101G1 **Mafeteng** Lesotho
109C3 **Maffra** Aust
99D3 **Mafia** *I* Tanz
101G1 **Mafikeng** S Africa
30G4 **Mafra** Brazil
92C3 **Mafraq** Jordan
32C2 **Magangué** Colombia
34D3 **Magdalena** Arg
24A1 **Magdalena** Mexico
26C4 **Magdalena** *R* Colombia
78D1 **Magdalena,Mt** Malay
7D5 **Magdalen Is** Can
56C2 **Magdeburg** Germany
31C6 **Magé** Brazil
78C4 **Magelang** Indon
47C1 **Maggia** *R* Switz
92B4 **Maghâgha** Egypt
45C1 **Magherafelt** N Ire
55A2 **Maglie** Italy
61J3 **Magnitogorsk** USSR
19B3 **Magnolia** USA
101C2 **Magoé** Mozam
15D1 **Magog** Can
23B1 **Magosal** Mexico
13E2 **Magrath** Can
7A3 **Maguse River** Can
76B1 **Magwe** Burma
90A2 **Mahābād** Iran
86B1 **Mahabharat Range** *Mts* Nepal
87A1 **Mahād** India
85D4 **Mahadeo Hills** India
101D2 **Mahajanga** Madag
100B3 **Mahalapye** Botswana
86A2 **Mahānadi** *R* India
101D2 **Mahanoro** Madag
16A2 **Mahanoy City** USA
87A1 **Maharashtra State,** India
86A2 **Māhāsamund** India
76C2 **Maha Sarakham** Thai
101D2 **Mahavavy** *R* Madag
87B1 **Mahbūbnagar** India
96D1 **Mahdia** Tunisia
87B2 **Mahe** India
85D4 **Mahekar** India
101D2 **Mahéli** *I* Comoros
86A2 **Mahendragarh** India
99D3 **Mahenge** Tanz
85C4 **Mahesāna** India
110C1 **Mahia Pen** NZ
85D3 **Mahoba** India
51C2 **Mahón** Spain
12J1 **Mahony L** Can
96D1 **Mahrés** Tunisia
85C4 **Mahuva** India
32C1 **Maicao** Colombia

47B1 **Maïche** France
43E4 **Maidstone** Eng
98B1 **Maiduguri** Nig
86A2 **Maihar** India
86C2 **Maijdi** Bang
76B3 **Mail Kyun** *I* Burma
84A1 **Maimana** Afghan
14B1 **Main Chan** Can
98B3 **Mai-Ndombe** *L* Zaïre
10D2 **Maine** State, USA
48B2 **Maine** *Region* France
44C2 **Mainland** *I* Scot
85D3 **Mainpuri** India
46A2 **Maintenon** France
101D2 **Maintirano** Madag
57B2 **Mainz** Germany
97A4 **Maio** *I* Cape Verde
29C2 **Maipó** *Mt* Arg/Chile
34D3 **Maipú** Arg
32D1 **Maiquetía** Ven
47B2 **Maira** *R* Italy
86C1 **Mairābāri** India
86C2 **Maiskhal I** Bang
107E4 **Maitland** New South Wales, Aust
108A2 **Maitland** S Australia, Aust
74D3 **Maizuru** Japan
70C4 **Majene** Indon
30B2 **Majes** *R* Peru
99D2 **Maji** Eth
72D2 **Majia He** *R* China
Majunga = Mahajanga
99D1 **Makale** Eth
70C4 **Makale** Indon
86B1 **Makalu** *Mt* China/Nepal
98B2 **Makanza** Zaïre
52C2 **Makarska** Yugos
61F2 **Makaryev** USSR
Makassar = Ujung Pandang
78D3 **Makassar Str** Indon
61H4 **Makat** USSR
97A4 **Makeni** Sierra Leone
60E4 **Makeyevka** USSR
100B3 **Makgadikgadi** *Salt Pan* Botswana
61G5 **Makhachkala** USSR
99D3 **Makindu** Kenya
88H5 **Makkah** S Arabia
7E4 **Makkovik** Can
59C3 **Makó** Hung
98B2 **Makokou** Gabon
110C1 **Makorako,Mt** NZ
98B2 **Makoua** Congo
85C3 **Makrāna** India
85A3 **Makran Coast Range** *Mts* Pak
96C1 **Makthar** Tunisia
93D2 **Mākū** Iran
98C3 **Makumbi** Zaïre
74C4 **Makurazaki** Japan
97C4 **Makurdi** Nig
79B4 **Malabang** Phil
87A2 **Malabar Coast** India
89E7 **Malabo** Bioko
77C5 **Malacca,Str of** S E Asia
32C2 **Málaga** Colombia
50B2 **Malaga** Spain
101D3 **Malaimbandy** Madag
107F1 **Malaita** *I* Solomon Is
99D2 **Malakal** Sudan
84C2 **Malakand** Pak
78C4 **Malang** Indon
98B3 **Malange** Angola
97C3 **Malanville** Benin
39H7 **Mälaren** *L* Sweden
34B3 **Malargüe** Arg
12F3 **Malaspina Gl** USA
93C2 **Malatya** Turk
101C2 **Malawi** Republic, Africa
Malawi,L = Nyasa,L
79C4 **Malaybalay** Phil
90A3 **Malāyer** Iran

70B3 **Malaysia** Federation, S E Asia
93D2 **Malazgirt** Turk
58B2 **Malbork** Pol
56C2 **Malchin** Germany
18C2 **Malden** USA
83B5 **Maldives Is** Indian O
104B4 **Maldives Ridge** Indian O
29F2 **Maldonado** Urug
47D1 **Male** Italy
85C4 **Malegaon** India
59B3 **Malé Karpaty** *Upland* Czech
101C2 **Malema** Mozam
84B2 **Mālestān** Afghan
61J3 **Maleuz** USSR
38H5 **Malgomaj** *L* Sweden
95B3 **Malha** *Well* Sudan
20C2 **Malheur L** USA
97B3 **Mali** Republic, Africa
78D1 **Malinau** Indon
99E3 **Malindi** Kenya
Malines = Mechelen
40B2 **Malin Head** *Pt* Irish Rep
86A2 **Malkala Range** *Mts* India
85D4 **Malkāpur** India
55C2 **Malkara** Turk
54C2 **Malko Tŭrnovo** Bulg
44B3 **Mallaig** Scot
95C2 **Mallawi** Egypt
47D1 **Málles Venosta** Italy
51C2 **Mallorca** *I* Spain
45B2 **Mallow** Irish Rep
38G6 **Malm** Nor
38J5 **Malmberget** Sweden
46D1 **Malmédy** Germany
43C4 **Malmesbury** Eng
100A4 **Malmesbury** S Africa
39G7 **Malmö** Sweden
61G2 **Malmyzh** USSR
79B3 **Malolos** Phil
15D2 **Malone** USA
101G1 **Maloti Mts** Lesotho
38F6 **Måløy** Nor
28A2 **Malpelo** *I* Colombia
34A2 **Malpo** *R* Chile
85D3 **Mālpura** India
8C2 **Malta** Montana, USA
53B3 **Malta** *Chan* Malta/Italy
53B3 **Malta** *I* Medit S
100A3 **Maltahöhe** Namibia
42D2 **Malton** Eng
39G6 **Malung** Sweden
87A1 **Mālvan** India
19B3 **Malvern** USA
85D4 **Malwa Plat** India
65F5 **Malyy Kavkaz** *Mts* USSR
61G4 **Malyy Uzen'** *R* USSR
61H2 **Mamadysh** USSR
99C2 **Mambasa** Zaïre
71E4 **Mamberamo** *R* Indon
98B2 **Mambéré** *R* CAR
98A2 **Mamfé** Cam
33D6 **Mamoré** *R* Bol
97A3 **Mamou** Guinea
101D2 **Mampikony** Madag
97B4 **Mampong** Ghana
94B3 **Mamshit** *Hist Site* Israel
100B3 **Mamuno** Botswana
97B4 **Man** Ivory Coast
21C4 **Mana** Hawaiian Is
101D3 **Manabo** Madag
33E4 **Manacapuru** Brazil
51C2 **Manacor** Spain
71D3 **Manado** Indon
25D3 **Managua** Nic
101D3 **Manakara** Madag
101D2 **Mananara** Madag
101D3 **Mananjary** Madag
111A3 **Manapouri** NZ
111A3 **Manapouri,L** NZ

56B2 **Meppen** Germany
78D2 **Merah** Indon
18B2 **Meramec** *R* USA
52B1 **Merano** Italy
71F4 **Merauke** Indon
8A3 **Merced** USA
22B2 **Merced** *R* USA
29B2 **Mercedario** *Mt* Chile
29C2 **Mercedes** Arg
29E2 **Mercedes** Buenos Aires, Arg
30E4 **Mercedes** Corrientes, Arg
29E2 **Mercedes** Urug
110C1 **Mercury B** NZ
110C1 **Mercury Is** NZ
4F2 **Mercy B** Can
6D3 **Mercy,C** Can
99E2 **Meregh** Somalia
76B3 **Mergui** Burma
76B3 **Mergui Arch** Burma
25D2 **Mérida** Mexico
50A2 **Mérida** Spain
32C2 **Mérida** Ven
11B3 **Meridian** USA
109C3 **Merimbula** Aust
108B2 **Meringur** Aust
95C3 **Merowe** Sudan
106A4 **Merredin** Aust
42B2 **Merrick** *Mt* Scot
14A2 **Merrillville** USA
13C2 **Merritt** Can
17B2 **Merritt Island** USA
109D2 **Merriwa** Aust
99E1 **Mersa Fatma** Eth
51B2 **Mers el Kebir** Alg
42C3 **Mersey** *R* Eng
42C3 **Merseyside** County, Eng
92B2 **Mersin** Turk
77C5 **Mersing** Malay
85C3 **Merta** India
43C4 **Merthyr Tydfil** Wales
50A2 **Mertola** Port
99D3 **Meru** *Mt* Tanz
60E5 **Merzifon** Turk
46D2 **Merzig** Germany
9B3 **Mesa** USA
46E1 **Meschede** Germany
93D1 **Mescit Dağ** *Mt* Turk
12C3 **Meshik** USA
99C2 **Meshra Er Req** Sudan
47C1 **Mesocco** Switz
55B3 **Mesolóngion** Greece
19A3 **Mesquite** Texas, USA
101C2 **Messalo** *R* Mozam
53C3 **Messina** Italy
100B3 **Messina** S Africa
55B3 **Messíni** Greece
55B3 **Messiniakós Kólpos** *G* Greece
54B2 **Mesta** *R* Bulg
52B1 **Mestre** Italy
32C3 **Meta** *R* Colombia
60D2 **Meta** *R* USSR
32D2 **Meta** *R* Ven
6C3 **Meta Incognito Pen** Can
19B4 **Metairie** USA
20C1 **Metaline Falls** USA
30D4 **Metán** Arg
101C2 **Metangula** Mozam
53C2 **Metaponto** Italy
44C3 **Methil** Scot
16D1 **Methuen** USA
111B2 **Methven** NZ
12H3 **Metlakatla** USA
18C2 **Metropolis** USA
87B2 **Mettür** India
49D2 **Metz** France
70A3 **Meulaboh** Indon
46A2 **Meulan** France
46C2 **Meuse** Department, France
49D2 **Meuse** *R* France
19A3 **Mexia** USA
24A1 **Mexicali** Mexico
24B2 **Mexico** Federal Republic, Cent America

24C3 **México** Mexico
23A2 **México** State, Mexico
18B2 **Mexico** USA
24C2 **Mexico,G of** Cent America
94B3 **Mezada** *Hist Site* Israel
23B2 **Mezcala** Mexico
64F3 **Mezen'** USSR
64G3 **Mezhdusharskiy** *I* USSR
85D4 **Mhow** India
23B2 **Miahuatlán** Mexico
11B4 **Miami** Florida, USA
18B2 **Miami** Oklahoma, USA
11B4 **Miami Beach** USA
90A2 **Miandowāb** Iran
101D2 **Miandrivazo** Madag
90A2 **Mīāneh** Iran
84C2 **Mianwali** Pak
73A3 **Mianyang** China
73C3 **Mianyang** China
73A3 **Mianzhu** China
72E2 **Miaodao Qundao** *Arch* China
73B4 **Miao Ling** *Upland* China
61K3 **Miass** USSR
59C3 **Michalovce** Czech
27D3 **Miches** Dom Rep
10B2 **Michigan** State, USA
14A2 **Michigan City** USA
10B2 **Michigan,L** USA
7B5 **Michipicoten I** Can
23A2 **Michoacan** State, Mexico
65F4 **Michunnsk** USSR
54C2 **Michurin** Bulg
61F3 **Michurinsk** USSR
104F3 **Micronesia** *Region* Pacific O
78B2 **Midai** *I* Indon
102F4 **Mid Atlantic Ridge** Atlantic O
46B1 **Middelburg** Neth
20B2 **Middle Alkali L** USA
16D2 **Middleboro** USA
100B4 **Middleburg** Cape Province, S Africa
16A2 **Middleburg** Pennsylvania, USA
101G1 **Middleburg** Transvaal, S Africa
16B1 **Middleburgh** USA
15D2 **Middlebury** USA
11B3 **Middlesboro** USA
42D2 **Middlesbrough** Eng
16C2 **Middletown** Connecticut, USA
16B3 **Middletown** Delaware, USA
15D2 **Middletown** New York, USA
14B3 **Middletown** Ohio, USA
16A2 **Middletown** Pennsylvania, USA
96B1 **Midelt** Mor
43C4 **Mid Glamorgan** County, Wales
104B4 **Mid Indian Basin** Indian O
104B4 **Mid Indian Ridge** Indian O
7C5 **Midland** Can
14B2 **Midland** Michigan, USA
9C3 **Midland** Texas, USA
101D3 **Midongy Atsimo** Madag
105G2 **Mid Pacific Mts** Pacific O
20C2 **Midvale** USA
105H2 **Midway Is** Pacific O
18A2 **Midwest City** USA
93D2 **Midyat** Turk
54B2 **Midžor** *Mt* Yugos

59B2 **Mielec** Pol
54C1 **Miercurea-Ciuc** Rom
50A1 **Mieres** Spain
16A2 **Mifflintown** USA
75A2 **Mihara** Japan
72D1 **Mijun Shuiku** *Res* China
65F4 **Mikhayiovka** USSR
54B2 **Mikhaylovgrad** Bulg
61F3 **Mikhaylovka** USSR
65J4 **Mikhaylovskiy** USSR
38K6 **Mikkeli** Fin
55C3 **Mikonos** *I* Greece
59B3 **Mikulov** Czech
99D3 **Mikumi** Tanz
74D3 **Mikuni-sammyaku** *Mts* Japan
75B2 **Mikura-jima** *I* Japan
32B4 **Milagro** Ecuador
Milan = Milano
51C2 **Milana** Alg
101C2 **Milange** Mozam
52A1 **Milano** Italy
92A2 **Milas** Turk
107D4 **Mildura** Aust
73A5 **Mile** China
93D3 **Mileh Tharthār** *L* Iraq
107E3 **Miles** Aust
8C2 **Miles City** USA
16C2 **Milford** Connecticut, USA
15C3 **Milford** Delaware, USA
15D2 **Milford** Massachusetts, USA
18A1 **Milford** Nebraska, USA
16B2 **Milford** Pennsylvania, USA
43B4 **Milford Haven** Wales
43B4 **Milford Haven** *Sd* Wales
18A2 **Milford L** USA
111A2 **Milford Sd** NZ
13E2 **Milk River** Can
49C3 **Millau** France
16C2 **Millbrook** USA
17B1 **Milledgeville** USA
12F2 **Miller,Mt** USA
61F4 **Millerovo** USSR
16A2 **Millersburg** USA
108A1 **Millers Creek** Aust
16C1 **Millers Falls** USA
16C2 **Millerton** USA
22C2 **Millerton L** USA
108B3 **Millicent** Aust
109D1 **Millmerran** Aust
45B2 **Milltown Malbay** Irish Rep
22A2 **Mill Valley** USA
15D3 **Millville** USA
6H2 **Milne Land** *I* Greenland
21C4 **Milolii** Hawaiian Is
55B3 **Milos** *I* Greece
107D3 **Milparinka** Aust
16A2 **Milroy** USA
111A3 **Milton** NZ
16A2 **Milton** Pennsylvania, USA
10B2 **Milwaukee** USA
51C2 **Mina** *R* Alg
93E4 **Mīnā' al Ahmadī** Kuwait
91C4 **Mīnāb** Iran
74C4 **Minamata** Japan
78A2 **Minas** Indon
29E2 **Minas** Urug
31B5 **Minas Gerais** State, Brazil
35C1 **Minas Novas** Brazil
25C3 **Minatitlan** Mexico
76A1 **Minbu** Burma
76A1 **Minbya** Burma
34A2 **Mincha** Chile
44A3 **Minch,Little** *Sd* Scot
44A2 **Minch,North** *Sd* Scot
40B2 **Minch,The** *Sd* Scot

12D2 **Minchumina,L** USA
47D2 **Mincio** *R* Italy
79B4 **Mindanao** *I* Phil
19B3 **Minden** Louisiana, USA
56B2 **Minden** Germany
108B2 **Mindona L** Aust
79B3 **Mindoro** *I* Phil
79B3 **Mindoro Str** Phil
45C3 **Mine Hd** *C* Irish Rep
43C4 **Minehead** Eng
30F2 **Mineiros** Brazil
19A3 **Mineola** USA
23B1 **Mineral de Monte** Mexico
16A2 **Minersville** USA
108B2 **Mingary** Aust
72A2 **Minhe** China
87A3 **Minicoy** *I* India
73D4 **Min Jiang** *R* Fujian, China
73A4 **Min Jiang** *R* Sichuan, China
22C2 **Minkler** USA
108A2 **Minlaton** Aust
72A2 **Minle** China
97C4 **Minna** Nig
10A2 **Minneapolis** USA
5J4 **Minnedosa** Can
10A2 **Minnesota** State, USA
50A1 **Miño** *R* Spain
8C2 **Minot** USA
72A2 **Minqin** China
72A3 **Min Shan** *Upland* China
60C3 **Minsk** USSR
58C2 **Minsk Mazowiecki** Pol
12E2 **Minto** USA
4G2 **Minto Inlet** *B* Can
7C4 **Minto,L** Can
63B2 **Minusinsk** USSR
72A3 **Min Xian** China
7E5 **Miquelon** Can
22D3 **Mirage L** USA
87A1 **Miraj** India
29E3 **Miramar** Arg
84B2 **Miram Shah** Pak
50B1 **Miranda de Ebro** Spain
47D2 **Mirandola** Italy
84B2 **Mir Bachchen Kūt** Afghan
78D1 **Miri** Malay
96A3 **Mirik,C** Maur
63A1 **Mirnoye** USSR
63D1 **Mirnyy** USSR
112C9 **Mirnyy** *Base* Ant
84C2 **Mirpur** Pak
85B3 **Mirpur Khas** Pak
55B3 **Mirtoan S** Greece
74B3 **Miryang** S Korea
86A1 **Mirzāpur** India
23B2 **Misantla** Mexico
84C1 **Misgar** Pak
14A2 **Mishawaka** USA
12B1 **Misheguk Mt** USA
75A2 **Mi-shima** *I* Japan
107E2 **Misima** *I* Solomon Is
30F4 **Misiones** State, Arg
59C3 **Miskolc** Hung
94C2 **Mismīyah** Syria
71E4 **Misoöl** *I* Indon
95A1 **Misrātah** Libya
7B5 **Missinaibi** *R* Can
20B1 **Mission City** Can
15C2 **Mississauga** Can
11A3 **Mississippi** State, USA
11A3 **Mississippi** *R* USA
19C3 **Mississippi Delta** USA
8B2 **Missoula** USA
96B1 **Missour** Mor
11A3 **Missouri** State, USA
10A2 **Missouri** *R* USA
10C1 **Mistassini,L** Can
30B2 **Misti** *Mt* Peru
109C1 **Mitchell** Aust
8D2 **Mitchell** USA
107D2 **Mitchell** *R* Aust

11B3	**Mitchell,Mt** USA
45B2	**Mitchelstown** Irish Rep
84C3	**Mithankot** Pak
55C3	**Mitilíni** Greece
23B2	**Mitla** Mexico
32C3	**Mitu** Colombia
99C3	**Mitumbar** *Mts* Zaïre
98C3	**Mitwaba** Zaïre
98B2	**Mitzic** Gabon
75B1	**Miura** Japan
72C3	**Mi Xian** China
69F3	**Miyake** *I* Japan
75B2	**Miyake-jima** *I* Japan
69E4	**Miyako** *I* Japan
74C4	**Miyakonojō** Japan
74C4	**Miyazaki** Japan
75B1	**Miyazu** Japan
74C4	**Miyoshi** Japan
72D1	**Miyun** China
99D2	**Mizan Teferi** Eth
95A1	**Mizdah** Libya
45B3	**Mizen Hd** *C* Irish Rep
54C1	**Mizil** Rom
86C2	**Mizo Hills** India
86C2	**Mizoram** Union Territory, India
94B3	**Mizpe Ramon** Israel
112B11	**Mizuho** *Base* Ant
74E3	**Mizusawa** Japan
39H7	**Mjolby** Sweden
100B2	**Mkushi** Zambia
101H1	**Mkuzi** S Africa
57C2	**Mladá Boleslav** Czech
58C2	**Mława** Pol
52C2	**Mljet** *I* Yugos
100B3	**Mmabatho** S Africa
84D2	**Mnadi** India
97A4	**Moa** *R* Sierra Leone
94B3	**Moab** Region, Jordan
9C3	**Moab** USA
98B3	**Moanda** Congo
98B3	**Moanda** Gabon
99C3	**Moba** Zaïre
75C1	**Mobara** Japan
98C2	**Mobaye** CAR
98C2	**Mobayi** Zaïre
10A3	**Moberly** USA
11B3	**Mobile** USA
11B3	**Mobile B** USA
8C2	**Mobridge** USA
101D2	**Moçambique** Mozam
76C1	**Moc Chau** Viet
100B3	**Mochudi** Botswana
101D2	**Mocimboa da Praia** Mozam
32B3	**Mocoa** Colombia
35B2	**Mococa** Brazil
34D2	**Mocoreta** *R* Arg
23B1	**Moctezuma** *R* Mexico
101C2	**Mocuba** Mozam
47B2	**Modane** France
101G1	**Modder** *R* S Africa
52B2	**Modena** Italy
46D2	**Moder** *R* France
8A3	**Modesto** USA
22B2	**Modesto Res** USA
53B3	**Modica** Italy
59B3	**Mödling** Austria
107D4	**Moe** Aust
47C1	**Moesa** *R* Switz
42C2	**Moffat** Scot
84D2	**Moga** India
35B2	**Mogi das Cruzes** Brazil
60C3	**Mogilev** USSR
60C4	**Mogilev Podolskiy** USSR
35B2	**Mogi-Mirim** Brazil
101D2	**Mogincual** Mozam
47E2	**Mogliano** Italy
34B2	**Mogna** Arg
68D1	**Mogocha** USSR
65K4	**Mogochin** USSR
50A2	**Moguer** Spain
110C1	**Mohaka** *R* NZ
86C2	**Mohanganj** Bang
15D2	**Mohawk** *R* USA
99D3	**Mohoro** Tanz
65J5	**Mointy** USSR
38G5	**Mo i Rana** Nor
48C3	**Moissac** France
21B2	**Mojave** USA
22D3	**Mojave** *R* USA
9B3	**Mojave Desert** USA
78C4	**Mojokerto** Indon
86B1	**Mokama** India
110B1	**Mokau** *R* NZ
22B1	**Mokelumne Aqueduct** USA
22B1	**Mokelumne Hill** USA
22B1	**Mokelumne North Fork** *R* USA
101G1	**Mokhotlong** Lesotho
96D1	**Moknine** Tunisia
86C1	**Mokokchūng** India
98B1	**Mokolo** Cam
74B4	**Mokp'o** S Korea
61F3	**Moksha** *R* USSR
23B1	**Molango** Mexico
55B3	**Moláoi** Greece
60C4	**Moldavskaya SSR** Republic, USSR
38F6	**Molde** Nor
54B1	**Moldoveanu** *Mt* Rom
100B3	**Molepolole** Botswana
53C2	**Molfetta** Italy
34A3	**Molina** Chile
30B2	**Mollendo** Peru
60C3	**Molodechno** USSR
112C11	**Molodezhnaya** *Base* Ant
21C4	**Molokai** *I* Hawaiian Is
61G2	**Moloma** *R* USSR
109C2	**Molong** Aust
100B3	**Molopo** *R* Botswana
98B2	**Molounddu** Cam
8D1	**Molson L** Can
71D4	**Molucca** *S* Indon
71D4	**Moluccas** *Is* Indon
101C2	**Moma** Mozam
31C3	**Mombaca** Brazil
99D3	**Mombasa** Kenya
98C2	**Mompono** Zaïre
56C2	**Mon** *I* Den
44A3	**Monach** *Is* Scot
49D3	**Monaco** Principality, Europe
44B3	**Monadhliath** *Mts* Scot
45C1	**Monaghan** County, Irish Rep
45C1	**Monaghan** Irish Rep
27D3	**Mona Pass** Caribbean S
13B2	**Monarch Mt** Can
5G4	**Monashee Mts** Can
41B3	**Monastereven** Irish Rep
47B2	**Moncalieri** Italy
31B2	**Monção** *R* Zaïre
38L5	**Monchegorsk** USSR
56B2	**Mönchen-gladbach** Germany
24B2	**Monclova** Mexico
7D5	**Moncton** Can
9C4	**Monctova** Mexico
50A1	**Mondego** *R* Port
52A2	**Mondovi** Italy
27H1	**Moneague** Jamaica
14C2	**Monessen** USA
18B2	**Monett** USA
52B1	**Monfalcone** Italy
50A1	**Monforte de Lemos** Spain
98C2	**Monga** Zaïre
98C2	**Mongala** *R* Zaïre
99D2	**Mongalla** Sudan
76D1	**Mong Cai** Viet
98B1	**Mongo** Chad
68B2	**Mongolia** Republic, Asia
100B2	**Mongu** Zambia
63D3	**Mönhhaan** Mongolia
21B2	**Monitor Range** *Mts* USA
98C3	**Monkoto** Zaïre
43C4	**Monmouth** Eng
18B1	**Monmouth** USA
13C2	**Monmouth,Mt** Can
97C4	**Mono** *R* Togo
21B2	**Mono L** USA
53C2	**Monopoli** Italy
51B1	**Monreal del Campo** Spain
19B3	**Monroe** Louisiana, USA
14B2	**Monroe** Michigan, USA
20B1	**Monroe** Washington, USA
18B2	**Monroe City** USA
97A4	**Monrovia** Lib
20D3	**Monrovia** USA
56A2	**Mons** Belg
47D2	**Monselice** Italy
16C1	**Monson** USA
58B1	**Mönsterås** Sweden
101D2	**Montagne d'Ambre** *Mt* Madag
96C1	**Montagnes des Ouled Naïl** *Mts* Alg
12E3	**Montague I** USA
49C3	**Mont Aigoual** *Mt* France
48B2	**Montaigu** France
53C3	**Montallo** *Mt* Italy
8B2	**Montana** State, USA
50A1	**Montañas de León** *Mts* Spain
49C2	**Montargis** France
48C3	**Montauban** France
15D2	**Montauk** USA
15D2	**Montauk Pt** USA
49D2	**Montbéliard** France
52A1	**Mont Blanc** *Mt* France/Italy
49C2	**Montceau les Mines** France
51C1	**Montceny** *Mt* Spain
49D3	**Mont Cinto** *Mt* Corse
46C2	**Montcornet** France
48B3	**Mont-de-Marsin** France
48C2	**Montdidier** France
30D2	**Monteagudo** Bol
33G4	**Monte Alegre** Brazil
52B2	**Monte Amiata** *Mt* Italy
47D2	**Monte Baldo** *Mt* Italy
15C1	**Montebello** USA
106A3	**Monte Bello Is** Aust
47E2	**Montebelluna** Italy
49D3	**Monte Carlo** Monaco
35B1	**Monte Carmelo** Brazil
34D2	**Monte Caseros** Arg
52B2	**Monte Cimone** *Mt* Italy
52A2	**Monte Cinto** *Mt* Corse
34B2	**Monte Coman** Arg
52B2	**Monte Corno** *Mt* Italy
27C3	**Montecristi** Dom Rep
52B2	**Montecristo** *I* Italy
23A1	**Monte Escobedo** Mexico
53C2	**Monte Gargano** *Mt* Italy
26B3	**Montego Bay** Jamaica
47D2	**Monte Grappa** *Mt* Italy
47C2	**Monte Lesima** *Mt* Italy
49C3	**Montélimar** France
53B2	**Monte Miletto** *Mt* Italy
50A2	**Montemo-o-Novo** Port
24C2	**Montemorelos** Mexico
26B5	**Montená** Colombia
54A2	**Montenegro** Region, Yugos
35D1	**Monte Pascoal** *Mt* Brazil
34A2	**Monte Patria** Chile
53C3	**Monte Pollino** *Mt* Italy
101C2	**Montepuez** Mozam
8A3	**Monterey** California, USA
15C3	**Monterey** Virginia, USA
8A3	**Monterey B** USA
32B2	**Montería** Colombia
30D2	**Montero** Bol
47B2	**Monte Rosa** *Mt* Italy/ Switz
24B2	**Monterrey** Mexico
31C5	**Montes Claros** Brazil
50B2	**Montes de Toledo** *Mts* Spain
29E2	**Montevideo** Urug
52A2	**Monte Viso** *Mt* Italy
27P2	**Mont Gimie** *Mt* St Lucia
11B3	**Montgomery** Alabama, USA
96C2	**Mont Gréboun** Niger
46C2	**Montherme** France
47B1	**Monthey** Switz
19B3	**Monticello** Arkansas, USA
16B2	**Monticello** New York, USA
9C3	**Monticello** Utah, USA
53A2	**Monti del Gennargentu** *Mt* Sardegna
47D2	**Monti Lessini** *Mts* Italy
53B3	**Monti Nebrodi** *Mts* Italy
7C5	**Mont-Laurier** Can
48C2	**Montluçon** France
7C5	**Montmagny** Can
46C2	**Montmédy** France
49C3	**Mont Mézenc** *Mt* France
46B2	**Montmirail** France
50B2	**Montoro** Spain
49D3	**Mont Pelat** *Mt* France
14B2	**Montpelier** Ohio, USA
10C2	**Montpelier** Vermont, USA
49C3	**Montpellier** France
7C5	**Montréal** Can
48C1	**Montreuil** France
52A1	**Montreux** Switz
47B1	**Mont Risoux** *Mt* France
8C3	**Montrose** Colorado, USA
40C2	**Montrose** Scot
48B2	**Mont-St-Michel** France
96B1	**Monts des Ksour** *Mts* Alg
51C3	**Monts des Ouled Neil** *Mts* Alg
51C2	**Monts du Hodna** *Mts* Alg
27E3	**Montserrat** *I* Caribbean S
12B1	**Monument Mt** USA
9B3	**Monument V** USA
98C2	**Monveda** Zaïre
76B1	**Monywa** Burma
52A1	**Monza** Italy
100B2	**Monze** Zambia
101H1	**Mooi** *R* S Africa
101G1	**Mooi River** S Africa
108B1	**Moomba** Aust
109D2	**Moonbi Range** *Mts* Aust
108B1	**Moonda L** Aust
109D1	**Moonie** Aust
109C1	**Moonie** *R* Aust
108A2	**Moonta** Aust
106A4	**Moora** Aust
106A3	**Moore,L** Aust
42C2	**Moorfoot Hills** Scot
8D2	**Moorhead** USA
22C3	**Moorpark** USA
7B4	**Moose** *R* Can

54B1 **Muntii Carpaţii Meridionali** *Mts* Rom
54B1 **Muntii Rodnei** *Mts* Rom
54B1 **Muntii Zarandului** *Mts* Rom
93C2 **Munzur Silsilesi** *Mts* Turk
64D3 **Muomio** Fin
76C1 **Muong Khoua** Laos
76D3 **Muong Man** Viet
76D2 **Muong Nong** Laos
76C1 **Muong Ou Neua** Laos
76C1 **Muong Sai** Laos
76C2 **Muong Sen** Viet
76C1 **Muong Sing** Laos
76C1 **Muong Son** Laos
38J5 **Muonio** Fin
38J5 **Muonio** *R* Sweden/Fin
99E2 **Muqdisho** Somalia
52B1 **Mur** *R* Austria
74D3 **Murakami** Japan
29B5 **Murallón** *Mt* Arg/Chile
61G2 **Murashi** USSR
93D2 **Murat** *R* Turk
53A3 **Muravera** Sardegna
75C1 **Murayama** Japan
90B3 **Murcheh Khvort** Iran
111B2 **Murchison** NZ
106A3 **Murchison** *R* Aust
51B2 **Murcia** Region, Spain
51B2 **Murcia** Spain
54B1 **Mureş** *R* Rom
46E2 **Murg** *R* Germany
65H6 **Murgab** *R* USSR
84B2 **Murgha Kibzai** Pak
109D1 **Murgon** Aust
86B2 **Muri** India
35C2 **Muriaé** Brazil
98C3 **Muriege** Angola
64E3 **Murmansk** USSR
61F2 **Murom** USSR
74E2 **Muroran** Japan
50A1 **Muros** Spain
74C4 **Muroto** Japan
75A2 **Muroto-zaki** *C* Japan
20C2 **Murphy** Idaho, USA
22B1 **Murphys** USA
18C2 **Murray** Kentucky, USA
108B2 **Murray** *R* Aust
13C2 **Murray** *R* Can
108A3 **Murray Bridge** Aust
71F4 **Murray,L** PNG
17B1 **Murray,L** USA
105J2 **Murray Seacarp** Pacific O
108B2 **Murrumbidgee** *R* Aust
109C2 **Murrumburrah** Aust
109D2 **Murrurundi** Aust
47B1 **Murten** Switz
108B3 **Murtoa** Aust
110C1 **Murupara** NZ
86A2 **Murwāra** India
109D1 **Murwillimbah** Aust
93D2 **Muş** Turk
54B2 **Musala** *Mt* Bulg
74B2 **Musan** N Korea
91C4 **Musandam** *Pen* Oman
Muscat = Masqat
91C5 **Muscat** Region, Oman
106C3 **Musgrave Range** *Mts* Aust
98B3 **Mushie** Zaïre
14A2 **Muskegon** USA
14A2 **Muskegon** *R* USA
18A2 **Muskogee** USA
15C2 **Muskoka,L** Can
95C3 **Musmar** Sudan
99D3 **Musoma** Tanz
8C2 **Musselshell** *R* USA
100A2 **Mussende** Angola
48C2 **Mussidan** France
55C2 **Mustafa-Kemalpasa** Turk
86A1 **Mustang** Nepal
109D2 **Muswelibrook** Aust
95B2 **Mut** Egypt
101C2 **Mutarara** Mozam
101C2 **Mutare** Zim
101C2 **Mutoko** Zim
101D2 **Mutsamudu** Comoros
100B2 **Mutshatsha** Zaïre
74E2 **Mutsu** Japan
74E2 **Mutsu-wan** *B* Japan
45B2 **Mutton** *I* Irish Rep
72B2 **Mu Us Shamo** *Desert* China
98B3 **Muxima** Angola
63D2 **Muya** USSR
38L6 **Muyezerskiy** USSR
99D3 **Muyinga** Burundi
98C3 **Muyumba** Zaïre
82A1 **Muyun Kum** *Desert* USSR
84C2 **Muzaffarābad** Pak
84C2 **Muzaffargarh** Pak
84D3 **Muzaffarnagar** India
86B1 **Muzaffarpur** India
64H3 **Muzhi** USSR
82C2 **Muztag** *Mt* China
82B2 **Muztagata** *Mt* China
100C2 **Mvuma** Zim
99D3 **Mwanza** Tanz
98C3 **Mwanza** Zaïre
98C3 **Mweka** Zaïre
98C3 **Mwene Ditu** Zaïre
100C3 **Mwenezi** Zim
99C3 **Mwenga** Zaïre
99C3 **Mweru** *L* Zambia
100B2 **Mwinilunga** Zambia
83D4 **Myanaung** Burma
59B3 **M'yaróvár** Hung
86D2 **Myingyan** Burma
76B1 **Myingyao** Burma
76B3 **Myinmoletkat** *Mt* Burma
82D3 **Myitkyina** Burma
76B3 **Myitta** Burma
86C2 **Mymensingh** Bang
69F3 **Myojin** *I* Japan
39F6 **Myrdal** Nor
38B2 **Myrdalsjökur** *Mts* Iceland
17C1 **Myrtle Beach** USA
20B2 **Myrtle Creek** USA
39G7 **Mysen** Nor
56C2 **Mysiloborz** Pol
64F3 **Mys Kanin Nos** *C* USSR
59B3 **Myślenice** Pol
69H1 **Mys Lopatka** *C* USSR
87B2 **Mysore** India
60D5 **Mys Sarych** *C* USSR
16D2 **Mystic** USA
61H5 **Mys Tyub-Karagan** *Pt* USSR
63G2 **Mys Yelizavety** *C* USSR
64H2 **Mys Zhelaniya** *C* USSR
77D3 **My Tho** Viet
20B2 **Mytle Point** USA
101C2 **Mzimba** Malawi
101C2 **Mzuzú** Malawi

N

21C4 **Naalehu** Hawaiian Is
39J6 **Naantali** Fin
45C2 **Naas** Irish Rep
75B2 **Nabari** Japan
61H2 **Naberezhnyye Chelny** USSR
12F2 **Nabesna** *R* USA
96D1 **Nabeul** Tunisia
94B2 **Nablus** Israel
101D2 **Nacala** Mozam
20B1 **Naches** USA
101C2 **Nachingwea** Tanz
19B3 **Nacogdoches** USA
76A3 **Nacondam** *I* Indian O
24B1 **Nacozari** Mexico
85C4 **Nadiād** India
50B2 **Nador** Mor
90B3 **Nadūshan** Iran
59C3 **Nadvornaya** USSR
56C1 **Naestved** Den
95B2 **Nafoora** Libya
75A2 **Nagahama** Japan
82D3 **Naga Hills** Burma
75B1 **Nagai** Japan
86C1 **Nāgāland** State, India
74D3 **Nagano** Japan
74D3 **Nagaoka** Japan
87B2 **Nāgappattinam** India
85C4 **Nagar Parkar** Pak
74B4 **Nagasaki** Japan
75B2 **Nagashima** Japan
75A2 **Nagato** Japan
85C3 **Nāgaur** India
87B3 **Nāgercoil** India
85B3 **Nagha Kalat** Pak
84D3 **Nagīna** India
74D3 **Nagoya** Japan
85D4 **Nāgpur** India
82D2 **Nagqu** China
59B3 **Nagykanizsa** Hung
59B3 **Nagykörös** Hung
69E4 **Naha** Japan
8A2 **Nahaimo** Can
84D2 **Nāhan** India
4F3 **Nahanni Butte** Can
94B2 **Nahariya** Israel
90A3 **Nahāvand** Iran
46D2 **Nahe** *R* Germany
72D2 **Nahpu** China
72E1 **Naimen Qi** China
7D4 **Nain** Can
90B3 **Nā'īn** Iran
84D3 **Naini Tai** India
44C3 **Nairn** Scot
99D3 **Nairobi** Kenya
90B3 **Najafābād** Iran
74C2 **Najin** N Korea
75A2 **Nakama** Japan
74E3 **Nakaminato** Japan
75A2 **Nakamura** Japan
75B1 **Nakano** Japan
75A1 **Nakano-shima** *I* Japan
74C4 **Nakatsu** Japan
75B1 **Nakatsu-gawa** Japan
95C3 **Nakfa** Eth
93E2 **Nakhichevan** USSR
92B4 **Nakhl** Egypt
74C2 **Nakhodka** USSR
76C3 **Nakhon Pathom** Thai
76C3 **Nakhon Ratchasima** Thai
77C4 **Nakhon Si Thammarat** Thai
12H3 **Nakina** Can
7B4 **Nakina** Ontario, Can
12C3 **Naknek** USA
12C3 **Naknek L** USA
4C4 **Nakrek** USA
39G8 **Nakskov** Den
99D3 **Nakuru** Kenya
13D2 **Nakusp** Can
61F5 **Nal'chik** USSR
87B1 **Nalgonda** India
87B1 **Nallamala Range** *Mts* India
95A1 **Nālūt** Libya
101H1 **Namaacha** Mozam
65G6 **Namak** *L* Iran
90C3 **Namakzar-e Shadad** *Salt Flat* Iran
65J5 **Namangan** USSR
101C2 **Namapa** Mozam
100A4 **Namaqualand** Region, S Africa
109D1 **Nambour** Aust
109D2 **Nambucca Heads** Aust
77D4 **Nam Can** Viet
82D2 **Nam Co** *L* China
76D1 **Nam Dinh** Viet
101C2 **Nametil** Mozam
74B4 **Namhae-do** *I* S Korea
100A2 **Namib Desert** Namibia
100A2 **Namibe** Angola
100A3 **Namibia** Dependency, Africa
82D3 **Namjagbarwa Feng** *Mt* China
71D4 **Namlea** Indon
109C2 **Namoi** *R* Aust
13D1 **Nampa** Can
20C2 **Nampa** USA
97B3 **Nampala** Mali
76C2 **Nam Phong** Thai
74B3 **Namp'o** N Korea
101C2 **Nampula** Mozam
38G6 **Namsos** Nor
76B1 **Namton** Burma
86D2 **Namtu** Burma
13B2 **Namu** Can
101C2 **Namuno** Mozam
46C1 **Namur** Belg
100A2 **Namutoni** Namibia
74B3 **Namwŏn** S Korea
13C3 **Nanaimo** Can
74B2 **Nanam** N Korea
109D1 **Nanango** Aust
74D3 **Nanao** Japan
75B1 **Nanatsu-jima** *I* Japan
73B3 **Nanbu** China
73D4 **Nanchang** China
73B3 **Nanchong** China
49D2 **Nancy** France
87B1 **Nānded** India
109D2 **Nandewar Range** *Mts* Aust
85C4 **Nandurbar** India
87B1 **Nandyāl** India
98B2 **Nanga Eboko** Cam
84C1 **Nanga Parbat** *Mt* Pak
78C3 **Nangapinoh** Indon
78C3 **Nangatayap** Indon
74B2 **Nangnim Sanmaek** *Mts* N Korea
86C1 **Nang Xian** China
67F3 **Nangzhou** China
87B2 **Nanjangūd** India
72D3 **Nanjing** China
Nanking = Nanjing
75A2 **Nankoku** Japan
73C4 **Nan Ling** Region, China
76D1 **Nanliu** *R* China
73B5 **Nanning** China
6F3 **Nanortalik** Greenland
73A5 **Nanpan Jiang** *R* China
86A1 **Nānpāra** India
73D4 **Nanping** China
6A1 **Nansen Sd** Can
99D3 **Nansio** Tanz
48B2 **Nantes** France
13E2 **Nanton** Can
72E3 **Nantong** China
10C2 **Nantucket** *I* USA
35C1 **Nanuque** Brazil
72C3 **Nanyang** China
72D2 **Nanyang Hu** *L* China
99D2 **Nanyuki** Kenya
74D3 **Naoetsu** Japan
85B4 **Naokot** Pak
22A1 **Napa** USA
12B2 **Napaiskak** USA
15C2 **Napanee** Can
65K4 **Napas** USSR
6E3 **Napassoq** Greenland
76D2 **Nape** Laos
110C1 **Napier** NZ
Naples = Napoli
17B2 **Naples** Florida, USA
19B3 **Naples** Texas, USA
73B5 **Napo** China
32C4 **Napo** *R* Peru/Ecuador
53B2 **Napoli** Italy
90A2 **Naqadeh** Iran
92C4 **Naqb Ishtar** Jordan
75B2 **Nara** Japan

45C2 **New Ross** Irish Rep
45C1 **Newry** N Ire
New Siberian Is =
Novosibirskye
Ostrova
17B2 **New Smyrna Beach**
USA
107D4 **New South Wales**
State, Aust
12C3 **New Stuyahok** USA
18A2 **Newton** Kansas, USA
16D1 **Newton**
Massachusetts, USA
19C3 **Newton** Mississippi,
USA
16B2 **Newton** New York,
USA
43C4 **Newton Abbot** Eng
45C1 **Newton Stewart** N Ire
42B2 **Newton Stewart** Scot
43C3 **Newtown** Wales
42B2 **Newtownards** N Ire
16A2 **Newville** USA
5F5 **New Westminster**
Can
10C2 **New York** State, USA
10C2 **New York** USA
110 **New Zealand**
Dominion, SW
Pacific O
105G6 **New Zealand Plat**
Pacific O
61F2 **Neya** USSR
91B4 **Neyriz** Iran
90C2 **Neyshābūr** Iran
98B3 **Nezeto** Angola
60D3 **Nezhin** USSR
98B3 **Ngabé** Congo
100B3 **Ngami** L Botswana
110C1 **Ngaruawahia** NZ
110C1 **Ngaruroro** R NZ
110C1 **Ngauruhoe,Mt** NZ
98B3 **Ngo** Congo
76D2 **Ngoc Linh** Mt Viet
98B2 **Ngoko** R Cam
68B3 **Ngoring Hu** L China
99D3 **Ngorongoro Crater**
Tanz
98B3 **N'Gounié** R Gabon
98B1 **Nguigmi** Niger
71E3 **Ngulu** I Pacific O
97D3 **Nguru** Nig
76D3 **Nha Trang** Viet
108B3 **Nhill** Aust
101H1 **Nhlangano** Swaziland
76D2 **Nhommarath** Laos
106C2 **Nhulunbuy** Aust
97B3 **Niafounké** Mali
14A1 **Niagara** USA
15C2 **Niagara Falls** Can
15C2 **Niagara Falls** USA
70C3 **Niah** Malay
97B4 **Niakaramandougou**
Ivory Coast
97C3 **Niamey** Niger
99C2 **Niangara** Zaïre
98C2 **Nia Nia** Zaïre
70A3 **Nias** I Indon
25D3 **Nicaragua** Republic,
Cent America
53C3 **Nicastro** Italy
49D3 **Nice** France
26B1 **Nicholl's Town**
The Bahamas
83D5 **Nicobar Is** Indian O
92B2 **Nicosia** Cyprus
25D3 **Nicoya,Pen de**
Costa Rica
58C2 **Nidzica** Pol
46D2 **Niederbronn** France
56B2 **Niedersachsen** State,
Germany
99C3 **Niemba** Zaïre
56B2 **Nienburg** Germany
46D1 **Niers** R Germany
97B4 **Niete,Mt** Lib
33F2 **Nieuw Amsterdam**
Surinam

33F2 **Nieuw Nickerie**
Surinam
46B1 **Nieuwpoort** Belg
92B2 **Niğde** Turk
97C3 **Niger** Republic, Africa
97C4 **Niger** R Nig
97C4 **Nigeria** Federal
Republic, Africa
55B2 **Nigríta** Greece
75C1 **Nihommatsu** Japan
74D3 **Niigata** Japan
74C4 **Niihama** Japan
75B2 **Nii-jima** I Japan
75A2 **Niimi** Japan
74D3 **Niitsu** Japan
94B3 **Nijil** Jordan
56B2 **Nijmegen** Neth
64E3 **Nikel'** USSR
97C3 **Nikki** Benin
74D3 **Nikko** Japan
60D4 **Nikolayev** USSR
61G4 **Nikolayevsk** USSR
63G2 **Nikolayevsk-na-Amure**
USSR
61G2 **Nikol'sk** RSFSR, USSR
61G3 **Nikol'sk** USSR
60D4 **Nikopol** USSR
92C1 **Niksar** Turk
91D4 **Nīkshahr** Iran
54A2 **Nikšić** Yugos
71D4 **Nila** I Indon
80B3 **Nile** R N E Africa
14A2 **Niles** USA
87B2 **Nilgiri Hills** India
85C4 **Nimach** India
49C3 **Nîmes** France
109C3 **Nimmitabel** Aust
99D2 **Nimule** Sudan
83B5 **Nine Degree Chan**
Indian O
104C4 **Ninety-East Ridge**
Indian O
109C3 **Ninety Mile Beach**
Aust
73D4 **Ningde** China
73D4 **Ningdu** China
68B3 **Ningjing Shan** Mts
China
76D1 **Ningming** China
73A4 **Ningnan** China
72B2 **Ningxia** Province,
China
72B2 **Ning Xian** China
73B5 **Ninh Binh** Vietnam
107D1 **Ninigo Is** PNG
12D2 **Ninilchik** USA
8D2 **Niobrara** R USA
98B3 **Nioki** Zaïre
97B3 **Nioro du Sahel** Mali
48B2 **Niort** France
5H4 **Nipawin** Can
7B5 **Nipigon** Can
7B5 **Nipigon,L** Can
7B5 **Nipissing** R Can
14B1 **Nipissing,L** Can
87B1 **Nirmal** India
86B1 **Nirmāli** India
54B2 **Niš** Yugos
81C4 **Nisāb** Yemen
69F4 **Nishino-shima** I
Japan
75A1 **Nishino-shima** I
Japan
75A2 **Nishiwaki** Japan
12G2 **Nisling** R Can
12H2 **Nisutlin** R Can
7C4 **Nitchequon** Can
31C6 **Niterói** Brazil
42C2 **Nith** R Scot
59B3 **Nitra** Czech
14B3 **Nitro** USA
78C2 **Niut** Mt Malay
46C1 **Nivelles** Belg
49C2 **Nivernais** Region,
France
38L5 **Nivskiy** USSR
87B1 **Nizāmābād** India
94B3 **Nizana** Hist Site Israel

61J2 **Nizhniye Sergi** USSR
61F3 **Nizhniy Lomov** USSR
65G4 **Nizhniy Tagil** USSR
63B1 **Nizhnyaya Tunguska**
R USSR
93C2 **Nizip** Turk
60D4 **Nizmennost** USSR
100B2 **Njoko** R Zambia
99D3 **Njombe** Tanz
98B2 **Nkambé** Cam
101C2 **Nkhata Bay** Malawi
98B2 **Nkongsamba** Cam
97C3 **N'Konni** Niger
86C2 **Noakhali** Bang
12B1 **Noatak** USA
12C1 **Noatak** R USA
74C4 **Nobeoka** Japan
47D1 **Noce** R Italy
23A1 **Nochistlán** Mexico
23B2 **Nochixtlán** Mexico
19A3 **Nocona** USA
24A1 **Nogales** Sonora,
Mexico
9B3 **Nogales** USA
23B2 **Nogales** Veracruz,
Mexico
47D2 **Nogara** Italy
75A2 **Nogata** Japan
60E2 **Noginsk** USSR
34D2 **Nogoyá** Arg
34D2 **Nogoyá** R Arg
84C3 **Nohar** India
75B2 **Nojima-zaki** C Japan
98B2 **Nola** CAR
61G2 **Nolinsk** USSR
16D2 **Nomans Land** I USA
12A2 **Nome** USA
46D2 **Nomeny** France
72B1 **Nomgon** Mongolia
5H3 **Nonacho L** Can
76C2 **Nong Khai** Thai
101H1 **Nongoma** S Africa
12B1 **Noorvik** USA
13B3 **Nootka Sd** Can
98B3 **Noqui** Angola
7C5 **Noranda** Can
46B1 **Nord** Department,
France
64D2 **Nordaustlandet** I
Barents S
13D2 **Nordegg** Can
38F6 **Nordfjord** Inlet Nor
39F8 **Nordfriesische** Is
Germany
56C2 **Nordhausen** Germany
56B2 **Nordrhein Westfalen**
State, Germany
38J4 **Nordkapp** C Nor
6E3 **Nordre** Greenland
38H5 **Nord Stronfjället** Mt
Sweden
1B9 **Nordvik** USSR
45C2 **Nore** R Irish Rep
43E3 **Norfolk** County, Eng
8D2 **Norfolk** Nebraska,
USA
11C3 **Norfolk** Virginia, USA
107F3 **Norfolk I** Aust
18B2 **Norfolk L** USA
105G5 **Norfolk Ridge**
Pacific O
1C10 **Noril'sk** USSR
18C1 **Normal** USA
19A2 **Norman** USA
48B2 **Normandie** Region,
France
107D2 **Normanton** Aust
12J1 **Norman Wells** Can
4B3 **Norne** USA
15C2 **Norristown** USA
39H7 **Norrköping** Sweden
39H6 **Norrsundet** Sweden
39H7 **Norrtälje** Sweden
106B4 **Norseman** Aust
63F2 **Norsk** USSR
102J2 **North** S N W Europe
42D2 **Northallerton** Eng
106A4 **Northam** Aust

102E3 **North American Basin**
Atlantic O
106A3 **Northampton** Aust
43D3 **Northampton** County,
Eng
43D3 **Northampton** Eng
15D2 **Northampton** USA
4G3 **North Arm** B Can
17B1 **North Augusta** USA
6D4 **North Aulatsvik** I Can
13F2 **North Battleford** Can
7C5 **North Bay** Can
20B2 **North Bend** USA
44C3 **North Berwick** Scot
7D5 **North,C** Can
7G4 **North C** NZ
11B3 **North Carolina** State,
USA
20B1 **North Cascade Nat Pk**
USA
14B1 **North Chan** Can
42B2 **North Chan** Ire/Scot
8C2 **North Dakota** State,
USA
43E4 **North Downs** Eng
14C2 **North East** USA
102H2 **North East Atlantic**
Basin Atlantic O
4B3 **Northeast C** USA
40B3 **Northern Ireland** UK
27L1 **Northern Range** Mts
Trinidad
106C2 **Northern Territory**
Aust
44C3 **North Esk** R Scot
16C1 **Northfield**
Massachusetts, USA
12D2 **North Fork** R USA
110B1 **North I** NZ
74B3 **North Korea** Republic,
S E Asia
North Land =
Severnaya Zemlya
19B3 **North Little Rock** USA
1B4 **North Magnetic Pole**
Can
17B2 **North Miami** USA
17B2 **North Miami Beach**
USA
8C2 **North Platte** USA
8C2 **North Platte** R USA
27R3 **North Pt** Barbados
14B1 **North Pt** USA
40B2 **North Rona** I Scot
44C2 **North Ronaldsay** I
Scot
13F2 **North Saskatchewan**
R Can
40D2 **North Sea**
N W Europe
4D3 **North Slope** Region
USA
109D1 **North Stradbroke** I
Aust
110B1 **North Taranaki Bight**
B NZ
9C3 **North Truchas Peak**
Mt USA
44A3 **North Uist** I Scot
42C2 **Northumberland**
County, Eng
107E3 **Northumberland Is**
Aust
7D5 **Northumberland Str**
Can
20B1 **North Vancouver** Can
43E3 **North Walsham** Eng
12F2 **Northway** USA
106A3 **North West C** Aust
84C2 **North West Frontier**
Province, Pak
7D4 **North West River** Can
4F3 **North West Territories**
Can
42D2 **North York Moors Nat**
Pk Eng
12B2 **Norton B** USA
12B2 **Norton Sd** USA

112B1 **Norvegia,C** Ant
16C2 **Norwalk** Connecticut, USA
14B2 **Norwalk** Ohio, USA
39F6 **Norway** Kingdom, Europe
5J4 **Norway House** Can
6A2 **Norwegian B** Can
102H1 **Norwegian Basin** Norewegian S
64A3 **Norwegian S** N W Europe
16C2 **Norwich** Connecticut, USA
43E3 **Norwich** Eng
16D1 **Norwood** Massachusetts, USA
14B3 **Norwood** Ohio, USA
54C2 **Nos Emine** *C* Bulg
74D2 **Noshiro** Japan
54C2 **Nos Kaliakra** *C* Bulg
44E1 **Noss** *I* Scot
91D4 **Nostrābād** Iran
101D2 **Nosy Barren** *I* Madag
101D2 **Nosy Bé** *I* Madag
101E2 **Nosy Boraha** *I* Madag
101D3 **Nosy Varika** Madag
58B2 **Notéc** *R* Pol
5G4 **Notikeuin** Can
53C3 **Noto** Italy
39F7 **Notodden** Nor
75B1 **Noto-hantō** *Pen* Japan
7E5 **Notre Dams B** Can
43D3 **Nottingham** County, Eng
43D3 **Nottingham** Eng
6C3 **Nottingham** *I* Can
6C3 **Nottingham Island** Can
96A2 **Nouadhibou** Maur
97A3 **Nouakchott** Maur
107F3 **Nouméa** Nouvelle Calédonie
97B3 **Nouna** Burkina
107F3 **Nouvelle Calédonie** *I* S W Pacific O
98B3 **Nova Caipemba** Angola
100B2 **Nova Chaves** Angola
35A2 **Nova Esperança** Brazil
35C2 **Nova Friburgo** Brazil
100A2 **Nova Gaia** Angola
35B2 **Nova Granada** Brazil
35B2 **Nova Horizonte** Brazil
35C1 **Nova Lima** Brazil
Nova Lisboa = Huambo
35A2 **Nova Londrina** Brazil
101C3 **Nova Mambone** Mozam
47C2 **Novara** Italy
7D5 **Nova Scotia** Province, Can
22A1 **Novato** USA
35C1 **Nova Venécia** Brazil
60D4 **Novaya Kakhovka** USSR
64G2 **Novaya Zemlya** *I* Barents S
54C2 **Nova Zagora** Bulg
31C2 **Nove Russas** Brazil
54A1 **Nové Zámky** Czech
60D2 **Novgorod** USSR
47C2 **Novi Ligure** Italy
54C2 **Novi Pazar** Bulg
54B2 **Novi Pazar** Yugos
54A1 **Novi Sad** Yugos
61J3 **Novoalekseyevka** USSR
61F3 **Novoanninskiy** USSR
61E4 **Novocherkassk** USSR
60C3 **Novograd Volynskiy** USSR
58D2 **Novogrudok** USSR
30F4 **Novo Hamburgo** Brazil
65H5 **Novokazalinsk** USSR
65K4 **Novokuznetsk** USSR
112B12 **Novolazarevskaya** *Base* Ant
52C1 **Novo Mesto** Yugos
60E3 **Novomoskovsk** USSR
60E5 **Novorossiysk** USSR
65K4 **Novosibirsk** USSR
1B8 **Novosibirskiye Ostrova** *I* USSR
61J3 **Novotroitsk** USSR
61G3 **Novo Uzensk** USSR
59C2 **Novovolynsk** USSR
61G2 **Novo Vyatsk** USSR
60D3 **Novozybkov** USSR
64J3 **Novvy Port** USSR
58C2 **Novy Dwór Mazowiecki** Pol
61K2 **Novyy Lyalya** USSR
64J3 **Novyy Port** USSR
61H5 **Novyy Uzem** USSR
58B2 **Nowa Sól** Pol
18A2 **Nowata** USA
86C1 **Nowgong** India
12D2 **Nowitna** *R* USA
109D2 **Nowra** Aust
90B2 **Now Shahr** Iran
84C2 **Nowshera** Pak
59C3 **Nowy Sącz** Pol
12H3 **Noyes I** USA
46B2 **Noyon** France
97B4 **Nsawam** Ghana
99D1 **Nuba** *Mts* Sudan
81B3 **Nubian Desert** Sudan
34A3 **Nuble** *R* Chile
9D4 **Nueces** *R* USA
5J3 **Nueltin L** Can
26A2 **Nueva Gerona** Cuba
34A3 **Nueva Imperial** Chile
9C4 **Nueva Laredo** Mexico
34D2 **Nueva Palmira** Urug
24B2 **Nueva Rosita** Mexico
26B2 **Nuevitas** Cuba
24B1 **Nuevo Casas Grandes** Mexico
24C2 **Nuevo Laredo** Mexico
99E2 **Nugaal** Region, Somalia
6E2 **Nûgâtsiaq** Greenland
6E2 **Nugssuag** *Pen* Greenland
6E2 **Nûgussaq** *I* Greenland
108A2 **Nukey Bluff** *Mt* Aust
93D3 **Nukhayb** Iraq
65G5 **Nukus** USSR
12C2 **Nulato** USA
106B4 **Nullarbor Plain** Aust
97D4 **Numan** Nig
75B1 **Numata** Japan
98C2 **Numatinna** *R* Sudan
74D3 **Numazu** Japan
71E4 **Numfoor** *I* Indon
108C3 **Numurkah** Aust
12B2 **Nunapitchuk** USA
84D2 **Nunkun** *Mt* India
53A2 **Nuoro** Sardegna
91B3 **Nurābād** Iran
47C2 **Nure** *R* Italy
108A2 **Nuriootpa** Aust
84C1 **Nuristan** *Upland* Afghan
61H3 **Nurlat** USSR
38K6 **Nurmes** Fin
57C3 **Nürnberg** Germany
108C2 **Nurri,Mt** Aust
93D2 **Nusaybin** Turk
12C3 **Nushagak** *R* USA
12C3 **Nushagak B** USA
12C3 **Nushagak Pen** USA
84B3 **Nushki** Pak
7D4 **Nutak** Can
12F2 **Nutzotin Mts** USA
86A1 **Nuwakot** Nepal
87C3 **Nuwara-Eliya** Sri Lanka
6C3 **Nuyukjuak** Can
16C2 **Nyack** USA
99D2 **Nyahururu** Kenya
108B3 **Nyah West** Aust
4C3 **Nyai** USA
68B3 **Nyainqentanglha Shan** *Mts* China
99D3 **Nyakabindi** Tanz
98C1 **Nyala** Sudan
86B1 **Nyalam** China
98C2 **Nyamlell** Sudan
100C3 **Nyanda** Zim
64F3 **Nyandoma** USSR
98B3 **Nyanga** *R* Gabon
101C2 **Nyasa L** Malawi/ Mozam
76B2 **Nyaunglebin** Burma
61J2 **Nyazepetrovsk** USSR
39G7 **Nyborg** Den
39H7 **Nybro** Sweden
64J3 **Nyda** USSR
6D1 **Nyeboes Land** *Region* Can
99D3 **Nyeri** Kenya
101C2 **Nyimba** Zambia
82D3 **Nyingchi** China
59C3 **Nyíregyháza** Hung
99D2 **Nyiru,Mt** Kenya
38J6 **Nykarleby** Fin
39F7 **Nykøbing** Den
39G8 **Nykøbing** Den
39H7 **Nyköping** Sweden
100B3 **Nylstroom** S Africa
109C2 **Nymagee** Aust
39H7 **Nynäshamn** Sweden
109C2 **Nyngan** Aust
47B1 **Nyon** Switz
98B2 **Nyong** *R* Cam
49D3 **Nyons** France
59B2 **Nysa** Pol
20C2 **Nyssa** USA
63D1 **Nyurba** USSR
99D3 **Nzega** Tanz
97B4 **Nzérékore** Guinea

O

6F3 **Oaggsimiut** Greenland
8C2 **Oahe Res** USA
21C4 **Oahu** *I* Hawaiian Is
108B2 **Oakbank** Aust
22B2 **Oakdale** USA
109D1 **Oakey** Aust
21A2 **Oakland** California, USA
20B2 **Oakland** Oregon, USA
14A3 **Oakland City** USA
14A2 **Oak Lawn** USA
22B2 **Oakley** California, USA
20B2 **Oakridge** USA
14C2 **Oakville** Can
111B3 **Oamaru** NZ
112B7 **Oates Land** Region, Ant
109C4 **Oatlands** Aust
23B2 **Oaxaca** Mexico
23B2 **Oaxaca** State, Mexico
65J3 **Ob'** *R* USSR
75B1 **Obama** Japan
111A3 **Oban** NZ
44B3 **Oban** Scot
75C1 **Obanazawa** Japan
47D1 **Oberammergau** Germany
46D1 **Oberhausen** Germany
47D1 **Oberstdorf** Germany
71D4 **Obi** *I* Indon
33F4 **Obidos** Brazil
74E2 **Obihiro** Japan
98C2 **Obo** CAR
99E1 **Obock** Djibouti
58B2 **Oborniki** Pol
60E3 **Oboyan** USSR
20B2 **O'Brien** USA
61H3 **Obshchiy Syrt** *Mts* USSR
64J3 **Obskava Guba** *B* USSR
97B4 **Obuasi** Ghana
17B2 **Ocala** USA
32C2 **Ocana** Colombia
50B2 **Ocaño** Spain
12G3 **Ocean C** USA
15C3 **Ocean City** Maryland, USA
16B3 **Ocean City** New Jersey, USA
5F4 **Ocean Falls** Can
22D4 **Oceanside** USA
19C3 **Ocean Springs** USA
61H2 **Ocher** USSR
44C3 **Ochil Hills** Scot
17B1 **Ochlockonee** *R* USA
27H1 **Ocho Rios** Jamaica
17B1 **Ocmulgee** *R* USA
17B1 **Oconee** *R* USA
14A2 **Oconto** USA
23A1 **Ocotlán** Jalisco, Mexico
23B2 **Ocotlán** Oaxaca, Mexico
97B4 **Oda** Ghana
75A1 **Oda** Japan
38B2 **Ódáðahraun** Region, Iceland
74E2 **Odate** Japan
74D3 **Odawara** Japan
39F6 **Odda** Nor
50A2 **Odemira** Port
55C3 **Ödemiş** Turk
101G1 **Odendaalsrus** S Africa
39G7 **Odense** Den
56C2 **Oder** *R* Pol/Germany
9C3 **Odessa** Texas, USA
60D4 **Odessa** USSR
20C1 **Odessa** Washington, USA
97B4 **Odienné** Ivory Coast
59B2 **Odra** *R* Pol
31C3 **Oeiras** Brazil
106B1 **Oekusi** Indon
53C2 **Ofanto** *R* Italy
94B3 **Ofaqim** Israel
45C2 **Offaly** County, Irish Rep
49D1 **Offenbach** Germany
49D2 **Offenburg** Germany
74D3 **Oga** Japan
99E2 **Ogaden** Region, Eth
74D3 **Ogaki** Japan
8C2 **Ogallala** USA
69G4 **Ogasawara Gunto** *Is* Japan
97C4 **Ogbomosho** Nig
8B2 **Ogden** Utah, USA
15C2 **Ogdensburg** USA
17B1 **Ogeechee** *R* USA
12G1 **Ogilvie** Can
4E3 **Ogilvie Mts** Can
17B1 **Oglethorpe,Mt** USA
47D2 **Oglio** *R* Italy
47B1 **Ognon** *R* France
97C4 **Ogoja** Nig
98A3 **Ogooué** *R* Gabon
58C1 **Ogre** USSR
96B2 **Oguilet Khenachich** *Well* Mali
52C1 **Ogulin** Yugos
111A3 **Ohai** NZ
110C1 **Ohakune** NZ
96C2 **Ohanet** Alg
111A2 **Ohau,L** NZ
10B2 **Ohio** State, USA
14A3 **Ohio** *R* USA
100A2 **Ohopoho** Namibia
57C2 **Ohre** *R* Czech
55B2 **Ohrid** Yugos
55B2 **Ohridsko Jezero** *L* Yugos/Alb
110B1 **Ohura** NZ
33G3 **Oiapoque** French Guiana
68B2 **Oijiaojing** China
14C2 **Oil City** USA
21B2 **Oildale** USA

46B2 **Oise** Department, France
49C2 **Oise** *R* France
74C4 **Ōita** Japan
22C3 **Ojai** USA
24B2 **Ojinaga** Mexico
23B2 **Ojitlán** Mexico
75B1 **Ojiya** Japan
30C4 **Ojos del Salado** *Mt* Arg
23A1 **Ojueloz** Mexico
60E3 **Oka** *R* USSR
100A3 **Okahandja** Namibia
20C1 **Okanagan Falls** Can
13D2 **Okanagan L** Can
20C1 **Okanogan** USA
20C1 **Okanogan** *R* USA
20B1 **Okanogan Range** *Mts* Can/USA
84C2 **Okara** Pak
100A2 **Okavango** *R* Angola/Namibia
100B2 **Okavango Delta** *Marsh* Botswana
74D3 **Okaya** Japan
74C4 **Okayama** Japan
75B2 **Okazaki** Japan
17B2 **Okeechobee** USA
17B2 **Okeechobee,L** USA
17B1 **Okefenokee Swamp** USA
97C4 **Okene** Nig
85B4 **Okha** India
69G1 **Okha** USSR
86B1 **Okhaldunga** Nepal
62J3 **Okhotsk,S of** USSR
69E4 **Okinawa** *I* Japan
69E4 **Okinawa gunto** *Arch* Japan
74C3 **Oki-shoto** *Is* Japan
9D3 **Oklahoma** State, USA
18A2 **Oklahoma City** USA
18A2 **Okmulgee** USA
98B3 **Okondja** Gabon
98B3 **Okoyo** Congo
97C4 **Okpara** *R* Nig
61J4 **Oktyabr'sk** USSR
61H3 **Oktyabr'skiy** Bashkirskaya, USSR
74D2 **Okushiri-tō** *I* Japan
38A2 **Olafsvik** Iceland
39H7 **Öland** *I* Sweden
108B2 **Olary** Aust
18B2 **Olathe** USA
29D3 **Olavarría** Arg
53A2 **Olbia** Sardegna
12G1 **Old Crow** Can
56B2 **Oldenburg** Niedersachsen, Germany
56C2 **Oldenburg** Schleswig-Holstein, Germany
15C2 **Old Forge** USA
42C3 **Oldham** Eng
12D3 **Old Harbor** USA
41B3 **Old Head of Kinsale** *C* Scot
16C2 **Old Lyme** USA
13E2 **Olds** Can
15C2 **Olean** USA
63E2 **Olekma** *R* USSR
63D1 **Olekminsk** USSR
38L5 **Olenegorsk** USSR
58D2 **Olevsk** USSR
69F2 **Ol'ga** USSR
100A3 **Olifants** *R* Namibia
55B2 **Ólimbos** *Mt* Greece
35B2 **Olímpia** Brazil
23B2 **Olinala** Mexico
31E3 **Olinda** Brazil
34C2 **Oliva** Arg
29C2 **Olivares** *Mt* Arg
35C2 **Oliveira** Brazil
13D3 **Oliver** Can
30C3 **Ollague** Chile
30C3 **Ollagüe** *Mt* Bol
18C2 **Olney** USA
68E1 **Olochi** USSR

39G7 **Olofstrom** Sweden
98B3 **Olombo** Congo
59B3 **Olomouc** Czech
60D1 **Olonets** USSR
79B3 **Olongapa** Phil
48B3 **Oloron Ste Marie** France
68D1 **Olovyannaya** USSR
46D1 **Olpe** Germany
58C2 **Olsztyn** Pol
47B1 **Olten** Switz
54B2 **Oltul** *R* Rom
20B1 **Olympia** USA
20B1 **Olympic Nat Pk** USA
Olympus = Ólimbos
20B1 **Olympus,Mt** USA
65J4 **Om'** *R* USSR
75B1 **Omachi** Japan
75B2 **Omae-zaki** *C* Japan
45C1 **Omagh** N Ire
18A1 **Omaha** USA
20C1 **Omak** USA
91C5 **Oman** Sultanate, Arabian Pen
91C4 **Oman,G of** UAE
98A3 **Omboué** Gabon
99D1 **Omdurman** Sudan
23B2 **Ometepec** Mexico
13B1 **Omineca** *R* Can
13B1 **Omineca Mts** Can
75B1 **Omiya** Japan
12H3 **Ommaney,C** USA
4H2 **Ommanney B** Can
99D2 **Omo** *R* Eth
65J4 **Omsk** USSR
74B4 **Omura** Japan
74C4 **Ōmuta** Japan
61H2 **Omutninsk** USSR
78D3 **Onang** Indon
14B1 **Onaping L** Can
100A2 **Oncócua** Angola
100A2 **Ondangua** Namibia
59C3 **Ondava** *R* Czech
68D2 **Öndörhaan** Molgolia
83B5 **One and Half Degree Chan** Indian O
64E3 **Onega** USSR
64E3 **Onega** *R* USSR
15C2 **Oneida L** USA
8D2 **O'Neill** USA
69H2 **Onekotan** *I* USSR
98C3 **Onema** Zaïre
15D2 **Oneonta** USA
64E3 **Onezhskoye Ozero** *L* USSR
100A2 **Ongiva** Angola
74B3 **Ongjin** N Korea
72D1 **Ongniud Qi** China
87C1 **Ongole** India
15C2 **Onieda L** USA
101D3 **Onilahy** *R* Madag
97C4 **Onitsha** Nig
68C2 **Onjüül** Mongolia
75B1 **Ono** Japan
75B2 **Ōnohara-jima** *I* Japan
74C4 **Onomichi** Japan
106A3 **Onslow** Aust
17C1 **Onslow B** USA
75B1 **Ontake-san** *Mt* Japan
22D3 **Ontario** California, USA
20C2 **Ontario** Oregon, USA
7A4 **Ontario** Province, Can
15C2 **Ontario,L** Can/USA
51B2 **Onteniente** Spain
106C3 **Oodnadatta** Aust
106C4 **Ooldea** Aust
18A2 **Oologah L** USA
46B1 **Oostende** Belg
46B1 **Oosterschelde** *Estuary* Neth
87B2 **Ootacamund** India
13B2 **Ootsa L** Can
69H1 **Opala** USSR
98C3 **Opala** Zaïre
87C3 **Opanake** Sri Lanka
61G2 **Oparino** USSR
59B3 **Opava** Czech

17A1 **Opelika** USA
19B3 **Opelousas** USA
12C2 **Ophir** USA
58D1 **Opochka** USSR
59B2 **Opole** Pol
Oporto = Porto
110C1 **Opotiki** NZ
17A1 **Opp** USA
38F6 **Oppdal** Nor
110B1 **Opunake** NZ
54B1 **Oradea** Rom
38B2 **Oraefajökull** *Mts* Iceland
85D3 **Orai** India
96B1 **Oran** Alg
30D3 **Orán** Arg
109C2 **Orange** France
22D4 **Orange** California, USA
49C3 **Orange** France
19B3 **Orange** Texas, USA
100A3 **Orange** *R* S Africa
17B1 **Orangeburg** USA
101G1 **Orange Free State** Province, S Africa
17B1 **Orange Park** USA
14B2 **Orangeville** Can
56C2 **Oranienburg** Germany
79C3 **Oras** Phil
54B1 **Orăstie** Rom
54B1 **Oravita** Rom
52B2 **Orbetello** Italy
109C3 **Orbost** Aust
46B1 **Orchies** France
47B2 **Orco** *R* Italy
106B2 **Ord** *R* Aust
106B2 **Ord,Mt** Aust
93C1 **Ordu** Turk
39H7 **Örebro** Sweden
8A2 **Oregon** State, USA
14B2 **Oregon** USA
20B1 **Oregon City** USA
39H6 **Oregrund** Sweden
60E2 **Orekhovo Zuyevo** USSR
60E3 **Orel** USSR
61H3 **Orenburg** USSR
34D3 **Orense** Arg
50A1 **Orense** Spain
56C1 **Oresund** *Str* Den/Sweden
111A3 **Oreti** *R* NZ
55C3 **Orhaneli** *R* Turk
68C2 **Orhon Gol** *R* Mongolia
23B2 **Oriental** Mexico
108B1 **Orientos** Aust
51B2 **Orihuela** Spain
15C2 **Orillia** Can
33E2 **Orinoco** *R* Ven
86A2 **Orissa** State, India
53A3 **Oristano** Sardegna
38K6 **Orivesi** *L* Fin
33F4 **Oriximiná** Brazil
23B2 **Orizaba** Mexico
35B1 **Orizona** Brazil
44C2 **Orkney** *I* Scot
35B2 **Orlândia** Brazil
17B2 **Orlando** USA
48C2 **Orléanais** *Region* France
48C2 **Orléans** France
63B2 **Orlik** USSR
82A3 **Ormara** Pak
79B3 **Ormoc** Phil
17B2 **Ormond Beach** USA
46C2 **Ornain** *R* France
47B1 **Ornans** France
48B2 **Orne** *R* France
38H6 **Örnsköldsvik** Sweden
32C3 **Orocué** Colombia
94B3 **Oron** Israel
Orontes = 'Āşī
79B4 **Oroquieta** Phil
59C3 **Orosháza** Hung
21A2 **Oroville** California, USA

20C1 **Oroville** Washington, USA
47B1 **Orsières** Switz
65G4 **Orsk** USSR
38F6 **Ørsta** Nor
48B3 **Orthez** France
50A1 **Ortigueira** Spain
47D1 **Ortles** *Mts* Italy
27L1 **Ortoire** *R* Trinidad
93E2 **Orūmīyeh** Iran
30C2 **Oruro** Bol
61J2 **Osa** USSR
18B2 **Osage** *R* USA
75B1 **Osaka** Japan
25D4 **Osa,Pen de** Costa Rica
18C2 **Osceola** Arkansas, USA
18B1 **Osceola** Iowa, USA
20C2 **Osgood Mts** USA
15C2 **Oshawa** Can
75B2 **Ō-shima** *I* Japan
10B2 **Oshkosh** USA
97C4 **Oshogbo** Nig
7B5 **Oshosh** USA
98B3 **Oshwe** Zaïre
54A1 **Osijek** Yugos
65K5 **Osinniki** USSR
58D2 **Osipovichi** USSR
18B1 **Oskaloosa** USA
60A2 **Oskarshamn** Sweden
39G7 **Oslo** Nor
92B2 **Osmaniye** Turk
56B2 **Osnabrück** Germany
30F4 **Osório** Brazil
29B4 **Osorno** Chile
50B1 **Osorno** Spain
20C1 **Osoyoos** Can
13C1 **Ospika** *R* Can
107D5 **Ossa,Mt** Aust
16C2 **Ossining** USA
60D2 **Ostashkov** USSR
Ostend = Oostende
38G6 **Østerdalen** *V* Nor
38G6 **Östersund** Sweden
56B2 **Ostfriesische Inseln** *Is* Germany
39H6 **Östhammär** Sweden
53B2 **Ostia** Italy
47D2 **Ostiglia** Italy
59B3 **Ostrava** Czech
58B2 **Ostróda** Pol
58B2 **Ostroleka** Pol
60C2 **Ostrov** USSR
64J2 **Ostrov Belyy** *I* USSR
64H1 **Ostrov Greem Bell** *I* Barents S
64F3 **Ostrov Kolguyev** *I* USSR
74F2 **Ostrov Kunashir** *I* USSR
64F2 **Ostrov Mechdusharskiy** *I* Barents S
90B2 **Ostrov Ogurchinskiy** *I* USSR
64G1 **Ostrov Rudol'fa** *I* Barents S
64G2 **Ostrov Vaygach** *I* USSR
1B7 **Ostrov Vrangelya** *I* USSR
58B2 **Ostrów** Pol
59C2 **Ostrowiec** Pol
58C2 **Ostrów Mazowiecka** Pol
50A2 **Osuna** Spain
15C2 **Osweg** USA
15C2 **Oswego** USA
43C3 **Oswestry** Eng
59B2 **Oświęcim** Pol
75B1 **Ota** Japan
111B3 **Otago Pen** NZ
110C2 **Otaki** NZ
74E2 **Otaru** Japan
32B3 **Otavalo** Ecuador
100A2 **Otavi** Namibia
75C1 **Otawara** Japan
20C1 **Othello** USA

8C2 **Platte** *R* USA
15D2 **Plattsburgh** USA
18A1 **Plattsmouth** USA
57C2 **Plauen** Germany
60E3 **Plavsk** USSR
23A2 **Playa Azul** Mexico
32A4 **Playas** Ecuador
23B2 **Playa Vicente** Mexico
50A1 **Plaza de Moro Almanzor** *Mt* Spain
22B2 **Pleasanton** California, USA
16B3 **Pleasantville** USA
14A3 **Pleasure Ridge Park** USA
76D3 **Pleiku** Viet
110C1 **Plenty,B of** NZ
58B2 **Pleszew** Pol
7C4 **Pletipi,L** Can
54B2 **Pleven** Bulg
54A2 **Pljevlja** Yugos
52C2 **Ploče** Yugos
58B2 **Płock** Pol
48B2 **Ploërmel** France
54C2 **Ploieşti** Rom
60B3 **Płońsk** Pol
54B2 **Plovdiv** Bulg
20C1 **Plummer** USA
12C2 **Plummer,Mt** USA
100B3 **Plumtree** Zim
22B1 **Plymouth** California, USA
43B4 **Plymouth** Eng
14A2 **Plymouth** Indiana, USA
16D2 **Plymouth** Massachusetts, USA
15C2 **Plymouth** Pennsylvania, USA
43B4 **Plymouth Sd** Eng
43C3 **Plynlimon** *Mt* Wales
57C3 **Plzeň** Czech
58B2 **Pniewy** Pol
38K6 **Pnyäselkä** *L* Fin
97B3 **Pô** Burkina
47E2 **Po** *R* Italy
97C4 **Pobé** Benin
69G2 **Pobedino** USSR
8B2 **Pocatello** USA
15C3 **Pocomoke City** USA
35B2 **Pocos de Caldas** Brazil
47D2 **Po di Volano** *R* Italy
63B1 **Podkamennaya** *R* USSR
60E2 **Podolsk** USSR
59D3 **Podol'skaya Vozvyshennost'** *Upland* USSR
60D1 **Podporozh'ye** USSR
61F1 **Podyuga** USSR
100A3 **Pofadder** S Africa
74B3 **P'ohang** S Korea
112C9 **Poinsett,C** Ant
108C2 **Point** Aust
27E3 **Pointe-à-Pitre** Guadeloupe
48B2 **Pointe de Barfleur** *Pt* France
98B3 **Pointe Noire** Congo
98A2 **Pointe Pongara** *Pt* Gabon
108B3 **Point Fairy** Aust
27L1 **Point Fortin** Trinidad
4B3 **Point Hope** USA
4G3 **Point L** Can
12B1 **Point Lay** USA
16B2 **Point Pleasant** New Jersey, USA
14B3 **Point Pleasant** W Virginia, USA
47B2 **Point St Bernard** *Mt* France
48C2 **Poitiers** France
48B2 **Poitou** Region, France
46A2 **Poix** France
85C3 **Pokaran** India
109C1 **Pokataroo** Aust
63E1 **Pokrovsk** USSR
58B2 **Poland** Republic, Europe
92B2 **Polatli** Turk
78D3 **Polewali** Indon
47A1 **Poligny** France
55B2 **Políyiros** Greece
87B2 **Pollāchi** India
79B3 **Polollo Is** Phil
59D2 **Polonnye** USSR
58D1 **Polotsk** USSR
60D4 **Poltava** USSR
52C1 **Pölten** Austria
64F3 **Poluostrov Kanin** *Pen* USSR
61H5 **Poluostrov Mangyshlak** *Pen* USSR
38L5 **Poluostrov Rybachiy** *Pen* USSR
64H2 **Poluostrov Yamal** *Pen* USSR
38L5 **Polyarnyy** Murmansk, USSR
1B8 **Polyarnyy** Yakutskaya, USSR
105H3 **Polynesia** *Region* Pacific O
32B5 **Pomabamba** Peru
35C2 **Pomba** *R* Brazil
22D3 **Pomona** USA
18A2 **Pomona Res** USA
17B2 **Pompano Beach** USA
16B2 **Pompton Lakes** USA
18A2 **Ponca City** USA
27D3 **Ponce** Puerto Rico
17B2 **Ponce de Leon B** USA
87B2 **Pondicherry** India
6C2 **Pond Inlet** Can
50A1 **Ponferrade** Spain
98C2 **Pongo** *R* Sudan
101H1 **Pongola** *R* S Africa
87B2 **Ponnāni** India
86C2 **Ponnyadoung Range** *Mts* Burma
13E2 **Ponoka** Can
64F3 **Ponoy** USSR
48B2 **Pons** France
35D1 **Ponta da Baleia** *Pt* Brazil
96A1 **Ponta Delgada** Açores
98B3 **Ponta do Padrão** *Pt* Angola
35C2 **Ponta dos Búzios** *Pt* Brazil
30F4 **Ponta Grossa** Brazil
35B2 **Pontal** Brazil
46D2 **Pont-à-Mousson** France
30E3 **Ponta Pora** Brazil
49D2 **Pontarlier** France
19B3 **Pontchartrain,L** USA
52B2 **Pontedera** Italy
52A2 **Ponte Leccia** Corse
50A1 **Pontevedra** Spain
18C1 **Pontiac** Illinois, USA
14B2 **Pontiac** Michigan, USA
78B3 **Pontianak** Indon
48B2 **Pontivy** France
46B2 **Pontoise** France
19C3 **Pontotoc** USA
43C4 **Pontypool** Wales
43C4 **Pontypridd** Wales
43D4 **Poole** Eng
Poona = Pune
108B2 **Pooncarie** Aust
108B2 **Poopelloe,L** *L* Aust
12C2 **Poorman** USA
32B3 **Popayán** Colombia
46B1 **Poperinge** Belg
108B2 **Popilta L** Aust
18B2 **Poplar Bluff** USA
19C3 **Poplarville** USA
107D1 **Popndetta** PNG
23B2 **Popocatepetl** *Mt* Mexico
98B3 **Popokabaka** Zaïre
71F4 **Popondetta** PNG
54C2 **Popovo** Bulg
85B4 **Porbandar** India
13A2 **Porcher I** Can
12F1 **Porcupine** *R* Can/USA
52B1 **Poreč** Yugos
35A2 **Porecatu** Brazil
39J6 **Pori** Fin
111B2 **Porirua** NZ
38H5 **Porjus** Sweden
69G2 **Poronaysk** USSR
47B1 **Porrentruy** Switz
38K4 **Porsangen** *Inlet* Nor
39F7 **Porsgrunn** Nor
45C1 **Portadown** N Ire
8D2 **Portage la Prairie** Can
13C3 **Port Alberni** Can
50A2 **Portalegre** Port
9C3 **Portales** USA
7C5 **Port Alfred** Can
100B4 **Port Alfred** S Africa
13B2 **Port Alice** Can
19B3 **Port Allen** USA
20B1 **Port Angeles** USA
26B3 **Port Antonio** Jamaica
45C2 **Portarlington** Irish Rep
19B4 **Port Arthur** USA
108A2 **Port Augusta** Aust
26C3 **Port-au-Prince** Haiti
14B2 **Port Austin** USA
108B3 **Port Campbell** Aust
86B2 **Port Canning** India
7D5 **Port Cartier** Can
111B3 **Port Chalmers** NZ
17B2 **Port Charlotte** USA
16C2 **Port Chester** USA
15C2 **Port Colborne** Can
15C2 **Port Credit** Can
109C4 **Port Davey** Aust
26C3 **Port-de-Paix** Haiti
77C5 **Port Dickson** Malay
100C4 **Port Edward** S Africa
35C1 **Porteirinha** Brazil
14B2 **Port Elgin** Can
100B4 **Port Elizabeth** S Africa
27N2 **Porter Pt** St Vincent
21B2 **Porterville** USA
107D4 **Port Fairy** Aust
98A3 **Port Gentil** Gabon
19B3 **Port Gibson** USA
12D3 **Port Graham** USA
20B1 **Port Hammond** Can
89E7 **Port Harcourt** Nig
13B2 **Port Hardy** Can
7D5 **Port Hawkesbury** Can
106A3 **Port Hedland** Aust
Port Heiden = Meshik
43B3 **Porthmadog** Wales
7E4 **Port Hope Simpson** Can
22C3 **Port Hueneme** USA
14B2 **Port Huron** USA
50A2 **Portimão** Port
109D2 **Port Jackson** *B* Aust
16C2 **Port Jefferson** USA
16B2 **Port Jervis** USA
109D2 **Port Kembla** Aust
14B2 **Portland** Indiana, USA
10C2 **Portland** Maine, USA
109C2 **Portland** New South Wales, Aust
20B1 **Portland** Oregon, USA
108B3 **Portland** Victoria, Aust
27H2 **Portland Bight** *B* Jamaica
43C4 **Portland Bill** *Pt* Eng
109C4 **Portland,C** Aust
13A1 **Portland Canal** Can/USA
110C1 **Portland I** NZ
27H2 **Portland Pt** Jamaica
45C2 **Port Laoise** Irish Rep
108A2 **Port Lincoln** Aust
97A4 **Port Loko** Sierra Leone
101E3 **Port Louis** Mauritius
108B3 **Port MacDonnell** Aust
13B2 **Port McNeill** Can
109D2 **Port Macquarie** Aust
12B3 **Port Moller** USA
107D1 **Port Moresby** PNG
100A3 **Port Nolloth** S Africa
16B3 **Port Norris** USA
89E7 **Port Novo** Benin
50A1 **Porto** Port
30F5 **Pôrto Alegre** Brazil
33F6 **Pōrto Artur** Brazil
35A2 **Pôrto 15 de Novembro** Brazil
30F3 **Pôrto E Cunha** Brazil
52B2 **Portoferraio** Italy
27E4 **Port of Spain** Trinidad
47D2 **Portomaggiore** Italy
97C4 **Porto Novo** Benin
20B1 **Port Orchard** USA
20B2 **Port Orford** USA
96A1 **Porto Santo** *I* Medeira
31D5 **Pōrto Seguro** Brazil
53A2 **Porto Torres** Sardegna
53A2 **Porto Vecchio** Corse
33E5 **Pôrto Velho** Brazil
111A3 **Port Pegasus** *B* NZ
108B3 **Port Phillip B** Aust
108A2 **Port Pirie** Aust
44A3 **Portree** Scot
20B1 **Port Renfrew** Can
27J2 **Port Royal** Jamaica
17B1 **Port Royal Sd** USA
45C1 **Portrush** N Ire
92B3 **Port Said** Egypt
17A2 **Port St Joe** USA
100B4 **Port St Johns** S Africa
7E4 **Port Saunders** Can
100C4 **Port Shepstone** S Africa
13A2 **Port Simpson** Can
27Q2 **Portsmouth** Dominica
43D4 **Portsmouth** Eng
14B3 **Portsmouth** Ohio, USA
11C3 **Portsmouth** Virginia, USA
109D2 **Port Stephens** *B* Aust
95C3 **Port Sudan** Sudan
19C3 **Port Sulphur** USA
38K5 **Porttipahdan Tekojärvi** *Res* Fin
50A2 **Portugal** Republic, Europe
14A2 **Port Washington** USA
77C5 **Port Weld** Malay
32D6 **Porvenir** Bol
39K6 **Porvoo** Fin
30E4 **Posadas** Arg
50A2 **Posadas** Spain
47D1 **Poschiavo** Switz
6B2 **Posheim Pen** Can
90C3 **Posht-e Badam** Iran
71D4 **Poso** Indon
58D1 **Postavy** USSR
14B2 **Post Clinton** USA
7C4 **Poste-de-la-Baleine** Can
100B3 **Postmasburg** S Africa
52B1 **Postojna** Yugos
74C2 **Pos'yet** USSR
101G1 **Potchetstroom** S Africa
19B2 **Poteau** USA
53C2 **Potenza** Italy
100B3 **Potgietersrus** S Africa
97D3 **Potiskum** Nig
20C1 **Potlatch** USA
15C3 **Potomac** *R* USA
30C2 **Potosi** Bol
30C4 **Potrerillos** Chile
56C2 **Potsdam** Germany
16B2 **Pottstown** USA
16A2 **Pottsville** USA
16C2 **Poughkeepsie** USA
35B2 **Pouso Alegre** Brazil
110C1 **Poverty B** NZ
61F3 **Povorino** USSR
7C4 **Povungnituk** Can
8C2 **Powder** *R* USA

106C2 **Powell Creek** Aust
9B3 **Powell,L** USA
13C3 **Powell River** Can
8C2 **Power** *R* USA
43C3 **Powys** County, Wales
73D4 **Poyang Hu** *L* China
92B2 **Pozantı** Turk
23B1 **Poza Rica** Mexico
58B2 **Poznań** Pol
30E3 **Pozo Colorado** Par
53B2 **Pozzuoli** Italy
97B4 **Pra** *R* Ghana
76C3 **Prachin Buri** Thai
76B3 **Prachuap Khiri Khan** Thai
59B2 **Praděd** *Mt* Czech
49C3 **Pradelles** France
35D1 **Prado** Brazil
Prague = Praha
57C2 **Praha** Czech
97A4 **Praia** Cape Verde
33E5 **Prainha** Brazil
18B2 **Prairie Village** USA
76C3 **Prakhon Chai** Thai
35B1 **Prata** Brazil
35B1 **Prata** *R* Brazil
Prates = Dongsha Qundao
49E3 **Prato** Italy
16B1 **Prattsville** USA
17A1 **Prattville** USA
48B1 **Prawle Pt** Eng
78D4 **Praya** Indon
47D1 **Predazzo** Italy
63B2 **Predivinsk** USSR
58C2 **Pregolyu** *R* USSR
76D3 **Prek Kak** Camb
56C2 **Prenzlau** Germany
76A3 **Preparis** *I* Burma
76A2 **Preparis North Chan** Burma
59B3 **Přerov** Czech
23A2 **Presa del Infiernillo** Mexico
9B3 **Prescott** Arizona, USA
19B3 **Prescott** Arkansas, USA
15C2 **Prescott** Can
30D4 **Presidencia Roque Sáenz Peña** Arg
35A2 **Presidente Epitácio** Brazil
112C2 **Presidente Frei** *Base* Ant
23B2 **Presidente Migúel Aleman** *L* Mexico
35A2 **Presidente Prudente** Brazil
30F3 **Presidenté Vargas** Brazil
35A2 **Presidente Venceslau** Brazil
59C3 **Prešov** Czech
55B2 **Prespansko Jezero** *L* Yugos
10D2 **Presque Isle** USA
42C3 **Preston** Eng
8B2 **Preston** Idaho, USA
18B2 **Preston** Missouri, USA
42B2 **Prestwick** Scot
31B6 **Prêto** Brazil
35B1 **Prêto** *R* Brazil
101G1 **Pretoria** S Africa
55B3 **Préveza** Greece
76D3 **Prey Veng** Camb
8B3 **Price** USA
13B2 **Price I** Can
60D4 **Prichernomorskaya Nizmennost'** *Lowland* USSR
27M2 **Prickly Pt** Grenada
58C1 **Priekule** USSR
100B3 **Prieska** S Africa
20C1 **Priest L** USA
20C1 **Priest River** USA
61G4 **Prikaspiyskaya Nizmennost'** *Region* USSR
55B2 **Prilep** Yugos
60D3 **Priluki** USSR
34C2 **Primero** *R* Arg
39K6 **Primorsk** USSR
60E4 **Primorsko-Akhtarsk** USSR
13F2 **Primrose L** Can
5H4 **Prince Albert** Can
4F2 **Prince Albert,C** Can
4G2 **Prince Albert Pen** Can
4G2 **Prince Albert Sd** Can
6C3 **Prince Charles I** Can
112B10 **Prince Charles Mts** Ant
7D5 **Prince Edward I** Can
13C2 **Prince George** Can
4H2 **Prince Gustaf Adolp** *S* Can
5E4 **Prince of Wales** *I* USA
71F5 **Prince of Wales I** Aust
4H2 **Prince of Wales I** Can
4G2 **Prince of Wales Str** Can
4F2 **Prince Patrick I** Can
6A2 **Prince Regent Inlet** *Str* Can
13A2 **Prince Rupert** Can
107D2 **Princess Charlotte B** Aust
13B2 **Princess Royal I** Can
27L1 **Princes Town** Trinidad
13C3 **Princeton** Can
18C2 **Princeton** Kentucky, USA
18B1 **Princeton** Missouri, USA
16B2 **Princeton** New Jersey, USA
4D3 **Prince William** USA
12E2 **Prince William Sd** USA
97C4 **Principe** *I* W Africa
20B2 **Prineville** USA
12E1 **Pringle,Mt** USA
6F3 **Prins Christian Sund** *Sd* Greenland
112B12 **Prinsesse Astrid Kyst** Region, Ant
112B12 **Prinsesse Ragnhild Kyst** Region, Ant
64B2 **Prins Karls Forland** *I* Barents S
25D3 **Prinzapolca** Nic
58D2 **Pripyat'** *R* USSR
54B2 **Priština** Yugos
56C2 **Pritzwalk** Germany
61F3 **Privolzhskaya Vozvyshennost'** *Upland* USSR
54B2 **Prizren** Yugos
78C4 **Probolinggo** Indon
5G5 **Procatello** USA
87B2 **Proddatūr** India
25D2 **Progreso** Mexico
20B2 **Project City** USA
61F5 **Prokhladnyy** USSR
65K4 **Prokop'yevsk** USSR
61F4 **Proletarskaya** USSR
64G2 **Proliv Karskiye Vorota** *Str* USSR
83D4 **Prome** Burma
31D4 **Propriá** Brazil
20B2 **Prospect** Oregon, USA
107D3 **Prosperine** Aust
59B3 **Prostějov** Czech
6E2 **Prøven** Greenland
49D3 **Provence** Region, France
16D2 **Providence** USA
15D2 **Provincetown** USA
49C2 **Provins** France
8B2 **Provo** USA
13E2 **Provost** Can
4D2 **Prudhoe Bay** USA
6D2 **Prudhoe Land** Greenland
58C2 **Pruszkow** Pol
60C4 **Prutul** *R* USSR
58C2 **Pruzhany** USSR
18A2 **Pryor** USA
59C3 **Przemys'l** Pol
55C3 **Psará** *I* Greece
60C2 **Pskov** USSR
58D2 **Ptich** *R* USSR
55B2 **Ptolemaïs** Greece
32C5 **Pucallpa** Peru
73D4 **Pucheng** China
34A3 **Pucón** Chile
38K5 **Pudasjärvi** Fin
87B2 **Pudukkottai** India
23B2 **Puebla** Mexico
23B2 **Puebla** State, Mexico
50A1 **Puebla de Sanabria** Spain
50A1 **Puebla de Trives** Spain
9C2 **Pueblo** USA
34B3 **Puelches** Arg
34B3 **Puelén** Arg
23A2 **Puenta Ixbapa** Mexico
34B2 **Puente del Inca** Arg
32A5 **Puerta Aguja** Peru
30B2 **Puerta Coles** Peru
34B2 **Puerta de los Llanos** Arg
31D3 **Puerta do Calcanhar** *Pt* Brazil
32C1 **Puerta Gallinas** Colombia
23B2 **Puerta Maldonado** *Pt* Mexico
32A2 **Puerta Mariato** Panama
29C5 **Puerta Médanosa** *Pt* Arg
23A2 **Puerta Mongrove** Mexico
25E4 **Puerta San Blas** *Pt* Panama
23A2 **Puerta San Telmo** Mexico
29B5 **Puerto Aisén** Chile
25D4 **Puerto Armuelles** Panama
33F6 **Puerto Artur** Brazil
32B3 **Puerto Asis** Colombia
32D2 **Puerto Ayacucho** Ven
25D3 **Puerto Barrios** Guatemala
32C2 **Puerto Berrio** Colombia
32D1 **Puerto Cabello** Ven
25D3 **Puerto Cabezas** Nic
32D2 **Puerto Carreño** Colombia
25D4 **Puerto Cortes** Costa Rica
25D3 **Puerto Cortés** Honduras
96A2 **Puerto del Rosario** Canary Is
30F3 **Puerto E Cunha** Brazil
32C1 **Puerto Fijo** Ven
31B3 **Puerto Franco** Brazil
32D6 **Puerto Heath** Bol
25D2 **Puerto Juarez** Mexico
33E1 **Puerto la Cruz** Ven
50B2 **Puertollano** Spain
27C4 **Puerto Lopez** Colombia
29D4 **Puerto Madryn** Arg
32D6 **Puerto Maldonado** Peru
23B2 **Puerto Marquéz** Mexico
29B4 **Puerto Montt** Chile
30E3 **Puerto Murtinho** Brazil
29B6 **Puerto Natales** Chile
24A1 **Puerto Peñasco** Mexico
29D4 **Puerto Pirámides** Arg
27C3 **Puerto Plata** Dom Re
79A4 **Puerto Princesa** Phil
32B3 **Puerto Rico** Colombi
27D3 **Puerto Rico** *I* Caribbean S
27D3 **Puerto Rico Trench** Caribbean S
23A2 **Puerto San Juan de Lima** Mexico
33G4 **Puerto Santanga** Brazil
30E2 **Puerto Suárez** Bol
24B2 **Puerto Vallarta** Mexico
29B4 **Puerto Varas** Chile
30D2 **Puerto Villarroel** Bol
61G3 **Pugachev** USSR
84C3 **Pugal** India
51C1 **Puigcerdá** Spain
111B2 **Pukaki,L** *L* NZ
74B2 **Pukch'ŏng** N Korea
110B1 **Pukekobe** NZ
111B2 **Puketeraki Range** *Mt* NZ
52B2 **Pula** Yugos
15C2 **Pulaski** New York, USA
71E4 **Pulau Kolepom** *I* Indon
70A4 **Pulau Pulau Batu** *Is* Indon
58C2 **Pulawy** Pol
87C2 **Pulicat,L** India
84B1 **Pul-i-Khumri** Afghan
87B3 **Puliyangudi** India
20C1 **Pullman** USA
71E3 **Pulo Anna Merir** *I* Pacific O
79B2 **Pulog,Mt** Phil
38L5 **Pulozero** USSR
58C2 **Pultusk** Pol
30C4 **Puna de Atacama** Arg
86B1 **Punakha** Bhutan
84C2 **Punch** Pak
87A1 **Pune** India
23A2 **Punéper** Mexico
98C3 **Punia** Zaïre
34A2 **Punitaqui** Chile
84C2 **Punjab** Province, Pak
84D2 **Punjab** State, India
30B2 **Puno** Peru
24A2 **Punta Abreojos** *Pt* Mexico
53C3 **Punta Alice** *Pt* Italy
34C3 **Punta Alta** Arg
29B6 **Punta Arenas** Chile
24A2 **Punta Baja** *Pt* Mexico
34A2 **Punta Curaumilla** *Pt* Chile
100A2 **Punta da Marca** *Pt* Angola
101C3 **Punta de Barra Falsa** *Pt* Mozam
29F2 **Punta del Este** Urug
24A2 **Punta Eugenia** *Pt* Mexico
25D3 **Punta Gorda** Belize
17B2 **Punta Gorda** USA
34A3 **Punta Lavapié** *Pt* Chile
34A2 **Punta Lengua de Vaca** *Pt* Chile
53B2 **Punta Licosa** *Pt* Italy
34A1 **Punta Poroto** *Pt* Chile
9B4 **Punta San Antonia** *Pt* Mexico
34A2 **Punta Topocalma** Chile
73C4 **Puqi** China
64J3 **Pur** *R* USSR
19A2 **Purcell** USA
12C1 **Purcell Mt** USA
13D2 **Purcell Mts** Can
34A3 **Purén** Chile

Rushville

18B1 **Rushville** Illinois, USA
108B3 **Rushworth** Aust
19A3 **Rusk** USA
17B2 **Ruskin** USA
110B1 **Russell** NZ
18B2 **Russellville** Arkansas, USA
18C2 **Russellville** Kentucky, USA
21A2 **Russian** R USA
60B3 **Russian Socialist Federated Soviet Rep** USSR
93E1 **Rustavi** USSR
101G1 **Rustenburg** S Africa
19B3 **Ruston** USA
99C3 **Rutana** Burundi
46E1 **Rüthen** Germany
23B2 **Rutla** Mexico
15D2 **Rutland** USA
84D2 **Rutog** China
Ruvu = Pangani
101D2 **Ruvuma** R Tanz/ Mozam
99D2 **Ruwenzori Range** Mts Uganda/Zaïre
101C2 **Ruya** R Zim
59B3 **Ružomberok** Czech
99C3 **Rwanda** Republic, Africa
60E3 **Ryazan'** USSR
61F3 **Ryazhsk** USSR
60E2 **Rybinsk** USSR
60E2 **Rybinskoye Vodokhranilishche** Res USSR
13D1 **Rycroft** Can
43D4 **Ryde** Eng
43E4 **Rye** Eng
20C2 **Rye Patch Res** USA
60D3 **Ryl'sk** USSR
61G4 **Ryn Peskt** Desert USSR
74D3 **Ryōtsu** Japan
59D3 **Ryskany** USSR
69E4 **Ryūkyū Retto** Arch Japan
59C2 **Rzeszów** Pol
60D2 **Rzhev** USSR

S

91B3 **Sa'ādatābād** Iran
56C2 **Saale** R Germany
47B1 **Saanen** Switz
46D2 **Saar** R Germany
46D2 **Saarbrücken** Germany
46D2 **Saarburg** Germany
39J7 **Saaremaa** I USSR
46D2 **Saarland** State, Germany
46D2 **Saarlouis** Germany
34C3 **Saavedra** Arg
54A2 **Šabac** Yugos
51C1 **Sabadell** Spain
75B1 **Sabae** Japan
78D1 **Sabah** State, Malay
26C4 **Sabanalarga** Colombia
70A3 **Sabang** Indon
87C1 **Sabari** R India
94B2 **Sabastiya** Israel
30C2 **Sabaya** Bol
93C3 **Sab'Bi'ār** Syria
94C2 **Sabhā** Jordan
95A2 **Sabhā** Libya
101C3 **Sabi** R Zim
24B2 **Sabinas** Mexico
24B2 **Sabinas Hidalgo** Mexico
19A3 **Sabine** R USA
19B4 **Sabine I** USA
91B5 **Sabkhat Maṭṭi** Salt Marsh UAE
94A3 **Sabkhet El Bardawîl** Lg Egypt
79B3 **Sablayan** Phil

7D5 **Sable,C** Can
17B2 **Sable,C** USA
7D5 **Sable I** Can
90C2 **Sabzevār** Iran
20C1 **Sacajawea Peak** USA
10A1 **Sachigo** R Can
57C2 **Sachsen** State, Germany
56C2 **Sachsen-Anhalt** State, Germany
4F2 **Sachs Harbour** Can
47B1 **Säckingen** Germany
22B1 **Sacramento** USA
22B1 **Sacramento** R USA
21A1 **Sacramento** V USA
9C3 **Sacramento Mts** USA
81C4 **Sa'dah** Yemen
54B2 **Sadanski** Bulg
82D3 **Sadiya** India
50A2 **Sado** R Port
74D3 **Sado-shima** I Japan
85C3 **Sādri** India
Safad = Zefat
84A2 **Safed Koh** Mts Afghan
39G7 **Saffle** Sweden
92C3 **Safi** Jordan
96B1 **Safi** Mor
90D3 **Safidabeh** Iran
94C1 **Şāfītā** Syria
93E3 **Safwān** Iraq
75A2 **Saga** Japan
76B1 **Sagaing** Burma
75B2 **Sagami-nada** B Japan
85D4 **Sāgar** India
16C2 **Sag Harbor** USA
14B2 **Saginaw** USA
14B2 **Saginaw B** USA
26B2 **Sagua de Tánamo** Cuba
26B2 **Sagua la Grande** Cuba
7C5 **Saguenay** R Can
51B2 **Sagunto** Spain
94C3 **Sahāb** Jordan
50A1 **Sahagún** Spain
96C2 **Sahara** Desert N Africa
84D3 **Saharanpur** India
84C2 **Sahiwal** Pak
93D3 **Şaḥrā al Hijārah** Desert Region Iraq
23A1 **Sahuayo** Mexico
107D1 **Saibai I** Aust
96C1 **Saïda** Alg
94B2 **Saïda** Leb
91C4 **Sa'īdabad** Iran
51B2 **Saidia** Mor
86B1 **Saidpur** India
84C2 **Saidu** Pak
75A1 **Saigō** Japan
76D3 **Saigon** Viet
86C2 **Saiha** India
68D2 **Saihan Tal** China
75A2 **Saijo** Japan
74C4 **Saiki** Japan
42C2 **St Abb's Head** Pt Scot
43D4 **St Albans** Eng
15D2 **St Albans** Vermont, USA
14B3 **St Albans West** Virginia, USA
43C4 **St Albans Head** C Eng
13E2 **St Albert** Can
46B1 **St Amand-les-Eaux** France
48C2 **St Amand-Mont Rond** France
101D2 **St André** C Madag
17A2 **St Andrew B** USA
44C3 **St Andrews** Scot
17B1 **St Andrew Sd** USA
27H1 **St Ann's Bay** Jamaica
7E4 **St Anthony** Can
108B3 **St Arnaud** Aust
17B2 **St Augustine** USA
43B4 **St Austell** Eng
46D2 **St-Avold** France
42C2 **St Bees Head** Pt Eng

47B2 **St-Bonnet** France
43B4 **St Brides B** Wales
48B2 **St-Brieuc** France
15C2 **St Catharines** Can
27M2 **St Catherine,Mt** Grenada
17B1 **St Catherines I** USA
43D4 **St Catherines Pt** Eng
49C2 **St Chamond** France
18B2 **St Charles** Missouri, USA
14B2 **St Clair** USA
14B2 **St Clair,L** Can/USA
14B2 **St Clair Shores** USA
49D2 **St Claud** France
10A2 **St Cloud** USA
47B1 **Ste Croix** Switz
27E3 **St Croix** I Caribbean S
43B4 **St Davids Head** Pt Wales
46B2 **St Denis** France
101E3 **St Denis** Réunion
46C2 **St Dizier** France
12F2 **St Elias,Mt** USA
12G2 **St Elias Mts** Can
48B2 **Saintes** France
49C2 **St Étienne** France
18B2 **St Francis** R USA
100B4 **St Francis,C** S Africa
47C1 **St Gallen** Switz
48C3 **St-Gaudens** France
109C1 **St George** Aust
17B1 **St George** South Carolina, USA
9B3 **St George** Utah, USA
17B2 **St George I** Florida, USA
20B2 **St George,Pt** USA
15D1 **St-Georges** Can
27E4 **St George's** Grenada
45C3 **St George's Chan** Irish Rep/Wales
46A2 **St Germain-en-Laye** France
47B2 **St-Gervais** France
47C1 **St Gotthard** P Switz
43B4 **St Govans Head** Pt Wales
22A1 **St Helena** USA
103H5 **St Helena** I Atlantic O
100A4 **St Helena B** S Africa
17B1 **St Helena Sd** USA
109C4 **St Helens** Aust
42C3 **St Helens** Eng
20B1 **St Helens** USA
20B1 **St Helens,Mt** USA
48B2 **St Helier** Jersey
47B1 **St Hippolyte** France
46C1 **St-Hubert** Belg
7C5 **St-Hyacinthe** Can
14B1 **St Ignace** USA
43B4 **St Ives** Eng
18B2 **St James** Missouri, USA
5E4 **St James,C** Can
15D1 **St Jean** Can
48B2 **St Jean-d'Angely** France
47B2 **St-Jean-de-Maurienne** France
10C2 **St Jean,L** Can
15D1 **St-Jérôme** Can
20C1 **St Joe** R USA
7D5 **Saint John** Can
7E5 **St John's** Can
14B2 **St Johns** Michigan, USA
17B2 **St Johns** R USA
15D2 **St Johnsbury** USA
15D1 **St-Joseph** Can
19B3 **St Joseph** Louisiana, USA
14A2 **St Joseph** Michigan, USA
18B2 **St Joseph** Missouri, USA
27L1 **St Joseph** Trinidad

14B2 **St Joseph** R USA
14B1 **St Joseph I** Can
7A4 **St Joseph,L** Can
47B1 **St Julien** France
48C2 **St-Junien** France
46B2 **St-Just-en-Chaussée** France
4B2 **St Kilda** I Scot
27E3 **St Kitts** I Caribbean S
47A1 **St-Laurent** France
7D5 **St Lawrence** R Can
7D5 **Saint Lawrence,G of** Can
4A3 **St Lawrence I** USA
15C2 **St Lawrence Seaway** Can/USA
48B2 **St Lô** France
97A3 **St Louis** Sen
11A3 **St Louis** USA
27E4 **St Lucia** I Caribbean S
101H1 **St Lucia,L** S Africa
44E1 **St Magnus** B Scot
48B2 **St Malo** France
101D3 **Ste Marie** C Madag
20C1 **St Maries** USA
27E3 **St Martin** I Caribbean S
108A2 **St Mary Peak** Mt Aust
109C4 **St Marys** Aust
15C2 **St Marys** USA
17B1 **St Marys** R USA
46C2 **Ste-Menehould** France
12B2 **St Michael** USA
16A3 **St Michaels** USA
47B2 **St-Michel** France
46C2 **St-Mihiel** France
47C1 **St Moritz** Switz
48B2 **St-Nazaire** France
46C1 **St-Niklaas** Belg
46B1 **St-Omer** France
13E2 **St Paul** Can
10A2 **St Paul** Minnesota, USA
97A4 **St Paul** R Lib
17B2 **St Petersburg** USA
7E5 **St Pierre** Can
15D1 **St Pierre,L** Can
46B1 **St-Pol-Sur-Ternoise** France
59B3 **St Pölten** Austria
46B2 **St Quentin** France
49D3 **St Raphaël** France
101D2 **St Sébastien** C Madag
17B1 **St Simons I** USA
17B1 **St Stephen** USA
14B2 **St Thomas** Can
49D3 **St-Tropez** France
46C1 **St Truiden** Belg
46A1 **St-Valéry-sur-Somme** France
101D3 **St Vincent** C Madag
27E4 **St Vincent** I Caribbean S
108A2 **St Vincent,G** Aust
46D1 **St-Vith** Germany
46D2 **St Wendel** Germany
71F2 **Saipan** I Pacific O
84B2 **Saiydabad** Afghan
30C2 **Sajama** Mt Bol
74D4 **Sakai** Japan
75A2 **Sakaidi** Japan
75A1 **Sakaiminato** Japan
93D4 **Sakākah** S Arabia
10C1 **Sakami,L** Can
100B2 **Sakania** Zaïre
101D3 **Sakaraha** Madag
60D5 **Sakarya** R Turk
58C1 **Sakasleja** USSR
74D3 **Sakata** Japan
97C4 **Saketél** Benin
69G1 **Sakhalin** I USSR
69E4 **Sakishima gunto** Is Japan
97A4 **Sal** I Cape Verde
61F4 **Sal** R USSR

25D3 **San Juan del Norte** Nic
27D4 **San Juan de los Cayos** Ven
23A1 **San Juan de loz Lagoz** Mexico
23A1 **San Juan del Rio** Mexico
25D3 **San Juan del Sur** Nic
20B1 **San Juan Is** USA
23B2 **San Juan Tepozcolula** Mexico
29C5 **San Julián** Arg
34C2 **San Justo** Arg
98C3 **San Kuru** R Zaïre
22A2 **San Leandro** USA
32B3 **San Lorenzo** Ecuador
34C2 **San Lorenzo** Arg
22B2 **San Lucas** USA
34B2 **San Luis** Arg
34B2 **San Luis** State, Arg
23A1 **San Luis de la Paz** Mexico
21A2 **San Luis Obispo** USA
23A1 **San Luis Potosi** Mexico
22B2 **San Luis Res** USA
53A3 **Sanluri** Sardegna
33D2 **San Maigualida** Mts Ven
34D3 **San Manuel** Arg
34A2 **San Marcos** Chile
23B2 **San Marcos** Mexico
52B2 **San Marino** Republic, Europe
34B2 **San Martin** Mendoza, Arg
112C3 **San Martin** Base Ant
47D1 **San Martino di Castroza** Italy
23B2 **San Martin Tuxmelucan** Mexico
22A2 **San Mateo** USA
30E2 **San Matias** Bol
72C3 **Sanmenxia** China
25D3 **San Miguel** El Salvador
22B3 **San Miguel** I USA
23A1 **San Miguel del Allende** Mexico
34D3 **San Miguel del Monte** Arg
30C4 **San Miguel de Tucumán** Arg
73D4 **Sanming** China
9B3 **San Nicolas** I USA
34C2 **San Nicolás de los Arroyos** Arg
101G1 **Sannieshof** S Africa
97B4 **Sanniquellie** Lib
59C3 **Sanok** Pol
26B5 **San Onofore** Colombia
22D4 **San Onofre** USA
79B3 **San Pablo** Phil
22A1 **San Pablo B** USA
34D2 **San Pedro** Buenos Aires, Arg
97B4 **San Pédro** Ivory Coast
30D3 **San Pedro** Jujuy, Arg
30E3 **San Pedro** Par
22C4 **San Pedro Chan** USA
9C4 **San Pedro de los Colonias** Mexico
25D3 **San Pedro Sula** Honduras
53A3 **San Pietro** I Medit S
24A1 **San Quintin** Mexico
34B2 **San Rafael** Arg
22A2 **San Rafael** USA
22C3 **San Rafael Mts** USA
49D3 **San Remo** Italy
34D2 **San Salvador** Arg
26C2 **San Salvador** I Caribbean S
32J7 **San Salvador** I Ecuador

30C3 **San Salvador de Jujuy** Arg
51B1 **San Sebastian** Spain
53C2 **San Severo** Italy
30C2 **Santa Ana** Bol
25C3 **Santa Ana** Guatemala
22D4 **Santa Ana** USA
22D4 **Santa Ana Mts** USA
34A3 **Santa Bárbara** Chile
24B2 **Santa Barbara** Mexico
22C3 **Santa Barbara** USA
22C4 **Santa Barbara** I USA
22B3 **Santa Barbara Chan** USA
22C3 **Santa Barbara Res** USA
22C4 **Santa Catalina** I USA
22C4 **Santa Catalina,G of** USA
30F4 **Santa Catarina** State, Brazil
26B2 **Santa Clara** Cuba
22B2 **Santa Clara** USA
22C3 **Santa Clara** R USA
29C6 **Santa Cruz** Arg
30D2 **Santa Cruz** Bol
34A2 **Santa Cruz** Chile
79B3 **Santa Cruz** Phil
29B5 **Santa Cruz** State, Arg
22A2 **Santa Cruz** USA
22C4 **Santa Cruz** I USA
35D1 **Santa Cruz Cabrália** Brazil
22C3 **Santa Cruz Chan** USA
96A2 **Santa Cruz de la Palma** Canary Is
26B2 **Santa Cruz del Sur** Cuba
96A2 **Santa Cruz de Tenerife** Canary Is
100B2 **Santa Cruz do Cuando** Angola
35B2 **Santa Cruz do Rio Pardo** Brazil
22A2 **Santa Cruz Mts** USA
34D2 **Santa Elena** Arg
33E3 **Santa Elena** Ven
34C2 **Santa Fe** Arg
34C2 **Santa Fe** State, Arg
9C3 **Santa Fe** USA
35A1 **Santa Helena de Goiás** Brazil
73B3 **Santai** China
29B6 **Santa Inés** I Chile
34B3 **Santa Isabel** La Pampa, Arg
34C2 **Santa Isabel** Sante Fe, Arg
107E1 **Santa Isabel** I Solomon Is
21A2 **Santa Lucia** Ra USA
21A2 **Santa Lucia Range** Mts USA
97A4 **Santa Luzia** I Cape Verde
9B4 **Santa Margarita** I Mexico
22D4 **Santa Margarita** R USA
30F4 **Santa Maria** Brazil
26C4 **Santa Maria** Colombia
21A3 **Santa Maria** USA
96A1 **Santa Maria** I Açores
23B1 **Santa Maria** R Queretaro, Mexico
23A1 **Santa Maria del Rio** Mexico
32C1 **Santa Marta** Colombia
22C3 **Santa Monica** USA
22C4 **Santa Monica B** USA
29E2 **Santana do Livramento** Brazil
32B3 **Santander** Colombia
50B1 **Santander** Spain
51C2 **Santañy** Spain
22C3 **Santa Paula** USA
31C2 **Santa Quitéria** Brazil
33G4 **Santarem** Brazil

50A2 **Santarém** Port
22A1 **Santa Rosa** California, USA
25D3 **Santa Rosa** Honduras
34C3 **Santa Rosa** La Pampa, Arg
34B2 **Santa Rosa** Mendoza, Arg
34B2 **Santa Rosa** San Luis, Arg
22B3 **Santa Rosa** I USA
24A2 **Santa Rosalía** Mexico
20C2 **Santa Rosa Range** Mts USA
31D3 **Santa Talhada** Brazil
35C1 **Santa Teresa** Brazil
53A2 **Santa Teresa di Gallura** Sardegna
22B3 **Santa Ynez** R USA
22B3 **Santa Ynez Mts** USA
17C1 **Santee** R USA
47C2 **Santhia** Italy
34A2 **Santiago** Chile
27C3 **Santiago** Dom Rep
32A2 **Santiago** Panama
79B2 **Santiago** Phil
32B4 **Santiago** R Peru
50A1 **Santiago de Compostela** Spain
26B2 **Santiago de Cuba** Cuba
30D4 **Santiago del Estero** Arg
30D4 **Santiago del Estero** State, Arg
22D4 **Santiago Peak** Mt USA
31C5 **Santo** State, Brazil
35A2 **Santo Anastatácio** Brazil
30F4 **Santo Angelo** Brazil
97A4 **Santo Antão** I Cape Verde
35A2 **Santo Antonio da Platina** Brazil
27D3 **Santo Domingo** Dom Rep
35B2 **Santos** Brazil
35C2 **Santos Dumont** Brazil
30E4 **Santo Tomé** Arg
29B5 **San Valentin** Mt Chile
34A2 **San Vicente** Chile
98B3 **Sanza Pomba** Angola
30E4 **São Borja** Brazil
35B2 **São Carlos** Brazil
33G5 **São Félix** Mato Grosso, Brazil
35C2 **São Fidélis** Brazil
35C1 **São Francisco** Brazil
31D3 **São Francisco** R Brazil
30G4 **São Francisco do Sul** Brazil
35B1 **São Gotardo** Brazil
99D3 **Sao Hill** Tanz
35C2 **São João da Barra** Brazil
35B2 **São João da Boa Vista** Brazil
35C1 **São João da Ponte** Brazil
35C2 **São João del Rei** Brazil
35B2 **São Joaquim da Barra** Brazil
96A1 **São Jorge** I Açores
35B2 **São José do Rio Prêto** Brazil
35B2 **São José dos Campos** Brazil
31C2 **São Luis** Brazil
35B1 **São Marcos** R Brazil
35C1 **São Maria do Suaçui** Brazil
35D1 **São Mateus** Brazil
35C1 **São Mateus** R Brazil
96A1 **São Miguel** I Açores
49C2 **Saône** R France

97A4 **São Nicolau** I Cape Verde
35B2 **São Paulo** Brazil
35A2 **São Paulo** State, Brazil
31C3 **São Raimundo Nonato** Brazil
35B1 **São Romão** Brazil
35B2 **São Sebastia do Paraiso** Brazil
35A1 **São Simão** Goias, Brazil
35B2 **São Simão** Sao Paulo, Brazil
97A4 **São Tiago** I Cape Verde
97C4 **São Tomé** I W Africa
97C4 **São Tomé and Principe** Republic, W Africa
96B2 **Saoura** Watercourse Alg
35B2 **São Vicente** Brazil
97A4 **São Vincente** I Cape Verde
55C2 **Sápai** Greece
78D4 **Sape** Indon
97C4 **Sapele** Nig
74E2 **Sapporo** Japan
53C2 **Sapri** Italy
18A2 **Sapulpa** USA
90A2 **Saqqez** Iran
10C2 **Saquenay** R Can
90A2 **Saráb** Iran
54C1 **Sarata** USSR
54A2 **Sarajevo** Yugos
90D2 **Sarakhs** Iran
61J3 **Saraktash** USSR
63A2 **Sarala** USSR
15D2 **Saranac L** USA
15D2 **Saranac Lake** USA
55B3 **Sarandë** Alb
79C4 **Sarangani Is** Phil
61G3 **Saransk** USSR
61H2 **Sarapul** USSR
17B2 **Sarasota** USA
15D2 **Saratoga Springs** USA
78C2 **Saratok** Malay
61G3 **Saratov** USSR
61G3 **Saratovskoye Vodokhranilishche** Res USSR
67F4 **Sarawak** State, Malay
92A2 **Saraykoy** Turk
90C3 **Sarbisheh** Iran
47D1 **Sarca** R Italy
95A2 **Sardalas** Libya
90A2 **Sar Dasht** Iran
52A2 **Sardegna** I Medit S
Sardinia = Sardegna
38H5 **Sarektjåkkå** Mt Sweden
84C2 **Sargodha** Pak
98B2 **Sarh** Chad
90B2 **Sārī** Iran
94B2 **Sarida** R Isreal
93D1 **Sarikamis** Turk
107D3 **Sarina** Aust
47B1 **Sarine** R Switz
84B1 **Sar-i-Pul** Afghan
95B2 **Sarir** Libya
95A2 **Sarir Tibesti** Desert Libya
74B3 **Sariwön** N Korea
48B2 **Sark** I UK
92C2 **Sarkišla** Turk
71E4 **Sarmi** Indon
29C5 **Sarmiento** Arg
39G6 **Särna** Sweden
47C1 **Sarnen** Switz
14B2 **Sarnia** Can
58D2 **Sarny** USSR
6E2 **Saroaq** Greenland
84B2 **Sarobi** Afghan
78A3 **Sarolangun** Indon
55B3 **Saronikós Kólpos** G Greece
47C2 **Saronno** Italy
55C2 **Saros Körfezi** B Turk
39G7 **Sarpsborg** Nor

Serrana Bank

46D2 **Sarralbe** France	84B1 **Sayghan** Afghan	94B3 **Sedom** Israel	52C2 **Senj** Yugos
46D2 **Sarrebourg** France	72B1 **Sayhandulaan**	100A3 **Seeheim** Namibia	69E4 **Senkaku Gunto** *Is*
46D2 **Sarreguemines** France	Mongolia	111B2 **Sefton,Mt** NZ	Japan
46D2 **Sarre-Union** France	91B5 **Sayhūt** Yemen	77C5 **Segamat** Malay	46B2 **Senlis** France
51B1 **Sarrion** Spain	61G4 **Saykhin** USSR	51B2 **Segorbe** Spain	99D1 **Sennar** Sudan
85B3 **Sartanahu** Pak	68D2 **Saynshand** Mongolia	97B3 **Ségou** Mali	7C5 **Senneterre** Can
53A2 **Sartène** Corse	61H5 **Say-Utes** USSR	**Segovia = Coco**	49C2 **Sens** France
48B2 **Sarthe** *R* France	16C2 **Sayville** USA	50B1 **Segovia** Spain	54A1 **Senta** Yugos
61H4 **Sarykamys** USSR	13B2 **Sayward** Can	51C1 **Segre** *R* Spain	98C3 **Sentery** Zaïre
65H5 **Sarysu** *R* USSR	57C3 **Sázava** *R* Czech	97B4 **Séguéla** Ivory Coast	13C2 **Sentinel Peak** *Mt* Can
86A2 **Sasarām** India	51C2 **Sbisseb** *R* Alg	96A2 **Seguia el Hamra**	85D4 **Seoni** India
74B4 **Sasebo** Japan	42C2 **Scafell Pike** *Mt* Eng	*Watercourse* Mor	**Seoul = Soul**
5H4 **Saskatchewan**	44E1 **Scalloway** Scot	34C2 **Segundo** *R* Arg	110B2 **Separation Pt** NZ
Province, Can	44C2 **Scapa Flow** *Sd* Scot	78D2 **Seguntur** Indon	76D2 **Sepone** Laos
5H4 **Saskatchewan** *R* Can	15C2 **Scarborough** Can	50B2 **Segura** *R* Spain	7D4 **Sept-Iles** Can
13F2 **Saskatoon** Can	42D2 **Scarborough** Eng	85B3 **Sehwan** Pak	95A2 **Séquédine** Niger
101G1 **Sasolburg** S Africa	27E4 **Scarborough** Tobago	46D2 **Seille** *R* France	21B2 **Sequoia** Nat Pk, USA
61F3 **Sasovo** USSR	44A2 **Scarp** *I* Scot	38J6 **Seinäjoki** Fin	71D4 **Seram** *I* Indon
97B4 **Sassandra** Ivory Coast	45B2 **Scarriff** Irish Rep	48C2 **Seine** *R* France	78B4 **Serang** Indon
97B4 **Sassandra** *R* Ivory	52A1 **Schaffhausen** Switz	46B2 **Seine-et-Marne**	78B2 **Serasan** *I* Indon
Coast	57C3 **Scharding** Austria	Department, France	54A2 **Serbia** Region, Yugos
53A2 **Sassari** Sardegna	46D1 **Scharteberg** *Mt*	99D3 **Sekenke** Tanz	61F3 **Serdobsk** USSR
56C2 **Sassnitz** Germany	Germany	20B1 **Selah** USA	77C5 **Seremban** Malay
47D2 **Sassuolo** Italy	7D4 **Schefferville** Can	71E4 **Selaru** *I* Indon	99D3 **Serengeti Nat Pk**
34C2 **Sastre** Arg	46B1 **Schelde** *R* Belg	78D4 **Selat Alas** *Str* Indon	Tanz
87A1 **Sātāra** India	10C2 **Schenectady** USA	78B3 **Selat Bangka** *Str*	100C2 **Serenje** Zambia
4G2 **Satellite B** Can	47D2 **Schio** Italy	Indon	59D3 **Seret** *R* USSR
78D4 **Satengar** *Is* Indon	46D1 **Schleiden** Germany	78A3 **Selat Berhala** *B* Indon	61G2 **Sergach** USSR
39H6 **Säter** Sweden	56B2 **Schleswig** Germany	71E4 **Selat Dampier** *Str*	65H3 **Sergino** USSR
17B1 **Satilla** *R* USA	56B2 **Schleswig Holstein**	Indon	31D4 **Sergipe** State, Brazil
61J2 **Satka** USSR	State, Germany	78B3 **Selat Gaspar** *Str*	78C2 **Seria** Brunei
84D2 **Satluj** *R* India	16B1 **Schoharie** USA	Indon	78C2 **Serian** Malay
86A2 **Satna** India	71F4 **Schouten** *Is* PNG	78D4 **Selat Lombok** *Str*	55B3 **Sérifos** *I* Greece
85C4 **Sātpura Range** *Mts*	7B5 **Schreiber** Can	Indon	47C2 **Serio** *R* Italy
India	21B2 **Schurz** USA	78D4 **Selat Sape** *Str* Indon	95B2 **Serir Calanscio** *Desert*
54B1 **Satu Mare** Rom	16A2 **Schuykill Haven** USA	78B4 **Selat Sunda** *Str* Indon	Libya
34D2 **Sauce** Arg	16B2 **Schuylkill** *R* USA	71D4 **Selat Wetar** *Chan*	46C2 **Sermaize-les-Bains**
39F7 **Sauda** Nor	57B3 **Schwabische Alb**	Indon	France
80C3 **Saudi Arabia**	*Upland* Germany	12B1 **Selawik** USA	71D4 **Sermata** *I* Indon
Kingdom,	57B3 **Schwarzwald** *Upland*	12C1 **Selawik** *R* USA	61H3 **Sernovodsk** USSR
Arabian Pen	Germany	12B1 **Selawik L** USA	65H4 **Serov** USSR
46D2 **Sauer** *R* Germany/Lux	12C1 **Schwatka Mts** USA	42D3 **Selby** Eng	100B3 **Serowe** Botswana
46D1 **Sauerland** Region,	47D1 **Schwaz** Austria	55C2 **Selçuk** Turk	50A2 **Serpa** Port
Germany	57C2 **Schweinfurt** Germany	12D3 **Seldovia** USA	60E3 **Serpukhov** USSR
38B1 **Sauðárkrókur** Iceland	101G1 **Schweizer Reneke**	100B3 **Selebi Pikwe**	35B2 **Serra da Canastra** *Mts*
14A2 **Saugatuck** USA	S Africa	Botswana	Brazil
16C1 **Saugerties** USA	56C2 **Schwerin** Germany	6H3 **Selfoss** Iceland	50A1 **Serra da Estrela** *Mts*
13B2 **Saugstad,Mt** Can	47C1 **Schwyz** Switz	95B2 **Selima Oasis** Sudan	Port
7B5 **Sault Sainte Marie**	53B3 **Sciacca** Italy	5J4 **Selkirk** Can	35B2 **Serra da Mantiqueira**
Can	14B3 **Scioto** *R* USA	42C2 **Selkirk** Scot	*Mts* Brazil
14B1 **Sault Ste Marie** Can	109D2 **Scone** Aust	13D2 **Selkirk Mts** Can	35A1 **Serra da Mombuca**
14B1 **Sault Ste Marie** USA	6H2 **Scoresby Sd**	22C2 **Selma** California, USA	Brazil
71E4 **Saumlaki** Indon	Greenland	50B2 **Selouane** Mor	35C1 **Serra do Cabral** *Mt*
48B2 **Saumur** France	103F7 **Scotia Ridge**	12H2 **Selous,Mt** Can	Brazil
98C3 **Saurimo** Angola	Atlantic O	78B3 **Selta Karimata** *Str*	33F5 **Serra do Cachimbo**
27M2 **Sauteurs** Grenada	103F7 **Scotia S** Atlantic O	Indon	*Mts* Brazil
54A2 **Sava** *R* Yugos	44B3 **Scotland** Country, UK	32C5 **Selvas** Region, Brazil	35A1 **Serra do Caiapó** *Mts*
97C4 **Savalou** Benin	112B7 **Scott** *Base* Ant	107D3 **Selwyn** Aust	Brazil
17B1 **Savannah** Georgia,	13B2 **Scott,C** Can	4E3 **Selwyn Mts** Can	35A2 **Serra do Cantu** *Mts*
USA	9C2 **Scott City** USA	78C4 **Semarang** Indon	Brazil
17B1 **Savannah** *R* USA	112C6 **Scott I** Ant	61E2 **Semenov** USSR	35C2 **Serra do Caparaó** *Mts*
76C2 **Savannakhet** Laos	6C2 **Scott Inlet** *B* Can	12C3 **Semidi Is** USA	Brazil
26B3 **Savanna la Mar**	20B2 **Scott,Mt** USA	60E3 **Semiluki** USSR	31C5 **Serra do Chifre** Brazil
Jamaica	106B2 **Scott Reef** Timor S	19A2 **Seminole** Oklahoma,	35C1 **Serra do Espinhaço**
7A4 **Savant Lake** Can	8C2 **Scottsbluff** USA	USA	*Mts* Brazil
76D2 **Savarane** Laos	17A1 **Scottsboro** USA	17B1 **Seminole,L** USA	35B2 **Serra do Mar** *Mts*
97C4 **Savé** Benin	109C4 **Scottsdale** Aust	65K4 **Semipalatinsk** USSR	Brazil
101C3 **Save** *R* Mozam	10C2 **Scranton** USA	79B3 **Semirara Is** Phil	35A2 **Serra do Mirante** *Mts*
90B3 **Sāveh** Iran	47D1 **Scuol** Switz	90B3 **Semirom** Iran	Brazil
46D2 **Saverne** France	**Scutari = Shkodër**	78C2 **Semitau** Indon	33G3 **Serra do Navio** Brazil
47B2 **Savigliano** Italy	5J4 **Seal** *R* Can	90B2 **Semnān** Iran	35B2 **Serra do**
46B2 **Savigny** France	108B3 **Sea Lake** Aust	46C2 **Semois** *R* Belg	**Paranapiacaba** *Mts*
49D2 **Savoie** *Region* France	18B2 **Searcy** USA	23B2 **Sempoala** Hist Site,	Brazil
49D3 **Savona** Italy	22B2 **Seaside** California,	Mexico	33F6 **Serra dos Caiabis** *Mts*
38K6 **Savonlinna** Fin	USA	32D5 **Sena Madureira** Brazil	Brazil
4A3 **Savoonga** USA	20B1 **Seaside** Oregon, USA	100B2 **Senanga** Zambia	35A2 **Serra dos Dourados**
38K5 **Savukoski** Fin	16B3 **Seaside Park** USA	19C3 **Senatobia** USA	*Mts* Brazil
71D4 **Savu S** Indon	20B1 **Seattle** USA	74E3 **Sendai** Honshū, Japan	33E6 **Serra dos Parecis**
76A1 **Saw** Burma	22A1 **Sebastopol** USA	74C4 **Sendai** Kyūshū, Japan	Brazil
85D3 **Sawai Mādhopur**	58D1 **Sebez** USSR	85D4 **Sendwha** India	35B1 **Serra dos Pilões** *Mts*
India	17B2 **Sebring** USA	15C2 **Seneca Falls** USA	Brazil
78A2 **Sawang** Indon	111A3 **Secretary I** NZ	97A3 **Senegal** Republic,	35A1 **Serra Dourada** *Mts*
76B2 **Sawankhalok** Thai	18B2 **Sedalia** USA	Africa	Brazil
75C1 **Sawara** Japan	46C2 **Sedan** France	97A3 **Sénégal** *R* Maur Sen	33F6 **Serra Formosa** *Mts*
95A2 **Sawknah** Libya	111B2 **Seddonville** NZ	101G1 **Senekal** S Africa	Brazil
12E1 **Sawtooth Mt** USA	94B3 **Sede Boqer** Israel	31D4 **Senhor do Bonfim**	55B2 **Sérrai** Greece
106B2 **Sawu** *I* Indon	94B3 **Sederot** Israel	Brazil	25D3 **Serrana Bank** *Is*
97C3 **Say** Niger	97A3 **Sédhiou** Sen	52B2 **Senigallia** Italy	Caribbean S

50B1	**Sierra de Guadarrama** *Mts* Spain
51B1	**Sierra de Guara** *Mts* Spain
51B1	**Sierra de Gudar** *Mts* Spain
23B2	**Sierra de Juárez** Mexico
34C3	**Sierra de la Ventana** *Mts* Arg
51C1	**Sierra del Codi** *Mts* Spain
34B2	**Sierra del Morro** *Mt* Arg
34B3	**Sierra del Nevado** *Mts* Arg
24B2	**Sierra de los Alamitos** *Mts* Mexico
50B2	**Sierra de los Filabres** Spain
23A1	**Sierra de los Huicholes** Mexico
23B2	**Sierra de Miahuatlán** Mexico
23A1	**Sierra de Morones** *Mts* Mexico
50A2	**Sierra de Ronda** *Mts* Spain
34B2	**Sierra de San Luis** *Mts* Arg
50B2	**Sierra de Segura** *Mts* Spain
50B1	**Sierra de Urbion** *Mts* Spain
34B2	**Sierra de Uspallata** *Mts* Arg
34B2	**Sierra de Valle Fértil** *Mts* Arg
23B2	**Sierra de Zongolica** Mexico
34C2	**Sierra Grande** *Mts* Arg
97A4	**Sierra Leone** Republic, Africa
97A4	**Sierra Leone,C** Sierra Leone
79B2	**Sierra Madre** *Mts* Phil
23A2	**Sierra Madre del Sur** *Mts* Mexico
24B2	**Sierra Madre Occidental** *Mts* Mexico
24C2	**Sierra Madre Oriental** *Mts* Mexico
34B2	**Sierra Malanzan** *Mts* Arg
9C4	**Sierra Mojada** Mexico
50A2	**Sierra Morena** *Mts* Spain
50B2	**Sierra Nevada** *Mts* Spain
21A2	**Sierra Nevada** *Mts* USA
32C1	**Sierra Nevada de Santa Marta** *Mts* Colombia
34B2	**Sierra Pié de Palo** *Mts* Arg
47B1	**Sierre** Switz
55B3	**Sífnos** *I* Greece
59C3	**Sighet** Rom
54B1	**Sighisoara** Rom
38B1	**Siglufjörður** Iceland
50B1	**Sigüenza** Spain
97B3	**Siguiri** Guinea
85E4	**Sihora** India
93D2	**Siirt** Turk
68B3	**Sikai Hu** *L* China
85D3	**Sīkar** India
84B2	**Sikaram** *Mt* Afghan
97B3	**Sikasso** Mali
18C2	**Sikeston** USA
55C3	**Síkinos** *I* Greece
55B3	**Sikionia** Greece
86B1	**Sikkim** State, India
50A1	**Sil** *R* Spain
47D1	**Silandro** Italy
23A1	**Silao** Mexico
79B3	**Silay** Phil
86C2	**Silchar** India
96C2	**Silet** Alg
86A1	**Silgarhi** Nepal
92B2	**Silifke** Turk
82C2	**Siling Co** *L* China
54C2	**Silistra** Bulg
39F7	**Silkeborg** Den
47E1	**Sillian** Austria
18B2	**Siloam Springs** USA
19B3	**Silsbee** USA
95A3	**Siltou** *Well* Chad
58C1	**Šilute** USSR
93D2	**Silvan** Turk
35B1	**Silvania** Brazil
85C4	**Silvassa** India
21B2	**Silver City** Nevada, USA
9C3	**Silver City** New Mexico, USA
20B2	**Silver Lake** USA
16A3	**Silver Spring** USA
13B2	**Silverthrone Mt** Can
108B2	**Silverton** Aust
47C1	**Silvretta** *Mts* Austria/Switz
78C2	**Simanggang** Malay
76C1	**Simao** China
90A3	**Simareh** *R* Iran
55C3	**Simav** Turk
55C3	**Simav** *R* Turk
15C2	**Simcoe,L** Can
70A3	**Simeulue** *I* Indon
60D5	**Simferopol'** USSR
55C3	**Sími** *I* Greece
84D2	**Simla** India
46D1	**Simmern** Germany
13B2	**Simoon Sound** Can
49D2	**Simplon** *Mt* Switz
47C1	**Simplon** *P* Switz
4C2	**Simpson,C** USA
106C3	**Simpson Desert** Aust
6B3	**Simpson Pen** Can
39G7	**Simrishamn** Sweden
69H2	**Simushir** *I* USSR
99E2	**Sinadogo** Somalia
92B4	**Sinai** *Pen* Egypt
32B2	**Sincelejo** Colombia
17B1	**Sinclair,L** USA
85D3	**Sind** *R* India
85B3	**Sindh** Region, Pak
55C3	**Sindirği** Turk
86B2	**Sindri** India
50A2	**Sines** Port
99D1	**Singa** Sudan
77C5	**Singapore** Republic, S E Asia
77C5	**Singapore,Str of** S E Asia
78D4	**Singaraja** Indon
99D3	**Singida** Tanz
78B2	**Singkawang** Indon
109D2	**Singleton** Aust
78A3	**Singtep** *I* Indon
76B1	**Singu** Burma
53A2	**Siniscola** Sardgena
93D2	**Sinjär** Iraq
84B2	**Sinkai Hills** *Mts* Afghan
95C3	**Sinkat** Sudan
82C1	**Sinkiang Autonomous Region**, China
33G2	**Sinnamary** French Guiana
92C1	**Sinop** Turk
54B1	**Sintana** Rom
78C2	**Sintang** Indon
50A2	**Sintra** Port
32B2	**Sinú** *R* Colombia
74A2	**Sinüiju** N Korea
59B3	**Siofok** Hung
47B1	**Sion** Switz
8D2	**Sioux City** USA
8D2	**Sioux Falls** USA
10A2	**Sioux Lookout** Can
79B4	**Sipalay** Phil
27L1	**Siparia** Trinidad
69E2	**Siping** China
112B3	**Siple** *Base* Ant
112B5	**Siple** *I* Ant
79B3	**Sipocot** Phil
70A4	**Sipora** Indon
79B4	**Siquijor** *I* Phil
87B2	**Sira** India
53C3	**Siracusa** Italy
86B2	**Sirajganj** Bang
13C2	**Sir Alexander,Mt** Can
91B5	**Sīr Banī Yās** *I* UAE
106C2	**Sir Edward Pellew Group** *Is* Aust
54C1	**Siret** *R* Rom
12J2	**Sir James McBrien,Mt** Can
87B2	**Sir Kālahasti** India
13D2	**Sir Laurier,Mt** Can
93D2	**Sirnak** Turk
85C4	**Sirohi** India
87B1	**Sironcha** India
85D4	**Sironj** India
55B3	**Síros** *I* Greece
91B4	**Sirri** *I* Iran
84D3	**Sirsa** India
13D2	**Sir Sandford,Mt** Can
87A2	**Sirsi** India
95A1	**Sirt** Libya
95A1	**Sirte Desert** Libya
95A1	**Sirte,G of** Libya
52C1	**Sisak** Yugos
76C2	**Sisaket** Thai
76C3	**Sisophon** Camb
46B2	**Sissonne** France
90D3	**Sistan** Region, Iran/Afghan
49D3	**Sisteron** France
63B2	**Sistig Khem** USSR
86A1	**Sītāpur** India
55C3	**Sitía** Greece
4E4	**Sitka** USA
12D3	**Sitkalidak** *I* USA
12D3	**Sitkinak** *I* USA
76B2	**Sittang** *R* Burma
46C1	**Sittard** Neth
86C2	**Sittwe** Burma
78C4	**Situbondo** Indon
92C2	**Sivas** Turk
93C2	**Siverek** Turk
92B2	**Sivrihisar** Turk
95B2	**Siwa** Egypt
84D2	**Siwalik Range** *Mts* India
86A1	**Siwalik Range** *Mts* Nepal
72D3	**Siyang** China
56C1	**Sjaelland** *I* Den
39G7	**Skagen** Den
39F7	**Skagerrak** *Str* Nor/Den
20B1	**Skagit** *R* USA
20B1	**Skagit Mt** Can
4E4	**Skagway** USA
39G7	**Skara** Sweden
59C2	**Skarzysko-Kamlenna** Pol
5F4	**Skeena** *R* Can
13B1	**Skeena Mts** Can
4D3	**Skeenjek** *R* USA
42E3	**Skegness** Eng
38H5	**Skellefte** *R* Sweden
38J6	**Skellefteå** Sweden
55B3	**Skíathos** *I* Greece
45B3	**Skibbereen** Irish Rep
5E4	**Skidegate** Can
58C2	**Skiemiewice** Pol
39F7	**Skien** Nor
96C1	**Skikda** Alg
74C4	**Skikoku** *I* Japan
42D3	**Skipton** Eng
55B3	**Skíros** *I* Greece
39F7	**Skive** Den
56B1	**Skjern** Den
6F3	**Skjoldungen** Greenland
14A2	**Skokie** USA
55B3	**Skópelos** *I* Greece
54B2	**Skopje** Yugos
39G7	**Skövde** Sweden
63E2	**Skovorodino** USSR
4C3	**Skwentna** USA
58B2	**Skwierzyna** Pol
40B2	**Skye** *I* Scot
39G7	**Slagelse** Den
45C2	**Slaney** *R* Irish Rep
54B2	**Slatina** Rom
78C4	**Slaung** Indon
5G3	**Slave** *R* Can
13E1	**Slave Lake** Can
65J4	**Slavgorod** Rossiyskaya, USSR
59D2	**Slavuta** USSR
60E4	**Slavyansk** USSR
44B3	**Sleat,Sound of** *Chan* Scot
12C2	**Sleetmute** USA
19C3	**Slidell** USA
16B2	**Slide Mt** USA
45C2	**Slieve Bloom** *Mts* Irish Rep
45B1	**Sligo County,** Irish Rep
41B3	**Sligo** Irish Rep
41B3	**Sligo** *B* Irish Rep
54C2	**Sliven** Bulg
54C2	**Slobozia** Rom
13D3	**Slocan** Can
58D2	**Slonim** USSR
43D4	**Slough** Eng
22B2	**Slough** *R* USA
59B3	**Slovensko** Region, Czech
56C2	**Slubice** Pol
59D2	**Sluch'** *R* USSR
68C1	**Sludyanka** USSR
58B1	**Słupsk** Pol
58D2	**Slutsk** USSR
58D2	**Slutsk** *R* USSR
41A3	**Slyne Head** *Pt* Irish Rep
63C2	**Slyudyanka** USSR
7D4	**Smallwood Res** Can
54B2	**Smederevo** Yugos
54B2	**Smederevska Palanka** Yugos
60D4	**Smela** USSR
15C2	**Smethport** USA
13E1	**Smith** Can
4F3	**Smith Arm** *B* Can
13B2	**Smithers** Can
7C3	**Smith I** Can
13B2	**Smith Sd** Can
15C2	**Smiths Falls** Can
109C4	**Smithton** Aust
13D1	**Smoky** *R* Can
109D2	**Smoky C** Aust
13E2	**Smoky Lake** Can
38F6	**Smøla** *I* Nor
60D3	**Smolensk** USSR
55B2	**Smólikas** *Mt* Greece
54B2	**Smolyan** Bulg
58D2	**Smorgon'** USSR
16B3	**Smyrna** Delaware, USA
17B1	**Smyrna** Georgia, USA
42B2	**Snaefell** *Mt* Eng
38B2	**Snafell** *Mt* Iceland
8B2	**Snake** *R* USA
8B2	**Snake River Canyon** USA
56B2	**Sneek** Neth
45B3	**Sneem** Irish Rep
22B2	**Snelling** USA
59B2	**Snĕžka** *Mt* Pol/Czech
38F6	**Snøhetta** *Mt* Nor
20B1	**Snohomish** USA
20B1	**Snoqualmie P** USA
76D3	**Snoul** Camb
43B3	**Snowdon** *Mt* Wales
43B3	**Snowdonia Nat Pk** Wales
4G3	**Snowdrift** Can
5H4	**Snow Lake** Can
108A2	**Snowtown** Aust
109C3	**Snowy Mts** Aust
9C3	**Snyder** USA
74B4	**Soan-kundo** *I* S Korea

99D2 **Sobat** *R* Sudan
31C2 **Sobral** Brazil
58C2 **Sochaczew** Pol
61E5 **Sochi** USSR
9C3 **Socorro** USA
24A3 **Socorro** *I* Mexico
34A2 **Socos** Chile
81D4 **Socotra** *I* Yemen
38K5 **Sodankylä** Fin
99D2 **Soddo** Eth
39H6 **Soderhamn** Sweden
39H7 **Södertälje** Sweden
99C1 **Sodiri** Sudan
46E1 **Soest** Germany
101C2 **Sofala** Mozam
Sofia = Sofiya
54B2 **Sofiya** Bulg
69G4 **Sofu Gan** *I* Japan
32C2 **Sogamoso** Colombia
39F6 **Sognefjorden** *Inlet* Nor
82D2 **Sog Xian** China
95C2 **Sohâg** Egypt
84D3 **Sohīpat** India
46B1 **Soignies** Belg
46B2 **Soissons** France
85C3 **Sojat** India
74A3 **Sŏjosŏn-man** *B* N Korea
92A2 **Söke** Turk
97C4 **Sokodé** Togo
61E2 **Sokol** USSR
58C2 **Sokołka** Pol
97B3 **Sokolo** Mali
6H3 **Søkongens Øy** *I* Greenland
99D1 **Sokota** Eth
97C3 **Sokoto** Nig
97C3 **Sokoto** *R* Nig
111A3 **Solander I** NZ
79B2 **Solano** Phil
87B1 **Solapur** India
47D1 **Solbad Hall** Austria
47D1 **Sölden** Austria
12D2 **Soldotna** USA
26C4 **Soledad** Colombia
43D4 **Solent** *Sd* Eng
46B1 **Solesmes** France
58D2 **Soligorsk** USSR
61J2 **Solikamsk** USSR
32C4 **Solimões** *R* Peru
46D1 **Solingen** Germany
65G4 **Sol'Itesk** USSR
38H6 **Sollefteå** Sweden
61H3 **Sol'lletsk** USSR
70B4 **Solok** Indon
105G4 **Solomon** *Is* Pacific O
47B1 **Solothurn** Switz
39F8 **Soltau** Germany
22B3 **Solvang** USA
42C2 **Solway Firth** *Estuary* Eng/Scot
100B2 **Solwezi** Zambia
75C1 **Sōma** Japan
55C3 **Soma** Turk
81C5 **Somalia** Republic, E Africa
54A1 **Sombor** Yugos
107D2 **Somerset** Aust
43C4 **Somerset** County, Eng
16D2 **Somerset** Massachusetts, USA
15C2 **Somerset** Pennsylvania, USA
100B4 **Somerset East** S Africa
6A2 **Somerset I** Can
16B3 **Somers Point** USA
16B2 **Somerville** USA
19A3 **Somerville Res** USA
54B1 **Somes** *R* Rom
46B2 **Somme** Department, France
46B2 **Somme** *R* France
46C2 **Sommesous** France
86A2 **Son** *R* India
74A3 **Sŏnch'ŏn** N Korea
39F8 **Sønderborg** Den
6E3 **Søndre Strømfjord** Greenland
47C1 **Sondrio** Italy
76D3 **Song Ba** *R* Viet
76D3 **Song Cau** Viet
101C2 **Songea** Tanz
73E3 **Songjiang** China
77C4 **Songkhla** Thai
74B3 **Songnim** N Korea
77C5 **Sông Pahang** *R* Malay
72A3 **Songpan** China
72C1 **Sonid Youqi** China
76C1 **Son La** Viet
85B3 **Sonmiani** Pak
85B3 **Sonmiani Bay** Pak
22A1 **Sonoma** USA
22B2 **Sonora** California, USA
24A2 **Sonora** *R* Mexico
9B3 **Sonoran Desert** USA
22C1 **Sonora P** USA
25D3 **Sonsonate** El Salvador
71E3 **Sonsorol** *I* Pacific O
10B2 **Soo Canals** Can/USA
13C3 **Sooke** Can
58B2 **Sopot** Pol
59B3 **Sopron** Hung
22B2 **Soquel** USA
53B2 **Sora** Italy
94B3 **Sored** *R* Israel
15D1 **Sorel** Can
109C4 **Sorell** Aust
92C2 **Sorgun** Turk
50B1 **Soria** Spain
38J5 **Sørkjosen** Nor
64C2 **Sørksop** *I* Barents S
61H4 **Sor Mertvyy Kultuk** *Plain* USSR
35B2 **Sorocaba** Brazil
61H3 **Sorochinsk** USSR
71F3 **Soroi** *I* Pacific O
60C4 **Sorok** USSR
71E4 **Sorong** Indon
71E4 **Sorong** Province, Indon
99D2 **Soroti** Uganda
38J4 **Sørøya** *I* Nor
53B2 **Sorrento** Italy
38K5 **Sorsatunturi** *Mt* Fin
38H5 **Sorsele** Sweden
79B3 **Sorsogon** Phil
38L6 **Sortavala** USSR
74B3 **Sŏsan** S Korea
59B2 **Sosnowiec** Pol
65H4 **Sos'va** USSR
64H4 **Sos'va** *R* USSR
98B2 **Souanké** Congo
97B4 **Soubré** Ivory Coast
16B2 **Souderton** USA
27P2 **Soufrière** St Lucia
27N2 **Soufrière** *V* St Vincent
48C3 **Souillac** France
96C1 **Souk Ahras** Alg
74B3 **Soul** S Korea
51C2 **Soummam** *R* Alg
Sour = Tyr
101G1 **Sources,Mt aux** Lesotho
31D3 **Sousa** Brazil
96D1 **Sousse** Tunisia
100B4 **South Africa** Republic, Africa
16B2 **South Amboy** USA
14B2 **Southampton** Can
43D4 **Southampton** Eng
16C2 **Southampton** USA
6B3 **Southampton I** Can
28F6 **South Atlantic O**
7D4 **South Aulatsivik I** Can
106C3 **South Australia** State, Aust
104E5 **South Australian Basin** Indian O
19C3 **Southaven** USA
17B2 **South Bay** USA
14B1 **South Baymouth** Can
14A2 **South Bend** Indiana, USA
20B1 **South Bend** Washington, USA
16D1 **Southbridge** USA
South Cape = Ka Lae
11B3 **South Carolina** State, USA
70C2 **South China S** S E Asia
8C2 **South Dakota** State, USA
16C1 **South Deerfield** USA
43D4 **South Downs** Eng
109C4 **South East C** Aust
111A2 **Southen Alps** *Mts* NZ
5H4 **Southend** Can
43E4 **Southend-on-Sea** Eng
111A2 **Southern Alps** *Mts* NZ
106A4 **Southern Cross** Aust
5J4 **Southern Indian L** Can
27H2 **Southfield** Jamaica
105G5 **South Fiji Basin** Pacific O
12D2 **South Fork** *R* Alaska, USA
22B1 **South Fork** *R* California, USA
28F8 **South Georgia** *I* S Atlantic O
43C4 **South Glamorgan** County, Wales
14A2 **South Haven** USA
5J3 **South Henik L** Can
104F3 **South Honshu Ridge** Pacific O
111A2 **South I** NZ
16C2 **Southington** USA
74B3 **South Korea** Republic, S E Asia
21A2 **South Lake Tahoe** USA
112C8 **South Magnetic Pole** Ant
17B2 **South Miami** USA
16A3 **South Mt** USA
4F3 **South Nahanni** *R* Can
26G1 **South Negril Pt** Jamaica
103F8 **South Orkney** *Is* Atlantic O
8C2 **South Platte** *R* USA
80E **South Pole** Ant
42C3 **Southport** Eng
27R3 **South Pt** Barbados
16B2 **South River** USA
44C2 **South Ronaldsay** *I* Scot
103G7 **South Sandwich Trench** Atlantic O
22A2 **South San Francisco** USA
5H4 **South Saskatchewan** *R* Can
42D2 **South Shields** Eng
110B1 **South Taranaki Bight** *B* NZ
44A3 **South Uist** *I* Scot
South West Africa = Namibia
107D5 **South West C** Aust
105J5 **South West Pacific Basin** Pacific O
103D5 **South West Peru Ridge** Pacific O
43D3 **South Yorkshire** County, Eng
58C1 **Sovetsk** RSFSR, USSR
61G2 **Sovetsk** RSFSR, USSR
98B3 **Soyo Congo** Angola
60D3 **Sozh** *R* USSR
46C1 **Spa** Belg
50A1 **Spain** Kingdom
Spalato = Split
43D3 **Spalding** Eng
14B1 **Spanish** *R* Can
26B3 **Spanish Town** Jamaica
21B2 **Sparks** USA
11B3 **Spartanburg** USA
55B3 **Spartí** Greece
69F2 **Spassk Dal'niy** USSR
27R3 **Speightstown** Barbados
12E2 **Spenard** USA
14A3 **Spencer** Indiana, USA
8D2 **Spencer** Iowa, USA
6A3 **Spencer Bay** Can
108A3 **Spencer,C** Aust
108A2 **Spencer G** Aust
6C3 **Spencer I** Can
111B2 **Spenser Mts** NZ
45C1 **Sperrin** *Mts* N Ire
44C3 **Spey** *R* Scot
57B3 **Speyer** Germany
27K1 **Speyside** Tobago
47B1 **Spiez** Switz
12F1 **Spike Mt** USA
20C1 **Spirit Lake** USA
5G4 **Spirit River** Can
Spitsbergen = Svalbard
57C3 **Spittal** Austria
38F6 **Spjelkavik** Nor
52C2 **Split** Yugos
47C1 **Splügen** Switz
20C1 **Spokane** USA
55C3 **Sporádhes** *Is* Greece
20C2 **Spray** USA
56C2 **Spree** *R* Germany
100A3 **Springbok** S Africa
18B2 **Springdale** USA
10B3 **Springfield** Illinois, USA
10C2 **Springfield** Massachusetts, USA
18B2 **Springfield** Missouri, USA
14B3 **Springfield** Ohio, USA
20B2 **Springfield** Oregon, USA
15D2 **Springfield** Vermont, USA
100B4 **Springfontein** S Africa
101G1 **Springs** S Africa
41D3 **Spurn Head** *Pt* Eng
13C3 **Squamish** Can
60E3 **Sredne-Russkaya Vozvyshennost** *Upland* USSR
63B1 **Sredne Sibirskoye Ploskogorve** *Tableland* USSR
61J2 **Sredniy Ural** *Mts* USSR
76D3 **Srepok** *R* Camb
68D1 **Sretensk** USSR
76C3 **Sre Umbell** Camb
83C5 **Sri Lanka** Republic, S Asia
84C2 **Srīnagar** Pak
87A1 **Srīvardhan** India
58B2 **Sroda** Pol
30H6 **Sta Clara** *I* Chile
32J7 **Sta Cruz** *I* Ecuador
56B2 **Stade** Germany
44A3 **Staffa** *I* Scot
43C3 **Stafford** County, Eng
43C3 **Stafford** Eng
16C2 **Stafford Springs** USA
Stalingrad = Volgograd
6A1 **Stallworthy,C** Can
59C2 **Stalowa Wola** Pol
32J7 **Sta Maria** *I* Ecuador
16C2 **Stamford** Connecticut, USA
16B1 **Stamford** New York, USA
100A3 **Stampriet** Namibia
101G1 **Standerton** S Africa
14B2 **Standish** USA
101H1 **Stanger** S Africa
22B2 **Stanislaus** *R* USA

Victorica

65J4 **Ust'Ishim** USSR
58B2 **Ustka** Pol
65K5 **Ust'-Kamenogorsk** USSR
63B2 **Ust Karabula** USSR
61J2 **Ust'Katav** USSR
63C2 **Ust'-Kut** USSR
61E4 **Ust Labinsk** USSR
63F1 **Ust'Maya** USSR
1C8 **Ust'Nera** USSR
63E2 **Ust'Nyukzha** USSR
63C2 **Ust'Ordynskiy** USSR
64G3 **Ust'Tsil'ma** USSR
63F2 **Ust'Umal'ta** USSR
75A2 **Usuki** Japan
25C3 **Usumacinta** R Guatemala/Mexico
101H1 **Usutu** R Swaziland
8B3 **Utah** State, USA
8B2 **Utah L** USA
58D1 **Utena** USSR
85B3 **Uthal** Pak
10C2 **Utica** USA
51B2 **Utiel** Spain
13D1 **Utikuma L** Can
56B2 **Utrecht** Neth
101H1 **Utrecht** S Africa
50A2 **Utrera** Spain
38K5 **Utsjoki** Fin
74D3 **Utsunomiya** Japan
76C2 **Uttaradit** Thai
86A1 **Uttar Pradesh** State, India
65H4 **Uval** USSR
107F3 **Uvéa** I Nouvelle Calédonie
99D3 **Uvinza** Tanz
99C3 **Uvira** Zaïre
6E2 **Uvkusigssat** Greenland
39J6 **Uvsikaupunki** Fin
68B1 **Uvs Nuur** L China
74C4 **Uwajima** Japan
72B2 **Uxin Qi** China
63B2 **Uyar** USSR
30C3 **Uyuni** Bol
80E1 **Uzbekskaya S.S.R.** Republic, USSR
48C2 **Uzerche** France
59C3 **Uzhgorod** USSR
60E3 **Uzlovaya** USSR
92A1 **Uzunköprü** Turk

V

101F1 **Vaal** R S Africa
101G1 **Vaal Dam** Res S Africa
100B3 **Vaalwater** S Africa
38J6 **Vaasa** Fin
59B3 **Vác** Hung
30F4 **Vacaria** Brazil
35C1 **Vacaria** R Minas Gerais, Brazil
21A2 **Vacaville** USA
85C4 **Vadodara** India
38K4 **Vadsø** Nor
47C1 **Vaduz** Leichtenstein
38D3 **Vágar** Føroyar
29E3 **Va Gesell** Arg
59B3 **Váh** R Czech
87B2 **Vaigai** R India
65K3 **Vakh** R USSR
60B4 **Vâlcea** Rom
29C4 **Valcheta** Arg
47D2 **Valdagno** Italy
60D2 **Valday** USSR
60D2 **Valdayskaya Vozvyshennost'** Upland USSR
32D2 **Val de la Pascua** Ven
50B2 **Valdepeñas** Spain
12E2 **Valdez** USA
29B3 **Valdivia** Chile
46B2 **Val d'Oise** Department France
17B1 **Valdosta** USA

20C2 **Vale** USA
13D2 **Valemount** Can
31D4 **Valença** Bahia, Brazil
35C2 **Valença** Rio de Janeiro, Brazil
49C3 **Valence** France
51B2 **Valencia** Region, Spain
51B2 **Valencia** Spain
32D1 **Valencia** Ven
45A3 **Valencia** I Irish Rep
50A2 **Valencia de Alcantara** Spain
46B1 **Valenciennes** France
47C2 **Valenza** Italy
32C2 **Valera** Ven
39K7 **Valga** USSR
64E4 **Valikiyo** USSR
54A2 **Valjevo** Yugos
39J6 **Valkeakoski** Fin
25D2 **Valladolid** Mexico
50B1 **Valladolid** Spain
47B2 **Valle d'Aosta** Region, Italy
27D5 **Valle de la Pascua** Ven
23A1 **Valle de Santiago** Mexico
47B2 **Valle d'Isére** France
32C1 **Valledupar** Colombia
97C3 **Vallée de l'Azaouak** V Niger
97C3 **Vallée Tilemis** V. Mali
30D2 **Valle Grande** Bol
22A1 **Vallejo** USA
30B4 **Vallenar** Chile
53B3 **Valletta** Malta
8D2 **Valley City** USA
20B2 **Valley Falls** USA
15D1 **Valleyfield** Can
13D1 **Valleyview** Can
47E2 **Valli di Comacchio** Lg Italy
51C1 **Valls** Spain
58D1 **Valmiera** USSR
35A2 **Valparaiso** Brazil
34A2 **Valparaiso** Chile
23A1 **Valparaiso** Mexico
17A1 **Valparaiso** USA
101G1 **Vals** R S Africa
85C4 **Valsåd** India
60E3 **Valuyki** USSR
50A2 **Valverde del Camino** Spain
38J6 **Vammala** Fin
93D2 **Van** Turk
63C1 **Vanavara** USSR
18B2 **Van Buren** Arkansas, USA
13C3 **Vancouver** Can
20B1 **Vancouver** Can
5F5 **Vancouver I** Can
12G2 **Vancouver,Mt** Can
18C2 **Vandalia** Illinois, USA
14B3 **Vandalia** Ohio, USA
13C2 **Vanderhoof** Can
106C2 **Van Diemen G** Aust
39G7 **Vänern** L Sweden
39G7 **Vänersborg** Sweden
101D3 **Vangaindrano** Madag
93D2 **Van Gölü** Salt L Turk
76C2 **Vang Vieng** Laos
9C3 **Van Horn** USA
15C1 **Vanier** Can
1C6 **Vankarem** USSR
38H6 **Vännäs** Sweden
48B2 **Vannes** France
47B2 **Vanoise** Mts France
100A4 **Vanrhynsdorp** S Africa
6B3 **Vansittart I** Can
105G4 **Vanuatu** Is Pacific O
14B2 **Van Wert** USA
47C2 **Varallo** Italy
90B2 **Varāmīn** Iran
86A1 **Vārānasi** India
38K4 **Varangerfjord** Inlet Nor
38K4 **Varangerhalvøya** Pen Nor
52C1 **Varazdin** Yugos

39G7 **Varberg** Sweden
39F7 **Varde** Den
38L4 **Vardø** Nor
58C2 **Varéna** USSR
47C2 **Varenna** Italy
47C2 **Varese** Italy
35B2 **Varginha** Brazil
38K6 **Varkaus** Fin
54C2 **Varna** Bulg
39G7 **Värnamo** Sweden
17B1 **Varnville** USA
35C1 **Várzea da Palma** Brazil
47C2 **Varzi** Italy
50B1 **Vascongadas** Region, Spain
60D3 **Vasil'kov** USSR
14B2 **Vassar** USA
39H7 **Västerås** Sweden
39H7 **Västervik** Sweden
52B2 **Vasto** Italy
65J4 **Vasyugan** R USSR
38B2 **Vatnajökull** Mts Iceland
38A1 **Vatneyri** Iceland
54C1 **Vatra Dornei** Rom
39G7 **Vättern** L Sweden
9C3 **Vaughn** USA
32C3 **Vaupés** R Colombia
13E2 **Vauxhall** Can
87C3 **Vavunija** Sri Lanka
39G7 **Växjö** Sweden
64G2 **Vaygach, Ostrov** I USSR
34C2 **Vedia** Arg
38G5 **Vega** I Nor
13E2 **Vegreville** Can
50A2 **Vejer de la Frontera** Spain
39F7 **Vejle** Den
52C2 **Velebit** Mts Yugos
35C1 **Velhas** R Brazil
39K7 **Velikaya** R USSR
60D2 **Velikiye Luki** USSR
61G1 **Velikiy Ustyug** USSR
54C2 **Veliko Tŭrnovo** Bulg
97A3 **Vélingara** Sen
87B2 **Vellore** India
61F1 **Vel'sk** USSR
87B3 **Vembanad L** India
34C2 **Venado Tuerto** Arg
35B2 **Vençeslau Braz** Brazil
49C2 **Vendôme** France
12E1 **Venetie** USA
47D2 **Veneto** Region, Italy
47E2 **Venezia** Italy
32D2 **Venezuela** Republic, S America
87A1 **Vengurla** India
12C3 **Veniaminof V** USA
Venice = Venezia
87B2 **Venkatagiri** India
56B2 **Venlo** Neth
58C1 **Venta** R USSR
101G1 **Ventersburg** S Africa
58C1 **Ventspils** USSR
32D3 **Ventuari** R Ven
22C3 **Ventura** USA
60D1 **Vepsovskaya Vozvyshennost'** Upland USSR
30D4 **Vera** Arg
51B2 **Vera** Spain
23B2 **Veracruz** Mexico
23B1 **Veracruz** State, Mexico
85C4 **Verāval** India
47C2 **Verbania** Italy
47C2 **Vercelli** Italy
35A1 **Verde** R Goias, Brazil
23A1 **Verde** R Jalisco, Mexico
35A1 **Verde** R Mato Grosso do Sul, Brazil
23B2 **Verde** R Oaxaca, Mexico
Verde,C = Cap Vert
35C1 **Verde Grande** R Brazil

34C3 **Verde,Pen** Arg
49D3 **Verdon** R France
46C2 **Verdun** France
101G1 **Vereeniging** S Africa
61H2 **Vereshchagino** USSR
97A3 **Verga,C** Guinea
34D3 **Vergara** Arg
50A1 **Verin** Spain
98C3 **Verissimo Sarmento** Angola
63D2 **Verkh Angara** R USSR
61J3 **Verkhneural'sk** USSR
63E1 **Verkhnevilyuysk** USSR
1C8 **Verkhoyansk** USSR
35A1 **Vermelho** R Brazil
13E2 **Vermilion** Can
10C2 **Vermont** State, USA
22B2 **Vernalis** USA
13D2 **Vernon** Can
46A2 **Vernon** France
9D3 **Vernon** USA
17B2 **Vero Beach** USA
54B2 **Veroia** Greece
47D2 **Verolanuova** Italy
47D2 **Verona** Italy
46B2 **Versailles** France
101H1 **Verulam** S Africa
46C1 **Verviers** Belg
46B2 **Vervins** France
46C2 **Vesle** R France
49D2 **Vesoul** France
38G5 **Vesterålen** Is Nor
38G5 **Vestfjorden** Inlet Nor
38A2 **Vestmannaeyjar** Iceland
53B2 **Vesuvio** Mt Italy
59B3 **Veszprém** Hung
39H7 **Vetlanda** Sweden
61F2 **Vetluga** R USSR
46B1 **Veurne** Belg
47B1 **Vevey** Switz
46A2 **Vexin** Region, France
47A2 **Veynes** France
50A1 **Viana do Castelo** Port
49E3 **Viareggio** Italy
39F7 **Viborg** Den
53C3 **Vibo Valentia** Italy
112C2 **Vice-commodoro Marambio** Base Ant
52B1 **Vicenza** Italy
51C1 **Vich** Spain
32D3 **Vichada** R Colombia
61F2 **Vichuga** USSR
49C2 **Vichy** France
19B3 **Vicksburg** USA
35C2 **Vicosa** Brazil
106C4 **Victor Harbour** Aust
34C2 **Victoria** Arg
13C3 **Victoria** Can
34A3 **Victoria** Chile
73C5 **Victoria** Hong Kong
78D1 **Victoria** Malay
108B3 **Victoria** State, Aust
9D4 **Victoria** USA
106C2 **Victoria** R Aust
107D4 **Victoria** State Aust
26B2 **Victoria de las Tunas** Cuba
100B2 **Victoria Falls** Zambia/ Zim
4G2 **Victoria I** Can
108B2 **Victoria,L** Aust
99D3 **Victoria,L** C Africa
112B7 **Victoria Land** Region, Ant
86C2 **Victoria,Mt** Burma
99D2 **Victoria Nile** R Uganda
111B2 **Victoria Range** Mts NZ
106C2 **Victoria River Downs** Aust
4H3 **Victoria Str** Can
15D1 **Victoriaville** Can
100B4 **Victoria West** S Africa
34B3 **Victorica** Arg

W